Disaster and
Human History

Disaster and Human History

Case Studies in Nature, Society and Catastrophe

BENJAMIN REILLY

McFarland & Company, Inc., Publishers

Jefferson, North Carolina, and London

LIBRARY OF CONGRESS CATALOGUING-IN-PUBLICATION DATA

Reilly, Benjamin, 1971–
Disaster and human history : case studies in nature, society and
catastrophe / Benjamin Reilly.
p.   cm.
Includes bibliographical references and index.

ISBN 978-0-7864-3655-2
softcover : 50# alkaline paper ∞

1. Natural disasters—History.   2. Natural disasters—Case studies.
3. Human beings—Effect of environment on—Case studies.   I. Title.
GB5014.R45   2009   363.3409 — dc22   2008052176

British Library cataloguing data are available

On the cover: San Francisco in ruins after the 1906 earthquake
(Library of Congress); tsunami inundation north of Phuket, Thailand,
on December 26, 2004 (NASA); human skeletal remains found after
the eruption of Mount Vesuvius in A.D. 79 (Parco Nazionale del Vesuvio);
Hurricane Katrina in the Gulf of Mexico on August 28, 2005 (NASA);
eruption of Mount St. Helens on May 18, 1980 (USGS)

Manufactured in the United States of America

*McFarland & Company, Inc., Publishers
Box 611, Jefferson, North Carolina 28640
www.mcfarlandpub.com*

Acknowledgments

Thanks to Anita Reilly, Vagel Keller, Mona Maher, Joe Trotter, David Hounshell, Joel Tarr, Florentina Bico, Mohammed Reswan Al Islam, John Robertson, Gary Warnock, Taghreed Hamada, Eleanore Adiong, Ikram Issa; Nicky Krysak, Isabelle Eula and the rest of the Carnegie Mellon University Qatar library staff; Barry Schles and his colleagues at Hunt Library on the Carnegie Mellon University main campus; Zeina Hamady, Fatma Abdel Aziz, and Valerie Jeremijenko at Virginia Commonwealth University in Qatar for their assistance with maps and diagrams; James Reardon-Anderson of Georgetown School of Foreign Service in Qatar for his feedback on section 6.1; John Bryant of the Engineering school of Texas A&M in Qatar for his advice on sections 3.1 and 3.3; Khaled Machaca of Weill Cornell Medical School in Qatar for his advice on chapter 8; Yan Gao from the Carnegie Mellon University Pittsburgh campus for her advice on sections 6.1 and 7.2; Dante Sell at the National Archives of Australia; Andre Gailani at Punch Ltd.; Carolyn McGoldrick and her colleagues at the Associated Press; and Chuck Thorpe.

Thanks also to Sir John Houghton, James Donnelly, Iain Stewart at IIASA, and Kerry Emanuel for allowing me to adapt their excellent maps and diagrams for use in this text.

A special thanks to the Qatar Foundation for their financial support for this project and for creating the global, interdisciplinary scholarly environment at Education City that inspired and enriched this book.

Table of Contents

Introduction

As a result of the events of 9/11 in 2001, which claimed nearly 3000 lives and resulted in at least $38 billion in economic damages, terrorism became the primary policy concern of the United States and many other nations in the opening years of the 21st century. In the ten months between December 2004 and October 2005, however, three catastrophic events served to refocus the world's attention on a far older threat to human society: natural disasters. First, in December 2004, the world was horrified by the ravages of the Asian Tsunami, which was brought directly to their TV screens by videos filmed by tourists or amateur photographers. By the time the deadly floodwaters receded, the Asian Tsunami had killed over 200,000 people in Indonesia, Thailand, Sri Lanka, and India. The world was equally shocked by the images of massive flooding and human misery in the American city of New Orleans, which was submerged in August 2005 by the powerful storm surge of Hurricane Katrina. Although Katrina only killed about 1,800 Americans—a little more than half of 9/11's death toll — Katrina's repair bill of $125 billion far overshadowed 9/11's more modest price tag. Soon after, in October 2005, the disaster-weary world was subjected to yet another catastrophe in the form of the Great Pakistani Earthquake. Although the TV images of the Pakistani Earthquake lacked the visceral punch of the Katrina and Asian Tsunami footage, the scale of the disaster was no less catastrophic: approximately 75,000 died and property damage topped $5 billion. Taken together, these events served as a needed reminder that natural disasters pose at least as much of a threat to human life as terrorism does.

Indeed, natural disasters have played an integral role in human history from the dawn of civilization to the present day. Volcanic eruptions have been credited with the fall of entire civilizations, such as the Minoan civilization of ancient Crete. Floods have changed the course of history, for example in 1970, when West Pakistani callousness towards the suffering caused by the massive Bhola cyclone in East Pakistan helped to trigger the independence movement that created the modern state of Bangladesh. Disease has been even more crucial in influencing human development. The pathogens brought by European explorers and soldiers to the Americas triggered the greatest epidemics in history, leading to the deaths of as much as 95 percent of the Amerindian population and the subsequent opening up of the Americas to European settlement. The Black Death of the Middle Ages, in turn, may have instigated the European technological revolution by both driving up the cost of labor, thus encouraging labor-saving new technologies, and by provoking Europeans to question some religious and philosophical beliefs that were inhibiting the development of European science. These disaster-related influences on humanity, however, may eventually pale in significance before the unfolding modern-day disaster of global warming, which threatens to transform both the world and the human species in the coming 21st century.

1

Natural disasters also affect history more indirectly by exerting a subtle influence over human culture and beliefs. The pessimistic mindset of the ancient Mesopotamians, who worshiped temperamental and wrathful gods, may be a consequence of the frequent floods of the Tigris and Euphrates Rivers. Indeed, the biblical story of Noah and the Ark, in which nearly all of mankind perishes as punishment for human wickedness, probably has Mesopotamian roots. By way of contrast, the relative optimism of ancient Egyptian religion is often explained by the relatively benign flood profile of the Nile River. Disease can exert a powerful influence over culture as well. Environmental historian William McNeill, for example, has linked the rise of Christianity and the increasing frequency of epidemic disease. As a result of the misery and uncertainty wrought by disease in the late Roman Imperial period, McNeill argues, Christianity's promise of a better life after death found fertile ground in the provinces of the Roman Empire. Similarly, McNeill claims that the "transcendental" or otherworldly nature of most Indian religions, most especially Buddhism and Hinduism, probably reflects a human desire to escape the miseries of the Indian subcontinent's disease-ridden climate. Natural disaster may influence the character of modern societies as well. According to Philippines specialist Greg Bankoff, for example, the many volcanoes, earthquakes, floods, and cyclones that periodically ravage the Philippines have profoundly shaped Filipino culture. Indeed, Bankoff claims that many characteristics of modern Filipino life — their pragmatism, their skepticism towards their government, their black sense of humor, their fatalism, and even their widespread belief in miracles— all reflect the frequency of natural disasters in the Philippine archipelago.

Natural disasters also exert a powerful influence over human economic and social relationships. One unfortunate effect of natural disasters is to exacerbate the modern trend of economic inequality, both between and within nations. Countries that are particularly prone to natural disasters, such as Bangladesh, are trapped in a vicious cycle: disasters lead to increased poverty, which in turn leads to increased vulnerability to disaster. The same phenomenon is visible within a given society as well. Since the poor are often compelled by their poverty to live in areas that are vulnerable to disasters, such as river floodplains, trailer parks, or disease-prone slums, they tend to suffer disproportionately from disasters when they occur, and these disasters serve only to make the poor poorer. The economically disadvantaged are also less likely to insure their property, making it far harder for them to recover financially in the disaster's aftermath. Natural disasters may even play a role in the formation of social class. McNeill, for example, argues that the rigid caste system of traditional India may represent an attempt at social quarantine, protecting high-caste Indians from contact with low-caste Indians, who are much more likely to carry diseases as a result of their poverty or unhealthy professions, such as street cleaning, butchering animals, or burying the dead.

Just as natural disasters influence human life, so too does human life affect natural disasters. In some disasters, such as volcanic eruptions and earthquakes, human beings do not contribute to causing the disaster, but can indirectly exacerbate the disaster through their poor decisions, such as building substandard housing or by locating communities near or upon fault lines. Similarly, humans play little role in producing cyclonic storms, but the impact of a given hurricane is inextricably tied to building construction codes, the existence of evacuation routes, availability of transportation, and the strength of the local flood control defenses. Other disasters are even more directly linked to human decisions; indeed, famine is almost invariably caused by war, rigid conformity to ideology, or flawed government policies, at least in the modern era.

As a result, many "natural disasters" are arguably anything but natural, but rather are partially or wholly the result of human agency. Indeed, American environmental historian Ted Steinberg has gone so far as to claim that the term "natural disaster" is often used as a form of

Albrecht Dürer's classic woodblock print, "The Revelation of St. John: The Four Riders of the Apocalypse." The riders are usually interpreted to represent War, Famine, Pestilence, and Death.

verbal whitewash. Social elites declare disasters to be "natural" in an attempt to conceal the class inequalities that make the poor more susceptible to disaster than the rich and to avoid responsibility for their own short-sighted and self-serving economic decisions, which often prove fatal in times of disaster. Furthermore, by stressing the "natural" component of disasters, elites can portray them as fluke occurrences that should not stand in the way of a quick return to business as usual. Consequently, the degree to which a given disaster is truly a "natural" disaster at all will be a recurrent theme in this textbook.

Just as natural disasters cannot be understood without considering the human element, so too natural disasters must also be considered within the context of other forms of disaster, which interact with each other in complex ways. One disaster may directly trigger another, such as famine causing disease; indeed, in nearly every famine, most deaths are directly attributable to opportunistic disease running riot through a famine-weakened populace. A given disaster may also worsen another disaster months or years later, such as when heavy volcanic ash deposits are transformed into deadly mudslides when loosened by heavy rain. Local disasters may also have trans-global effects. The 1816 eruption of Mount Tambora in the Indonesian archipelago, for example, spewed so much ash into the air that it lowered global temperatures by an appreciable amount, triggering famine and disease in distant Europe in the following year. In some cases, disasters may even serve as links in a deadly chain. Global warming, it is theorized, may influence the El Niño weather cycle, leading to extreme drought or heavy flooding in different regions worldwide. Both flooding and drought, in turn, can trigger deadly famine and disease.

The "disaster hierarchy" diagram below represents one attempt to summarize these com-

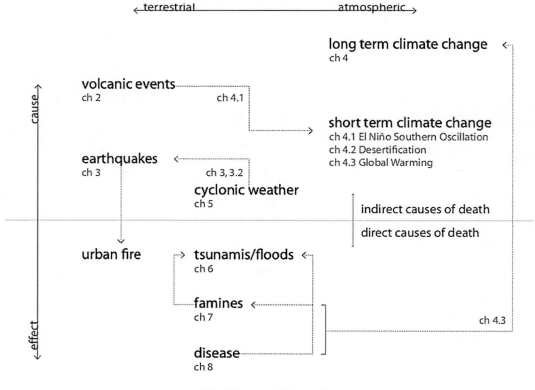

The Disaster Hierarchy

plex interrelationships between natural disasters. At the top of the diagram are the "indirect" causes of disasters, events such as climate change and volcanic activity, which are rarely the actual cause of the loss of human life. Events further down on the chart can be caused by the disasters immediately above. Volcanic activity can spawn earthquakes, for instance, and climate change can alter the El Niño cycle, which in turn can influence tropical cyclones and the famine. At the bottom of the chart are the "direct" causes of disasters, which are often the result of disasters higher on the chart. Cyclones, for instance, rarely kill directly through wind and rain, but the floods, disease, and famines they leave in their wake can cause considerable loss of life.

It is important to note, however, that disasters on the bottom of the chart can occasionally influence the indirect disasters at the top, occasionally in the form of a feedback loop. The social dislocation caused by disease, for example, can undermine food production or distribution networks, triggering famine. Disease can also drain resources from flood control systems, creating vulnerability to disastrous flooding. Furthermore, as we shall see in section 4.3, some scholars believe that disease can actually cause climate change, as the regrowth of forest in former farmland following a major epidemic drains the atmosphere of the greenhouse gas CO_2. The resulting cooler weather can lead to crop failures, famine, disease, and possibly still more expansion of forests and consequently even cooler global temperatures.

Structure of the Book

The two organizing themes described above — human agency in "natural" disasters, and the complex interrelations between disaster events — are reflected in the structure of this text. The introduction is followed by a brief history of the modern world, to provide historical context. The remaining chapters each focus on a specific type of disaster: volcanoes, earthquakes, environmental change, tropical cyclones, floods and tsunamis, famines, and disease. Each of these chapters begin with a "science and history" section, which in turn is divided into 5 parts. The first will consider the causes of the disaster, usually from the perspective of natural science, but occasionally from the perspective of social science as well if the disaster's causes are primarily human. The second will examine the disaster in a broad historical context, with a particular eye towards examining that disaster's role in shaping global history. The third part will examine the role that human beings play in either causing or exacerbating the given disaster. Part four of each "science and history" section will consider linkages to other forms of disaster, including both historically observed linkages and possible linkages that might occur in the future, such as the possible changes to the El Niño cycle due to global warming. Finally, all "science and history" sections conclude with study questions designed to test the reader's understanding of the factual content of the text. These can be used either as classroom discussion prompts or as written homework assignments.

Each science and history section will be followed by 3 or 4 "case studies." These case studies will serve two main purposes. First of all, each case study is designed to deepen the reader's theoretical understanding of a general disaster type by providing an in-depth example of how that disaster played out in a real world historical context. Secondly, each case study is designed to allow students to explore the broader themes of this textbook by applying them to a specific event. To what degree are humans responsible for the disaster described in the case study? How did other disasters contribute to a given disaster's outcome? Which theory of famine best describes a given food shortage? Which typology of disease best fits a given epidemic? To better explore these issues, each "case study" is followed by a number of study questions, and unlike the "science and history" study questions, these questions are open-ended and test a student's ability to apply theory or defend an argument.

Each section of the book concludes with a list of sources and suggested readings, which readers are encouraged to pursue if they want more detailed information about the topic.

Finally, the Conclusion considers to what degree the lessons of past natural disasters can serve as a guide to the future of the human species.

Scope of the Book

Unlike texts on disasters that are limited either to specific types of disasters or specific regions of the world, this book is intended to be comprehensive, considering all major types of natural disasters and all parts of the planet. What is more, while most books on natural disasters give disproportional weight to events in the United States, the case studies in this book are drawn from widely dispersed geographical regions, from Asia to North America, Africa to Europe, South America to Australia. This global perspective is designed to help readers appreciate that natural disasters do not look the same to everyone, but rather are appreciated quite differently by people from different cultural, religious, or ideological backgrounds. What is more, a comparative study of disasters in different regions underscores the human element of disasters. Indeed, disasters often play out in quite different ways depending on the beliefs of the people who are affected by the event.

However, while the geographical scope of the book is global, the chronological scope of the text is far more narrowly defined: all the case studies in this book occurred during or after the 1840's. There are several reasons why that is the case. First of all, since the disasters in this book occurred relatively recently, they are generally well documented, and thus can be sub-

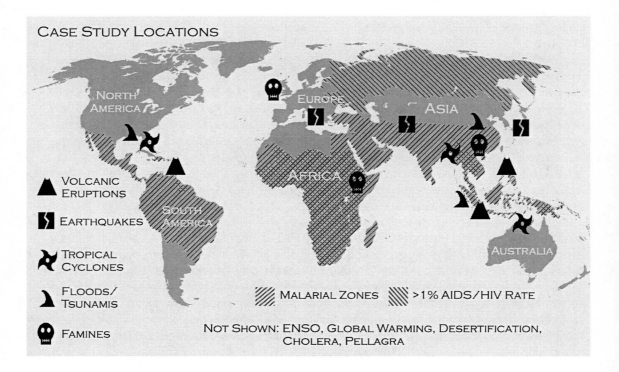

CASE STUDY TIMELINE

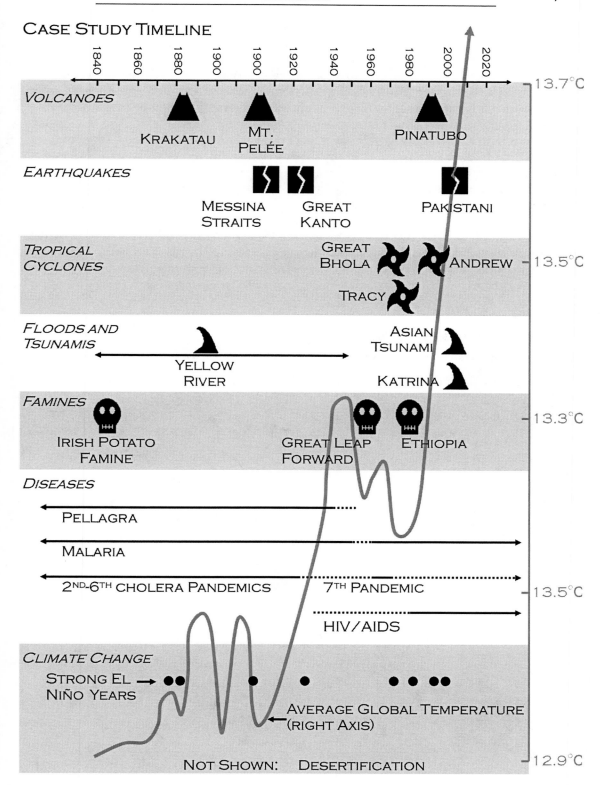

jected to more detailed scientific and historical analysis. Secondly, since they all occurred recently — some within the lifetimes of the reader — they will probably be of more interest and relevance to a modern student. Thirdly, and most importantly, the limited chronological scope of the book allows for constructive cross-disaster comparisons. There is little to be gained from comparing a volcanic eruption in ancient Indonesia with an eruption in the modern-day Caribbean, for instance, since the two events are widely separated in both time and space. However, it would be more fruitful to compare two geographically dispersed eruptions at a roughly similar time in world history — for instance, the Krakatau eruption of 1883 and the Mount Pelée eruption of 1902. In such an analysis, any similarities and differences between the two events are likely to be meaningful since they cannot simply be explained by distance in time.

This book's focus on the late modern era is useful in another way as well: it limits the amount of background information a reader needs to know in order to put the case studies into their proper historical context. Since not all readers of this text will have had previous exposure to the history of the past two hundred years, the next chapter will briefly summarize the history of the modern era. It is highly recommended that students who have not studied modern history read Chapter 1 before proceeding to the rest of the text, in order to understand the case study natural disasters — and the human beings affected by them — in a proper historical context.

Sources/Suggested Readings

Bankoff, Greg. *Cultures of Disaster: Society and Natural Hazard in the Philippines.* New York: RoutledgeCurzon, 2003.
Diamond, Jared. *Guns, Germs, and Steel: The Fates of Human Societies.* New York: W. W. Norton, 1997.
McNeill, William. *Plagues and Peoples.* New York: Anchor Books, 1976.
Ponting, Clive. *A Green History of the World: Nature, Pollution, and the Collapse of Societies.* New York: Penguin, 1991.
Steinberg, Ted. *Acts of God: The Unnatural History of Natural Disaster in America.* New York: Oxford University Press, 2000.

CHAPTER 1

A Brief History of
the Modern World

What is the "Modern World"? We all know when it ends—by definition, every moment that passes adds a new "final" chapter to the history of the modern age — though some academics have complicated matters by inventing the paradoxical notion of "postmodernism." But when does the modern era of history begin?

Historians of European history are trained to believe that the "modern" era of world history began in 1815, with the fall of Napoleon Bonaparte, the restoration of European political stability following the Congress of Vienna, and the definitive end of the French Revolutionary era. From the perspective of world history, however, this is a rather unsatisfactory starting point. True, Napoleon's definitive defeat would help establish the hegemony of the maritime nation of Great Britain within Europe, and thus would indirectly increase Europe's overseas prominence. On the whole, however, Napoleon's fall does little to explain the most important overall trend in recent world history: the decline of the large Asian land-based empires such as the Ottoman, Mughal, and Chinese states, and the increasing dominance of European nation-states over world affairs.

From a world history point of view, the roots of the modern world lie considerably farther back in time than the fall of Napoleon. Two dates in particular could lay claim to the beginning of the "modern" world: 1492, the start of European domination in the Americas, and 1712, the year of the development of the first economically viable steam engine.

The "Columbian Exchange"

The year 1492 is often heralded of the year of the "discovery" of the Americas by Europeans, which is rather unfair, since the Americas had been "discovered" previously by several groups, including the Asian ancestors of the Amerindians, the Vikings, and perhaps Polynesian or Chinese seafarers as well. In any case, Columbus was not out to discover anything; his real goal was to chart out a direct east-west connection to the trade markets of Asia across the Atlantic ocean, in order to outflank the Moslem states which sat astride the East-West trade route at that time. Columbus' goal was not to explore a new continent but rather to outdo the Portuguese, who had rounded the Cape of Good Hope in 1487/88, and thus were poised to begin direct trade with Asian powers. Indeed, if Columbus had not sailed west across the Atlantic in 1492, the Portuguese would today have the honor of "discovering" the Americas, since a Portuguese navigator sighted the coast of Brazil in 1500 by accident while trying to sail around Africa to India.

The real significance of 1492 was not the inauguration of an era of discovery, but rather the start of one of the most significant biological transformations ever to occur on our planet, which pioneering environmental historian Alfred Crosby dubbed the "Columbian Exchange." In the three hundred years following 1492, Eurasia, Africa, and the Americas would be bound together by reciprocal links of human, plant, and microorganism exchanges that would profoundly shape the course of future world history.

In the short run, the most significant exchanges occurred at a microscopic level: the transfer of Old World (Eurasian and African) diseases to the previously unexposed populations of the Americas. Before the arrival of Europeans in the Americas, Amerindian populations had reached impressive levels, in part because lack of domesticated animals and lack of long-distance trade with other cultures limited their exposure to epidemic diseases. The epidemiological innocence of the Amerindians, however, was shattered by the arrival of Europeans, who brought measles, chicken pox, and a multitude of other Old World infections. Europeans generally acquired these diseases during childhood and, if they survived to adulthood, had lifelong resistance to these ailments. Amerindians, however, had no such resistance, and thus suffered repeated waves of deadly epidemics once these diseases were introduced in the Americas. Once regular contact was established between the Americas and Africa, the epidemiological problems of the Amerindians were further compounded by African infections, including yellow fever and the more vicious strains of malaria.

As we shall see in greater detail in chapter 8, these Old World plagues would have profound consequences in the Americas. In the two centuries after European contact, the Amerindian population of the Americas plummeted by between 50–100 million, a decrease of as much as 90 or 95 percent. This dramatic drop in Amerindian numbers allowed Europeans, whose military technology and organization was moderately but not decisively superior to that of the Amerindian societies, to quickly seize the most desirable plots of land in the Americas. Once in control, European societies quickly remade the Americas in their own image. In areas with large remnant Amerindian populations, especially in Mexico and Peru, the natives were converted to Christianity and were integrated into a European-style hierarchical system that made their labor available to their colonial masters. Elsewhere, surviving natives were steadily evicted from desirable land through bloody conflicts more akin to genocide than war.

In the medium term, the "Columbian exchange" led to a vast increase in European trade. The great Empires of the Amerindians were plundered of their wealth, and once the easily accessible gold had been snatched up, Europeans herded subject Amerindians and African slaves into mines to extract the sizable mineral resources of the Americas. The resulting windfall of gold and silver significantly changed Europe's economic standing in the global economy. Before 1500, Europe had suffered from chronic trade imbalance in comparison to the established empires of Asia, for the simple reason that these Asian empires produced spices, porcelain, and other commodities that were in great demand in Europe, but Europe produced little of interest to the rest of the world, and its manufactures (other than perhaps weapons) were more expensive and of lower quality than what the great Asian states could produce. The influx of cheap cash from the Americas, however, allowed Europeans to purchase Asian commodities on more favorable terms, stimulating Europe's economy.

Europeans were also able to extract vast amounts of wealth from the Americas through agriculture. Some of these crops were of American origins, including tobacco, a drug that quickly became a valuable trade commodity in large part by virtue of its addictive characteristics. Other crops originated in Africa, such as African Rice, which became a staple crop in coastal North America. Still other crops grown profitably in the Americas were of Old World origin, most notably sugar, a valuable crop that grew well in few places in the Old World but

A brutal depiction of the treatment of American slaves, which appeared in a European publication in the 1830s.

could grow in great abundance in the American tropics. Indeed, the need for manpower to harvest this labor-intensive crop compelled Europeans to tap into African slave markets, further transforming the character of the Americas. What is more, American colonists were able to vastly increase the productive potential of American farmland by importing previously unknown Eurasian crops, animals, and farming techniques, most notably wheat, cattle, and the heavy iron-tipped plow. It is important to note that Europe was not the only area to benefit from these changes. American silver produced a commercial revolution in China, and coastal African kingdoms befitted considerably from the expansion of the African slave market. Nonetheless, Europe was the primary beneficiary of the transformation of the Americas, and consequently Europe's prominence on the world stage was substantially increased.

The Columbian exchange benefitted Europe in the longer term as well. The dense trade networks that linked Eurasia, Africa, and the Americas created what historians have called an "Atlantic economy," which in turn generated vast amounts of investment capital that fueled European economic transformation. The establishment of large overseas colonies inhabited by large and fairly affluent populations of European extraction created important markets for European goods, further stimulating the European economy. What is more, the gradual importation of American crops into the Old World had the unexpected long-term consequence of vastly increasing the Old World's population. In 1500, for instance, Europe's population only amounted to 80 million, which represented 19 percent of the total world population; by 1700 Europe's population had nearly doubled, reaching 140 million, or 23 percent of the world's population. Other parts of the Old World also benefitted enormously from American crops in the long run, particularly China and Africa, but since Europe was the initial place of importation Europe received the strongest initial bump from American plants.

Why were American crops so important in the Old World? In part because of their high caloric content; maize, manioc, and the potato, the three most important American crops imported to the Old World, all produce substantially more calories per acre than any Old World crop apart from rice. Even more importantly, however, American crops filled niches that Old World crops could not fill. The potato, for example, grew abundantly in cold, wet climates suitable for few Old World crops, which by and large were domesticated from species that originated in the warmer, dryer Middle East. Maize, on the other hand, came in many varieties suitable to a number of different rainfall and temperature ranges, allowing productive cultivation of previously marginal agricultural areas. The sweet potato, another American import, grew in poor quality soils unsuitable for existing Old World crops. For the most part, these crops did not supplant existing Old World crops, but rather supplemented them, increasing the amount of food available to societies while simultaneously mitigating the threat of famine by increasing the diversity of available foodstuffs.

As a result of the Columbian Exchange, Europe in the 18th century enjoyed a far stronger position relative to the rest of the world than had been the case in the 16th century. Europe's wealth had been vastly increased by infusions of American silver, American tobacco, American grown sugar, and other lucrative trade goods. European merchants could now tap into far larger markets, in part due to domestic population growth, but also due to the expansion of overseas colonial holdings. What is more, though all of the Old World eventually benefitted from the importation of American crops, only Europe was in a position to unlock the vast potential wealth of the Americas by importing proven Old World crops and advanced Old World technology to American soil.

It is important to note, however, that different parts of Europe benefitted to quite different degrees from contacts with the Americas. Italy probably lost ground to the rest of Europe as a result of the Columbian Exchange, since the shift of Europe's economic center of gravity from the Mediterranean to the Atlantic undermined their profitable role as middleman traders with the Moslem Middle East. Central and Eastern Europe, in turn, were only indirectly affected by the "Atlantic Economy" that the Columbian Exchange created. The European nations who benefitted the most were those along the Atlantic coast, with easy access to the new riches of the Americas. Initially, the European states to benefit the most were Spain and Portugal, who carved out the first American colonial empires in the Caribbean and Brazil respectively. Nonetheless, these nations gained only limited long-term advantage, in part because much of the wealth Spain acquired from the Americas was squandered in an unsuccessful attempt to dominate Europe, but also because massive gold and silver imports ruined domestic Spanish and Portuguese craft industries by making imports of goods far cheaper than domestic production.

In the long run, the chief beneficiaries of the Atlantic Economy were these states of Northern Europe, especially the Dutch, French and British. The Dutch became enormously successful as merchants of the new "Atlantic Economy," building up an immensely profitable set of trade routes, and even penetrated the Indian Ocean in the wake of the Portuguese, eventually replacing Portugal as the dominant European trade partner in Asia. However, Holland had too low a population, and was too vulnerable to land invasion, to remain a great power in the long run. Rather, for much of the 18th century, it appeared that France would become Europe's dominant power. Due to its large population, but also due to infusions of wealth from its colonial empire, most notably the sugar producing powerhouse of Saint Dominigue, France dominated the political history of the 18th century. At the same time, French Atlantic ports, such as Bordeaux, Nantes, and Rouen, became bustling cosmopolitan centers. Nonetheless, as French Revolutionary historian Bailey Stone points out, France was

HTTP://COMMONS.WIKIMEDIA.ORG/WIKI/IMAGE:NSR-SLIKA-085.PNG

Diagram of a potato plant from a late 19th century European botanical treatise. The potato was one of several American "supercrops" that lead to a sharp jump in Europe's population after 1500.

weakened by its desire to maintain a large colonial empire overseas while simultaneously fighting for dominance in continental Europe. The resulting strain on the French economy would be one of the primary causes of the French Revolution, which in turn plunged France into over two decades of draining civil and foreign warfare.

Britain, by way of contrast, was a much less populous nation than France, but as an island nation, it was not constantly drawn into costly entanglements on the European continent, and its large war and mercantile fleet meant that England was perfectly positioned to exploit the wealth of the Atlantic Economy. Britain also had another crucial advantage: It was the cradle of the industrial revolution, which in the long run would shape the world even more profoundly than the Columbian Exchange.

European Industrialization

It is beyond the scope of this book to fully explain why Europe, and not some other part of the world, was the first region to adopt industrialization. A number of theories have been posited for this phenomenon, ranging from Europe's political fragmentation to Europe's scientific legacy from the ancient Greeks. Other scholars point to the decline in the intellectual dominance of the Church in post Black Death Europe, which as we will see in chapter 8, may have loosened the mental reigns that had inhibited European science before 1500. Church hegemony over knowledge eroded further as a result of the Protestant Revolution of the 16th century, which effectively fragmented the once-unified West European Church.

Another influential explanation for Europe's industrial revolution lies in Europe's prevailing conception of the relationship between man and the natural world. As pointed out by Lynn White in an influential 1967 article, Europeans inherited the Judeo-Christian belief that God had placed mankind in a position of stewardship over nature, and that natural resources were created for humans to use. Europeans were also influenced by Greek philosophy, which placed man at the center of the universe and argued for a clear distinction between man and nature. The writings of later European thinkers, such as Karl Marx, clearly reflect these ideas; Marx and other economists assumed that mankind could and should fully exploit the world's natural resources in the name of human progress.

This European human-centered and progressive tradition stands in stark contrast to many non–Western schools of thought on the environment. Chinese Taoism calls upon mankind to live in harmony with the natural world, as do the belief systems of most Amerindian cultures. Furthermore, Indian Buddhism, Hinduism, and Jainism all stress that human beings are deeply embedded in the natural world — thus, overexploitation of resources and habitat destruction is an essentially self-obliterating act. This strand of thought, however, was weak in Europe, and the prevailing European ideology of dominance over the natural environment helps to explain why Europe was the first region of the world to adopt the environmentally destructive practices of industrialization.

However, the most convincing explanation for the industrial revolution in Europe was the boost that Europe received from the Atlantic Economy. The industrial revolution depended on four crucial inputs: capital to fund new ventures, plentiful raw materials, a large and cheap work force, and large domestic and overseas markets for finished goods. Thanks to the Atlantic Economy and the Columbian Exchange, which bolstered Europe's trade prosperity, population density, and overseas reach, of these pieces were in place by the beginning of the 18th century.

It is also beyond the scope of this book to fully explain why Great Britain was the first European nation to enter the industrial age. Part of the answer lies in Britain's early adoption of free market capitalism, perhaps in part because the ruling aristocrats of Britain were relatively open to the idea of investing in business ventures, as opposed to their more traditionalist counterparts in continental Europe. Furthermore, Britain benefited enormously from the opening of the Americas to European settlement, both directly (through its North American and Caribbean colonies) and indirectly (by siphoning off the wealth of the Spanish and Portuguese through piracy, smuggling, and trade concessions). Britain's ability to leverage the resources of the Americas to its advantage was, in turn, a consequence of the strength of its fleet. Britain's war fleet achieved naval dominance in Europe after the defeat of the Spanish Armada in 1588 and the decline of the Dutch fleet after 1674, and then total naval supremacy after the defeat of the combined French and Spanish fleets in the battle of Trafalgar in 1805 during French Revolutionary wars. What is more, the relative weakness of English guilds, which elsewhere in Europe actively inhibited entrepreneurship and technological change, also gave Britain a relative economic advantage.

Perhaps most importantly, the rise of British industrial might is intimately linked to changes in British agriculture. During the "Enclosure Movement" of the 18th and 19th centuries, British landlords divided the traditional "commons" or communally-owned land of English villages

HTTP://COMMONS.WIKIMEDIA.ORG/WIKI/IMAGE:HARTMANN_MASCHINENHALLE_1868_%28019629.JPG

A machine works in Saxony, c. 1868.

into small plots of privately-owned lands, increasing the wealth of rich farmers while simultaneously displacing many poor farmers who could no longer rely on the commons to sustain themselves. As a result, the enclosure movement not only created investment capital for industry, it also created a potential pool of low-cost workers.

Perhaps Britain's most crucial advantage in the race towards industrialization, however, was the substantial coal reserve located beneath its soil. The division of labor greatly increased the efficiency of energy used for craft production, but so long as human beings were limited by the energy of wood, wind, water, animal power, or human muscle power, the advantages gained from division of labor were limited. Traditionally, wood was the most important power source exploited by the British, but by 1700, British forests were becoming depleted, in part due to the population boost generated by the Columbian Exchange. As a result, the British were forced to turn to coal for domestic and industrial power, but British mines were becoming increasingly deep in order to keep pace with demand, meaning that ever more human or animal energy was required to work the pumps to keep them from filling with ground water. In 1712, however, Thomas Newcomen solved this conundrum by inventing a steam engine, which was able to convert the stored power of wood or coal to generate mechanical force.

Newcomen's engine represents a crucial breakthrough in human history. In previous ages of man, the amount of energy available was limited by the output of the sun. Wind, wood, animal, and human muscle power all originate, albeit through very different mechanisms, from sunlight striking the earth in the present or recent past. Coal and other fossil fuels, however, are a left-over remnant of ancient sunlight. When Newcomen's engine burnt coal, it was essentially consuming "buried sunlight," energy collected by ancient forest or swamp plants and then stored underground for millions of years. In the long run, the greenhouse gases released while burning these fuels would set the stage for the unprecedented disaster of global warming that we all face today. In the shorter run, however, Europe in general and Britain in particular were able to take advantage of their sudden superiority in available energy to achieve global dominance over the course of the 18th and 19th centuries. Indeed, during this time period, Europeans steadily sought to increase their political and economic control over overseas territories, a phenomenon that historians have termed European imperialism.

European Imperialism Declines in the Americas, Rises in Asia

Ironically, despite its early start down the road of industry, Britain suffered a major short term setback just as the industrial age was beginning to dawn. As discussed above, European states had dominated the Americas ever since the 16th and 17th centuries, largely due to the immunodeficiency of the native Amerindian populations. Over time, however, a powerful "Creole" class of American-born whites came to dominate Europe's American colonies, and these merchants and planters began to resent the political and economic domination of their mother countries. When Britain raised taxes on its colonies in the late 1760s and early 1770s, American Creole resentment boiled over into the American Revolution, leading to the formation of the United States of America.

The War of (North) American independence proved to be only the first act of a much longer drama. In part due to the inspiration of the American example, and in part because of European distraction during and after the wars of the French Revolution, the Spanish Creoles of Central and South America managed to win their independence in a series of wars between 1812 and 1828. Brazil gained its independence more peacefully, as a result of the flight of the Portuguese royal family to Brazil in 1807 during the Napoleonic Wars. The French colony of Haiti, in turn, gained its independence between 1791 and 1804 as a result of the only successful slave rebellion in history. It should be noted that all of the European imperial powers managed to retain control over one or more territories in the Americas, especially in the Caribbean islands, where European control over the sea helped to contain independence movements. Still, these territorial losses represented a major setback that, if not counterbalanced by Europe's growing industrial strength, may have signaled a decline in Europe's power relative to the rest of the world.

With the dawn of the industrial age, however, Europe quickly recovered its strength and embarked on a new imperial adventure, this time directed towards Asia and Africa. The British, thanks to their head start on industrialization, took an early lead. Britain's most important territorial acquisition was India, which Britain progressively subdued through a mixture of war and diplomacy. At the same time or soon after, Britain annexed the neighboring territories (Bengal, Burma, modern-day Pakistan, Malaysia, Singapore, and modern-day Sri Lanka) in order to defend the Indian "jewel" of the British Imperial crown. Fears concerning the security of British India were also a factor in Britain's seizure of Cape Colony on the southern tip of Africa from its Dutch masters, since this territory served as a crucial halfway point for sea voyages between Britain and her Indian possessions. In the meantime, Britain also established colonies in Australia and New Zealand, in part to settle convicted felons who could no longer be dumped along the North American seaboard colonies after the War of American Independence.

Britain's European rivals were slower to adopt an imperialist foreign policy, in part due to the slower pace of industrialization in those countries, but most major European states eventually followed Britain's lead. Portugal tried to make up for the loss of Brazil by expanding into the interior of Africa from its coastal footholds in Angola and East Africa. France attempted to build its own empire in India, but was repulsed by the British in the Seven Years war of 1756–63. As a result, France contented itself with stripping Algeria and other North African territories from the declining Ottoman Empire, which had dominated the Middle East and North Africa in the pre–industrial age. Other European nations gradually annexed the archipelagos north of Australia, with the Dutch taking control over the spice-producing islands of what is now called Indonesia, and Spain dominating the Philippines, which guarded Spain's profitable Pacific Ocean trade route with the Chinese Empire. In the meantime, Russia began to expand steadily into mostly–Muslim central Asia. Anxious to safeguard India, the British responded to the Russian threat with their own alliances, military campaigns, and clandestine dealings, a struggle that scholars have dubbed "the great game." In the end, this game concluded with a stalemate, with Britain dominating Asia south of the Himalayas, Russia dominating north of the Himalayas, and the independent states of Persia and Afghanistan set up as a buffer in between.

Punch cartoon depicting the division of China into European spheres of interest during the 1890s.

As European powers expanded, they increasingly undermined the large Empires that had long dominated the Asian continent. The Mughal Empire of northern India was already in decline before the British arrived, largely due to growing friction between the Muslim-run government and the majority Hindu populace. Indeed, the British conquest of India was greatly facilitated by the power vacuum left behind by the Mughal collapse. The Istanbul-based Ottoman Empire was also in decline, and although it continued to have a strong presence in the Middle East and a weaker presence in Southeast Europe and North Africa, it could do little to stop the European powers from scooping up distant provinces such as Algeria, Kuwait, Egypt, and Morocco. China, long the world's most populous and economically advanced state, entered the 1800s in a position of strength, but two disastrous wars with the technologically superior British from 1840–43 and 1856–60 gravely weakened the ruling Qing dynasty. As we will see in section 6.1, this military defeat contributed to the disastrous failure of China's increasingly under funded flood control measures, further accelerating China's decline. In the end, China was compelled to grant Europeans free access to a number of port towns, all but relegating China to the status of an economic dependency of the European powers. It is likely that only the self-interested objections of the increasingly powerful United States, which wanted to safeguard its own trading interests in China, prevented the European powers from carving up China into outright colonial possessions.

Imperialism Expands

The early wave of post-industrial imperialist conquests largely bypassed Africa, and with good reason: Prior to the 1850s, Europeans had no effective defense against the fevers and other diseases that decimated European armies in tropical climates. In addition, Europeans enjoyed only a limited technological advantage over African states, especially in inland areas out of the range of the guns of European sailing warships. In 1850, European colonies in Asia were restricted to French Algeria, Portuguese East Africa and Angola, a scattering of coastal forts left over from the slave trade, and Cape Colony, which was a British possession but largely populated by "Afrikaners" of Dutch descent. Only in Cape Colony did European control extend much beyond the coast, and only because Cape Colony was an anomaly. As Jared Diamond points out in his seminal work *Guns, Germs, and Steel,* South Africa's temperate climate was not suitable to African agricultural systems, so the Bantu-speaking tribes who occupied most of Central Africa were not able to effectively penetrate south of the Limpopo River. As a result, the Africans that Europeans encountered in this area were mostly scattered bands of hunter-gatherers, as opposed to the dense populations of iron-armed African agriculturalists who ruled north of the Limpopo, and these unfortunate people were soon pushed aside. The temperate climate of South Africa was also relatively free of the tropical diseases that were so deadly in Africa's tropical regions. Consequently, large numbers of Europeans settled in South Africa, and about 4 million of their descendents still reside there today.

After 1850, European technological advances opened up the rest of Africa to European domination. Europeans increasingly began to employ the drug quinine as an anti-malarial agent, and as a result, European armies could now march through Africa without excessive loss to disease. Europe's adoption of the germ theory of disease in around 1875 also opened Africa up to colonization, since it allowed doctors to locate and eliminate the sources of infectious diseases in formerly disease-prone areas. What is more, technological advances— most especially river-going steamships, rifles firing percussion cap bullets, and early forms of the machine gun— increasingly gave Europeans a decisive military advantage over native African forces.

As a result, Europeans began to enter Africa in larger numbers, first as explorers and missionaries, later as conquerors. Indeed, once the first blood of African imperialism was in the water, it lead to a veritable feeding frenzy, as European powers fought to annex as much territory within Africa as possible. During the "scramble for Africa" of 1885–1906, European armies raced into the African continent, establishing military posts at key strategic locations, and crushing the indigenous African states in the process. Indeed, Europeans nearly came to blows with each other over African territory: Competing French and British claims over Sudan almost precipitated a war between those powers in 1898, and France and Germany nearly went to war over Morocco in both 1905 and 1911. These tensions over Africa would contribute to the outbreak of the First World War in 1914. In any case, when the dust had settled, only the United States' African protectorate of Liberia and the ancient African Christian state of Ethiopia managed to remain free of the European yoke.

Another crucial element to the second wave of imperialism, from the mid 1850s onwards, was the entry of the United States and Japan into the imperialist frenzy. Up until the end of the 19th century, the United States expended most of its burgeoning resources on westward expansion. From the 1890s onwards, however, the United States began to expand outwards, seizing effective control of Hawaii in 1893, conquering Spanish Guam, Puerto Rico and the Philippines in 1898, and American Samoa in 1899. Japan, the only major non–Western participant of the Imperial game, entered fairly late, as might be expected given the fact that it only adopted European-style industrialization after the 1860s. Within a few decades, however, Japan rose to the

Scene from the 1884 Conference of Berlin, in which European powers agreed upon the ground rules for imperialism in Africa. Within 15 years of this Conference almost all of Africa would be under the thumb of European colonial powers.

status of a major imperial power, annexing the island of Formosa (now Taiwan) in 1895 and formally annexing Korea in 1912. From 1931 onwards, the Japanese turned their sights on China, leading to a bloody series of drawn-out conflicts that only ended with Japanese defeat in the Second World War.

Motivations for Imperialism

Why did Europeans, Americans, and Japanese spend so much blood and treasure on the acquisition of these Asian and African overseas colonies? National pride played a role; indeed, the era of industrialization and imperialism is also the acute era of European nationalism, and controlling a larger colonial empire than your rivals became a source of pride for many Europeans. Religious motivations played a role as well. Missionary groups facilitated colonization by preaching a gospel of imperialism, in hopes that the expansion of European military control into overseas territory would stifle resistance to the missionary's Christianization campaigns. More broadly, many Europeans and Americans were inspired by the goal of sharing Christianity and civilization — which were widely seen as synonymous terms — with backwards,

unenlightened peoples. Although ridiculed today, Rudyard Kipling's poem "White Man's Burden" captured a pervasive contemporary belief that it was Europe's sacred duty to bring the benefits of Christian civilization to the "half devil and half child" peoples of Africa and Asia.

Perhaps most importantly, industrialism provided not only the means for overseas conquests, it also provided a motive: As industrialization advanced, it required an increasingly large amount of raw materials and ever-larger consumer markets, both of which could be acquired by force through imperial conquest. The issue of raw materials was particular crucial for Japan, which lacked large domestic supplies of coal, metals, petroleum, or other industrial goods. Similarly, steam ships were a powerful tool of empire, but since these ships could not travel more than a couple of weeks before running out of coal, it was necessary for the industrial powers to establish a number of coaling stations around the world, further fueling the European and American impulse to expand. Indeed, Britain, Germany, and the United States nearly went to war in 1899 over the tiny and economically negligible Solomon Islands, since all three powers wanted to expand their network of coaling stations into the South Pacific.

Imperialism, Industrialization, and Social Change

The twin processes of European industrialization and European imperialism had a profound effect on how humans lived their lives worldwide. Because industrialization made labor far more efficient, the aggregate wealth of the human species rose markedly. At the same time, the gap between the rich and poor widened dramatically, both between imperial and colonized nations, and within individual nations. Overall, Europe and English-speaking North America gained the most, but at an enormous social cost. Early industrial workers labored 12 or more hours a day performing monotonous, mind-numbing tasks, and since their work no longer required much skill, the wages they received were barely above the subsistence level. Partially as a result of these low wages, early industrial cities were full of hastily-built, unsanitary, and heavily polluted slums, perfect breeding grounds for infectious disease. One contemporary eyewitness, Friederich Engels, was shocked by the miserable state of the English working class. As he wrote in the 1840s,

> If anyone wishes to see in how little space a human being can move, how little air — and such air — he can breathe, how little of civilization he may share and yet live, it is only necessary to travel [to Manchester, England].... The cottages are old, dirty and of the smallest sort, the streets uneven, fallen into ruts and in part without drains or pavement; masses of refuse, offal and sickening filth lie among standing pools in all directions; the atmosphere is poisoned by the effluvia from these, and laden and darkened by the smoke of a dozen tall factory chimneys.

Inspired by the misery of the industrial workers, Engels would later co-author the *Communist Manifesto* with German radical Karl Marx, and this pamphlet, which called for a revolution of industrial workers against the "bourgeois" oppressors, would prove to be one of the most influential documents of the 19th and 20th centuries. In the short run, however, the chance of a revolution declined as worker's wages began to rise over the course of the 19th century, in part due to the development of craft unions and workers' political parties, and in part due to growing state intervention to improve the well-being of the working class.

Opposite: **Scenes of French colonial possessions in East Asia. Note how the steamship occupies a central place in this picture.**

To these reasons should perhaps be added a third: The wages of European workers were supported in large part by the ruthless European exploitation of colonial Africa and Asia. Despite their "Christian civilization" rhetoric, European powers generally subordinated the interests of the colonial subjects to their own political and economic ends. In India, the British encouraged the cultivation of cotton, which was consumed in vast amounts by British textile factories, then resold to Indians at a huge profit in the form of textiles. In the process, the British destroyed the ancient Indian handicraft industry, which had long produced the world's highest-quality cotton cloth, and threw millions of people into poverty. India was also encouraged to become a food exporting country, mainly in order to lower the price of food to British factory laborers, thus enabling British employers to cut wages. Unfortunately for the Indians, the British insisted on exporting food from India even in times of drought, leading to horrific famines that will be discussed in chapter 7. India was also forced to pay high taxes which were used, not for the betterment of the Indians, but mainly to fund Britain's "great game" of military and diplomatic competition with Tsarist Russia. Largely due to such exploitative such policies, India's share of the world GDP declined by more than half from 1700–1890, while Europe's share nearly doubled over the same period.

Areas that were not directly controlled by Europeans, such as China, were also negatively impacted by Europe during this age of industrialization and imperialism. Britain made huge profits selling opium, an addictive drug, to the Chinese. When China went to war to stop this trade, it suffered humiliating defeat at the hands of the technologically superior British and was forced to pay huge yearly indemnities to the British Empire. As a result, the discredited and cash-starved Chinese government became locked in a downward cycle. As we will see in section 6.1, the financially straightened government lacked the funds to keep the Yellow River under control, and the Yellow River's change of course rendered inoperable China's Grand Canal, cutting a vital economic link between northern and Southern China. The government's decline was further accelerated by its financial inability to respond to the El Niño famines of the late 1870s and late 1890s. Popular cults and regional warlords arose to fill the resulting political vacuum, leading to the eventual collapse of the Imperial government in 1912. Due largely to this lethal blend of political, fiscal, and environmental chaos, China's per capita income actually dropped from 1820 to 1950, and China's share of the world GDP slid from 32.4 percent in 1820 to only 13.2 percent in 1900.

Of course, not everyone suffered in this age of imperialism and industrialization. A new aristocracy of industrial magnates joined, and generally surpassed, the old aristocracy of noble landlords that had long dominated Europe. Indeed the wealthiest families of Europe and North America enjoyed a level of opulence never before seen in world history. They were joined in both Europe and the United States by a new, numerous, and economically comfortable middle class of managers and professionals. European and American workers' wages rose steadily, if unevenly, over time. What is more, many traditional elite groups of the non-western world managed to retain their wealth in the age of imperialism, usually by collaborating with European authorities. However, since these gains came to some degree at the expense of the colonized Asians and Africans, world economic inequality widened dramatically. Historian Mike Davis goes so far as to claim that European imperialism and industrialization in the 1800s is chiefly responsible for the fracture of the world into Western "haves" and non–Western "have nots," a situation that remains true to the present day. As we will see repeatedly throughout this book, the relative impoverishment of the formerly colonized "third world" helps to make these countries particularly susceptible to natural disasters.

A second and perhaps equally disastrous legacy of the imperial and industrial era in the third world is the environmental degradation it left behind. Blinded by their belief in "progress,"

Europeans of this age prioritized extraction of resources and gave little thought to the long-term environmental consequences of their policies. As we shall see in section 4.2, for example, European colonial administrators in the Sahel region of Africa disregarded the traditional knowledge of the local African peoples and instituted intensive cash crop agriculture. This served their short term economic interests, but in the long run the deforestation and excessive animal grazing that this policy encouraged desertification, contributing enormously to West Africa's current levels of poverty. Worse yet, the rampant burning of fossil fuels during the age of industrialization raised CO_2 levels in the atmosphere worldwide, and as discussed in section 4.3, these emissions play a crucial role in the modern-day phenomenon of global warming.

The World Wars

By 1900, Europe all but dominated the planet, but Europe soon squandered this advantage in a series of fratricidal wars. In 1914, the assassination of Austrian Archduke Franz Ferdinand caused existing intra–European rivalries to boil over, and thanks to the industrial advances of the previous century, the resulting war produced unprecedented casualties. All told, 10 million Europeans were killed by artillery shells, suffocated by poison gas, cut down by machine guns, crushed by tanks, bombed from zeppelins or airplanes, or overcome by diseases in crowded and unsanitary military encampments. Worse yet, the defensive advantages provided by these new technologies ensured that the war would drag on a full 4 years, throwing Europe deep into debt. The war was unprecedented in another way as well: Though Europe had long meddled in Amer-

A Vickers Machine Gun crew equipped with gas masks. As a result of technological advances like poison gas and machine guns, the casualty figures of the First World War surpassed those of all previous wars.

ica, this war represented the first large-scale American intervention in European affairs. Indeed, the entry of the United States into the war on the side of France and Britain proved to be a vital tipping point of the conflict, contributing substantially to Germany's defeat.

In the short run, the First World War lead to the expansion of European imperialism on an even larger scale, as the victorious French and British carved up the Middle Eastern territory of the defeated Ottoman Empire between them. In the long run, however, the financial and manpower drain of the war greatly weakened Europe's hold on its far-flung imperial possessions. Worse yet, since the post–World War I settlement embittered Germany and did not satisfy the ambitions of either Italy or Japan, it proved only to be the prelude for an even more destructive war from 1939–1945. Once again, the United States entered the war on the side of France and Britain, and Germany and its allies were eventually defeated. Indeed, Germany suffered terribly from the war: Most of its cities were carpet bombed into near oblivion and the post-war settlement stripped it of territory and divided it in two. However, even the victors in Europe were crippled by this war. Britain had been heavily bombed and was deeply in debt, and France had been overrun and looted by Germany.

The destruction caused by the two World Wars, especially in Europe, would leave a lasting mark on world history. First of all, Europe's manpower and property losses lead to the progressive unraveling of the European colonial empires, since Europeans no longer had the resources or the will to maintain control over their vast and increasingly restless territories. What is more, Europe's weakness allowed two formerly peripheral powers to dominate world affairs: the United States and the Soviet Union. The conflict between these two states, and their diametrically opposed ideological systems, would dominate the next half century of world history.

The Cold War

The roots of the Cold War go as far back as 1917, when the Communist Party of Russia staged revolution and seized control of the state. The Russian revolution came as quite a surprise to most contemporaries, even those of the Marxist persuasion, since Russia's weak industrial sector seemed to make her an unlikely candidate for a working class revolution. The Russian Communists, however, benefited enormously both from disaffection with the army, which was in a mutinous state thanks to the relentless German advance, and from the strong leadership of Vladimir Lenin. Once in power the Bolsheviks, as the followers of Lenin are often called, proceeded to transform the country along Marxist lines, collectivizing agriculture and assuming state oversight of the industrial sector. The former project was an economic failure — it actually caused crop yields to drop by eliminating worker incentives — but a political success, as it all but eliminated peasant resistance to the Bolshevik regime. Indeed, as we shall see in chapter 7, Stalin deliberately employed man-made famine as a weapon to cow his own people into submission. In any case, Soviet plans to stimulate the industrial economy were more successful, at least in the strategically important heavy industry sector. Indeed, the Soviet Union's industrial output actually exceeded that of the heavily industrialized Germans during the Second World War, contributing heavily to Germany's defeat.

As a result of Soviet victory against the Germans in the Second World War, the Soviet

Opposite: **Although this poster was designed to promote war bonds, it indirectly expresses the fate of Europe during the First and Second world wars: Europe transformed its "silver into bullets," squandering enormous resources on bloody and destructive internal conflicts.**

COURTESY NATIONAL NUCLEAR SECURITY ADMINISTRATION/NEVADA SITE OFFICE

Nuclear bomb test at Bikini Atoll, 1946.

Union became a dominant player on the world stage. During the war the Soviets gained physical possession of nearly all of Eastern Europe and quickly transformed these territories into Communist states tied by treaty to the Soviet Union. Even a portion of Germany fell to Soviet control, becoming the Communist state of East Germany. However, Soviet influence was by no means limited to Europe. In 1949, the Soviet Union's strategic situation was vastly improved by the Chinese Communist Party's successful seizure of power in mainland China, meaning that the world's most populous state had apparently joined the Communist camp. What is more, the anti-capitalist, anti-imperialist message of the Soviet Union resonated strongly with the populace of the European colonial empires, as it promised a more equitable distribution of resources and an end to European oppression. Indeed, many colonial independence movements, such as the Vietnamese Viet Kong, ascribed to some form of Marxist political ideology.

These world developments deeply disturbed the United States, which as the world's most industrialized and most capitalist state felt vitally threatened by rapid global spread of Communist ideas. As a result, the United States adopted an activist foreign policy directed towards preventing the further spread of Communism in Europe, Asia, and elsewhere. Both the United States and the Soviet Union built up vast forces in Europe, though the existence of newly-developed nuclear weapons in both countries' arsenals made it unlikely that either would risk direct military conflict with the other. In addition, each superpower intermittently sent troops to support its allies or crush its ideological opponents, such as the Soviet use of force to crush a pro-democratic movement in Czechoslovakia in 1968 and the U.S. struggle to prop up the unpopular, pro–Western South Vietnamese government against communist North Vietnam and their insurgent allies in the South, the Vietcong.

For the most part, however, the two superpowers engaged each other indirectly by seeking allies in the Americas and in newly-independent Africa and Asia. In this new version of the "great game," each power attempted to support sympathetic governments—in other words, governments that claimed to be following the same socio-political ideology—while undermining governments adhering to the other ideology. As a result, the speed or scope of U.S. or Soviet relief efforts towards third world nations in times of disaster was often determined by ideological rather than humanitarian factors. Another negative side effect of this Cold War struggle was rise of dictatorships in much of the third world, either because of the seizure of power by Marxist parties following the Bolshevik tradition of authoritarian government, or because of American support for military strongmen who claimed to be bulwarks against communism. Indeed, U.S. allies during the cold war included the bloody Chilean dictator Augusto Pinochet and the repressive Shah of Iran, who was saved from a possible coup by U.S. spies in 1953 but was later overthrown by a coalition of Marxist and Islamist rebels in 1979. Even today, repressive regimes installed during the Cold War continue to rule countries worldwide. As we shall see in chapter 7, this is especially unfortunate from the perspective of famine, since autocratic regimes are less accountable to their subjects and more likely to adopt impractical, ideologically-driven economic policies.

Contemporary Developments

The Cold War ended rather abruptly, in 1989, when Soviet Premier Mikhail Gorbachev announced that the Soviet Union would no longer use military force to guarantee the existence of the Soviet satellite states in Eastern Europe. To a certain degree, this policy reflected Gorbachev's personal preference for a more open system of government. It also reflected the Soviet Union's increasing economic frailty, due to the inefficiencies inherent in communist economic systems, forcing the Soviet Union to scale back its expensive military program. Whatever Gorbachev's motives, this policy rapidly lead to the disintegration of Communist control over Eastern Europe, as one country after another adopted democracy in what is now called the "Velvet Revolution." This revolutionary spirit soon spread to the Soviet Union itself, which in 1991 splintered into its component national states, including a shrunken Russian Republic. It could be argued that the 1991 revolution changed relatively little in a political sense, since in recent years Russia and its former Soviet provinces have increasingly become authoritarian states ruled by communist–Era strongmen, and Russian influence remains strong in the region. However, in a geopolitical sense, the change has been dramatic: The abrupt collapse of Soviet military power signaled a shift from a bipolar to unipolar world, with the United States reigning as the sole superpower.

The dominion of the United States has not gone unchallenged, however. The end of the Cold War has opened the way for the incorporation of Europe into a single political entity, and if the dream of the "European Union" is fully realized, it might pose a significant economic if not political threat to U.S. world hegemony. China is a rising power as well, thanks largely to its enormous population and its abandonment of the Marxist economic model in favor of free-market capitalism. Perhaps most importantly, the September 2001 attacks on the World Trade Center and the Pentagon have focused attention on the threat posed by terrorist groups. The

PHOTOGRAPH BY DEREK JENSEN (TYSTO), 2004 SEPTEMBER 11

Photograph of the 2004 Memorial for the 2001 World Trade Center attacks. The columns of light mark where the Twin Towers once stood before the September 11th terrorist attacks.

most notable such group is Al-Qaeda, a radical Islamic organization directed to weakening the United States and Europe, largely because Al-Qaeda accuses these powers of exerting a negative cultural and political influence over the Islamic world. To combat Al-Qaeda and other terrorist organizations, the U.S. government and its allies launched a "war on terror," leading to the overthrow of the Al-Qaeda tied Taliban government in Afghanistan in October 2001 and, more controversially, the invasion and occupation of Iraq in March of 2003. However, as of the middle of 2008, these costly military actions had done little to curb the phenomenon of global terrorism.

In the meantime, a consensus seems to be forming that global warming, not global terrorism, ought to be the world's foremost concern. There is no doubt that terrorism poses a significant threat, but terrorism must be examined within the wider perspective of threats to mankind, and even the horrors of the September 11th terrorist attack seem tame compared with the crop failures, higher sea levels, and species extinctions that may be triggered by rising levels of atmospheric greenhouse gases. What is more, global warming has been projected to worsen already-occurring natural catastrophes, such as cyclones, floods, droughts, and tropical diseases. Furthermore, although terrorist actions tend to affect only a small area, global warming threatens the entire world community. Finally, while terrorism seems to defy solution, global warming is caused by a specific set of economic activities that human beings have the ability, though not necessarily the willingness, to change. Whether or not human beings will make the required sacrifices before global warming causes irreversible damage is still an open question. Hopefully, this book will give readers the necessary historical and scientific knowledge they need to make informed decisions about how to address global warming and other problems raised by mankind's often disastrous interaction with the natural environment.

Study Questions

1. According to this chapter, why was Europe the first region of the world to enter the industrial age?

2. "Europe's rise to a position of global domination after 1500 was primarily the result of good luck and good timing." To what degree do you agree with this statement? Base your argument on evidence from the text.

3. Based on this chapter, what role did European ideological beliefs play in European dominance of the world, 1815–1945?

4. "In simple terms, the 19th century was characterized mainly by European imperialism, the 20th for struggles over ideology, and the 21st for struggles vs. the natural environment." To what degree do you agree with this statement? Base your argument on evidence from the text.

Suggested Readings

Crosby, Alfred W. *Children of the Sun: A History of Humanity's Unappeasable Appetite for Energy.* New York: W. W. Norton, 2006.

Crosby, Alfred W. *The Columbian Exchange: Biological and Cultural Consequences of 1492.* Westport, CT: Praeger Publishers, 2003, originally published 1972.

Davis, Mike. *Late Victorian Holocausts: El Nino Famines and the Making of the Third World.* New York: Verso, 2001.

Diamond, Jared. *Guns, Germs, and Steel: The Fates of Human Societies.* New York: W. W. Norton, 1997.

Engels, Friedrich. *The Condition of the Working Class in England.* 1845. Reprint, New York: Oxford University Press, 1993.

Kipling, Rudyard. "White Man's Burden." (1899).

McNeill, William. *The Rise of the West: A History of the Human Community.* Chicago: University of Chicago Press, 1963.

McNeill, J. R. *Something New Under the Sun: An Environmental History of the Twentieth-Century World.* New York: W. W. Norton and Company, 2000.

Roberts, J. M. *A Short History of the World.* New York: Oxford University Press, 1993.

Stone, Bailey. *The Genesis of the French Revolution: A Global Historical Interpretation.* New York: Cambridge University Press, 1994.

White, Lynn Jr. "The Historical Roots of Our Ecologic Crisis." *Science*, Vol. 155, No. 3767 (March 10, 1967), pp. 1203–1207.

CHAPTER 2

Volcanoes

Science and History

Loud, showy, and dramatic, volcanic eruptions are among the most spectacular of natural disasters, and because of their theatrical nature, they have acquired the largely undeserved reputation of being amongst the most dangerous calamities to threaten mankind. In fact, only about a quarter of a million people have been killed directly by volcanic eruptions in the past 400 years, a figure that pales in comparison with the millions of lives reaped by disease, floods, and famines. Nonetheless, volcanoes have exerted an enormous indirect influence on human history. Volcanic eruptions can smother whole cities, but since the soil laid down during eruptions is often highly fertile, it can support large populations that unknowingly live and work on the same soil that shrouds the buried dead. Volcanoes are also intricately tied with nearly every other type of major environmental disaster. The same volcanic materials that lead to bumper crops on the ground, for instance, can cause global cooling if they penetrate the troposphere, perhaps triggering famine and disease.

Thankfully, due to scientific and technical advances, it is now possible to map out areas imperiled by volcanic eruptions and even to predict when a major eruption is likely to occur. Despite this knowledge, human beings are probably more vulnerable now to volcanic eruptions than ever before in history. In developing countries, population pressure is forcing more and more people to live and work on volcano slopes, while in wealthier countries, the mania for real estate with a scenic view is having roughly the same effect. Unfortunately, even the best early warning systems cannot completely safeguard the lives of those who live in the shadow of a volcano.

The Science of Volcanism

Volcano Origins

Volcanoes get their name from the Roman god Vulcan, a master blacksmith whose fiery underground labors reputedly caused mountains to erupt. During the European Renaissance, European scholars developed a more sophisticated understanding of volcanoes, realizing that they resulted from the eruption of molten underground materials due to pressure from below, though no one could adequately explain the underlying mechanism that produced the pressure. It took until the 1970s for scientists to develop a complete understanding of how and why volcanoes form. Before the 1970s, the prevailing scientific opinion imagined the surface of the world as stable and unchanging. During the 1960s and 1970s, however, this conception of the earth gave way to the new theory of plate tectonics, which holds that the surface of the earth consists of a number of rocky plates that rub, jostle, and collide with each other as they float on the earth's semi-liquid interior. The interaction of these plates, scientists came to realize, is the key to understanding volcanoes.

Tectonic plates interact with each other in three main ways, and two of these ways tend to produce volcanoes. When two plates grind alongside each other, their interaction creates a "transform" or "strike-slip" fault, such as the famous San Andreas Fault. In such faults, however, friction between the plates offers little opportunity for molten rock or "magma" to rise to the surface, inhibiting the growth of volcanoes. Volcanoes are much more likely to arise from so-called "normal" faults, in which two plates are moving apart from each other. Since this motion creates a gap in the earth's crust, magma tends to well up from below, and this process leads to the formation of approximately 85 percent of the world's volcanoes. Although very common, these volcanoes are rarely seen, since "normal" faults generally occur deep under the ocean, where they create vast volcanic mountain chains such as the Mid-Atlantic ridge. Only in a few places, most notably Iceland and the Rift Valley of Africa, have "normal" faults created volcanoes that sit atop dry land. Volcanoes created by normal faults are generally characterized by heavy flows of lava — the name that magma is given once it breaches the earth's surface — but relatively few explosive eruptions, for reasons that will be discussed below.

The third type of fault, "thrust" faults, produce relatively fewer volcanoes than "normal" faults. Unfortunately, however, the volcanoes they produce are by far the most dangerous and by far the most likely to impact mankind. In a thrust fault, two tectonic plates collide into each other, and the outcome of this collision depends on the type of plates involved. If both are "continental" plates, and thus are composed of rock of equivalent density, the two plates will crumple together to form a mountain range, such as the Himalaya range that marks the collision of the Indian and Asian plate. Faults of this type produce frequent earthquakes—for example, the Pakistani Earthquake of 2005 discussed in section 3.3 — but no volcanoes, as they provide no avenue for molten rock to reach the surface.

If an ocean plate meets a continental plate, however, a process called "subduction" generally takes place. The heavier rock of the ocean plate will be forced to dive below the continental plate, carrying water with it in the process. As the ocean plate descends below the earth's crust into the semi-molten layer below, called the mantle, part of the ocean plate melts and forms blobs of magma. Since these blobs are lighter than the mantle itself, in part because of the water and gas dragged down with the diving ocean plate, they tend to rise through the mantle like bubbles in soda water, eventually forming pools called magma chambers beneath the continental plate. About 90 percent of this magma eventually cools and remains below ground. The remaining 10 percent of the magma, however, will be propelled through fractures in the crust by pressure from below, and a volcano will form where it reaches the earth's surface. Indeed, many of the world's most impressive mountain ranges, such as the Andes in South America and the Cascades in North America, were created by subduction and resulting volcanic activity. Subduction also tends to produce the world's most explosive eruptions, since the magma expelled is rich in water and gas, causing it to burst like champagne from a well-shaken bottle when it reaches the earth's surface.

Although the majority of volcanoes occur at the junction of tectonic plates, volcanoes can also form in the middle of a plate as a result of a "hot spot" or "mantle plume." For reasons that are still poorly understood, a few areas in the mantle are particularly hot, and magma rising up from the mantle is able to melt its way through the crust and reach the earth's surface, forming volcanoes. The Hawaiian island chain, for example, was created over the course of millions of years as the Pacific plate passed slowly over a hot spot in the mantle, creating a string of volcanic islands in the process. Indeed, the next island in the chain, an underwater seamount called Loihi, is already rising towards the surface about 28 kilometers southeast of Hawaii's Big Island. Since the volcanic material ejected in Hawaii consists of relatively pure molten rock unadulterated by water or gasses, Hawaiian eruptions are rarely explosive. Rather, they generally take the form of slowly flowing flows of lava that pose little direct danger to mankind. Unfortunately, Hawaii's relatively docile and highly photogenic volcanoes have misled the public about the true danger that volcanism poses to mankind.

Just as volcanoes can result from a number of different geological processes, so too can they take a number of different physical forms. Technically, any aperture in the earth that produces volcanic material is a volcano, even if it consists of a simple gas-emitting vent. If the vent discharges large amounts of small rocks, a cinder cone might develop. These modest volcanoes, which resemble nothing so much as large anthills, are quite unstable, since large volcanic eruptions can easily scatter the loose rock that forms their structure. On the other end of the spectrum are shield volcanoes, shallow domes built out of layer upon layer of hardened lava. Although not steep, shield volcanoes can be staggeringly large in size. Hawaii's Mauna Loa Volcano measures 48 kilometers long, 96 kilometers wide, and 4 kilometers high, but that is just the tip of the iceberg: Mauna Loa's base is almost 13 kilometers below sea level, and indeed Mauna Loa's tremendous weight has produced a 8 kilometer deep depression on the floor of the Pacific Ocean. By way of contrast, Mount Everest only rises less than 9 kilometers above sea level.

The best known type of volcano, however, is the "composite volcano" or "stratovolcano." These shapely cones consist of alternate layers of cinders and lava flows, so the resulting volcano is characterized both by the steepness of a cinder cone and the solidity of a lava shield. Many of the best known volcanoes in the world, such as Mt. Fuji in Japan and Mt. Vesuvius in Italy, are stratovolcanoes. Stratovolcanoes are also amongst the most dangerous volcanoes, since compared with shield volcanoes, they tend to erupt less frequently but far more explosively.

Volcano Hazards

Although many people associate volcanoes mainly with lava flows, lava is the least of your problems if you find yourself near an erupting volcano. Even the fastest lava flows move more slowly than walking speed, so lava poses a threat mainly to property, not people. Far deadlier, though less well known, is the pyroclastic flow or "nuée ardente," a French term meaning "glowing cloud." Pyroclastic flows are ground-hugging, fast-moving clouds of vaporized magma and shattered rock. This type of volcanic event, which only came to the attention of science following the 1902 eruption of Mount Pelée, occurs when magma containing high concentrations of gas and water is released explosively from a volcano, shattering the magma and surrounding rock into small, hot fragments. Unlike ash, which is relatively light, pyroclastic flows tend to stay close to the ground the ground, traveling at up to 500 kilometers an hour, far faster than the winds of the strongest hurricanes. Worse yet, pyroclastic flows are blisteringly hot, reaching temperatures of up to 700 degrees Celsius. As a result, any building that stands in the way of a pyroclastic flow is likely to be simultaneously toppled and lit aflame, while nearly all people caught by the blast will be roasted alive, even if they have sought shelter in basements or fortified structures. Those caught on the edges of pyroclastic flows generally do not perish instantly, but often die of suffocation hours later due to severe burns to the throat and lungs. Thankfully, although pyroclastic flows can travel five or more kilometers, they generally only affect those living on or in the shadow of an erupting volcano.

Volcanoes can also kill through tremendous landslides, triggered when loose material on the side of a volcano is dislodged by a small earthquake, movement of magma, heavy rainfall, or a volcanic eruption. The scale of these landslides can be truly awe inspiring. When Mount Saint Helens erupted in 1983, the resulting landslide measured 2.5 cubic kilometers in volume, traveled 50–80 meters per second, and was powerful enough to force its way up a 400 meter tall ridge 5 kilometers away from the volcano. Volcanic landslides can be especially deadly if they strike a body of water, since the impact generally produces enormous waves, called tsunamis. The most notable such event in history occurred in 1792 when a huge landslide on Japan's Mt. Mayuyama struck the Ariaka Sea, generating a tsunami that killed 15,000 people on the coast of Japan's Kyushu Island. As we shall see in section 2.1, the eruption of Krakatoa triggered an even more deadly tsunami, though in this case it is unclear whether a landslide, eruption blast, or pyroclastic flow is to blame for the giant wave.

Similar to a landslide, but much more wide-ranging in effect, is the lahar, an Indonesian term describing a deadly mixture of water and volcanic rock. A lahar occurs when loose volcanic materials, ranging in size from miniscule particles of ash to enormous boulders, become waterlogged and slide downhill, generally following the contours of the land. Unfortunately for those living near a volcano, the water needed for the lahar can come from a number of different sources. Volcanoes themselves can spew out significant quantities of water, either because the magma itself contains large amounts of dissolved H_2O, or because underground water superheated by the magma boils up to the surface like steam escaping from a kettle. In other cases, the water comes from mountaintop lakes—a common occurrence, since volcanoes are often topped by bowl-like "calderas" left over from previous eruptions—or from glacial ice melted by magma. Other lahars are fueled by heavy rains, raising the frightening possibility that a lahar can be triggered days, months, or even many years after a volcanic eruption.

However they are formed, lahars pose a potentially devastating threat to communities downhill from the volcano. Depending on their composition, lahars can resemble anything from muddy water to boulder-choked avalanches, and they can travel tens of meters per second, fast enough to catch even a swift runner. When they strike a community, lahars will sweep poorly-built houses off their foundations, pummel well-built houses with boulders and tree trunks, and eventually bury everything under a blanket of mud that might be 60 or more meters in depth. The threat posed by a lahar is compounded by their tendency to choke on their own debris. A lahar can become so thick with sediment and other materials that it can actually dam itself up temporarily, leading to horrific flood crests minutes, hours, or even many days later when the dam collapses from backside pressure. Worse yet, lahars can actually gain in strength as they travel downhill, since they tend to pick up additional material through erosion and may eventually reach 10 times their original size. As a result, lahars have been observed to travel 100 kilometers from their source.

The lethal potential of lahars is best demonstrated by the Nevado Del Ruiz eruption in Colombia, which was actually relatively small as eruptions go, yet proved to be the second most deadly volcanic event of the 20th century. Although Ruiz is only 500 km from the equator, it is high enough to boast a permanent cap of snow and ice. When a mild eruption melted about 10 percent of this ice cap in 1985, the resulting water generated a large lahar. Three hours later and 48 kilometers away, when the lahar reached the town of Armero, it had ballooned enormously in size and swamped the town under 2 to 5 meters of sediment. Since the town received virtually no warning, largely due to lack of communications infrastructure and ineptitude of the local government, more than 23,000 people were killed, fully three quarters of the town's population. Not only that, Ruiz ultimately cost Colombia approximately $7.7 billion in damages and rebuilding costs, a sum that equals a full fifth of the country's Gross National Product.

Although pyroclastic flows, landslides, and lahars are the most deadly weapons in a volcano's arsenal, volcanoes can wreck human lives and property through other means as well. During eruptions, volcanoes launch volcanic rock called "tephra" high in the air, in sizes that range from tiny dust-like particles to truck-sized "lava bombs." Although physically more impressive, the larger chunks actually pose less of a threat to human life, since they tend to fall to earth close to the summit of the volcano. Volcanic dust and ash, however, can be carried by the wind over many kilometers, and when it settles, its weight can collapse building roofs and kill people who have sought shelter within. As we will see in section 2.3, roof collapses are particularly likely when ash mixes with rain, forming a paste with the consistency and weight of wet cement. Volcanic ash can also wreck the engines of jet airplanes that fly too closely to an erupting volcano, and although no planes have yet crashed due to ash, it is probably just a matter of time.

Volcanoes also emit large amounts of poisonous gasses, such as hydrogen dioxide and sulfur dioxide. Both can kill at ground level, but sulfur dioxide also poses a serious threat if it enters the upper layer of the atmosphere, where it reflects sunlight back into space and can lead to global cooling. Indeed, the colossal eruption of the Indonesian volcano Mount Tambora in 1815 released so much sulfur dioxide into the atmosphere that it caused Northern Hemisphere temperatures to dip as much as 10°C below normal in 1816, sparking famines and associated diseases worldwide. Closer to the ground, sulfur from Tambora poisoned the soil and water, causing deadly outbreaks of diarrhea for years after the eruption. Volcanoes can also kill by releasing large amounts of CO_2, a heavy gas that tends to hug the earth and collect in depressions near eruptions. In one of the more bizarre incidents recorded in the annals of vulcanology, Lake Nyos in Cameroon "erupted" in August of 1986, releasing a deadly cloud of CO_2. Scientists later determined the cause: Lake Nyos lies over an active volcanic vent, and interaction between magma and groundwater essentially "carbonized" the deep water of the lake, infusing it with CO_2. It is not entirely clear why the CO_2–rich deep water of the lake suddenly bubbled through the lighter layer of surface water in 1986, but the results are indisputable — 1,700 people in nearby river valleys were suffocated in a matter of hours by the odorless, colorless gas.

Even if a given volcanic event does not kill directly, volcanoes can lead to disastrous changes to the environment. Although volcanic materials can increase the fertility of soil, especially once they have been weathered by time, in the short run lahars, ash falls, landslides, and pyroclastic flows can bury huge tracts of productive soil under meters of sludge and rubble. Volcanic tephra that consists mainly of pumice, a common volcanic stone, poses a particular problem. Since pumice is so light that it actually floats on rather than mixes with water, soil containing large amounts of pumice is nearly useless for farming. Worse yet are lava flows, which can blanket soil with many meters of solid rock and take a very long time to weather away into cultivatable soil. Worse yet, it can take many decades for all the volcanic materials emitted by an eruption to stabilize, and until then, communities downstream of volcanoes suffer under the constant threat of sudden lahars following any earthquake or rainstorm. What is more, volcanoes tend to kill most of the nearby vegetation, which in turn reduces local rainfall and can contribute to desertification. Thankfully, nature does eventually recover from volcanic eruptions, and even solid lava flows will eventually be weathered into fertile soil — until the next eruption, of course.

Volcanoes in History

Unlike such disasters as famines, floods, and cyclones, which occur almost every year in some part of the world, volcanic eruptions have appeared less frequently in the historical record.

When they do occur, however, they tend to command considerable attention, a fact that reflects their cinematic effects as much as their rarity. One of the most consequential volcanoes in human history, however, is probably the least well known. As we shall see in more detail in chapter 4, the eruption of the Indonesian Mount Toba at about 72,000 B.C. emitted so much ash into the atmosphere that it probably caused global temperatures to dip by over 10°C for several years. In the process, it may have played a role in killing off all but about 10,000 of the human beings that were alive at that time, and very nearly drove the human race to extinction. Incidentally, scientists have developed a curiously unscientific term for eruptions on this scale: "humongous." Somewhat less powerful eruptions on Mount Tambora's scale, by way of contrast, are described by scientists as merely "colossal."

Much later, during Europe's Bronze Age, another "colossal" volcanic eruption once again left a tremendous mark on human history. At the time, the most advanced culture in Europe was Minoan civilization, which was based on the modern-day island of Crete. Sometime during the 17th century B.C., however, the nearby volcanic island of Thera exploded spectacularly, drowning Crete under hot ash and submerging its coastline under a tsunami that may have topped 9 feet in height. Either because of the hot ash, or because of oil lamps overturned by Thera's shock wave, nearly every Minoan palace burned to the ground, effectively beheading the Minoan government. What is more, the ash fall likely ruined the crop in the field and poisoned the soil with acid, reducing yields for years to come. As a result, Minoan civilization fell, and Minoan people scattered widely, especially to nearby Greece. Other bands of displaced Minoans fled to Tunisia, Egypt, or even Palestine, where they became the "Philistines" of the Bible.

Above and beyond its direct impact in terms of lives and property, the eruption of Thera exerted a tremendous influence on the culture of surrounding civilizations. The legend of the drowned city of Atlantis was probably inspired by the fall of Minoan civilization, and scholars have linked other myths, such as the legend of Noah's flood and the story of Jason and the Argonauts, to Thera's inspiration. What is more, some biblical scholars speculate that disastrous events described in the Hebrew book of Exodus may have been triggered by Thera's eruption, arguing that Thera's emissions could easily have altered the local climate and thus created both famine and floods. More concretely, Minoan refugees to Greece helped to enrich the local culture and thus helped to create classical Hellenic civilization, which in turn has greatly influenced the culture of the modern West.

Better known, but less consequential to human historical development, was the eruption of Mount Vesuvius in 79 A.D. Vesuvius buried two cities, Herculaneum and Pompeii, under a thick layer of ash, killing at least 2,000 in the process. Archeologists used to believe that Vesuvius' victims were smothered by the ash itself, but we now know that Vesuvius killed mainly through six successive pyroclastic flows, which eventually deposited 8 cubic kilometers of volcanic material over an area of 300 square kilometers surrounding the volcano. Unlike Thera, Vesuvius did not precipitate the fall of Roman civilization, which survived for hundreds of years after. Indeed, Vesuvius actually helped to preserve the Roman Empire, in a sense, by blanketing two of its cities under a preserving layer of ash. This heavy ash preserved invaluable examples of Roman mosaic and fresco art, as well as numerous artifacts of daily Roman life. Although the ash did not preserve the people themselves, it did the next best thing: As the bodies of Vesuvius' victims rotted away, they left hollow spaces within the ash, which subsequent archeologists have filled with plaster of Paris, creating perfect molds of what Vesuvius' victims were doing at the time of the catastrophe.

Vesuvius' eruption was typical of most eruptions of the next two millennia: Although dramatic, they generally had only a local impact, and did little to shift the direction of history.

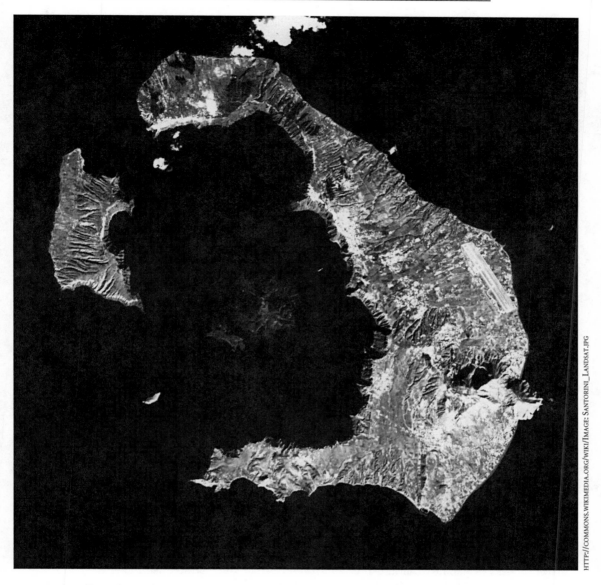

NASA satellite photograph of Santorini Island in Greece, clearly depicting the collapsed caldera of Mount Thera, which exploded catastrophically during the 17th century B.C. Thera's eruption is widely credited with precipitating the collapse of Minoan civilization.

Only a few volcanoes during this period have exerted more than a regional effect. The eruption of the Icelandic volcano of Laki in 1783 created a blue, sulfurous haze that wafted over most of Europe, leading first to an abnormally hot summer and then a series of frigidly cold winters. As a result, much of Europe was plunged into famine or near-famine for several years, creating popular misery that some scholars speculate may have helped to trigger the French revolution. It is important to take such claims with a grain of salt: After all, the French Revolution has also been linked to El Niño and even to ergot, a hallucinogenic fungus related to LSD that occasionally grows on cereal crops.

Since 1783, several other volcanoes have been identified as exerting more than a regional

Pompeii from the Southwest by German artist Friedrich Federer, 1850.

impact on climate. The Mount Tambora eruption, mentioned above, caused average temperatures to drop by as much as 10 degrees Celsius between 1816–1817, triggering famines throughout Europe, which was already reeling from the damage caused by the Napoleonic wars. Tambora's chill has also been implicated in causing floods in China and famine in India, not to mention an associated epidemic of cholera that subsequently spread to port cities worldwide. Japan suffered from bitterly cold temperatures, failure of the rice crop, and resultant famine. Tambora's touch even reached as far as New England in the United States, where 1816 was long remembered as the "year without a summer." Snow penetrated as far south as Saratoga, New York and Concord, New Hampshire in June of 1816, impoverishing many New England farmers and accelerating the ongoing migration from the "hardscrabble" farms of the Northeast to the Midwestern frontier. Pinatubo's 1991 eruption has also been implicated in causing global weather changes, as discussed in section 2.3.

Volcanoes and Other Disasters

As we have already seen repeatedly throughout this chapter, volcanoes can play a significant role in triggering other types of natural disaster. Volcanoes are most closely associated with earthquakes, and for good reason: As magma moves from underground chambers to the surface, it causes the surrounding rock to vibrate, producing characteristic long-duration, low intensity quakes. These quakes are rarely powerful enough to cause much damage, and indeed they sometimes do more good than harm, since they can alert people living near a volcano that it is awakening from its slumber. At the same time, earthquakes caused by the movement of magma can trigger catastrophic eruptions by shifting rock on the surface of the volcano, creating an opening for magma to burst into the atmosphere. Volcanoes can also be triggered by earthquakes unrelated to volcanic activity, such as those caused by plate tectonics. Since most volcanoes are located near the edges of tectonic plates, this is not an uncommon occurrence.

Volcanoes also play a significant role in triggering disastrous floods. The landslides and earthquakes associated with volcanoes can trigger tsunami waves ranging from a few meters to over a hundred meters in height. Because of their high velocity, pyroclastic flows that strike water often have the same effect. What is more, the volcanic material left behind by an eruption often triggers deadly lahars when mixed with water, and this threat can linger long after the actual eruption, until the volcanic tephra has either been stabilized by plant growth or else fully washed down into surrounding bottomlands. Volcanoes can also cause floods by heating water and driving it under pressure to the surface. Indeed, the well-known water eruptions of "Old Faithful," the star attraction of Yellowstone national park, are testimony to the presence of magma beneath northwestern Wyoming in the United States.

Although not commonly associated with volcanoes, famine often makes an appearance in the aftermath of a volcanic eruption, for a number of reasons. Croplands close to a volcanic eruption can be ruined by lava flows, ash falls, pyroclastic flows, and lahars, leading to food shortages and starvation. At medium range, sulfur emitted by volcanoes can mix with water vapor to form acid rain, killing crops and destroying the fertility of the soil. As we have already seen, sulfur dioxide in the upper atmosphere can cause global temperatures to drop precipitously, leading to crop-killing frosts in the northern hemisphere and the possible interruption of the rain-giving Asian monsoon cycle in the tropics. Indeed, approximately 10,000 people — ⅕ of the population of Iceland — starved during the "Haze Famine" triggered by Laki's eruption in 1783.

Bizarrely enough, volcanic events have been linked to changes in the El Niño cycle. Scientists at the National Center for Atmospheric Research have discovered a strong statistical link between El Niño and tropical volcanic eruptions: In the years following a major eruption, they argue, the chance of El Niño doubles compared with a standard year. It is not entirely clear at this point how volcanoes trigger El Niños, but the answer may lie in the global cooling that accompanies large eruptions. According to climatologist Michael Mann, the cooling effect of volcanoes would be more notable in the western part of the Pacific Ocean, thus reducing the temperature differential between the eastern and western Pacific and setting the stage for El Niño. Since the El Niño in turn influences the formation of tropical cyclones, these findings suggest that tropical volcanoes may play a role in cyclonic weather as well.

Finally, although it seems counterintuitive that something as large as a volcano can influence events on the microscopic level, volcanoes can play a role in causing disease. The sulfurous emissions of volcanoes can cause deadly diarrhea in both men and animals. Farm animals are also vulnerable to another volcanic emission, fluorine, which causes animals to develop "bone-sickness," leading to soft, tumor-riddled bones, the loss of their teeth, and eventual death. Volcanoes can also cause disease more indirectly, through the intermediary of famine: Indeed, as many as 100,000 Irish died following the Tambora eruption due to cold temperatures, crop failure, famine, and the subsequent explosion of epidemic typhus in the weakened Irish population. Furthermore, the physical injuries caused by pyroclastic flows and lahars can lead to fatal infections, especially tetanus and gangrene. Volcanoes can also indirectly trigger disease by displacing their victims into closely-packed refugee camps, which often suffer from poor hygiene and associated disease outbreaks. As we shall see in section 2.3, outbreaks of disease in refugee camps marred an otherwise effective Philippine government response to the 1991 eruption of Mount Pinatubo.

Volcanoes and Human Agency

Unlike some other disasters, especially famines, floods, and disease, human beings play no direct role in volcanic eruptions. Indeed, volcanic eruptions, like earthquakes, are the result of raw elemental forces that are far beyond the power of human beings to prevent, let alone trigger. However, people can and do greatly exacerbate the destructive potential of volcanoes by living within volcanic danger zones and by not taking the appropriate precautions.

To a certain degree, human beings and volcanoes are obliged to share space by sheer eco-

An 18th century painting by Japanese artist Ichiyusai Hiroshige depicting the extinct Ashita-kayama volcano, one of many volcanoes in Japan.

nomic necessity. The soil near active volcanoes can be enormously fertile, encouraging the development of large human populations. Consider for instance the neighboring Indonesian islands of Java and Sumatra. Both islands host numerous volcanoes, but Java's volcanoes are much younger, and thus have more recently enriched the island's soil. Sumatra's volcanoes are considerably older, and its soil is correspondingly less fertile. As a result, although Sumatra is over three times as large as Java, it hosts only about ⅓ of Java's population. What is more, because of the phenomenon of subduction, most terrestrial volcanoes occur on or near coastlines. Unfortunately, human beings tend to occupy the same land, since coastal settlements offer many advantages, most especially cheap sea transportation, access to ocean foods, and (in many cases) more rainfall and correspondingly better agricultural potential. Clearly, human beings and volcanoes will continue to cohabitate the same land for the foreseeable future.

That being said, in some areas, the closeness between volcanoes and human populations has reached ridiculous extremes. In Third World countries, settlement on volcano slopes is somewhat understandable: Due to poverty or land hunger, many people simply have nowhere else to go. Less explicable is why so many people in developed countries have chosen to live in harm's way. About a million people now live in the danger zone of Mount Vesuvius, despite the potential peril, and indeed despite Italian government regulations restricting construction on the flanks of Vesuvius. The nearby Sicilian volcano Mt. Etna, in turn, looms over the densest concentration of farms and dwellings on the island, many of which are luxury vacation homes of the rich. Even more people have chosen to live in the shadow of Washington State's volcanic Mt. Rainier, which lies only about 150 kilometers from the city of Portland and less than 100 miles from Seattle. Indeed, many people living near Mt. Rainier, including quite a few of the 200,000 inhabitants of the nearby city of Tacoma, dwell upon sediment deposited by previous Mt. Rainier lahars.

Unfortunately for people living so close to volcanoes, there is little that human beings can do to mitigate a volcanoes' destructive potential. Since no buildings can withstand the force and volume of lahar mudslides, the only way to escape destruction is to build all structures on hilltops and high slopes, but while this may be economically feasible for the rich few, it is beyond the means of the more numerous poor. It is possible to protect city harbors from volcanic tsunamis by building breakwaters, but this protection is far from complete and is far too expensive to extend to the entire coastline. As for pyroclastic flows, the only possible defense is to run to an underground room, grab a wet blanket, wrap it around yourself, try not to breathe, and hope for the best. Human beings have been marginally more successful in mitigating the danger of lava flows. Indeed, in 1973, enterprising Icelandic firemen helped to save the port of Vestmannaeyjar from threatening lava by selectively solidifying the flow with jets of water, forming a dike to channel the lava away from the town. Almost two decades later, a similar drama played out in Sicily. At the invitation of the Italian government, the U.S. military used explosives and concrete blocks to try to shift the course of a threatening lava flow emanating from Mt. Etna. However, according to volcano expert David Ritchie, "Operation Volcano Buster" was only "a partial success at best." Even this partial success should be qualified by the knowledge that lava flows are generally the least dangerous of earthquake hazards.

Human beings may be unable to prevent eruptions and their associated perils, but they do have two valuable tools at their disposal to avoid loss of life: hazard maps and early evacuations. We now know enough about volcanoes to anticipate what areas are likely to suffer from ash fall, lahars, landslides, and pyroclastic flows. What is more, a variety of monitoring devices have been developed to help predict the likelihood of volcanic eruption. Scientists use laser-mirror arrays and GPS sensors to detect bulges on the side of the volcano that may indicate the build-up of magma below the surface. Gas detectors can be used to monitor for changing levels of volcanic gas, especially sulfur dioxide and CO_2. Scientists are even able to use seismographs, which detect earthquakes, to obtain an "x-ray" picture of a volcano. Since seismic waves are slowed or blocked when they pass through magma, a network of seismographs on the side of a volcano can be used to predict how far magma has progressed towards the surface, and thus whether or not an eruption is immanent. These detection measurements are by no means perfect, but as we shall see in section 2.3, if a sophisticated early detection system is coupled with an efficient evacuation plan, thousands of lives can be saved. Human beings may not be able to prevent eruptions, therefore, but since we now have the ability to detect and prepare for their approach, mankind must shoulder some of the responsibility whenever people are still killed by volcanic eruptions.

Study Questions

1. Explain, in your own words, the mechanisms through which volcanoes are created.

2. Why do volcanoes tend to kill many fewer people than other forms of natural disaster? Your answer should include a discussion of specific earthquake hazards.

3. "Although they get bad press, volcanoes on the balance are probably more helpful than harmful to mankind." To what degree does this section support this statement?

4. Based on the text, do you think that the death toll from volcanoes is likely to become greater or lesser over time? Explain your answer with evidence from the text.

Sources/Suggested Readings

De Boer, Jelle Zeilinga, and Theodore Donald Sanders. *Volcanoes in Human History*. Princeton, NJ: Princeton University Press, 2002.

Kerr, Richard A. "Volcanic Blasts Favor El Nino Warmings." *Science* 17 January 2003, 336–337.

McPhee, John. *The Control of Nature*. New York: Farrar, Straus and Giroux, 1989.

Prager, Ellen. *Furious Earth: The Science and Nature of Earthquakes, Volcanoes, and Tsunamis*. New York: McGraw-Hill, 2000.

Ritchie, David. *The Encyclopedia of Earthquakes and Volcanoes*. New York: Facts on File, 1994.

Savino, John, and Marie D. Jones. *Supervolcano: The Catastrophic Event That Changed the Course of Human History*. Franklin Lakes, NJ: New Page Books, 2007.

Scarth, Alwyn. *Vulcan's Fury: Man Against the Volcano*. New Haven, CT: Yale University Press, 1999.

Stommel, Henry, and Elizabeth Stommel, *Volcano Weather: The Story of 1816, the Year Without a Summer*. Newport, RI: Seven Seas Press, 1983.

"Volcano Hazards Program." *United States Geological Service*. Available from http://volcanoes. usgs.gov/

2.1: Krakatau, 1883

The eruption of Krakatau (often misspelled Krakatoa) on August 27, 1883, was far from the most violent eruption in history. Indeed, it was not even the most powerful volcanic event of the 19th century, a distinction that belongs to the 1816 eruption of nearby Mount Tambora. However, several factors conspired to make Krakatau the best known eruption in recent memory. Unlike Tambora, which erupted in relative obscurity in a more remote part of the Indonesian archipelago, Krakatau was located in the middle of the well-traveled Sunda Straits and less than 200 km from Batavia, the populous capital of the Dutch East Indies. As a result, even though Krakatau's eruption and the resulting tsunami killed as many as 40,000 people, many witnesses to the eruption survived, and these included a large number of literate Europeans who recorded their observations. These observations quickly became front page news world-wide thanks to telegraph cables, which linked Batavia to the rest of the world by the 1880s. Thanks in part to the telegraph, the Dutch quickly brought disaster relief to those devastated by the eruption. However, despite the rapidity of the response, at least one historian has speculated that the Krakatau disaster probably helped to create the anti–Dutch resistance movement that eventually helped give birth to the modern day state of Indonesia.

Like most of the volcanoes of the Indonesian archipelago, Krakatau owes its existence to the process of subduction. Each year, the Indo-Australian plate moves about 7.5 centimeters to the north northeast, where it grinds against the lighter material of the Eurasian Plate. As a result, the rock of the Indian-Australian plate is forced to dive beneath the Eurasian plate, carrying with it water and gas from the floor of the Indian Ocean. When this rock melts, it forms blobs of magma which work their way to the surface, forming volcanoes. Indeed, the Indonesian archipelago can claim the dubious distinction of hosting the densest concentration of volcanoes on Earth, including at least 132 volcanoes that have erupted in the last 10,000 years. The same plate movements have also triggered a large number of earthquakes, including the Pakistani Earthquake of 2005 and Indian Ocean Earthquake of 2004, an event better known as the Asian Tsunami. These disasters will be treated in sections 3.3 and 6.2 respectively.

Unfortunately for those living nearby, Krakatau occupies a particularly active point on an already volatile plate collision zone. Krakatau lies in the center of the Sunda Strait, an area of extremely high tectonic activity due to uneven rates of movement within the Eurasian plate: While the island of Java is moving in a roughly eastern direction, the neighboring island of Sumatra is being pushed more northeasterly, creating a fissure in between. The growing gap between these islands leads to fractures in the crust that provide an easy avenue for magma to reach the surface. This explains not only Krakatau's physical location, but the catastrophic power of its eventual eruption.

At the time of the Krakatau eruption, the Indonesian archipelago was largely under the control of the Dutch, who had been slowly expanding their dominion over this politically fractured and ethnically diverse island chain since 1605. Indeed, as of the 1883 eruption, this process was not yet complete, and the Dutch had still not established effective control over some islands that would later become the state of Indonesia. The Dutch presence was very strong in the vicinity of Krakatau, however, since the island of Java was not only the most densely populated part of the Indonesian archipelago, it was also the location of Batavia, the capital of the Dutch East Indies (hereafter DEI).

Why did the Dutch decide to colonize such a large and diverse territory so far from Europe? The answer, simply put, was the spice trade. Under Dutch economic control, the various islands of Indonesia were transformed into plantation complexes, growing cloves, mace, nutmeg, and cinnamon and other commodities that commanded high prices in European markets. Other islands, such as Java itself, were directed to grow food crops, which were then sold to the spice-producing islands, to the profit of the Dutch. The Dutch further greased the wheels of commerce by importing silver from the Americas, which commanded far higher prices in the DEI than in Europe. Unsurprisingly, these trade transactions favored the Dutch and impoverished the Indonesians, who also groaned under the weight of heavy taxation, including a land tax that amounted to one-fifth the crop. By the time of Krakatau's eruption, the system was improving: Under a new "Ethical Policy," the Dutch government began to take more interest in improving the education, public health, and economic situation of native Indonesians. However, the post-eruption period would prove that the native Indonesians still harbored a great deal of antipathy for their Dutch oppressors.

Despite the popular discontent brewing below the surface, the DEI were enjoying a period of relative peace in the early 1880s, outside of an ongoing war between the Dutch and the fiercely independent northern Sumatran Sultanate of Aceh. Krakatau, however, was about to upset this apparent stability. Starting in 1877, a series of earthquakes rocked Sunda Straits, which in retrospect probably indicated that magma was beginning to rise to the surface beneath the volcano. By early 1883, ships passing through the straits reported seeing smoke and steam rising from Krakatau, though at this point Krakatau's activity was still so mild that nearby residents of Java and Sumatra mistook these portents for clouds. Any doubt about Krakatau's volcanism was removed on May 20th of 1883, when the peace of the region was rocked by what one observer called a "tremendous eruption, with continual shaking and heavy rain of ashes." Although this eruption was actually rather mild by volcanic standards, and deposited only a small quantity of ash on land, it was a clear warning of things to come.

Clear warning though it might have been, the Dutch largely ignored it. Few precautions were taken to prepare the islands against more serious eruptions to come. Indeed, the Dutch treated the awakened Krakatau as a sideshow rather than a threat, and enterprising local businessmen even organized an "agreeable excursion" of 87 sightseers to the volcano on May 27th. Why the Dutch were so complacent is a matter of conjecture. Although the Indonesian natives retained folk memories of previous Krakatau explosions—indeed, they associated Krakatau with the god Orang Alijeh, who hurled down ash and lava if provoked by mankind's misdeeds— Krakatau had been dormant during most of the European presence in the region, except for a rather modest eruption in 1680 that was too insignificant an event even to be recorded in the DEI record books. The Dutch may also have thought that, since Krakatau itself was uninhabited and lay 25 km from either Java or Sumatra, it was too remote to pose a threat to anyone. This attitude may have been compounded by the fact that Batavia, where the bulk of the Dutch lived, was fully 160 km away from the volcano. If the majority of Krakatau's immediate neighbors were Dutch rather than Indonesians, it is likely that the authorities of DEI would have taken more of an interest.

The Dutch may also have been lulled into complacency by Krakatau's behavior; after the initial explosion of May 20th, Krakatau's violence seemed to taper off, though it never ceased entirely. Appearances, however, were deceptive. Underneath the Sunda Straits, pent up pressure was building steadily, kept in check only by the sheer bulk of the mountain itself. On August 26th, the pressure exerted by the subterranean magma had become unstoppable. With a tremendous roar, Krakatau launched a titanic column of black ash twenty-five kilometers into the sky. This proved to be just the first of a series of violent eruptions, most of them accompanied by pyroclastic flows, which would surge from the mountain over the course of the next few days. These culminated in a tremendous explosion at 10:02 A.M. on August 27th, which not only destroyed most of Mount Krakatau, but was actually heard clearly as far as 4,775 km away. Indeed, the main Krakatau explosion was so powerful that it created a sort of aerial earthquake, which bounced and rebounded through the world's atmosphere several times and was recorded on barometers globally. Krakatau's explosion also disturbed seas worldwide, kicking 1 meter breakers in distant South Africa, and even producing measurable swells in Northern European harbors. These rogue waves were not mere curiosities. Indeed, a sudden ocean swell crashed into a fisherwoman in Ceylon [modern day Sri Lanka], killing her and giving her the dubious distinction of being the most distant known victim of the Krakatau eruption.

Much closer to ground zero, the Krakatau eruption terrified the residents of the Dutch capital of Batavia. Europeans in the city on the 26th reported hearing the sound of thunder, and assumed the awaited monsoon rains were coming, though it was a cloudless day. These rumblings grew progressively louder, to the point that Batavia's night cannon, fired every evening at 8 o'clock, was all but drowned out by the noise. Few slept in Batavia that night, due to

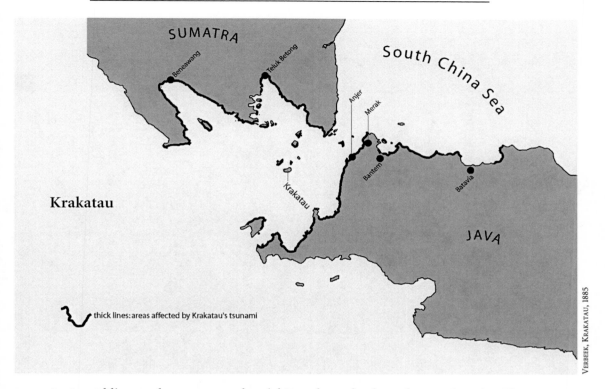

VERBEEK, KRAKATAU, 1885

constant rumbling, and many spent the night outdoors for fear of an earthquake. The next morning was overcast and rather cold — indeed, temperatures dropped to an unheard of 65 degrees F. — and a light-colored ash began to rain from the sky to the point that one eyewitness observed that Batavia resembled "a country in Europe after a heavy snowstorm." Sometime after 9:30 many Batavia residents reported a "strange pressure" in their ears, and when they checked their barometers, they discovered that the air pressure had begun to fluctuate wildly, no doubt because of Krakatau's aerial earthquake. Then, without warning, a "tidal wave" raced up the long canal that connected Batavia with the sea and swamped the city's wharves with several feet of water, wrecking the brickwork of the canal and killing several people.

Although they had no way of knowing it at the time, Batavia got off lightly: 160 kilometers of distance shielded the city from the eruption's direct effects, and the protruding northwest tip of Java island deflected the worst of Krakatau's tsunami. Those living along Sunda Strait, however, were not so lucky. The coast of Sumatra, which lay downwind of Krakatau, suffered from repeated pyroclastic flows. The family of the Dutch official Beyernick, for example, was overtaken by a pyroclastic flow on the morning of the 27th, which gushed up between the floorboards of the house in which they had sought shelter. They were so seriously burnt that their skin hung from their flesh and their limbs swelled up to several times their normal size, but they survived. Many more did not, however; indeed, pyroclastic flows probably claimed about 4,000 of the volcano's 36,000-odd victims.

Far more deadly, however, were the tsunamis generated by Krakatau's cumulating explosions on the morning of the 27th. Volcano scholars do not agree whether these tsunamis were spawned by Krakatau's deadly pyroclastic flows, by underwater landslides, or by the cataclysmic explosion of the island of Krakatau itself. However they were formed, they left an unmistakable mark on the shores of the Sunda Straits. Unfortunately for those who dwelled there, local geographic conditions conspired to increase the perils posed by Krakatau's tsunami waves. On

A dramatized illustration based on contemporary rumors about Krakatau tsunami victims washed out to sea.

E. COTTEAU, *KRAKATAU ET LE D'ETROIT DE LA SONDE. LE TOUR DU MONDE* 51, P. 125

The Dutch gunboat Berouw's resting place after being washed 2 kilometers inland by Krakatau's tsunami.

the Java coast, the sea was separated from the interior hills by a nearly flat and 6–8 km wide coastal plain which offered little resistance to the incoming tsunami. Nearby Sumatra was somewhat more mountainous, but two funnel-shaped bays, the Teluk Lampung and Teluk Semangka, channeled the tsunami straight toward the major population centers of Telok Betong and Beneawang (now called Kotaagung and Bandar Lampung respectively).

As a result of this natural geographic vulnerability, most towns along the Sunda Straits were all but wiped from the map. In Anjer (today spelled Anyar), the largest town on the Java side of the Straits, the coming tsunami wave was described as a "low range of hills rising out of the sea," and that wave was just the first amongst many. Indeed, survivors agreed that the second wave, which was so high that it managed to overtop a knoll that rose more than 35 meters over sea level, probably accounted for the most deaths. Only a few people survived, either by racing the tsunami wave to higher ground, or — in the case of one elderly Dutch pilot — by clinging to one of the few palm trees to withstand the flood until the wave receded. The waves were even higher in Merak, located about 8 km north of Anjer, where the Sunda Straits narrowed and became shallower. Here the wave was described as "a great black thing ... very high and strong," and when it struck land, "trees and houses were washed away as it came along." There was high ground near Merak, but so many people rushed to a single path up the slopes that they became entangled with each other, forming a desperate, screaming, struggling mass. One native Javanese survivor later speculated that many of those who drowned at Merak were actually dragged to their deaths by those farther down the slopes, much like crabs in a bucket pull each other down in their struggles to climb to safety.

Communities on the Sumatra side of the Straits were similarly affected. At Telok Betong, a European observer reported that, other than a few buildings that happened to be about 35 meters in elevation, "nothing has been spared, not even a single tree." Luckily, the office of a Dutch high official was located atop a 37 meter hill, so many Europeans survived, though observers reported the deaths of an "immense number" of Indonesian people living farther down the slopes. Also killed at Telok Betong were the 28 sailors aboard the Dutch gunboat *Berouw*, which suffered an astonishing fate: After the tsunami, it was found stranded in a river valley about 2 kilometers inland and 10 meters above sea level. About 60 kilometers away, at Beneawang, a European eyewitness named Le Sueur reported that the sea crashed into town at 7:00, leading to a mass rush to houses on higher ground, but these structures were later swamped and detached from their foundations by subsequent tsunami waves. Le Sueur himself was nearly crushed between two floating houses, and only survived the floods by grabbing the trunk of a banana tree and holding on for dear life.

Perhaps the most awe-inspiring accounts of the eruption, however, were penned by passengers of ships at sea that happened to be in the Sunda Straits at the time of the paroxysm. The Dutch mail steamer *Governor General Loudon* was anchored in deep water off Telok Batong when the tsunami waves struck, and as a result the ship rode out the tsunami with relative ease, since tsunami waves are generally harmless to boats offshore. The *Loudon* was close enough to land, however, for her crew and passengers to watch as the tsunami crashed into Telok Betong, wrecking the town and washing the *Berouw* up the valley of the Kuripan River. Unable to give any assistance, and fearful of their own safety, the crew of the *Loudon* set out for Anjer. However, due to heavy ash fall, which turned the morning pitch black and reduced visibility to nil, the *Loudon* was obliged to drop anchor before reaching Anjer. Rising winds and monstrous waves— one observer reported "seas as high as the heavens"— later obliged them to drop both anchors and to power up the ship's propeller to keep the bow into the oncoming swells. Lightning, probably generated by friction between the ash particles in the air, struck the ship six or seven times, and a layer of pumice stones and mud covered the deck to a depth of 10 centimeters. To top things off, *Loudon*'s masts and spars began to glow with Saint Elmo's Fire, and although this static energy phenomenon was harmless, the superstitious Indonesian sailors on board worked desperately, but unsuccessfully, to extinguish the flames.

Sailing conditions not did improve appreciably until the morning of the 28th, when the *Loudon* set out for Anjer. On the way, however, they ran across an unexpected wall of apparently solid land, which turned out to be a 2 or 3 meter deposit of floating pumice stone. When the morning brightened, they discovered to their amazement that the island of Krakatau had all but disappeared — in one observer's evocative phrase, the "island had spit itself out"— and that new islands had appeared in the surrounding seas, most likely created by Krakatau's falling fragments. Due to resulting navigational difficulties, the *Loudon* did not reach Anjer until 4 o'clock, whereupon they discovered that the shore where Anjer had once stood had become an "even, gray plain ... not even a ruin remained; everything was wiped away and leveled to the ground." The shocked crew of the *Loudon* picked up what survivors they could find and headed north to the port of Bantam to report the scale of the catastrophe.

In the post-disaster period rumors spread like wildfire, not only within Batavia, but in the overseas press. "Great chasms had opened in the earth," the *San Francisco Chronicle* reported, "and streams of lava poured incessantly down the sides of the mountains into the valleys, sweeping everything before them." The same paper also reported a "most singular" phenomenon: "the carrying in the midst of molten lava a bed of solid ice of enormous size, which has been emitted from one of the craters." This ice, the paper went on to say, must have formed "the crust of some underground lake," and it probably survived in the midst of the lava since it was "surrounded by a thick envelope of sand and scoria [a light volcanic rock], which are non-conductors of heat." In Batavia itself, the paper reported, "it is hardly probable that more than 5,000 managed to save their lives," at least in the low-lying port district of the town. The *Chronicle* made no mention of pyroclastic flows or tsunamis, and for good reason: These tales were based not on actual observations of the eruption, but rather on popular misconceptions about volcanoes, especially the erroneous belief that volcanoes kill mainly through lava flows. As we shall see in section 2.2, this tendency to assume that future volcanic eruptions will follow the same patterns set by past eruptions can have fatal consequences.

Although the *Chronicle*'s flights of fancy had little to do with reality, the actual situation in Java and Sumatra was desperate enough. According to the Reverend Tenison-Woods, who visited the Java coast within a week of the catastrophe, "nothing was left. Not a house, scarcely a tree, not a road. All the divisions between the fields were obliterated, and the boundaries of properties destroyed." Only a narrow strip of flat coastal land was inundated by the tsunami, Tenison-Woods explained, but since "on it mainly was settled the whole, or very near the whole, population of that part of the country," the loss of life was enormous. Indeed, Dr. Sollewyn Gelpke, the first government observer sent to the ruins of Anjer, reported that "thousands of corpses of human beings and also carcasses of animals still await burial, and there presence is apparent by an indescribable stench. They lie in knots and entangled masses impossible to unravel." Gravediggers had been hired to dispose of the dead, Dr. Gelpke continued, but they were forced to contend with gangs of looters, who were prospecting for valuables amidst the "carrion fields" and "pools and lagoons of rotting sea water."

The situation in Sumatra was just as grim. Urgent telegraphs sent to Batavia from Telok Betong reported "thousands of corpses floating about, many scorched to death, desolation over mainland extends three miles from beach." Another account of Telok Betong painted a picture of "rotting and foul smelling corpses, a few survivors all suffering from burns, the country around laid waste, and the houses gone." The same report bemoaned the plight of the European community, which had been "reduced to destitution" by the tsunami, though it made no mention of the situation of the surviving Indonesian natives. What is more, the entire geography of Lampong Bay was fundamentally altered. "The shores both of the islands and mainland, to a height of 10 to 120 ft above sea level," a Dutch official reported, "are quite bare and covered with a grey colored muddy deposit probably left behind there by the tidal wave. Where formerly hundreds of white sails on fishermen's prahus [small boats] and crafts were charmingly reflected upon the blue surface of the water," he continued, "the only living creature now visible is a solitary water bird which wanders by itself along the grayish plain."

The volcanic eruption left a lasting mark on the sea as well. The entire seafloor of the Sunda Straits was fundamentally altered, since there was now an undersea caldera where Krakatau had once stood, and the scattered remnants of the exploded mountain formed dangerous reefs in areas that had once been deep water. Vast rafts of volcanic pumice also posed a threat to navigation, since they blocked up harbors, damaged steam engine coolant systems, and slowed the progress of ships at sea. Daring (or perhaps foolhardy) sailors discovered that these pumice rafts, if thick enough, could support the weight of a man. They were also sturdy enough to carry the corpses of tsunami victims as far as Africa, where students at a mission school in Zanzibar found a large quantity of skulls and bones, along with pumice, "all along the beach at high-water mark." Indeed, ships passing through or near the Sunda Straits reported encountering masses of human bodies, in "groups of 50 to 100 all passed together, most of them naked," along with innumerable carcasses of animals.

In the aftermath of the Krakatau eruption, the Dutch government did a reasonably good job providing disaster assistance, though critics charged that it was more concerned with providing succor to the tragedy's white survivors than with assisting afflicted Indonesian natives. Money was raised for disaster relief measures, food and blankets were distributed, roads were cleared, and temporary shelters were reopened. Luckily for the Dutch, Mother Nature assisted in the recovery effort. Within a month of the eruption, heavy monsoon rains had cleared most of the ash from the ground, and new coconut and banana trees were pushing their way through the volcanic debris. Although the flooded coastal regions were initially so barren that they resembled "a row of dunes stretched [...] along the coast," within just eight weeks "everything had become green again" What is more, the ash deposited by Krakatau exerted stimulating effect on local agriculture, not only by adding nutrients to the soil, but by making the soil more porous and thus better suited to plow cultivation. One European observer in Sumatra less than 6 months after the eruption noted that "all the growing crops bore a luxuriant appearance, particularly the pepper."

Despite the speed of both the Dutch relief effort and the natural ecological revival, the Krakatau disaster stirred up deep wells of resentment amongst the native Indonesian peoples. This resentment was apparent even during the eruption, when Europeans reported hearing complaints that the Krakatau eruption was divine retribution for the Dutch war against Aceh. In the hills above Anjer, Dutch survivors of the tsunami reported that Indonesians refused to shelter Europeans in their houses, since the "exceedingly superstitious" natives "attributed their misfortune to us." Indeed, Krakatau historian Simon Winchester has argued that Java's population, though Islamic, was still profoundly influenced by pre–Islamic beliefs which ascribed volcanic eruptions to divine anger. As a result, "Krakatau's almighty act of self-immolation in August 1883 was seen locally as possessing the most profound of inner meanings."

Intriguingly, there is evidence that Indonesia's Islamic leadership had made dire prophesies linking Dutch occupation with volcanic eruptions well before the eruption even took place. Winchester discusses the case of Hajii Abdul Karim, a Javanese Islamic leader, who predicted long before the eruption that the "Mahdi," or "guided one," would appear before the end of days to purify the godless world. His arrival would be foretold by signs, including "diseases of cattle," "floods," "blood-colored rain." Most tellingly, Abdul Karim foresaw that "volcanoes would erupt, and people would die." These were not particularly daring prophesies to make — thanks to El Niño and plate tectonics, floods and volcanic eruptions are inevitable events in the Indonesian archipelago. Nonetheless, many Indonesians no doubt interpreted the Krakatau eruption as fulfillment of Abdul Karim's apocalyptic vision, and believed that the fall of Dutch rule in Indonesia was at hand.

As a result, Winchester argues that Krakatau's eruption encouraged some Indonesian Muslims to cross the line from passive resentment to active resistance. Just five weeks after the eruption, a Dutch soldier was brutally stabbed in a marketplace by a bearded man dressed in white robes. The assailant apparently said nothing, but his dress and appearance suggested he was a *hajji*— in other words, a Muslim who had completed the religiously mandated "*Hajj*" pilgrimage to Mecca. Six weeks after that, a similarly-dressed man attacked and wounded a sentry at a Dutch military base. He was captured, but when the military police questioned him, they were "bewildered by the man's confusing answers" and eventually concluded that he had acted out of "extreme religious zeal." The military police were not even able to determine if the assailant in custody had acted alone, or was working in conjunction with a larger organization.

In fact, a strong anti–Dutch resistance group was being organized in Java, but it would be another 5 years before they were confident enough to strike. The resulting rebellion was called the "Bantem Peasants' Revolt," but this name is misleading, since the rebellion's causes were as much religious as social. The principle organizers and leaders of the revolt were almost all *hajjis*, and like the earlier rebels, they wore white robes of religious purity. Their actions, however, were anything but pure: On July 9th of 1881, they swarmed into the northeast Javan village of Sandeja and slaughtered both its European inhabitants and some natives who were collaborating with the Europeans. Ultimately 24 people died before Dutch soldiers arrived and mowed down the rebels with repeating rifles. Due to the efficiency of the Dutch response, the rebellion lasted less than 24 hours.

So was the Bantem Peasants' Revolt a direct result of post–Krakatau religious fanaticism, as Winchester contends? Other scholars of Indonesia are doubtful. Merle Ricklefs, an expert on Indonesian history, charges that Winchester has all but ignored the existence of a long tradition of anti-colonialism in Java, inspired by concrete social and economic grievances. These deeply seated problems inspired a series of rebellions in the 75 years before the Krakatau blast, most of which were both larger in scale and more significant than the post–Krakatau peasant revolt. Indeed, a six-year rebellion from 1825 to 1830 killed 8,000 Europeans and an estimated 200,000 Javanese. What is more, Winchester's focus on the Islamic fundamentalist causes of the rebellion probably reflects his post September 11th mentality — his book was published in 2003 — rather than the reality of the situation. Winchester has also been accused of failing to establish a clear link between the Krakatau eruption and the events of 1888. He has no documentary evidence of any links, other than a long quote taken from a book by hydraulic engineer R. V. van Sandick written 4 years after the rebellion, and this text probably tells us more about the Dutch attitude towards the 1888 revolt than about the mindset of the Indonesians themselves. Winchester also fails to explain why the Bantem Peasants' Revolt occurred a full 5 years after Krakatau, rather than in its immediate aftermath, when passions were running highest.

Indeed, the most important lessons that we can draw from the Krakatau eruption concern not Indonesia's past, but its future. Unfortunately for the Indonesian people, the islands of the Indonesian archipelago that boast the most fertile soils — and hence the highest populations — are also the areas most affected by volcanic activity. As a result, in the past 10,000 years, Indonesia has accounted for only 17 percent of all volcanic eruptions, but 33 percent of the eruptions that produced known human fatalities. Thanks to the burgeoning growth of Indonesia's population, which soared to nearly a quarter of a billion in 2006, it is likely that the same trend will continue or become even more pronounced in the future. Indonesia would be well advised, therefore, to draw lessons from Krakatau as it prepares to contend with future volcanic eruptions.

Study Questions

1. To what degree was the damage and destruction caused by the Krakatau eruption worsened by other forms of natural disaster?

2. To what degree ought the Dutch be blamed for the massive loss of life following the Krakatau eruption?

3. "The death and destruction caused by the Krakatau eruption owed more to the location of the volcano than to the inherent strength of the eruption itself." To what degree does the evidence in this section support this contention?

4. How convincing do you find Winchester's contention that the Krakatau eruption interacted with Indonesian ideological beliefs to spark the Bantem Peasant's Revolt?

Sources/Suggested Readings

De Boer, Jelle Zeilinga, and Theodore Donald Sanders. *Volcanoes in Human History*. Princeton, NJ: Princeton University Press, 2002.

Scarth, Alwyn. *Vulcan's Fury: Man Against the Volcano*. New Haven, CT: Yale University Press, 1999.

Simkin, Tom, and Richard S. Fiske. *Krakatau 1883*. Washington, DC: Smithsonian Institution Press, 1983.

Winchester, Simon. *Krakatoa: The Day the World Exploded August 27, 1883*. New York: HarperCollins, 2003.

2.2: Mount Pelée, 1902

The eruption of Mount Pelée on the French Island of Martinique on May 8, 1902, was far from the most powerful volcanic eruption of the 20th century. Indeed, Mount Pelée's blast rates only 4 (large) on the 1–8 scale of the volcanic explosivity index. Despite this, Mount Pelée wreaked havoc on Martinique far out of proportion to its size. In all, an estimated 27,000 people fell victim to Pelée's pyroclastic flows and lahars, and the bustling city of St. Pierre, "Pearl of the West Indies," was essentially wiped off the map. To a certain degree, these deaths were inevitable, given the logistical impossibility of evacuating a city of St. Pierre's size with the means available. Nonetheless, the failure of the French authorities to understand the full threat that Mount Pelée represented, largely because of the primitive state of volcanology at the time, did play a contributing role in the disaster. So too did racism and cost-cutting pressures, which lead to a premature French government attempt to resettle refugees on the volcano slopes. However, some good did arise from the Mount Pelée eruption: Scientists working in the aftermath of the eruption made enormous strides in understanding volcanism, and indeed, it is no exaggeration to say that the Mount Pelée eruption created the modern science of volcanology.

The island of Martinique lies near the center of the Lesser Antilles, a string of islands created by the collision of the North American plate and the lighter materials of the Caribbean plate. Since the rate of movement of the North American plate is relatively slow — only about 2 cm a year — the Lesser Antilles is characterized by less frequent volcanic activity than other hot zones in the world, such as Siberia and the Japanese archipelago. However, since the volcanoes of the Lesser Antilles are formed by subduction of oceanic plate material, the resulting magma tends to be high in dissolved gasses, leading to highly dangerous eruptions. The peril posed by these volcanoes is exacerbated by the high population densities of the Lesser Antilles islands, and by the very fact that they are islands, which seriously complicates evacuation efforts. In case of a fast-developing eruption, the inhabitants of the Lesser Antilles often have nowhere to go.

At the time of the eruption, Martinique had been a French colonial possession for approximately 250 years. For almost 200 of those years, Martinique's economy had been based on slavery, since Martinique's main sources of income — sugar cane cultivation, refining of cane into sugar, and distilling rum from molasses — were backbreaking and dangerous tasks that free men generally refused to do. Slavery had been abolished in 1848, but the island's social system still reflected its legacy. For the most part, wealth and power was held by a small minority of elite whites, who owned much of the land as well as most of the island's industrial enterprises. The bulk of the population, however, was made up either of ex-slaves and their decedents or "mulattos" of mixed black-white heritage. By and large these groups were poor and uneducated — nearly half of the 1900 population was illiterate — though some mulattos rose to positions of power through hard work or white patronage. At the time of the eruption, white dominance in Martinique was being challenged at the ballot box by mulatto or black candidates, most notably by Amédee Knight, the first black man to be elected senator to the French Parliament. This political dispute would have unfortunate consequences in the aftermath of the eruption as we shall see below.

The largest town on Martinique at the time of the eruption was St. Pierre, variously described as the "Pearl of the West Indies" or even the "Paris of the West Indies," though this reputation reflects post-disaster nostalgia as much as pre-eruption realities. St. Pierre was not the political capital of the island, nor was it the island's main military base — the rival city of Fort-de-France, located in the center of the island, enjoyed both of these distinctions. St. Pierre was, however, the center of everything else that mattered: culture, wealth, and religious life. It was also far more attractive than Fort-de-France, in part because the capital city, which lay on low-lying, marshy soil, had been periodically damaged by earthquakes and associated tsunamis. In contrast, St. Pierre stood on solid rock, and had the reputation of being a much safer place to live than Martinique's official capital. As St. Pierre's 26,011 citizens would learn in May of 1902, however, this reputation was quite undeserved.

St. Pierre's problem, though few were aware of it at the time, was its close proximity to Mount Pelée, a volcanic peak that dominated the landscape of the northern half of Martinique. At 200,000 years of age, Mt. Pelée is a relatively young volcano, though it appears far older, since the Caribbean's stormy weather has eroded away the once-pristine shape of Mt. Pelée's composite cone. In the period before the eruption, few people in Martinique even knew that it was a volcano, and most of those who did know assumed that it had long gone extinct. In fact, the volcano's last major eruption had occurred only 600 years before, but since the French had all but wiped out the native Amerindians of the island, there was no one to maintain folk memories of the mountain's earlier eruptions. Admittedly, there had been a sizable eruption in 1851 which killed all vegetation at the peak of the mountain. Indeed, this eruption gave Pelée its name, which means "bald" or "peeled" in French. Nonetheless, news of this eruption was overshadowed by the ongoing turmoil caused by the liberation of slaves and by fears of a Yellow Fever epidemic. As a result, according to volcano scholar Alwyn Scarth, "all that local folklore remembered [of the '51 eruption] was the pleasant little plume of fumes and steam" that rose above the otherwise undistinguished mountain.

St. Pierre's complacency towards their volcanic neighbor was underscored by the local tradition of day trips to Mount Pelée's summit. A few times a year, mostly-white expeditions left from St. Pierre and made a leisurely climb to the top of Mt. Pelée, from which they could cast their eyes over a full ⅔ of the island of Martinique. These expeditions then generally picnicked by the Lac des Palmistes, a pond that had formed inside an old volcanic crater just below the summit. It was also traditional for hikers to "inscribe their impressions of the scene" on the walls of a nearby chapel, Notre Dame de l'Etang. Why these day trippers felt compelled to carry out this customary vandalism to a religious structure is a mystery. In any case, the practice was discontinued following the May 1902 eruption.

It was in June of 1900, during one of these day trips to Pelée's summit, that the people of Martinique first learned that the "extinct" volcano was re-awakening. Hikers noticed that two new fumaroles, or volcanic vents, had formed in the Etang Sec, a "dry pond" (really an old volcanic crater) on the side of Mount Pelée. Most plants within 40 meters of the vents had been killed and the ground was covered with sulfur deposits, clear signs of volcanic activity. Another day trip to the summit in 1901 noted that the number of vents had multiplied to 5 or 6, and a sulfurous, rotten egg stink now hung in the air. By early 1902, the smell of sulfur had wafted over to nearby villages and even as far downhill as coastal settlements, especially Le Prêcheur, the seaside town closest to the volcano. Nonetheless, locals remained unconcerned. "It was only like an old man snoring," it was said in Martinique, "nothing to worry about. Just his last fling."

Despite these hopeful predictions, Mount Pelée refused to go back to sleep. As winter gave way to spring in 1902, still more sulfur vents opened on the Etang Sec crater, and earthquakes became more frequent, which probably indicates that magma was beginning to rise to the surface below Mount Pelée. On April 23rd, columns of steam and ash rose high into the air above Mount Pelée, indicating (though no one in Martinique knew it) that water percolating through the rocks of Mount Pelée was beginning to react with the molten magma moving up from below. According to contemporary witnesses, this ongoing eruption was strong enough to "juggle with boulders several cubic meters [sic] in diameter." Still, observers were not much concerned, and dismissed the eruption as the mountain's April Fool's joke. Indeed, as late as April 30th, the citizens of St. Pierre were busily planning one of their traditional May expeditions to the summit. The organizers promised participants a splendid first-hand view of the "gaping hole" atop Mt. Pelée — assuming, of course, that "the gendarmes [police] don't take it into their heads to arrest the crater!"

In the following days, however, the main flow of people was not up to the summit, but rather down from mountain villages to the supposed safety of St. Pierre. This mass movement of humanity was triggered by a sudden escalation of Mount Pelée's violence starting on the first of May. By May 2nd, thick clouds of ash were billowing out of Pelée's crater, bringing gloom to St. Pierre and pitch black darkness to Le Prêcheur. Ash covered houses and snapped tree branches, creating a "winter landscape without the cold." In the mountain village of Le Morne-Rouge, relatively close to the crater, people were so frightened by the escalating eruption that they fought with each other over who was the bigger sinner in order to get first crack at the confessional. What is more, despite lack of rain, the normally dry Etang Sec was filling with water. In addition, the Rivière Blanche or "White River," which debouched about 3 km north of St. Pierre, began to flow spasmodically, alternately drying up and then rushing to the sea at many times its normal capacity.

Indeed, the Rivière Blanche formed the means by which Mount Pelée claimed its first casualties. Groundwater pushed upwards by the heat of the magma bubbled up in the normally dry Etang Sec and put increasing pressure on the thin southeastern wall of the Etang Sec crater. The steadily rising number of earthquakes further weakened this fragile natural dam. Finally, on May 5th, the crater's rim gave way catastrophically, releasing a massive lahar that raged down the valley of the Rivière Blanche. Witnesses to the lahar reported hearing a "an immense noise," followed close behind by a "black avalanche ... full of huge blocks, more than 10m high and at least 150m wide." The lahar leveled a rum factory near the mouth of the Rivière Blanche and killed a total of 25 people, including a mother and baby who were on boats offshore near where the lahar struck the sea. In fact, the lahar impacted the ocean with such force that it created a tsunami wave. Observers in St. Pierre reported that the sea first retreated 30–60m, then rushed back, submerging parts of St. Pierre under a 4m wall of water. Luckily, no one in St. Pierre was killed.

The Rivière Blanche lahar alerted the inhabitants of Martinique that the Mount Pelée eruption had the potential to kill, but unfortunately, they drew entirely wrong conclusions from the event. Some people assumed that, now that the volcano had "blown out its stopper," it would settle down, "just as it did in 1851." Even if more eruptions did occur, it was widely believed that Mount Pelée's "lava" would follow river valleys, thus sparing St. Pierre. This view was reinforced by news of the Rivière Blanche lahar, which was confused with a lava flow in the popular mind. The same popular mind assumed that the true danger to St. Pierre came from the sea, in the form of a tsunami wave, rather than the volcano itself.

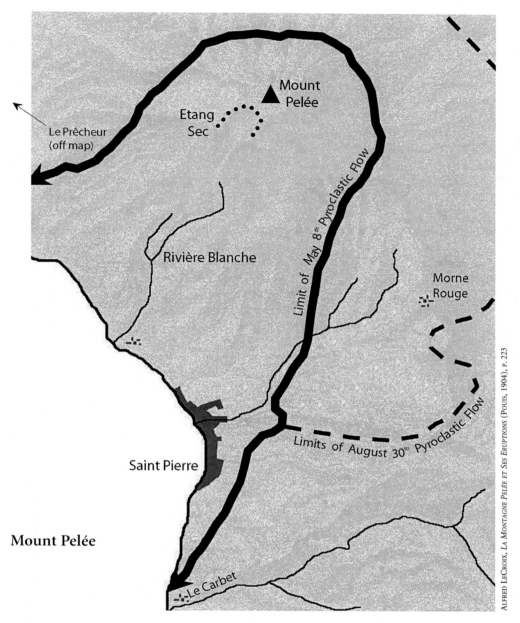

Mount Pelée

ALFRED LECROIX, *LA MONTAGNE PELÉE ET SES ERUPTIONS* (POUIS, 1904), P. 223

These mistaken views were reinforced by evidence from previous natural disasters. Although the fate of Pompeii was well known, most people in St. Pierre embraced the comforting myth that Vesuvius buried Pompeii with slow-moving lava flows and that most of the surrounding population had time to escape. More recent events mislead the inhabitants of St. Pierre as well. It was widely believed that earthquakes, such as the 1839 quake that had leveled Fort-de-France, were far more of a threat in the Caribbean than volcanic eruptions. What is more, many elites in St. Pierre must have been well informed about the Krakatau eruption, which had occurred less than 20 years before, and which had wreaked most of its destruction in the form of a tsunami wave. In addition, the city of Galveston in Texas had been nearly obliterated by a hurricane-driven tidal wave in 1900, further convincing Martinique's citizens that the true danger was the sea rather than the mountain. On the basis of these "facts," the mayor assured his citizens in a widely distributed poster that the volcano posed "no immediate danger" to the city of St. Pierre.

If the citizens of St. Pierre had paid closer attention to the mountain itself rather than these government pronouncements and misleading historical precedents, they might have come to a different conclusion about the danger they faced. By May 6th, it was clear that the column of ash pumping out of the volcano was "lit up by the fire inside," indicating that magma had now reached the surface of the earth. They might have also noted that the recent collapse of the south-western rim of the Etang Sec had created a large notch that would channel any volcanic explosions directly towards St. Pierre. Nonetheless, comforted by the government's calming declarations, few people chose to leave St. Pierre immediately before the climactic eruption. Indeed, many people in St. Pierre were more concerned with the theatrics of the ongoing election to the French assembly than they were about the distant rumbling of Mount Pelée. Radical politician Amédée Knight even tried to link the two events: "The mountain will only sleep," he told his constituents, "when the whites are out of office!"

It is important to note that the complacency of St. Pierre's citizens in the face of Mount Pelée's dangers was informed by fatalism as much as ignorance; in reality, a large-scale evacuation of the city was simply impossible given the situation. There was a road of sorts between St. Pierre and Fort-de-France, but it was rough and poorly maintained, entirely unsuitable for a large-scale evacuation. The route north was blocked by the Rivière Blanche lahar, and in any case, the towns north of St. Pierre were even closer to the volcano than St. Pierre itself. In effect, the only way out of St. Pierre was by sea, but the vessels at hand only had the capacity to move a few hundred people at a time, and thus were entirely inadequate for the fast and orderly evacuation of a city of over 26,000. The best the government could do, under these circumstances, was to try to keep the citizens of St. Pierre calm and hope for the best.

As a result, when the volcano did erupt catastrophically on May 8th, the loss of life was staggering. At 8:02 in the morning, a massive explosion that was heard as far away as distant Venezuela shattered a lava dome that had formed atop the Etang Sec and released a huge cloud of superheated vapors. As witnesses watched, this glowing cloud collapsed and started running downhill at a terrible velocity. Moving at over 500 km/hour, the pyroclastic flow covered the 7 km between Mount Pelée and St. Pierre in less than two minutes, giving its victims almost no time to react. A businessman in Fort-de-France later remembered how the pyroclastic flow had struck in the middle of phone conversation with a friend in St. Pierre: "He had just finished his sentence when I heard a dreadful scream, then another much weaker moan, like a stifled death rattle. Then silence." Another Fort-de-France resident on the phone to St. Pierre at the time of the eruption suffered a violent shock that "threw me from the telephone."

The destruction wrought by this pyroclastic flow in the city of St. Pierre was nothing short of astounding. Every single building in the northern Fort district of the city was razed to the ground; indeed the new Fort marketplace, built to withstand hurricane-strength winds, vanished completely in the face of the onslaught. The St. Pierre cathedral, though one of the most stoutly built structures on the island, lost its dome instantly and then collapsed upon itself, crushing the many people who were worshiping within. Weaker structures, like houses, were all but vaporized. Some large machines that were too heavy to shift survived the blast, but were twisted and bent by the heat and violence of the flow. The flow did not limit itself to land, but even fanned out into St. Pierre's harbor, sinking or crippling every ship in the vicinity and killing most of their crewmembers. The explosive blast was so powerful, in fact, that it created a vacuum near the crater that, in turn, generated a "return wind," stopping the pyroclastic flow near the southern outskirts of St. Pierre. If not for the return wind, the pyroclastic flow may well have reached the villages of Beauregard, Le Carbet, and Lajus, and the death toll might have been even higher.

Obviously, given sheer power of the pyroclastic flow, human beings engulfed by the glowing cloud had little hope of survival. Those caught in the street were bludgeoned by the winds or roasted alive by temperatures that ranged from 200–450 degrees Celsius. People in more sheltered locations were either asphyxiated by the fiery gasses, which sucked the oxygen out of the atmosphere, or else choked to death when they "swallowed the fire," since the same gasses scorched the throat and lungs when they were inhaled. In the aftermath of the eruption, the rumor spread that only a single man, who was lucky enough to be incarcerated in a vault-like prison cell, managed to survive the blast in St. Pierre. This is not quite true. Some people caught at the edge of the pyroclastic flow did survive the blast, although many were terribly burned and some died within a few days of the eruption. Others probably survived the initial blast in St. Pierre, but were killed in the subsequent fire: As it rushed through town, the superheated gas set off a number of fires, and thanks to the presence of many casks of highly flammable rum in St. Pierre warehouses, these fires soon raged through the entire town, incinerating almost everything and everyone that managed to withstand the initial blast.

As a result, when would-be rescuers arrived by sea from Fort-de-France, they were faced with an almost indescribable scene of destruction. "The whole city of Saint-Pierre was ablaze," wrote an observer aboard the steamship *Rubis*, "and formed a colossal inferno, 4km long ... our little steamer was floating in the midst of the half-charred bodies of the unfortunate sailors from the vessels that had been consumed by fire." Although the crew of the *Rubis* scanned the coast intently, they "did not see a living soul," and they were soon forced to turn back by the intense heat of the conflagration along the shore, which probably reached 900 degrees Celsius. Next on the scene was the naval vessel *Suchet*, which managed to collect a number of burn victims who either had been on offshore ships or else caught in the very edge of the pyroclastic flow. Nine of these survivors were so badly hurt that they did not survive the trip back to Fort-de-France. As for the city of St. Pierre itself, no effort was made to search it for survivors because the captain of the *Suchet* was convinced that no one could possibly have survived the blast and the subsequent inferno. Upon returning to Fort-de-France, the *Suchet*'s captain informed the top civilian official in town that "the whole city had been destroyed ... it would be hard to imagine a more complete catastrophe."

News of the "complete catastrophe" in St. Pierre soon spread to the world via the telegraph, and in the days following the eruption, charity organizations and private individuals sent large donations of money and goods to the survivors. The Emperor of Germany, the King of England, the Pope, and President Theodore Roosevelt of the United States all sent handsome donations. However, this influx of material aid was soon cut short by a vicious media campaign started by French conservatives. According to Ferdinand Clerc, a right wing white politician and an opponent of Amédee Knight, the radically-inclined Governor of the island had refused to evacuate St. Pierre and even placed troops around the city to ensure that the citizenry stayed put. Why? Because of electoral politics: The city of St. Pierre was expected to cast votes mainly for radical candidates for public office, especially given the influx of poor farmers into the city from their villages on the slopes of the volcano. These charges were utterly without foundation, but were widely believed, perhaps in part because, in the words of volcano scholar Alwyn Scarth, they resonated with mankind's "psychological need to explain the disaster and, if possible, to blame someone for it." What is more, an even more damaging story reached the international press alleging that black aid recipients in Martinique were shirking work and "dancing and partying" on the international community's dime. There was not a shred of truth to this rumor, but since it matched the widespread contemporary stereotype of the lazy, childish black man,

ALFRED LACROIX, *LA MONTAGNE PELÉE ET SES ERUPTIONS* (1904), P. 294

The ruins of St. Pierre only a few days after the first eruption.

this tale seemed plausible to most would-be donors. As a result, the international relief funds to Martinique dried up shortly after May 17th, when these stories began to hit the French press.

These false rumors were unfortunate, as relief funds were desperately needed in post-eruption Martinique. Indeed, the island's misery had by no means ended with the May 8th eruption. In the aftermath of the disaster, the French government made the belated decision to evacuate people from villages in northern Martinique which lay below the still active volcano. As a result, the city of Fort-de-France was inundated with approximately 25,000 poor and mostly black refugees within a few weeks of the eruption. At first, the government opened its heart and its coffers to these misplaced people, granting them generous aid in terms of cash, food, and clothing. However, this humane policy soon came under attack. Some critics, influenced by the prevailing liberal ethos of the day, worried that these cash handouts would destroy the moral character of Martinique's laboring class. Others opposed the policy on racist grounds, arguing that it was "disgraceful" for the government to distribute good food to "these negroes" at a time when many white Frenchmen were still mired in poverty.

These ideological arguments against the government's relief policy were reinforced by the practical realities of the situation. The administration feared that the presence of so many refugees in the small city of Fort-de-France would create fertile ground for disease outbreaks, and their fears were seemingly confirmed by a typhoid fever epidemic in the capital shortly after the eruption. What is more, public relief on this scale was too expensive to continue indefinitely, especially in light of the abrupt discontinuation of international relief funds. As a result, the government caved into pressure and adopted a new policy: Despite the continued eruptions of Mount Pelée, the former inhabitants of Northern Martinique would have to return to their homes. If they did so before August 15th, they would continue to receive some governmental assistance, but if not, their relief funds would be shut off and the government would assume no further responsibility for their welfare. Thus, although this new policy of returning the refugees to their homes was theoretically voluntary, the government essentially gave the poor villagers no choice. In one of the disaster's bitterest ironies, the naval vessel *Suchet*, which had earlier performed fine service in rescuing people from Mount Pelée's blast zone on the 8th, was now used to ferry terrified villages back under the shadow of the volcano.

Ruins of St. Pierre after the pyroclastic flow. Notice that buildings parallel to the flow survived more intact than buildings which received Mt. Pelée's broadside blast.

ANGELO HEILPRIN, *MONT PELÉE AND THE TRAGEDY OF MARTINIQUE* (1903), P. 38

For the mostly black inhabitants of the town of Le Morne-Rouge, the government's resettlement policy proved to be a death sentence. Almost as soon as the villagers returned to their mountain town, located barely 5 km from Mount Pelée's crater, the volcano roused itself from a month-long nap and resumed activity, spewing pyroclastic flows down the already-ruined valley of the Rivière Blanche. At the same time, a dome of congealed lava began to form in Pelée's crater, and to the villagers' horror, it eventually rose so high that its top peeked over the crater's rim and was visible in Le Morne-Rouge below. A frantic delegation sent to the Governor's office was met with callous indifference — the citizens of Le Morne-Rouge were informed that they had to stay put if they wished to continue receiving their food allowance, which they could not do without because of ash falls and livestock loss in the agricultural lands near the volcano. As a result, when faced with the choice of starving or taking their chances with Pelée, most villagers chose to do the latter. Indeed, they could hardly do otherwise.

Thanks to this hard-hearted and most likely racially motivated decree, Mount Pelée was allowed to claim an additional 1085 victims. On August 30, with a tremendous roar, another massive pyroclastic flow exploded from the volcano. Unlike the May 8th flow, however, this one did not limit itself to the sector southwest of the crater, but flowed due south as well, reaching as far as the town of Le Morne-Rouge. This superheated volcanic cloud had small silver lining: The August 30th pyroclastic flow was not as powerful as the May 8th cataclysm, and as a result some people survived, especially those who found themselves in strongly-built and relatively airtight houses at the time of the eruption. Even so, the carnage was immense. Every structure in town was either damaged or destroyed, corpses littered the streets, and hot ash covered everything in a funerary shroud. Some of those who survived the initial blast succumbed later to their injuries, especially those who "swallowed the fire" and thus slowly asphyxiated. Remarkably, the French authorities in Martinique managed to avoid censure for their part in the disaster — perhaps because Le Morne-Rouge was a small town with a large black popula-

ALFRED LACROIX, *LA MONTAGNE PELÉE ET SES ERUPTIONS* (1904), P. 223

The ruins of St. Pierre after repeated pyroclastic flows.

tion, and thus very different from the wealthy, populous, and disproportionably white town of St. Pierre.

Although Mount Pelée continued to erupt for over a year, no casualties occurred following the August 30th eruption. Nonetheless, the eruptions left a lasting mark on both local and global history. Although St. Pierre was eventually rebuilt on a much smaller scale, the economic, cultural, and social center of gravity of Martinique shifted permanently south to Fort-de-France, which at 100,000 people can now boast nearly 20 times St. Pierre's population. Even more importantly, Mount Pelée became the first eruption of the 20th century to be intensely studied by the scientific community. Scientists marveled at the remarkable "Tower of Pelée"— a huge but fragile skyscraper of solidified lava that eventually towered over 570 meters above the crater floor before collapsing. Far more importantly, scientists identified two previously unknown volcanic phenomena: pyroclastic flows, which were dubbed "nuées ardentes" or "glowing clouds" by French-speaking scientists, and "mud torrents," which are now called lahars. The Mount Pelée eruption also convinced scientists that different volcanoes could exhibit markedly different patterns of behaviors, and as a result scientists created a rich vocabulary of new terms— such as Peléan, Hawaiian, and Plinian — allowing them to classify eruptions according to observed historical types. Consequently, the Mount Pelée eruption marked the death of old St. Pierre, but the birth of a new branch of science: volcanology.

Study Questions

1. Based on this reading, to what degree was the damage inflicted by the Mount Pelée eruption exacerbated by other types of natural disaster?

HTTP://COMMONS.WIKIMEDIA.ORG/WIKI/IMAGE:MOUNT_PEL%C3%A9E_1902.JPG

Mt. Pelée's eruption as seen from Morne Rouge.

2. To what degree did French racism play a role in worsening the Mount Pelée disaster?

3. In your opinion, was the carnage caused by the Mount Pelée eruption unavoidable? Your answer should both reflect the physical location of the eruption and the state of volcanology at the time of the disaster.

Sources/Suggested Readings

De Boer, Jelle Zeilinga, and Theodore Donald Sanders. *Volcanoes in Human History*. Princeton, NJ: Princeton University Press, 2002.

Scarth, Alwyn. *La Catastrophe: The Eruption of Mount Pelée, the Worst Volcanic Disaster of the 20th Century.* New York: Oxford University Press, 2002.

Scarth, Alwyn. *Vulcan's Fury: Man Against the Volcano.* New Haven, CT: Yale University Press, 1999.

Zebrowski, Ernest Jr. *The Last Days of St. Pierre: The Volcanic Disaster That Claimed Thirty Thousand Lives.* New Brunswick, NJ: Rutgers University Press, 2002.

2.3: *Mount Pinatubo, 1991*

The story of Mount Pinatubo in 1991 is not really a tale of disaster, but rather of disaster averted. Although the Pinatubo eruption was the second most powerful of the 20th century, and though it occurred on the densely populated Philippine island of Luzon, the eruption lead to only a little over a thousand deaths, and many of those casualties were as much the fault of a coincidental tropical storm as they were of Pinatubo itself. This low casualty toll largely reflects advances in volcanology over the 20th century, especially the use of sophisticated equipment to forecast likely eruptions and the creation of hazard maps to identify areas at risk from pyroclastic flows, lahars, and other volcanic phenomena. However, the Pinatubo eruption also highlights the limits of modern volcanology in mitigating volcanic disasters. Volcanologists were able to minimize the loss of life at a local level but unable to do anything more than observe as Pinatubo's emissions caused a noticeable drop in global temperatures. What is more, volcanologists were powerless to prevent Pinatubo's eruption from turning the world of the nearby Aeta tribesmen upside-down. Indeed, the eruption severed the powerful economic, cultural, and religious ties that bound the semi-nomadic Aeta to Mount Pinatubo, which was both their home and their deity. Even today, the Aetas struggle to adapt to the changed reality following the 1991 Pinatubo eruption.

Mount Pinatubo, as with all volcanoes in the Philippines, owes its existence to the interaction of the Philippine Sea plate with neighboring plates. The eastern side of the plate abuts the heavier Pacific Ocean plate, which is sliding beneath the Philippine plate at a rate of over 5 cm a year. This process of subduction has created the deepest known undersea valley on the planet — the 10.6 km deep Mariana Trench — as well as the Mariana chain of volcanic islands, which includes the U.S. territory of Guam. In the meantime, the western end of the Philippine Sea plate is being pinched into a V-shaped cleft of the Eurasian continental plate. The complex interaction between these two plates means that part of the Philippine Sea plate is diving under the Eurasian plate at the northern end of the Philippine Islands, while the Eurasian Plate is sliding under the Philippine Sea plate at the south end. The result of this double process of subduction is an island chain studded with more than 200 identified volcanoes, ten of which have erupted over the course of the last century. Unfortunately for the Filipinos, these volcanoes have historically been very destructive, in part because the subduction of sea plates produces magma rich in dissolved water and gas, and in part because the Philippines receives heavy rainfall, which aggravates the problem of lahars.

To mitigate the problem posed by volcanoes, the Philippine government has established PHIVOLCS, the highly professional Philippine Institute of Volcanology and Seismology. Nonetheless, the reawakening of the Pinatubo volcano was an unexpected surprise. Few people who lived in western Luzon Island were even aware of its existence, since Pinatubo was a relatively modest peak nestled with and nearly indistinguishable from the other crests of the low-lying Zambales mountain chain. The last eruption of Pinatubo had occurred in about A.D.

1500, almost half a century before the Philippines were annexed by Spain. Since then, the forested slopes and fertile flatlands surrounding Pinatubo had become the home to over half a million people, including 30,000 who lived on the slopes of the volcano itself.

For the most part, the inhabitants of this vulnerable region were ethnic Filipinos, with two notable exceptions: the 16,000 American servicemen and dependants at Clark Air Force base and the 35,000-strong Pinatubo Aeta ethnic minority, both of whom would play a major role

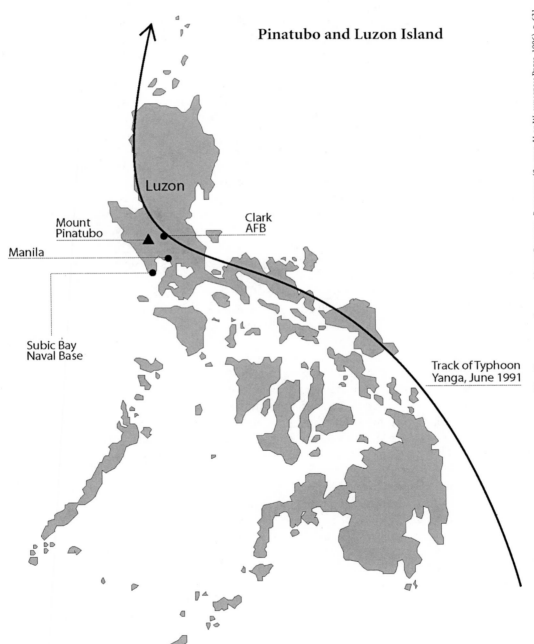

Pinatubo and Luzon Island

Luzon

Mount
Pinatubo

Clark
AFB

Manila

Subic Bay
Naval Base

Track of Typhoon
Yanga, June 1991

CHRISTOPHER G. NEWHALL AND RAYMONDO S. PUNONGBAYAN, EDS., *FIRE AND MUD: ERUPTIONS AND LAHARS OF MOUNT PINATUBO, PHILIPPINES* (SEATTLE: U OF WASHINGTON PRESS, 1996), P. 631

in the unfolding Pinatubo eruption. Clark Air Force Base, which lay only about 20 km from the volcano, was a long-standing fixture of the region, though its future at the time of the eruption was uncertain due to ongoing lease negotiations between the U.S. and Philippine governments. The Pinatubo Aetas lived even closer to the volcano, in many cases on the slopes of the mountain itself. This group was a local branch of a more widespread ethnic minority group, the Aetas, which had occupied Luzon Island since around 28,000 B.C., when low sea levels probably created land bridges allowing their ancestors to migrate to the Philippines from an as yet unidentified ancestral homeland. Dark skinned, curly haired, and small of stature, the Aetas have more in common with New Guinea highlanders and the Australian aborigines than they do with the Filipinos, who are descendants of Austronesian seafarers who came to the Philippines from the island of Taiwan at around 5000–2,500 B.C. The Aetas originally occupied the entire island of Luzon, but were gradually displaced by the Austronesian Filipinos and driven into mountains. Although the Aetas retreated to the highlands only under duress, over time the Aetas became acclimated to mountain life. Indeed, for the Pinatubo Aetas, Mount Pinatubo served simultaneously as a food source, an anchor of their spirituality, and a visible reminder of their historical development.

Pinatubo first gave notice that it was coming back to life in July of 1990, when a 7.8 magnitude earthquake occurred 100 km northeast of Pinatubo. Only a few weeks later, a landslide accompanied by billows of steam disturbed the peace of Mount Pinatubo's northwest flank. In the following year, this volcanic activity escalated: A series of earthquakes rocked the Pinatubo area, followed by a series of small eruptions in April that were probably the result of water superheated by magma reaching the mountain's surface. At this point, PHIVOLCS deployed a team of volcanologists to watch for further increases in volcanic activity, and these researchers were joined by a group of volcanologists from the United States Geological Survey, which had a special interest in Pinatubo due to its proximity to Clark AFB. The joint PHIVOLCS and USGS team quickly went to work, setting up a network of seismographs to monitor the mountain, and investigating the area around Pinatubo to determine how Pinatubo had behaved during past eruptions as a guide for the future. What they discovered was sobering: In past Pinatubo eruptions, pyroclastic flows had reached as far as 20 km from the mountain peak, and lahars spawned by previous eruptions had traveled over 40 km from the volcano, reaching almost the outskirts of the Philippine capital of Manila. Indeed, it was discovered that Clark AFB was built upon debris left behind by prehistoric pyroclastic flows.

In the weeks after the first eruptions, the joint PHIVOLCS/USGS team detected signs that Pinatubo was gearing up for a big eruption. Hundreds of small, high frequency earthquakes were detected in April and May, and as the epicenter of these quakes was generally close to Pinatubo, they were interpreted as evidence that magma was moving to the surface below the mountain. This analysis was confirmed by a steady increase of sulfur dioxide emissions from Pinatubo's crater. As May turned to June, earthquake activity increased, but sulfur dioxide emissions decreased, suggesting that a plug of magma was now blocking the escape of volcanic gasses to the surface. At around the same time, the slope of the east flank of the volcano began to deform due to internal pressure, and just days later, a lava dome was spotted on the northwest side of the summit. Then, on June 8, Pinatubo launched a major column of ash into the atmosphere, raising the fears of scientists that a pyroclastic flow was imminent. As a result, PHIVOLCS raised the volcanic alert level to its highest level, announced an eruption was in progress, and ordered the evacuation of all civilians living within 20 km of the volcano. The wisdom of this move was confirmed by a major explosive eruption on June 12, after which the evacuation zone was extended to 30 km.

These progressive evacuation orders were met with resistance by the affected populations.

The evacuation of Clark AFB was initially opposed by General Adams, the regional air force commander, who believed than an evacuation of Clark AFB would probably claim more lives than Pinatubo's eruption. He based this belief on his observation of lava flows on Hawaiian volcanoes, where "you see the molasses coming down the volcano when it finally erupts ... [and] it takes days and days for it to finally get down to the ocean." Thankfully for the servicemen at Clark AFB, volcanologists from the USGS managed to convince him that pyroclastic flows of the composite volcanoes of the Philippines were more dangerous that Hawaii's rivers of creeping lava, and on June 10th, all but 1,500 soldiers evacuated Clark. In the meantime, the Filipino mayor of Angeles City accused the Americans of overreacting to the threat of Pinatubo, probably because he feared the impact the closure of Clark AFB would have on the economy of his city. His skepticism was shared by many Filipinos, but it began to evaporate after a film graphically showing the hazards of a volcanic eruption was distributed by the volcanologists to local communities.

The group most affected by the evacuations, however, was the Pinatubo Aetas. Before the eruption, the Aetas of Pinatubo had practiced a semi-nomadic lifestyle in the mountain forests of Luzon, in which the cultivation of root crops was supplemented by wild foods such as edible plants, fish, and small game. So successful was this lifestyle, in fact, that the American military had employed Pinatubo Aetas to train soldiers in jungle survival during the Vietnam War. As a result of this economic system, which was self-contained and utilized multiple sources of food, the Pinatubo Aetas had been relatively unaffected by natural disasters up until 1991, even during periods when lowlander Filipinos on the island of Luzon were in the grip of famine. The evacuation of Pinatubo, therefore, meant the abandonment of an entire way of life, since the area around Pinatubo was one of very few forest areas remaining within overpopulated Luzon.

The exodus of the Aetas from the slopes of Mount Pinatubo was also a moment of intense cultural crisis. Since the Pinatubo Aetas are almost entirely illiterate, they remembered past events chiefly in reference to the geographical features of the mountain where they occurred. Anthropologist Hiromu Shimizu, writing just three years before the eruption, declared that, for the Aetas, "their own surroundings are the silent witnesses that gives realism to their history ... with their environment ever present in their sight, they see their own history all the time." The forced evacuation from Pinatubo, therefore, cut the Aetas from their own past. Worse yet, the abandonment of the slopes of Pinatubo lead to an enormous religious rupture for the Pinatubo Aeta. Although most Aeta Pinatubo were nominally Christian at the time of the eruption, the Aeta world view was still predominantly informed by pre–Christian beliefs. As a consequence, most Aetas regarded Mount Pinatubo as the center of the universe, the home of the spirits, and for some tribes, the resting place for the souls of the deceased. All prayers were spoken in the direction of Pinatubo, and offerings to the spirits were always given while facing the mountain. Most important amongst these spirits was *Apo Namalyari*, the supreme being and creator of the universe, who could punish mankind if disturbed or insulted. As a result, the reawakening of Mount Pinatubo was seen by the Aetas not as a natural event but rather as physical manifestation of divine rage. Indeed, most Pinatubo Aetas believed that *Apo Namalyari* had been provoked to anger by the recent drilling into Pinatubo's side by a firm seeking to construct a geothermal power plant.

Given Pinatubo's profound importance to the Aeta people, it is not surprising that a few Aetas resisted being evacuated from their sacred mountain. Some Aeta claimed to be physically unable to make the journey to lowland evacuation camps, while others wanted to stay on the mountain until the harvest was ready. Still others simply refused to believe that *Apo Namalyari* wanted to hurt his people. Nonetheless, most Aetas consented to leave the mountain for refugee camps. The fate of these Pinatubo Aetas depended largely on where they lived before the eruption. Pinatubo Aeta families living on the north and west slopes of the volcano, for instance, were transported into Aeta-only resettlement camps relatively close to the mountain. Although these camps were nearby familiar territory, they suffered from inadequate water supplies, extreme overpopulation, and lack of good farmland. The poor quality of the roads to neighboring lowland towns helped shelter the Pinatubo from lowlander interference, but also hindered relations with would-be lowlander Filipino employers or trade partners. To complicate matters, the best plots of land near these camps were the property of Filipino farmers, and this led to territorial disputes, as Aeta culture did not recognize the principle of private land ownership. What is more, the full-time agricultural lifestyle the Aeta were forced to embrace in the camps was hard to reconcile with the Aetas' hunter-gatherer sensibilities. Relying solely on agricultural produce made the Aetas feel tied down and vulnerable, and the Aetas, whose former lifestyle required flexibility and opportunistic utilization of immediately available resources, found it hard to embrace the long-term discipline required by agriculture, especially saving a portion of the crop to eat in the months between harvests.

Nonetheless, the condition of these Aetas was vastly preferable to those unlucky enough to live on the southern flanks of Pinatubo. Aetas living to the south of the peak were initially mixed with the displaced Filipino population and deposited in crowded tent cities with up to 25,000 occupants. For the Aetas, used to living in small groups in sparsely inhabited woodlands, moving to the camps proved to be a traumatic experience. Food was a problem as well: While the resourceful Aetas could feed themselves easily in the tropical uplands, they had problems with lowlander food—for example, they were completely unfamiliar with canned foodstuffs. The resulting malnutrition, combined with overcrowding, created a perfect stalking ground for disease, and the unvaccinated Aetas proved to be easy prey. Overall, 77 Aetas perished from respiratory infections, 101 to diarrhea, and 108 to measles. These diseases disproportionably affected Aeta children, 150 of whom died in refugee camps within a month of the eruption. The problem of disease was compounded by the lack of health care, in part because of lack of resources, but also because of the cultural gap between the Aeta and the lowland Filipinos, which sometimes manifested itself in outright anti–Aeta racism.

As miserable as the plight of the Aeta proved to be, it would have been far worse had they remained on the slopes of the mountain. On June 14th, following several days of major eruptions, Mount Pinatubo essentially exploded. A column of ash reached 30,000 meters into the sky, and pyroclastic flows once again rushed down the flanks of the volcano, this time coming within 400 meters of the "Hill Housing" residential complex at Clark AFB. During this eruption, Pinatubo disgorged as much as 10.4 cubic kilometers of volcanic debris into the atmosphere and surrounding lowlands, a volume equal, in the words of Eddee Castro, "to 71 million 10-wheeler trucks filled with sand." When the crest of Pinatubo finally became visible again in the days after the culminating blast, scientists discovered that an enormous new caldera had formed atop Pinatubo. This caldera would later fill with water and become a new lake nearly 2 km long.

Because of the enormous volume of volcanic materials emitted by Pinatubo, including an estimated 17 megatons of sulfur dioxide, the Pinatubo eruption exerted a marked impact on global weather. In the northern hemisphere, average temperatures actually fell by about half a degree Celsius. By happenstance, this drop in temperature was partially offset by global warming, which had begun in earnest by 1991, and thus did not trigger any large-scale crop failures, though early snowfalls were reported throughout the northern hemisphere and the pack ice failed to melt in Canada's Hudson Bay. Pinatubo's aerosol emissions also had a profound effect on "hole" in the ozone layer above the southern hemisphere, which increased to a record 27 million square kilometers in 1992.

Photograph of the Pinatubo eruption taken from Clark Air Force Base before its abandonment.

Photograph of Clark Air Force Base following the Pinatubo ashfall.

Given the global influence of the Pinatubo eruption, it is a tribute to the vigilance of the PHIVOLCS /USGS team and efficiency of the pre-eruption evacuations that only about 200–300 people died during the eruption itself. Many of those who did die perished because of an unforeseen circumstance: the arrival of the first rain bands of Typhoon Yunya at precisely the moment of the climactic eruption. As a result, Pinatubo's waterlogged ash had the consistency and weight of wet cement. This ash covered the land around Pinatubo to a depth of up to 15 cm, and the galvanized steel roofs of many structures near the volcano proved unable to withstand its smothering weight. In all, 98 hospitals, 18 public markets, 83 administrative buildings, and an unknown number of schools suffered roof collapses on the 14th. Clark AFB suffered extensive damage — visitors to the base after the storm described it as "a lumpy, grey blanket as far as the eye could see." Overall 110 buildings at the base were flattened, including the base's large gymnasium, which eyewitness C. R. Anderegg described as resembling nothing so much as "a crumpled piece of wastepaper" after the eruption. Luckily, Filipino private homes survived the wet ash mostly intact, since the walls of private dwellings in the Philippines are generally less than 5 meters apart and thus provided adequate support for the weight of even an ash-covered galvanized steel roof.

Although the June 14th blast marked the climax of Pinatubo's eruptions, it by no means signaled the end of the danger that Pinatubo posed to surrounding communities. Further volcanic eruptions, though smaller in scale, continued to issue from the mountain in the following months. Worse yet, the Pinatubo eruption took place shortly before the arrival of the rainy

AP/WIDE WORLD PHOTOS

The 1996 breach in the "Megadike" designed to restrain lahars of Pinatubo Ash.

season in the Philippines, and scientists warned that the combination of heavy rains and ash deposits would lead to deadly lahars. These fears were soon proven correct. During the 1991 rainy season, about 200 lahars, some with a discharge volume of up to 1,000 cubic meters per second, raged down Pinatubo's river valleys at up to 30 km/hour. By 1993, these mudflows had deposited almost two cubic kilometers of ash and pumice on the plains surrounding Pinatubo, burying some villages beneath 5 meters of mud, killing an estimated 100 people, and ruining vast stretches of agricultural land. The danger posed by lahars was reduced somewhat by the construction of the so-called "megadike" in the mid-1990s, a massive lahar-control structure that cost over $30 billion dollars to complete. Unfortunately, the breach of the megadike mere months after its completion in 1996 demonstrated that lahars would continue to pose problems for years to come.

Pinatubo's combined lahars, ash fall, and pyroclastic flows ultimately inflicted considerable economic damage on central Luzon. Damage to crops and property was estimated at $374 million in 1991, and continued lahars raised that total by a further $69 million in 1992. An estimated 8,000 houses were destroyed and 75,000 more suffered severe damage. Mudflows ultimately affected 42 percent of the cropland around Pinatubo, dealing a major blow to the region's agricultural economy. What is more, the volcanic eruption helped to convince American lease negotiators that Clark AFB was more trouble than it was worth, especially given the fact that a pyroclasic flow had all but filled in Crow Valley, the location of Clark's bombing range. The closure of the base, in turn, created enormous unemployment in surrounding Filipino communities, which had depended heavily on the jobs and trade opportunities that the air base provided. As for the Pinatubo Aetas, they discovered that a full ⅔ of the upland forests where they had once dwelled had been obliterated, dashing hopes for a quick return to the slopes of their sacred mountain.

In the aftermath of the Pinatubo eruption, the various parties that had once coexisted in the shadow of Mount Pinatubo were forced to adapt to the new post-eruption realities. For the Americans at Clark AFB, the transition was relatively painless—the United States soon found an alternative site in Singapore. Nonetheless, the U.S. Air Force retains a presence in the region in the form of nearly 2000 retired military veterans, as of 1998, who chose to remain in the area despite the base closure. For Filipinos, who did not have the luxury of abandoning the country following the eruption, the transition to post-eruption life was considerably more difficult. Continued lahars posed a constant threat to downstream settlements every rainy season, especially since the volcanic material that choked the upper river valleys had a tendency to dam up rivers for days or weeks at a time before giving way and releasing catastrophic mudflows. Filipino farmers compensated for these lahars in several ways. On the advice of the government, some villagers constructed 4 meter earthen platforms near their homes as a refuge from lahars. What is more, in order to mitigate the risk of a lahar wiping out a year's crop, many Filipinos near Pinatubo began to grow quick ripening crops, such as peanuts, tomatoes, cassava, and sweet potatoes, which can be harvested before the arrival of the late summer rainy season and the threat of lahars.

On the other hand, some lowlander Filipinos have found ways not only to survive, but also to prosper, in the aftermath of Pinatubo. With the closure of Clark, the Philippine government found itself in possession of a large, flat, and reasonably well developed piece of land, surrounded by a population that, thanks to the long-time presence of Clark AFB, was generally better educated and more proficient in English than the rest of the Philippines. To capitalize on these assets, and to assist the region's post-volcano recovery, the Philippines government created the Clark Development Corporation, a free trade zone designed to attract both industry and tourism to the region. By and large it has succeeded: The former site of Clark now hosts over 672 businesses, including factories, duty-free shops, resort hotels, and several golf courses featuring hills and slopes sculpted out of Pinatubo's ash. Only the "Hill Housing" complex, which lies closest to the path of Pinatubo's 1991 pyroclastic flows, remains in its original, unrenovated state.

As for the Pinatubo Aetas, they have adjusted to post-eruption realities with various degrees of success. Those who lived in the Aeta-only camps to the east of Pinatubo tended to be better off, in part because they can migrate seasonally back to unspoiled areas on Pinatubo's slopes, and in part because they have been taken under the wing of various NGO's (non-governmental organizations), which provide food, resources, and job training. Elsewhere, the Aeta have fared worse, in part because non–Aeta Filipinos, attracted by the new facilities built by the government, have increasingly moved into resettlement camps, marginalizing or displacing the Aetas. This process is perhaps best seen as the most recent manifestation of the long historical trend of Filipino infiltration into Aeta land. But Filipino-Aeta relations are by no means uniformly confrontational. The new proximity of the Aeta to the Filipino Christians has created excellent economic opportunities for some Aetas, who have earned good income collecting roof thatching and firewood for lowlander Filipinos. Other Aetas have adopted entirely new professions, such as weaving rattan furniture or molding adobe bricks, or else are turning traditional skills into commercial advantages, for instance producing bows and arrows for the tourist market. The sharp recent increase in Filipino-Aeta intermarriage further demonstrates the pragmatic flexibility of the Aeta people in the aftermath of the Pinatubo eruption. Nonetheless, it is unclear at this point whether the Pinatubo Aeta's unique culture, as opposed to the Aeta people themselves, will be able to survive the loss of Mount Pinatubo.

Overall, there can be no doubt that the Mount Pinatubo eruption lead to considerable destruction, death, and misery, particularly on the part of the Pinatubo Aetas, who experienced the eruption as a spiritual as well as a physical event. Nonetheless, it could have been far worse. Thanks to the early detection, hazard mapping, well coordinated evacuations, and public education campaigns, Pinatubo's death toll (both direct and indirect) has been tabulated at only 1,202 — a mere drop in the bucket, given that as many as a million people lived within the possible hazard radius of Pinatubo before the eruption. Indeed, volcano authority Alwyn Scarth estimates that PHIVOLCS and the USGS probably saved somewhere between 20,000 and 50,000 lives. Thus, the Pinatubo eruption of 1991 is notable as much for its severity as for the fact that, in Scarth's words, "the biggest volcanic disaster of the twentieth century ... did not take place."

Study Questions

1. Based on the text above, to what degree did the 1991 eruption of Pinatubo mark a major discontinuity, or turning point, in the history of the island of Luzon?

2. What factors conspired to make the Pinatubo Aetas most vulnerable to the Mount Pinatubo eruption?

3. To what degree was volcanic eruption of Mount Pinatubo worsened by its interaction with other forms of natural disaster?

4. "The low death toll of the Pinatubo eruption of 1991 demonstrates that modern technology has effectively tamed the threat posed by volcanic eruptions." Based on the evidence provided in this and the previous three sections, how compelling do you find this statement?

Sources/Suggested Readings

Anderegg, C. R. *The Ash Warriors.* Washington, DC: Air Force History and Museums Program, 2005.

Castro, Eddee. *Pinatubo: The Eruption of the Century.* Quezon City, Philippines: Phoenix Publishing House, 1991.

Fondevilla, Emma F. Sr. *Eruption and Exodus: Mt. Pinatubo and the Aytas of Zambales.* Quezon City, Philippines: Claretian Publications, 1991.

Newhall, Christopher G., and Raymondo S. Punongbayan, eds., *Fire and Mud: Eruptions and Lahars of Mount Pinatubo, Philippines.* Seattle, WA: University of Washington Press, 1996.

Scarth, Alwyn. *Vulcan's Fury: Man Against the Volcano.* New Haven, CT: Yale University Press, 1999.

Seitz, Stefan. "Coping Strategies of an Ethnic Minority Group: The Aeta of Mount Pinatubo." *Disasters*, Vol. 22(1) 1998, 76–90.

Shimizu, Hiromu. *Pinatubo Aytas: Continuity and Change.* Manila, Philippines: Ateno de Manila University Press, 1989.

Soriquez, Tessa, and Ruben Maria Soriquez. *Mount Pinatubo and the Saga of the Megadike.* Quezon City, Philippines: Jade Asia Group Publishing Inc., 2006.

Chapter 3

Earthquakes

Science and History

Although less theatrical in their effects than volcanoes, which arise from similar tectonic forces, earthquakes pose a much greater overall threat to human lives and property. In part, this is because earthquakes are far more common — indeed, an earthquake occurs somewhere in the world approximately every 30 seconds, and 120 large, destructive earthquakes occur on average each year. The high death toll reaped by earthquakes also reflects the fact that, unlike volcanoes, earthquakes tend to strike with little or no forewarning. Not surprisingly, given their abrupt and disastrous consequences, catastrophic earthquakes have repeatedly left an imprint on the historical record. Some earthquakes have even changed the course of human history: The Lisbon Earthquake of 1755, it has been argued, profoundly influenced the contemporary European intellectual movement called the Enlightenment. Thankfully, due to advances in earthquake detection and preparedness, modern earthquakes are less likely to have such world-changing effects. Nonetheless, as the Pakistani Earthquake of 2005 and the Indian Ocean Earthquake of 2004 vividly demonstrated, modern technology still has a long way to go before it catches up with the awesome destructive power of earthquakes.

The Science of Earthquakes

Earthquake Origins

Although human beings have long been aware of the dangers posed by earthquakes, only very recently has the process that causes them been fully understood. Pre-modern man tended to blame earthquakes on the anger of the gods. The first group to develop a "scientific" explanation for earthquakes was the ancient Greeks, who devised the theory that quakes are the result of wind trapped in underground caves. As a result, in the following centuries, Europeans widely believed that earthquakes could be predicted by changes in the weather, though exactly what constituted "earthquake weather" was a matter of debate. American scientist Benjamin Franklin later speculated that the earth's surface was a solid "shell" floating upon a dense interior fluid, and that "the surface of the globe" was therefore "capable of being disordered by any violent movements of the fluid on which it rested," thus producing earthquakes. Franklin's insight was actually remarkably accurate, but it would not be until the 1970s, when the theory of plate tectonics became widely accepted, that science was able to discover a mechanism to explain the "violent movements" that Franklin had imagined.

To understand plate tectonics, it is vital to first understand the composition of the earth.

Plate Tectonics and Convection

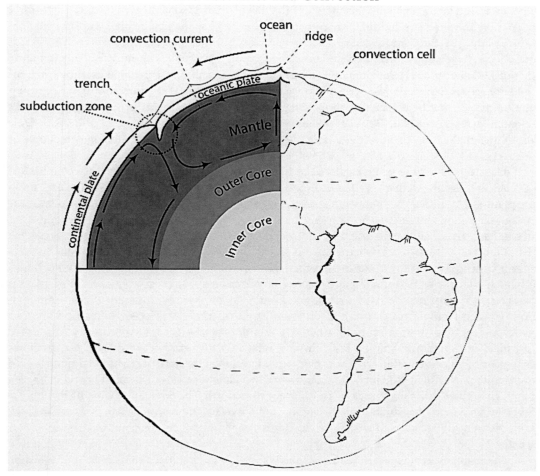

Although the ground we walk on seems solid enough, in reality the hard crust of the earth is merely skin-deep. Below the earth's solid outer layer, which is only about as thick as the coat of paint on a wooden croquet ball, lies a vast layer of semi-molten rock called the mantle. The rock of the mantle is constantly moving, albeit very slowly, as a result of convection: The rock at the bottom of the mantle is very hot, so it tends to rise, while the rock near the surface is cooler and tends to fall, forming a circular current resembling the movement of the colored globs in a lava lamp. These currents in the mantle, though slow, are strong enough to shift the continental and oceanic crust plates that float upon them. As a result, the crust of the world is in constant motion, but in different directions and at different speeds, depending on the mantle currents underneath. The interaction of these plates as they abrade and collide with each other, scientists now realize, is what gives rise to earthquakes.

If tectonic plates moved smoothly alongside each other, earthquakes would never occur, since the vast forces involved would be released slowly over a long period of time. However, the interaction between two plates is rarely smooth. Indeed, most of the time, tectonic plates seem motionless in respect to each other as friction keeps them locked in place. This motionlessness is deceiving, however, since the movement of the semi-fluid mantle layer under the crust exerts enormous pressure on the plates, causing one or both of them to buckle and deform.

In the process, energy is stored in the plate, much like energy can be stored in a bow by pulling back on the string. Eventually the energy in the plate becomes so great that it exceeds the force of friction and the plate suddenly snaps back to its normal shape. In the process, force that has been building up for years, decades, or even centuries is suddenly released. The resulting earthquakes can have almost unimaginable power: A strong earthquake can release energy equal to that of 12,000 or more Hiroshima-type atomic bombs. Thankfully, earthquakes of that magnitude are relatively rare, occurring only once a year on average. Far more common are minor quakes that cannot be detected without sensitive instruments—in any given year, earthquake scientists record over 600,000 such quakes, which make up almost ⅔ of all earthquakes. Only about one quake out of a hundred is actually strong enough to inflict any damage on people or property.

The strength of any given earthquake is determined by a number of factors. One important variable is the relative speed and direction of the interacting tectonic plates. "Fast" moving plates—plates that are in motion at an average speed of over 5 cm/year—store up far more energy than slow moving plates. The length of time since the last eruption also determines the strength of earthquakes. Since each earthquake represents a release of energy, it can be expected that a fault which has recently experienced an earthquake will have less potential energy than a fault which has not moved for many years. The size of a fault is also important: Long faults, in which a large portion of one plate is locked by friction against a sizable portion of another plate, can store up more energy than smaller faults. What is more, different types of interaction between tectonic plates produce different levels of friction. Friction is lowest if the two plates are moving apart from each other. The faults that result from such interaction, called "normal" or "spreading" faults, tend to have relatively low-grade earthquakes but frequent eruptions of volcanic materials, since they create fissures in the earth's crust. Earthquakes tend to be more powerful at "slip strike" faults, where two plates are moving roughly parallel to each other, though at different speeds or in different directions. The San Andreas Fault in California, the movement of which caused the San Francisco earthquake of 1906, is a well-known example of a slip strike fault. At slip-strike faults, earthquakes can reach a magnitude of 8 or greater.

The strongest earthquakes, with a magnitude of 9 or greater, occur at "thrust faults," when two plates collide. If both plates are continental plates composed of relatively light rock, the impact will cause both plates to crumple, forming ranges of mountains. The Himalaya Mountains, for example, were created by the violent collision of the Indian-Australian plate and the Eurasian plate. An even better example is the Zagros Mountains of Iran, which consist of a series of parallel ridges formed by the buckling of the Eurasian plate under pressure from the Arabian plate. On the other hand, if one or both plates are ocean plates, the heavier plate will dive under the lighter plate and be drawn by gravity back into the semi-molten rock of the mantle. As we learned in chapter 2, this process is called "subduction" and produces about 15 percent of the world's volcanoes. The process of subduction also produces frequent and very powerful earthquakes, as the direct collision of plates stores up enormous amounts of energy that is eventually released in massive jolts. The 2004 Asian Tsunami and the 2005 Pakistani Earthquake, discussed in sections 3.3 and 6.2 respectively, are both the result of the impact of the Indian-Australian and Eurasian plates.

It is important to realize that the "magnitude" of a quake, as measured by scientists, is not a linear measurement. Each new level of magnitude represents a geometric rather than arithmetic increase in power. A magnitude 7 quake, therefore, is somewhere between 30 and 40 times as powerful as a magnitude 6 earthquake. A magnitude 8 quake, in turn, is approximately a million times more powerful than a magnitude 4 quake. As a result, slip-strike faults like the faults of California are far more limited in their potential strength than their thrust fault cousins. Why, then, does San Andreas get such a disproportional share of attention? The answer, simply enough, is that the location of an earthquake matters as much as its strength. Consider for example the different situations of California and Alaska, both major locations for North American earthquakes. Although the slip-strike faults of California release far less overall energy than the thrust faults of Alaska, the far greater population density of California virtually assures that California earthquakes will reap much more damage in terms of lives and property.

The location of earthquakes is closely related to their power: Areas capable of producing the strongest earthquakes also tend to produce earthquakes more frequently. As a result, fully 75 percent of all earthquakes are produced along the boundaries of the vast Pacific Plate, which has numerous thrust faults on its western side and slip-strike faults along its northeast rim. Another 23 percent of the world's earthquakes occur along a line starting in the Straits of Gibraltar, passing through the Mediterranean and the Persian Gulf, continuing through the Himalayas, skirting the islands of Sumatra and Java, and terminating near the north coast of Australia. Along this line, the African/Arabian plates and the Indian-Australia plate are crunching against the lighter Eurasian plate, producing a jagged line of thrust and slip-strike faults. Only 2 percent of earthquakes occur elsewhere in the world.

For the most part, earthquakes occur along the fault lines between tectonic plates, but there are a few exceptions. Some quakes occur in mid-plate, usually along the lines of old fractures in the earth's crust. The most notable example of such a mid-plate fracture lies under the central valley of the Mississippi River, which in 1811 gave rise to an earthquake with an estimated 8 point magnitude. Luckily, the area was only sparsely settled at the time and the quake did relatively little damage to people and property, though it was strong enough to force the Mississippi River to reverse flow for a brief period of time. Another mid-plate fracture that produces frequent quakes in the North American continent follows the path of the St. Lawrence River between Canada and the United States. Even more mid-plate earthquakes occur along the Great Rift Valley of Africa, where the African plate is slowly pulling itself apart, creating a bizarre chain of volcanic mountains and vast lakes stretching from Ethiopia to Mozambique. Indeed, if present trends continue along the Great Rift Valley, East Africa will eventually separate itself entirely from the rest of Africa and will form a new continent. One can only imagine the magnitude of the earthquakes that would accompany such a momentous event.

Earthquake Hazards

For those who have lived through them, earthquakes are an unforgettable experience. Depending on the severity of the quake, the earth trembles, shudders, or bucks beneath your feet. Pictures fall off the walls, dishes shatter, and furniture skitters across the floor, or even spins in place. Tall buildings sway and bend like reeds in the wind. In severe quakes, fissures open in the ground, buildings collapse, and clouds of dust blot out the sun. All of these phenomena have the same cause: the seismic waves radiating out from the epicenter of the quake. These waves are not like the waves in the sea, which are caused by the wind, but rather like the ripples a thrown rock creates in a still pool. Successive crests and troughs spread outward from where the rock impacted the water, causing a great deal of turmoil where the rock struck, but quickly losing height and strength as they spread outward. As we shall see below, this analogy is far from perfect: The earth's crust, being a solid, has different characteristics than water, and earthquakes tend to originate deep underground, while the ripples in the pond begin on the surface. Nonetheless, it does highlight the fact that earthquakes consist of waves traveling through the crust of the earth. Indeed, many people caught in quakes suffer from something akin to seasickness, caused by the undulations of the ground beneath their feet.

Of course, if you are caught in a major earthquake, seasickness is the least of your concerns. Far more dangerous is the possibility that the structure you occupy will collapse around you, crushing you in the process. To return to the ripple analogy, imagine small model buildings floating on the surface of a still pond. If a rock hits the pool nearby the building, the ridges and troughs produced by the splash will alternatively raise one side of the building, then the other, like a ship rocking on waves in a storm. If the model is poorly built, it will likely fall apart due to the strain. Alternatively, if the model building is relatively tall, it will rock and sway until it collapses.

Once again, this analogy is slightly oversimplified. In actuality, earthquakes produce not one type of wave, but several: P or "primary" waves, S or "secondary" waves, and surface waves, which are the main cause of earthquake-induced seasickness. A further flaw in the rock-and-pond analogy is that earthquakes do not normally originate from a single source. The "epicenter" of an earthquake is not the only source of earthquake waves, and in some cases it is not even the strongest source. Rather, it is the location where the earthquake started, or more properly, the surface location above the true underground source of the earthquake, called the "hypocenter" or "focus." Once pressure is released in one place, the resulting seismic waves can trigger chain reactions, creating secondary sources of seismic waves up and down the fault. To truly simulate this, you would have to throw numerous rocks into a pond at several second intervals. The ridge and trough patterns thus created in the pond would be very complex: In some cases two waves would add to each other's strength, in other cases they will cancel each other out, thus sparing one structure while obliterating similar houses in the area.

Those people who do not die immediately during an earthquake due to falling masonry may be killed by a common secondary effect of earthquakes: urban fires. Earthquakes create a fertile field for fires in several ways. First of all, by reducing buildings into piles of loose rubble, quakes create an enormous amount of ready-made kindling for fire. Secondly, earthquakes can topple oil lamps, upend candles, spill fireplace embers, and otherwise scatter fire sources into the post-earthquake rubble. Furthermore, earthquakes tend to disable fire protection infrastructure, such as water mains, and block roads, preventing the quick passage of firefighters. At the same time, earthquakes in modern cities tend to cut electrical wires, creating hot sparks, and cause leaks in gas lines, creating the possibility of fiery explosions. As a result, fire can spread out of control after an earthquake, and indeed can account for more lost lives and destroyed property than the quake itself.

Earthquakes can also create carnage by triggering tsunamis, a Japanese term meaning "harbor waves." Often misnamed tidal waves, tsunamis have nothing to do with the tides. Rather, tsunamis are set in motion by earthquakes, either because the movement of tectonic plates leads to the sudden displacement of water, or due to underwater landslides triggered by the quake. Tsunamis can reach 30 meters or more in height, though even much smaller tsunamis have enormous potential for death and destruction depending on the vulnerability of the coastal communities where they hit. As suggested by the Japanese term "harbor wave," tsunamis are often most deadly in enclosed harbors and inlets, where arms of land channel the wave and focus its destructive power. Tsunamis are also particularly deadly in conjunction with urban fire. In a number of documented cases, earthquake victims have clustered along the shoreline of a coastal city to escape the raging flames triggered by the earthquake, only to fall victim to the crashing waves of a post-earthquake tsunami. We will discuss tsunamis further in chapter 6, which considers water disasters such as tsunamis and floods.

Finally, although there is little truth to the popular belief that earthquakes can swallow people up through fissures in the ground, there have been cases in which earthquakes have killed people by temporarily transforming soil into quicksand. A case in point is the Port Royale earthquake in 1692, which all but destroyed the city of the same name on the island of Jamaica. Port Royale, a notorious pirate haven of the day, was built on an offshore sandbar. Shortly before the earthquake, hurricane waves and rains had drenched this vulnerable spit of land. As a result, when the earthquake struck, its seismic waves essentially liquefied the moist, sandy soil beneath Port Royale. Every building of the island collapsed, and many people reportedly sunk to their chest or their head in the suddenly soft soil, only to suffocate when the earthquake ended and the soil reconsolidated around them. All told, as many as 2000 of Port Royale's 6000 inhabitants perished, and the city itself was abandoned. Not surprisingly, many people of the day assumed that Port Royale's unusual demise was divine punishment for its inhabitants' piratical ways. As we shall see below, however, many less sinful locations suffer from the same vulnerability as Port Royale, and face catastrophic damage from earthquake-induced soil liquefaction.

Earthquakes in History

Like volcanoes, earthquakes have made a continuous appearance in the annals of human history. The Old Testament of the Bible, which most scholars regard as an unparalleled historical source as well as a religious text, makes numerous references to earthquakes, which are usually portrayed as signs of God's anger against mankind. The book of Isaiah, for example, foretold that earthquakes would be sent as punishments against the supposedly overly-materialistic and impious Jews of the 8th century B.C. Because the Jews had "transgressed the laws ... broken the everlasting covenant," Isaiah predicted, God would cause the following to pass: "[T]he foundations of the earth do shake. The earth is utterly broken down, ... the earth is moved exceedingly. The earth shall reel to and from like a drunkard." That the authors of the Bible would use earthquake imagery to describe God's wrath comes as no surprise to geologists, who have identified more than 40 devastating earthquakes with magnitudes between 6.7 and 8.3 in the last 2,500 years. In any case, despite Isaiah's fear of quakes, earthquake experts Sanders and de Boer believe that these quakes probably benefited the Israelite tribes on the whole, since they threw down the walls protecting the nomadic Israelites' town-dwelling enemies. Earthquakes are also suspected to have destroyed the allegedly sinful cities of Sodom and Gomorrah, though the exact location of these Biblical cities has not been determined.

The Holy Land's frequent quakes are the result of the complicated interaction of the Eurasian, Middle Eastern, and African plates, which converge in the area of Palestine. Indeed, Palestine itself occupies a mini-plate, which is gradually separating from the faster-moving Arabian plate. The growing gap between plate and mini-plate has shaped the face of the lands of the Bible. The River Jordan flows southwards through the resulting rift valley before emptying itself into the Dead Sea, which incidentally has the distinction of being the lowest point on the surface of the earth. Even more astoundingly, the combination of low elevation, extreme aridity, and plate tectonics has created a unique geographical feature in Palestine — salt domes. Palestine's salt domes form when salt layers under the earth, formed by the evaporation of ancient seawater, are put under pressure by overlying strata of rock. As a result, the salt gradually squeezes up from below through fault lines along the east end of the Palestine sub-plate, forming low hills composed primarily of salt. The erosion of these mountains has created striking pillars of salt, some almost human in appearance, which are thought to be the inspiration for the famous story of Lot's wife.

Earthquake scholars de Boer and Sanders have identified a number of other instances when powerful quakes may have altered the course of human history. A disastrous earthquake in

Greece's Peloponnesian Peninsula 464 B.C. killed as many as 20,000 Spartans, triggered a massive rebellion, soured the Spartan-Athens alliance, and thus played a contributing role in the Peloponnesian war, a fratricidal war within Greece which ended Athens' Golden Age and opened the way for outside invasion. According to de Boers and Sanders, the Great Lisbon Earthquake exerted an even greater impact on human history. On November 1st of 1755, a quake with a magnitude of perhaps 8.5, generated by subduction of the African plate beneath the Eurasian continental plate, rocked the modern-day nations of Portugal and Morocco. The quake was felt as far away as western France, where the radiating seismic waves rang church bells. Closer to the quake's epicenter, the Moroccan cities of Fez and Casablanca were severely damaged.

In Lisbon, the prosperous capital of the Portuguese Empire, the damage was nothing short of cataclysmic. Much of the city's staunchly Catholic population was in church at the time of the quake celebrating All Saint's Day. Devotional candles had been lit throughout the city to commemorate the holiday. When the quake struck, witnesses watched in horror as "the whole tract of the country about Lisbon was seen to heave like the swelling of billows in a storm." Church roofs collapsed and crushed worshipers throughout Portugal, while upturned candles and fireplace embers sparked a tremendous inferno in Lisbon that lasted more than a week. Worst of all, about an hour after the first shock, a tremendous tsunami, "rising ... like a mountain, ... foaming and roaring," washed into Lisbon's shoreline. It raged up Lisbon's Tagus River, raising it to nearly 10 meters above normal water level, and then just as quickly receded, sucking many thousands of quake survivors to their deaths as it did. The overall death toll from all of these calamities is thought to be between 15,000 and 90,000 in Lisbon alone, plus many thousands more killed elsewhere in coastal Portugal and in North Africa, where tsunami waves may have topped 15 meters.

In the short run, the Lisbon tsunami dealt a severe blow to the power and prestige of Portugal, hastening Portugal's gradual decline from Great Power status into the ranks of second-rank European states. Even more significant was the Great Lisbon Earthquake's impact on European intellectual thought. Before the Lisbon earthquake, the main thrust of the European Enlightenment was an optimistic belief in human progress and perfectibility. This attitude was epitomized by German philosopher Leibnitz, who argued that an omnipotent god must have considered all possibilities before making the world and chosen the best one for mankind — thus we are all living in "the best of all possible worlds." Followers of Leibnitz strained to fit the Great Lisbon Earthquake into this schema. The French *philosophe* Rousseau, for example, blamed the citizens of Lisbon themselves for the disaster, since they had abandoned "nature" when they gathered together in "twenty thousand houses of six or seven stories," and went on to insist that earthquake victims become food for worms and wolves, ensuring that "the particular ill of one individual contributes to the general good."

This sort of twisted logic infuriated the Enlightenment philosopher Voltaire, who responded by writing *Candide*, one of his masterworks. In this tale, which takes place in part in earthquake-ravaged Lisbon, Voltaire ridicules Leibnitz and Rousseau's optimism, presenting instead a world in which human beings are prey to forces beyond their control and where lust, greed, and the quest for power inspire terrible acts of inhumanity. Voltaire concludes *Candide* with the advice that human beings should not devise elaborate philosophic systems that clash with the world's observed realities but rather "work without theorizing" and "cultivate one's garden." Voltaire's influence is clearly seen in the more skeptical turn taken by the Enlightenment in the second half of the 18th century, when philosophers increasingly subjected well-established truths, especially religious truths, to the light of reason. It should be noted that the Great Lisbon Earthquake also exerted a profound influence on the physical sciences, since it inspired widespread theorizing about the natural forces behind the destructive quake. Indeed, Immanuel

Kant's popular pamphlet on the likely causes of the Lisbon disaster — he theorized that the earthquake had resulted from winds passing though huge subterranean caverns full of hot gasses — has been credited with laying the foundations of the new science of seismology.

The Great Lisbon Earthquake became notorious in part because of its severity, but also because of its location: The epicenter was less than 300 kilometers away from Lisbon, the wealthy and populous capital of one of Europe's richest states. Less well known are two other pre-modern earthquakes, both located in North America, which were less important for their impact on the past than their implications for the future. In 1700, an enormous earthquake with an estimated magnitude of 8.7–9.2, caused by subduction of the small Juan de Fuca plate beneath the North American plate, rocked the region that would later become Oregon and Washington State. The resulting tsunamis reached as far as Japan, but damage was much worse along the North American coast, as demonstrated by tree ring data from submerged red cedar forests. Similarly, the central Mississippi valley was thrown into turmoil in 1811 by a massive mid-plate earthquake that was powerful enough to change the course of the mighty Mississippi River. In both of these quakes, damage to people and property was minimal due to the low population density at the time. Both areas are much more thickly settled today, however, so if similar quakes occur — as they almost certainly will — the resulting damage will likely be catastrophic.

Although these two quakes, which have been dubbed the Cascadia Earthquake and the New Madrid Earthquake respectively, were far stronger than the San Francisco Earthquake of 1906, the 1906 quake has received the lion's share of attention. Once again, the reason is location. San Francisco in 1906 was the largest city on the U.S. west coast, with a population of approximately 400,000. Unfortunately for its inhabitants, a number of factors conspired to render it particularly vulnerable to earthquake damage. Much of the city's waterfront was built on "made land," composed of loose soil and debris created by earlier quakes, and thus was particularly prone to earthquake-induced soil liquefaction. What is more, as a frontier town, much of the city's structures were built of timber, rendering them vulnerable to post-earthquake fire. To compound matters further, San Francisco's once-elite fire department had deteriorated by 1906, since political corruption had drained it of funds. Fire Chief Dennis Sullivan had recently begged for funding to build a saltwater pumping system for use if the water mains failed, and had also sought money to train his men to use dynamite to create firebreaks. Both requests had been denied.

Largely as a result, the 1906 earthquake caused atrocious damage. One witness to the quake later claimed that he could "see it coming up Washington Street. The whole street was undulating. It was as if the waves of the ocean were coming towards me, billowing as they came." These seismic waves caused severe damage to much of the city, most especially in waterfront areas constructed on "made land," but also in San Francisco's poorer districts, where building construction standards were particularly shoddy. Only a few buildings specifically designed to resist earthquakes, like the Palace Hotel, survived the quake intact. Unfortunately, the Palace Hotel could not withstand the second phase of the disaster, the post-quake inferno. For six days, fires raged out of control through the ruins of San Francisco, consuming the entire city outside of a few lucky or well-protected neighborhoods. The fire department fought the flames as best they could, but their efforts were hampered by the lack of water, since the water mains had been disrupted just as Chief Sullivan had predicted. The firemen were also hampered by their inexperience using dynamite as a fire-fighting tool, and probably caused as many fires as they stopped. Although vindicated by events, Chief Sullivan was not around to say "I told you so" to the administration; like many other San Francisco residents, Sullivan was killed by building collapses in the first moments of the quake.

Although the San Francisco Earthquake killed relatively few people — estimates range from

San Francisco, April 18, 1906. Note the rubble in the foreground and billowing smoke from the fires in the distance.

300 to 3000 — it inflicted unprecedented property damage on the city of San Francisco. Damage estimates for the quake top $300 million, or over $6 billion in 2006 dollars. This figure represents damage to structures alone: Many more millions of dollars in furniture, jewelry, and cash also perished in the flames. As many as a quarter million people were rendered homeless, and gravitated to the city's parks, which became vast refugee camps. Many more abandoned the city entirely for the nearby city of Oakland, which grew substantially after 1906. The quake did have one positive outcome for San Francisco, however. In the following years, the corrupt administration which had helped to exacerbate the effects of the 1906 earthquake was turned out of office.

Despite the change of government, San Francisco soon forgot the lessons of the 1906 earthquake. The city did belatedly establish a system of saltwater pumping stations and beefed up the building codes. These codes, however, were often minimally followed or else ignored due to cost concerns or tight construction deadlines. Advice from experts to establish height restrictions for San Francisco buildings was not followed. Even more structures were built on fill land. Indeed, rubble from the 1906 quake was dumped into the harbor in order to extend San Francisco's shore line still further into San Francisco Bay. As we shall see in section 3.3, San Francisco's lackadaisical post-earthquake attitude contrasts strongly with Japan's more practical and thoughtful response to the lessons of the Great Kanto Earthquake of 1923.

Although San Francisco's earthquake history continues to capture the popular mind, the 1906 quake was far from the most destructive earthquake disaster of the last 100 years. Only two years after the San Francisco quake, the Italian city of Messina was leveled by a catastrophic earthquake that killed as many as 80,000 people, making it by far the deadliest earthquake disaster in European history. Even more people would die in the Great Kanto Earthquake of 1923, which severely damaged the city of Tokyo and all but leveled the prosperous port city of Yokohama. Indeed, one historian has blamed the rise of Japanese militarism, in part, on the devastation caused by the Great Kanto Earthquake. Unfortunately, earthquake death tolls on this enormous scale are by no means a thing of the past. Indeed, the Great Pakistani Earthquake killed a comparable number of people as recently as 2005. These three major earthquakes will be the subject matter of section 3.1, 3.2, and 3.3 respectively.

Earthquakes and Other Disasters

Earthquakes quite often play an important causative role in triggering other forms of natural disaster. This is most obviously true in the case of volcanic eruptions. By opening gaps between tectonic plates, earthquakes can facilitate the passage of magma to the surface of the earth, thus helping volcanoes to form. Indeed, most volcanoes are located upon fault zones in the earth's crust. What is more, earthquakes can directly trigger volcanic eruptions by causing rock slides, thus releasing the pressure holding magma in check. The explosive eruption of Washington State's Mount St. Helens in 1980, for example, was triggered by a landslide that effectively popped the cork of the mountain, releasing the magma contained in the volcano to the open air. It should also be noted that volcanoes actually create their own earthquakes, as the movement of magma towards the surface produces characteristic long duration, low intensity earthquakes.

Powerful earthquakes have also been linked to disastrous flooding. As we have already discussed in the earthquake hazards section above, offshore quakes often produce tsunamis, enormous waves that can top 30 meters in height. The exact triggering mechanism for any given tsunamis is often a matter of conjecture. It is widely agreed that displacement of tectonic plate material triggers tsunamis; in this case, the sudden rise or fall of one plate relative to another leads to the displacement of a large volume of water, generating waves that radiate from the epicenter of the earthquake. More recently, however, earthquake researchers have argued that the strongest tsunamis are actually the result of underwater landslides triggered by earthquakes. These tremendous landslides displace far more water than the movement of the plates themselves and thus have the potential to create far larger tsunami waves. Interestingly enough, there is evidence that displacement tsunamis, though potentially weaker than landslide tsunamis, tend to travel much farther through the water, while landslide-generated tsunamis dissipate fairly quickly. One reason for the scholarly uncertainty on this matter is the difficulty of studying underwater landslides. The only effective way to detect them is to compare pre-earthquake sea floor topography to post-quake topography, but this is often impossible, as to this date only a small fraction of the sea floor has been fully charted. Further oceanic exploration should shine more light on this subject.

Earthquakes are also strongly linked to famine. Strong quakes tend to destroy buildings, including food storage structures. Food stored in household pantries may be inaccessible beneath a thick layer of debris. In the modern world, where perishable food is commonly preserved through refrigeration rather than canning, salting, or smoking, earthquakes can destroy food stores by cutting off the electricity needed to run refrigerators. Earthquakes also imperil food availability by wrecking transportation infrastructure — collapsing bridges, undermining roads, and warping train tracks — and thus hampering the efficient distribution of existing food supplies. Thankfully, since earthquakes tend to inflict only limited damage on agricultural land, famines triggered by earthquakes tend to be brief in duration.

What is more, earthquakes can also create a fertile breeding ground for disease. In the aftermath of a destructive earthquake, tens of thousands of people are often displaced from their homes and congregate in relief camps or other temporary shelters. Since these quickly-fabricated and often poorly planned camps generally have only rudimentary sanitary facilities, they provide ideal habitats for diseases transmitted through fecal matter, such as cholera. The crowded conditions prevalent in refugee camps also favor the spread of diseases linked to poor hygiene, such as typhus, which is transmitted by human body lice. Refugee camps also tend to suffer high rates of malnutrition, and malnourished people are much less able to fight off disease. Finally, earthquakes can contribute to the transmission and spread of diseases by damaging the hospitals and clinics that normally serve the residents of the effected area.

In each of the above cases, with the partial exception of volcanic eruptions, earthquakes have played a causative role in their interaction with other natural disasters. But can earthquakes be the result, and not the trigger, of natural disasters as well? One disaster authority, Weather Bureau meteorologist C. F. Brooks, believes that cyclonic weather played a strong causative role in the catastrophic Great Kanto Earthquake of 1923. At the time of the earthquake, a powerful typhoon was approaching southern Japan, and the low air pressure at the center of the storm effectively lessened the weight of the atmosphere on the land by about two million tons per square mile of land. At the same time, the storm surge of wind-whipped water at the front edge of the storm probably increased the load on the earth by approximately nine million tons. The resulting pressure differential, Brooks has argued, might have stressed the fault line and released the seismic energy stored between the Philippine, Pacific, and Eurasian plates. This is mere speculation, however. More concretely, the swirling winds of the same typhoon played an indisputable role in fueling and spreading the fires triggered by the Great Kanto Earthquake, which as we shall see in section 3.2, eventually burned most of Tokyo and Yokohama to the ground.

Finally, earthquakes are strongly linked to urban fires, which commonly accompany earthquake devastation. Since urban fires are anything but "natural," however, they are not treated as a distinct natural disaster type in this volume.

Earthquakes and Human Agency

Unlikely as it may seem, human beings can play a direct role in inducing earthquakes. Quakes are relatively common in the years after the construction of large dams, since the artificial lakes created behind the dam exert new stresses on the continental plates. The detonation of nuclear devices can cause plate movement as well, as demonstrated by underground nuclear tests in the U.S. What is more, earthquakes have occurred in areas where human beings have deliberately pumped fluid underground. For example, in 1962 U.S. Army disposed of a large volume of liquid nerve gas by injecting it underground near Denver, Colorado. In the months after pumping began, earthquakes began to become more frequent, and seismographs showed that nearly all the quakes originated in the area directly below the drill hole. Scientists now believe that the liquid nerve gas penetrated and activated old fault lines by reducing the friction that was keeping the crust fracture boundaries locked in place.

These examples, however, are exceptions that prove the rule: Human beings do not cause earthquakes. In each of these cases, human beings helped to induce earthquakes by jolting or lubricating existing fault lines. Most if not all of the actual energy released during the earthquakes was the result of plate tectonics, not human behavior. Human beings may have pulled the trigger, therefore, but plate tectonics loaded the gun. In any case, most quakes that are associated with human activities have been modest in scale, with the possible exception of a deadly 1967 earthquake near Mumbai, India that may have been induced by the construction of the nearby Konya Dam.

Nonetheless, human agency does play an important role in earthquake disasters. Human beings may not load the gun, to stretch the analogy, but they often place themselves in the line of fire. Billions of human beings live in areas that are known to be seismically active. To a certain degree this is unavoidable: As we have seen, most earthquakes occur on the edges of tectonic plates, particularly in subduction zones, where continental and oceanic plates meet. Population in such areas tends to be high despite the earthquake risk, largely because of the availability of sea resources and cheap transportation costs. What is more, as we saw in chapter 2, subduction zones are often characterized by high levels of volcanic activity, and consequently high levels of soil fertility. Nonetheless, in some areas, human proximity to known earthquake zones has reached absurd extremes. According to disaster scholars de Boer and Sanders, a number of California towns have been built alongside or even directly on top of fault lines. "It is not unusual to find schools, churches, banks, supermarkets, oil refineries, bridges, dams, freeways, and water reservoirs located along the trace of the San Andreas Fault," these authors observe. In the nearby California city of Berkeley, the University of California football stadium, built directly atop Hayward Fault, is actually pulling apart at the rate of more than a centimeter a year. Worst of all, thirteen schools have been built directly atop the Hayward fault. De Boer and Sanders have pronounced such reckless building practices as "inexcusabl[e]," and given the Bay Area's notorious earthquake history, it is difficult to disagree.

Human beings also set themselves up for disaster by building structures on unconsolidated "fill" soil, which is particularly vulnerable to damage during earthquakes. San Francisco's fill land proved especially vulnerable to the 1906 earthquake, and since rubble from the 1906 earthquake was used to further extend the city into the Bay, San Francisco's vulnerability has only grown over time. Fill soil also played a key role in the horrific destruction caused by a Great Hanshin Earthquake of 1995 in Kobe, Japan. Since the harbor and port districts of Kobe were built atop two artificial islands composed largely of gravel and silt, the Great Hanshin Earthquake caused widespread soil liquefaction in Kobe; indeed, in some areas the soil subsided a full half meter. The liquefaction of the soil, combined with widespread post-earthquake fires, lead to atrocious casualties. In all, 6,434 people lost their lives in the Great Hanshin Earthquake, and $200 billion dollars worth of property was destroyed, a sum equal to 2.5 percent of Japan's 1995 GDP. As a consequence, Kobe enjoys the dubious distinction of being the site of what is arguably the single most destructive natural disaster in human history.

The Kobe disaster was made even worse by post-disaster problems that slowed the flow of relief workers to the devastated areas. In part, this delay was caused by the destruction of Kobe's transportation infrastructure. Rail lines passing near the area were twisted and unusable, a number of bridges had collapsed, and the elevated expressway that formed the main artery into and out of the city suffered extensive damage, having collapsed in ten places. Disaster relief was also delayed by the Japanese government's reluctance to call on outside support, in part because first reports underplayed the scale of the catastrophe, but also out of national pride. To accept outside help would have been an admission that Japan lacked the resources to deal with the disaster itself, and for a country that values self-reliance and prides itself on disaster preparedness, such an admission would have involved an unacceptable loss of face on the part of the government. Japan's reluctance to accept assistance after the Great Hanshin Earthquake was by no means unprecedented: As we shall see in section 3.2, the Japanese government was just as reluctant to accept outside help in the aftermath of the Great Kanto Earthquake of 1923, with even more tragic results.

Finally, human beings contribute to earthquake disasters through bad building design or poor construction practices. In the best of all possible worlds, most dwellings in earthquake zones would be houses made of fireproofed wood, which tend to withstand earthquakes rela-

"Reclaiming" land along Hong Kong's waterfront, June 2008.

tively well as they are lightweight and somewhat flexible. Larger buildings would be anchored on solid rock, which is less affected by quakes, or else constructed on metal coils or other supports capable of dampening seismic waves. Tall buildings would be constructed mainly of steel, and would feature numerous cross braces to prevent the building from shaking horizontally during earthquakes. Unfortunately, most structures in earthquake zones do not meet these standards. In undeveloped countries, most dwellings are built out of bricks, stones, adobe, or cinderblocks, since wood is too expensive or unavailable. Reinforced concrete, another popular building material in the developing world, is also vulnerable to seismic waves. Such buildings generally collapse into piles of rubble when exposed to the horizontal forces of seismic waves, just as a child's block tower will topple when tapped by a finger. Indeed, as we shall see in section 3.3, building collapses in Pakistan and India claimed the lion's share of lives lost in the 2005 Pakistani Earthquake.

Structures in developed countries tend to be built to higher quality standards, which helps explain why the industrialized world generally suffers a much lower death toll from comparable earthquakes than the developing world. Nonetheless, earthquakes can lead to disastrous building collapses in the developed world as well. Older buildings, constructed before more stringent modern earthquake-"proof" building codes were adopted, are only rarely retrofitted to modern standards. Builders often ignore building regulations or else use substandard building materials in an attempt to cut costs and maximize their profits. Some architects continue to give a higher value to aesthetic concerns or functionality than to earthquake preparedness when designing buildings. Furthermore, due to the high value of seaside land, builders continue to construct houses on "fill" soil, which is most vulnerable to damage during earthquakes. It is perhaps inevitable that such abuses occur: Capitalist societies often prioritize short-term economic gain over human life. To a certain degree, these abuses are kept in check by governmental oversight. Unfortunately, government agencies often enforce building codes most vigorously after destructive earthquakes, when the damage has already been done, and not before the earthquakes, when more foresight could have saved more lives.

Study Questions

1. Explain, in your own words, the mechanism by which earthquakes are created.

2. "When it comes to earthquakes, the 'power' of the quake often has little relation to the 'damage' inflicted by the quake." To what degree do you agree with this statement? Explain your answer.

3. "Earthquakes rarely kill directly; most of the death toll they 'cause' is produced by other forms of natural disaster." To what degree do you agree with this statement? Explain your answer.

4. Based on this text, in what ways can human beings exacerbate the damage caused by earthquakes?

Sources/Suggested Readings

De Boer, Jelle Zeilinga, and Theodore Donald Sanders. *Earthquakes in Human History*. Princeton, NJ: Princeton University Press, 2005.

Fradkin, Philip L. *The Great Earthquake and Firestorms of 1906*. Berkeley: University of California Press, 2005.

Friedrich, Otto. *The End of the World*. New York: Coward, McCann and Geoghegan, 1982.

Kedrick, T. D. *The Lisbon Earthquake*. New York: J. B. Lippincott Company, 1955.

Prager, Ellen. *Furious Earth: The Science and Nature of Earthquakes, Volcanoes, and Tsunamis*. New York: McGraw-Hill, 2000.

Ritchie, David. *The Encyclopedia of Earthquakes and Volcanoes*. New York: Facts on File, 1994.

3.1: Messina Strait, 1908

On December 28 of 1908, the city of Messina in Sicily was all but leveled by the most powerful recorded earthquake in European history. To a certain degree, the Messina disaster was inevitable. Messina's strategic location ensured that the site of the tragedy would be densely settled, while Messina's proximity to the intersection of the Eurasian and African tectonic plates meant that earthquakes were an unavoidable eventuality. However, Messina's inherent vulnerability to earthquakes was greatly exacerbated by poor human architectural and cultural choices. As a result of this grim collusion between mankind and nature, the Messina Strait earthquake became arguably the worst single-event natural disaster in European history.

The city of Messina lies alongside the Straits of the same name, which separate Sicily from the toe of the Italian boot. Since Messina hosts the best harbor along this crucial strategic waterway — indeed, perhaps the best harbor in Italy — the site has hosted a fairly large settlement since ancient times. The harbor was first occupied by seafaring Greeks in the 8th century B.C., but only remained under Greek control until the 3rd century, when it fell to the Romans. In the

Postcard from the 1910s depicting the straits of Messina. Messina is on the western (left) side of the strait, Reggio on the right, and Mount Vesuvius is visible in the distance to the north.

following millennia, Messina changed hands repeatedly, falling to the German Goths, the Byzantines, the Arabs, the Normans, the British (briefly), Spanish, and finally the newly-unified Italian state. Indeed, any power with ambitions of controlling the Mediterranean was almost obliged by dint of geography to have a presence in Messina. By 1908, Messina was long past its heyday, since advances in sailing technology meant that ships no longer needed to keep sight of land while navigating, allowing them to pass through the Mediterranean via the more direct route of the Sicilian Chanel. Nonetheless, Messina remained an important Mediterranean city, with a population of roughly 150,000. Many of these people were employed by Messina's port, though others worked the tourism industry, since Messina was widely renowned for its architectural beauty. Ironically, as we shall see below, Messina's architecture would be a contributing factor in the city's violent downfall.

Human strategic and economic concerns, therefore, made Messina an attractive site for human habitation. However, from a geological standpoint, Messina's location was far from ideal. Sicily and the south of Italy lie along the zone of intersection between the Eurasian and African continental plates, an extremely complex region from the standpoint of plate tectonics. Although the overall interaction of these plates is best described as the subduction of the African plate under the lighter Eurasian plate, the boundary between the two continental plates is mediated by a number of smaller "platelets" which move somewhat independently of the continental plates. One of these platelets, the Apulian platelet, is actually pushing into Italy from the west-northwest, and its subduction under the Tyrrhenian platelet is responsible for producing an arc of volcanoes, including Vesuvius, on the western coast of Italy. At the same time, the African continental plate is also pushing under the Tyrrhenian platelet, fueling Mount Etna, one of Europe's most continuously active volcanoes. Messina lies along a major fault line near the conjunction of these two plate movements, about 390 kilometers south of Vesuvius and only 75 kilometers northeast of Etna. Although all of these plates move relatively slowly, by world standards, Messina's lynchpin location between these fault zones ensures that powerful earthquakes are inevitable in this region.

What is more, the underlying geology of the Messina Straits ensures that when earthquakes do occur, they strike with devastating effect. The Straits of Messina are bounded by relatively steep mountains composed primarily of shale and sandstone, relatively soft rocks that crumble easily. As a result, the coastal margins of both sides of the Straits consist primarily of gravel flats, unconsolidated material that is particularly vulnerable to seismic waves. These gravel flats drop off rather sharply into the deep water of the Straits, making them particularly prone to subsidence: During an earthquake, this land tends to slump into deeper water, pulled down by gravity and pushed down by the rocky material higher up that had more recently broken from the coastal mountains. Rather than build structures suited to the inherent instability of this coastal gravel, the inhabitants of Messina actually worsened the problem by extending the harbor into the sea using gravel and rubble from old buildings, creating fill land that was particularly subject to liquefaction during earthquakes.

Worse yet, the coastal gravel was incorporated directly into the city's buildings, which consisted on the main of thick-walled, massive structures built of cobblestone-sized rocks cemented together with poor-quality mortar and faced with stucco or concrete. Although imposing in appearance, buildings of this type prove particularly vulnerable to earthquakes, since they have little flexibility when shaken by seismic waves. What is more, the general practice in Messina was to build multi-story buildings in which a heavy tile floor was laid on floorboards that in turn rested on niches carved into the building's walls. If the floorboards had been more securely fastened to the wall, they might have given the buildings additional lateral support in times of earthquakes. Instead, since the walls supported the floorboards rather than vice versa, Messina's ceilings collapsed as readily as the walls that that held them up, and the walls often fell into the void the collapsing ceilings left behind. Consequently, Messina's "man trap" architecture, and not the quake itself, was responsible for most of the earthquake mortality. Seismologist W. H. Hobbs pointed out in the immediate aftermath of the disaster that "if an army in tents had been camped on the site of Messina on the morning of the 28th of December last, the loss to life and property would have been insignificant." Since the local inhabitants chose to live in unstable multi-story houses rather than light, flexible tents, Hobbs reasons, the Messina disaster was "largely of man's own making."

The lack of foresight on the part of Messina's architects might be more forgivable if Messina was not known to be in an earthquake prone area, but this is not the case: Indeed, Messina's history is punctuated by frequent and destructive earthquakes. A terrifying quake rocked Messina and the surrounding area in 1169, creating widespread misery that may have contributed to the eventual overthrow of Norman power on the island of Sicily. Another devastating quake struck in 1693, and killed as many as 93,000 in Sicily and Calabria, the Italian province that makes up the toe of the Italian boot. Messina was luckier in 1783, when a horrific quake killed as many as 40,000 in the mainland city of Naples, but only 700 in Messina, which was farther from the quake epicenter. Nonetheless eyewitnesses in Messina reported that some parts of the city center were "totally ruined," and that parts of the quay sunk below sea level, probably due to the subsidence of the gravel shelf upon which Messina rested. The 1783 quake also spawned secondary disasters that added to the death toll: Famine and associated diseases claimed another 10,000 lives, while a destructive tsunami claimed over 1,000 more. Following this devastating quake, local authorities instituted building codes to prevent future earthquake deaths, but these regulations were largely ignored by Messina's architects and builders.

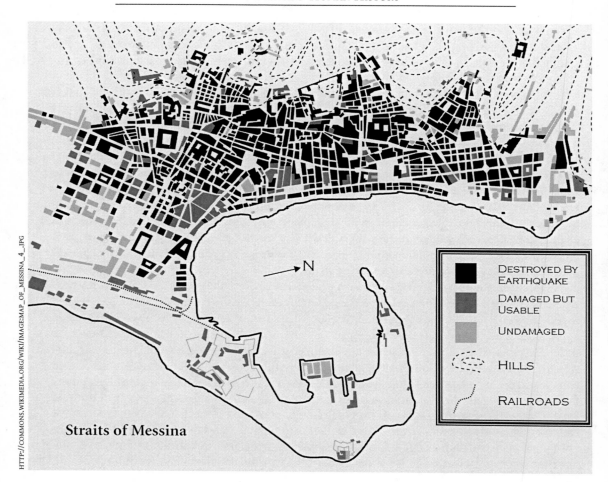

Map of Messina showing damage to the city as a result of the earthquake. Note the buildings on the rocky hills fared relatively better than the buildings constructed atop the gravel, rubble, and fill of the coastal plain. In addition, the newer buildings built in former agricultural land along the edges of the city survived the quake somewhat better than the older buildings of the tightly packed city center.

Nor were destructive earthquakes a mere memory from Messina's past: In the years up to 1908, Messina had suffered frequent quakes that should have alerted Messina to its peril. A moderately powerful earthquake killed over 100 people in Sicily and Calabria in 1894, and lead to the partial collapse of 200 houses in Messina and property damage to 10,000 more. Another quake in 1905 killed 529 people and inflicted over $10 million in damage upon the region. Still another quake, this one in 1907, killed 175 and caused significant property damage throughout the region. It is quite probable that these recent quakes weakened the masonry of those buildings that remained standing, and thus contributed indirectly to the almost total destruction of the 1908 quake. These earlier earthquakes inflicted another indirect injury on Messina as well: Following each of these quakes, rumors spread through Italy that Messina and its sister city Reggio on the Italian toe had been utterly destroyed, rumors that of course turned out to be vastly exaggerated. Indeed, many Italians believed that Reggio had been wiped off the map by the 1905 quake, when in fact Reggio emerged virtually unscathed, with not a single building suffering significant earthquake damage. These repeated exaggerations may have trained northern Italians to be skeptical of tales of earthquake catastrophe in Sicily and Calabria, which in turn may help explain the somewhat slow response to the 1908 disaster.

As it turned out, the actual facts of the 1908 disaster surpassed all but the most outlandish rumors. The rumbling began at 5:23 in the morning of December 28th, shortly before dawn, at a time when most people were still indoors sleeping in their beds. The quake itself measured 7.5 on the Richter scale—certainly a significant quake, though by no means unprecedented. About 18 quakes of this magnitude occur each year, and in a relative sense, the Messina Straits earthquake only packed about ⅒ of the punch of the earthquake that triggered the Asian Tsunami in 2004. Nonetheless, since the epicenter of the quake was located less than 10 kilometers from Messina, on the very tip of the Italian toe, the relative effect of the Messina Straits earthquake was immense. In his excellent summary of the quake, Charles W. Wright of the U.S. Geological Survey reports that survivors remembered "being lifted up and swayed back and forth in the air, only to be left down again by jerks and by jars." The shaking lasted for about 30 to 40 seconds, and caused the collapse of nearly every masonry building in the city. Tens of thousands in Messina were killed instantly by falling rubble. Thousands more suffered serious injuries, and the pre-dawn darkness was filled with their cries of pain as soon as the rumble of the earthquake subsided. Still other citizens of Messina were trapped, hurt or unhurt, inside tombs of fallen masonry.

As a result of this catastrophic structural damage, the end of the quake signaled the beginning of a desperate struggle to save buried Messinians from death by thirst or starvation. Unfortunately, in the quake's immediate aftermath, most Messinians had to struggle just to save their own lives. It was raining when the earthquake ended — indeed, many survivors had vivid memories of the fine, cold "earthquake rain" that was falling that morning — but with most buildings ruined or close to collapse, there was little shelter to be had. Making matters worse, most survivors were stark naked, since it was a widespread Italian custom at the time to sleep unclothed, and their garments were buried between the rubble. Even if clothes had been readily available, they would have been difficult to find in the pitch black of the early morning. Survivors also had to contend with a tsunami wave that topped 2 meters in height which swept over the breakwater in the harbor, wrecking Messina's fishing fleet in the process. The only silver lining to this dark cloud was lack of fire: Messina boasted few wooden buildings, and thus was spared the raging firestorms that characterized San Francisco's 1906 quake. Those fires that did occur tended to flare up near gas pipe breaks, and were quickly doused by the rain, which fell in a fine drizzle for days after the earthquake.

In most other respects, however, the situation was dire. The water lines had been cut, depriving the city of fresh water, and most food was buried under tons of debris. Nor was any fresh food likely to reach the city any time soon, since the quake had blocked the rail lines in the mainland Calabria province, and much of the city's fleet of fishing boats had been wrecked by the post-quake tsunami. What is more, the telegraph lines had been damaged, preventing Messina from getting quick word of the disaster to the central government in Rome. The sanitation system had been destroyed as well — a serious problem, given that Messina had lost 16,000 of its citizens to an epidemic of sewage-borne cholera only fifty years before. As it turned out, the illness that most plagued the quake survivors was probably Post Traumatic Stress Disorder, which would explain why so many observers describe the quake survivors as "childlike" in their bearing and behavior. Furthermore, many of the survivors sported serious injuries, but the hospitals and clinics had been all but obliterated by the quake.

Making matters worse, a number of Messinians who were unhurt by the quake turned their efforts, not towards rescuing the wounded and trapped, but towards looting valuables from the ruined city. These local looters were soon joined by would-be treasure hunters from throughout Italy, forcing first responders to spend some of their effort protecting buried property (mainly by executing looters) rather than rescuing buried Messinians. As a result, the death toll from the quake soon began to mount, as the number of people who died directly of injury during the earthquake was augmented further by victims perishing of injury, hunger, thirst, or exposure to the elements.

It is important to note that Messina was not the only part of southern Italy to be affected by the Straits Earthquake. The mainland port of Reggio, Messina's sister city on the Straits, also suffered catastrophic damage due to the quake, and at Reggio the earthquake destruction was compounded by a considerably higher tsunami wave, which may have reached three meters in height. Damage was also severe in the mountain villages alongside the straits, which may seem surprising, since such villages were both farther from the quake epicenter and built on ground that was more solid than the gravel flats of the coast. However, the normal construction practices of the mountain villages ensured that even a moderate quake would prove deadly. Most mountain homes were constructed of weak masonry, topped by roofs consisting of tiles mounted upon wooden poles. Even moderate seismic waves were sufficient to rattle these roofs, dropping cascades of heavy tile upon the villagers within. What is more, the plight of the mountain villages was exacerbated by their sheer remoteness, which made it far more difficult to get word of their plight out and relief supplies in.

Nonetheless, it was Messina that suffered most heavily from the 1908 quake. Out of a pre-quake population of 150,000, as few as 50,000 Messinians survived the quake, meaning that the Straits earthquake inflicted an almost unheard-of 66 percent mortality rate in Messina. More conservative estimates put the death rate at 40 percent, which is still a remarkable figure.

The toll of dead was compounded by the misery of the living. The 50,000-odd survivors of the quake were in desperate straits, in immediate need of material assistance. Unfortunately, getting large-scale and immediate assistance to Messina proved to be beyond Italy's capacity. To their credit, the King and Queen of Italy arrived at Messina the day after the disaster, and their presence reportedly raised the spirits of the survivors, though by themselves the King and Queen could offer little more than emotional assistance. Material aid was hampered by red tape and an overstrained postal and telegraph system, as well as corruption, which outside observers claimed was endemic in the Italian civil service. Worse yet, the Italian railroad system proved woefully inadequate to the task of providing for the survivors. Due to lack of track capacity, railroad cars full of relief supplies were shunted for weeks or even months into side tracks or freight houses. It is telling that the first rescuers on the scene were not Italians at all, but Russian sailors from three warships that happened to be cruising off the coast of Calabria at the time of the disaster.

The response by international institutions to the disaster was no better. The Red Cross organization had been established about 50 years earlier, but it had not yet been put to a test as severe as the Messinian earthquake. It would be too strong a statement to say that the Red Cross failed the test, but its response was weakened by severe disunity within the organization. American nurse Alice Fitzgerald, who was in Naples in the aftermath of the quake, found that the Red Cross, "instead of being one large body of workers with the same interests and aims, is divided into as many branches as there are cities, and there is but little if any connection between them at all." As a result, generous donations of supplies given to one Red Cross branch were not distributed to others that may have needed them more, and information concerning the wounded was not widely shared, hampering the reunion of scattered families. Indeed Fitzgerald described the city of Naples, where the Red Cross response was headquartered, as a scene of "absolute confusion." Thankfully, the Red Cross had profited from the lessons of Messina by the time of the First World War, which broke out less than 6 years later.

However, the biggest obstacle blocking rescue and relief efforts was not institutional disorganization, but rather the sheer task of the undertaking itself. In all, an estimated 98 percent of the buildings of Messina had been damaged or destroyed entirely, creating a million tons of debris. This debris entombed thousands who survived the earthquake itself; indeed, living victims were still being pulled out of the rubble 18 days after the earthquake. However, the vast majority of those caught in the rubble were dead, and their removal proved to be time consuming, disgusting task. Contemporary observers described Messina as a "corpse-mine," a "vast tomb," or even a "fantastically horrible necropolis." The quick removal of these bodies was seen as essential, however, since Italian authorities of the time clung to the "miasmic" theory of disease, believing that illness was caused by foul odors. Despite this urgency, progress on corpse removal was slow. More than three weeks after the disaster, the military governor of the area reported that only 4,000 corpses had been recovered and that another 50,000 still lay under the debris. The full clearing of the city, it was estimated, might take as long as 2–3 years.

As a result of these difficulties, many Italians seriously questioned whether Messina could,

Downtown Messina with body recovery efforts underway.

HTTP://COMMONS.WIKIMEDIA.ORG/WIKI/IMAGE:CLEARING_AWAY_THE_RUINS_ON_ROUTE_TO_CANTANIA_-_SICILY_(AFTER_EARTHQUAKE).JPG

Clearing rubble after the Messina earthquake.

or should, rise up again from its ruins. Some believed that what remained of the city should be shelled by battleships until the "last walls crumble, fall, and bury together the city and its dead." Other contemporaries suggested moving the city three miles to the south, where the underlying gravel shelf was not as thick. In the end, however, it was decided that Messina's strategic location and world-class harbor made it too valuable to be abandoned. As a result, rebuilding efforts began almost immediately, assisted by both the Red Cross and large-scale American donations. The metropolis that arose from Messina's ruins was in many ways a quite different city. The largely medieval plan of narrow, winding streets gave way to a more modern urban grid. Perhaps most importantly, Messina's multi-story masonry structures were largely replaced by one-story wooden houses, especially in the "American village," built by the U.S. Navy in former farmland south of Messina as a model for local Italian builders to emulate. Although these humble wooden buildings lacked the picturesque appearance of old Messina's masonry edifices, they at least had the virtue of being more resistant to the seismic waves of a South Italian earthquake.

Study Questions

1. This section begins with the proposition that the Messina earthquake disaster of 1908 was to some degree "inevitable." Given the evidence presented, how convincing do you find this contention? Explain.

2. Which do you think contributed more to the death toll from the 1908 quake, Messina's underlying geography, or human error?

3. In the aftermath of the Messina earthquake, the newspapers were filled with sensational stories, such as the rumor that young Messina girls, orphaned by the quake, were being taken as sex slaves to the brothels of Naples. What effect do you think such stories might have had on the earthquake relief effort?

Sources/Suggested Readings

Belknap, Reginald Rowan. *American House Building in Messina and Reggio*. New York: G. P. Putnam's Sons, 1910.

Benjamin, Sandra. *Sicily: Three Thousand Years of Human History*. Hanover, NH: Steerforth Press, 2006.

Dickie, John. "The Smell of Disaster: Scenes of Social Collapse in the Aftermath of the Messina-Reggio Calabria Earthquake, 1908." In John Dickie, John Foot, and Frank Snowden eds., *Disastro! Disasters in Italy since 1860*. New York: Palgrave, 2002.

Fitzgerald, Alice. "Experiences in Naples After the Messina Disaster." *The American Journal of Nursing*, Vol. 9, No. 7 (Apr. 1909), pp. 482–492.

Hamilton, William. "An Account of the Earthquakes Which Happened in Italy..." *Philosophical Transactions of the Royal Society of London*, Vol. 73. (1783), pp. 169–208.

Hobbs, W. H. "The Messina Earthquake." *Bulletin of the American Geographical Society*, Vol. 41, No. 7 (1909), pp. 409–422.

Howe, Maud. *Sicily in Shadow and in Sun: The Earthquake and the American Relief Work*. Boston, MA: Little, Brown, and Company, 1910.

Oldham, R. D. "The Italian Earthquake of December 28, 1908." *The Geographical Journal*, Vol. 33, No. 2 (Feb. 1909), pp. 185–188.

Wright, Charles W. "The World's Most Cruel Earthquake." *National Geographic*, Vol. 20 (1909), pp. 373–396.

3.2: Great Kanto Earthquake, 1923

Like the Messina Straits Earthquake of 1908, the Great Kanto Earthquake was notable not for its strength, but rather for its close proximity to major urban centers, in this case the Japanese cities of Tokyo and Yokohama. In almost every other respect, however, the Great Kanto quake was quite different from the 1908 disaster on the Messina Straits. Unlike the Messina Straits Earthquake, few people died as a result of the quake itself, but tens of thousands perished in the fire storm that followed, while fire was only a minor cause of death in 1908. What is more, although the two events killed a comparable number of people, the Great Kanto quake actually killed a far smaller percentage of the people affected. On the other hand, while the Messina Straits Earthquake rocked the periphery of the Italian state, the Great Kanto quake struck the very center of the Japanese body politic. Perhaps for this reason the Great Kanto quake left a more lasting imprint on history: The Great Kanto Earthquake not only triggered an outpouring of anti–Korean racial hatred that presaged the massacres of World War II, but may have even played a role in the fueling the Japanese-American tensions that cumulated in the attack on Pearl Harbor, launching both Japan and the U.S. into the second World War.

Perhaps more than any other place on earth, Japan's history has been molded by climatic and tectonic forces. Indeed, Japan owes its very existence to the phenomenon of plate tectonics. The Japanese Archipelago consists almost exclusively of volcanic islands, which are fueled by the subduction of the Pacific and Philippine oceanic plates beneath the Eurasian continental plate. This helps to explain why Japan is such a mountainous country, with only small patches of flat land suitable for farming. However, other climatic factors combine to ensure that this mountainous island chain can support a large human population. Thanks to the emissions of its many volcanoes, Japan is blessed with quite fertile soil, constantly renewed from upstream sources. Japan also receives a considerable amount of rainfall — about 100 to 200 centimeters a year — most of which blows into Japan from the tropical Pacific Ocean during the summer and autumn typhoon season.

As a result of this combination of mountainous land but fertile, well-watered soils, Japan's has traditionally hosted a large but highly concentrated population, most of which is clustered into a small number of arable coastal plains. The largest such flatland, Japan's Kanto Plain, is only 13,000 square kilometers, or about the size of Connecticut. Nonetheless, Japan's Kanto plain boasts a population of about 40 million people as of 2008, while Connecticut — though it is the fourth most densely populated American state — only has 3.5 million inhabitants. Population density on this scale has obliged the inhabitants of Japan's coastal plains to live in closely packed communities, often built upon marginal land such as river beds, coastal alluvial soil, or upon land reclaimed from the sea. Unfortunately, it is precisely such settlements that are most vulnerable to the effects of an earthquake.

The Kanto Plain also is notable not only for its population density, but also for lying nearby one of the most seismically active regions of the world. Just south of Kanto is Sagami Bay, which sits upon the juncture of three tectonic plates: the Eurasian Plate, which is moving quite slowly to the east, and the Philippine and Pacific plates, which are subducting beneath the Eurasian plate. Both of the subducting plates are moving rather quickly — 4 centimeters a year in the case of the Philippine plate, and 10 centimeters a year for the Pacific Plate, which is the world's fastest moving plate. What is more, the two subducting plates are moving at slightly different directions — north-northwest in the case of the Philippine plate and west-northwest in the case of the Pacific plate — creating enormous stress at the point of juncture. This process of subduction has created a number of volcanoes, most notably Japan's famous Mount Fuji, which sits near the mouth of Sagami Bay and directly to the west of Kanto Plain. Subduction forces also mean that powerful earthquakes are a common occurrence in this part of Japan.

Unfortunately, the morning of September 1, 1923 found the inhabitants of the Kanto Plain woefully unprepared for an earthquake disaster. Indeed, recent historical trends had exacerbated the danger that the Kanto Plain faced in 1923. Both Tokyo and Yokohama — the two chief cities of the Kanto Plain — had recently experienced massive but somewhat disorganized growth. In the case of Tokyo, this growth was a byproduct of the transfer of the capital from the old imperial center of Kyoto to Tokyo in 1869, a transfer that also symbolized the new Meiji government's desire to modernize. Tokyo was already a very large city before this point, but in the second half of the 19th and early 20th century its population ballooned to over 2 million. Indeed, Tokyo's population swelled by an estimated 300,000 between 1908 and 1920 alone, an extraordinary rate of urban expansion.

Unfortunately, despite the Meiji government's official rhetoric of modernization, most of

Tokyo was constructed using traditional techniques poorly suited to an urban environment. According to earthquake scholars de Boer and Sanders, Tokyo in 1923 was "essentially a gigantic village of wooden buildings built close together in a warren of narrow streets and alleys." Traditional Japanese buildings consisted of timber, tile, and oiled paper panels, light but sturdy structures with some resilience against both earthquakes and typhoons. Houses of this sort were extremely vulnerable to fire, but in Japan's rural villages, this is only a minor problem, as houses were generally far enough apart that a single house fire was unlikely to ignite a general conflagration. However, once these village-style houses began to be constructed *en masse* in a closely-packed city, large-scale fires became a common occurrence. Indeed, urban fires were so common in Tokyo that they were popularly dubbed "flowers of Edo" by the Japanese, Edo being the original name of Tokyo before it became the seat of government.

Yokohama was, if anything, even less prepared for a disastrous earthquake in 1923. Although a much smaller city than Tokyo in 1923 — it boasted only half a million inhabitants as compared with Tokyo's estimated 2.26 million — Yokohama's relative growth was much faster. Indeed, while Tokyo was already a large city by the mid–19th century, Yokohama was just a sleepy fishing village in 1859, the year of American Commodore Matthew Perry's visit to Japan. Using a combination of persuasion and intimidation, Perry compelled the Japanese to open their ports to foreign trade, and Yokohama soon became one of the centers of that trade. In part, this was because Yokohama's harbor was capacious enough to accommodate the deep keels of American sailing vessels. Just as important was the Imperial government's fear that trade with the West might exert a corrupting influence over Japanese society, a concern that made remote Yokohama a far more desirable trade hub than populous and politically sensitive Tokyo. Observers to Yokohama's birth were struck by the remoteness and bleakness of the site; a British envoy described it in 1859 as "a marsh by the edge of a deserted bay." By the 1860s, however, Yokohama's population had begun to boom, in part because a fortuitous stroke of luck: The European silkworm industry had been all but obliterated by an epidemic disease in the late 1850s, creating a lively demand for the Japanese product. Indeed, by the early 20th century, Japan was producing 60 percent of the world's raw silk, and much of that silk passed through the port of Yokohama.

Buoyed by trade, Yokohama quickly developed into one of Japan's most cosmopolitan cities. According to Yokohama expert Joshua Hammer, by the 1920s, Yokohama had become "packed with adventurers, millionaires, fugitives and drifters from every corner of the world." In Yokohama, Hammer continues, "Bengali shopkeepers, Lebanese jewelers, Chinese moneychangers, Russian optometrists, French diplomats, Korean laborers, English silk merchants, Spanish missionaries, American tea traders ... jostled along the Bund, Water Street, and Main Street." The most exotic expatriate community was probably the Russians, most of whom were former nobles who had been driven into exile by the Bolshevik Revolution of 1917, and were now trying to make ends meet as "barmaids, dance instructors, or piano teachers." Various entertainments sprung up to entertain these foreign sojourners, most notably the "Gaiety Theatre on the Bluff," which attracted touring companies from both Europe and America. Beneath the international veneer, however, Yokohama remained a distinctly Japanese city, and like Tokyo, most buildings were small wooden structures packed tightly together along hastily improvised streets and alleys. What is more, since the original site of Yokohama was quite swampy, much of the city was built on reclaimed or fill land, which in the words of de Boer and Sanders "shakes like jelly" when impacted by seismic waves. Other parts of Yokohama were built atop former rice paddy fields, which are similarly vulnerable to liquefaction when earthquakes strike.

Admittedly, some structures within the Great Kanto Plain had been built with earthquakes and urban fires in mind. Case in point was Tokyo's imperial hotel, designed by renowned American architect Frank Lloyd Wright. The Imperial was built upon a concrete slab atop thousands of short cement piles, and was designed to "float" atop the undulating soil below in case of an earthquake. As further assurance, Lloyd reinforced the concrete walls with steel bars, and gave the building a light copper roof and a low center of gravity, further reducing the chance of earthquake damage. Finally, as a precaution against fire, Wright ordered the construction of an enormous outdoor pool at the hotel's entrance court and made sure it was connected to the hotel's water system, giving the hotel a huge reserve of water to combat fire even if the city water mains were severed. Nor was Wright's Imperial Hotel alone in its precautions: Other modern structures within the city had been provided with various degrees of earthquake and fire protection. Nonetheless, taken as a whole, prosperity and population growth had rendered the city more, and not less, vulnerable to earthquake and fire disasters.

The rapid urban growth leading up to 1923, then, helped to render the cities of the Great Kanto Plain more vulnerable to earthquake disaster. Short term happenstance helped to increase Japan's vulnerability as well. Japan's recognized expert on earthquakes at the time of the disaster was Professor Fusakichi Omori, who correctly forecast that Sagami bay would be the site of an enormous future earthquake, but who incorrectly predicted that great quakes would not occur "for at least some sixty or seventy years to come." Omori's younger colleague Professor Tetsuzo Inumaru believed a quake could be expected much sooner, but his warnings were not heeded due to Omori's ascendency in the field. Japan was equally unprepared for the earthquake from a political standpoint. At the time of the earthquake, Japan was still in the midst of a regime change, as the previous prime minister of the country had died only a week earlier, and the new prime minister was still organizing his cabinet. The resulting confusion blunted the governmental response to the disaster. Perhaps most crucially, the quake occurred at precisely 11:58 A.M., at a time when housewives throughout the city had lit fires to cook lunch over gas or charcoal stoves. When the earthquake struck, it scattered red-hot coals and upended kerosene stoves, triggering fires. These fires, in turn, were worsened by another unfortunate happenstance: On the same day as the quake, a powerful typhoon was passing to the north of Tokyo, and although Tokyo received little rain from the storm, it was whipped by gale-force winds, which would nurture and then spread the growing fires, creating a general conflagration.

Indeed, the simultaneous occurrence of earthquake and typhoon may have been more than just a coincidence. In the 1920s, the respected meteorologist C. F. Brooks speculated that the Great Kanto Quake may have been triggered by the typhoon itself. The typhoon, Brooks reasoned, brought with it unusually low atmospheric pressure, allowing a bulge of water to form where the pressure was lowest. Since this bulge of water would have been enormously heavy — Brooks estimated that it would have added a net 7 million tons of pressure to the sea floor below — it may have pushed an already straining fault line to a breaking point and triggered an earthquake. What is more, at the same time that the sea floor was experiencing greater pressure the surrounding land would have borne less weight than normal due to the typhoon's low barometric pressure, creating a pressure differential that would have put further strain on the undersea fault lines. Although this thesis remains unproven, it is intriguing to speculate about the subtle but important links that may exist between the quick-moving atmosphere and hydrosphere and the slow moving tectonic forces.

Thus, on the first of September of 1923, all the elements were in place on the Kanto Plain for disaster. In terms of location, the quake not only rocked one of the most densely populated locations in the world, it also disproportionally affected the waterlogged seacoast margins, which due to the explosive expansion of Japan's overseas trade were also amongst the most densely settled zones. In terms of time, the Kanto quake struck at the end of a period of dramatic but disorganized population growth and at precisely the most vulnerable time in terms of Japanese weather, politics, and even daily routine. Small wonder, then, that the results of the 1923 quake were so tragic.

The immediate effects of the quake were perhaps best described by Professor Inumaru, who had the misfortune of being in his office at Tokyo's Imperial University at the time of the trembler. Imamura reported that the quake began with "slow and feeble" vibrations, then escalated rapidly, to the point that the building he occupied was "shaken to an extraordinary extent." By the 12th second of the quake, the vibrations had escalated still further, becoming "slower but bigger," until they finally began to recede, eventually becoming an "undulatory movement like that ... on a boat in windy weather." Professor Inamaru did not feel that it was safe to stand until a full 5 minutes after the start of the quake, a duration that suggests that the Great Kanto quake was a major seismic event. Indeed, estimates of the Great Kanto quake's strength vary, but the evidence indicates that the quake measured between 7.9 and 8.3 on the Richter scale.

Given the magnitude of the Great Kanto Earthquake, it is hardly surprising that the communities located closest to the epicenter suffered atrocious damage. Fishing villages alongside Sagami Bay were devastated by the earthquake, and this destruction was compounded by towering tsunami waves that might have reached 13 meters in height. In the fishing town of Atami, 100 boats were pushed 200 meters inland by the waves, which then carried away 300 wooden houses when they returned to sea. Sixty people were killed by the wave at the town of Atami, and 100 bathers were washed out to sea at Kamakura. In nearby Nebukawa, a train that had just left a railroad station was knocked of its tracks by a mudflow triggered by the earthquake, killing another 200 people. Similar tragedies unfolded in the mountain towns west of Sagami bay, which were inundated by flash floods triggered by the collapse of temporary dams of rubble which briefly choked up rivers higher in the mountains. As in the Messina Straits Earthquake, the damage in the mountain towns was exacerbated by the fact that relief was slow to reach such remote locations.

In Tokyo and Yokohama, which were farther from the earthquake epicenter and protected from tsunami waves by the Miura peninsula, the immediate effects of the quake were somewhat less severe. Many poorly reinforced masonry structures, which were most common in the Western quarter of Yokohama, collapsed immediately, killing many of their occupants. However, the lighter wooden houses of the Japanese did a better job weathering the seismic waves. In general, houses built in the inland heights—an area called the "high city" Tokyo—fared better than lowland houses constructed on waterlogged coastal alluvial soil or fill. Experts later estimated that the earthquake's force was three times greater in the area built on alluvial soil and man-made ground than elsewhere. "High city" houses had a double advantage: Not only were they built upon earthquake-resistant bedrock, they tended to be of better construction than low-city homes, since the demarcation between high city and low city was one of rich and poor as much as highland and coast. Nonetheless, even in the most badly effected zones, the immediate damage inflicted by the quake was quite light: In Yokohama, only about 12.4 percent of structures collapsed due to the quake, and in Tokyo, which was farther from the epicenter, the percentage was probably under 1 percent. As a result, relatively few people were killed by the earthquake itself.

This is not to imply that damage to Tokyo and Yokohama was in any sense "mild." Telephone poles were down, roads were blocked by fissures large enough to swallow automobiles, and blinding clouds of dust filled the air. In the Yokohama harbor, ships that had become unmoored during the shock drifted and collided in the newly turbulent water. Worst of all, thousands of people had died instantly, and thousands more lay pinned beneath the rubble of col-

Top: Damage to Tokyo's Nihonbashi district. *Bottom:* Earthquake damage in a Tokyo residential neighborhood.

lapsed buildings, pleading for assistance. The first job of the survivors was to try to dig free friends, neighbors, and family members who were pinned under the ruins.

The struggle to save the trapped soon became a race against time. Throughout both Tokyo and Yokohama, the earthquake had triggered small fires, and due to the mostly-wood construction of traditional Japanese houses, these were soon stoked to formidable blazes by the whipping typhoon winds. The spread of the fires was further facilitated by damage inflicted by the earthquake, since many stone roof tiles had been dislodged from traditional Japanese homes by the quake, exposing wooden beams to falling cinders from nearby blazes. The fire department was largely helpless to contain the growing conflagration, since the water mains they depended upon had largely been broken by the storm. Firemen tried to compensate by pumping water out of local sources using pumps, but this approach enjoyed only limited success, and was accomplished only through great injury and loss of life. As a result, the fires engulfed approximately 80 percent of Tokyo and nearly 50 percent of Yokohama. Witnesses to the scenes described "a veritable sea of fire," and declared that "hell was indeed let loose on earth." In both cities, survivors were driven from their neighborhoods and pursued by the flames, which jumped from building to building with terrible speed, impelled both by the typhoon winds and the force of their own updrafts.

So ferocious were the Tokyo fires that they spawned a "dragon-twist," also known as a fire tornado. These rarely seen phenomena require a very specific set of conditions to form, but unfortunately for the inhabitants of Tokyo and Yokohama, those conditions fell into place on September 1st, 1923. The raging fires created intense updrafts, or ascending columns, of superheated air. What is more, the smoke from the flames created what Joshua Hammer has termed an "artificial cumulous formation" above both cities. When the howling updrafts encountered these turbulent clouds, they created a tornado-like vortex funnel stretching from the clouds to the ground, sucking up all available oxygen and incinerating everything in its path. Indeed, evidence collected by Professor Akitsune Imamura suggests that the Great Kanto Earthquake may have triggered the largest dragon twist ever recorded — a monstrous cyclone of smoke and flame that reached nearly 300 meters in width when it touched down in post-earthquake Tokyo.

Tragically, the Tokyo dragon-twist struck the city in precisely the place where it was most vulnerable. Near the center of Tokyo, on the banks of the Sumida River, lay a 15-acre open space in the midst of Tokyo's densely settled sprawl. Until recently, the site had hosted an huge army clothing depot, but the facilities had been dismantled only a year before, leaving a open-air void in the heart of Tokyo that had not yet been filled by the expanding city. Naturally, this open space attracted refugees from throughout Tokyo, especially since the prevailing winds pushed the fire away from the army depot site for most of the afternoon. Indeed, the local police actively encouraged people to take shelter in the army clothing depot grounds, mistakenly believing that the absence of buildings would protect its occupants from the raging fires. As a result, the army depot grounds were soon jammed with over 44,000 people and their intimate belongings, so closely packed together that there was barely room to move.

At around 6:00 P.M., the winds that had previously shunted the fires away from the army clothing depot grounds suddenly changed direction, possibly due to changes in the location of the central low pressure mass of the typhoon passing over northern Japan. The result of this wind shift was catastrophic. Horrified witnesses could do nothing so save themselves as the dragon twister, a "fire extend[ing] up to the sky," emerged from the thick smoke that shrouded the depot grounds. The twister only lingered over the army depot for about 3 minutes, but the damage it inflicted in that time was horrific. Some people were burnt alive by the superheated winds and red-hot embers. Others were hurled into the air by the dragon twister or else killed by flying debris, such as fragments of corrugated metal roofs, which sliced through the assembled crowd with lethal effect. Still other victims in the army depot grounds were simply suffo-cated, since the firestorm consumed nearly all of the oxygen from the atmosphere, replacing it with carbon dioxide and carbon monoxide. In the end, only about 300 of the estimated 44,000 refugees who had packed the army depot grounds managed to survive the holocaust.

When rescuers arrived at Tokyo's army depot in the aftermath of the fires, they encoun-tered a scene worthy of a horror movie. Corpses were stacked one atop the other, "ten, twenty people on top of one another." Henry W. Kinney, an American reporter who arrived early to the scene, described the bodies as "twisted and contorted, naked or with only rags clinging to them, covering acre upon acre." In some places the bodies were so thickly concentrated that they did not even lay on the ground, but remained standing, "the dead rubbing elbows with the dead." Worse yet, the bodies of the killed were so badly charred that only about 6,000 of the 44,000-odd victims could be identified by sex, much less as individuals. These hecatombs of corpses soon began to rot in the warm, humid late summer weather, creating clouds of flies and writhing masses of maggots. Ultimately rescuers gave up burying the dead in the army depot individually and decided to burn the corpses where they lay, finishing the job that the dragon twister had started. As for the local police official who had ordered his men to herd the refugees into the former army clothing depot grounds, he took his own life out of grief and remorse, disemboweling himself with a sword in the traditional Japanese samurai fashion.

It is important to note that mass mortality was by no means limited to the army depot grounds. In Tokyo, hundreds of people tried to survive the firestorm by clustering upon the bridges crossing the Sumida River, only to discover to their horror that the iron arches and tres-tles of these bridges supported planks of highly flammable wood. Those who sought safety in the rivers themselves perished in huge numbers as well, suffocated by lack of oxygen or boiled alive by the superheated river water. In Yokohama, many survivors of the quake sought shel-ter from the flames in the waters of the port, but perished due to collisions with ships or debris in the turbulent waters or else were killed when slicks of oil or other flammable materials float-ing on the harbor water exploded into flame. However, the majority of the dead suffered a less dramatic demise: Unable to leave their own homes due to injury or infirmary, they were burnt by the fires or succumbed to suffocation where they lay. A small number died because they were trapped in their homes by human hands, including many of Tokyo's prostitutes, who had been locked inside their brothels by their madams for fear they might take the opportunity to escape from their state of virtual slavery.

Overall, the Great Kanto Earthquake and firestorm killed approximately 100,000 people. Another 40,000 or so were reported missing by friends and family, probably bringing the death toll to near 150,000. As Joshua hammer rightfully points out, "rarely outside the battlefield had human beings died in such numbers." What is more, the plight of the living was little better than the fate of the dead. As many as 150,000 people had been injured by the quake and the fires, some severely. There was little food to be had, and little water, since the water mains had been broken and most bodies of fresh water were tainted by the rotting corpses of the dead. Some traumatized survivors, often severely burned, wandered amidst the ruins and the after-shocks seeking missing family members. Others fled the city in droves; indeed, an estimated 1.5 million people were homeless in Tokyo alone. Many of these people sought temporary shel-ter in the sprawling grounds of Tokyo's imperial palace or other large open areas not touched by the firestorm. For assistance, they turned to the government, but in the short run at least the Japanese state had little to offer. The recent change of prime minister bred confusion, the telegraph lines were down, and railroads had been disabled throughout the Great Kanto Plain, and newspapers had been knocked out of service. There were plenty of resources for relief in Japan's other provinces, which were untouched by the earthquake, but provincial officials relied

Tokyo's metropolitan police station survived the earthquake only to be lost to the post-quake fires.

on the central government in Tokyo for direction, and in the wake of the crisis clear direction was not forthcoming. Indeed, it would take until September 8th for the Japanese army to assemble a sizable military force in the Kanto with which to provide large-scale humanitarian relief.

In the meantime, human misery and helplessness on such a vast scale provided combustible material for a different sort of fire, wild rumors. By 1923, Japan's booming industries had attracted a relatively small population of Korean guest workers, who even before the fire had been widely distrusted and reviled by many Japanese. In the earthquake's aftermath, rumors circulated that Koreans were starting fires, poisoning wells, looting the ruins, or raising an insurrection against the government. To counter this imagined threat, surviving Japanese in both the Kyoto and Yokohama area formed vigilante groups that often lynched Koreans they encountered. Witnesses to the massacres reported that many Koreans were tortured horribly before being killed, though the rape of Korean women was apparently rare. When army and police forces began to retake control over the ruined cities, they did little to stop the killings but rather became active participants, systematically hunting down and publically executing "enemy" Koreans. Overall, as many as 6,000 Koreans were killed in Tokyo and its environs out of a pre-quake Korean population of about 20,000. Not surprisingly, given the atmosphere of blind rage and hysteria, non–Koreans were accidentally killed in these massacres as well. In one verified incident, two teenage boys were killed and impaled on bamboo spears after being unable to answer the questions shouted at them by Japanese vigilantes. As it turned out, these boys were not Korean at all, but deaf Japanese.

Why did the stricken cities compound their earthquake and fire disaster with man-made atrocities? Various theories have been postulated, ranging from economic competition between native Japanese and Korean workers to anti-colonial racism to anti–Bolshevik hysteria. More recently, anthropologist Sonia Ryang has speculated that the Japanese behavior after the quake may have been informed by an older Japanese tradition of designating certain groups as "outcasts," and thus outside of the normal body politic. According to Ryang, this theory explains not only why the Koreans were targeted in the days after the massacre, but also why few Korean women were raped — sex with "outsiders" was taboo.

Be that as it may, Ryang's theory does less to explain what exactly triggered the massacres in the first place. On that point, it may be fruitful to examine the 1923 massacre of Koreans in the context of other catastrophic natural disasters. In the aftermath of the Lisbon Earthquake of 1755, "outsiders"— mainly foreign sailors— were publically executed, though in that case the killings were carried out by the state. Krakatau's eruption, as we have already seen in section 2.1, may have worsened a prevailing climate of anger against the colonial Dutch. Nor is this phenomenon limited to tectonic events. As we shall see in chapter 8, the mass death of the Black Death inspired bloody pogroms against Jews, the classic "outsiders" of Medieval Europe. Interestingly, Europe's Jews were widely accused of poisoning wells, one of the same crimes attributed to the Koreans in the aftermath of the Great Kanto Earthquake.

So do disasters provoke an instinctive xenophobia in the societies that experience them? Some disasters scholars believe that they do. The reason for this is simple: Major disasters are almost inevitably followed by disease, and distrust of outsiders is an effective method of avoiding pathogenic disease. In a recent paper published in the *Group Processes and Intergroup Relations* journal, Jason Faulkner et al. claim that "temporarily-heightened vulnerability to disease amplifies negative reaction to foreigners." The study's authors suggest that xenophobia can be provoked by something as mundane as a news article about a disease occurring elsewhere or a foul-smelling garbage can. After the Kanto Earthquake and fire, by way of context, bodies were rotting in the streets— the magnitude of the xenophobic impulse must have been correspondingly greater.

Traumatic disasters, therefore, may predispose their survivors to a nationalistic reaction, lashing out against the "other" as an instinctive communal reflex. Unfortunately, that same reflex also helped to poison U.S.–Japanese relations in the quake's aftermath. Indeed, Joshua Hammer argues that the Great Kanto Earthquake played a pivotal role in fueling the tensions that would lead to the Second World War. The Japanese were so suspicious of American intentions in the immediate aftermath of the disaster that they downplayed the event, perhaps even to the point of jamming American wireless radio transmissions from American vessels in the harbor.

Although Japan's reluctance to accept outside assistance probably worsened the overall death toll, it is quite understandable given the prevailing historical circumstances. Japan was one of very few non-colonized nations in the non–Western world in the 1920s, so it is perhaps not entirely unreasonable that Japan might have feared that America and other western powers might take advantage of Japan's crisis for their own advantage. Western powers quite frequently employed the language of "progress" and "uplift" to justify flatly imperial ventures. Who is to say that the hand of friendship extended to post-earthquake Japan might not conceal a weapon or a shackle?

Despite this hesitation to receive American assistance, the Japanese did eventually accept enormous material relief from the government and private sector of the United States. Nonetheless, continued suspicion and obstructionism on the part of the Japanese — perhaps exaggerated by scandal-seeking American journalists— turned American opinion against the Japanese.

So to did emerging rumors of the massacre of the Koreans. In America, rising Japanophobic sentiment helped to speed the passage of the National Origins Act, which limited Japanese immigration into the United States. This in turn infuriated the Japanese, who felt stigmatized as an inferior race. Hammer also argues that the earthquake greatly strengthened the political clout of the army and the Emperor, helping to fuel Japanese military ambitions on the Asian mainland and elsewhere. Thus, Hammer concludes, the earthquake helped to place Japan's feet on the path to global war.

Hammer's argument should be taken with a grain of salt; by his own admission, U.S.–Japanese tension was strong even before the Great Kanto quake, and most historians would argue that economic motives played a more important role in impelling resource-poor Japan onto the resource-rich Asian mainland. Nonetheless, it could be argued that the Great Kanto earthquake and fire contributed indirectly to the outbreak of war by scattering the expatriate community of Yokohama. This substantial group of foreigners served a double role in Japan in the era before the Great Kanto earthquake, not only introducing Japan to Western people and ideas, but also serving as a window into Japanese culture for the West. During the earthquake and firestorm, however, nearly 3,000 Yokohama expatriates (including many Chinese) died or went missing, and most survivors fled the ruins as soon as the opportunity became available. With their passing, a valuable window between Japan and the outside world closed, helping to exacerbate both Japanese nativism and Western anti–Japanese prejudices.

Perhaps the only silver linings to the thick smoke clouds produced by the Great Kanto Earthquake were the lessons learned for the future. Well aware that earthquakes and fires on the scale of the Great Kanto quake would occur again, the Japanese were determined to be better prepared for the next disaster, and to this end, the Japanese have enacted the most comprehensive natural hazards mitigation legislation in the world. By law, entire districts of modern Tokyo are required to be constructed of fireproof materials, such as reinforced concrete, and these districts are distributed throughout the cities to serve as firebreaks to contain raging fires. What is more, the Japanese government has actively constructed urban parks and has provided tax incentives to prevent urban sprawl into farming areas near the cities, in hopes such open areas will provide safe haven from fire. What is more, the Japanese have pioneered the construction of earthquake-resistant structures, and have spent considerable resources educating citizens about how to react to earthquake and fire disasters. Finally, knowing that preplanning is essential to effectively combat disasters, the Japanese have constructed a number of "disaster-prevention" bases, well-stocked and strategically located points from which rescue efforts will be launched. In the meantime, disaster-prevention bases are centers of disaster preparation, including such tasks as education and training.

Japan's stringent anti-earthquake and anti-fire measures have by no means prevented disaster mortality in Japan, as the deaths of over 4,500 people during the Kobe quake of 1995 graphically demonstrated. What is more, some experts worry that the sheer size of modern Tokyo, which is now the world's largest city, will likely foil even the best disaster preparedness plans. Should the Great Kanto Quake recur, the damage toll could top $1.2 trillion, and since Japan is an international trade and financial center, the consequences of such a quake could send destructive waves through the world's economy. Nonetheless, thanks to diligent preparation and education, the Japanese today are far better prepared to face the geographic challenges that threaten them than they were eight decades ago, on that fateful September day in 1923.

Study Questions

1. Based on your readings of the text, what role did Japan's underlying geology play in ensuring the Great Kanto Earthquake would be so destructive in lives and property?

2. What links exist between the Great Kanto quake and other forms of natural disaster?

3. How convincing do you find the statement, above, that "traumatic" natural disasters "may predispose their survivors to a nationalistic reaction, lashing out against the 'other' as an instinctual communal reflex?" Your answer should reflect your readings of earlier chapters, as well as your own knowledge, and should address the fact that not all disasters lead to massacres.

4. Although nearly all disaster scholars praise Japan's disaster prevention programs, some wonder if the Japanese model can realistically be followed elsewhere. After all, Japan is a highly centralized state with a fairly homogeneous population. Based on this reading, other readings, and your personal experience, how convincing do you find this argument?

Sources/Suggested Readings

Davison, Charles. "The Japanese Earthquake of 1 September 1923." *The Geographical Journal*, Vol. 65, No. 1. (Jan. 1925), pp. 41–61.

De Boer, Jelle Zeilinga, and Theodore Donald Sanders. *Earthquakes in Human History*. Chapter 8, "Japan's Great Kanto Earthquake: 'Hell Let Loose on Earth'" Princeton, NJ: Princeton University Press, 2005.

Faulkner, Jason, Mark Schaller, Justin H. Park, and Lesley A. Duncan. "Evolved Disease-Avoidance Mechanism and Contemporary Xenophobic Attitudes." *Group Processes and Intergroup Relations*, Vol. 7, No. 4 (2004), pp. 333–353.

Hammer, Joshua. *Yokohama Burning: The Deadly 1923 Earthquake and Fire That Helped Forge the Path to World War II*. New York: Free Press, 2006.

Kumagai, Yoshio, and Yoshiteru Nojima. "Urbanization and Disaster Mitigation in Tokyo." In James K. Mitchell, ed., *Crucibles of Hazard: Mega-Cities and Disasters in Transition*. New York: United Nations University Press, 1999.

Larson, Erik. *Isaac's Storm*. New York: Vintage Books, 1999.

Ryang, Sonia. "The Great Kanto Earthquake and the Massacre of Koreans in 1923: Notes on Japan's Modern National Sovereignty." *Anthropological Quarterly*, Vol. 76, No. 4. (Autumn 2003), pp. 731–748.

Seidensticker, Edward. *Low City, High City: Tokyo from Edo to the Earthquake*. New York: Alfred A. Knopf, 1983.

3.3: Pakistani Earthquake, 2005

On October 8, 2005, the north of Pakistan and the northwest of India was struck by a powerful earthquake, triggering the single most deadly natural disaster of the year. As earthquakes go the Pakistani earthquake was fairly strong, though it was by no means the highest magnitude quake of the year. What made the Pakistani Earthquake into a "disaster" was not its inherent strength but rather the vulnerability of the people living nearby. The region struck by the earthquake was mountainous, fairly densely populated, and relatively impoverished, all of which magnified the scale of the disaster. What is more, the Pakistani Earthquake took place along a political fault line as well as a seismic fault zone. The epicenter of the quake was near Kashmir, a heavily militarized and politically unstable region in which Pakistan and India have rival claims. As a result, political and military considerations of the belligerent parties would further complicate an already difficult recovery and relief mission, worsening the misery caused by the earthquake itself.

As with many recent natural disasters, there is no consensus on what the October 8th earth-

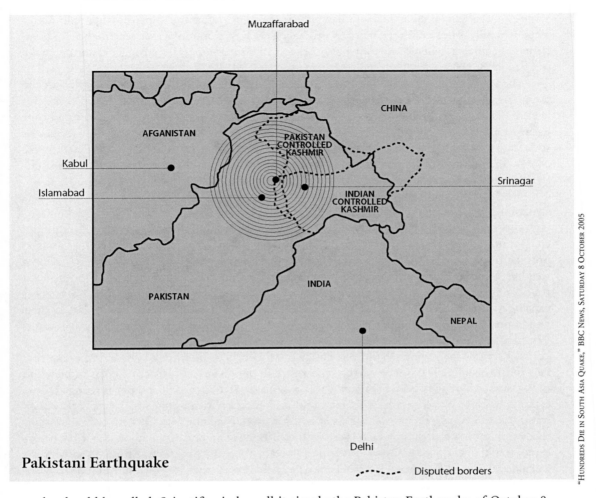

Muzaffarabad

CHINA

AFGANISTAN

PAKISTAN CONTROLLED KASHMIR

Kabul

Islamabad

Srinagar

INDIAN CONTROLLED KASHMIR

INDIA

PAKISTAN

NEPAL

Delhi

Pakistani Earthquake

╌╌╌╌╌ Disputed borders

"Hundreds Die in South Asia Quake," BBC News, Saturday 8 October 2005

quake should be called. Scientific circles call it simply the Pakistan Earthquake of October 8. In popular parlance, the quake has been given a number of different names, including the Great Pakistani Earthquake, the Kashmiri Earthquake, and the South Asia Earthquake. Of these terms, the South Asia quake generated the most Google hits in the spring of 2008, though many of these hits resulted from the search engine's inability to disentangle references to the Pakistani Earthquake from the quake that caused the Asian tsunami during the previous year. In any case, since "South Asia" is a vast area, this name is unacceptably imprecise. The name "Kashmiri Quake," in turn, is misleading, as the epicenter of the quake was located in Pakistan's North West Frontier Province rather than Kashmir. Therefore, the remainder of this section will adopt the term common among seismologists: the Pakistani Earthquake.

By whatever name it is known, the 7.6 magnitude Pakistani Earthquake was not the strongest quake of the 2005. That title belongs to an 8.6 magnitude undersea quake off the coast of Sumatra. Although this quake struck in the same general vicinity as the late 2004 earthquake that had triggered the Asian tsunami, the 2005 quake caused little damage in Sumatra or else-where. The Pakistani Earthquake was not even the second strongest seismic event of 2005, a distinction that belongs to a 7.8 magnitude quake that struck a sparsely populated region of northern Chile and killed only 11 people. What is more, despite its high death toll the "Great" Pakistani Earthquake was far less catastrophic than it could have been. The earthquake occurred along a subduction fault where the Indian plate is grinding against the somewhat lighter Eurasian plate. Not only is this collision currently producing the largest mountains on earth, the Himalaya Range, it can also generate earthquakes in excess of 8 magnitude, far stronger than the quake of October 8, 2005.

The Pakistani Earthquake may not have been exceptionally powerful, but that is beside the point. As we have already seen repeatedly in this text, natural events like earthquakes are not necessarily disasters; rather, they are natural "hazards" which may or may not cause significant harm to human life and property. Hazards only become disasters if they impact a society or social sub-group that is vulnerable to their effects. Unfortunately, as the Pakistani Earthquake convincingly proved, the inhabitants of northern Pakistan and northwest India were particularly vulnerable to seismic shocks.

Probably the factor that contributed most to worsening the tragedy was local building construction practices. Northern Pakistan experiences severe winters, so most homes and buildings were designed with sturdy roofs capable of bearing the weight of heavy snowfall. In addition, cold winter temperatures encouraged builders in the region to construct thick exterior walls to provide insulation. At the same time, since Northern Pakistan is well out of range of cyclonic weather, buildings were not designed to withstand the impact of high winds. As a result, most residential buildings in this part of Pakistan were thick-walled, rigid structures with heavy roofs capable of supporting the dead weight of snow but not the dynamic horizontal forces, such as wind impact or the horizontal sheering forces produced by the undulating seismic waves of the Pakistani earthquake.

Why were the region's buildings designed so poorly against inevitable seismic hazards? Part of the problem is poverty; earthquake-resistant design and construction costs money, and in Pakistan, where the per capita income was only about $2,600 in 2006, money is scarce. Deforestation has also played a role. Wooden buildings tend to withstand seismic waves better than masonry structures, since wood is lighter and has more inherent flexibility. However, wood is in short supply in Pakistan, which is currently suffering from one of the highest rates of deforestation in the world and may well run out of forest entirely by the 2030s. Although some wood in Pakistan is used for house construction, especially in woodcutting communities, most wood is burnt as fuel during north Pakistan's harsh winters, since Pakistan as a whole has only modest fossil fuel reserves. But the important reason that buildings were designed so poorly against earthquakes was sheer complacency. Although this region of Asia is subject to powerful quakes, the relatively slow movement of the Eurasian and Indian plates means that these quakes occur relatively infrequently. As a result the local building standards were not designed with earthquakes in mind, and although independent seismic design guidelines had been drawn up by the government, they were both outdated and unenforced.

Surveys conducted by seismologists in the stricken area soon after the event offered clear testimony to the vulnerability of prevailing building styles to earthquake damage. Researchers identified two basic types of rural dwellings in the region: the *Katcha* or non-permanent house, constructed of mud or stone rubble walls with a flat, heavy roof of thatch and mud, and the *Pucca* or permanent house, with stone rubble or brick walls and a slightly tilted sheet metal or reinforced concrete slab roof. Despite the differences between these building styles, they suffered similar fates during the quake. When shaken by the earthquake's seismic waves, the exterior walls cracked and buckled. Since the roofs were often poorly connected to the walls — in many cases the roofs were held in place only by the force of gravity — the heavy roofs tended to collapse down upon the house and the occupants within. Since many walls were, in turn, held in place partially by the weight of the roof, the roof's failure caused further wall collapses, completing the destruction.

Larger buildings in the region were constructed with more sophisticated techniques and as a result suffered relatively less damage during the quake. Nonetheless, poor design did lead to many catastrophic building collapses. In general, larger buildings in the quake zone consisted of frames of reinforced concrete filled in with cinderblock or brick, with a decorative coating of plaster. Whether or not structures of this type survived the quake was generally a reflection of how well they had been designed or constructed. Buildings constructed with concrete reinforced using smooth rebar fared worse than those using ribbed rebar, which was more likely to bind to and reinforce the concrete within which it was imbedded. Buildings constructed of several different types of materials, either to cut costs or because of later additions to the structure, fared much worse than buildings of homogenous construction because the different materials reacted non-uniformly to seismic shocks. Many large buildings in the area with a ground floor "soft story"—a first floor where the concrete frame is not supported by masonry—fared particularly poorly. In such buildings, where the first floor was used for commercial space (with non load-bearing glass storefronts) or for parking, the columns of the first story often collapsed totally, causing the upper floors to cascade down into the void.

Other factors contributed to building collapses as well. Many well-built buildings suffered partial damage or total destruction because of the collapse of poorly-built structures nearby. The heavy water tanks on the roofs of many large buildings also increased the loads that buildings were obliged to bear during the quake. What is more, many otherwise well constructed structures collapsed due to poor quality concrete that easily shattered during the quake. Other structures were weakened by "cold joints," vulnerable seams in the building's concrete created when concrete is poured at different times rather than all at once. Sometimes builders incorporate cold joints into the structure of a building by design—for instance to allow the building to expand or contract due to temperature fluctuations without cracking—in which case they can strengthen the structure. However, unplanned cold joints left in the masonry by incompetent or cost-cutting construction companies can create weak areas in a building's structure or else allow water into the building, leading to dangerous cracks. Other buildings suffered damage when unsupported masonry walls built within the concrete frames collapsed, and either tumbled outwards into the streets or nearby buildings or inwards upon the occupants. Poor construction practices of this sort are dangerous in any building but particularly so in an earthquake zone.

The damage caused by design and construction flaws was compounded by the exceptionally hilly terrain of the affected region. As might be expected at the impact zone of two continental plates the terrain surrounding the quake's epicenter is characterized by steep slopes, some of which are heavily settled. Unfortunately, buildings constructed upon sloping terrain are particularly vulnerable to damage during earthquakes. In part, this is because quakes can set off major landslides, especially in deforested terrain where there is less vegetation to hold the soil in place. What is more, the effect of earthquakes can be magnified by the "ridge effect," a phenomenon where the geometry of the hills amplifies and focuses the quake's seismic waves. Indeed, Investigators believe that a small community on a hill near the town of Balakot fell victim to the "ridge effect"; several hundred reinforced concrete and masonry structures collapsed entirely and partially tumbled down the hill towards the town below. The hilly terrain also complicated post-quake rescue and relief, since bridges were damaged and roads were blocked by landslides throughout the quake area. On the other hand, the mountainous nature of the local terrain meant that there was very little alluvial soil within the affected area. Thus, there were few recorded instances of soil liquefaction, which would have further exacerbated the damage inflicted by the quake.

Thanks to this fatal combination of design flaws, faulty construction, and geographical factors, the Pakistani earthquake inflicted enormous structural damage throughout the region. The city suffering by far the worst damage was Muzaffarabad, home to 1 million people and capital of Pakistan's Azad Jammu Kashmir Province. In Muzaffarabad, 115,211 buildings collapsed entirely, including 929 educational buildings and 103 medical facilities. Damage was particularly bad within the city center, where the buildings smashed together and fell atop each other during the quake. Overall, 183,000 buildings were completely destroyed by the quake in Azad Jammu Kashmir, and another 72,000 buildings suffered some damage. In the less densely populated North West Frontier province, located even closer to the quake epicenter, nearly 89,000 buildings were completely destroyed and another 110,000 partially damaged. In all, the earthquake inflicted approximately $5 billion dollars of damage upon the region. This figure pales before the damage inflicted by major disasters in the West: By way of comparison, Hurricane Katrina had caused $125 billion to damage just months before in the United States. Keep in mind, however, that the U.S.'s GDP annual is about 86 times larger than that of Pakistan. Thus, the damage inflicted by the Pakistani Earthquake was the relative equivalent of a $430 billion dollar disaster in the United States, a truly staggering amount.

Not surprisingly, such a damaging quake also inflicted an enormous human death toll. According to official government statistics 29,342 people perished in Pakistan's North West Frontier Province, while 43,362 died in Azad Jammu Kashmir, including 33,724 in the city of Muzaffarabad alone. A roughly similar number of people in both areas were injured to a greater or lesser degree. In neighboring India the death toll was only 1,216, largely because this region was further away from the epicenter. Nonetheless, the quake in India was strong enough to damage as many as 200,000 houses and injure another 6,240 people. The earthquake even killed 4 people in relatively distant Afghanistan, though fairly little damage was reported there. It is important to note that these are the officially documented figures; the unofficial death estimate for the quake is closer to 100,000.

One of the greatest tragedies of the Pakistani earthquake was the terrible toll it exacted on children. In part this is because children were less likely to be able to free themselves from the debris of collapsed structures. To a greater degree, however, the high mortality rate among children is a function of timing. The Pakistani Earthquake occurred at 8:30 on a weekday morning, meaning that the majority of the region's young people were in school. Unfortunately, school buildings seem to have been especially susceptible to earthquake damage; a total of 3,424 school and college buildings were destroyed and 2,751 damaged in Pakistan alone. As a result at least 18,000 school students perished during the earthquake along with 835 teachers and other school workers. The estimated cost of restoring normal educational facilities in Pakistan has been calculated at nearly half a billion U.S. dollars, an astronomical sum for such an impoverished country.

While the loss of so many school children was a tremendous blow to Pakistan's future, in the shorter run the bigger problem was the damage inflicted upon the region's medical infrastructure. According to official government figures, nearly 74,397 people were in urgent need of medical attention in Pakistan and India in the days after the quake, but in reality the total was probably higher. Unfortunately, due to damage to the region's medical infrastructure, local medical officials were in no position to meet the quake zone's needs. The earthquake destroyed 262 medical buildings in Pakistan outright, and partially damaged another 161 hospitals, clinics, and other health care facilities. In India, the tally was 35 medical buildings destroyed and another 99 damaged. Overall 75 percent of the region's health care facilities were either destroyed or damaged, including all five of Pakistan's District Headquarters' Hospitals in the quake area. The loss to health care personnel was probably high as well, though this is less clear from the available statistics.

As a result of the damage inflicted by the earthquake on the region's residential and medical infrastructure, Pakistan and India faced a serious humanitarian crisis in the days after the quake. Tens of thousands of people had life-threatening injuries, and few medical resources were available to assist them. In addition, the breakdown of normal medical services, sanitation, and water supply infrastructure created a potential opportunity for epidemic disease. Furthermore, the destruction of so much residential property so close to the onset of winter created the possibility of even greater loss of life to hypothermia, pneumonia, and exposure when the temperature dropped. International observers worried that half a million homeless people might succumb to the cold when northern Pakistan's bitter winter arrived. Damage inflicted by the earthquake to the region's communication and transportation infrastructure further compounded the problem. The quake damaged 4,427 kilometers of roadway in Pakistan alone and damaged or destroyed a number of bridges as well. Furthermore, the quake damaged up to 40 percent of the telephone exchanges and 15 percent of the telephone lines in the worst affected region in Pakistan. The only good news for the region was that the Tarbela Dam on the Indus River, which is the largest earth-filled dam in the world, was not damaged by the quake. Despite this silver lining the overall picture was grim, and the region faced a double crisis; massive outside assistance was needed because of the earthquake, but the same earthquake ensured delivering this assistance to the people in need would be extremely problematic.

Clearly, a vigorous and concerted response was needed to alleviate the suffering of the quake survivors. Unfortunately, due to tension between Pakistan and India the governmental response to the disaster was neither vigorous nor concerted. To understand why, it is necessary to back up a bit and discuss the history of Kashmir, a disputed territory on the India-Pakistani border. In 1947, when the United Kingdom granted British India independence, the formerly unified colony was divided into a majority Hindu territory (India) and majority Moslem territory (Pakistan, now subdivided into Pakistan and Bangladesh, for reasons discussed in section 5.1). During the partition process, the ruler of the state of Kashmir chose to cede his province to India despite the fact that approximately 75 percent of his subjects were Moslems. The United Nations decreed that Kashmir's entry into India ought to be ratified by its populace, and India promised to do so, but once the Indian military had taken control of most of Kashmir India broke its vow. As a result the Pakistanis resorted to force to defend their own claim to the territory and fought inconclusive wars with India over Kashmir in 1947–48, 1965, and 1999. War nearly broke out again between the two countries in 2001–2002 over an attack by Pakistani sponsored militants on the Indian parliament. What is more, since 1989 groups Kashmiri separatist have launched bloody attacks against Indian targets within Kashmir and elsewhere in India, killing thousands. At the time of the earthquake, Pakistani-Indian tension had receded somewhat due to 2003–2004 peace talks. Nonetheless, the political situation along the Indian-Pakistani border remained extremely tense at the time of the Pakistani Earthquake in 2005.

At first, there were hopes that the Pakistani Earthquake might further defuse tensions between the two nations. India delivered 300 tons of food, medical supplies, and tents into Pakistani territory within weeks of the disaster and consented to allow Pakistani helicopters to operate along the Indian-Pakistani border, which was normally a no-fly zone. The two governments pledged to open a limited number of border crossings to facilitate the transfer of aid personnel and supplies between the two states and discussed establishing a "peace bus" to facilitate transportation between Indian and Pakistani Kashmir. The Indian government even offered Pakistan the use of its helicopters for Pakistani rescue and relief missions. These helicopters would have been enormously useful to Pakistan, since they would have given the Pakistani army access to remote areas cut off by bridge collapses and rock slides. What is more, had Pakistan consented to allow Indian helicopters into their territory, it is not unreasonable to believe that this show of mutual cooperation might have given further impetus to ongoing peace talks.

However, because of lingering mutual suspicions, this did not happen. Citing "military sensitivities," Pakistan's government — a military dictatorship under General Pervez Musharraf — declared it would allow Indian aircraft into its territory only on the condition that they were flown by Pakistani pilots. India would not agree to this condition. What is more, mutual suspicion between the two countries lead to exaggerated security precautions that reduced the flow of civilians through the newly-opened border crossings to a mere trickle. As a result, the relief and recovery effort was compromised, especially in Pakistan, increasing the human misery of the disaster and probably adding to the death toll as well.

Mutual suspicions between Pakistan and India compromised internal rescue and relief efforts as well. In both nations the army was the primary instrument for providing immediate disaster relief to the stricken population. This made sense in theory; both India and Pakistan maintain large armed forces, and since the zone of the earthquake was a disputed area, many of those troops were already stationed nearby. In practice, however, the military character of the relief effort seriously hampered its effectiveness. In Pakistan especially, the army "reacted as if they were in a state of war, not faced with a natural disaster" in the opinion of the International Crisis Group, a non-governmental organization that participated in recovery efforts. Civilian leaders were not consulted about the distribution of relief supplies, leading to widespread inefficiency as well as charges that the regime had peculated some of the $6.2 billion aid donated by an International Donors' Conference of November 19th. In addition, there is evidence that the Pakistani army sought to politicize the disaster by channeling relief funds through anti–India extremists groups such as the Lashkar-e-Tayyaba and Jaishe Mohammed in hopes of bolstering popular support for these groups in Kashmir. Charges were also made that both the Indian and Pakistani armies used relief supplies in a political manner, giving preferential access to those with political connections.

Thankfully, the task of providing relief did not rest solely with the Indian and Pakistani armed forces. The United States sent two helicopters to the area within 24 hours of the earthquake, and by mid–November 24 U.S. helicopters were in operation in the quake zone, where they participated in such missions as air dropping emergency food and shelter supplies in remote areas. Approximately 1000 American servicemen participated in relief efforts on the ground, including a handful of soldiers from Louisiana whose home towns had just suffered at the hands of another natural disaster, Hurricane Katrina. These soldiers helped to clear roads, organize air traffic, and provide medical care to the many survivors wounded by the earthquake. The United States also provided spare parts to Pakistan's large but ill-equipped helicopter force, further facilitating the relief effort. In part because of the assistance of the U.S. and other members of the international community, post-earthquake recovery occurred faster than most observers anticipated. Earlier fears of half a million deaths during the winter proved unfounded. Instead the recovery effort began to shift from rescue and relief to reconstruction by February 2005.

Nonetheless, even if the medium term effects of the Pakistani Earthquake did not live up to the worst fears of some observers, the long term prospects for the quake-stricken region remain fairly grim as of 2008. The earthquake offered a brief opportunity for India and Pakistan to collaborate constructively for the good of the disputed region, but this opportunity was lost, and the status quo quickly returned to mutual hostility. As a result, Kashmir's fate remains in a state of limbo, and both India and Pakistan continue to squander scarce national resources on military expenditures rather than economic growth or disaster preparedness. In the meantime, seismic energy continues to build along the fault line between the Indian and Eurasian plates. It is only a matter of time before this region is shaken once again by a major earthquake, and when that occurs it is likely that the continuing political standoff between India and Pakistan will once again worsen an already bad situation.

Study Questions

1. Based on your readings in this section, to what degree was the Pakistani Earthquake really a "natural" disaster?

2. "The Pakistani earthquake clearly demonstrates that disasters are economic and political problems which require economic and political solutions." To what degree do you agree with this statement?

Sources/Suggested Readings

Ali, Tanvir, Babar Shahbaz, and Abid Suleri. "Analysis of the Myths and Realities of Deforestation in Northwest Pakistan." *International Journal of Agriculture and Biology*, 2006.

Banerjee, Dipankar, and D. Suba Chadran eds., *Jammu and Kashmir After the Earthquake*. New Delhi, India: Samskriti, 2007.

Durrani, Jan Ahmad, Amr Salah Elnashai, Youssef M. A. Hashash, Sung Jig Kim, and Arif Masud. *The Kashmiri Earthquake of October 8, 2005: A Quick Look Report*. Urbana-Champaign, IL: Mid-America Earthquake Center, 2005.

"Pakistan Earthquake: International Response and Impact on U.S. Foreign Policies and Programs." Staff Trip Report to the Committee of Foreign Relations, United States Senate. Washington, DC: U.S. Government Printing Office, 2005.

Renner, Michael, and Zoë Chafe. *Beyond Disasters: Creating Opportunities for Peace*. Washington, DC: Worldwatch Institute, 2007.

"Significant Earthquakes of the World, 2005." *United States Geological Service*, Available From http://earthquake.usgs.gov/eqcenter/eqarchives/significant/sig_2005.php

Chapter 4

Environmental Changes

Science and History

The climate of the planet earth is in a constant state of change, both in the short turn and the long run. Temperatures fluctuate in nearly every part of the planet daily, as the world rotates and day gives way to night. Ocean tides flood coastal land twice a day, and the intensity of the tides is tied to the 28-day lunar cycle, with the strongest floods occurring during the "spring tides" when the moon is in its new and full phases. Each year, the tilting of the planet brings hot and cold seasons to most areas in the temperate zones, and alternate rainy and dry seasons to much of the tropics.

Other weather-making systems have a multi-year cycle, such as the North Atlantic Oscillation and El Niño. On an even longer scale, changes to the earth's orbit lead to predictable cycles of warming and cooling, and plate tectonics alters the climate by thrusting up mountains and shifting the location of the world's land and water. Still other influences on the earth's climate occur at unpredictable intervals, such as volcanic eruptions, sunspot activity, changes to the composition of the atmosphere, and even impacts by extraterrestrial objects such as meteors and comets.

As a result, current fears about the dangers of irreversible climate change need to be placed in perspective: Climate change is a constant on our planet, and the human species has already survived several episodes of dramatic environmental change in the past. Nonetheless, there are some indications that future changes to our climate may have unprecedentedly disastrous consequences for humans.

Because of the dramatic expansion of the human population in the last 100 years, more people are stretching the planet's natural resources than ever before, meaning that even normal changes to the climate may have major consequences. Human demographic expansion also means that more and more fragile marginal lands are being exploited by farmers and woodcutters, while fertile land is being intensively used and potentially degraded in an attempt to fulfill the material needs of mankind's burgeoning numbers. Perhaps most importantly, the runaway pace of human technological and economic activity now threatens not only to significantly alter the world's climate, but to do so in a matter of mere centuries or even decades, far quicker than most previous instances of climate change, and perhaps faster than human beings or the species they are dependent upon can adapt. Indeed, in the coming century, human-induced global warming may very well cause the most dangerous "natural" disasters that the human species has ever faced.

The Science of Environmental Change

As climate researchers have recently discovered while attempting to design climate modeling software, the number of variables that go into determining the climate of any particular patch of the world's surface is simply staggering. A modeler would first examine a location's latitude and its altitude, which together would help to determine both the likely average temperatures and the temperature extremes, both on a daily and yearly basis. However, temperature is also influenced by a variety of other factors, such as local ocean currents, which can pump warmth into normally chill latitudes. A second crucial determiner of climate, annual rainfall, is even more regionally variable. Areas close to strong warm water currents or else on the windward slopes of tall mountains often receive far more rainfall than other areas at the same latitude, while regions near cool water currents or on the leeward side of imposing mountain ranges can be unusually dry. Both heat and moisture are, in turn, strongly impacted by the large-scale atmospheric convection systems, such as the "Hadley Circulation," a large-scale atmospheric convection phenomenon that creates pockets of moist, rising air at the equator and dry, sinking air at the edge of the tropical zones.

Even the jigsaw layout of the world's continents themselves can strongly impact climate. Landlocked areas far from the ocean can have particularly dry climates, since most moisture will have been squeezed out of the atmosphere by the time it reaches the distant interior of the continents. The presence or absence of land can exert a powerful influence on the world's natural weather cycles; as we shall see in section 4.1, for example, the ENSO weather phenomenon could not exist without the Indonesian Archipelago, which bottles up and concentrates the sun-heated waters of the equatorial Pacific. Similarly, Europe would be a significantly cooler place if not for the existence of the Isthmus of Panama, which deflects westward-flowing ocean currents towards the north. Furthermore, the fact that most of the world's land mass is concentrated in the northern hemisphere has a profound influence on global climate, since land masses both heat up and cool down much faster than the world's ocean, helping to drive seasonal weather patterns.

Even if all of the factors above were constant, the climate of a given location would still vary over time due to other inputs. One such input is volcanic activity, which alters climate both in the short run and the long run. In the short term, volcanoes fill the atmosphere with ash and sulfides, reflecting the sun's radiation back into space and thus lowering world temperatures. In the longer term, volcanic activity can change climate by emitting temperature-raising greenhouse gasses like CO_2 and by altering the world's landforms, and thus influencing ocean current and rainfall patterns. Another crucial input is solar energy, which can vary in significant ways over time. For reasons that are not fully understood, sunspot activity is positively linked with high levels of solar radiation, leading to relatively higher temperatures while sunspots are present, and lowered temperatures when sunspots are absent. Sunspot activity has a short cycle of approximately 11 years, which influences the temperature of a given year in minor ways. What is more, there is evidence that long-term lulls in sunspot activity can lead to global cooling for decades or even centuries at a time. Indeed, as we shall see below, some climate scientists believe that the "Little Ice Age" of the 14th–19th centuries may be linked to the "Maunder Minimum," a period of time when little sunspot activity was evident.

The effect of solar radiation on the earth's climate is also influenced by two long-term natural cycles, the "eccentricity" or deviation from true orbital circularity over time, and "precession," subtle changes to the tilt of the earth's axis. Both cycles can affect how much sunlight the earth receives, particularly in the northern hemisphere, which both absorbs and releases heat quicker than the southern hemisphere due to its disproportionally high land mass. As a result,

WILLIAM F. RUDDIMAN, *PLOWS, PLAGUES, AND PETROLEUM* (PRINCETON, NJ: PRINCETON UNIVERSITY PRESS, 2005), PP. 29, 30

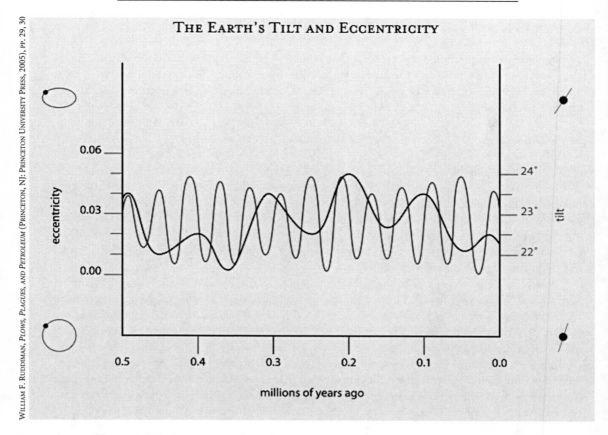

the world as a whole is warmer when the northern hemisphere is tilted more towards the sun, and cooler when the southern hemisphere tilts more in the sun's direction. Similarly, if the northern hemisphere experiences summer when the earth is orbiting relatively close to the sun, due to high eccentricity, the world will experience more temperature extremes. Since these two cycles are out of phase, they occasionally counteract each other, but just as frequently reinforce each other, leading to exceptionally high or low global temperatures. Currently, these forces are in a state of near equilibrium, tending towards gradually lower global temperatures. Indeed some climate scientists believe that our planet is still in the midst of an "ice age," and our current relative warmth is just a natural lull between periods of glacier formation. However, this natural cooling trend is being profoundly disrupted by "anthropogenic climate change," better known as global warming.

Finally, the phenomenon of "feedback mechanisms" ensures that even relatively small variations in solar radiation, or short-term volcanic particle emissions, can have a strong long-term impact on climate. One such mechanism is surface albedo, or reflectivity. Snow and ice, for example, are extremely reflective, bouncing back nearly all solar energy back into space, preventing it from being absorbed and transformed into heat. As a result, a slight increase in the amount of snow and ice cover due to a very small variation in solar radiation reaching the ground may trigger a self-perpetuating process, in which more snow and ice means more reflection of sunlight back into space, still cooler temperatures, and yet more snow and ice. The same process works in reverse; as snow and ice begins to melt, it means yet more land area of the world is exposed to sunlight, more absorption of solar radiation by the land, higher temperatures, and thus even less snow.

Although polar albedo is the best known and best understood feedback mechanism that can lead to climate change, scientists have identified other potential feedback mechanisms as well. As we shall see in more detail in section 4.2, vegetation loss can potentially lead to higher levels of surface albedo, since bare ground reflects much more solar radiation back into space than forested land. Increases in atmospheric water vapor can also trigger a feedback mechanism. As temperatures rise, there is increased evaporation of water into the atmosphere, and since water is a potent greenhouse gas, capable of absorbing a considerable amount of solar radiation, this may trigger yet higher temperatures and still more atmospheric water vapor. In this case, however, the heating effect of higher water vapor levels may be reduced or negated by increased cloud formation, since many types of clouds reflect solar radiation back into space. As we shall see in section 4.3, much of the uncertainty about the possible future effects of global warming on the earth's climate stem from uncertainty about how atmospheric water vapor and other feedback mechanisms will affect future climates.

Environmental Change in History

Humanity, like every other animal species, has been profoundly affected by both short-term and long-term climate change. Indeed, some scholars believe that humanity as we know it today owes its genetic makeup to a catastrophic climate event that occurred approximately 71,000 years ago, the eruption of the Indonesian volcano Mount Toba. According to anthropologist Stanley Ambrose, Toba disgorged a phenomenal 800 cubic kilometers of magma, 16 times as much as was released during the colossal Mount Tambora eruption discussed in chapter 2. Up to 4 meters of ash settled as far away as India, and deep sea sediment core samples indicate that significant amounts of ash settled planet wide. Destruction was especially dramatic close to the volcano itself; the evidence suggests that Toba's direct and indirect effects led to the complete deforestation of southeast Asia close to the blast. Some of Toba's ash reached the upper atmosphere, where it probably caused global temperatures to drop by 10 degrees Celsius for a period of approximately 6 years. Soon after, the global environment what Ambrose has called an "instant ice age;" a sharp and sustained cooling phase triggered by Mount Toba ash.

Not surprisingly, this enormous eruption had a profound impact on the human beings alive at the time. Genetic evidence compiled by Ambrose suggests that the human species was probably reduced to as few as 10,000 human beings, and that entire lines of human evolution were wiped out. Since tropical Africa was less affected by the post–Toba chill than elsewhere, more Africans survived to transmit their genetic heritage to modern humanity, which may explain why the continent of Africa hosts the world's most genetically diverse population. Elsewhere, only scattered pockets consisting of relatively few individuals survived, which helps to explain the division of humanity into seven genetically differentiated clusters including Asian, European, African, New Guinean, and Native American subtypes. In a very real sense, then, we are all children of post–Toba environmental change.

While Toba's eruption and subsequent chill had a profound effect on our genetic heritage, a much later warming period probably helps to explain an even more important milestone in human history, the adoption of agriculture. Approximately 13,000 years ago, global temperatures began to warm appreciably, and glaciers, which at their maximum had stretched as far south as the British Isles, began to retreat. The end of this ice age posed considerable problems for the human species, since during the glacial period mankind has become adept at hunting the large mammals which occupied the ice age woodlands. The end of the ice age meant reduced rainfall, and with it the gradual replacement of forests by grassland, reducing the range of the large animals on which human beings depended. Human beings probably helped this process along considerably by intensively hunting the animals that remained using their increasingly sophisticated tool technology, leading to local or even global extermination of certain animal species.

To compensate for these lost calories, hunter-gatherers in the Near East gradually turned to more and more plant foods, especially grains, which grew abundantly and well in the grasslands the forests left behind. Driven by climate change and population pressure, hunter-gatherers gradually adopted agricultural techniques, such as deliberately clearing fields, gathering and sowing seeds, and storing food over the winter. These techniques eventually gave farmers considerable advantages over their hunter-gatherer neighbors, leading to the gradual spread of agriculture by a process of imitation, assimilation, or outright conquest. Nonetheless, agriculture most likely originated, not as a deliberate choice for a better life, but as a series of makeshift survival tactics by people living in a changing environment that offered dwindling animal resources.

Other milestones in human history have been marked by climate change as well. In a recent book, archeologist and writer David Keys has made the claim that a single violent volcanic eruption and subsequent cooling period in the 6th century A.D. exerted a major impact on subsequent world historical development. In 535, Keys argues, the Krakatau volcano erupted so explosively that it split apart the formerly conjoined islands of Java and Sumatra. The Indonesian Book of Kings, a source that gives scholars crucial information about that period, reported "a great glaring fire which reached the sky ... the whole world was greatly shaken," a passage that Keys interprets as proof of the eruption. The blast was heard as far away as China, where chroniclers reported that "yellow dust rained down like snow" soon after. At the same time, Roman observers noted that the sun "gave forth its light without brightness like the moon during this whole year," undoubtedly because of the massive amount of ash that Krakatau projected into the atmosphere. Exceptionally cold weather and famine afflicted areas as far-flung as Central America, Great Britain, and Korea. Because of the blocked solar radiation, the climate cooled dramatically for a period of years across the globe; indeed, tree ring analysis worldwide shows profoundly stunted tree growth from 536 to 543.

The consequences of this environmental catastrophe were both global and profound. Krakatau's blast precipitated the fall of the Teotihuacan civilization in Central Mexico, where drought and malnutrition apparently lead to popular insurrection. In the process, the 535 eruption may have indirectly aided Mayan civilization, which up to that point had been kept under the thumb of Teotihuacan, the local superpower. Dramatic weather fluctuations after 535 contributed to the collapse of the enormous dam of the Marib in Yemen and the mass migration of a number of families into central Arabia, including the ancestors of the future founders of the Islamic Empire. In China, disastrous drought led to a horrific famine, which in turn lead to the collapse of the southern Chinese state, opening the door to the eventual reunification of China by the ruling family of northern China, the Sui. The Japanese suffered a major famine in 536 as well, also fueled by drought, and Keys links this famine to the adoption of Buddhism by the Japanese. What is more, since the Turkish mountain peoples of Asia were less impacted by the famines than horse-breeding nomads like their Avar neighbors, the climate shift probably facilitated the rise of the Turks as a major force in world history.

Perhaps most importantly, the erratic climate probably triggered an explosion in the population of the bubonic plague-carrying rodents in East Africa, and overpopulation forced these rodents out of their native ranges and into human habitations. Since East Africa had trade connections with the Mediterranean at the time, merchants soon carried the plague across the Suez isthmus and into Byzantium, the Greek-speaking remnant of the Roman Empire. Weakened by pre-plague famines, and with no previous exposure to the epidemic, the Byzantine populous proved enormously vulnerable to the ravages of the disease. Plague first decimated Alexandria in Egypt, and then spread to the Byzantine capital of Constantinople, where the casualty rate probably reached 50 percent. Observers in the early 540s reported seeing "corpses rotting and lying in corners and streets and in the porches of courtyards and in the churches," and even ghost ships at sea, "whose sailors were suddenly attacked by [God's] wrath," turning their ships into "tombs adrift on the waves." Worst yet, now that the plague was firmly established in Europe, it continuously recurred, not petering out entirely until at least 717, and exerting a constant drain on the Byzantine state. As a result, Keys argues, climate change can be indirectly linked to the Slavic invasion of Eastern Europe, the Lombard invasion of Northern Italy, and more indirectly, the fall of the Levant, North Africa, and Anatolia to the Arabs, who expanded in the 7th century under the banner of Islam.

Climate change would again play a major role in history during the so-called "Little Ice Age" of the late medieval-early modern period of history. Exactly what triggered the Little Ice Age is unclear. Some scholars have attempted to explain the Little Ice Age as a consequence of sunspot activity, and indeed, it is suggestive that the Maunder Minimum — a period of negligible sunspot activity — occurred near the nadir of the Little Ice Age. This theory is further supported, albeit indirectly, by ice core samples which suggest that similar cooling events have occurred fairly regularly since the last Ice Age at approximately 1,500 year intervals. On the other hand, as we shall see in greater detail in chapter 8, climate scholar William Ruddiman has argued that the Little Ice Age was the indirect consequence of epidemic disease in the Americas, which lead to massive depopulation, resultant reforestation of formerly agricultural lands, a consequent reduction of the amount of CO_2 in the atmosphere, and finally global cooling.

Not surprisingly, given these various origin theories, historians and climatologists give various dates for the Little Ice Age's start. Some date it to 1250 when more pack ice began to form in the Atlantic, perhaps triggering greater surface albedo and a gradual cooling trend. Others date it to 1315–1317, years of wild weather, agricultural disaster, and widespread famine throughout Europe. Still other scholars date its start to 1550, when glaciers began to expand in mountains in both Europe and South America.

One fact is clear: The Little Ice Age exerted an important, though often subtle, impact on world history. This is most especially true in Europe, where the previous Medieval Warm Period, a half-millennium era of relatively mild weather in the high latitudes of the northern hemisphere, was replaced by centuries of colder and much more erratic weather. As might be expected, temperatures were on average lower during the Little Ice Age — by a little less than 1 degree Celsius on average — than in periods before and afterwards. Although this does not sound like much, it was enough to profoundly alter Europe's environment, especially at high altitude and in the higher latitudes. Glaciers throughout Europe began to march downhill, often by hundreds of feet per year, advancing over and destroying highland farms. Worse yet, these glaciers had the unfortunate habit of partially melting in the summer months, creating temporary lakes within the mass of the glaciers which occasionally burst out and flooded communities below the ice. Cold weather so damaged the 1696–1697 harvest that famine and associated diseases broke out throughout Europe, most notably in Finland where as much as a third of the population perished. The Scandinavian settlements in Iceland and Greenland suffered terribly; harvest failures and iced-locked ports brought horrific famine to the former, and entire settlements on the latter had to be abandoned since the changed climate had rendered them unsuitable to European livestock.

However, the effects of the Little Ice Age were not limited to cooling. During this period, a natural weather cycle called the "North Atlantic Oscillation" began to behave erratically, leading to weather extremes. The North Atlantic Oscillation, or NAO for short, is an important ocean/atmosphere climate system that significantly impacts European weather. The NAO cycle is determined by the relative strength and location of the permanent low pressure system north of Europe and the permanent high pressure system to Europe's south, both of which are produced by global convection cells like the Hadley circulation. In "positive" NAO years, both pressure systems are strong, and together they drive strong westerly winds into the North of Europe. Since the water they pass over is relatively warm, thanks to the presence of the warm-water Gulf Stream off of the American East Coast, these winds bring both heat and moisture to northern Europe, leading to mild winters and rainy summers. Indeed, the combination of the westerly winds and the Gulf Stream keeps Europe's weather much warmer than it ought to be, given its latitude; without these ameliorating influences, northern Europe's weather would more resemble that of Canada's Newfoundland province, which lies at the same latitude. In a "Negative" NAO year, however, the high and low pressure systems are weak, leading to weaker westerly winds. As a result, much of Northern Europe suffers dry conditions, abnormally cold winters, and (paradoxically) exceptionally hot summers.

It is important to note that the NAO weather patterns are far from absolute. Indeed, there are often periods of "weak positive" or "weak negative" NAOs, when the weather tends towards the average. During the Little Ice Age, however, the climate of Europe tended to jump from extreme to extreme. At the start of the Little Ice Age, for instance, Europe seems to have suffered through several years of strong "negative" NAO conditions, leading to extreme cold and dry conditions and three successive poor harvests. In 1315 and 1318, however, the NAO shifted to an extreme positive mode, leading to unseasonably cool and exceptionally wet summers. Farmers hoped the rains would lead to a life-saving harvest following three poor years, but instead the rains turned fields into bogs and washed the topsoil from hillside farms. The problem was exacerbated by acute European overpopulation. The hospitable climate of the Medieval Warm Period had allowed Europe's population to rise almost past the point of sustainability, and land-hungry farmers had been forced to colonize mountains, hills, floodplains, and bogs, precisely the types of land most badly affected by climate extremes. The result was one of the worst famines in European history; Europe's poor reportedly turned to cannibalism and grave robbing to survive, and up to 10 percent of Europeans perished.

Extreme NAO conditions caused other problems during the Little Ice Age as well. In 1362, hurricane-force winds, probably the result of an extremely "positive" NAO cycle, created powerful storm surges that inundated much of the low-lying Netherlands. So many people died that the storm was dubbed *Grote Mandrenke*, the "Great Drowning of Men." The Grote Mandrenke etched a lasting mark on the Dutch landscape; along with other storms from the 13th to 15th centuries, the Grote Mandrenke carved out the *Zuider Zee* or "inland sea" of the Netherlands, which remains today the low-lying nation's most distinguishing natural feature. Similar storms struck Europe repeatedly throughout the period, including highly destructive floods in 1413, 1421, 1446, and 1570. Other areas were overwhelmed not by water, but by sand. Relentless gales blew coastal dunes inland in England and elsewhere, transforming rich farmlands into virtual desert, and forcing the abandonment of a number of coastal villages.

As might be expected, poor weather on this scale left a powerful mark on the historical record. The period between 1560 and 1600 was characterized by particularly bad weather, most notably in 1588, when the Spanish launched their famous Armada against England only to have their invasion foiled by an unseasonable August storm. During the same period England's fledgling Roanoke colony in North Carolina vanished, most likely a casualty to the worst drought suffered in the American east coast in 800 years. Brian Fagan also draws indirect links between the extreme NAO cycles of the period to the Great London Fire of 1666, the Irish Potato Famine, and the French Revolution.

On a more positive note, Fagan argues that the climate uncertainty of the period, much like the unsettled period following the end of the last Ice Age, served as an impetus for agricultural improvements. During this period Northern Europeans, who were most affected by the changing climate, pioneered such innovative agricultural techniques as crop rotation, land reclamation, enclosures, fodder crops for livestock, and water meadows. Together, these new practices substantially raised European crop production, paving the way for European industrial development, especially in Britain. Indeed, Fagan goes so far as to argue that Europe's Little Ice Age had the paradoxical effect of transforming the British, who were disproportionally affected by its ravages, into a world power.

If Fagan is correct, then the Little Ice Age sowed the seeds of its own destruction: The industrial innovations that the British unleashed on the world played a crucial role in ending the Little Ice Age. One of the byproducts of the industrial revolution was the vastly increased use of fossil fuels, which release carbon dioxide, a potent greenhouse gas, when burned. As a result, Europe's 500-year cold snap finally ended by around 1850, for reasons that will be discussed in greater detail in section 4.3.

Environmental Change and Other Disasters

As we have seen repeatedly throughout this chapter, climate change is intimately connected with other forms of natural disaster. Volcanic eruptions, for instance, can trigger both short term and long-term climate change. Eruptions can even exacerbate climate change that is already occurring; for instance the eruption of the Laki Volcano of Iceland, already mentioned in chapter 2, may have aggravated the cooling effects of the Little Ice Age in the years before the French Revolution. Volcanism also contributes to climate change by influencing the content of the atmosphere, both in the short term and the long term. Indeed, most of the water vapor, carbon dioxide, and nitrogen that makes up the atmosphere today owes its origins to five billion years of volcanic eruptions; without volcanoes, our atmosphere might still consist of a primordial mixture of methane, ammonium, helium, and hydrogen. Volcanoes also emit vast quantities of sulfides into the atmosphere, where they reflect solar radiation back into space and thus cool the earth's climate. However, sulfides have a short life span in the atmosphere, so this effect is only temporary.

Environmental change is also strongly correlated with famine, especially in societies that have adopted agriculture. In such societies, human beings tend to be dependent on a relatively small number of plant and animal crops for survival, and these crops and animals are selected because they grow well under local environmental conditions. In so doing, agriculturalists are taking an informed gamble, placing all of their chips on a small number of crops and livestock that have won repeatedly in the past. If the climate changes, animals and plants that formerly were proven winners might go bust, leading to the total or near total failure of the food supply. The effect that this failure has on society depends on the duration of the environmental change. If the environment experiences dramatic but short term fluctuations, such as those accompanying an El Niño event, the damage to human society may be severe though short lived. Long-term climate change, however, may force the permanent abandonment of established human settlements. Case in point is the ancient Syrian city of Tell Leilan, which grew from a farming village in 5000 B.C. to a city of 30,000 by 2600 B.C., only to be completely abandoned by 2,200 B.C. Many archeologists believe that Tell Leilan fell victim to an earlier Little Ice Age, which desiccated the local environment and forced the complete abandonment of the site. The Tell Leilan story also serves to demonstrate how quickly climate change can occur:

Excavators discovered that a layer of soil showing signs of vibrant human activity was covered with three feet of soil containing few signs of any animal life at all. Indeed, so severe was the drought that overwhelmed Tell Leilan that even the earthworms died out.

Environmental change is also strongly linked to disease-related disasters. In part, this is because disease is a common companion of famine; as we shall see in chapters 7 and 8 the great majority of deaths that occur during famine are directly attributable to viral, bacterial, or mal-nutritional disease. Environmental change also tends to disorder human societies: Political systems break down, health care suffers, and normal sanitation and hygienic practices are neglected. Disease tends to thrive in precisely such conditions. Furthermore, environmental change tends to favor what ecologists term "r-selection" species (which survive through fast growth and many mutations) over "K-selection" species (which survive by being extremely well-adapted to specific ecologies). Disease-causing microorganisms like bacteria and viruses are quintessential r-selection species, as are common disease carriers such as mosquitoes and rats. Human beings, on the other hand, are quintessential K-selection species; we have relatively few offspring, who grow slowly to adulthood while being rigorously trained to compete and prosper in specific environmental conditions. Thus, disease agents are far more likely to thrive when faced with environmental change than their human hosts.

Environmental change is linked, albeit more indirectly, to other forms of disaster as well. Rising or falling temperatures are intimately linked to the rate of cyclone formation, as well as the strength of given cyclones. Since environmental change can lead to more extreme weather, it can contribute to flood disasters, as we have already seen in 13th–15th century Holland. Environmental change is also linked to multi-year climate oscillation systems. As discussed above, the environmental change of the Little Ice Age wreaked havoc with the NAO cycles, seriously worsening Europe's weather. Furthermore, as we shall see in section 4.1, long-term environmental change can seriously impact the El Niño/Southern Oscillation cycle. The only form of natural disaster with no clear links to environmental change is earthquakes, which arise almost exclusively from tectonic forces and have only tenuous connections to either the atmosphere or the hydrosphere.

Environmental Change and Human Agency

To some degree the ability of human beings to alter their natural environment is limited. Human beings can exert little influence over many of the long-term forces that govern global climate; we cannot alter sunspot cycles, planetary tilt, the eccentricity of the planet's orbit, or emissions by volcanoes. However, humans can play an important role in environmental change locally by influencing vegetation patterns and globally by changing the composition of the atmosphere, especially in terms of the concentrations of "greenhouse" gasses.

On a local level, humans can alter local ecologies by changing the density or the consistency of plant cover. It seems likely that even hunter-gatherers created environmental change to some degree, as evidenced by the pre-agriculture aborigines of Australia, who set brushfires in order to encourage the natural growth of useful plant species. With the advent of agriculture human beings began to alter the environment more systematically, actively uprooting plant and animal species they found undesirable in favor of more useful staple crop and livestock species. In their quest for resources human beings adopted ever more intensive agricultural strategies, such as damming rivers for agriculture, draining swamps, terracing hillsides, and the like. Unfortunately, over the long run these survival strategies could profoundly and perhaps permanently alter local ecosystems. Deforested hillsides are subject to severe erosion, which can not only reduce sloping land to bare rock but can choke nearby productive land with sterile subsoil, greatly reducing its capacity to support life. As we shall see in section 4.2, the rocky slopes of modern-day Greece bear grim testament to the dire consequences of practicing intensive agriculture in arid, hilly terrain. Intensive agriculture using irrigation can also lead to soil salinization — the accumulation of salt deposits over time — a process that severely impedes the capacity of an area to support vegetation.

Deforestation also plays a role in the second way humans can alter the environment: by changing the composition of the atmosphere. As we shall see in detail in section 4.3, the global climate is strongly influenced by the volume of "greenhouse gasses" in the atmosphere, which trap solar radiation and transform it into heat. One of these gasses is carbon dioxide, which a number of human behaviors can introduce into the atmosphere. When land is cleared for agriculture, for instance, most of the carbon stored in the vegetation is released into the atmosphere in the form of CO_2. Indeed, the esteemed climate scientist William Ruddiman goes so far as to suggest that human beings have exerted a slow warming trend ever since the dawn of agriculture, and that without this mild anthropogenic influence on the climate, world temperatures may have dropped low enough during the "Little Ice Age" to trigger a real Ice Age via surface albedo feedback.

The impact of agriculture on climate change, however, pales in comparison to the projected impact of the Industrial Revolution of the modern era. Since the Industrial Revolution, human beings have been consuming ever-rising quantities of fossil fuels, and in the process are releasing unprecedented levels of CO_2 and other greenhouse gasses into the atmosphere. As we shall see in section 4.3, the scientific community is united in its assessment that these emissions will exert a powerful impact on the world's future climate. Indeed, the main source of debate in the scientific community is not whether global warming exists, or whether human beings are causing it. Rather, the debate now centers on the speed and magnitude of change to the environment that mankind has thoughtlessly set into motion.

Study Questions

1. Explain, in your own words, how feedback mechanisms relate to climate change.

2. How compelling do you find Keys and/or Fagan's attempts to relate historical events to climate change? Explain.

3. "Climate change may be natural, but it is by no means a 'disaster,' since it is the normal state of the world rather than an exception to the norm." To what degree do you agree with this statement?

Sources/Suggested Readings

Ambrose, Stanley H. "Late Pleistocene human population bottlenecks, volcanic winter, and differentiation of modern humans." *Journal of Human Evolution*, Vol. 34, No. 6 (1998), pp. 623–651.
Cohen, Mark Nathan. *The Food Crisis in Prehistory: Overpopulation and the Origins of Agriculture.* New Haven, CT: Yale University Press, 1997.
Denham, Tim and Peter White. *The Emergence of Agriculture: A Global View.* New York: Routledge, 2007.
Fagan, Brian. *The Great Warming: Climate Change and the Rise and Fall of Civilizations.* New York: Bloomsbury Press, 2008.
Fagan, Brian. *The Little Ice Age: How Climate Made History, 1300–1850.* New York: Basic Books, 2000.
Fleming, James Rodger. *Historical Perspectives on Climate Change.* New York: Oxford University Press, 1998.
Keys, David. *Catastrophe: An Investigation into the Origins of the Modern World.* New York: Ballantine Books, 1999.
Linden, Eugene. *The Winds of Change: Climate, Weather, and the Destruction of Civilizations.* New York: Simon and Schuster, 2006.
Overpeck, Jonathan, Julia Cole, and Patrick Bartlein. "A 'Paleoperspective' on Climate Variability and

Change." In Thomas E. Lovejoy and Lee Hannah, eds., *Climate Change and Biodiversity*. New Haven, CT: Yale University Press, 2005.

Ruddiman, William F. *Plows, Plagues, and Petroleum: How Humans Took Control of Climate*. Princeton, NJ: Princeton University Press, 2005.

Weiss, Harvey. "Beyond the Younger Dryas: Collapse as Adaption to Abrupt Climate Change in Ancient West Asia and the Eastern Mediterranean." In *Environmental Disaster and the Archeology of Human Response*. Albuquerque, NM: Maxwell Museum of Anthropology, 2000, pp. 75–98.

4.1: *El Niño Southern Oscillation (ENSO)*

If natural disasters are dated by when they are first identified by human beings, the El Niño/Southern Oscillation weather phenomenon is a relative newcomer to the world scene. The term was coined only in 1891, when it was used to describe a warm water counter current that occasionally washed against the western coast of South America, drastically changing the local climate. For much of the following century El Niño was regarded as a local curiosity, but subsequent research demonstrated that El Niño was part of a much wider weather system, the "Southern Oscillation," with important worldwide consequences. What is more, we now know that ENSO is an ancient phenomenon that has exerted a crucial, though subtle, influence on world history since at least the time of the Pharaohs. Nonetheless, it may turn out that ENSO's greatest influence on mankind is still to come, since ENSO may be intimately linked to the greatest environmental threat of the next century: global warming.

Since "El Niño" is the atypical phase of a multi-year climate cycle, the Southern Oscillation, it is important to first understand how that cycle looks during a "normal" part of the cycle. In most years, the equatorial Pacific comes under the influence of the westerly-flowing trade winds, which bunch up the equatorial pacific's warm surface water on the western side of the Pacific, forming a vast dome of warm water near the Indonesian Archipelago. This warm water dome leads to profound atmospheric consequences: low air pressure, high humidity, and generous rainfall, much to the delight of Indonesian farmers. In the meantime, on the South American side of the weather system, cold water wells up from the deep ocean to replace the surface water pushed eastward by the trades. As a result, the "normal" weather in coastal South America is generally very dry, since the cold ocean water inhibits evaporation and thus lowers humidity, while the Andes Mountains restrict moisture from reaching the region through the westward blowing trade winds. Though South American coastal farmers suffer from the chronic dry conditions, fishermen thrive, since the coastal waters of South America are enriched by an upwelling of nutrient-rich deep ocean water capable of supporting one of the world's densest fish populations.

During an El Niño year, however, this "normal" state of affairs is effectively reversed. For reasons that will be discussed below, the trade winds slacken and the warm water "bulge" near Indonesia migrates to the west, eventually reaching the South American coast. In the Indonesian area, the cooler surface waters lead to lower atmospheric humidity and rising air pressure, hampering rain cloud formation. Farmers may suffer from drought, and wildfires, often set by farmers trying to clear land for agriculture, rage through tinder-dry forests. Meanwhile, on the other side of the Pacific, unusually high water temperatures lead to increased atmospheric humidity, bringing rare downpours to this normally dry region. One North American witness to this phenomenon wrote a letter from the Chilean coast in 1891 that "the rain fell in inconceivable torrents for weeks ... the desert became a garden." Bolstered by the sudden bounty,

This 1997 satellite image shows the typical temperature abnormalities in the Pacific during an El Niño phase of ENSO. The light area in the Pacific near South America denotes unusually warm seas, while the dark area in the Western Pacific indicates a pocket of unusually cool water.

insect life flourished: "almost every evening we were pestered by insects of ever-changing variety and of every size and shape imaginable ... [and] even more remarkable were the spiders that came into the house, dozens of species we had never seen before and never saw afterward." Such generous rainfall may be good for farmers, assuming they can counter the consequent flooding and soil erosion. At the same time, El Niño brings hard times to Chilean and Peruvian fishermen, since the thick layer of warm surface water brought by El Niño prevents the upwelling of nutrient-rich deep ocean water, transforming a fertile fishery into an aquatic desert. Indeed, the 1925 El Niño so depleted the fish population off South America that seabirds, which normally feasted on the ocean's bounty, died in such huge numbers that their carcasses festered in the ocean and blackened the bottoms of fishermen's boats.

As might be expected, ENSO's ability to transfer vast quantities of warm water between the western and eastern side of the Pacific has profound planetary consequences. El Niño generally causes a high pressure system to entrench itself over East Asia, diverting moisture-laden winds away from North China. El Niño can also disrupt the monsoon winds that normally bring seasonal rains to the Indian subcontinent, Australia, the Horn of Africa, and even the Nordeste of Brazil. Other areas suffer unexpectedly heavy rains during an El Niño event. Normally dry islands in the Central Pacific are deluged with rain, and Pacific storms that prevailing winds typically shunt north to Alaska strike the Californian coast instead, bringing downpours and mudslides to this normally arid region. Similarly, El Niño can divert the normal monsoon rains of China up the western Pacific coast instead, causing deluges in Japan. El Niño can wreck havoc on global temperatures as well, chilling normally warm areas and heating other regions far above average. During the 1977 El Niño, for instance, the American East Coast suffered from record cold during January just as Alaska was enjoying temperatures far above the seasonal norm. What is more, the heat from the El Niño in the eastern Pacific Ocean can bleed over into the Atlantic, suppressing rainfall and bringing drought to the Sahel region of Africa.

El Niño produces these profound global effects, in part, by shifting the normal location of the Inter-tropical Convergence Zone, or ITCZ. The ITCZ is formed by the convergence of wind currents from the northern and southern hemisphere, both of which are trying to fill the relative vacuum of the equator, where the heat of the sun causes a constant column of air to rise into the atmosphere. The area where these wind currents meet is characterized by significant climatic instability, often in the form of tropical thunderstorms; indeed, the ITCZ can sometimes be discerned clearly from space as a belt of clouds encircling the earth. As the planet tilts over the course of the year, this belt meanders north or south of the equator, following the relative vacuum where the sun's rays fall most directly on the earth's surface. Because of the yearly shift of the ITCZ, many tropical regions are characterized by distinct wet and dry seasons—wet when the ITCZ is in the area, dry when it has shifted elsewhere. Indeed, some areas close to the equator have two distinct wet seasons each year as the ITCZ passes overhead twice during its yearly peregrinations. El Niño is generally not strong enough to completely displace the ITCZ, but during an El Niño year, the ITCZ is forced to shape itself around the unusual highs and lows created by El Niño. As a result, in the words of El Niño expert J. Madeleine Nash, El Niño causes the ITCZ to "shortchange[...] some areas in favor of lingering over others," skewing normal precipitation patterns.

In higher latitudes, El Niño alters the weather not by shifting the ITCZ but by altering the location of seasonal "anticyclones," long-term high pressure systems that influence the world's weather by altering the location of the air currents in temperate latitudes. Anticyclones, which often appear on weather maps in the form of "highs," are accumulations of high pressure air characterized by relatively low humidity. Unlike cyclones, which spin in a counterclockwise direction in the northern hemisphere, anticyclones spin clockwise direction, drawing weather systems to the north and east. As we shall see in chapter 5, anticyclones play a tremendously important role in determining the trajectories of cyclonic weather, causing storms to "recurve," hooking away from the equator and eventually back around in a clockwise direction. Since El Niño changes the location of anticyclones, it can vastly change the trajectory of cyclonic weather. Indeed, a 1991 El Niño was implicated in channeling a series of devastating typhoons into Japan by shifting the anticyclone that normally diverts typhoons away from Japan.

Although we now know quite a bit about how El Niño can influence the world's weather, climate scientists do not yet fully understand the exact mechanism that triggers a given El Niño event. El Niño events tend to follow close on the heels of the slacking of the trade winds, but it is not clear whether El Niño causes the winds to die, or vice versa. Some scientists suspect that El Niño can be caused by tropical cyclones, which can disrupt the normal east-to-west flow of the trades and thus release the hot water dome near Indonesia. However, other meteorologists believe that it is the eastward shift of the warm water pool that itself causes the winds to slacken, since the easterly spread of warm water reduces the temperature differential that normally fuels the wind. El Niño has also been linked to volcanic activity. Researchers have observed that major volcanic eruptions in the tropics often trigger three years of El Niño conditions. Still other climate scientists believe that El Niño functions as a heat transfer mechanism, periodically releasing built-up equatorial heat into higher latitudes. The continued inability of researchers to reliably predict El Niño events, not to mention the variability of El Niño from one event to another, suggests that a given El Niño is probably triggered by a constellation of factors rather than a single cause.

Whatever the cause of the El Niño phenomenon, there can be no doubt that El Niño has left a heavy footprint on human history. In a recent book entitled *Floods, Famines, and Emperors*, Brian Fagan has compiled an impressive list of historical events that have been linked to El Niño. Between 2180 and 2160 B.C., for instance, a series of powerful El Niños prevented the ITCZ from passing over the Ethiopian highlands. The normally dependable Nile flood failed almost completely, which in turn provoked an unprecedented series of famines in ancient Egypt. In desperation, the Egyptians hoarded what little water passed down the Nile and even tried to cultivate mid-river sandbars revealed by the low water levels, but such measures did not prevent mass starvation. Popular unrest lead to political chaos — according to the ancient Greek historian Manetho, during this period 70 Pharaohs reigned for only 70 days each before being deposed — and eventually brought down the "Old Kingdom" of Egypt. This unprecedented disaster permanently changed the Egyptian style of governance; during the subsequent period, called the "Middle Kingdom" by historians, the pharaohs adopted a more paternalistic style of government, building granaries and water reservoirs rather than lavish temples and royal tombs. Nonetheless, Egypt continued to suffer badly from El Niño droughts, most notably from 1768 to 1740 B.C. and A.D. 1220–1221, during the period of Islamic rule.

Fagan has linked El Niño to the collapse of other civilizations as well, especially in the Americas. By the 6th century A.D., for instance, the coast of Peru was ruled by a people called the Moche, who survived in this arid region by diverting the waters of local rivers into sophisticated irrigation schemes and by fishing the nutrient-rich waters of the Pacific. Between A.D. 550 and 600, however, the El Niño cycle began to behave bizarrely, possibly due to the A.D. 535 Krakatoa eruption. For a number of years the Peruvian coast suffered extreme drought due to the exacerbation of "normal" conditions: Coastal Peru became even more cool and arid than usual, a phenomenon that scientists call "La Niña." The rivers failed, plunging the Moche into famine, though exceptionally rich fishing probably alleviated some of the hunger. Then sometime before A.D. 600 La Niña gave way to what some scholars have called a "Super El Niño," which brought unprecedented floods to the Peruvian coast. Normally gentle rivers became torrents, and the Moche's extensive irrigation systems, constructed by generations of human labor, were washed away by the relentless rains. Worse yet, the coastal waters became warm and sterile, and fishermen began to return empty handed. Moche civilization managed to survive for another 200 years after these twin disasters of famine and flood, but in a greatly weakened state. Fagan argues that El Niño was the undoing of other Amerindian civilizations as well, most notably the classical Mayans and the Pueblo Indian civilization of the American southwest.

Interestingly, Fagan argues that the collapse of the Moche was not purely due to El Niño, and attributes it at least partially to Moche leadership's inability or unwillingness to compromise with the climatic variability that El Niño imposes on the region. The large-scale irrigation systems of the Moche, Fagan contends, were driven in part by ideology. Like the pharaohs of the Old Kingdom, the Moche lords insisted on passing into the next world in style, and much of the Moche economy was geared towards building the tombs and providing the burial goods that Moche lords needed for a successful afterlife. The commoners consented to this exaction in part because of coercion but also because they were convinced that the Moche lords were sacred beings whose rituals ensured prosperity and the orderly cycles of the seasons. If this is the case — and many South American archeologists believe that it was — El Niño would have posed a severe ideological threat to the Moche as well as an economic threat, since its disruption to the weather would have undermined the Moche lords' claim to be semi-divine beings.

Ideology played an even more crucial role in worsening the most destructive El Niño famines known to history, the so-called "Late Victorian Holocausts" of the second half of the 19th century. According to Mike Davis strong El Niños repeatedly caused the Indian monsoon winds to fail in the 19th century, and because the monsoon accounts for nearly all the annual rainfall in these regions the result was famine on an enormous scale. Unfortunately for the Indian people these El Niños struck during the period of British rule in India, and British imperial policy served to greatly exacerbate the loss of life. As we shall see in greater detail in chapter 7, the British adhered to the policy of free trade even in the depths of the famine, resisting price controls on food that might have saved lives and even permitting the export of hundreds of tons of grains from a starving country. What is more, in keeping with the "Malthusian" economic beliefs of the time the British resisted instituting large-scale relief programs to counter the famine, arguing instead that state-funded relief would only perpetuate Indian "overpopulation" and create still worse problems for the future. Ultimately, Davis argues, the "Late Victorian Holocausts" were at least as much a product of British imperial priorities, which focused on resource extraction and ensuring a favorable trade balance for Britain, as they were of the weather effects of El Niño.

Mike Davis goes so far as to argue that, while El Niño itself did not create the modern-day "Third World," it interacted with European Imperial policies in ways that have left an indelible mark upon the developing world today. In the period before European economic penetration into the tropics, most areas under the influence of El Niño weather shifts had evolved economic and political strategies to cope with the climate fluctuations of El Niño years. In Mughal India, for example, the government offered tax subsidies to promote water conservation projects, such as reservoirs and wells. The Mughals also closely controlled the grain market in famine years, forbidding food exports from regions of dearth, distributing free food, and forbidding price gouging even to the point of amputating the limbs of merchants who shortchanged hungry peasants. What is more, recognizing that famine can result from a lack of money as well as a lack of food, the Mughals commonly remitted the rents and taxes of poor farmers working in drought-stricken regions. These practices effectively reduced the ravages of El Niño droughts to a minimum, but when these sensible laws were repealed during the era of British rule in the name of free trade El Niño took a heavy toll on the lives and livelihoods of the Indian people. Indeed, India suffered from 31 serious famines in the 120 years of British rule, as opposed to only 17 recorded famines in the 2000 years prior to British occupation of India. Even some British officials recognized that their rule had impoverished India. As the magnificently-named British colonial official Mountstuart Elphinstone noted in one of his books about the region, in the period before British control, the Indian people "seem to have been exempt from some of the evils which exist under our more perfect Government." One imagines that he used the term "perfect" with a certain amount of irony.

Nor was India alone. According to Mike Davis, European economic pressure exerted a similar impact on China, Ethiopia, West Africa, and Brazil, areas where the weather was strongly tied to the caprices of El Niño. In each region, European economic policy directly or indirectly encouraged the integration of the local economy into the world market. As a result, more traditional economic practices, often designed with famine mitigation in mind, gave way to new economic systems geared towards producing a single crop for the export market, such as coffee, cotton, or cocoa. Since these crops were quite often non-native plants which coped poorly with drought, their adoption on a large scale increased the nation's vulnerability to El Niño. What is more, these new crops gradually edged out food production. In the name of economic efficiency, many formerly food producing regions became food importers and raw material exporters, further predisposing these regions to disastrous famine in times of drought. European economic policy also discouraged the development of industry in colonial or post-colonial states, preventing them from developing a source of income capable of mitigating famine.

The end result of this dual attack by European imperialism and El Niño was spectacular. According to Davis' numbers, China, India, and Europe each controlled a roughly equal share of the world's economy in 1700, but China had declined to only 5.2 percent of world GDP in 1952 while India had dropped to 3.8 percent. On a personal level, the per capita income of Europeans rose from slightly below the world's average in 1800 to many times above average by 1900. The relative increase in the fortunes of Europe was the result not only of European economic progress, but also non–European economic decline. Indeed, Davis argues that China's per capita income actually declined by about 9 percent between 1820 and 1950, while Europe's PCI rose by a staggering 374 percent. As a result, El Niño and imperialism conspired to create a vast economic disparity between the wealthy imperial states and the colonial world, an inequality that survives as the division of the world into "developed" and "developing" economies today.

In the modern era, of course, "developing" nations like China and India are beginning to gain ground economically on the developed world, in part because the end of Empire meant that the non–Western world was free once again to adopt economic policies capable of countering the economic impacts of El Niño. In India, for instance, "Green Revolution" economic policies geared towards making India agriculturally self-sufficient have successfully staved off famine in the post–Imperial period. Nonetheless, the benefits of independence to the developing world have been undermined to some degree by the work of western-dominated international financial institutions, most notably the World Bank and the International Monetary Fund (IMF). Both institutions were supposedly established to "develop" the impoverished countries of the Third World. Unfortunately, the loans they grant generally have a number of strings attached that not only favor the economic interests of the developed world but also have had the unintended effect of rendering the recipients more vulnerable to El Niño.

Indeed, the IMF and World Bank insists that loan recipients agree to a number of economic conditions, given the euphemistic title "Structural Adjustment Policies" (SAPs) that are potentially counterproductive in areas that suffer from El Niño effects. SAPs usually demand that money recipients balance their budgets. Although a laudable principle in general, budgetary stringency often compels developing nations to cut back on government programs, like investment into agricultural infrastructure or water conservation, which might mitigate the ravages of El Niño and thus save the state money in the long run. Most SAPs require recipient states to adopt free market economic policies, preventing them from countering famine by embargoing food exports or imposing price controls. Furthermore, in a throwback to the era of European imperialism SAPs tend to promote the monoculture of "cash crops," agricultural products grown for export to international commodity markets. This may be in the economic interest of the developed world, which is hungry for cheap raw materials, but since these cash crops are often imported plants ill-suited to El Niño conditions, and since they take the place of edible crops, they greatly increase the third world's vulnerability to El Niño droughts.

Worst of all, thanks to the globalization of the world's food trade in the modern era, countries that have developed cash crop monoculture can fall victim to El Niño even if they are not directly impacted by the event. During the 1972-73 El Niño, for example, warm surface waters off the South American coast devastated the region's anchoveta industry. This was bad news for livestock raisers in the United States, Europe, and Japan, who for years had used ground anchoveta as a high-protein animal feed. As a result, livestock producers were forced to purchase protein-rich soybeans for animal feed instead, driving up prices. Not surprisingly, during the next year many American farmers planted more soybeans and less grain. However, the timing was terrible; the 1973 El Niño also caused atrocious droughts and crop failures in major grain producing regions such as the Soviet Union, the Indian subcontinent, Australia, and Africa's Sahel region. Consequently, world food reserves plummeted and world food prices spiked. In the developed world, where food costs represented only a sliver of the household budget, this rise in prices was at most an annoyance. However, in the developing world — especially in monoculture countries dependent on food imports— the 1972-1973 El Niño was an unmitigated disaster. High food prices there lead to widespread malnutrition or even starvation outright starvation.

Future developments would demonstrate that the global scope of the1972-1973 El Niño was no fluke. In 1982 El Chichón volcano erupted explosively, creating a caldera a full mile wide and releasing a huge amount of ash into the upper atmosphere. The global cooling effect of this atmospheric ash may have triggered and almost certainly exacerbated the intense 1982-1983 El Niño, one of the biggest on record. Severe drought conditions afflicted the American Midwest, southern Russia, and much of Australia, three important grain-exporting regions. What is more, the South American anchoveta harvest failed once again, driving up food prices. In South Africa, where grain production dropped by 44 percent in 1982 and 46 percent in 1983, more than a third of rural children suffered malnutrition during these years. In the Nordeste of Brazil, which frequently suffers drought during El Niño, agricultural production dropped 16 percent but food prices rose as much as 300 percent, in part due to a spike in food prices on world markets. As a result the Brazilian government was forced to provide work relief to fully 2.8 million people, seriously depleting the Brazilian treasury. In all, the 1982-1983 El Niño caused an estimated $13 billion dollars in economic damage and contributed to the deaths of 2,000 people worldwide. Thanks to the global scale of its impact, the 1982-1983 ENSO event earned the nickname of "the Mother of El Niños," and it spawned intense research into the ENSO phenomenon.

Despite this research, however, the El Niño phenomenon remains poorly understood. Perhaps the most important unanswered question as we head into the 21st century is the exact link between global warming and the ENSO cycle. The severity of some recent El Niños has convinced some scientists that global warming is likely to have an exacerbating effect on ENSO events, and the available evidence seems to support this contention. Indeed, the 1972-1973 and 1982-83 El Niños were among the worst known, and the 1997-1998 El Niño had such severe worldwide consequences that it killed approximately 16 percent of the world's temperature-sensitive coral reefs. There are also indications that El Niño has become more common in the modern era, occurring once every 5 years or so rather than one out of roughly every 7. Indeed, climate scientist George Philander has speculated that the world might be headed towards a permanent El Niño state in the future, just as it was 3 million years ago, when the world was far hotter and crocodiles and palm trees could be found at the poles. These speculations, however, are not supported well by computer modeling, which has so far yielded highly contradictory results about likely future interactions between global warming and El Niño. What is more, there are indications that global warming may impact El Niño in beneficial ways. The link between El Niño and the failure of the Indian monsoon, for example, seems to have weakened over the course of the 20th century. Scientists speculate that global warming is causing the

Eurasian landmass to warm earlier in the year, creating a strong temperature imbalance between land and sea that favors monsoon formation even in El Niño years.

Nonetheless, one fact is certain. El Niño's impacts are felt most harshly by the poor, who are more likely to be negatively impacted by rises in food prices and more likely to be dependent on agriculture for their livelihood. Since global warming is likely to increase worldwide income imbalance and poverty, and thus vulnerability to El Niño, it is almost certain that El Niño will be an even more potent agent of human misery in the future.

Study Questions

1. "ENSO occupies a crucial middle position in the disaster hierarchy, since it is both influenced by, and strongly influences, other forms of disaster." To what degree does the information in this section support this statement?

2. Based on the material presented in this section, to what degree do you think that El Niño is really a "natural" disaster, and to what degree do you think that human beings have created a disaster out of a naturally occurring climate phenomenon?

3. If you were appointed to run a moderately-funded UN program to deal with the global consequences of El Niño, what actions would you take? Explain and defend your answer.

Sources/Suggested Readings

Chapdelaine, Claude. "Struggling for Survival: The Urban Class of the Moche Site, North Coast of Peru." In *Environmental Disaster and the Archeology of Human Response*. Albuquerque, NM: Maxwell Museum of Anthropology, 2000, pp. 121–142.

Davis, Mike. *Late Victorian Holocausts: El Nino Famines and the Making of the Third World*. New York: Verso, 2001.

Fagan, Brian. *Floods, Famines, and Emperors: El Niño and the Fate of Civilizations*. New York: Basic Books, 1999.

Federov, Alexey V. and S. George Philander. "Is El Niño Changing?." *Science*, Vol. 288, No. 5473. (June 16, 2000), pp. 1997–2002.

Kumar, K. Krishna, Balaji Rajagopalan, and Mark A. Cane. "On the Weakening Relationship Between the Indian Monsoon and ENSO." *Science*, Vol. 284, No. 5423. (June 25, 1999), pp. 2156–2159.

Linden, Eugene. *The Winds of Change: Climate, Weather, and the Destruction of Civilizations*. New York: Simon and Schuster, 2006.

Nash, J. Madeleine. *El Niño: Unlocking the Secrets of the Master Weather-Maker*. New York: Warner Books, 2002.

Philander, George S. *Our Affair With El Niño*. Princeton, NJ: Princeton University Press, 2004.

Reycraft, Richard Martin. "Long-Term Human Response to El Niño in South Coastal Peru." In *Environmental Disaster and the Archeology of Human Response*. Albuquerque, NM: Maxwell Museum of Anthropology, 2000, pp. 99–118.

4.2: Desertification

If you asked a well-informed person thirty years ago about climate change, the conversation would likely have revolved around desertification, not global warming. Indeed, back in the 1970s and 1980s scholars and laypeople alike feared that Africa's Sahara desert was marching relentlessly and irreversibly to the south due to overgrazing and overuse by impoverished African farmers and pastoralists. Over the last 30 years, however, it has become clear that desertification is a much more nuanced phenomenon than was previously thought. Desertification is now seen as a fundamentally local problem, inextricably tied to specific geographical zones and specific

The World's Drylands

NICK MIDDLETON, *DESERTIFICATION* (NEW YORK: OXFORD UNIVERSITY PRESS, 1991), PP. 10

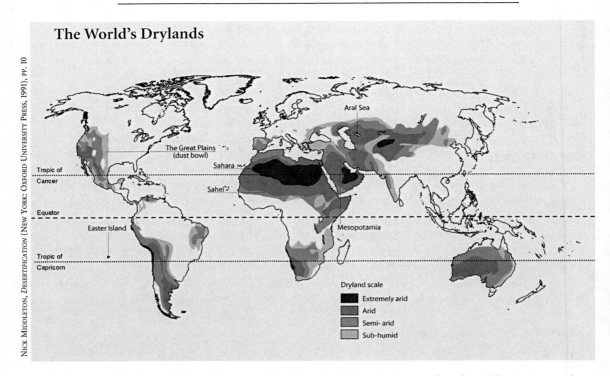

patterns of land usage as well as to natural long-term environmental cycles. What is more, the focus of study has shifted away from Africa and towards Asia, where ill-conceived political and economic policies are leading to increased degradation of formerly productive land. In any case, although the actual course of desertification has not lived up to the worst fears of the 1970s and 1980s, the growing phenomenon of global warming may very well reestablish desertification in the public mind as an important "natural" disaster in the coming decades.

The story of desertification is intimately tied to the story of aridity, since desertification almost exclusively occurs in the world's dry lands. Overall as much as 41 percent of the world's surface is categorized as dry, depending on your exact definition. Part of the problem in defining aridity is that dryness can occur due to a variety of different natural processes. Probably the most important factor overall in producing drylands is the constant circulation of air between the tropics and subtropics. At the equator the fierce sun constantly heats the surface air, causing it to rise into the upper atmosphere, where it cools and loses its moisture. Since more warm air is constantly rising from below, this dry air is forced outwards to the north and south and eventually descends to the earth near the Tropics of Cancer and Capricorn in the northern and southern hemispheres respectively. As a consequence the latitudes between approximately 15° and 30° both north and south are characterized by dry conditions, though in some cases local aridity may be ameliorated by other natural forces. Well known deserts of the subtropical high pressure zone include the Sahara and Kalahari deserts of Africa, the Arabian and Thar deserts of Asia, and the Great Sandy Desert of Australia.

Other deserts owe their origins to very different forces. Deserts in the mid-latitudes, between 30° and 50° latitude, are generally located in the interior of large continents, which are deprived of moisture by sheer distance from oceanic sources of water. Such deserts include the Gobi desert of Mongolia and the Karakum desert of Central Asia. Deserts can also form in the "rain shadow" on the leeward side of mountain ranges. In drylands of this type, such as those found in Western Oregon and Washington in the USA, the air is dry because most moisture

GLOBAL ATMOSPHERE AND WATER CIRCULATION

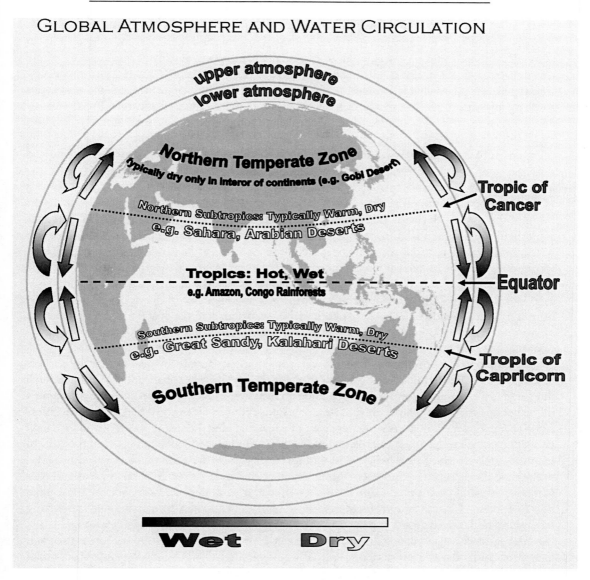

upper atmosphere
lower atmosphere

Northern Temperate Zone
Typically dry only in interor of continents (e.g. Gobi Desert)

Northern Subtropics: Typically Warm, Dry
e.g. Sahara, Arabian Deserts

Tropics: Hot, Wet
e.g. Amazon, Congo Rainforests

Southern Subtropics: Typically Warm, Dry
e.g. Great Sandy, Kalahari Deserts

Southern Temperate Zone

Tropic of Cancer

Equator

Tropic of Capricorn

Wet   Dry

precipitated out in the form of rain and snow as the prevailing winds passed over tall mountains. Still other deserts, such as the Namib desert of Southwestern Africa and Baha California's *Desierto de Vazcaíno*, form in areas where the ocean currents touching the land are extremely cold, inhibiting the evaporation of water into the atmosphere. These desert-forming forces are by no means mutually exclusive. Chile's hyperarid Atacama Desert, for example, owes its origin to the combined force of cold water currents and rain shadows.

Of course, whether or not a given area is a "desert" is not really an absolute determination but rather a matter of degree. Geographers usually classify the world's drylands into three sub-categories depending on annual precipitation: hyperarid, arid, and semiarid. Hyperarid lands are defined as receiving less than 25 millimeters of rain a year, and host little or no vegetation for most of the year, though a rare rainstorm may trigger a short-lived flourish of grasses and other quick-growing plants. Arid regions receive up to 350 millimeters or rain per year, but low humidity and high yearly rainfall variation ensures that plant cover is sparse or scattered. As a result, arid regions are best suited for animal grazing and can only support farms if water is provided through irrigation. Semi-arid regions, on the other hand, may receive up to 800 millimeters of rain a year, enough to support hardy grasses, thorny shrubs, and drought-resistant trees. Sufficient rain falls in semi-arid regions to make non-irrigated farming a possibility, though relatively high yearly rainfall variation can make agriculture in semi-arid zones a risky proposition. Geographers often add a fourth climate type, "sub-humid," to the list of drylands. Here, rainfall is sufficient to host grasslands and forests, but yearly rainfall variation renders this climate zone highly susceptible to drought. The North American prairie, with its thick carpet of green grass that withers to brown in times of drought, epitomizes the sub-humid zone. So does the "Mediterranean" climate region, an area of wet winters and hot, dry summers stretching from modern-day Spain to Syria.

It is important to realize that "arid" is by no means synonymous with "unproductive." Because the world's drylands receive only low to moderate precipitation they are far less susceptible to the problem of mineral nutrients leaching out of the soil, a common phenomenon in the world's well-watered tropical zones. As a consequence, if drylands can be supplied with water, they can be remarkably productive. Indeed, civilization originated in the Tigris, Euphrates, and Nile river valleys, dryland areas that are watered and enriched by seasonal flooding. The most productive agricultural region in the world today is also a dryland: the sub-humid American Midwest. These vast grain fields export an average of 100 million metric tons of grain each year, enough food to feed approximately 250 million people. Overall, the world's drylands host as many as 2 billion people — nearly a third of the world's population.

Although often productive, drylands can also be highly fragile and are frequently subject to some degree of desertification. Scientists disagree on exactly what constitutes "desertification," but there is a general consensus that it means a reduction in the ability of the land to support life either due to loss of soil or loss of water. Forested land may give way to thorny shrubs, grasslands to hard-packed or stony soil. Deprived of vegetable cover, the soil may dry out and blow away, or may be crisscrossed by erosion gullies that ruin the productive potential of the soil. In extreme cases "sandification" will occur, and formerly productive land will be choked by shifting dunes. Desertification can occur in all types of drylands—even hyperarid areas can lose what little vegetation they have due to further environmental degeneration. For the most part, however, desertification is a problem mainly in semi-arid and sub-humid regions supporting reasonably high population densities and thus have more to lose from desertification.

Dry lands are also particularly vulnerable to desertification because of the low rate of soil formation under dry conditions. Soil is actually a surprisingly complex substance, and very long in the making. The best way to understand soil is to imagine it as the layer of interaction between living matter and inanimate rock. Plant roots and microorganisms "weather" the rock below them, breaking it down into increasingly small particles, which by virtue of greater overall surface area are better at retaining the moisture needed to support plant life. The weathering process is helped along by tunneling animals, such as moles, ants, termites, and worms. When these plants and animals die, their decomposition adds important organic material to the mineral matter below. In ideal circumstances, this process is a positive feedback loop. As soil accumulates, it can support more and more living organisms, leading in turn to yet more soil accumulation. In fragile environments such as drylands, however, soil builds up far more slowly due to lower plant volume and higher potential rates of erosion. As a result, in dryland environments the accumulated soil of thousands of years can be lost in centuries, or even decades, to desertification.

Desertification often occurs due to natural weather cycles. The Sahara, for example, has undergone profound transformations in recent millennia. During the last ice age, over 10,000 years ago, the desert extended ever farther south than it does today. Between 10,000 and 8,000 years ago the melting of the ice sheet covering most of Europe brought a wetter climate to the Sahara, since during this period Europe was covered with a perpetual low pressure zone. When this low pressure zone dissipated with the disappearing ice sheet the Sahara began to dry out again, especially the northern portion. The southern Sahara, however, remained fairly wet, since high levels of solar energy created a column of rising air in the Sahara that in turn drew in moisture-laden air from the Atlantic Ocean. By around 4,500 years ago, however, solar radiation levels lowered to about where they are today, and as a result, the annual monsoon winds that formerly watered the Southern Sahara gradually petered out. The growth and decline of regional deserts, therefore, is intricately linked with global climate cycles.

Nonetheless, human beings can exacerbate or even directly cause desertification in dryland climates. This process can be seen with particular clarity on islands, which due to their small size and isolation can serve as models for desertification in practice. Easter Island, for instance, was heavily wooded when it was discovered by Polynesian seafarers around A.D. 900. As the population of the island expanded the trees were systematically cut down to make way for agricultural land. Deforestation, however, lead to increasing erosion of Easter Island's soils, which were now vulnerable to the island's powerful winds. Loss of trees also meant that Easter Island's soils dried out easily, which not only reduced crop yields but also further worsened the erosion problem. As a result, Easter Islanders were forced to cut down ever more forest to acquire fresh farmland, and by 1650 or so the last tree on Easter Island was chopped down.

With no more trees to break the wind or shade the soil, Easter Islanders turned to desperate measures to retain what little soil they had, often covering it with rocks to conserve its moisture, or else cultivating gardens in deep pits to shelter crops from the desiccating wind. But these measures could not prevent demographic collapse; by the 1700s the population had fallen to 30 percent of previous levels, and the remaining islanders resorted to cannibalism to supplement their meager agricultural production. As a result, when Europeans first found the island they described it as a barren wasteland covered with brown and scorched grass and inhabited by people who were "small, lean, timid, and miserable."

Indeed, the historical record is well stocked with examples of human societies which have suffered from the desertification of their natural environment. As we already saw in chapter 4 human beings probably adopted agriculture as a response to naturally occurring desertification: During the last ice age (12,900–11,500), the forests of the Middle East gave way to dryer grasslands, forcing the hunter-gatherers of the region to gradually adopt farming of wild cereals to supplement the fading productivity of hunting and foraging. However, farming proved to be a flawed survival tactic from the start, as agriculture not only drained nutrients from the soil but also fostered erosion of the soil from wind and rain and hampered new soil formation by interfering with the natural ecology of the region.

As a result, most early agriculturalists were obliged to adopt the "swidden" system of agriculture. Swidden farmers adopt a semi-nomadic lifestyle, cultivating a patch of land for a few years and then moving on once the land degraded and yields began to fall. The alternative to the swidden system was to allow land to stand fallow once every two or three years and to fertilize the soil with animal manure, but this tactic worked only so long as population levels remained relatively stable. If population rose too high rising subsistence demands forced societies to abandon fallowing the land and reduce the number of livestock, a strategy that sacrificed future food production for the needs of the present. In extreme cases the degradation of the land can trigger a "Malthusian collapse," a dramatic demographic decline. We will explore this issue in greater depth in chapter 7.

There were some notable exceptions to this pattern of soil degradation and resultant social collapse, most notably the Mesopotamian, Egyptian, and Chinese civilizations, all of which enjoyed the benefit of annual deposits of sediment washed downstream from the Tigris and Euphrates, Nile, and Yellow Rivers respectively. As a result, these societies managed to practice dryland agriculture over a long period of time. Even in these areas, however, desertification gradually became a problem. In Mesopotamia, for example, long-term agriculture was possible on the same plots of land by diverting sediment-filled water from the rivers into agricultural fields, but lack of drainage meant that salt gradually built up in the fields as river water evaporated. What is more, poorly-drained Mesopotamian fields suffered from "waterlogging," the raising of the water table due to repeated irrigation. Once the water table was permeated with salty water, adding new water to the field served only to exacerbate the problem of salinization, since it brought more salt to the surface by capillary action.

The destructive effects of waterlogging and salinization are most clearly seen in Mesopotamia. By 2000 B.C. Mesopotamian documents complain that "the earth turned white," rendered infertile by a thick deposit of mineral salts. The consequences of Mesopotamian salinization were dramatic. In a seminal article, Thorkild Jacobsen and Robert Adams argued that the output of Mesopotamian irrigated farms fell by as much as ⅘ between 2400 B.C. and 1700 B.C., relegating this former cradle of human civilization to the status of a neglected backwater dominated by stronger neighbors. The ecology of Mesopotamia had recovered somewhat by the 8th century A.D., when it became the economic and political center of the Moslem Abbasid Caliphate. Once again, however, extensive irrigation led to rampant salinization and resulting loss of agricultural fertility, which helps to explain the rapid unraveling and eventual collapse of the Abbasid state. What is more, as we shall see in section 6.1, the fertile sediment washed down the Yellow River in Chinese civilization proved to be a mixed blessing at best, leading to disastrous long-term environmental consequences.

In the meantime, civilizations based on dryland agriculture without the benefit of annual sediment deposits proved far more ephemeral than these river valley civilizations. By the time of the greatest flowering of Greek civilization, for example, thousands of years of agriculture had transformed Greece from a heavily wooded and fertile peninsula into a land of barren, rocky slopes with only tiny patchworks of remaining forest. As a consequence by the end of the 5th century B.C. Greece was importing somewhere between a third and three-quarters of its food from Egypt or the more unspoiled island of Sicily. Some Greeks were well aware of their country's environmental problems, and tried to slow the loss of soil fertility by forbidding the cultivation of steep slopes vulnerable to erosion or by plowing manure or burnt stubble into fields to slow the loss of soil fertility. This advice when largely unheeded, however, and as consequence Greek agriculture declined over time. Indeed, two foods which are today regarded as quintessentially Greek, olives and grapes, were adopted by necessity rather than choice, since they were among the few crops that could be planted successfully in Greece's rocky, degraded soil.

The Roman Empire, which absorbed Greek civilization after the 2nd century B.C., faced even worse problems from land degradation and desertification. In an attempt to feed the burgeoning city of Rome, the Romans transformed the forested slopes of North Africa into cultivated fields, leading to extensive erosion and land degradation in a formerly fertile region. After the fall of Rome the desertification in North Africa was continued by Berber and (later) Arab pastoralists, whose flocks overgrazed the increasingly sparse vegetation of North Africa. As a consequence, the ruins of formerly prosperous Roman cities can now be found in the midst of sterile deserts in Tunisia and Libya, vivid testimonies to fragility of dryland ecosystems. A similar process played out in Roman Asia Minor and Syria, where some regions have lost nearly two meters of soil since Roman times. Even Italy itself, which receives considerably more water each year than typical dryland zones, suffered severe problems from environmental degradation over the course of the Roman Republican and Imperial periods. Indeed, as we shall see in section 8.2, deforestation and erosion, along with the proliferation of malaria in the alluvial coastal plains, played a profoundly important role in the unfolding of Roman history.

Not surprisingly, given the severe environmental problems of the drylands areas that were the cradle of human civilizations, the centers of gravity in human societies gradually shifted towards areas where agriculture was more sustainable over the long term. The demographic and economic center of Chinese civilization, for example, eventually migrated southwards towards the humid subtropical Yangtze River valley, where a sustainable economy based on the high-yield crop rice increasingly became the backbone of China's prosperity. In Europe, the economic and population center shifted northward, towards the fertile grain lands of northern France, northern Germany, the Low Countries, and England. Crucial to this development was the development of the heavy plow sometime in the 6th century A.D., an farm implement so massive that it had to be pulled by as many as eight oxen connected by yokes but which was much better suited to the heavy soils of Northern Europe than the light plows employed by Mediterranean civilizations. Although northern European soils had to be left fallow once or twice every three years to maintain their fertility, ample rainfall precluded the possibility of desertification. What is more, agricultural improvements such as crop rotation, mineral fertilizers, and land reclamation projects allowed Europe to increase its yields at a time that other civilizations, most especially the Islamic states, were suffering from increased desertification due to salinization, overgrazing, and deforestation in their arid lands.

Europe's heavy and well-watered soils gave it some advantages against rival civilizations, but the real key to the rise of European power on the world stage was the accidental discovery of the Americas in 1492. Although the first explorers and conquerors of the Americas were mainly interested in acquiring American gold, in the long run it was the America's virgin soils that did the most to enrich the Europeans who exploited the American continents. American soil was still fertile in 1492 largely because Amerindian farmers had not exploited it to nearly the same extent as the Old World's soils. Some desertification had occurred by 1500 due to intensive agriculture in the Mexican highlands, and Mayan civilization had already collapsed due to overexploitation of the fragile semi-humid tropical forest environment of the Yucatan peninsula. For the most part, however, Amerindian population lacked the grazing animals and the metal tools needed to ruin their environment on the scale of the Old World. Rather, in much of the New World, Amerindians practiced a mixture of hunter-gathering and swidden agriculture using varieties of maize (Indian corn) suited to local climate conditions, economic practices that left a relatively light long-term imprint on American ecosystems.

Vastly strengthened by American resources, especially its virgin soils, Europeans swiftly moved into a position of dominance not only over the world's various peoples, but also over the world's various soils. Convinced that the European model of agriculture was both superior and universally applicable, Europeans subjected dryland soils to the intensive agricultural practices that were applied in Europe, with frequently disastrous consequences. The irrigation systems that Britain constructed in both India and Egypt without proper drainage by engineers ignorant of indigenous environmental factors quickly resulted in soil salinization. India's irrigation canals also fostered malaria and cholera, as we shall see in sections 8.2 and 8.3 respectively. Intensive European-style farming quickly exhausted Australia's dry and nutrient weak soils, while overgrazing by European farm animals and exotic wild animal species brought by Europeans resulted in widespread desertification. What is more, the Europeans tended to force the native peoples of their colonies to abandon traditional patterns of cultivation, which often included growing a number of different crops to retain soil fertility and hedge against famine. Rather, native farmers were encouraged or compelled to adopt monoculture farming for export, producing crops such as coffee, sugar, bananas, tea, groundnuts, cotton, or tobacco. Repeated cultivation of the same crops, however, led to rapid exhaustion of the soil. Indeed, European agricultural policy in their colonies often amounted to "soil mining," destroying the long-term fertility of the land in exchange for short-term economic gain. This was especially true in arid lands, which were particularly unsuited to European agricultural practices.

However, since the people affected by this human-induced desertification were relatively voiceless and marginalized, the world paid little attention to the threat desertification posed to human society. The Dust Bowl of the 1930s, however, brought desertification firmly into the center stage of the world's attention. Although the soil of the western U.S. and Canada is amongst the most fertile in the world decades of intensive farming of crops without the use of fallowing or crop rotation had severely degraded the soils of the Great Plains. What is more, western farmers had put a great deal of marginal land under cultivation by the 1930s, first to exploit high food prices during World War I and later to survive the economic vicissitudes of the Great Depression. As a result, when drought struck between 1933 and 1938, the soil suffered from unheard-of levels of wind erosion. The topsoil of entire farms blew away, forming vast clouds of dust that reached two miles into the sky and traveled as far as Boston on the American east coast. As a result, a region that had been one of the most prosperous in the United States only a few years earlier was now utterly impoverished, and a total of 2.5 million people were forced to migrate out of the Western United States alone. Thousands more fled the Canadian grain belt, migrating to cities such as Toronto in search of work. The horrors of the Dust Bowl served as a red flag that human misuse of the land could transform fertile fields into sterile desert.

The lessons of the Dust Bowl seemed to be confirmed by the unprecedented ecological catas-

UNITED STATES DEPARTMENT OF AGRICULTURE

A 1936 photograph of agricultural machinery buried by wind-blown soil during the American Dust Bowl.

trophe that struck the Sahel region of Africa during the 1970s. The word "Sahel" comes from an Arabic term meaning "shore," though the sea in this case is actually a sea of sand: the Sahara desert, which laps up against the Sahel's northern edge. The Sahel is a classic dryland zone, mostly arid or semi-arid, which receives seasonal rains that vary in volume from year to year. During the 1950s and 1960s, for instance, the Sahel had enjoyed abundant rain, and as a result farmers of the Sahel, encouraged by government incentives designed to maximize export earnings, were moving steadily northwards into areas once considered fit only for cattle grazing. The cattle herders, in turn, were pushed northward to the very edge of the Sahara, which had been opened up for cattle grazing by the construction of deep artesian wells.

As a consequence, when a prolonged drought struck in the 1970s, it proved disastrous for both herders and farmers. Each well built in the Sahel became the focal point of a miniature desert, as the too-numerous cattle consumed every scrap of vegetation in a wide radius around the well. The bare soil around these wells was then stamped by cattle hooves into a hard, sun-baked crust or else ground into powder and blown away. In the meantime, farmers who had gotten out of the habit of leaving fallow land during the good years found their overworked fields becoming increasingly sterile. Hundreds of thousands of farmers were thus forced to abandon their land, migrating to urban centers like Nouakchott in Mauritania, which exploded from a city of 4,000 in 1959 to half a million in the early 1990s. As many as 200,000 people simply starved to death.

Worst of all, many scientists became convinced that the desertification of the Sahel was no short-term setback, but a potentially permanent change in the region's ecology. Some scientists believed that the loss of the Sahel's vegetation would become progressive due to a steady rise in the albedo, or the reflectivity, of the earth's surface. As the theory goes, the greater surface albedo of bare soil would lead to lowered ground temperatures, leading to fewer columns of rising air and thus less rain, since rainstorms only develop where rising columns of air are present. With less rain there would be even less surface vegetation and higher albedo, and as a result, the Sahel would be locked in a feedback loop leading to inevitable desertification. Other feedback processes were implicated in the desertification of the Sahel as well. Large dust storms, it was believed, would suppress rainfall by disrupting the formation of the convective air currents needed for rain cells to form. As desertification increased, so would the potential for dust storms, leading to another self-strengthening loop. It was also believed that lack of surface vegetation would mean less water vapor released into the atmosphere, lowering humidity and thus the chance of rainfall. As a result, many people feared that the Sahel region was doomed to progressive desertification. One scientist even made the sensational claim that dunes of sand were advancing into some parts of the Sahel at a rate of 5 or 6 kilometers a year.

The world community was so concerned about the phenomenon of desertification, in fact, that the UN created the United Nations Convention to Combat Desertification in the mid–1990s. In part due to the stimulus exerted by the UNCCD, the subject of desertification has been subject to intense academic study in recent years. Ironically, some of this research has undermined the principles of feedback loops and irreversible desertification that the UNCCD was founded to combat. Recent studies have not supported the surface albedo/desertification hypothesis. What is more, most of the evidence on atmospheric dust suggests that it is the effect of desertification, not the cause; in addition, there are indications that atmospheric dust can have highly variable effects on local climate depending on cloud cover and other factors. The recent greening of the Sahel in the first decade of the 21st century due to generous rainfall has further undermined the "irreversible desertification" argument. Indeed, the scholarly consensus now holds that long-term decadal cycles of rainfall in the Sahel region, and not human activity, play the determining role in governing the ebb and flow of vegetation in the African Sahel.

Desertification scholars learned three important lessons from their false prophesies about irreversible Sahel desertification. First, scientists now generally have greater respect for the knowledge and traditional habits of dryland peoples, who they now see as a potential ally against desertification rather than its cause. When desertification does occur, it is usually the work of outsiders applying inappropriate practices of intensive or market-driven agriculture rather than local people more interested in subsistence and long-term sustainability. Second, scientists now believe that natural environments are more resilient than was earlier believed, especially in dryland areas where the animals and plants have evolved to withstand considerable climate variability. Finally, scholars now recognize that desertification is predominantly a local affair, determined by specific combinations of socioeconomic factors, political priorities, soil conditions, atmospheric trends, and other forces, rather than immutable laws true in all places and all times.

Indeed, after surveying hundreds of case study monographs about desertification in six different continents, desertification scholar Helmut Geist has identified five main regionally specific "pathways" of desertification in the modern world. In Africa, Geist argues, desertification is almost always local, linked to commercial farming and agriculture and often focused around specific infrastructure features, such as artesian wells, irrigated farms, or villages founded by the government to resettle nomadic or displaced populations. African farmers who employ more traditional subsistence-oriented practices, such as seasonal nomadism and intricate networks of mutual obligations between farmers and herders, rarely cause land degradation. When desertification does occur, it is often the indirect result of war or civil unrest, which can disrupt African migration and exchange routes. In any case, the resilience of native African flora and fauna means that desertification is rarely irreversible.

A second pathway of desertification is common in areas where European farming and herding was introduced into newly colonized dryland environments, such as the Americas and Australia. In these areas, drylands were generally used as animal pastures, and in times of ample rainfall herds grew to unsustainable levels. When drought comes these huge herds cause heavy environmental degradation, especially in the infertile soils of Australia, which are particularly predisposed to desertification as compared to the American Southwest. To make matters worse, Australian soils are poorly drained and thus suffer from high potential rates of salinization. However, the resilience of the native vegetation in both Australia and the Americas has largely prevented desertification, except in a few areas where poverty and governmental policies are encouraging overuse of the land, such as Mexico and Patagonia. Even in these areas, however, desertification is only relative; grasses are disappearing due to overgrazing but are replaced by thorny shrubs that are unpalatable to grazing animals rather than true desert. If irreversible desertification is occurring in these areas, it is happening in only a few areas that have a geological predisposition to desertification due to the lithography of the underlying rock. In Australia and the United States, by way of contrast, desertification has been curbed by governmental policy and by land use changes, for example, by shifting land use of dryland areas from herding to tourism.

In Europe, a third pattern predominates: soil erosion leading to land degradation. Desertification in Europe is limited mainly to the Mediterranean climate zone, which receives moderate seasonal rain that varies considerably from year to year. There, once soil is eroded down to a certain depth soil loss increases and soil formation is curbed, processes that can potentially turn productive land to gravel or bare rock. However, research demonstrates that this occurs quite infrequently, and only in a few areas where a geological predisposition exists. Desertification in Europe is also kept in check by the resiliency of local drought-adapted plants and by Europe's relative economic prosperity, which allows Europeans to simply abandon degraded

A ship stranded by the dramatic decline of Central Asia's Aral Sea.

land, allowing it to return to its natural state. When desertification does occur it tends to be driven by fire, which can destroy nearly all the biomass of a given plot of land. On the whole, however, Europe does not face the specter of irreversible desertification.

It is Asia, most especially Central Asia, where desertification poses the greatest threat today. Geist has identified two main pathways of Asian desertification, both of which can lead to potentially irreversible sandification or salinization. In the cold highland areas of China, for instance, governmental policy has encouraged the large-scale transfer of ethnically Han (Chinese) citizens into frontier dryland zones in order to increase the dominance of the Chinese government and encourage the economic development of these marginal reasons. To accomplish both ends, large areas of dryland in both northern China and Tibet have been converted from pasture land into cultivated fields watered by irrigation. As a result, herders were forced to try to sustain their herds on greatly reduced range lands. When yields from both cropland and pasture dropped due to land degradation, the farmers and herders were forced to adopt even more intensive forms of land exploitation, worsening the problem. As a result, both farmland and pasture land has been subject to heavy erosion, loss of biomass, and eventual sandification, as former grasslands are progressively reduced to gravel or even bare rock. Scientists believe that local rock chemistry, combined with the inherent fragility of the high steppe grassland ecosystem of Central Asia, significantly predisposed this area to irreversible desertification. Also, there is evidence that Central Asia is becoming naturally dryer due to climate change.

AP/WORLD WIDE PHOTOS

Dunes encroaching on farmland in Northwest China.

In other Asian areas, a second desertification pathway predominates: the misuse of water resources in arid lowland plains. In this region, stretching from China through the former Soviet Union, formerly dry plains came under intensive cultivation in the 20th century thanks to government supported large-scale hydraulic engineering projects. Most of the crops thus grown were cash crops like cotton, grain, and rice, all of which required enormous amounts of water to cultivate. The result was increasing soil salinization, an increase in groundwater salinity, depletion of soil nutrients, and eventual sandification. The problem was and remains most dire in the vicinity of the Aral Sea, where a long-standing Soviet policy of converting dry grassland to cotton fields using water diverted from nearby rivers has led to the dramatic contraction the Aral, which lost .5 meters in depth and 1000 km^2 in surface area from 1960 to 1995. As a consequence, shifting dunes of sand and salt deserts are becoming increasingly common in contemporary Central Asia. Since this area is also becoming naturally dryer due to climate change, it is quite likely that much of the recent desertification in Asia will be of long duration, if not irreversible.

With the exception of Central Asia, however, recent research on desertification does not support the thesis of irreversible human-caused desertification throughout the world's drylands. Nonetheless, the phenomenon of global warming does give cause for concern. As we will see in section 4.3, global warming is projected to lower the rainfall of some parts of the world, thus increasing the range of the world's drylands. Higher global temperatures will also increase the rate of evaporation, further desiccating the soil. What is more, future rainfall events are likely to be more intense and therefore far more likely to lead to soil erosion. Furthermore, global warming may have a disproportional impact on plants with long growing cycles, such as trees, since they will be less able to shift their location to compensate for changing temperatures than can perennial species like grass. As a result, global warming is likely to worsen deforestation, and thus erosion, soil loss, and desertification. Deforestation, in turn, could trigger the release of yet more carbon dioxide into the atmosphere, creating a feedback loop of more deforestation, more CO_2 emissions, and yet higher levels of global warming. Since scientists still disagree on both the scale of global warming and on the effect that global warming will have on the world's ecosystems, it is difficult to say for sure how desertification and global warming might be linked in the future.

So will global warming, like the desertification of the 1970s, later to be proved to be a less serious threat to the human species than originally feared? Or alternatively, will global warming finally bring about the dire warnings of irreversible desertification issued by the climate scientists of the 1970s? Only time will tell.

Study Questions

1. Is desertification "natural," a "disaster," or both? Defend your answer.

2. Based on this reading and previous chapters, how interconnected is desertification to other forms of natural disaster?

3. Based on this section, if you were an official in the UNCCD program, how would you spend your limited budget to combat desertification? Defend your answer.

Sources/Suggested Readings

Diamond, Jared. *Collapse: How Societies Choose to Fail or Succeed.* New York: Penguin Books, 2005.
Fagan, Brian. *Floods, Famines, and Emperors: El Nino and the Fate of Civilizations.* New York: Basic Books, 1999.
Geist, Helmut. *The Causes and Progression of Desertification.* Burlington, VT: Ashgate Publishing Company, 2005.
Jacobsen, Thorkild, and Robert M. Adams. "Salt and Silt in Ancient Mesopotamian Agriculture." *Science,* Vol. 128, No. 3334 (Nov. 21, 1958), pp. 1251–1258.
Johnson, Marc Pierre, Karel Mayrand, and Marc Paquin, eds., *Governing Global Desertification.* Burlington, VT: Ashgate Publishing Company, 2005.
Middleton, Nick. *Desertification.* New York: Oxford University Press, 1991.
Montgomery, David R. *Dirt: The Erosion of Civilizations.* Berkeley: University of California Press, 2007.
Ponting, Clive. *A Green History of the World: Nature, Pollution, and the Collapse of Societies.* New York: Penguin, 1991.
Runnels, Curtis. "Anthropogenic Soil Erosion in Prehistoric Greece." In Garth Bawden and Richard Martin Reycraft, eds., *Environmental Disaster and the Archeology of Human Response.* Albuquerque, NM: Maxwell Museum of Anthropology, 2000, pp. 11–20.

4.3: Global Warming

Although global warming has only recently come to the attention of the world public, the phenomenon of atmospheric warming by so-called "greenhouse gases" is of ancient pedigree. Since the dawn of life on earth, greenhouse gases have exerted a warming effect on the climate, rendering the world more hospitable to living things. Even man-made global warming may be a fairly old phenomenon: If environmental historian William Ruddiman is correct, humans have been interfering with greenhouse gases since the dawn of agriculture ten millennia ago. What is new, and frightening, about modern global warming is not the phenomenon itself, but rather the breakneck speed at which it now seems to be occurring. The industrial revolution trans-

SIR JOHN HOUGHTON, *GLOBAL WARMING: THE COMPLETE BRIEFING*, 3RD ED. (NEW YORK: CAMBRIDGE UNIVERSITY PRESS, 2004), PP. 14–53.

Greenhouse Gas Summary

greenhouse gases	produced by	lifespan	natural effect on GW	human-made effect on GW
Carbon Dioxide (CO₂)	• defrostation • animal respiration • burning biomass • burning fossil fuels	100 yrs.	25%	70%
Methane (CH₄)	• wetlands agriculture livestock	12 yrs.	little	24%
Nitrous Oxide (N₂O)	• fertilizer use • chemical industry	115 yrs.	little	6%
Ozone (O₃)	• industry • natural processes in upper atmosphere	short	8%	O₃ levels are dropping due to CFCs
Chloroflorocarbons (CFC)	• man-made • used in consumer goods	1000 yrs.	none	potentially high, but destroys O₃
Water (H₂O)	• evaporation at the rate linked to temperature	constant circulation	60%	unclear – see text

formed the way that the human species lived, but in the process it unleashed phenomenal quantities of greenhouse gases into the world, threatening us with a dramatic spike in global temperatures over the next 100 years. If the worst case scenarios prove to be correct, this rapid heating will exacerbate almost every form of disaster that currently plagues mankind, from cyclonic weather to floods, famines to disease. Indeed, the climate changes that mankind faces in the next few hundred years may very well pose the greatest threat the human species has yet encountered.

Almost all discussions of global warming begin with a lesson about the "greenhouse effect." However, this oft-used term is misleading. Actual greenhouses function by breaking the normal convection cycle, preventing sun-warmed surface air from rising and being replaced by cooler high-altitude air, forcing warm air to accumulate at ground level instead. "Greenhouse" gases, on the other hand, produce warmth by absorbing solar radiation and storing it in the form of heat. This process is not a "disaster" per se; in fact, the greenhouse gases are crucial to life on earth, and the exact temperature of our planet at any given point has always been largely determined by the chemical composition of the atmosphere. Nearly 80 percent of our atmosphere consists of nitrogen, almost all locked in N_2 molecules, but two-atom molecules like N_2 are generally poor absorbers of solar energy. Another 20 percent of our atmosphere consists of oxygen in the form of O_2, which is vital for terrestrial life but which similarly absorbs little incoming radiation. The atmospheric molecules that play by far the most important role in absorbing solar radiation are those with three or more atoms, most notably H_2O (water vapor), CO_2 (carbon dioxide), O_3 (ozone), CH_4 (methane), N_2O (Nitrous Oxide), and CFCs (Chlorofluorocarbons). These complex molecules, which have a more flexible structure than rigid two-atom gases, react to solar radiation by vibrating, creating collisions that heat the surrounding gases.

In terms of relative importance to the functioning of the climate system water vapor is by far the most important greenhouse gas, contributing to as much as ⅔ of our atmosphere's heat absorption. Carbon dioxide ranks a distant second in terms of overall influence on the global climate, though as we shall see carbon dioxide is the most important greenhouse gas in terms of man-made climate change. Methane is the third most important gas, accounting for about 4 to 9 percent of the greenhouse effect, followed by nitrous oxide and ozone. Although collectively these gases make up only a little more than 1 percent of the composition of our atmosphere, without them the global temperature would be slightly below freezing as opposed to its present average global temperature of 15 degrees Celsius.

As the amount of greenhouse gas in the atmosphere has changed over time, global temperatures have fluctuated accordingly. 100 million years ago, during the mid–Cretaceous period, CO_2 concentrations in the atmosphere rose above 1,000 parts per million — three times the present-day level — and temperatures were at least 5 degrees Celsius higher than those of today, possibly much higher. At that time, dinosaurs roamed a much warmer Earth, even colonizing the ice-free poles. On the other hand, about 350 million years ago, during the Carboniferous period of the Paleozoic era, carbon dioxide levels plummeted to unprecedented lows, and the world experienced at least one major Ice Age. Of course, global temperatures are affected by more than just the composition of the atmosphere, so the relationship between greenhouse gases and temperature is not purely linear. Nonetheless, at any given point in time during past eras the level of atmospheric greenhouse gases played an important role in determining the climate.

The exact amount of greenhouse gases in the atmosphere at any given point is the result of a bewildering array of variables. Dying plant matter gives off a great deal of carbon dioxide and methane, while living plants absorb carbon dioxide. Indeed, most of the biomass of any given tract of land consists of carbon and other elements drawn from the atmosphere, not from the soil. The ocean also acts as an important carbon dioxide sink, and in fact contains about 50 times as much CO_2 as the atmosphere. Nonetheless, since rising temperature limits water's ability to absorb CO_2, the sea can also exhale carbon dioxide into the atmosphere under certain conditions. Ozone occurs naturally in the upper atmosphere, and since it is created by solar radiation the overall amount of ozone reflects the solar output at any given time. At the same time, the amount of ozone in the atmosphere can be reduced dramatically by increasing quantities of atmospheric nitrogen, chlorine, bromine, and hydrogen.

Plate tectonics has an even more complicated relationship with greenhouse gases. Much of the CO_2 and water in our atmosphere was exhaled from the planet's interior by volcanic eruptions, and volcanoes still belch millions of tons of carbon dioxide into the atmosphere each year. At the same time, however, plate subduction carries vast quantities of carbon and water underground and back into the earth's crust, removing it from the world's surface — though as we saw in chapter 2, some of this subducted material bubbles back to the surface as a component of volcanic magma. Further complicating matters is the fact that nearly all greenhouse gases last only a limited amount of time in the atmosphere before breaking down into their component parts or reverting to liquid form. Carbon dioxide has a highly variable atmospheric lifetime, for example, while methane persists for only 12, and water is constantly being precipitated into and out of the atmosphere due to the water cycle and respiration by living things.

Human behaviors must also be factored in to the greenhouse gas equation. Indeed, climate historian William Ruddiman has gone so far as to argue that human beings have exerted a significant influence over greenhouse gas concentrations since the dawn of agriculture. Ruddiman contends that methane levels have been on the increase for the past 5,000 years, ever since agricultural man began keeping livestock (which produce methane "at both ends," as Ruddiman delicately puts it), burning forests to create farmland, and most importantly, practicing wet-field (paddy) agriculture, which releases a great deal of methane into the atmosphere. Carbon dioxide levels began to climb even earlier (about 8,000 years ago) as forests were steadily cleared for agriculture, greatly reducing the biomass per square unit of soil. In the process human beings released enough carbon to hold CO_2 levels at about 280 parts per million. Without mankind's additional input, Ruddiman contends, CO_2 levels would have declined to 240 ppm.

These man-made greenhouse gas emissions may actually have staved off an overdue Ice Age. In the natural course of things, the earth's temperature should have dropped below the "glaciation threshold" sometime between 4,500 and 4,000 years ago. Permanent year-round ice caps should have formed, and once established, increasingly higher levels of surface albedo would have made glaciation a self-feeding process. What is more, Ruddiman argues, mankind came very close to triggering another Ice Age in approximately A.D. 1500 as an unexpected side effect of the European discovery of the Americas. As we shall see in chapter 8, European contact with the previously isolated Amerindian population lead to the deaths of up to 95 percent of the Amerindians by 1500, and since many of these Amerindians were agriculturalists the result must have been widespread reforestation and the absorption of considerable quantities of CO_2 from the atmosphere. Indeed, Ruddiman points to evidence of a historical die-off of lichens on Canada's Baffin Island, probably produced by limited ice cap formation c. 1500, to illustrate how close mankind came to a human-induced Ice Age at the time of Columbus. Fortunately, Ruddiman argues, the heightened CO_2 levels produced by over seven millennia of human agricultural activity prevented these Canadian glaciers from becoming established and initiating a self-perpetuating albedo feedback mechanism.

Ruddiman's theories are controversial, but mankind's second major influence on the climate — the burning of fossil fuels following the industrial revolution — is now an established scientific fact. Prior to the industrial revolution human beings burned fuels for a variety of purposes, but for the most part this fuel was wood, peat, animal waste, or other organic compounds. Consequently the absolute amount of carbon on the planet's biosphere and atmosphere stayed nearly constant. Fossil fuels, however, are the remains of forest and swamp plants that died approximately 200 million years ago and were later transformed into carbon or hydrocarbon compounds by heat and pressure within the earth's crust. Thus, when we burn fossil fuels we are essentially consuming energy laid down by ancient sunlight, reinserting carbon into the atmosphere that had settled out millions of years ago. In that sense modern man is burning the candle at both ends, exploiting present-day solar energy for agriculture while simultaneously consuming ancient solar energy for industry. The world standard of living has soared as a result, but so too have greenhouse gas levels.

Interestingly, this sort of thing may have happened before. Two hundred and forty-five million years ago, an unprecedented natural calamity known by scientists as the Permo-Triassic extinction fundamentally altered the course of life on earth. The exact origins of this event are obscure, but one theory holds that a massive outpouring of CO_2 from volcanoes in what is now Siberia may have warmed global temperatures by about 6 degrees Celsius, enough to thaw the poles. As the polar ice melted, it released billions of tons of trapped CO_2 and CH_4 from the polar tundra and the ocean floor. In effect this meant that the atmospheric carbon and methane of the Permo-Triassic era was suddenly supplemented with greenhouse gases that had settled out during earlier ages of terrestrial life. Global temperatures rose even higher, and oxygen levels in the atmosphere seem to have dropped, most likely because CH_4 in the atmosphere tends to combine with O_2 to form H_2O and CO_2. The results were dramatic: Approximately 90 percent of the world's species were driven to extinction, especially the dominant mammal species of the age, which proved most vulnerable to the radical climate changes. As we shall later in this section, some researchers worry that the thawing of the poles due to modern-day global warming might pose a similar threat to the dominant mammal of the present day: mankind.

Even if this nightmare scenario proves unfounded, the carbon dioxide that mankind is currently releasing into the atmosphere may itself be sufficient to trigger catastrophic long-term effects. Most of this CO_2 enters the atmosphere as the result of burning fossil fuels: coal, oil, and natural gas. All three materials are thought to be the result of the decomposition of ancient biomass deep under the earth's surface, though a minority scientific view holds that oil and natural gas may be of non-organic origin.

Coal is by far the most common fossil fuel and also the easiest to extract from the ground, which explains why coal was the first fossil fuel to be used on a large scale. It is important to note that human beings generally turned to coal not out of choice, but out of necessity. Indeed, coal is overall an inferior fuel to mankind's preferred fuel throughout history: wood, which is both more readily available and generally burns cleaner. Wood also has the benefits of being a renewable resource, and of not adding ancient carbon back into the atmosphere when burned. However, the world's forests came under a double squeeze in recent history. Growing human populations created a greater demand for wood as a fuel and building material, but also greater demand for farmland, a need that can often only be satisfied by cutting down forests. Since demand for forest exceeded supply, the world's forests dwindled steadily throughout historical time. The Chinese began to run out of forests as early as A.D. 900, and were forced to turn to coal rather than wood in their iron smelting industry. Coal was definitely in widespread use in China by the end of the 13th century, when Marco Polo described seeing "black rocks" that were burned for fuel while exploring the Chinese Yuan Dynasty. Europe reached this point somewhat later, only using coal on a large scale during the mid–19th century, by which time coal was widely used not only as an industrial fuel but also as a heating source for urban homes.

Thanks to ample supplies of timber, the United States turned to coal even more recently; indeed, some American steam trains still ran on wood, not coal, after the turn of the 20th century.

The good news about coal is that it is extremely plentiful — current known reserves would last mankind over a century at the present rate of consumption. The bad news is that coal, when burned, releases much more carbon dioxide than other fossil fuels. The amount of CO_2 produced when any fossil fuel is burned depends largely on the ratio of carbon to hydrogen in the fuel. In the case of coal, that ratio is roughly 10:1 in favor of carbon, though the composition of specific types of coal varies considerably. Thus, when oxygen combines with the combustible materials in coal, it produces a relatively large amount of CO_2 and relatively little H_2O. Once again, however, there is good news: Coal currently accounts for a declining percentage of all fossil fuels burned. To some degree, this declining consumption reflects a growing realization about the dangers of greenhouse gases in the atmosphere. To a greater extent, however, this shift reflects changes in machine technology. Most of the first engines of the industrial revolution consisted of a heat source, a water boiler, and a series of pistons driven by steam pressure. Coal was well suited to this form of technology, since although coal takes a while to build up heat it releases that heat non-explosively and for a considerable period of time. However, the pistons of the internal combustion engines in today's machinery are driven not by steam but by a series of miniature explosions, requiring a more volatile form of fuel. This has favored the increasing use of gasoline and natural gas, though coal continues to dominate certain industries, especially the production of electricity.

The second major form of fossil fuel is oil, but unlike coal oil is rarely used directly as a fuel. Indeed, "mineral oil," or petroleum, consists of a mixture of compounds that must be separated at a refinery. The first such compound to be developed commercially was kerosene, which was mass marketed after 1850 to fuel the oil lamps of the day. Kerosene was a good choice for this purpose, as it created considerable light but only moderate heat when burned and rarely ignited explosively. One by-product of the kerosene manufacturing process was the far more volatile fluid gasoline. However, early chemists initially found few uses for this potentially dangerous compound, and it was sold in limited amounts on the market as a hair louse treatment and stain remover. With the development of an economically viable internal combustion engine in around 1900, however, the demand for gasoline grew to the point that it remains the most widely used byproduct of mineral oil today.

As an energy source gasoline has both advantages and disadvantages when compared to coal. Gasoline, a "hydrocarbon," contains twice the amount of hydrogen as coal, meaning that less carbon dioxide is produced per unit of energy generated. As a result, gasoline and diesel fuel, a similar compound also derived from mineral oil, contribute proportionally less CO_2 to the atmosphere than coal when consumed, though this advantage is reduced somewhat when you consider the energy expended to refine the gasoline from mineral oil in the first place. On the other hand, it could be argued that the convenience of gasoline as a fuel — gasoline is high in energy, easily portable, combustible at low temperatures — has indirectly done more harm to the environment than less versatile coal. Gasoline and diesel made possible two key transportation technologies which we now take for granted in the modern world, automobiles and aircraft. Without these technological marvels we might be much more dependent on animal or wind power for our transportation, and although travel would be slower it would be driven to a greater extent by renewable power sources that release no greenhouse gases.

The third member of the fossil fuel triad, natural gas, is a relatively recent addition to the hydrocarbon scene. Natural gas is a mixture of gases that are found trapped in rock domes underground, often in the presence of either coal or (more commonly) mineral oil reserves. About 97 percent of natural gas consists of methane (CH_4), but any given volume of natural gas contains an array of other materials, including heavier hydrocarbons (ethane and propane), hydrogen sulfide, carbon dioxide, helium, and sometimes even mercury. For much of human history natural gas was not used by mankind, in part because the technology for separating the methane from the other compounds was not available and in part because the capture, storage, and transportation of the natural gas posed insurmountable problems. Indeed, up until about the middle of the 20th century, oil companies considered natural gas an annoyance and deliberately burned it at their wells, a practice called flaring.

Paradoxically, during the same period, some western countries manufactured "artificial" natural gas by subjecting coal to heat to release hydrocarbon gas and then removing contaminants, creating a product variously called "coal gas" or "town gas." Although somewhat expensive to produce, such gas was economically viable because it burned with a bright, steady light, unlike the flickering candles and oil lamps of the day. During the second half of the 19th century virtually every city of note in the West constructed a gas plant in order to provide gas for public lighting systems and even to residential homes. After the turn of the century, however, "town gas" steadily lost ground to an emerging rival technology: electric lighting.

True "natural gas" only began to be exploited on a large scale after 1959, when British petroleum engineers demonstrated that natural gas could be exported economically if transformed into a more compact liquid through refrigeration technology. Since that time the demand for natural gas has skyrocketed, as it burns cleaner and produces far less pollution than conventional fuels, and since it is particularly well adapted for use in cheap, small-scale electricity generation plants. Perhaps most important to the present discussion, natural gas produces considerably less carbon dioxide when burned than other fossil fuels when burned — about 30 percent less than petroleum and 45 percent less than coal. As a result, some scientists and politicians have argued that the global warming problem could be alleviated by weaning our economy away from coal and petroleum and adopting natural gas wholesale as a source of energy.

However, natural gas is unlikely to solve the world's greenhouse problems. For one thing, methane is itself a greenhouse gas, and in fact is about 70 times more potent per unit of volume than carbon dioxide in trapping solar radiation. Thus, any benefit gained from burning natural gas could easily be offset by the accidental leakage of methane into the atmosphere, where it would act strongly as a greenhouse gas, and as more and more of the economy is switched over to natural gas, the opportunities for leakages are likely to rise accordingly. What is more, any large-scale shift towards natural gas is bound to be temporary, since known world supplies of natural gas are limited. Indeed, at the current rate of usage, the natural gas supply is expected to peak in around 2030 and then decline afterwards. Some entrepreneurs, in response, have suggested production of natural gas through "gassification" — essentially a revival of the "town gas" of the 19th century — to convert coal into cleaner burning hydrocarbon gases. However with current technologies the gassification process itself produces so much carbon dioxide that it might on balance cause more rather than less global warming than simply burning the coal for energy.

Thus, the consumption of fossil fuels is responsible for most of the man-made climate change the world is currently experiencing. Nonetheless, human beings have worsened global warming by releasing other gases into the atmosphere as well. One is nitrous oxide (N_2O), more commonly known by the general public as "laughing gas." About 90 percent of nitrous oxide is emitted into the atmosphere naturally by bacteria living in the soils and oceans. However, humans account for another 10 percent, mainly by using nitrogen fertilizers and rearing livestock, and since the net greenhouse effect of a given volume of nitrous oxide is about 300 times that of carbon dioxide, even this small amount contributes appreciably to global climate change. Human beings are also responsible for emitting a purely artificial gas, chlorofluorocarbon (CFC).

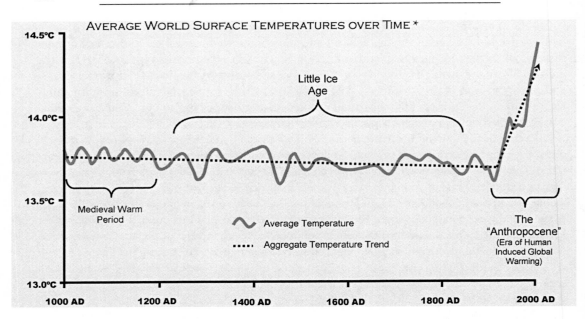

CFC, along with chemically related gases HCFC and HFC, are non-reactive molecules marketed as fire suppressants and refrigerants. However, these convoluted molecules cause approximately 12,000 times the greenhouse gas effect as carbon dioxide, and as a result, these compounds are now being phased out of the world economy. Incidentally, the effect of both nitrous oxide and CFCs on global warming is complicated by the fact they destroy atmospheric ozone (O_3), a greenhouse gas produced naturally in the upper atmosphere.

So much for the causes of global warming — what about the effects? How are human emissions of greenhouse gases likely to alter future climate, and what impacts will these changes have on the human species?

Unfortunately, at the present time it is not possible to give a clear and unambiguous answer to this question, as the answer depends both on uncertain human inputs and on unclear scientific propositions. We will consider the human inputs at the conclusion of the chapter when we discuss what can be done about the global warming problem. As for science, although no reputable scientist now doubts that global warming is occurring, there is some uncertainty about issues such as surface albedo, cloud albedo, the effect of CO_2 on tundra biomass, and the like. In terms of surface albedo, for example, there is wide agreement that polar ice sheets are melting, especially the north polar ice cap, where the average area covered by winter sea ice at its maximum extent is down about 18 percent since the 1980s. Since water absorbs much more solar energy than ice, this could trigger higher temperatures and yet more melting, a process called a "positive feedback loop." Melting polar glaciers also move faster than those that are not melting, which will encourage the "calving" of glaciers into icebergs, further decreasing the albedo of the polar regions. Worse yet, warmer polar temperatures may trigger the thawing of the permafrost and undersea ice deposits, releasing enormous amounts of methane and carbon dioxide from frozen underground sinks and perhaps triggering catastrophic climate change such as that which occurred during the Permo-Triassic era. Melting ice caps might also trigger dangerous rises in sea level, as we shall discuss below.

*COMPILED FROM DATA PUBLISHED IN P.D. JONES & M.E. MANN (2004): "CLIMATE OVER PAST MILLENNIA," REVIEWS OF GEOPHYSICS, 42, ARTICLE NUMBER RG2002, AND P.D. JONES, D.E. PARKER, T.J. OSBORN & K.R. BRIFFA (2005), "GLOBAL AND HEMISPHERIC TEMPERATURE ANOMALIES—LAND AND MARINE INSTRUMENTAL RECORDS," TRENDS: A COMPENDIUM OF DATA ON GLOBAL CHANGE. CARBON DIOXIDE INFORMATION ANALYSIS CENTER, OAK RIDGE NATIONAL LABORATORY, U.S. DEPARTMENT OF ENERGY, OAK RIDGE, TN

However, other considerations complicate this clear picture of steadily decreasing polar ice and correspondingly rising temperatures. For one thing, there is considerable dispute as to how robust the arctic albedo process will be and also about whether pools of water will form atop the polar ice during the summer, pools that might significantly alter the ice's surface albedo. Secondly, higher temperatures may allow existing subarctic forests to shift their range northwards, potentially trapping a great deal of atmospheric carbon dioxide, though the death of subarctic forests now growing in unsuitably warm areas may counteract this process. What is more, some scientists believe that increased temperatures will lead to increased precipitation and thus more ice formation, especially in Antarctica, potentially counteracting the melting of the edges.

Perhaps most controversially, no one knows for sure what effect the melting of polar ice will have on the North Atlantic thermohaline circulation. In the North Atlantic, salt-laden surface water tends to sink when cooled by frigid North Atlantic temperatures, forming a column of "downwelling" (descending) water. As it descends, it draws in more water from the tropics, perpetuating the cycle. This "thermohaline" or "heat-salt" current is one of the primary pumps of a great global circulation system researchers have called the "Great Ocean Conveyor Belt," an oceanic circulation system ensures that deepwater nutrients are constantly being circulated back into shallower depths. More important for the present discussion is that the Atlantic leg of this current helps to draw warmth from the American tropics into western Eurasia, making the temperature of Northern Europe warmer than it ought to be given its high latitude. If the infusion of fresh water disrupts this saltwater sink the North Atlantic thermohaline circulation may fail, temperatures in the northern hemisphere may plunge precipitously, and glaciation may recur.

The North Atlantic thermohaline's failure is the inspiration of the film *The Day After Tomorrow*, which depicted the virtually instantaneous glaciation of much of Europe and North America. In reality, the consequences of this failure would be far less rapid, though perhaps no less significant. Scientists believe that the "Younger Dryas," a thousand-year period of extremely cold conditions that ended about 10,000 years ago, may very well have been triggered by the rapid draining of the now-vanished freshwater lake Agassiz into the North Atlantic. This sudden infusion of fresh water likely shut down the North Atlantic thermohaline, and with it the transfer of tropical heat to high northern latitudes. Temperatures dropped, glaciers reformed, and the resulting increase of surface albedo caused temperatures to drop still further. It is precisely this sort of scenario—the prospect that rising global temperatures will actually trigger a feedback mechanism that causes some local temperatures to drop—that makes forecasting the likely extent of global warming so difficult to predict precisely.

Other potential feedback mechanisms further complicate easy predictions about the probable effects of global warming. Higher levels of heat will likely lead to greater evaporation of water into the atmosphere, and since water vapor is a potent greenhouse gas, this may trigger still higher temperatures and begin a self-perpetuating feedback mechanism. At the same time, higher humidity will likely lead to greater cloud cover, and since many types of clouds are highly reflective to solar radiation it is unclear whether higher water vapor levels will cause more or less warming on the balance. Similarly, deforestation causes global warming directly by releasing more CO_2 into the atmosphere. In addition, deforested land respires less water into the atmosphere, leading to less local humidity, less local rain, and (potentially) still more deforestation due to loss of vegetation cover. On the other hand, land that has been deforested generally has a higher surface albedo than forested land, thus reflecting more solar radiation back into space. What is more, rising CO_2 levels are likely to favor the growth of many plants worldwide due to what scientists call the "carbon dioxide fertilization effect," and this plant growth

GLOBAL WARMING POSSIBLE FEEDBACK LOOPS

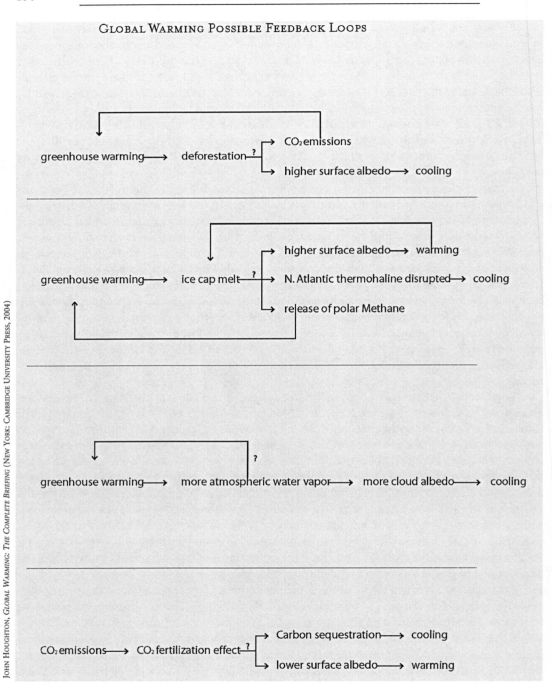

JOHN HOUGHTON, GLOBAL WARMING: THE COMPLETE BRIEFING (NEW YORK: CAMBRIDGE UNIVERSITY PRESS, 2004)

might paradoxically withdraw carbon from the atmosphere, reducing global warming. However, the carbon dioxide fertilization effect may in turn be counteracted by large scale plant die-offs due to climate change. The net result of these countervailing trends is impossible to predict.

Feedback mechanisms are not mere scientific curiosities but rather lie at the heart of the global warming phenomenon. According to climate writer Elizabeth Kolbert, as much as ⅔ of the anticipated "greenhouse effect" will be caused by these feedback mechanisms rather than by greenhouse gases themselves. Small wonder, then, that scientists are divided over the impact of global warming. It is important to point out, however, that these disagreements are over degree, not over the phenomenon itself. Contrary to the rhetoric of U. S. President George W. Bush, who presented global warming as a disputed and unproven theory for most of his presidency, global warming is a matter of consensus in the scientific community. What is debated, rather, are the parameters of the changes we are likely to expect.

The most important parameter, not surprisingly, is the exact extent of global temperature increase. There is widespread agreement that global temperatures have already begun to go up: Average global temperatures have risen by about 0.6 degrees Celsius since 1800 and record high temperatures were recorded regionally or globally in 1998, 2002, 2005, and 2006. There is less agreement on how high temperatures will continue to rise. Depending on the assumptions used by scientists, temperatures may go up by as little as 1.5° Celsius or as much as 6° Celsius by 2100. An average global heat rise of 1.5° Celsius does not sound like much, but keep in mind that most animal and plant species have evolved to live within fairly narrow temperature ranges, so even such a small temperature rise will likely lead to the widespread re-distribution of life. Indeed, some species with nowhere suitable to go, such as species trapped in patches of forest surrounded by human settlement, will be doomed to extinction. Even the best case scenario suggests that many large forests, which cannot migrate quickly in response to climate change, are likely to die off. Such a die off would harm local economies and trigger the release of even more greenhouse gases into the atmosphere. What is more, such a minimal rise is one of the most unlikely scenarios, as it assumes the feedback mechanisms will behave in an optimal fashion and that mankind will take all necessary steps in the short run to curb greenhouse gas emissions.

What about the mid-range estimates? In a recent study, William R. Cline at the Center for Global Development has examined the likely effect that moderate global warming is likely to have on world agriculture, and his findings are sobering. Cline calculated that overall agricultural harvests will drop by 3.2 percent by the end of the 21st century, even if the carbon fertilization effect is factored in. Since global population is slated to increase by as much as 50 percent by the same time, such a drop in agricultural production would be an unmitigated disaster. However, the damage that global warming will inflict on agriculture will not be equally distributed worldwide. A number of northern hemisphere countries, most notably the United States, Russia, China, and Northern Europe will actually enjoy better harvests than before because a rise in global temperatures will make parts of these countries more hospitable to agricultural production. In the tropical world, however, even minor temperature increases will reduce the number of crops that can be profitably grown, and higher rates of evaporation will require more extensive — and expensive — irrigation systems that these relatively impoverished countries can ill afford.

The high end of the spectrum, a 6° Celsius temperature spike in the next 100 years, is almost too terrible to contemplate. Such a dramatic change in temperature is nearly unprecedented in the history of the Earth; only catastrophic events, such as meteor strikes or colossal volcanic eruptions, have the potential to change global climate so strongly and so quickly, and events of this kind are almost always accompanied by mass extinctions. What is more, diseases that are currently confined to the tropics, such as Malaria, Dengue Fever, and Yellow Fever, may reach well into areas that currently have temperate climates. It is possible that humans may find ways to adapt to the worst case scenario. Food crops could be genetically engineered to survive in higher temperatures, for example, and humans could take advantage of temperature changes to push agriculture into higher latitudes or further up mountain slopes. Making

Changes to the Climate by 2071–2100

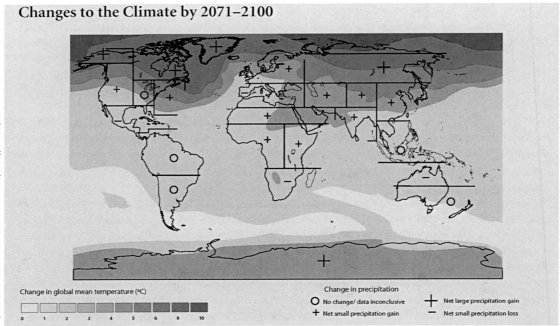

Change in global mean temperature (°C)

0   1   2   3   4   5   6   8   10

Change in precipitation

○ No change/ data inconclusive
+ Net small precipitation gain
+ Net large precipitation gain
– Net small precipitation loss

JOHN HOUGHTON, *GLOBAL WARMING: THE COMPLETE BRIEFING* (NEW YORK: CAMBRIDGE UNIVERSITY PRESS, 2004), PP. 126, 127

these changes would expend an enormous amount of capital, however, not to mention international cooperation — both of which might be scarce commodities in a chaotic, global warming world.

Another unknown, though crucial, parameter is the likely rise of ocean levels. Even without input from melting ice, ocean levels will rise by virtue of the fact that water, like virtually all substances, expands when heated. Indeed, it appears that average global sea level has already risen by about 10 to 20 cm over the course of the last 100 years, and much of this rise is attributable to simple thermal expansion. If the world's mountain glaciers melt completely — a process already well underway — that would raise world sea levels by another 23 cm. This increase in volume will almost certainly be augmented by the thawing of the polar ice caps, though there is less agreement on how much melting we ought to expect. If the Antarctic ice cap melted entirely, global oceans would rise by 200 meters — a catastrophic but also rather unlikely scenario, at least in the foreseeable future. Even a partial melt of the Antarctic Ice sheet would have significant consequences to world sea levels, and northern portions of the Antarctica are already beginning to thaw. An even more likely event is the melting of the Greenland ice sheet, which would add another 7 meters to the elevation of the ocean if it were to completely thaw. It is important not to sensationalize the danger; even in the worst case scenario, it would take hundreds of years for these massive ice sheets to completely melt. Nonetheless, it is estimated that melting polar and glacial ice plus thermal expansion will increase sea levels by an additional 9 to 90 centimeters by 2100.

Although the rise of global sea levels by less than a meter does not sound very threatening, experts predict that even a moderate rise in sea levels will pose a considerable challenge to mankind. About half a million people live in low-lying coral atolls, which will either be submerged entirely or rendered unsafe for habitation by even a slight rise in sea level. Millions more live in low-lying coastal delta land, such as the Ganges Delta in Bangladesh, the Nile Delta in Egypt, the Mississippi Delta in the United States, and the Rhine Delta in Europe, all of which are particularly vulnerable to rises in sea level. Indeed, it is estimated that 20 percent of

LIKELY CHANGES TO WORLD'S WEATHER AS A RESULT OF GLOBAL WARMING

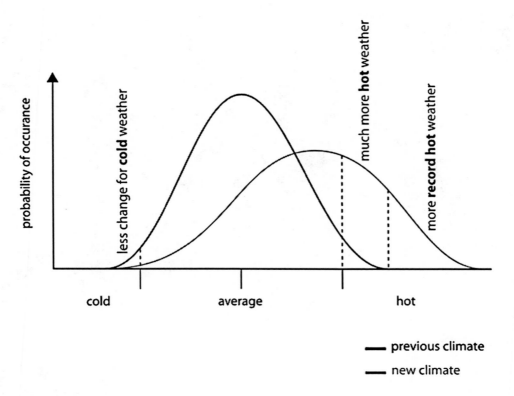

JOHN HOUGHTON, *GLOBAL WARMING: THE COMPLETE BRIEFING* (NEW YORK: CAMBRIDGE UNIVERSITY PRESS, 2004), P. 129

Bangladesh's arable land would be lost to a one meter sea level rise, and 15 million would be displaced. The figures for Egypt are comparable: An extra meter of sea elevation would drown 12 percent of the country's farmland and affect 7 million people. Nor would people on higher ground be immune to the effects of sea level changes. A one meter rise in sea level would vastly increase the destructive power of ocean floods such as storm surges and tsunamis, leading to exponential increases both in the scope and damage potential of such events. What is more, higher sea levels would lead to greater infiltration of coastal water tables by seawater, threatening the water supply of coastal cities worldwide. Since a full half of the world's population lives along the sea coast, the exact amount of likely sea level rise is a matter of vital concern.

Global warming will not only cause the sea level to rise, it will cause the sea to heat up, though by how much and with what effects is a matter of scholarly debate. Some scientists have contended that rising ocean temperatures will augment the power of future tropical cyclones. As we shall see in more detail in chapter 5, since even a slight increase in cyclone wind speed can lead to a proportionally greater increase in the storm's destructive potential, global warming could potentially raise the power of cyclonic storms exponentially. Warmer overall seas may also expand the range of tropical cyclones into higher latitudes, and may increase the frequency of these events. On the other hand, some scholars believe that other effects of global warming, in particular an increase in wind sheer, might actually dampen tropical cyclone formation. As we shall see in more detail in chapter 5, the scientific community is far from a consensus on how global warming will impact tropical cyclones. Warmer Pacific Ocean temperatures are also

AP/WORLD WIDE PHOTOS

The disappearance of the Boulder Glacier Ice Cave in Glacier National Park between 1932 and 1988.

likely to increase the frequency, if not the strength, of the El Niño weather phenomenon, thus increasing the occurrence of economically destructive droughts. As mentioned above, it is likely that a warmer ocean might serve as a less effective carbon sink, further increasing atmospheric CO_2 levels.

It is even possible that a warmer ocean would be a more sterile ocean, since a thick layer of warm, low-density surface water would inhibit the upwelling of nutrient-rich deep ocean water. If this were to occur it would reduce the overall biomatter of the ocean, and since ocean life absorbs considerable quantities of CO_2 from the atmosphere the result might be a positive feedback loop leading to even higher sea temperatures and even more atmospheric carbon dioxide. Higher sea temperatures will also lead to the "bleaching," or mass death, of many coral reefs, and since these reefs are extremely important to tropical sea life, the death of these reefs might also trigger a destructive downward cycle of higher temperatures and yet more coral bleaching. Coral reefs also serve as fish nurseries, so their loss could reduce the availability of seafood and thus worsen the problem of agricultural losses in a global warming world.

Scientists also disagree as to exactly how much impact global warming will have on the world's rainfall. One indisputable fact is that higher temperatures will lead to greater evaporation of water into the atmosphere creating more cloud formations and rainfall on average. However, this rain will not be distributed equally around the world, and while some areas (such as the high northern latitudes) will likely receive more rain in the future, other areas (such as Southern Europe and Central America) are expected to dry out considerably in a global warming world. Even in areas that receive more rain, higher temperatures will mean that soil will dry out more quickly, perhaps negating the value of increased rainfall as far as agriculture is concerned. What is more, the existing evidence suggests that precipitation in a global warming world will likely become more episodic, with short-duration but powerful storms interspersed with longer dry periods. Since short bursts of heavy rain are absorbed into the soil much less efficiently than long periods of moderate rain, heavier rain may paradoxically lead to less rainwater reaching the water table, reducing fresh water supplies and contributing to famine. Worse yet, heavy bursts of rain are more likely to lead to disastrous flooding and will almost certainly lead to large-scale soil erosion. As we will see in chapter 9, irreversible soil loss poses a serious future threat to mankind.

So what can be done to stave off the threat of global warming? In one sense, not much. Global warming is already leading to profound changes in the lives of people worldwide, especially those living in extreme climates like Alaska's Inuit. What is more, the earth's climate is slow to react to new inputs, which means that much of the eventual global warming that will result from present-day greenhouse gas levels is still to come; even if today's greenhouse gas levels were somehow stabilized, warming would continue for decades into the future. However, mankind does have the ability to limit future global warming if it acts now to curb greenhouse emissions. Basically, two choices are available: 1) removing existing greenhouse gases from the atmosphere, or 2) preventing further greenhouse gases from being produced. However, both choices are fraught with difficulties.

The main problem with removing greenhouse gases from the atmosphere, simply put, is that we currently lack an effective means to do so. One obvious option is reforestation, which would remove carbon from the atmosphere by locking it inside plant matter. However, to accomplish this on a significant scale would require a level of global resolve that simply does not exist. Indeed, the overall global trend is towards increased deforestation, driven mainly by population pressure and poverty in the world's tropical regions. Many developed countries have called for the preservation of these forests, and for good reason, but it would be unethical to expect the poor to give up a possible means of feeding their families for the good of future generations on distant continents. In any case, reforestation would decrease the earth's surface albedo, counteracting somewhat the cooling effect of removing carbon dioxide from the atmosphere. As a result, a number of other schemes have been proposed to extract carbon from the atmosphere, ranging from carbon dioxide "scrubbers" to deliberate fertilization of oceanic biomass to pumping CO_2 into oil empty oil wells to the submersion of carbon-rich agricultural waste into the deep ocean. However, none of these methods holds much chance of success.

The second means of curbing global warming, reducing greenhouse gas emissions into the atmosphere, is no less problematic. One obvious means would be to wean the global economy off of fossil fuels and adopt renewable energy such as wind, solar, and geothermal power instead, but these energy sources are currently far less plentiful and far less efficient than fossil fuels. Nuclear energy is more economically competitive with fossil fuels, and produces virtually no greenhouse gas emissions. Nonetheless, nuclear waste poses its own risks of environmental disaster and in any case nuclear power reactors remain deeply unpopular with the general public. Some politicians have embraced hydrogen fuel cells as an alternative to fossil fuels, but hydrogen is not a power source so much as an energy storage mechanism: Energy must be expended to extract free hydrogen from water, so unless renewable energy is used to produce that hydrogen, it would be more efficient to burn fossil fuels.

Perhaps the most promising way to produce energy while reducing greenhouse gas emissions would be to adopt "biofuels," hydrocarbons derived not from fossil sources but rather from grown vegetable matter such as corn, sugar, switchgrass, and the like. These fuels have the benefit of manufacturing energy from current sunlight rather than releasing greenhouse gases from ancient sunlight back into the atmosphere. However, current technology levels mean that some biofuels, such as corn-based ethanol, are grossly inefficient, requiring such a large expenditure of energy to manufacture that they end up releasing more greenhouse gases into the atmosphere than their fossil fuel counterparts. Indeed, ethanol would probably be driven from the market if not for the U.S. farm lobby's success in winning substantial ethanol subsidies from the U.S. government. Other forms of biofuel are more considerably efficient, but formidable technological problems must be overcome before biofuels can pose a significant challenge to the world's fossil fuels. Perhaps most importantly biofuels pose a moral dilemma, since converting food into fuel tends to drive up food prices, and spikes in food prices have a disproportional impact upon the poor.

A final way to reduce the release of greenhouse gases is to cut the consumption of fossil fuels. In a sense this is the easiest option, requiring no technological innovations: We simply need to consume less. In another sense, this is the least likely option, since it is extremely difficult to convince people to give up a standard of living they are accustomed to and adopt an environmentally friendly but austere lifestyle. However, were the political will available there are a number of changes we could make that could seriously increase the efficiency of our energy consumption. Adopting fluorescent light bulbs in place of conventional filament bulbs, as has recently been decreed by the state government of California, would significantly reduce energy consumption and reduce greenhouse emissions. Recycling programs hold out the same promise, since they mean that new goods could be created from semi-finished materials obtained locally rather than raw materials exported with great energy expenditure from far away. Houses could be designed to be more energy efficient, as could cars, and sin taxes could be placed on low-efficiency vehicles like SUVs. What is more, since the global warming problem can only be solved with an international effort, the United States could embrace global treaties like the Kyoto accords that, however flawed, do hold out prospect for limited reductions in greenhouse gases.

So far, despite the threat of global warming, most of the developed world has adopted a

"business as usual" approach, refusing to adopt even minimally painful economic drawbacks or concessions that could make a big difference in greenhouse gas emissions. The problem is not really one of technology or knowhow — as S. Pacala and R. Socolow point out in a recent article, mankind already has at its disposal proven techniques that, taken together, could stabilize carbon emission increases. However, in both America and the world at large, the real problem is mankind's unwillingness to make the economic sacrifices needed to reduce greenhouse gas emissions. It remains to be seen if our generation's selfish refusal to alter the status quo today will lead to dramatic changes to the world that our children and grandchildren will live in tomorrow.

Study Questions

1. It is often suggested that a "business as usual" approach is the best solution to global warming, since free market capitalism leads to technological progress, and technology can solve the global warming problem. How compelling do you find this argument? Explain.

2. "Global warming is the 'master disaster' of the modern age, capable of exacerbating every other type of disaster we face." To what degree do you agree with this statement? Explain.

3. One of the main U.S. objections to the Kyoto accords, which would have called for caps or reductions in future greenhouse gas emissions, is that it curbed greenhouse emissions of the developed world immediately, but gives the undeveloped world decades before they have to do the same. Do you think that this is a valid reason to reject the treaty?

4. Curbing greenhouse gas emissions globally will effectively prevent most of the population of the developing world from achieving the "first world" style of living that they aspire to. What moral obligations, if any, does this impose on the nations of the developed world?

Sources/Suggested Readings

Bourne, Joel K. Jr. "Green Dreams." *National Geographic*, Oct. 2007, pp. 41–59.

Cline, William R. *Global Warming and Agriculture: Impact Estimates by Country*. Washington, DC: Center for Global Development, 2007.

Del Moral, Roger, and Lawrence R. Walker. *Environmental Disasters, Natural Recovery, and Human Responses*. New York: Cambridge University Press, 2007.

Dow, Kirstin, and Thomas E. Downing. *The Atlas of Climate Change: Mapping the World's Greatest Challenge*. Berkeley: University of California Press, 2006.

Dressler, Andrew E., and Edward A. Parson. *The Science and Politics of Global Climate Change: A Guide to the Debate*. New York: Cambridge University Press, 2006.

Flannery, Tim. *The Weather Makers: How Man Is Changing the Climate and What It Means for Life on Earth*. New York: Atlantic Monthly Press, 2005.

Glick, Daniel. "The Big Thaw." *National Geographic*, Sept. 2004, pp. 13–33.

Houghton, John. *Global Warming: The Complete Briefing*. New York: Cambridge University Press, 2004.

Kolbert, Elizabeth. *Field Notes from a Catastrophe: Man, Nature, and Climate Change*. New York: Bloomsbury, 2006.

Kunstler, James Howard. *The Long Emergency*. New York: Grove Press, 2006.

McKibben, Bill. "Carbon's New Math." *National Geographic*, Oct. 2007, pp. 33–37.

Palaca, S. and R. Socolow. "Stabilization Wedges: Solving the Climate Problem for the Next 50 Years with Current Technologies." *Science*, Vol. 305 (August 13, 2004), pp. 968–972.

Ruddiman, William F. *Plows, Plagues, and Petroleum: How Humans Took Control of Climate*. Princeton, NJ: Princeton University Press, 2005.

Weinhold, Bob. "Infectious Disease: The Human Costs of Our Environmental Errors." *Environmental Health Perspectives*, Vol. 112, No. 1 (Jan. 2004), pp. A32–A38.

Chapter 5

Tropical Cyclones

Science and History

Although known by regional names, such as hurricane or typhoon, the terrifying tropical cyclone is a truly global phenomenon that reaps an annual harvest of death and destruction over large sections of our planet. While the forces that create cyclones—heat, evaporation, and the earth's rotation—are well known, the scientific laws governing their behavior are extremely complex and make the task of forecasting their strength and trajectory very difficult. Worse yet, tropical cyclones are linked in little-known ways to long-term weather phenomena, such as El Niño and global warming, making long-term forecasts of the severity of future hurricane seasons problematic. Only two facts are certain: Tropical cyclones pose an enormous danger to human lives and property, and on a number of occasions hurricanes have arguably altered the course of human history.

The Science of Cyclones

Origins and Categorization

The generic term used by meteorologists to describe spinning tropical storms of great intensity is "tropical cyclone" in reference to the circular movement of winds of such storms. Indeed, the term "cyclone" is derived from a Greek word meaning "coiled like a snake." If the tropical cyclone happens to form north of the equator in the Central or Eastern Pacific, it is labeled a typhoon. On the other hand, if the storm develops in the North Atlantic or the west coast of Mexico, it is dubbed a hurricane, mostly likely as a tribute to *Hurakan*, the Mayan god of destructive storms. Only tropical cyclones born in the Indian Ocean and near Australia are actually called "cyclones," in popular speech, though some Australians prefer the local moniker of "willy-willies." All of these different names, however, describe the same phenomenon.

Like almost all terrestrial weather events, tropical cyclones owe their origin to the energy of the Sun. Between June and October in the northern hemisphere, and between December and April south of the equator, the Sun beats down relentlessly on the tropics, which lie between 0 and 23.5 degrees latitude in both the northern and southern hemispheres. Since heated air is less dense than cooler air, the Sun's heat creates small pockets of low air pressure, called tropical waves, just north and south of the equator. These tropical waves generally migrate to the west in both the northern and southern hemispheres, following the prevailing trade winds of the tropics. Most tropical waves eventually dissolve into scattered rainstorms, but some strengthen, drawing energy and moisture from the warm tropical seas over which they pass.

caglecartoons.com/español

This cartoon, drawn shortly after the extraordinarily active 2005 hurricane season, graphically illustrates the link between cyclonic storms and human mortality.

Although these disorganized depressions are still nothing more than blips on a meteorologist's radar screen, each one contains the seeds of a possible tropical cyclone.

At this point things become interesting. Since these tropical waves are bowls of low pressure, they draw towards them any moisture-filled clouds that happen to be nearby. The straight-line force of air pressure, however, is counteracted by the Coriolis Effect, a weak force generated by the rotation of the earth and popularly believed to cause water to spin counterclockwise in northern hemisphere toilets. In reality, the schoolyard scientists have it wrong: The Coriolis Effect is far too weak too exert any significant influence on the workings of bathroom water fixtures. It does, however, impart a slight spin — counterclockwise in the northern hemisphere, clockwise in the southern hemisphere — to weather formations that cover a significant portion of the earth's surface such as tropical waves. As a result of the slight twist provided by the Coriolis Effect, the cloud formations drawn towards the low pressure of the tropical wave never quite get there, and instead are deflected into orbit around the center of the developing storm like electrons orbiting an atom's nucleus.

Once the storm has been set to spinning, it can strengthen quite rapidly, if conditions are favorable. The most important factor to a storm's development its ability to absorb heat and moisture from warm-water seas. In a well-organized system, the central area of low pressure serves as a siphon, drawing up evaporated moisture from the ocean and sending it spiraling upward and outwards into the body of the storm system. Once this moisture reaches a certain height, the colder temperatures of the upper atmosphere cause the moisture to condense into towering cumulonimbus clouds, which might rise five miles into the sky over the developing tropical disturbance, higher than the summit of Everest. As it condenses, the moisture releases heat, fueling the storm's strengthening cyclonic winds. In turn, these winds kick up waves and spray on the sea below, further increasing the rate of evaporation at the base of the storm and perpetuating the cycle.

Although the forces that produce cyclones are self-strengthening and naturally produce a process of intensification over time, there are a number of external factors that might cut short the life of the young cyclonic storm. Upper level wind "shear," or winds running at an angle to the movement of the storm, might interrupt the transfer of moisture from sea to atmosphere, effectively beheading the developing weather system. The storm might stray over a patch of cool water or might stumble onto dry land, short-circuiting the constant flow of seawater evaporation necessary to sustain the storm.

If the storm manages to weather these possible perils, it will continue to gather size and strength, passing in the process through a number of different stages of categorization. At first, the storm will qualify only as a humble tropical depression, with low sustained winds and no definable eye. Once the sustained winds reach 64 kilometers per hour, the weather system is upgraded to the status of a full-fledged tropical storm, and meteorologists will assign it a name based on the order in which it appeared (the first hurricane of a season might be named Albert, the second Betty, and so on).

Although fearsome in their own right and characterized by gusting winds and torrential rains, tropical storms are just a stepping stone in the process of cyclone development. If conditions remain favorable and sustained winds top 117 kilometers per hour, the storm will officially rise to the rank of a cyclone, hurricane, or typhoon, depending on its region of origin. Even then there are further gradations of storm strength, each of which represents an exponential increase of destructive power over the previous ranking. At the bottom end of the scale, called the Saffir-Simpson scale after its creators, is the category 1 hurricane with sustained winds below 152 kilometers per hour and relatively modest barometric readings. Storms of this intensity generally cause only minor damage — limbs will be blown off of trees, power lines will be felled, and the odd shutter will be torn from a house. On the other end of the spectrum looms the category 5 tropical cyclone, a true meteorological monster and arguably the most destructive disaster of the natural world. Only three such storms have ever struck North America in recorded history — the 1935 Labor Day Hurricane, Hurricane Camille, and Hurricane Andrew — and each left catastrophic damage in its wake. When Hurricane Camille made landfall on the

KERRY EMANUEL, *DIVINE WIND: THE HISTORY AND SCIENCE OF HURRICANES* (NEW YORK: OXFORD UNIVERSITY PRESS, 2005), P. 16.

STRUCTURE OF A NORTHERN HEMISPHERE CYCLONIC STORM

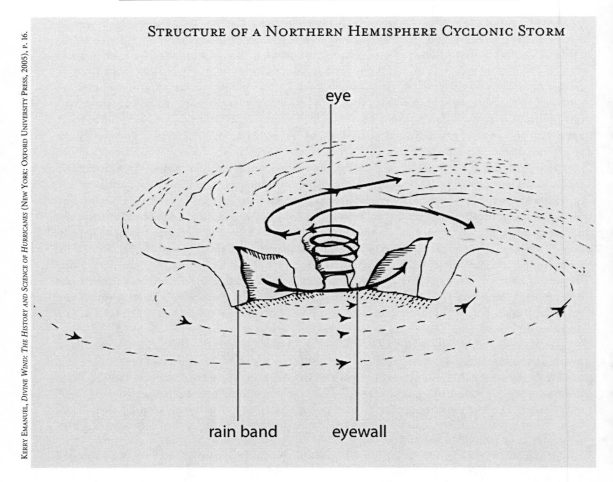

eye

rain band   eyewall

Louisiana and Mississippi coasts in 1969, for instance, it killed 256 people and inflicted 6.1 billion dollars worth of damage, prompting meteorologists to dub it "the greatest storm of any kind ever to have affected the mainland of the United States." As we will see in section 5.3, however, Camille's swath of destruction pales before that of Hurricane Andrew, which struck Florida and Louisiana in 1992. It is fortunate that the severity of such storms is matched by their rarity; if the 20th century is any indication, category-five storms make landfall in the United States only once every 33 years.

Whether it be category 1 or 5, the defining characteristic of a well-developed tropical cyclone is its eye, an oasis of clear skies and gentle winds at the heart of the hurricane. While the eye is passing overhead the once-raging winds die down to a mere breeze, the temperature becomes pleasantly warm, and the rays of the Sun or moon glitter upon the storm-wrecked landscape. Ironically this deceitful calm at the center of the storm often produces many of its casualties by tempting hopeful survivors to venture out of their hiding places, only to fall victim to the returning winds of the second half of the cyclone.

The hurricane's eye is no freak, nor is it a trap laid by the natural world for those who would underestimate the fury of Mother Nature. The eye, rather, is the dynamo that powers the storm. As anyone who has boiled an egg at high altitudes knows, water evaporates (and thus boils) much more quickly in areas of low atmospheric pressure. As a result the eye's abnormally low barometric pressure greatly facilitates the extraction of water vapor from the seawater below, providing yet more fuel for the developing storm. The eye also strengthens the storm by acting as a chimney of sorts, allowing moisture to be drawn efficiently into higher elevations, where it condenses into billowing cumulonimbus clouds and releases heat that further strengthens the storm. Indeed, the ring of towering clouds surrounding the eye, called the eyewall by meteorologists, generally encompasses the storm's most powerful winds and drenching rains. Since this eyewall ring ranges from 50 to 240 kilometers in diameter, the damage potential of the eyewall is immense.

Although the eye and eyewall of a mature tropical cyclone are its defining features, these structures make up only a small portion of the storm's diameter. Most of the pinwheel structure of the storm is made up of spiraling rain bands, which are best described as tendrils of moisture cast off by the sucking eye of the cyclone. Although these rain bands do not usually have the same intensity of rainfall and wind speed that characterizes the eyewall they can still prove extremely destructive, and since rain bands pass over much more territory than the eye and eyewall proper they account for a sizable portion of the damage inflicted by a given storm. The power of rain bands depends largely on their nearness to the storm's center. Far-flung rain bands at the distant edges of the storm might prove no more severe than a garden-variety thunderstorm. At the same time, only a few dozen miles closer to the center of the storm, the rain band's fury might match that of the eyewall, and people could be losing their lives.

Movement

The meteorological factors that account for the movement of tropical cyclones are just as complicated as those that explain the storm's formation. As a general rule, the starting point of tropical cyclones is quite predictable; nearly all cyclones are born between 10–20 degrees latitude in the northern and southern hemispheres. Cyclones rarely form farther north, as the sea temperatures are too cold to favor their formation. The Coriolis Effect, in turn, prevents cyclones from being born farther to the south; near the equator, the Coriolis Effect is not strong enough to deflect clouds away from the low pressure at the center of a tropical wave, meaning that any bowls of low pressure are quickly filled and negated. As a result, the equatorial region tends to be quite uniform in terms of barometric pressure, which hampers the formation of winds. In the age of sail, mariners avoided the "doldrums" of zero degrees latitude, fearing that their ships might be stalled for weeks or months at a time in the equator's windless seas. It should be noted however that typhoons and cyclones tend to be born closer to the equator than hurricanes, probably because the warm waters of the Pacific and Indian Oceans are a more favorable environment for cyclone development than the relatively cooler waters of the Atlantic.

Once cyclones form they generally wander westward, following a worldwide pattern of prevailing tropical winds that owes its origin, once again, to the Coriolis Effect. However, this westward orientation is only a general tendency that can be influenced by a bewildering array of meteorological variables. One such force is the Coriolis Effect itself, which generally causes the cyclone to "recurve" to the north-northeast (or south-southwest in the southern hemisphere) at a rate proportional to the cyclone's distance from the equator, with this tendency increasing as the cyclone moves into higher latitudes. This tendency is often counteracted by the influence of temperate "anticyclones," clockwise rotating masses of high-pressure air that are constantly being generated north of the subtropics in the northern hemisphere. Since these high-pressure air masses are impenetrable to low-pressure storm systems like cyclones, anticyclones can prevent recurvature and ensure that a cyclone continues to track westward. At the same time, however, the clockwise-rotating winds of the anticyclone can catch passing cyclones and cause them to hook dramatically to the north or even back towards the east, thus exacerbating a storm's natural tendency to recurve. Since anticyclones tend to be stable, long-term meteorological events, their existence helps to explain why successive cyclones in the same hurricane season such as Katrina and Rita in 2005 tend to follow roughly similar paths.

Other factors can influence the velocity and direction of tropical cyclones as well. The path taken by a cyclone is influenced by differentials in the rotation of the earth at different latitudes and at different altitudes of the storm, which tend to nudge the storm in subtle and highly complex ways. Cyclonic movement is also influenced by the location and strength of other storm systems; indeed, when two cyclonic storms approach each other, they often lock into a majestic meteorological dance called the Fujiwhara Effect, named after the Japanese meteorologists who first described it. Hurricane speed and direction can also be affected by surface conditions; indeed cyclones tend to "jump" over mountains, breaking apart and then reforming somewhere other than on the forecasted track. Given all of these variables, it is hardly surprising that the science of hurricane prediction is still so frustratingly inexact.

As a result of these interacting forces, some tropical cyclones journey quite far from their ocean of origin, ending their lives spinning over cooler waters far from the warm tropical seas that spawned them. Nearly every year hurricanes recurve their way as far north as Virginia and the Carolinas, and typhoons wreck havoc on the Korean Peninsula and Japan. Although the phenomenon is rare, cases do exist where hurricanes of Caribbean origin have followed the Gulf Stream up the U.S. coast, spun eastwards over the north Atlantic, and then smashed into Great Britain. Similarly, some Pacific typhoons travel as far as Alaska before sputtering out in the frigid waters of the Bering Sea. Such anomalies are few and far between, however, and most cyclonic storms follow roughly predictable paths on their way to familiar destinations.

Destructive Power

Unfortunately for those caught in their serpentine spirals, cyclonic storms spread death and destruction in a number of different ways. Some of these ways are terrifyingly straightforward: sandblasting winds, roaring floodwaters, and razor-sharp flying debris. Other forms of hurricane destruction are far more indirect. The death toll can continue to mount for days even after a relatively minor hurricane, as people are electrocuted by fallen wires, cut to death by their own chainsaws while clearing hurricane-downed tree limbs, or sent into cardiac arrest by post-storm heat or stress. Damage totals can continue to climb days or even weeks after a hurricane as well; if a house has been deprived of its roof, even a gentle shower can cause irreparable water damage to property that managed to survive the first storm. What is more, devastating flooding can occur even days after a cyclone if further rain falls into rivers and streams already swollen by a cyclonic storm.

Indirect damage of this sort is a constant headache for civil authorities in hurricane-prone areas. Nonetheless, meteorologists claim that the vast preponderance of cyclone death and desolation is caused directly by the passage of the storm itself. Three aspects of a tropical cyclone are especially destructive: rain, storm surge, and wind.

When accounting for a hurricane's destruction, few people give much thought to the power of rain, but this is a mistake; even low-intensity storms can prove devastating if accompanied by drenching downpours. Hurricane Agnes of 1972 was a relatively weak category 1 hurricane which only boasted hurricane force winds for two days during its nine-day stroll up the American east coast. Nonetheless, Agnes ranks as one of the most destructive hurricanes in U.S. history due to the massive floods that it brought to coastal America. Rivers all up and down the eastern seaboard reached record floodwater crests, and in Virginia alone, 10,000 people were driven from their homes by the relentless flooding. The most notable "achievement" of the storm, however, occurred on June 22nd, when an 8-foot wall of water rushing down the Susquehanna River gutted the ground floor of the governor's mansion in Harrisburg, Pennsylvania.

By the time the floodwaters finally receded 122 people had drowned, making puny little Agnes one of the most deadly hurricanes in the history of the United States.

As bad as Agnes was, it was just a drop in the bucket compared with Hurricane Mitch, whose drenching downpours nearly washed away the entire nation of Honduras in October of 1998. Mitch trundled ashore in Honduras on October 26, then stopped dead in its tracks and gradually lost its ferocity. By the 29th, in fact, this former category 5 monster had declined to mere tropical storm intensity. As it died out, however, Mitch dumped an unbelievable quantity of water on the hapless nation of Honduras. Some locations received over half a meter of rain per day for 6 days. As a result, rivers and streams that normally trickled their way to the ocean became raging rapids that swept away everything in their path. Waterlogged by the week-long deluge, whole hillsides melted into mud and sloughed downhill, burying entire towns under hundreds of tons of muck. When civil authorities in Central America finally tallied up the damage statistics for Mitch, the numbers were staggering. Between 9,000 and 12,000 had died, mostly by drowning, and hundreds of thousands of survivors — including a full 25 percent of the inhabitants of Honduras — were rendered homeless by the storm. The storm also inflicted a devastating 5.5 billion dollars of property damage in the states of Central America, a sum that represents nearly a third of Honduras' pre–Mitch yearly GDP.

As bad as flooding due to rainfall might be, it generally does not cause the lion's share of death and destruction in a typical cyclonic storm. That dubious distinction belongs to the "storm surge," the deadly floodwaters that often accompany a hurricane's landfall. The storm surge owes its origin in part to the exceptionally low pressure of the storm's siphoning eye, which actually causes seawater to well up from below, as nature tries to fill the eye's relative vacuum. This mound of water is further augmented by a hurricane's whipping winds, which stacks the seawater upon itself, especially near the front right quadrant of the storm where a northern hemisphere cyclone's counterclockwise-turning winds are augmented by the storm's forward momentum. The height of the storm surge depends on many factors, but by far the most important one is the storm's overall strength. In a category 1 hurricane, this bulge is relatively modest in size, generally rising only a meter or so above the surrounding seawater. On the other hand, category 5 storms can produce a terrifying saltwater dome many kilometers wide and five meters or more in height, and since each cubic meter of water in the dome weighs about ¾ of a ton, the potential destructive power of such a storm surge is unimaginable. If a storm surge crest of this size is driven onto dry land — especially at high tide — the results can be catastrophic.

One of the most terrifying storm surges of modern American meteorological history accompanied the Galveston, Texas, hurricane of 1900. Because of the inadequate hurricane warning system of the time — not to mention the arrogance of the U.S. Weather Bureau, which ignored the warnings of Cuban meteorologists that the storm was headed towards Texas — Galveston received virtually no forewarning of the coming of the storm. As a result, Galveston's 30,000 residents were subjected to a disaster almost unmatched in American history. Although the Great Galveston Hurricane did not quite reach the status of a category 5 behemoth, its 5 meter storm surge was more than sufficient to level the low-lying island city, leaving demolished buildings and as many as 8,000 casualties in its wake.

When rescuers arrived in Galveston to assess the damage they discovered a scene worthy of Armageddon. The ruins of the town were strewn with so many drowned corpses that rescue workers had to resort to mass cremations and burials at sea to dispose of the rapidly decomposing dead. What is more, almost every building within 3 blocks of the Gulf of Mexico had been obliterated, and nearly every other building in town was damaged, if not entirely destroyed. One particularly hard-hit neighborhood was scraped clean by a long wooden streetcar trestle pushed inland with bulldozer force by the relentless power of the storm surge. All told, the Great

Galveston Hurricane inflicted $40 million in damage, the equivalent of nearly half a billion dollars in modern U.S. currency. This horrifying storm would remain the most destructive single hurricane in U.S. history until the Great Miami Hurricane of 1926. In the modern day, of course, Katrina has set a whole new standard for hurricane destruction, as we shall see in section 6.3.

Despite the severity of these historical storm surges, America should count itself lucky: With the exception of the Labor Day Hurricane's monstrous "tidal wave" in 1935, the storm surges that have struck the United States cannot compare with the almost biblical force of the storm surges of Asian meteorological history. Far larger storm surges routinely smash into the Indian subcontinent, especially the small nation of Bangladesh at the northern tip of the Bay of Bengal. Unfortunately for the poor Bengali people, in the battle between man and nature in Bangladesh nature holds all the cards. Bangladesh is a low-lying, densely populated nation, almost impossible to evacuate and difficult even to warn of oncoming disaster due to the undeveloped state of Bangladesh's communications systems. What is more, the extreme poverty that haunts Bangladesh limits its ability to construct large-scale public works that might facilitate evacuation or hold off the floodwaters of a storm. As we shall see in section 5.1, Bangladesh's unprecedented level of vulnerability to cyclones has resulted in catastrophic levels of destruction from storm surge.

Although there are a few exceptions, such as the freshwater storm surges of Lake Okeechobee during the Florida hurricanes of 1926 and 1928, for the most part inland areas have little to fear from the terrors of the storm surge. Almost nowhere is safe, however, from a cyclonic storm's last damage vector: destructive winds. A mere tropical storm can still topple power lines and produce tree-toppling gales. The winds of a category 4 or 5 tropical cyclone, by way of contrast, can exceed those of all but the strongest tornadoes, and often cover hundreds of square kilometers of territory. Small wonder, then, that the raw power of the wind is often the most damaging feature of cyclonic storms.

A tropical cyclone's strongest winds are located in the eyewall, the ring of towering clouds and vicious air currents that surrounds the tranquil expanse of the eye. The eyewall winds of a category 1 storm, though formidable, tend to cause only minimal destruction. According to the creators of the Saffir-Simpson scale, a category 1 hurricane's passage ought to cause "no damage to building structures," though it might wreck destruction upon "unanchored mobile homes, trees, and signs." As the wind quickens, however, the destructive power of a storm increases exponentially. During a category 5 storm, Saffir and Simpson tell us, "intense winds" cause "complete roof failures on many residences and buildings," while other structures suffer "complete building failures," and are destroyed in their entirety. In a category 5 storm the eyewall winds generally reach a sustained speed of 248 kilometers per hour with occasional blasting gusts of 320 kilometers per hour. Winds of such extreme velocity strike with the force of a battering ram, and the resulting debris can be as deadly as the shrapnel of a bomb.

In addition to the punishing power of the wind, those struck by the eyewall of a powerful cyclonic storm often suffer a devastating one-two punch. The winds of the first eyewall generally blow consistently from one direction, usually the east or north in northern-hemisphere storms. After the calm, however, the winds shift dramatically, and now approach from precisely the opposite direction as before. As a result, areas that were safe during the first eyewall's passage can prove to be dangerously exposed to the second eyewall's shrieking gusts. Furthermore, buildings that withstood the pounding of the first eyewall's winds often fall victim to those of the second, as already-weakened structures are beset by an entirely new set of structural stresses. Not surprisingly, then, a tropical cyclone's zone of greatest death and destruction is generally marked by the diameter of the storm's sightless eye.

Although all tropical cyclones cause wind damage to some degree, some boast more destruc-

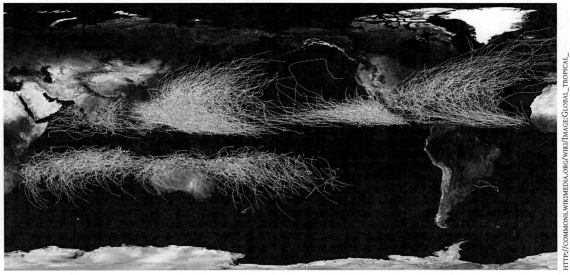

HTTP://COMMONS.WIKIMEDIA.ORG/WIKI/IMAGE:GLOBAL_TROPICAL_
CYCLONE_TRACKS–EDIT.JPG

Map depicting the tracks for all cyclonic storms from 1985 to 2005.

tive gusts than others, and no storm in recent memory has even come close to matching the horrific wind damage produced by the passage of Hurricane Andrew in 1992. As we shall see in section 5.3, Hurricane Andrew's raging winds all but obliterated the communities on the Florida peninsula south of Miami, and inflicted a staggering $30 billion in damages, well more than triple the damage total of any previous American hurricane.

Cyclones in History

Cyclonic weather has long influenced human life, and not always for the worse. Many areas in the tropics and subtropics owe their lush greenery and their ability to sustain dense human populations in large part to the rainwater deposited by seasonal cyclonic storms. For example, it is estimated that 47 percent of the rain that falls in the Philippines yearly owes its origin to typhoons. In Australia the figure is between 10 and 15 percent.

In other cases, cyclonic weather has been a disaster for some people but a positive boon for others. Perhaps the best such example is provided by the Hakata Bay typhoon of medieval Japan. The year was 1281, and Japanese samurai were engaged in a desperate struggle against the forces of the Mongol Emperor Kublai Khan, grandson of the great Genghis. Kublai had already subjugated the Chinese. Now he set his sights on Japan, which had refused to offer sufficient signs of respect to the all-conquering Khan. Determined to bring the stubborn Japanese to heel, Kublai assembled a massive 4,500-ship fleet manned by 145,000 soldiers and armed with all the latest technological innovations, including crossbows and gunpowder-fired cannons. Up to this point no nation had yet successfully fended off the mighty Mongols, and Japan's situation seemed hopeless.

For all his might, however, the great Khan could not control the weather, and to his dismay his assembled fleet was all but destroyed by the onslaught of a ferocious north Pacific typhoon. The death toll was appalling — historians believe that between 45,000 and 100,000 Mongol soldiers perished in a single night — and the Mongol commander was forced to call off the invasion and return his shattered fleet to the mainland. Ecstatic over their good fortune the

Japanese people dubbed the storm the *kamikaze*, or "divine wind," believing that this heavenly gift had spelled salvation to the beleaguered Japanese people in their hour of greatest need. If not for the 1281 typhoon, then, Japanese history would likely have turned out quite differently and would have forever borne the stamp of Mongol occupation.

The story of the *kamikaze*, incidentally, has a curious modern postscript. In mid–December of 1944, during the American invasion of the Japanese-occupied Philippine archipelago, the American Third Fleet had its own bitter taste of the unbelievable destructive power of a tropical cyclone. Although the fleet's navigators knew that a typhoon was in the vicinity, they were relayed misleading weather reports, and as a result the fleet's attempt to escape the storm served only to bring it directly to the typhoon's raging center. According to one historian, "destroyers, cruisers, battleships, and carriers were tossed about like corks," and the American battle fleet was eventually scattered over an area of 2,500 square miles. Although the big ships rode out the storm tolerably well, the smaller destroyers were in serious peril, and three of them eventually succumbed to the tempest's heaving seas carrying 790 sailors into a watery grave.

The loss of the destroyers was tragic, but from a military standpoint the most damaging impact of the storm was the destruction of the 150 aircraft that were washed off the decks of the aircraft carriers. Since aerial squadrons were the crucial combat units in the Pacific theatre of World War II, the hurricane dealt a serious potential blow to American fighting effectiveness against Japan. As it turned out, the loss of these planes turned out to be less than crucial since by 1944 the tide of the war had already turned against the Japanese. If this new *kamikaze* had struck a major American fleet in 1941–1942, when the Japanese enjoyed a temporary military superiority over the unprepared American forces, the results could very well have been disastrous for the United States. As it was, the steady build-up of American naval forces in the Pacific after 1942 forced the Japanese to resort to a man-made *kamikaze*—the use of suicide attacks against American ships—a tactic inspired by and named after the great "divine wind" that saved Japan during the Mongol war. Unlike the 1281 incarnation of the *kamikaze*, however, these desperate suicide attacks could not save Japan from eventual defeat.

Hurricanes can also influence the course of human events in more subtle ways. One historian has argued, for example, that the 17 major hurricanes that struck the Spanish West Indies from 1766 to 1778 may have contributed to American independence. As the theory goes, the repeated ravages of the 1760s and 1770s hurricanes all but obliterated the food-producing capacity of these Caribbean islands, forcing Spanish colonial authorities to import ever-larger supplies of foodstuffs from British North America. British mercantilist policy strictly forbade such direct trade, however, insisting instead that all North American trade pass through the British mother country. As a result, Spain had a vested interest in breaking Britain's monopolistic power over North American trade, and when the thirteen colonies were swept up by a tide of revolution, Spain became an enthusiastic and self-interested supporter of the struggling United States, encouraging stronger powers like France to intervene as well.

Perhaps the most notable example of cyclonic weather's ability to change the course of history, however, occurred during the Great Cyclone of 1970. As we shall see in section 5.1, the Great Cyclone reaped an unprecedented harvest of human lives and misery in what was then East Pakistan, yet provoked little in the way of assistance or even sympathy from the West Pakistani government. The resulting feelings of outrage and betrayal helped to fuel a resistance movement that eventually resulted in the creation of the independent state of Bangladesh.

In more recent years, cyclonic weather disasters have exerted a powerful influence on American presidential politics. Many attribute George Herbert Walker Bush's loss to Bill Clinton in the November 1992 in part to the federal government's inability to adequately or swiftly assist those ravaged by Hurricane Andrew in the summer of the same year. Twelve years later president George Walker Bush, son of the former president, suffered similar political fall out following the disastrous failure of the levees guarding New Orleans. We will consider these cases in more detail in section 5.3 and 6.3 respectively.

Cyclones and Other Disasters

Perhaps no other natural disaster is so intricately intermeshed with other natural processes, and natural disasters, as cyclonic storms. Indeed, cyclones occupy a central place in the natural disaster hierarchy. Tropical cyclones can influence a number of direct causes of disaster, especially floods and famines. At the same time, cyclones are themselves influenced by more long-term weather phenomena and cycles, most especially ENSO and global warming. In rarer cases, cyclonic weather can be tied indirectly to disease and even earthquakes or volcanic activity.

According to meteorologists, the El Niño/Southern Oscillation cycle exerts a powerful influence over cyclonic weather. In El Niño years hurricane activity in the Atlantic Ocean tends to drop off remarkably, perhaps because El Niño tends to suppress the westerly winds that normally carry tropical waves over the warm waters of the South Atlantic. Indeed, hurricanes are statistically nearly six times as likely to hit North America in a weak phase of the El Niño (La Niña) than when El Niño is strong. In the Pacific Ocean, El Niño's influence on typhoons is more complex. During El Niño years, typhoons tend to originate in the central Pacific rather than the western Pacific, closer to the equator, a matter of obvious concern for inhabitants of Micronesia and other central Pacific islands. ENSO's influence on Indian Ocean cyclones is less certain.

Turning to global warming, at this point no one can say for sure what effect it will have on cyclonic storms, but climate models do give cause for concern. The extraordinarily active 2005 hurricane season notwithstanding, there is no evidence that global warming will increase the frequency of future cyclonic storms. However, there is some evidence that global warming will increase cyclonic weather intensity. According to a study by climate scientists Thomas R. Knutson and Robert E. Tuleya, cyclones in the CO_2–rich future world will have 10 percent stronger winds, 14 percent lower central air pressures, and 31 percent more precipitation on average than those of today's world. This may not seem like much of a change, but keep in mind that as the wind strength of a cyclonic storm increases, the destructive force of the storm rises exponentially. Indeed, although the winds in a category 4 cyclonic storm might only be about 50 percent stronger than the winds of a category 1 storm, a category 4 hurricane packs 10,000 percent of the destructive potential of its category 1 counterpart.

Have we already reached the threshold when global warming triggers more devastating cyclonic storm disasters? Some scientists believe that we have. In August of 2005, hurricane expert Kerry Emanuel published an influential paper in *Nature* magazine predicting that hurricanes were becoming more intense as the Earth warmed. Just weeks later, New Orleans was swamped by Hurricane Katrina, convincing scientists and laypeople alike that Emanuel was correct. Not all meteorologists are convinced, however. Even Kerry Emanuel himself has recently backed away from any blanket statements that rising word temperatures will lead to a proportional increase in hurricane strength. In his latest article, Kerry argues that the best climate modeling to date suggests only a very moderate increase in tropical cyclone intensity in a warmer world, and perhaps even a decrease in tropical cyclone frequency. Hopefully future scientific research will bring the link between hurricanes and tropical cyclones into better focus.

Moving from proximate causes of disasters to direct causes there can be no doubt that cyclonic weather plays an important, if not causative, role in major flooding events. Indeed, aside from a small number of people killed by the power of the wind, most cyclone victims fall prey to floodwaters in the form of storm surge, river flooding, landslides, or "lake eruptions," which occur when a body of water at high elevation breaches or overflows its banks in a sudden, catastrophic deluge of water. Cyclones can also cause flooding by overwhelming flood control structures, as we shall see in detail when discussing Katrina in section 6.3.

The link between tropical cyclones and famine is less obvious but no less real. The extraordinarily heavy rains brought by cyclonic weather can wash out entire crops, especially if they strike at vulnerable times in the harvest cycle. Cyclonic winds can blow fruit off trees and level field crops. The salt water pumped inland by storm surges not only kills standing crops in coastal agricultural land, but can leave a salty residue that reduces crop yields for years to come. In addition, cyclonic storms can damage a country's storage and transportation infrastructure, preventing food from reaching areas where it is desperately needed. Perhaps most importantly, the death and property damage inflicted by recurrent tropical cyclones can help trap a region in poverty. As we shall see in chapter 7, poverty can breed a lack of "entitlement" to food supplies and starvation even without a crop failure.

Although the linkages are more indirect, hurricanes can be implicated in fostering disease as well. The refugee camps often established for the victims of powerful tropical cyclones can serve as potent breeding grounds for disease if sanitary conditions break down, as they often do. Storm victims can also suffer from malnourishment, increasing their vulnerability to disease. The flooding caused by tropical cyclones can facilitate the spread of waterborne diseases, such as cholera. Finally, the rains deposited by tropical cyclones can lead to an explosion both of the mosquito population and of mosquito-carried diseases such as Malaria, Yellow Fever, and Dengue.

Tropical cyclones can also combine with volcanic activity in tragic ways. Active volcanoes often produce a large amount of tephra, volcanic mineral material, ranging in size from particles of ash to massive boulders. In the aftermath of a volcanic eruption large deposits of this material can coat the sides of nearby mountains and settle in gorges and valleys. Months or years later the torrential rains brought by a tropical cyclone can loosen this volcanic detritus and trigger deadly lahars. As we saw in section 2.3, this deadly one-two punch of rain and volcanism lead to tragic consequences in the aftermath of the Mt. Pinatubo eruption.

Finally, although the science is speculative at best, some scholars have speculated causal links between cyclonic weather and earthquakes. As we already saw in section 3.1, American meteorologist C. F. Brooks speculated in the 1930s that the low pressure which accompanies cyclonic storms might create pressure differentials that could trigger the movement of an already strained fault line. What is more, other scholars have speculated that the high waves piled up by cyclonic winds might actually cause the sea bed to vibrate, and may once again lead to the catastrophic release of built-up pressure along a fault line. Although these theories are unproven, they suggest the existence of subtle but important links between the atmosphere, hydrosphere, and lithosphere that could lead to disastrous consequences.

Cyclones and Human Agency

As with all "natural" disasters, tropical cyclones are natural processes that only constitute a "disaster" when they inflict damage to human lives and property. In principle, human beings ought to be able to take appropriate steps to protect themselves from the onslaughts of tropical cyclones. After all, the risks posed by cyclonic weather are well understood, and cyclones tend to follow familiar paths to very predictable destinations. Typhoons roar yearly through the South China Sea, cyclones plow consistently into Bangladesh, India, and Pakistan, and hurricanes wreck an annual reign of terror in the Caribbean, Gulf of Mexico, and the U.S. East Coast. Given the known hazard that tropical cyclones represent to human life one may very well ask: Why are humans in these vulnerable areas often so poorly prepared when storms do arrive?

Part of the answer lies in the economic and demographic problems of the nations in the regions most frequented by tropical cyclones. Full protection of human life against cyclones requires expensive infrastructure—flood control projects, early warning systems, evacuation routes, emergency shelters, etc.—which are well beyond the financial means of many developing countries. Overpopulation in developing nations also exacerbates the effects of cyclonic weather. Deforestation of highland areas due to population pressure tends to lead to soil erosion, raising levels of sediment in the rivers and thus worsening floods caused by tropical cyclone rainfall. What is more, population pressure and poverty can force humans to live in marginal lands that are extremely vulnerable to cyclonic storms, such as exposed coastal fishing communities in the Philippines and low-lying *char* islands in Bangladesh's Ganges Delta.

Human economic activities can worsen the risk of disaster as well. As we will see in section 6.3, the booming Louisiana petroleum industry played a contributing role to the Katrina disaster by damaging the coastal wetlands that normally protect the New Orleans area from storm surge. On the other end of the economic spectrum poor fishermen in the Philippines are increasingly replacing coastal mangrove forests with fish ponds, thus eliminating natural vegetation that can blunt the impact of storm surge. Finally, even human economic activity far from the coasts can exacerbate the effect of tropical cyclones if that activity generates large amounts of CO_2, thus aggravating the effect of global warming.

Human political and ideological choices can also exacerbate vulnerability to cyclonic weather. As we will see in section 5.3, the slow federal government response to the unprecedented destruction wrought by Hurricane Andrew was due in part to a shift of government funding from natural disaster preparedness to Cold War military projects. Similar ideological and political blinders helped to hamper the federal response to Hurricane Katrina. As we shall see in section 6.3, a post 9/11 shift from disaster preparedness to terrorism preparedness led to a similar level of governmental inability when faced with natural disaster. Finally, as we shall see in section 6.2, the mania for seacoast property in the United States and other places in the developed world can serve to place thousands of souls in the danger zone in times of tropical cyclones.

Study Questions

1. Explain in your own words the scientific principles that explain the formation of tropical cyclones.

2. What factors influence the movement of tropical cyclones?

3. What factors make tropical cyclones so destructive to human lives and property?

4. Why do cyclones occupy a "central place" in the disaster hierarchy?

5. "Both developed and developing nations make choices that place them at risk during tropical cyclones, but while developed nations make these choices out of ideology or cultural values, developing countries make them out of poverty or desperation." To what degree do you agree with this statement?

Sources/Suggested Readings

Barnes, Jay. *Florida's Hurricane History*. Chapel Hill: University of North Carolina Press, 1998.

Davies, Pete. *Inside the Hurricane: Face to Face with Nature's Deadliest Storms*. New York: Henry Holt, 2000.

Emanuel, Kerry. *Divine Wind: The History and Science of Hurricanes*. New York: Oxford University Press, 2005.

Emanuel, Kerry. "Increasing Destructiveness of Tropical Cyclones over the Past 30 Years." *Nature*, Vol. 436, No. 4 (August 2005), pp. 686–688.

Emanuel, Kerry, Ragoth Sundararajan, and John Williams. "Hurricanes and Global Warming: Results from Downscaling IPCC AR4 Simulations." *Bulletin of the American Meteorological Society* (2008).

Knutson, Thomas R., and Robert E. Tuleya. "Impact of CO_2–Induced Warming on Simulated Hurricane Intensity and Precipitation." *Journal of Climate*, Vol. 17, No. 18 (Sept. 15, 2004), pp. 3477–3495.

Longshore, David. *Encyclopedia of Hurricanes, Typhoons, and Cyclones*. New York: Checkmark Books, 2000.

Murnane, Richard J., and Liu, Kam-Biu, eds., *Hurricanes and Typhoons: Past, Present, and Future*. New York: Colombia University Press, 2004.

Pielke, R. A. Jr., C. Landsea, M. Mayfield, J. Laver, and R. Pasch. "Hurricanes and Global Warming." *American Meteorological Society* (Nov. 2005), pp. 1571–1575.

Toomey, David M. *Stormchasers: The Hurricane Hunters and Their Fateful Flight into Hurricane Janet*. New York: W. W. Norton and Company, 2003.

5.1: Great Bhola Cyclone, 1970

The Great Bhola cyclone, which struck the Ganges River delta on November 13th of 1970, was by no means the strongest cyclone ever recorded. Far stronger tropical cyclones raged through the Pacific Ocean during the same year, and the Great Bhola cyclone was not necessarily even the strongest storm of the 1970 North Indian Ocean cyclone season. What made the Bhola cyclone "Great" was not the force of nature, but the force of circumstances: simply put, the Bhola cyclone struck in the worst possible place at the worst possible time. The 1970 cyclone struck the *char* islands of the Ganges delta, densely populated but extremely flat tracts of land composed of unstable river sediment. Worse yet, the Ganges delta lies at the very tip of the Bay of Bengal, a northward-pointing funnel of warm, tropical water that spawns frequent tropical cyclones and then concentrates the power of their storm surge. In terms of timing, the Bhola cyclone was unfortunate as well: Not only did it strike during a full moon night, it came ashore in the midst of a political crisis that magnified the effect of the catastrophe. These and other exacerbating factors ensured that the fairly modest Great Bhola Cyclone would be remembered as the most deadly cyclonic storm in world history.

The scene of the Bhola Cyclone tragedy, the Ganges River delta, has the unfortunate distinction of being one of the most disaster-prone regions on the planet. This disaster vulnerability is largely a function of the region's unique topography. Ironically, the flat lowland Ganges delta owes its very existence to the distant Himalayas, the world's most imposing mountain range. Each year, the north-flowing winds of the Indian Ocean monsoon are forced to climb this imposing wall of mountains, and as the rising winds cool, they discharge most of their moisture in the form of rain or snow. The resulting torrents give rise to four of the world's greatest rivers, the Yangtze, Bramhaputra, Mekong, and Ganges, respectively the world's 3rd, 7th, 11th, and 12th mightiest rivers in terms of discharge volume. Two of these rivers, the Bramhaputra and Ganges, merge shortly before the coast, briefly supplanting the Yangtze's title as the world's third river by volume in the process. The combination of these two rivers also creates the world's largest river delta, the Ganges Delta, which consists mainly of ground-up sand and soil particles weathered away from the distant Himalaya Mountains.

NOAA

Satellite photograph of Great Bhola Cyclone during its approach to East Pakistan, now Bangladesh.

The Ganges delta's origins have left an indelible imprint on its topography. In simple terms, the Ganges delta is a broad fan of alluvial soil crisscrossed with river channels. These channels change constantly over time, since each channel plants the seeds of its own destruction. As a river channels floods they deposit sediment, raising the level of the channels and eventually obliging the rivers to seek lower and easier routes to the Bay of Bengal. The sum result of these constant river shifts is that the region as a whole is flat as an ironing board, with no part of the delta rising more than a few meters above sea level. The topography of the region is also profoundly impacted by yearly sediment deposits, which if heavy can create entirely new midstream islands, called *char* in the local parlance. The same yearly floods that build one *char* can wear away another, ensuring that the average lifespan of a given *char* is only about 4 years and only 10 percent of *chars* remain intact 20 years after their formation.

The same yearly sediment deposits that create the *char* islands also bring rich alluvial soil deposits to the region, allowing high crop yields with minimal effort and rudimentary agricultural practices. Unfortunately, as is common in an agricultural region where birth control is rare, the region's inherent fertility has historically led, not to high incomes, but rather to a large and impoverished population. Indeed, at the time of the Great Bhola Cyclone, the Ganges River Delta boasted a population density of nearly 400 people per square kilometer, rivaling the modern-day Netherlands, one of Europe's most densely populated states. Overall, Bangladesh's population jumped by about 17 million between 1961 and 1971, an increase of over 30 percent. To accommodate this swelling population, delta farmers pushed progressively to the south, clearing land for farms in the Sunderband forest, a vast expanse of coastal mangroves which used to act as a buffer against storm surges. Despite this colonization, Ganges delta farmers continued to suffer from chronic malnutrition and other diseases, such as cholera, which fester in an overpopulated, underfed populace. High rates of population growth before 1970 also meant that a disproportionate number of the Ganges Delta's inhabitants were young children, who not as economically productive as adults and are more vulnerable to natural disasters.

The problems of overpopulation are compounded by extreme climate variability. Each year the Ganges delta is inundated by the seasonal melting of the Himalaya snowpack or else by heavy rains falling during the summer rainy season. In most years, these floods do more good than harm because of the river sediment they deposit in the delta. Unfortunately, during peak water years the floods can prove deadly, drowning thousands and displacing millions. River flooding can also trigger horrific famines by drowning crops in the fields and washing away food reserves, and can lead to disease by contaminating drinking water and providing breeding opportunities for disease-carrying mosquitoes. In extremely low-flood years, on the other hand, agriculture can suffer either because of lack of fresh water for farming or because of infiltration by saltwater into the delta's rivers.

More importantly for the present discussion, saltwater flooding is also a serious problem in the Ganges delta. Low-lying and intersected by river channels, the region offers little resistance to cyclonic storm surge, which can reach many kilometers inland. What is more, the geographical circumstances of the nearby Bay of Bengal ensure that destructive storm surges will be a frequent occurrence. The Bay of Bengal is a fairly warm sea, with water temperatures reaching or exceeding 26 degrees Celsius throughout the year. What is more, the Bay of Bengal is quite shallow. This is important, since elsewhere in the world cyclones weaken themselves by stirring up cooler water from the ocean depths, a rare circumstance in the shallow waters of the Bay of Bengal. The bay's shallowness also prevents the formation of a deep water countercurrent that might allow wind-stacked floodwaters to return to open sea, thus reducing the height of a cyclonic storm surge. Furthermore, the topography of the bay itself is conducive to storm surge development. The Bay of Bengal is shaped like a northward-pointing funnel which channels and focuses the power of water passing towards its tip. As a result, if the right conditions are present, storm surges from tropical cyclones in the Bay of Bengal can reach truly terrifying proportions. What is more, the extreme flatness of the terrain and the relatively flimsy quality of most houses, especially those built on temporary *char* islands, ensures that cyclonic winds can strike with devastating effect.

In the face of these threats from land, air, and sea, the inhabitants of the Ganges Delta have adopted a number of tactics designed to minimize the risks posed by their treacherous environment. To protect against flooding residents did drainage channels around their homes and use the excavated soil to raise the level of their house and yard above the elevation of normal floodwaters. In addition, in order to hedge their bets against possible damage by cyclonic storm surge, most delta farmers grow some salt-resistant crops, like millet, water melon, and mug, a locally grown bean. Delta farmers also try to minimize risk by cultivating two or more disconnected strips of land, often with different soil qualities and different elevations above water level, thus hoping to gain some cushion against both price fluctuations and natural disasters. What is more, local farmers tended to cultivate thick stands of coconut palms, water chestnuts, bananas, and other quick-growing plants surrounding their *bari*, a extended family farming community of several houses sharing a common courtyard. Not only do these plants provide food, fuel, and building materials for the inhabitants of the *baris*, they help protect the home from wind damage in case of a tropical cyclone. Finally, farmers in the Ganges delta are accustomed to building fairly large-scale flood control works, such as earthen dams connecting two or more islands, in order to channel the flow of the waters.

Delta farmers have one last weapon in their arsenal against the region's difficult climate: mobility. Islands that are particularly vulnerable to weather extremes may be occupied only seasonally, for instance during the summer rainy season, and then abandoned in mid–September, shortly before the normal tropical cyclone season reaches its peak. If inhabited islands begin to disappear, which often happens with *char* islands due to erosion, farmers will simply pull up stakes and seek better conditions elsewhere. Houses can be dismantled, transported, and reconstructed piece-by-piece, or else key building components, such as corrugated iron roofs, could be salvaged and reused. Livestock can be moved long distances as well — indeed the water buffalo, one of the staple farm animals of the region, is an excellent swimmer. To a certain degree, the ability of farmers to migrate from place to place is limited by social convention. Many farmers are in fact sharecroppers on land owned by other people, and their ability to pull up stakes is limited by debt or contractual obligations. What is more, given the region's high population density, delta farmers who move away from threatened territories might have had trouble finding land or work elsewhere. As a result, a constant stream of displaced or landless farmers moves annually to Dhaka or to one of the other growing urban centers of the Ganges Delta. Nonetheless, other farmers are always willing to take their place, attracted by the region's high agricultural fertility.

Tactics such as tree planting, raised home sites, and migration generally suffice to mitigate loss of life and property in normal years, but they are of little defense when the Ganges delta is struck by extreme weather. Unfortunately, disastrous weather afflicts the region with depressing regularity. Heavy upstream rains or rapid melt of snow pack brings repeated flooding to the Ganges delta, most recently in 1998, when almost 70 percent of Bangladesh was submerged. This flood led to relatively few casualties, largely because of a vigorous international food relief effort, but as we shall see in chapter 6 historical river floods in what is now Bangladesh have lead to atrocious death tolls. Cyclonic weather has left an even more profound stamp upon the region. In 1737, for instance, a strong cyclone struck the Hooghly River region in the western portion of the Ganges delta, submerging the area under a storm surge that may have reached 13 meters in height. In all, as many as 350,000 people perished in the floodwaters. A similar storm washed into the Ganges delta in 1876, and although it only killed 100,000 or so directly, another 100,000 died of cholera shortly afterward when drinking water became contaminated with cholera bacteria. Still other cataclysmic storms struck the region in 1897 and again in 1942, killing 175,000 and 42,000 respectively.

In terms of overall power, the Bhola cyclone did not quite match up to these earlier cyclonic events. Scientists believe that its storm surge only reached about 3 meters in height in 1970 — an impressive surge but nothing compared to earlier cyclonic storm surges in the Bay of Bengal. Had the Bhola cyclone come ashore at low tide the Bay of Bengal's unusually extreme tidal swing might have cancelled the storm surge entirely. As luck would have it, however, the Bhola cyclone came ashore at almost the peak of high tide, which meant the net height of the storm surge actually reached 6 meters, more than enough to completely inundate even the raised houses in the Ganges delta's *char* islands. The fact that the cyclone struck during a full moon, when tides are exceptionally high due to the moon's gravitational pull, further worsened a bad situation.

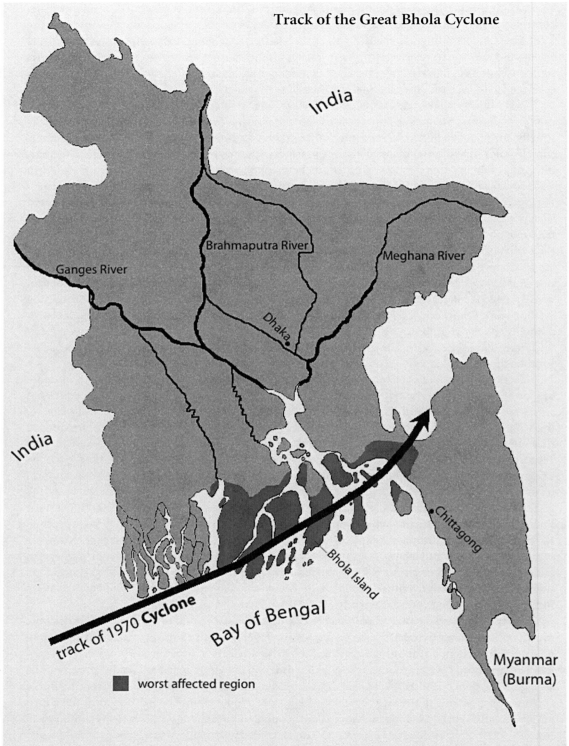

Track of the Great Bhola Cyclone

India

Brahmaputra River

Meghana River

Ganges River

Dhaka

India

Chittagong

Bhola Island

track of 1970 **Cyclone**

Bay of Bengal

Myanmar
(Burma)

worst affected region

The timing of the Bhola cyclone was unfortunate in other ways as well. The storm struck shortly after the first week of November, a time when tropical cyclones were normally quite infrequent, so many delta farmers no doubt dropped their guard. This problem was compounded by the fact that the storm made landfall in the early morning hours when people were asleep in their beds. Furthermore, the cyclone impacted the region right before the start of the November rice harvest season. This was doubly unfortunate since not only were food stocks in the region fairly low at this point in the agricultural cycle, but also the harvest itself had attracted as many as a half-million migrant workers from farther north in Bangladesh hoping to make some cash as day laborers. These migrant farmers, who often slept in the open alongside the fields they harvested, were particularly vulnerable to the cyclone's storm surge.

Finally, the Great Bhola Cyclone had the misfortune to strike at a politically sensitive moment. At the time, the delta was under the sovereignty of the nation of Pakistan, which had two constituent parts: West Pakistan (today Pakistan) and East Pakistan (now Bangladesh), separated from each other by the nation of India. Relations between the two halves were somewhat strained, in part because many in East Pakistan believed that their interests were being neglected in favor of more populous West Pakistan. Tensions were further fueled by an upcoming vote, scheduled for December, which was expected to lead to gains by pro-independence parties in East Pakistan. These political machinations did not affect the storm itself but would impact the storm's aftermath, as we shall see below.

News of the impending cyclone was first delivered to Indian and West Pakistani authorities on November 11th, when U.S. weather satellites spotted a storm of at least category 1 intensity tracking up the Bay of Bengal. Neither nation apparently did much initially to prepare for the coming disaster. On November 12th, when the cyclone began to approach land, Indian radio stations began to broadcast storm warnings which were then taken up by East Pakistani authorities. However, these warnings tended to be heard by those least in need of hearing them. Radio ownership was most common in and near urban centers, while inhabitants of the coastal provinces and *char* islands, who were in much greater peril from the storm, also had the least access to electricity or radios. In any case, even if the Pakistani authorities had gotten out word about the storm's impending landfall it is unlikely that much could have been done to save lives. In most of the threatened area, there was simply no high ground to which to flee, and lack of roads or motorized water transport made large-scale evacuation into the interior impractical.

As a result, most families in the Ganges delta had little warning of the upcoming storm until howling winds began to batter their rudimentary houses shortly before midnight. Sustained winds of approximately 210 km/hour snapped trees and systematically dismantled local houses, which were mostly of thatched grass, palm frond, or rope-lashed bamboo construction. Soon after, the storm surge began to force its way over the Ganges Delta, continuing the destruction started by the wind. Witnesses disagreed about the character of the advancing floods. Some remembered the floods building up slowly, at a rate of only a half-meter or more an hour, while other witnesses claimed the storm surge was a single wall of water that approached with the sound of "100 planes flying together." Desperate to avoid being drowned by the swirling floods, many delta farmers clambered atop their houses, though their roofs rarely survived for long in the teeth of the water and winds. After their homes shattered, the only recourse for most storm victims was to climb the tallest tree they could find to avoid drowning. Unfortunately, humans were not the only animals to seek shelter in the treetops. After the cyclone had passed, a number of survivors remembered being forced to share their perches with poisonous snakes. On the other hand, one survivor in the delta, a fortunate Mrs. Karim, reported being saved by a constrictor snake that apparently wrapped her unconscious body in its coils during the storm. Most likely the snake was just trying to hold on tight to whatever it could touch in its

AP/WORLD WIDE PHOTOS

Cyclone damage in Manpura, a village located about 180 kilometers south of Dhaka.

treetop storm shelter, but its actions saved the lives of Mrs. Karim and her newborn infant in the process.

When the waters finally receded, those who had clung to safety atop trees or upon the rare rooftop that survived the floods descended into a world transformed. In the most badly-affected districts, such as the southern tip of Bhola Island and the *char* islands to its southwest, all that remained was a few half-broken trees and weathered mounds which hinted at where *baris* compounds might have been. Only a few houses, mostly big, reinforced structures with heavy tin roofs, managed to survive more or less intact, though in some cases the inhabitants had been obliged to cut holes through the roofs to escape the rising water. Overall, 85 percent of the housing in the worst affected area suffered some reported damage. As for agricultural losses, the crop in the ground was wiped out in most areas flooded by the storm surge; in fact, the paddies and fields where crops had been planted were often unrecognizable. Crop losses elsewhere, though not total, were severe. Rice crops were wiped out, even in areas where the saltwater surge had not penetrated, since rice at this stage of the harvest was extremely vulnerable to high winds. Other crops, such as sugarcane and banana, had been heavily damaged. Many nut trees, such as cocoanuts, did manage to survive the storm, but the nuts themselves had been blown away, costing the farmers much of a year's harvest.

Damage to crops and property, however, paled in comparison to the human harvest extracted by the storm. The official death toll published in the days after the storm was 225,000, representing 17 percent of the population in the area most strongly impacted by the cyclone. In all likelihood, however, this is a gross underestimate. The official death toll reflects only the deaths of people known to the government before the storm struck. In fact, the records probably seriously undercounted the region's population due to poor record keeping, a very high birth rate, and the inherent difficulty of keeping close tabs on the shifting lands and peoples of

Close-up view of cyclone damage in Manpura.

the Ganges delta. What is more, the state's ability to keep accurate population tallies was likely undermined by the delta people's distrust of the government, seen by many delta farmers as a corrupt, parasitical entity. The death figure also does not include an unknown number of migrant workers who were in the Ganges delta at the time of the Bhola Cyclone. Since most of the storm victims were washed to sea, and their bodies were never recovered, an exact or even approximate death toll for the Great Bhola Cyclone will probably never be known. Under such circumstances, the widely-given figure of 500,000 overall casualties is probably as good a guess as any.

As is generally true in natural disasters, the death toll varied by age, gender, and class. Young children and the elderly, two groups that were least able to protect themselves from storm surge, died at a much higher rate than the general population: 29.2 percent of those under four and 20.7 percent of those over 70 were killed in affected areas, compared with only 6.1 percent of 35–39 year olds. Men tended to survive at a higher rate than women, most likely because they had the physical strength to reach and then hang on to safe perches on rooftops and trees. What is more, the rich tended to weather the storm better than the poor. In part, this is because their houses were built of higher quality materials, such as metal sheeting, rather than the thatch or bamboo construction common to the region. What is more, the *char* islands were disproportionally inhabited by the poorest farmers, who were obliged by their impecunious circumstances to try to scratch out a living from these potentially fertile but inherently unstable coastal flatlands.

In any case, following the cyclone, the plight of the living was nearly as deplorable as the fate of the dead. The surging floodwaters destroyed most or all food stocks in the affected regions, meaning that storm survivors faced the specter of post-cyclone starvation. This problem was exacerbated by the fact that the cyclone struck almost on the eve of the rice harvest,

AP/WORLD WIDE PHOTOS

Bodies of storm surge victims washed back to shore in the days after the 1970 Great Bhola Cyclone.

meaning food supplies were at low ebb even before the storm struck. Nor was there any prospect of growing much food in the immediate future, since most of the seed crop and farm tools had been washed away by the storm surge. In any case the paddies and fields had been rendered temporarily sterile by saltwater contamination. Shelter against the sun and rain was also in short supply. Indeed, even months after the cyclone some survivors were still living in "tiny grass and straw huts, three or four feet wide and perhaps six feet long, each housing a family of two to eight persons," a situation that relief workers Alfred Sommer and W. Henry Mosley pronounced "pathetic." In addition, many survivors sported serious post-storm injuries. The most common ailment was what Sommer and Mosley dubbed "cyclone syndrome"—severe abrasions of the chest, arms, and thighs—which was "grim evidence of the tenacity with which the survivors had clung to the trees to withstand the buffeting of the waves." Many others suffered broken bones and suppurating, infected wounds. What is more, the cyclone created perfect conditions for the proliferation of disease, especially cholera, which was endemic to the Ganges delta and had erupted explosively after past cyclones.

Clearly, fast action was needed to succor the living and prevent a bad disaster from becoming even worse. Nonetheless, the central government in West Pakistan seemed to turn a deaf ear to East Pakistan's suffering. The first material aid given to this region came not from Pakistan, but rather Pakistan's supposed enemy India, which immediately provided cash for disaster relief. Soon after, the United States dispatched $10 million in relief supplies, Great Britain pledged $7.2 million for reconstruction efforts, and China offered $1.2 million in rice, blankets, and medicine. In the meantime, the Western Pakistani-dominated central government did fairly little. In a move reminiscent of George W. Bush's fly-over of New Orleans following Hurricane Katrina, Pakistani President Khan reportedly passed over the delta in Fokker Friendship aircraft, declared that the damage to the region had been exaggerated, and then assigned a subordinate to direct relief efforts rather than tackling the issue himself. Only after the world press began publishing pictures of bodies dangling in tree tops and hollow-eyed, traumatized children did the West Pakistani government stir to action.

By then, however, the political damage had been done. On November 23rd, East Pakistani officials sent a letter to President Khan charging him with "gross neglect, callous inattention, and utter indifference." The war of words was soon joined with weapons, as outraged East Pakistanis rose in armed rebellion against the West Pakistani-dominated government. Of course, not all East Pakistani grievances revolved around the 1970 cyclone. Pakistan's political system gave disproportional influence to West Pakistan, which also claimed the lion's share of the state's revenues. The decision to make Urdu the official language of all of Pakistan, although it was not widely spoken in the East, further heightened tensions. The fact that Khan was a military leader installed in government by a coup further undermined the legitimacy of the regime, as did the fact that West Pakistanis dominated the military establishment, a legacy of the British imperial era. It took the trauma of the 1970 cyclone, however, to ignite these latent grievances into a general firestorm of insurrection against the West Pakistani government.

If it is accepted that the 1970 cyclone played a crucial role in the 1971 insurrection, then the cyclone must bear some indirect blame in the atrocious human suffering triggered by the Bangladesh Liberation War. West Pakistani strategy during this conflict is best summarized by President Khan's supposed advice to his generals, "kill 3 million of them and the rest will eat out of our hands." The actual casualty figures produced by the war are a matter of heated debate, but are almost certainly in the hundreds of thousands, with intellectuals and Hindu residents of East Pakistan particularly singled out for massacre by West Pakistani troops and allied East Pakistani militia forces. Indeed, the targeted nature of the killings, not to mention that most victims belonged to the civilian population, has inspired some authors to term the killings a "selective genocide." These massacres were probably intended to depopulate the country of "undesirable" people, and in the short run they had the desired effect; approximately 10 million East Pakistanis fled the fighting to neighboring India.

This heavy toll of human misery was further augmented by disease and famine, which as we shall see in chapters 7 and 8 are the constant accompaniment to both natural and man-made disasters. Cholera, endemic in Pakistan, found fertile ground in the unsanitary conditions of the hastily-built and overcrowded refugee camps in India. Approximately 10,000 succumbed to cholera in these camps, though as cholera can be difficult to distinguish from other gastrointestinal diseases the true death toll is probably higher. Thousands more died of smallpox, which was on the verge of eradication in East Pakistan before the war but not in neighboring India where the camps were located. When East Pakistani refugees in Indian camps returned to their home villages after the cessation of hostilities, they often brought smallpox with them. Thankfully, as regional disease specialists Alfred Sommer, Nilton Arnt, and Stanley Foster have pointed out, this smallpox epidemic was limited by two factors: 1) the high rate of pre-war smallpox vaccinations amongst East Pakistan's populace, and 2) the *bari* system of East Bangladeshi settlement patterns, which effectively quarantined smallpox cases within particular extended family groups. What is more, many in East Pakistan also suffered from food shortages, and per-capita grain intake dropped from 16.2 ounces/day in 1970 to 14.8 ounces in 1971. However, according to nutritional scholars Lincoln C. Chen and Jon E. Rohde, East Pakistan avoided outright famine during the war years largely because the number of people in the region had been sharply reduced due to mass death within East Pakistan and mass migration to the outside.

Following Bangladesh's successful bid for independence, one of the first goals of the new-born state was to take steps to protect delta farmers from future storm surges on the scale of the 1970 Bhola Cyclone disaster. The new government established 38 data relaying stations and 3 radar stations to scan the Bay of Bengal for potential cyclonic storms. If a storm was detected, information would immediately be conveyed to the Red Crescent Society of Bangladesh, which would activate a network of 57 radio transmitters and 20,000 volunteers to warn endangered communities about the incoming threat. To mitigate storm surges, some earthen embankments were constructed on particularly vulnerable islands. The capstone of the Bangladeshi storm surge protection program, however, was the construction of cyclone shelters built of reinforced concrete on high stilts capable of riding out even a severe cyclonic storm surge.

As subsequent events were to prove, however, this cyclone protection system was far from foolproof. In 1991, another powerful cyclone made landfall in Bangladesh, this time near the major port city of Chittagong. Like the Bhola Cyclone, the 1991 storm surge coincided with high tide, and since the 1991 storm boasted even higher winds than the 1970 storm, the storm surge it kicked up was at least as high as the 1970 storm. Overall 138,000 people perished during the storm itself, another 460,000 were injured, and thousands more died of gangrene, diarrhea, and respiratory disease in the storm's aftermath. It is no surprise that fewer people died in 1991 than 1970; this time, the storm struck the mainland rather than the islands, so evacuation inland was a much more viable option for the majority of the affected population. However, given the possibility of inland evacuation, 138,000 remains a shockingly high number of deaths. Clearly, two decades of preparation for the next big storm surge had produced few meaningful results.

Why did Bangladesh's storm surge protection system fail in 1991? Cyclone researchers C. Emdad Haque and Danny Blair subsequently pinpointed a number of flaws in the system. Despite the hard work of the Bangladeshi Red Crescent, many people did not receive warning until it was too lake to take effective action, especially in rural areas where radios remained a relative rarity. Some Bangladeshis who did receive the warnings dismissed them, distrusting the honestly or competence of a government still widely seen as corrupt. Other storm survivors claimed that evacuation routes were choked with people before the storm, while others feared the storm less than they feared the loss of their property to looting. What is more, urban authorities in Chittagong and elsewhere had done little to prevent the construction of vast slums in river floodplains which were particularly vulnerable to the impact of storm surges.

Perhaps most importantly, the cyclone shelters proved to be unequal to the task of preparing coastal residents for the impact of the 1991 storm. In all, only 302 shelters had been constructed in the two decades since 1970, and these shelters provided refuge for only a maximum of a half-million people nationwide, a far cry from the 4.5 million people affected by the storm in the landfall area alone. Worse yet, there are reasons to believe that the cyclone shelters would not be fully utilized even if they existed in sufficient numbers to house the entirety of Bangladesh's coastal population. Some Bangladeshis interviewed in the storm's aftermath claimed that they feared unscrupulous local government officials might force them to pay "rent" for the privilege of using the shelter. Others feared the break-up of their families if forced into shelters — a concern as much economic as social, since extended family networks in Bangladesh traditionally provide post-storm assistance beyond the capability of the financially strapped government. What is more, more recent research has indicated that many Bangladeshi women were hesitant to enter crowded cyclone shelters for fear of violating *purdah*, the traditional Moslem practice that forbids women from revealing themselves to men outside of the family.

Perhaps the most disconcerting finding of the Haque and Blair survey is that a number of respondents failed to move from their homes because of religious scruples. When asked why they did not evacuate their homes in the face of the cyclone, 15.7 percent or respondents in rural areas replied that the cyclone was "Allah's will," and that to seek escape from it was sacrilege. One villager demanded of interviewers, "what can you do against Allah? Cyclone happens because of our sin." What is more, fully 89 percent of interviewed villagers reported praying to Allah as one of the measures they took to prepare for the oncoming storm. So did religiously-informed fatalism worsen the cyclone death toll in 1991, if not 1970? Perhaps, but disaster researcher Hanna Schmuck believes that the apparent Bangladeshi fatalism towards disaster is really a healthy reaction to an unstable environment, a "self-help strategy to overcome crises as quickly as possible," preventing victims from "wasting time and energy asking why disasters happen to them and not others." What is more, Schmuck asserts that Bangladeshi farmers tend to be anything but fatalistic in actual practice and take whatever realistic steps that are available to them to mitigate loss of life and property during disasters. Haque and Blair's own research bears this out: Respondents to their survey on pre-storm preparations were allowed to pick more than one category of behavior, and although "prayed to Allah" was by far the most common preparation made by rural farmers, "no measures taken" was by far the least common response, asserted by only 4 percent of respondents.

Unfortunately, if fatalism is a useful reaction to an uncertain environment, the inhabitants of the Ganges River delta are likely to have even more need of it in the years to come. Indeed, Bangladesh's vulnerability to cyclonic storm surge is expected to grow ever higher with the passage of time, especially as we move into the age of global warming. As sea levels rise, more and more of the Ganges delta will be submerged. This will undoubtedly concentrate Bangladesh's population in urban areas, most notably the burgeoning capital city of Dhaka, which boasts 11 million residents and a yearly growth rate of nearly 4 percent. Dhaka lies on alluvial soil deposits only 3–6 meters above sea level, and as the city continues to grow the only available territory for expansion is downhill in river floodplains. This is not to say that Dhaka will be exposed to oceanic storm surge any time soon — Dhaka lies about 200 kilometers from the sea and would likely take a century or more of rising sea level to seriously threaten the city. However, future storm surges will seriously impact the food supply of Bangladesh as a whole, which is already a food importing region despite its fertile soils. What is more, the concentration of more and more people into poorly-built slum cities in the flood plains surrounding Dhaka will render the region even more vulnerable to river flooding. Either famine or flood will likely trigger horrible epidemics of disease in a country where health care resources are already in short supply. It remains to be seen if the 1970 cyclone foreshadows even more calamitous disasters in the Ganges River delta in our greenhouse warming future.

Study Questions

1. "In terms of both location and timing, the Great Bhola cyclone was a 'perfect storm,' and could not have been better designed to cause mass mortality." To what degree do you agree with this statement?

2. Given the information presented in this section, to what degree was a disaster on the scale of the Great Bhola cyclone inevitable?

3. Based on the information presented here, to what degree did local culture worsen and/or lessen the impact of the 1970 Great Bhola cyclone?

4. Bangladesh's horrific vulnerability to cyclone and other forms of disaster raises the question: Does the global community have a responsibility to continuously provide relief

aid to people who knowingly live in such a disaster-prone region? Explain and defend your answer.

Sources/Suggested Readings

Chen, Lincoln C. and Jon E. Rohde. "Civil War in Bangladesh: Famine Averted?" In Lincoln C. Chen, ed., *Disaster in Bangladesh: Health Crises in a Developing Nation.* New York: Oxford University Press, 1973, pp. 190–205.

Choudhury, A. M. "Cyclones in Bangladesh." In K. Nizamuddin, ed., *Disaster in Bangladesh: Selected Readings.* Dhaka, Bangladesh: Graphtone Printers, 2001. pp. 61–76.

Emanuel, Kerry. *Divine Wind: The History and Science of Hurricanes.* New York: Oxford University Press, 2005.

Haque, C. Emdad, and Danny Blair. "Vulnerability to Tropical Cyclones: Evidence from the April 1991 Cyclone in Coastal Bangladesh." *Disaster,* Vol. 16, No. 3 (Sept. 1992), pp. 217–229.

Haque, C. Emdad. *Hazards in a Fickle Environment: Bangladesh.* Boston, MA: Kluwer Academic Publishers, 1997.

Huq, Saleemul. "Environmental Hazards in Dhaka." In James K. Mitchell, ed., *Crucibles of Hazard: Mega-Cities and Disasters in Transition.* New York: United Nations University Press, 1999.

Longshore, David. *Encyclopedia of Hurricanes, Typhoons, and Cyclones.* New York: Checkmark, 2000.

Mosley, Henry W., and Monowar Hossain. "Population: Background and Prospects." In Lincoln C. Chen, ed., *Disaster in Bangladesh: Health Crises in a Developing Nation.* New York: Oxford University Press, 1973, pp. 8–17.

Nizamuddin, Khondakar. "Global Warming and Its Impact on Bangladesh." In K. Nizamuddin, ed., *Disaster in Bangladesh: Selected Readings.* Dhaka, Bangladesh: Graphtone Printers, 2001. pp. 61–76.

Rosenberg, Irwin H. "Nutrition: Food Production, Dietary Patterns, and Nutritional Deficiencies." In Lincoln C. Chen, ed., *Disaster in Bangladesh: Health Crises in a Developing Nation.* New York: Oxford University Press, 1973, pp. 31–51.

Samad, M. A. *Cyclone of 1970 and Agricultural Rehabilitation.* Dacca, Bangladesh: Agricultural Information Service, 1971.

Schmuck, Hanna. "'An Act of Allah': Religious Explanations for Floods in Bangladesh as Survival Strategy." *International Journal of Mass Emergencies and Disasters,* Vol. 18, No. 1 (March, 2000), pp. 85–95.

Sommer, Alfred, and W. Henry Mosley. "The Cyclone: Medical Assessment and Determination of Relief and Rehabilitation Needs." In Lincoln C. Chen, ed., *Disaster in Bangladesh: Health Crises in a Developing Nation.* New York: Oxford University Press, 1973, pp. 119–132.

Sommer, Alfred, Nilton Arnt, and Stanley O. Foster. "Post–Civil War in Bangladesh: the Smallpox Epidemic." In Lincoln C. Chen, ed., *Disaster in Bangladesh: Health Crises in a Developing Nation.* New York: Oxford University Press, 1973, pp. 225–240.

5.2: Cyclone Tracy, 1974

Cyclone Tracy, which struck Darwin, Australia, on Christmas day of 1974, is an interesting case study about what happens when tropical cyclones strike the developed rather than the developing world. The death toll inflicted by Tracy was relatively low, especially when compared to the hundreds of thousands slain by the Great Bhola Cyclone in Bangladesh only three years before. What is more, in the aftermath of the disaster, the state of Australia was able to bring considerable resources to bear for relief and recovery, which is rarely the case when disastrous cyclones strike the developing world. On the other hand, Cyclone Tracy caused destruction to property on a scale rarely seen in underdeveloped nations. Indeed, witnesses in post-storm Darwin likened the scene to a nuclear holocaust, and overall property damage amounted to nearly $5 billion in modern American currency. Small wonder, then, that Tracy is still remembered as the worst natural disaster in Australian history.

Australia is a land threatened by numerous natural hazards. The weather is quite variable, subject to sharp seasonal variations as well as multi-year cycles such as El Niño. This problem is exacerbated by the region's old, nutrient-poor soils, which increase the likelihood that poor weather will trigger crop failures. What is more, cyclonic weather is fairly common in the north of Australia, since the southwest Pacific Ocean basin produces an average of over 10 tropical storms per year, about half of which develop into full-fledged cyclones. Worse yet, disastrous brush fires, often triggered by lightning strikes, are a constant problem in arid Australia. Nonetheless, in Australian history these natural hazards have only rarely triggered "disasters," if disaster is defined as large-scale loss of human life and property. In the period before European colonization of the continent, Australia's Aborigine peoples lived in small, widely-scattered nomadic groups. Because of their small numbers and high mobility, the Aborigines were resilient against environmental disasters. When Australia became a European colony the importation of sophisticated British agricultural and engineering technology, combined with a relatively high standard of living and relatively low population density, further mitigated the effects of natural hazards. Indeed, the disasters most vividly remembered by Australians prior to 1974 were man-made, such as the high casualty figures suffered by Australia in both World War I and World War II.

Interestingly, the man-made disaster of war played an important contributory role in the developments leading up to the Cyclone Tracy. Before 1940, the remote Australian city of Darwin was known only for its brief 1870s gold rush and its importance as a station for the intercontinental telegraph system. With the outbreak of World War II, however, Darwin became a crucially important strategic center for the Allied war effort against Japan, since it boasted the best port site in the thinly populated northern frontier of Australia. Not surprisingly, Darwin itself was bombed repeatedly by the Japanese during the war, most notably in February 19th of 1942, when at least 243 people were killed. Despite this wartime trauma many of the 10,000-odd Australian servicemen stationed in Darwin during the war chose to stay, attracted by the city's pleasant tropical climate. Darwin's growth was further encouraged by Australian military spending, as even after the end of World War II, Darwin remained an important naval and air station for the Australian military. The post-war discovery of uranium deposits about 200 kilometers from Darwin brought a further infusion of wealth, bringing back the gold rush atmosphere that Darwin had enjoyed a hundred years earlier. Still other residents of Darwin were hippies, attracted by the city's warm temperature and laid-back social atmosphere. This influx of people by no means made Darwin a large city—on the eve of Tracy, Darwin still boasted only 43,500 inhabitants. Nonetheless, Darwin was by far the largest urban center in Northern Australia.

Darwin's architecture strongly reflected the origins of the city. Many early houses were short, utilitarian structures crafted of brick or stone seemingly built to withstand Japanese bombs rather than house human beings in comfort. By the 1970s, however, this style of building was somewhat out of fashion, increasingly replaced by high-set "government houses," which were essentially single-level houses erected upon 10-foot stilts. Since the main building material in these houses was fibrocement, a cement/asbestos composite that is cheap and easy to work with, these homes were fairly inexpensive to build. Most private dwellings had roofs of corrugated iron, a light and inexpensive building material often used in the tropics where roofs do not have to withstand the weight of snow. What is more, the 10-foot stilts ensured that the house was high enough to catch the tropical breezes, providing natural cooling for the home. As a further defense against the tropical heat, most government houses were fitted with louvres, windows consisting of parallel slats that could be cranked open to various angles to allow the desired amount of outside air to circulate within the house. Furthermore, the bulk of the houses were built close to the ocean, where they could catch as much sea breeze as possible.

A typical Darwin "Government House."

These houses made Darwin a pleasant and attractive place to live, but as we shall see below, Darwin's government houses proved particularly vulnerable to cyclonic winds. Worse yet, Darwin's government houses were actually getting more vulnerable over time. In the period leading up to 1974, the louvres windows of the town were becoming larger and larger, while an increasing number of homes were being built or refitted with large sliding glass doors leading into the living room. This style of construction certainly fit well with Darwin's warm climate and casual social atmosphere, but it was an unwise design choice given Darwin's location in the western South Pacific cyclone zone. Indeed, only a month before Tracy's arrival local architect Peter Dermoudy, who had become concerned about the city's trend towards large windows, went television to warn people to stay away from large plate glass doors and windows in case of a cyclonic storm.

Despite this most of Darwin's residents were skeptical that a cyclone was likely to hit their tropical paradise. Many of Darwin's residents were relative newcomers from Australia's temperate south, with little or no experience with tropical cyclones. What is more, cyclone Selma had prowled the waters outside of Darwin earlier that same December, producing a flurry of storm warnings but little adverse weather. As a result, many Darwin residents were still somewhat skeptical of cyclone storm warnings at December's end. Barbara James, a Darwin resident and Tracy survivor, later told storm chronicler Bill Bunbury that "you started to almost think that it was never going to happen in Darwin even though you had cyclone warnings on the radio all the time." In any case, it was Christmas Eve, one of the busiest days of the year in Darwin's social calendar. Many refrigerators were crammed with holiday foods, many cupboards were well-stocked with alcohol, and many people were loathe to break plans made well in advance of the storm. This fatal combination of inexperience and wishful thinking lead many in Darwin to disregard the danger that Tracy posed to their seaside community.

The inhabitants of Darwin ought to have known better, because powerful tropical cyclones of the past had already left their mark on Darwin's history. In 1877, Darwin suffered a direct hit by a major cyclone, and 100 people were reportedly killed outright, while 700 more suffered injuries. Only 11 years later, another powerful cyclone struck Darwin, and according to cyclone scholar David Longshore, this storm "ravaged the city, claiming an estimated 139 lives and collapsing nearly every structure—from piers to warehouses—along the waterfront." Darwin was struck yet again by cyclones in 1897, 1917, and 1937. Still another tropical cyclone exerted a more indirect, but no less devastating, impact on Darwin in 1875. In February of that year, the ship SS *Gothenburg* was following the north coast of Australia en route to Adelaide on Australia's south coast. On board were 112 or so passengers and crewmen, including many of Darwin's best and brightest such as government officials and judges, as well as miners who had struck it rich in Darwin's gold rush. As the ship rounded Queensland, it was wrecked by a cyclonic storm, and all but 22 passengers perished. Given Darwin's tiny size at the time, this represented a sizable proportion of the town's population, and a major setback to Darwin's fortunes. Nonetheless, the 1875 and other cyclones had largely been forgotten by Christmas of 1974.

At first, Tracy's behavior seemed to justify the city's lack of concern. Like many Australian cyclones, Tracy started off as a low pressure mass in the warm Arafura Sea, which lies between Australia's north central coast and the Indonesian Archipelago. Meteorologists quickly identified this tropical low as a potential cyclone in the making but anticipated that if it made landfall at all it would strike far to the east of Darwin in a relatively unpopulated region called Arnhem Land. Tracy defied these predictions, wandering instead almost due west, to the point that some meteorologists suspected it might wander harmlessly into the Indian Ocean. On December 24th, however, Tracy began a fatal recurvature to the south and east. In the process, Tracy passed over the sun-warmed waters of the Timor Sea and quickly strengthened to the status of a category 5 cyclone. However, even at this point, some meteorologists remained hopeful. Cyclone Selma had drifted quite close to Darwin earlier that month only to abruptly turn north and then veer away to the west before sputtering out over the Indian Ocean. To the surprise and dismay of meteorologists, however, Tracy continued to recurve southwards and eastwards, a course that would eventually take it directly over the city of Darwin.

Even after meteorologists accepted and announced the reality of Tracy's imminent arrival, the reaction of Darwin's citizens was decidedly mixed. Some took what steps they could to prepare for the storm, for instance securing lawn furniture and filling bathtubs in expectation of post-storm water supply failures. Boat owners generally moved their vessels away from the quay and took up position in the harbor or open water to better ride out the expected storm. On the other hand, quite a few residents of Darwin essentially ignored the storm. In his interviews with Tracy survivors, Gary McKay found that some Darwinians had hung laundry out to dry before the storm, danced at a local disco, or done their nails rather than storm preparations. What is more, although some Christmas parties were cancelled for fear of Tracy, others were held in defiance of the approaching weather, meaning that quite a few residents of Darwin faced Tracy in a state of extreme inebriation. Worse yet, many went to bed on Christmas night wearing their normal sleeping outfits—which in laid-back, tropical Darwin was often nothing at all. As we shall see below, lack of clothing posed real problems during and after Tracy's arrival.

When Tracy did arrive, it struck with a ferocity that even the most pessimistic meteorologists had not anticipated. Like many category-5 cyclones, Tracy was a very compact storm, but this only augmented its strength as the air pressure gradient at the storm's center was

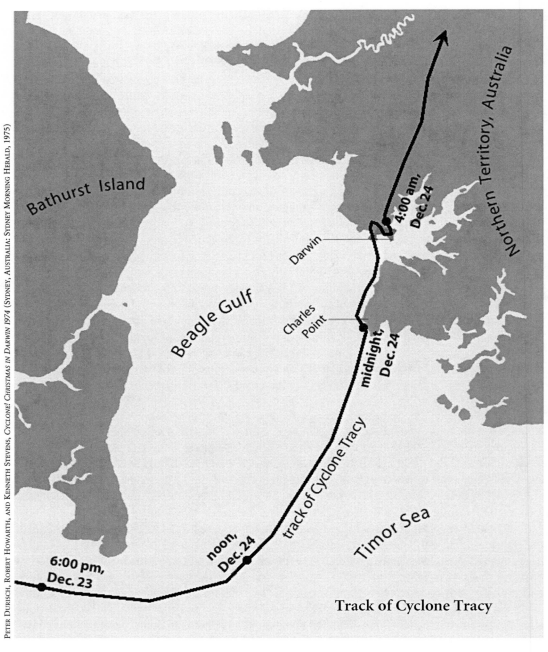

PETER DURISCH, ROBERT HOWARTH, AND KENNETH STEVENS, *CYCLONE! CHRISTMAS IN DARWIN 1974* (SYDNEY, AUSTRALIA: SYDNEY MORNING HERALD, 1975)

Bathurst Island

4:00 am,
Dec. 24

Northern Territory, Australia

Darwin

Beagle Gulf

Charles
Point

midnight,
Dec. 24

track of Cyclone Tracy

Timor Sea

noon,
Dec. 24

6:00 pm,
Dec. 23

Track of Cyclone Tracy

extremely steep. As a result, Tracy's winds may have reached 300 km/hour in velocity, a wind speed normally only achieved in tornadoes. Indeed, there is evidence to suggest that, unlike most southern hemisphere cyclones, Tracy did indeed spawn tornadoes as it passed over Darwin. Tracy also dropped as much as 28 centimeters of rain in the 24 hours between 9:00 am Christmas Eve and 9:00 Christmas Day, an impressive amount. The only good news for Darwin was that the cyclone's storm surge was quite modest, perhaps because Tracy's path took it around Bathurst Island and over the tip of Charles Point as it approached Darwin, blunting the surge's force. Furthermore, Tracy's landfall did not coincide perfectly with high tide, which would have augmented the storm surge's height. In any case, much of Darwin was built atop coastal bluffs that rose slightly but appreciably over the surrounding ocean, providing some protection against storm surge.

The lack of significant storm surge was little comfort to Darwin's residents, who faced a harrowing Christmas morning in the wee hours of December 25th. Since the power went out early in much of the city Darwinians were forced to await Tracy's passing in inky darkness alleviated intermittently by the flicker of multiple lightning strikes. Most houses weathered the "first wind" of the storm tolerably well, though loose materials such as unsecured corrugated iron roofs, solar panels, and tree limbs were deposited everywhere throughout the town. When the second wind arrived, however, all hell broke loose. Thanks to the steepness of Tracy's pressure gradient, the back-side wind of the cyclone struck Darwin with terrible suddenness, almost like the blade of a bulldozer. Survivor Chris Kingston-Lee later told storm chronicler Gary McKay that the second wind sounded like a "hundred" semi-trailers, "coming at us flat out, revving their guts out." Another Tracy survivor, Rowan Charrington, described the same sound as "a squadron of tanks starting to drive all over the wreckage."

Indeed, by all accounts, the storm's second wind was worse than the first. This makes Tracy something of an anomaly: since cyclonic weather is fueled by evaporation of ocean water, most cyclones weaken after making landfall. What made Tracy seem different was the zigzag path that it took as it passed over Darwin. On its initial approach, Darwin passed to the north of Darwin proper, meaning that Darwin itself lay in the front right quadrant of the cyclone — and since Tracy was a clockwise-turning southern hemisphere cyclone, the front right quadrant suffered less ferocious winds than the front left. However, after tearing over Darwin's northern suburbs, Tracy did an abrupt about-face directly towards downtown Darwin. As a result, the backside winds of the storm were now traveling in the same direction as the storm itself, augmenting the power of Tracy's gusts. Once it reached downtown, Tracy apparently switched direction again, and this time Darwin was subjected to the devastating front left quadrant winds of the cyclone. Small wonder, then, that most of Tracy's damage occurred during the second half of the storm.

Tracy's second winds triggered an awful chain reaction of destruction. The first winds had filled the streets with scraps of corrugated iron, timbers, tree limbs, solar panels, and other debris. When the wind strengthened and shifted direction following the passage of the eye, the first wind's detritus battered Darwin's homes. This was especially true of government houses, which had been built high to catch the breeze and thus were now fully exposed to the second wind's wrath. Flying debris shattered sliding glass doors, blasted open louvres windows, and sheered off window boxes and other extruding architectural features. Cyclone winds then penetrated the interior of houses through the damaged exterior, which meant that Darwin's many corrugated iron roofs were now under attack from below as well as above. As a result, most corrugated iron roofs in Darwin peeled off or were lifted away, which in turn compromised the structural integrity of the rest of the house. Once deprived of their roofs most houses disintegrated, torn apart either piece by piece or all at once by Tracy's gusts. The windblown fragments of corrugated iron, lumber, fibrocement paneling, and other materials then collided with still-standing houses, starting the cycle over again. Of course, this simple scenario does not describe all of Tracy destruction. Some houses collapsed during the first wind, while others were untouched by the second wind since they sat in a protected valley or depression. Such occurrences were the exception rather than the rule, however, and the debris propelled by the second wind accounted for the majority of the storm's devastation.

As a result of widespread building failures, most of Darwin's residents suffered through a terrifying ordeal on Christmas Eve of 1974. Tracy's penetrating winds forced them to seek ever more secure locations within their houses—living rooms were abandoned in favor of bedrooms, and bedrooms for back halls, interior bathrooms, closets, or even cabinets and freestanding wardrobes. When the wind direction changed following the passage of the eye, formerly safe locations suddenly became perilous, obliging storm victims to struggle through the darkness and battering winds in search of shelter. Quite often this meant clambering through twisted corrugated iron sheets or across floors strewn with broken glass—and remember, many of Darwin's residents were completely naked. Some sought shelter in the relative safety of their cars, which were often parked in the hollow beneath Darwin's raised government houses, only to have the house collapse atop them. Most terrifying of all was the broken glass, which whirled through houses once the wind penetrated windows, shredding anything it touched. In the words of Gary McKay, some post-storm house interiors "resembled the inside of a blender that had just chopped up half a ton of glass."

Those caught outside of their houses were even worse off. Some who braved the open streets were killed instantly, sliced in half by flying bits of corrugated iron roofing. Tracy survivor Laurie Gwynne was luckier: The piece of corrugated iron that struck him in the street was upright, and although it did fling him 40 meters down the road, it only broke his toes in the process. The situation was even worse in the harbor, where sailors who remained in their boats were obliged to fight for their lives against the storm-tossed seas and the howling winds, which progressively drove them closer and closer to the rocky north Australian shore. In the end, 29 boats were sunk during Tracy, and the number of people killed at sea was officially listed at 22. This was fewer than the 49 Tracy victims killed on the mainland but proportionally far more in terms of the percentage of those caught up in the storm.

When the winds relented, survivors emerged into an almost unrecognizable world. 70 percent of Darwin's homes were uninhabitable, and nearly every structure sustained some damage. The fragments and the contents of damaged homes lay strewn across the landscape to the point that one survivor, Rick Conlon, described Darwin as resembling "a 250-square mile rubbish dump." Most food had been destroyed during Tracy or rotted soon after in refrigerators left without power, as the electrical grid was a casualty of the storm. Survivors described how some food had actually been driven into solid wood beams by storm gales or else imbedded with windblown glass. Water lines had been cut, and some of the standing water was contaminated with saltwater blown overland by the storm; indeed, it would take several months before enough rain fell to restore fertility to Darwin's salted soil. Since all songbirds had been blown away by the storm along with nearly all the leaves of the plants and trees, there were no sounds to drown out the cries of the 1000-odd people injured by the storm. When the injured were brought to the hospital, they encountered a terrifying sight: several centimeters of standing rainwater, tinted with the blood of earlier arriving victims, covered the floors of the hospital and gave the appearance that hospital employees were working ankle-deep in blood.

Obviously, the post-storm situation in Darwin was dire, but Australians soon pitched in at the local, regional, and national levels to provide effective relief. First on the ball was Darwin's own hippie community, who in the words of cyclone survivor William Walsh, were "accustomed to a fairly high level of confusion and uncertainty [and] didn't seem too disturbed by the fact that everything was different." As a result, some of Darwin's hippies spearheaded the establishment of emergency kitchens throughout the city to feed the survivors. Those with access to a bulldozer immediately set about clearing Darwin's rubble-strewn streets. Furthermore, Tracy survivors who happened to live in undamaged homes took in the newly homeless. On a more regional level, the nearby city of Alice Springs raised $100,000 Australian dollars for disaster relief within 24 hours of the storm, and a number of nearby communities, including Alice Springs, Katherine, and Tennant Creek, set up reception centers to receive approximately

Courtesy the National Archives of Australia

Post-Tracy wreckage in Darwin.

9,000 Darwin residents who had bundled into cars and driven out of the ruins of their city. If anything, the other municipalities of Australia provided too much assistance; Gary McKay reports one incident when 14 doctors were made available to an incoming batch of Tracy refugees, only 3 of whom were actually injured.

As for Australian state disaster relief, it was slightly longer in coming in part because of the timing: since Tracy struck during the Christmas holiday, both the government and the media were operating with skeleton crews. Once the country had been alerted to the scale of the damage, however, the government sprang quickly into action. The national recovery efforts were facilitated by the establishment of the National Disasters Organization, founded only two months before. Like FEMA, which was established in the U.S. five years later, the NDO was designed to coordinate cooperation between the armed services, government agencies, and civilians. With the assistance of the NDO, massive resources were quickly assigned to the task of recovery. Indeed, the post–Tracy recovery efforts stand out as one of the success stories in the history of modern national disaster response.

One of the critical problems facing the Tracy recovery effort was headquartering the relief operation; since Darwin was by far the largest city in Northern Australia, and since Darwin had effectively ceased to exist, from where would the relief operations be directed? The solution to this problem was to send the Australian navy as first responders, since each ship was effectively an individual city with its own power plant, food stores, medical facilities, and communications equipment. The navy men were quickly joined by Australian Federal Police, Northern Territory Police, and police units on loan from other cities. Together, these servicemen distributed food and water, assisted in clearing the roads, cracked down on post–Tracy looting, and got started with the grim task of searching ruined houses for bodies. They also worked quickly to get the airport back in operation, recognizing that only airplanes could provide the fast, bulk relief that Darwin desperately needed.

Once the air link was restored, the civil authorities made the decision to evacuate the bulk of Darwin's population out of the disaster zone. After all, why provide rudimentary food, shelter, and medical services in the ruins of Darwin when better services could be provided more quickly and cheaply elsewhere in Australia? To this end, the government organized a series of airlift flights out of Darwin. These flights were intended mainly for women and children, though there are reports that some of Darwin's men dressed in drag in an attempt to get aboard. In all, a total of 20,000 people were evacuated from Darwin by air in only 6 days, a remarkable achievement. Airlifted refugees were not allowed to carry much in the way of baggage, but they were allowed to take small pets with them, a sensible and humane step given the magnitude of the trauma that Tracy had inflicted on Darwin's citizens.

National authorities also offered comprehensive disaster mitigation services for those who remained. To prevent malaria-carrying mosquitoes from gaining a toehold in the swampy conditions created by Tracy's passage authorities employed crop-dusting aircraft and fogging machines to spread insecticide throughout Darwin. Federal authorities also built public latrines to mitigate the problem of cholera, a disease carried by human waste. In the meantime the NDO rounded up volunteers to carry out the unpleasant but unnecessary tasks needed to get the city back up and running, including breaking into abandoned houses and removing rotting food, which was seen as a disease risk. In the longer term, city and federal authorities designed more stringent (and more expensive) building codes to guide the reconstruction of the city, but also provided various subsidies and financial incentives to lure back Darwin's scattered population. Thanks to the hard labor of the national authorities and the men left behind in Darwin, women and children began to return to the city by early 1975, and the city returned to its pre–Tracy population level by 1978.

Although Cyclone Tracy was undoubtedly Australia's worst natural disaster it has not materially affected the growth of the city of Darwin, which remains Northern Australia's largest urban center. Indeed, Darwin today is perhaps even wealthier than ever before, since the income it receives from the air base and uranium industries has now been supplemented by the discovery of oil and gas reserves in the Timor Sea, the development of a strong tourism industry, and the recent construction of a railway link to the rest of Australia. As a result, Darwin now boasts over 100,000 residents and is one of the fastest growing cities in Australia. Nonetheless, some fear that Darwin's new boom has blinded the city to the persistent threat of tropical cyclones. According to architect Peter Dermoudy, who Bill Bunbury interviewed in 1994, Darwin has become a better-built city, but it still lacks comprehensive emergency plans to deal with the next big blow. Nonetheless, as the Cyclone Tracy experience demonstrates, developed nations which make speedy and effective use of their considerable resources can provide effective relief and recovery services even in the case of a catastrophic cyclone disaster.

Study Questions

1. Clearly, Cyclone Tracy had a very different impact than the Great Bhola Cyclone of just 4 years previous. Do you believe that the differences between the two storms is best explained by different geographies, different characteristics of the storms themselves, or else socioeconomic differences between the two effected societies? Explain.

2. Why do you think that Cyclone Tracy spawned no secondary disasters (famine, disease, etc.) unlike other historical tropical cyclones? Explain.

Sources/Suggested Readings

Bunbury, Bill. *Cyclone Tracy: Picking Up the Pieces*. South Freemantle, Australia: Freemantle Arts Press Centre, 1994.
Durisch, Peter, Robert Howarth, and Kenneth Stevens. *Cyclone! Christmas in Darwin 1974*. Sydney, Australia: Sydney Morning Herald, 1975.
Longshore, David. *Encyclopedia of Hurricanes, Typhoons, and Cyclones*. New York: Checkmark, 2000.
Lourensz, R. S. *Tropical Cyclones in the Australian Region July 1909 to June 1980*. Canberra, Australia: Australian Government Publishing Service, 1981.
McKay, Gary. *Tracy: The Storm That Wiped Out Darwin on Christmas Day 1974*. Crows Nest, Australia: Allen and Unwin, 2001.
Terry, James P. *Tropical Cyclones: Climatology and Impacts in the South Pacific*. New York: Springer, 2007.

5.3: Hurricane Andrew, 1992

In 1992 four decades of relatively mild hurricane seasons in the North Atlantic came to an abrupt end. And what an end it was: Hurricane Andrew, which struck South Florida on August 24th, was a category 5 hurricane and the third most powerful storm to strike the United States in recorded history. Thanks to a fortuitous combination of geography and luck Andrew's storm surge inflicted only limited damage on the coast, helping to ensure that the storm itself would produce few casualties. On the other hand, Andrew surprised even hurricane experts by wrecking unprecedented wind damage through South Florida. The misery inflicted by the storm was exacerbated by a federal government response which was so ineffectual that observers believe it may have impacted George H. W. Bush's 1992 bid for reelection. Local officials made a poor showing as well, despite the fact that previous hurricanes in the Miami area should have alerted governments to the threat they faced from cyclonic weather. The consequence of this deadly combination of natural disaster and human incompetence was a mass human migration that would not be surpassed within the United States until 2004, when Hurricane Katrina set and even worse U.S. record for hurricane destruction and sheer human misery.

Hurricane Andrew was far from the first tropical cyclone to wreck havoc in the Miami area. Indeed, the Great Miami Hurricane of 1926, which researchers believe was a category 4 cyclone, inflicted a more direct hit on the city by Biscayne Bay. A storm surge that topped 4 meters in height washed over Miami Beach and raged up the Miami River, sinking all but one vessel in the process. About 200 people died in the greater Miami area, primarily due to floods and structural collapses. At least 150 people — possibly many more — died in the town of Moore Haven on nearby Lake Okeechobee, where water stacked up by the hurricane on the lake's southern bank overtopped the levees that protected the town from flooding.

To a certain degree the high death toll in the 1926 storm reflected the inexperience of Miami's populace, which consisted mainly of recent northern transplants to the tropics with little knowledge of, and no experience with, the full power of an Atlantic Hurricane. As the 1926 storm proved, hurricane inexperience could be deadly. A high proportion of the fatalities in 1926 occurred as a result of the passage of the hurricane's eye; many people left their homes during this deceptive calm, only to be exposed to the resurging winds of the hurricane's rear eye wall.

However, an even larger share of the blame for the 1926 death toll belongs to Miami's real estate industry. Shortly before the 1926 storm Miami had been the epicenter of an unprecedented real estate boom during which hastily built, poorly reinforced structures were erected on coastal flats or even on artificial islands, such as the Venetian Islands, constructed with marine sediment in the middle of Bay Biscayne. One of the ironies of the 1926 storm was that newly-built houses constructed of modern materials fared worse during the hurricane than the driftwood shacks of the original Miami pioneers, who had learned from hard experience how to design homes to withstand the ravages of the Atlantic hurricane.

The correlation between shoddy building practices and the death toll of the 1926 storm did not go unnoticed by contemporaries. Indeed, Stella Crossley, who wrote a damning article for *The Nation* magazine several weeks after storm, blamed Florida realtors for the bulk of the storm mortality. "Florida is on the edge of the tropics," she informed readers, "and hurricanes are to be reckoned with in the tropics. The best man can do there is to admit calmly to himself and others that such things are always likely to happen and to take such precautions as are possible. But in Florida," Crossley charged, "the realtor's cupidity ... forbade this. So a land where human habitations should be constructed for strength they are generally constructed flimsily for huge profits." The consequence, she concluded, was written unmistakably in "Death's black letters over Florida today." Whoever was to blame, the hurricane propelled Miami into a profound economic downturn, which grew still worse during the Great Depression of 1929, and which only relented in the aftermath of the Second World War.

Shamed by the national publicity of their hurricane misfortune and hoping to recover the boom-time prosperity Miami had enjoyed in the early 1920s, Florida lawmakers passed a slate of new building construction standards designed to ensure that Miami fared better in the next major hurricane. As Andrew was to prove, however, these building codes were not up to the task. The codes were designed to protect houses from winds of up to 120 miles per hour (about 190 km/hr) but Andrew's gales were far stronger, with gusts of 320 km/hr or higher near the eye wall. Miami's codes allowed practices such as attaching shingles with staples — a particularly dubious practice in a hurricane-prone zone — and did not mandate storm shutters, which provide fairly good protection against hurricane winds. In addition, those inadequate regulations that did exist did not apply to mobile homes, which as we shall see were particularly vulnerable to Andrew's raging winds.

What is more, in the period immediately before 1992, a new real estate boom had swept through southern Florida. Unlike the boom of the 1920s, which functioned essentially as a pyramid scheme centered around the purchase and resale of real estate, the new boom that began in the mid–1970s was based largely on narcotics: Thanks to the Miami area's close proximity to Latin America and innumerable small coves and inlets, Miami became the importation site of an estimated 70 percent of the nation's cocaine and heroin supply. Local drug kingpins and their bankers tried to launder their money by investing heavily in real estate, helping to fuel a boom. The mid–1970s real estate boom was also driven by financial instability in Latin Amer-

COURTESY NOAA/NATIONAL CLIMATIC DATA CENTER

Satellite photograph of Andrew shortly before landfall.

ica. To safeguard their assets Latin American elites invested their money in the dependable American real estate market, and since Miami was becoming increasingly Hispanic in composition by the mid–1970s Miami received a disproportional amount of these investment dollars.

Although the reasons for the post–1970s boom were quite different from the Miami boom of the 1920s, the result was the same: a substantial reduction in building standards. The pre–Andrew boom brought a bevy of outside building contractors to South Florida, some of whom were not well informed on local building standards let alone the realities of constructing homes in a hurricane zone. What is more, in the heady days of the new real estate boom profit-minded builders frequently cut corners in their haste to put houses on the market, and county building inspectors were unable to keep up with the volume of houses that required their attention. Not surprisingly, then, many of Miami's homes were in no shape to withstand Andrew's category 5 winds.

Furthermore, as with Miami boom of the early 1920s, the pre–Andrew boom brought many northern transplants to South Florida and the relative hurricane inexperience of these newcomers further exacerbated the damage inflicted by the hurricane. Miamians had ample warming about Andrew's approach days in advance; indeed forecasts by the U.S. Weather Bureau in the days before Andrew's landfall were exceptionally accurate despite the fact that Andrew was a fast-moving storm. Nonetheless, even with significant forewarning many Miami-area people simply did not know what to do. Some people taped up their windows—a useless precaution—rather than nailing plywood over their doors and windows, a measure that does mitigate storm damage. Other people left lawn furniture or other such items in their yards, objects that would become airborne battering rams when Andrew arrived. Even many relatively well-informed Miami residents neglected to properly brace their garage doors, which was doubly unfortunate. Not only were unsecured doors likely to detach from the garage and become dangerous flying projectiles, but a garage without its door provided a possible means for hurricane winds to infiltrate the house, possibly resulting in the loss of the roof or other major structural damage.

Local demographics also played a crucial role in increasing South Florida's vulnerability to Andrew. The Miami area hosts a sizable population of "snowbirds," retirees who wintered in Florida and summered in the northern states. Since Andrew struck on August 24th, fairly early in the hurricane season, most snowbirds had not yet returned from their summer sojourn in the cooler northern states. As a result their empty houses were often poorly prepared for the storm. Furthermore, snowbird houses could be a threat to the entire neighborhood, since even the houses of even well-prepared Miami residents could be damaged by debris blown off an unprepared snowbird dwelling. An even greater proportion of the Miami area population con-

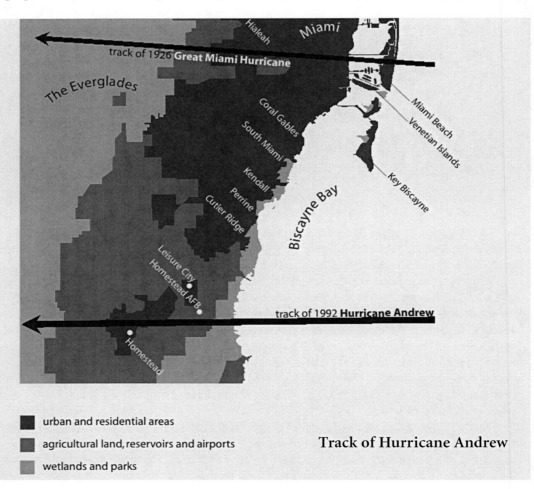

urban and residential areas

agricultural land, reservoirs and airports

wetlands and parks

Track of Hurricane Andrew

sists of an even more vulnerable group: immigrants from Latin America. By 1992 Miami had become the unofficial capital city of the Caribbean basin, hosting substantial populations of Cubans, Haitians, Nicaraguans, Colombians, Dominicans, and Mexicans. With the exception of the earliest Cuban immigrants, who were largely upper-class exiles from Castro's communist revolution, most of these immigrants were economic migrants who had come to the United States to escape the crushing poverty of their homelands. Unfortunately, the bulk of these immigrants remained mired in poverty on the eve of Andrew's arrival. As a result a disproportionate number of Haitians and Hispanics rode out Andrew's winds in substandard quality, uninsured homes.

Clearly, lack of hurricane experience, poor preparedness, and material deprivation played a strong contributing role in the Andrew disaster. Nonetheless, no amount of preparation could have fully mitigated the risk posed by a storm as powerful as Andrew. Indeed, local atmospheric and geographic forces combined to make Andrew a true meteorological monster. Andrew approached Florida following an almost perfectly strait westward course as it approached Miami, staying within a few degrees of 25 degrees north latitude. In most cases, storms that reach this latitude are weakened by wind sheer, a phenomenon in which winds close to the earth's surface flow in a somewhat different direction than upper-level winds. As Andrew approached Florida, however, both upper and lower-level winds at 25 degrees north were blowing the same direction. With nothing to hinder its formation, Andrew rapidly intensified as it passed over the warm waters off the east coast of the Bahamas, growing from a mere tropical storm into a category 5 hurricane in the process. Andrew did weaken somewhat as it passed over the Bahamas themselves but then rapidly strengthened once again as it passed over the warm waters of the Gulf Stream off the east Florida coast. What is more, Andrew touched down at the Everglades, one of the largest marshlands in the world. Since the warm waters of the marsh sustained the convection cell within the eye Andrew did not suffer rapid diminution of strength, which is the normal fate of hurricanes that pass over land.

The impact of this ferocious storm would have been even worse if South Florida hadn't benefited from a few strokes of luck. Andrew was a relatively fast moving storm, and although this worsened the ferocity of the wind in the right front quadrant of the hurricane, it also limited the amount of time during which South Florida was buffeted by hurricane-force winds. Andrew was also an unusually compact storm for its strength, with hurricane winds extending out only about 55 kilometers away from its center. What is more, Andrew was a remarkably dry hurricane and thus caused little flooding outside of its storm surge. Finally, and most importantly, Dade County benefited from a last-second wobble in the storm track that deflected Andrew away from the center of Miami and towards the southern suburbs. As a result, the Miami area received only a glancing blow from Andrew's category 5 winds. Furthermore, Andrew's eye touched ground on a protected national park shoreline which in turn backed up to a sparsely populated area and the Homestead Air Force Base, which was operating at only partial capacity due to the draw-down of the U. S. Air Force since the end of the Cold War in 1990. Thus relatively few people were affected by Andrew's 5-meter peak storm surge, and the more densely populated Miami and Miami Beach experienced storm surges of only about 2.5 meters and 2 meters respectively. Closer to the point of impact, Andrew's storm surge was prevented from penetrating far into Dade County by Cutler Ridge, the remnant of an ancient coral reef rising 7 meters in places. Had Andrew drifted just twenty or so miles to the north, researchers estimate, the damage and death toll would likely have been two or three times higher.

The fact that Andrew could have been worse, however, should not detract us from how bad it actually was. Unlike most cyclonic storms Andrew inflicted the bulk of its damage not

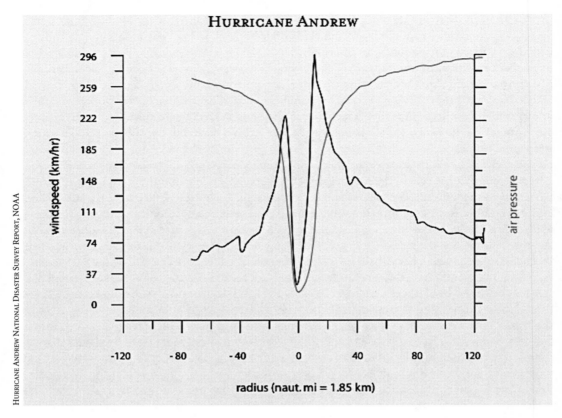

HURRICANE ANDREW NATIONAL DISASTER SURVEY REPORT, NOAA

Graph of Andrew's wind speeds and air pressure, based on measurements taken by reconnaissance aircraft shortly before landfall. Note how sharply Andrew's barometric pressure drops near the storm's center; this helps to explain the power of Andrew's winds. Note also that wind speeds were highest to the right of Andrew's eye, as is typical of a northern hemisphere cyclonic storm.

through storm surge and flooding, but rather through its winds. Interestingly, until 2004 Andrew was thought to be a category 4 hurricane, largely because recorded sustained wind speeds fell below the 250 km/hr threshold. In retrospect, the National Hurricane Center concluded that Andrew's winds probably did exceed this threshold, but were not properly recorded, in part because the very same winds that were being measured destroyed the measuring equipment before Andrew's maximum strength could be established. Although Andrew's upgrade from a strong cat-4 storm to a weak cat-5 storm may seem like a matter of only academic interest, remember that the destructive power of winds rises exponentially, not linearly, with increases in wind speed. Thus, Andrew's upgrade helps to explain the awesome destructive power of its eye wall winds.

As for those actually caught within the eye wall, they had no doubts that Andrew was a storm of extraordinary ferocity. Eyewitness accounts collected by Eugene and Asterie Provenzo offer vivid testament to Andrew's muscular fury. Survivors described how the night grew inky dark as Andrew passed overhead, sporadically illuminated only by lightning bolts and flashes of light from exploding electrical transformers. Those trapped in their homes listened while their windows exploded and their homes were systematically torn apart by the winds. The sound was "much worse than a freight train, between the howling and whistling of the wind ... it was

COURTESY BOB EPSTEIN AND FEMA

Andrew inflicted extensive wind damage on Southern Florida.

an incredible, indescribable noise." Making matters worse, Andrew blew down the electrical power grid within the first few hours of its landfall, and in the absence of air conditioning the survivors remember how the terror of Andrew was augmented by the suffocating August heat, which particularly oppressed those who tried to seal themselves within cramped closets or bathrooms inside their besieged houses. Those few to venture outside during the storm were stunned by what they saw. Michael Tang, a police officer patrolling the streets of lower Dade Country, remembered "trees coming down and you could see cables slapping together and falling," all lit by the weird green light of exploding transformers. Mr. Tang finally gave up his patrol and sought shelter when the winds began to lift his car off the street.

When the winds subsided and survivors emerged from their hiding places they encountered further testimonies to Andrew's awful power. Indeed, South Dade residents described the scene that greeted them as "like a surrealistic movie ... the whole thing was *not real.*" Others likened the scene to a "battlefield" or a "holocaust." The air was extraordinarily clear, as the hurricane had blown away all the dust, but this served only to bring Andrew's destruction into more vivid focus. It was unnaturally quiet, too, since South Florida's birds had been blown away by the storm. Entire neighborhoods were "just flat ... it was just like someone had dropped a bomb in our vicinity." In some hard-hit areas, Andrew had descended like a whirling scythe, toppling everything above eye level. Formerly painted walls had been stripped to bare wood by scouring wind-blown sand. Every yard was strewn with a bizarre mixture of shredded building materials, trash, and household knick-knacks from shattered homes. Wind-blown debris was later found a mile from where it had originated, if it was found at all. Boats were stacked upon each other at quays "like dominoes," wrecked planes littered airports, and mangled cars choked parking lots. Even heavy trucks were lifted up or toppled by Andrew's winds. Most

Damage to a mobile home community near Florida City.

astounding of all, a number of palm trees that somehow managed to survive the storm were found impaled by wind-blown planks and pieces of plywood. Simply put, in the area encompassed by Andrew's eye wall winds the scene was one of almost unimaginable devastation.

Needless to say, Andrew's winds caused extensive damage to residential structures in South Florida. Andrew destroyed or rendered uninhabitable nearly as many as 80,000 private homes, and caused significant damage to over 50,000 more. The entire town of Homestead, a blue-collar community of 26,000 in South Dade, was "razed beyond recognition." Interestingly, as with the 1926 storm, older houses tended to withstand the hurricane better than newly-built homes, in this case because older homes tended to be modest structures of concrete and masonry, while newer houses were more grandiose edifices of timber and pressed wood. As for mobile homes, which under the best of conditions can withstand sustained winds of only up to about 128 km/h, they suffered catastrophic losses during Andrew. An astounding 97 percent of Dade County's mobile homes essentially disintegrated during Andrew, transformed by the storm into deadly clouds of shrapnel. Not surprisingly, mobile home communities accounted for a disproportional number of Andrew's deaths.

Nor did Andrew limit its fury to private dwellings. An estimated 8,000 businesses were damaged or completely wrecked by the storm. Losses to South Florida's truck farming industry, still sizable despite Miami's advancing urban sprawl, amounted to approximately $1.5 billion. Homestead Air Force base was "virtually destroyed" by Andrew, its runways strewn with debris from mangled hangers and wrecked airplanes. What is more, old ships that had been laden down with concrete blocks and deliberately sunk offshore to form artificial reefs were shifted by Andrew, and some were even washed onto dry land. The overall area damaged by Andrew in South Florida was larger than the city of Chicago.

Because the destruction produced by Andrew was so total, especially in what authorities called "damage streaks," there was speculation after the storm that Andrew might have spawned tornadoes as it raged across Florida. Such a phenomenon is by no means unknown with hurricanes, and indeed Andrew would spin off tornadoes when it eventually crashed into Louisiana. Nonetheless, there were no reports of tornadoes as Andrew passed over Dade County. What meteorologists now suspect is that Andrew created "miniswirls" or "micro bursts," which occur when a small wind vortex forms within the hurricane itself. In the portion of the vortex moving in the same direction as the cyclone's dominant wind, the net force of the winds can be substantially increased, to the point that meteorologists believe that some of Andrew's winds may have reached an astounding 340 km/hr. Even outside of such intense local zones of destruction, however, Andrew's impact was severe. In all Andrew caused an estimated $30 billion in damages, mostly in South Florida. Andrew also left South Dade county buried under 35 million tons of debris, which is more trash than the Miami area produces in 30 normal years. As always in a major disaster the damage was exacerbated by post-storm looters, who began scrounging from ruined homes and businesses as soon as the winds began to relent.

The human toll inflicted by Andrew was no less staggering. True, relatively few people died directly because of Andrew: Only 15 deaths have been directly ascribed to Andrew's winds and floods, while another 28 people perished indirectly from the storm as a result of accidental electrocution, heat stroke, and the like. The number of people rendered homeless by the storm, however, was vastly higher — approximately a quarter of a million people in Dade County lost their homes. Only 80,000 could be accommodated by local hurricane shelters, leaving about 175,000 without housing. Eventually, 100,000 former Dade residents left the county for good, the largest mass migration triggered by a natural disaster since the American Dust Bowl. In recent times, only Hurricane Katrina would force a larger human exodus in the United States.

As always in natural disasters, the damage inflicted by Andrew was by no means equally apportioned between different socioeconomic groups. According to Andrew researchers W. G. Peacock and C. Girard, blacks and Hispanics were far less likely than the general population to have insurance on their homes: 8.7 percent of blacks and 9.2 percent of non–Cuban Hispanics had no insurance coverage, compared to only 4.1 percent of Cubans and 2.7 percent of whites. The same authors also discovered that blacks and non–Cuban Hispanics generally received less money in settlement from their insurers: 38.1 percent of blacks and 41.3 percent of non–Cuban Hispanics report receiving less from their insurers than their properties were worth, compared to only 24.7 percent for Cubans and 16.1 percent for whites. To a certain degree this disparity was the result of market forces in the insurance world. Non-white groups tended to poorer than whites, and thus more likely to seek the services of cut-rate insurance providers which did not have the cash reserves for an event of Andrew's magnitude. In this case, however, market forces may have been unfairly stacked against Miami's poor, especially the black population. The "top three" insurance providers, Peacock and Girard claim, practiced a form of indirect racial segregation by systematically refusing to issue policies to homeowners living in "black" communities, forcing them to turn instead to second-tier insurance providers with shallower pockets. What is more, language barriers between Hispanic disaster victims and insurance adjusters, who rarely knew other languages than English, also prevented immigrant groups from getting an equal share of insurance settlements.

Women were disproportionally impacted by Andrew as well. In most American families, particularly immigrant families, women take the lead in domestic affairs such as provisioning the home and supervising the children. Despite this fact most hurricane relief organizations followed a "head of household" model when apportioning relief funds, and the "head of household" was generally assumed to be male. According to Andrew researchers Betty Hearn Morrow and Elaine Enarson, the unfortunate result of this policy was that some male recipients squandered the government money on cars, jewelry, stereos, or other personal items which did little to benefit the women and children of the family. Worse yet, some men cashed the government relief checks and then left the state, abandoning part or all of their families in the process. Poor immigrant women were also disproportionally targeted by unscrupulous landlords and contractors who took advantage of the post–Andrew misery to squeeze money out of desperate storm survivors. Furthermore, women were more likely to lose their jobs as a result of Andrew, since more women than men in the Miami area worked for small-scale, local businesses, which were more likely to fail in Andrew's aftermath. At the same time, women were less likely to benefit from the economic opportunities that opened up during the recovery effort, for instance construction work. Last, but certainly not least, women were disproportionally affected by the crime wave that washed over the Miami in the wake of Andrew.

One form of crime that soared after Andrew was domestic violence, and this in turn was connected with another form of damage that Andrew inflicted upon South Florida: mental disorder and distress. According to a joint publication by members of the federal Centers for Disease Control and Prevention and the Florida Department of Health and Rehabilitative Services, Hurricane Andrew's psychological effects were as profound as its physical effects, especially in lower Dade country where Andrew exerted its greatest impact. In the community of Cutler Ridge for instance, 35 percent of all households reported having at least one member suffering from stress and anxiety in late 1992, while nearly 55 percent reported someone suffering from depression and anxiety. By way of contrast, the Dade county district of Hialeah, which was far less affected by both the storm surge and winds, reported figures of only 15 percent for anxiety and depression and less than 10 percent for depression and anxiety. Even more disturbingly, Andrew's impact on the mental health of Dade Country proved to be relatively long-lasting. Thirteen months after the hurricane, nearly 20 percent of respondents still reported stress or anxiety in Cutler Ridge, and fully 35 percent still reported suffering from anxiety or depression. What is more, given the fact that the mentally distressed were probably more likely to leave lower Dade County after the hurricane, it is probable that this limited improvement was produced as much by a change of address as by a change of mind.

Lingering mental health problems hindered the post–Andrew recovery in a number of ways. Depressed or anxious adults were less likely to find, or keep, a job in the aftermath of Andrew. Traumatized children, who feared that every minor cloudburst heralded the return of "the monster," put tremendous strain on their already stressed parents. As a result of these pressures families in post–Andrew Dade County suffered disproportionally from domestic violence, substance abuse, divorce, and/or suicide. As always the poor suffered the most, since they were least likely to have insurance to cover the treatment of mental disease. Recognizing the problem, FEMA made an attempt to address the situation by sending mental health outreach teams to the effected areas. However, the same study discussed above concluded that FEMA's door-to-door mental health outreach effort was generally a failure, offering aid to as few as 25 percent of all needy respondents in lower Dade County.

Indeed, FEMA's inability to help the mental health victims of Dade County was symptomatic of the agency's larger failings following the Andrew disaster. To his credit, President George H. W. Bush made an immediate visit to the Dade County and promised federal help. However, Federal assistance proved slow in coming, in large part because FEMA, the American agency charged with disaster relief assistance, was in no way up to the task.

Indeed, despite his sincere sentiments towards the victims of Andrew, President Bush himself bears some of the responsibility for FEMA's problems. During the presidency of Ronald Reagan (1981— 89) FEMA's core mission of natural disaster preparedness had been compromised as a result of the Reagan administration's almost single-minded purpose to end the Cold War with the defeat of the Soviet Russia. As part of a general policy of rearming an obsolete U.S. military and ratcheting up the diplomatic and economic pressure on the USSR, FEMA's resources were redirected from natural disaster recovery to Civil Defense. Natural hazards such as hurricanes and earthquakes were marginalized within the agency, which retooled itself to fight domestic insurgency, terrorism, or strategic nuclear attack. As Reagan's vice president (and a former Director of Central Intelligence), George H. W. Bush should have been well aware that the FEMA he inherited as president had become, in the words of Christopher Cooper and Robert Block, "a two-headed" agency: A group of well funded "doomsday workers" obsessed about possible human disasters, and the natural hazards wing, a "withered appendage" with only about one-twelfth the financial resources of the "security cult" that essentially ran the agency. Despite the generally peaceful world situation that occurred during his presidency, George H. W. Bush did not return the priority of FEMA to that of managing recovery operations from natural disasters.

Not surprisingly, the lopsided monster that FEMA had become was in no shape to deal with a natural disaster on Hurricane Andrew's scale. In the days after Andrew news reporters televised vivid scenes of desolation and suffering in Dade County. On national television survivors scoured the ruins for food and water with no federal agents in sight. Local officials pleading for resources received mostly promises, requests for paperwork, and impenetrable red tape. On the third day after Andrew, Dade County emergency director Kate Hale made an emotional TV appeal, declaring that "enough is enough," and demanding to know, "where the hell is the cavalry on this one? For God's sake, where are they?" An embarrassed President Bush responded by essentially bypassing FEMA entirely and ordering the Army and Navy to begin immediate relief efforts in Dade county. Eventually 20,000 American troops were dispatched to the scene, where they distributed food and water and sent up vast tent cities for the homeless. However, the political damage had been done. President Bush, who was up for re-election in the fall after Andrew, was unable to emerge from the shadow that Andrew and a faltering economy inflicted on his reputation.

As for FEMA, the Andrew debacle convinced many frustrated congressmen argued that it ought to be abolished altogether. FEMA survived, however, in large part thanks to incoming president Clinton, who not only increased its funding, but hired an experienced disaster expert, James Lee Witt, to head the agency. Witt immediately began dismantling the "doomsday" wing of FEMA even to the point of remodeling "Mount Weather," a nuclear shelter established by the previous FEMA directors, into a state of the art disaster response training facility. Perhaps more importantly, understanding that preplanning and rapid response were the keys to mitigating natural disasters, Witt channeled FEMA money into natural disaster preparedness and prevention efforts. The result was an agency that even Clinton's detractors praised for its swift and efficient response to major crises. Unfortunately, as we shall see in section 6.3, the second President Bush would allow FEMA to revert to Cold War habits after he became president in 2000, leading to disastrous consequences when Hurricane Katrina struck the New Orleans area in 2004.

In the meantime the Miami area remains profoundly vulnerable to future hurricanes on the scale of Andrew. Florida remains today what it has always been: a low spit of land wedged between the Gulf of Mexico and the Gulf Stream, both of which are warm enough to nurture very powerful hurricanes. What is more, Florida's population has rebounded dramatically since Andrew. By 2008, Florida's population stood at 18 million, an increase of nearly four million in just ten years. About two-fifths of these inhabitants live in coastal areas vulnerable to storm surge. What is more, virtually all residents in low-lying Florida are vulnerable to winds on

Andrew's scale. Florida's current road system is inadequate to a widespread evacuation, as is Florida's hurricane shelter system. Finally, although Florida once again upgraded its building codes in the wake of Andrew, building codes are only as strong as community enforcement, which almost always relaxes after a dozen years or so of mild hurricane seasons. Thus, it is all but inevitable that disasters even worse than Andrew will strike an increasingly crowded Florida as we move deeper into the age of global warming.

Study Questions

1. Based on the information presented in this section, to what degree was the devastation caused by Hurricane Andrew inevitable?

2. Natural disasters are sometimes argued to be merely the magnification of existing inequalities and problems following a triggering event. To what degree does the Andrew disaster support this view?

3. Overall, given the dangers presented by Florida's geographical location, what do you think the federal government's role should be before, during, and after Florida hurricane disasters? Does the federal government have a responsibility to spend resources to protect people who live in a vulnerable region, or rather ought the Federal government discourage people from living in such dangerous areas? Defend your answer.

Sources/Suggested Readings

Barnes, Jay. *Florida's Hurricane History.* Chapel Hill: University of North Carolina Press, 1998.

Cooper, Christopher, and Robert Block. *Disaster: Hurricane Katrina and the Failure of Homeland Security.* New York: Henry Holt and Company, 2006.

Crossley, Stella. "Real Estate vs. Human Lives in Florida," *The Nation,* Oct. 13 (1926), pp. 341–342.

Gore, Rick. "Andrew Aftermath." *National Geographic,* Vol. 183, No. 4 (April 1993), pp. 1–37.

Gross, Eric. "Somebody Got Drowned, Lord: Florida and the Great Okeechobee Hurricane Disaster of 1926." Ph.D. Thesis, Florida State University, 1995.

Hopkins, Richard. "Long-Term Effects of Hurricane Andrew: Revisiting Mental Health Indicators. *Diasters,* Vol. 19, No. 3 (Sept. 1995), pp. 235–245.

"Hurricane Andrew: South Florida and Louisiana, August 23–26, 1992." National Disaster Survey Report, U.S. Department of Commerce, National Oceanic and Atmospheric Administration, National Weather Service, Silver Spring, Maryland, November 1993. Available online at http://www.nws.noaa.gov/om/assessments/dfs/andrew.pdf

McDonnell, Sharon, Richard P. Troiano, Nancy Barker, Eric Noji, W. Gary Hlady, and Richard Hopkins. "Long-Term Effects of Hurricane Andrew: Revisiting Mental Health Indicators. *Diasters,* Vol. 19, No. 3 (Sept. 1995), pp. 235–245.

Monastersky, R. "Unusual Weather Spurred Andrew's Growth." *Science News,* Vol. 142, No. 19 (Sept. 5, 1992), p. 150.

Morrow, Betty Hearn, and Elaine Enarson. "Hurricane Andrew Through Women's Eyes: Issues and Recommendations." *International Journal of Mass Emergencies and Disasters,* Vol. 14, No. 1 (March 1996), pp. 5–22.

Peacock, Walter Gillis, and Chris Girard. "Ethnic and Racial Inequalities in Hurricane Damage and Insurance Settlements." In Peacock, Walter Gillis, Betty Hearn Morrow, and Hugh Gladwin, eds., *Hurricane Andrew: Ethnicity, Gender, and the Sociology of Disasters.* Chapter New York: Routledge, 1997.

Provenzo, Eugene F. Jr., and Asterie Baker Provenzo. *In the Eye of Hurricane Andrew.* Gainesville: University Press of Florida, 2002.

Reardon, Leo Francis. *The Florida Hurricane and Disaster.* Coral Gables, FL: Arva Parks and Company, 1986 edition, originally published 1926.

Reese, Joe Hugh. *Florida's Great Hurricane.* Miami, FL: Lysle E. Fesler, 1926.

Reilly, Benjamin. *Tropical Surge: A History of Ambition and Disaster on the Florida Shore.* Sarasota, FL: Pineapple Press, 2005.

Smith, Stanley K., and Christopher McCarty. "Demographic Effects of Natural Disasters: A Case Study of Hurricane Andrew." *Demography,* Vol. 33, No. 2 (May, 1996), pp. 265–275.

Solecki, William D. "Environmental Hazards and Interest Group Coalitions: Metropolitan Miami after Hurricane Andrew." In James K. Mitchell, ed., *Crucibles of Hazard: Mega-Cities and Disasters in Transition.* New York: United Nations University Press, 1999.

Steinberg, Ted. *Acts of God: The Unnatural History of Natural Disaster in America.* New York: Oxford University Press, 2000.

CHAPTER 6

Floods and Tsunamis

Science and History

Water is crucial to life on our planet. Unfortunately, water is also a potent agent of destruction. As we already saw in chapter 4 and will see in greater detail in chapter 7, various forms of climate change can lead to reductions in the water supply, leading to short-term famine or perhaps even long-term desertification. Excess water can also contribute to catastrophe. As discussed in chapter 2, the interaction between water and volcanic tephra can lead to devastating lahars, and water plays a secondary role in generating pyroclastic flows. Earthquakes can interact with water disasters as well, particularly if they destroy dams or create temporary landslide dams which release floods when they collapse.

At the very time this chapter was written, in fact, Chinese officials were evacuating thousands of people living downstream of a river that had been dammed up by a powerful May 12, 2008, earthquake in Sichuan province. The same quake weakened man-made dams throughout the region, requiring frantic repair efforts by Chinese authorities. What is more, as discussed in chapter 5, cyclonic weather can also lead to watery disasters, most notably through the storm surge associated with powerful cyclones.

Water disasters can take other forms as well. Frozen water, in the form of glaciers, can also exert tremendous forces and fundamentally alter the landscape, though usually on the scale of geological rather than human time. The geologic record also suggests the occasional occurrence of "superfloods," world-changing deluges caused by the emptying of prehistoric seas or lakes. Such superfloods may have had a flow volume matched only by that of ocean currents and might even have influenced the planet's climate.

Pre-historical meteorite and comet strikes have been implicated as causing superfloods as well, in the form of "mega tsunamis." Water disasters can also take somewhat more modest forms, ranging from freshwater flash floods, lake eruptions, lake seiches and river floods to tsunamis and other forms of oceanic coastal flooding. What is more, some floods are partially or completely man-made, triggered by the catastrophic failure of human alterations to the natural landscape.

Obviously, the number of disasters with a flooding component is too vast to be covered in detail in a single chapter. Rather than try to treat each of these various forms of water-related disasters individually, this chapter will break from the pattern followed by other introductory chapters and confine itself to two particularly damaging forms of flooding, river floods and tsunamis.

The Science of Water

Not all floods consist of water, or at least water alone. In 1919, the city of Boston, Massachusetts, was the site of a bizarre molasses flood after a gigantic storage tank ruptured, releasing a sticky wave of semi-refined sugar that killed 21 residents of Boston's North End. What is more, nearly all floods contain some amount of debris or suspended sediment. However, since the common element of both floods and tsunamis is water, we should first look into the scientific properties that make water so vital to yet so dangerous to life on earth.

Perhaps the most important property of water, as far as natural disasters go, is its weight. Each liter of water weighs exactly one kilogram, which is no coincidence — the weight of a kilogram is defined as the mass of one liter of water. A similar volume of air, by way of contrast, weighs only about .0013 kilograms at sea level pressure and at 0 degrees Celsius. Nonetheless, despite the fact that air is a featherweight substance, air moving at velocity is capable of exerting tremendous force. As we saw in sections 5.2 and 5.3, cyclone winds are capable of systematically dismantling houses and driving heavy wooden boards through trees and brick walls. Imagine, then, the potential destructive power of water, a substance that is 750 times heavier. The Amazon River, for example, has an average discharge of 119 million kilograms of mass every second, an astounding cumulative force. Not surprisingly, given the vast energy potential of the Amazon and other Brazilian rivers, Brazil obtains approximately 80 percent of its energy from hydroelectric dams. Not all countries are so richly supplied with water as Brazil, but nonetheless, 19 percent of the world's energy is supplied by harnessing the power of water — or more correctly, the power of gravity, which constantly pulls water downhill along the path of least resistance. However, the same kinetic energy that humans tap for power can also wreck destruction during disastrous flooding.

The weight of water brings us to its second property: its ability to carry an enormous volume of solid material as it moves downhill. Although heavy on its own, water can exert even greater force if it carries rocks, trees, and debris within its flow. Indeed, some floods nearly choke themselves with the material they carry. The waters of the deadly Johnstown flood of 1889, the worst disaster in the history of the United States to that time, became so clogged with debris that observers likened it to a "hill of rubbish." Debris imbedded the Johnstown floodwaters not only caused enormous immediate damage, but actually caught fire shortly after the floodwaters themselves receded. Water can also carry much smaller particles in the form of sand, silt, and sediment. Although these sediment particles can be so small as to be individually indistinguishable by the human eye, they can be just as deadly over the long run as large chunks of debris, since sediment deposits can choke up river beds and lead to disastrous alterations in a river's course. As we shall see in section 6.1, millions have perished in China because of the steady build-up of sediment in the extraordinarily silt-rich Yellow River.

Another life giving but potentially deadly property of water is the fact that it readily changes its state at temperatures that occur relatively frequently on the earth's surface. Water freezes at 0 degrees Celsius and turns into vapor at 100 degrees Celsius, which is again no coincidence: The Celsius temperature system was designed by a Swedish scientist who experimented primarily in the properties of water. Water's propensity to change from solid to liquid at 0 degrees Celsius is especially important in temperate climates or at high altitudes. The rapid melt of river ice can lead to "ice floods," while rapid glacial melt can lead to a *jökulhlaup*, also known as a glacial lake outburst flood, where the ice dam holding in a lake of melt water gives way and a torrent of water rushes suddenly downhill. *Jökulhlaup* floods have also occurred when volcanic activity rapidly melts a mountaintop glacier. Such was the case during the Nevado Del Ruiz eruption of 1985, discussed in some detail in chapter 2.

Water's propensity to transform into vapor is even more important to life, and sometimes death, on the planet earth. Although water's formal "boiling point" is 100 Celsius, water in fact begins to turn into vapor at much lower temperatures. At or below 0 degrees Celsius, relatively little liquid water evaporates, but at temperatures of 20 degrees Celsius or above, the amount of evaporation of water into the atmosphere increases dramatically. Indeed, meteorologists consider 25 degrees Celsius to be a crucial temperature threshold after which water evaporates far more readily than at lower temperatures. This phenomenon that helps to explain the sudden onset, and then rapid end, of typical tropical cyclone seasons worldwide. The evaporation rate of water also depends somewhat on altitude and humidity, which is why we feel hotter during humid days than dry days: Our body cools itself by perspiration, and sweat evaporates less efficiently if there is already a lot of water vapor in the atmosphere.

Once in the atmosphere, water vapor tends to rise, since it is lighter than dry air. Wind currents can then carry the water vapor far from its place of origin. Eventually, atmospheric water vapor returns to the earth's surface by a reversal of this process: Colder temperature or higher altitudes causes it to revert to a liquid (dew or rain) or a solid (hail or snow). Taken together, this process is called the water cycle, and it is crucial to the existence of terrestrial life on Earth. At the same time, the water cycle's ability to deposit enormous volumes of water many kilometers from its origin in a short period of time can set the stage for disastrous floods. The water cycle's ability to cause flooding is likely to increase in the future as global warming increases average world temperatures farther towards the all-important tipping point of 25 degree Celsius.

One final property of water that must be considered is the fact that water is a fluid, and thus bodies of water readily deform when impacted by physical shocks. As a result, water is a fairly efficient transmitter of kinetic energy. When water is displaced by a powerful physical force, such as the blast of a volcanic pyroclastic flow or the void created by a submarine landslide, the displaced water is quickly snapped back into place by gravity but in the process ripples are created that transmit the force of the original impact far from its source of origin. The same process occurs during earthquakes, especially along subduction faults, which can either push up or pull down huge columns of ocean water. Once again, gravity acts immediately to restore equilibrium to the ocean surface, but in the process the vertical deformation caused by the earthquake spreads out horizontally, creating tsunami waves.

River Flooding

With the possible exception of volcanoes, river valleys are perhaps the most geologically active parts of our planet. Since river systems collect rainwater and melt water from large watersheds, river flow is strongly influenced by short-term weather changes and can vary considerably from season to season and from year to year. At the same time, rivers can determine the shape of their own watersheds, especially silt-laden rivers like China's Yellow, North America's Mississippi, Mesopotamia's Tigris and Euphrates, and India's Ganges-Brahmaputra-Meghna river system. In these river systems, enormous quantities of silt and sand are washed downstream each year, creating vast deltas where the rivers meet the sea. What is more, silt deposits along a river's lower stretches constantly build up the river's bed, causing the river to change course repeatedly as gravity pulls it along the path of the least resistance towards the sea. The net result of these constant changes to the course of the river is a large, flat floodplain consisting primarily of sediment washed downstream from distant highlands.

Floodplains have historically served as cradles of human civilization. Indeed, rivers offer a number of advantages to those who would farm their banks. Rivers, for example, offer unmatched transportation advantages. Boats can pass up and down the river as far up as the "fall line" where rapids begin, facilitating communication and trade. Land travelers benefit from the flat and relatively open flood plains located along the river's margin. What is more, since nearly all rivers discharge into seas or oceans, rivers can serve as vital arteries of seaborne trade into the interior, enriching the people who live along their banks. What is more, the ecology of flood plains inherently nurtured agriculture. River ecosystems favor the local proliferation of plants that grow quickly on newly cleared soil — precisely the characteristics preferred by early farmers. In addition, the fine-grained sediment found along flood plains is quite often suitable for agriculture, so long as it contains sufficient organic content.

Perhaps most importantly, the annual sediment deposits left behind by rivers allowed some early farming societies to break free of the inherit limitations imposed by land degradation. Most early farming societies were obliged to leave significant portions of the cropland "fallow" (uncultivated) each year to allow it to regain its fertility, or to adopt "swidden" (slash and burn) agriculture, where farmers cut new agricultural land out of the forest, plant it for a few years until it loses its fertility, and then move to another patch of forest. Because swidden farmers are only cultivating a fraction of the available land at any time, overall population density tends to be low. Swidden agriculture also produces a great deal of soil erosion, to the detriment of swidden farmers, though perhaps to the advantage of riverside farmers downstream. It should come as no surprise therefore that most of the early centers of human civilization were centered around rivers: The civilizations of the Fertile Crescent and China, for instance, originated in the Nile and Tigris-Euphrates and Yellow-Yangtze River systems respectively.

Sediment-laden rivers may be the mothers of human civilization, but the same characteristics that nourish human societies also threaten those societies with disaster. A river that deposits life-bringing sediments during a "normal" flood year may bring deadly floods the next, or may shrivel to a trickle and deny both fertility-replenishing silt and water to riverside farmers. What is more, when a river shifts its course dramatically, it might drown farmlands or even human settlements downstream, while leaving former riverside areas high and dry, forcing their abandonment. A given river's geomorphic instability depends largely on local topography, climate, and geology. Rivers with only a moderate silt load and a relatively steep slope, like the Nile, only rarely experience devastating floods. In addition, the Nile's headwaters in Ethiopia and the Central African plateau lie thousands of kilometers away from the river's mouth, meaning that there is plenty of time for even a heavy mountain downpour to flatten out into a more even flow before the downpour's water reaches downstream. The Tigris and Euphrates, on the other hand, feature high silt loads and shallow slopes, a combination that frequently causes the rivers to shift course. These same river characteristics ensure that the Tigris and Euphrates drain slowly after heavy foods, severely disrupting the Mesopotamian agricultural cycle in high water years. What is more, the headwaters of the Tigris and Euphrates are close enough to the rivers' mouths that heavy rain upstream flows down in high, coherent crests, vastly increasing the danger of flooding to Mesopotamian civilization.

The different characteristics of the Nile and Tigris-Euphrates river systems may even have left a fundamental mark upon Egyptian and Mesopotamian culture. Perhaps in part because of the fickleness of their rivers, Mesopotamian civilizations generally had a fairly pessimistic worldview, featuring hostile gods associated with primordial chaos, natural disasters, the ubiquity of death, and a gloomy vision of the afterlife. Mesopotamian civilization is also credited with writing the first flood myth, which later found its way into the Christian Bible in the form of the story of Noah's ark. The weaving course of the Tigris and Euphrates rivers also served to subdivide Mesopotamia into a number of sub-regions, which may in turn help to explain why Mesopotamian society was long divided into many warring city-states rather than a unified regional empire. The Nile, on the other hand, seems to have inspired a more optimistic set of religious beliefs. Egyptian Gods were envisioned as allies of mankind, who provided human beings with what they needed to live, most especially the life giving waters (and sediments) of the Nile. What is more, the ancient Egyptians were optimistic about the afterlife as well, and developed elaborate funerary practices—including the construction of monumental tombs—to ensure an untroubled afterlife for their dead. The straight and generally unchanging course of the Nile probably also helps to explain Egypt's long tradition of political stability and centralization, as opposed to their more politically decentralized Mesopotamian neighbors.

In order to deal with seasonal and yearly river fluctuations, populations living alongside rivers are obliged to develop sets of practices designed to maximize the benefits and minimize the risks of their fickle environment. Such is the case of the farmers in the Ganges Delta, the outlet of the vast Ganges, Brahmaputra, and Meghana river systems that together have the second highest discharge outflow of any river system in the world. As discussed in section 5.1, the Ganges Delta is immensely fertile, due to seasonal deposits of silt; indeed, virtually the entire modern nation of Bangladesh lies upon soil laid down by prehistorical sediment deposits. However, the same rivers that essentially created the territory of Bangladesh overflow their banks almost every year during the June–September monsoon season, when swelling rivers typically inundate between one-fifth and one-third of the country's territory. In years of extremely high river levels, or during years of heavy rainfall within Bangladesh itself, the floodwaters might inundate 70 percent of the country. Worse yet, Ganges River system takes on the characteristics of a "braided" river as it passes through Bangladesh, meaning that the river is constantly shifting in its bed, creating new channels while abandoning others. For the most part these river shifts are the result of sediment accretion, but Bangladesh flood scholars Hofer and Messerli suggest that the catastrophic flood of 1787 may have been triggered by an earthquake that dramatically changed the Brahmaputra River's course. River bed shifts in the Ganges river system can affect enormous numbers of people: In 1983, these yearly channel shifts were estimated to affect nearly a million people a year. Bangladesh's population has soared in the interim, so the figure is undoubtedly considerably higher today.

Bangladeshi farmers have adopted a number of strategies to maximize the advantages and mitigate the drawbacks of their fertile but fickle environment. As discussed in section 5.1, farmers on the *char* islands, which are most vulnerable to flooding, dig drainage canals around their home sites and used the excavated soil to provide raised crop beds. Bangladeshi farmers also tend to farm multiple strips of land in different areas or different elevations to mitigate risk from flooding. Farmers close to the ocean and thus vulnerable to storm surge plant salt-resistant crops like millet and watermelon, while Bangladeshi farmers everywhere tend to plant an assortment of different crops to mitigate the chance of total harvest failure. In areas where freshwater river flooding is more likely, however, farmers tend to grow *aman*, a type of rice that grows quickly enough to keep pace with rising flood waters. When low river levels are expected, on the other hand, entirely different crops are grown, including jute (used to make burlap) and *aus*, a drought tolerant variety of rice. Nearly all types of crops are harvested soon before the wet season to mitigate possible flood damage to the crop. Farmers in the Ganges Delta take even greater care with the livestock. Chickens and ducks are either sold off or moved indoors shortly before the flood season, while cattle and other large livestock are herded onto platforms made of layers of straw, water hyacinth, bamboo, and banana trucks, which not only can float atop the floods, but can also provide food for the animals, since the straw and water hyacinth are edible. If flood waters are exceptionally high, or their home site suffers from extreme erosion, the last resort of Ganges Delta farmers is simply to pull up stakes and move elsewhere. One scholar of Ganges Delta *char* communities found that almost 62 percent of respondents to surveys had relocated their homes between 5 and 10 times in previous 16 years.

Practices such as this make the Ganges Delta inhabitable during normal years—indeed, the Ganges Delta has one of the highest populations per square kilometer of any rural area in the world. Nonetheless, even the most meticulous preparations cannot fully mitigate the disastrous effect of exceptionally high floods. According to historical records, a serious flood and subsequent famine in 1769 killed as much as ⅓ of the population of Bengal, as Bangladesh was called at the time. The 1787 flood, which may have been worsened by an earthquake, was even more destructive. Millions of people were forced from their homes by the water, but many had nowhere to go, as even the regional capital of Dhaka was inundated. What is more, food prices soared 300–400 percent at a time when many people had lost their livelihoods, leading to widespread famine. Serious floods occurred again in 1871 and 1885, and then ten more times during the 20th century, including a horrific flood in 1998 that inundated almost 68 percent of the country. Interestingly, widespread poverty is so pervasive in Bangladesh that even the mere rumor of a flood can prove deadly. As we shall see in chapter 7, the 1974 Bangladesh flood was fairly mild, and food production was actually up over previous years, but fear of flooding lead to artificially inflated food prices which in turn lead to widespread starvation among land-poor farmers and wage laborers.

Bangladesh, then, is a land whose character has been profoundly shaped by the rivers that flow through it. However, just as rivers can leave a mark on the civilizations that rise up on their banks, so to do civilizations leave marks of their own upon rivers. The very first known permanent human settlement, Jericho, constructed an elaborate system of ditches and walls to prevent the Jordan River from running riot through their houses and farms. Mesopotamians built a variety of flood control measures ranging from simple earthen dikes to elaborate stone dams braced by metal bars to control their rivers. As we shall see in section 6.1, the Chinese took this process to such an extreme that the existence of various Chinese dynasties was inextricably linked to that dynasty's commitment to flood control measures on the Yellow River. However, these flood control measures often proved self-defeating. Dikes—long restraining walls built alongside the river—may control the water in the short run. However, the steady build up of the river bed ensures it will overcome human defenses over the long run, unless escalating amounts of resources are expended on taming the river. Significantly, the civilization with the best record of "controlling" its river was the ancient Egyptians, who according to environmental historian Clive Ponting, were obliged to construct only minor flood control measures to tap the Nile's bounty. As a result, most river-related disasters in Egypt occurred not during floods but during low water years, when the absence of the silt-rich floods to replenish the soil and irrigate the crops brought the specter of famine to the region.

Flood control measures can prevent loss of life along the river's banks and harness the river's water for agriculture, transportation, or even power generation, but they come at a high price. By interfering with the natural ecology of river systems, flood control systems can contribute to water pollution and salinization of surrounding soils. Even more importantly, when dams and dikes fail the downstream impact is often catastrophic. By their very nature flood control measures impound a vast quantity of water, which exerts an enormous weight on the dikes and dams themselves. The accretion of sediment worsens the problem by raising the level of the water trapped within the dike or dam and increasing the chance that the water can escape its bonds. What is more, since sediment is no longer being deposited normally within the river's floodplain and delta, the soil level outside of the diked region can actually decrease, as semi-fluid river sediment gradually flattens out and slumps into the sea. These twin processes—sedimentation within the constraints of the flood control measures and the subsidence of the soil in supposedly "protected" areas— often conspire to create a "hanging" river, held dangerously above low-lying residential or agricultural land by man-made structures. As we shall see in both sections 6.1 and 6.3, the phenomenon of hanging rivers contributed profoundly to both Yellow River flooding of 19th–20th centuries and the 21st century tragedy of Hurricane Katrina, which are widely considered the worst natural disasters to have occurred in Chinese and American history respectively.

Other floods are almost completely man-made. Perhaps the best example of this was the Johnstown Flood of 1889 that all but obliterated the Pennsylvania factory town of the same name. Johnstown was built upon the flood plain of the Conemaugh River, which predisposed it for a flooding catastrophe, but its real misfortune was to lay downstream of the South Fork Dam. The South Fork Dam was originally constructed as part of a complex scheme to build a canal system across the Allegheny Mountains to link Pittsburgh and Philadelphia, in hopes of matching the economic success of the Eire Canal. However, the dam was rendered obsolete almost as soon as it was finished by the construction of a Philadelphia to Pittsburgh railway, so it never served its intended purpose. Instead, the abandoned dam was taken over by a group of wealthy Pittsburgh industrialists, including Andrew Carnegie and Henry Clay Frick, who were attracted to the large mountain lake that formed behind the dam. Dubbed Lake Conemaugh, the South Fork Dam reservoir offered splendid fishing and boating opportunities for the "South Fork Fishing and Hunting Club," a secretive group of elite Pittsburghers who owned the dam and surrounding land and consequently could enjoy the rare privilege of sailboating amid the mountains.

Unfortunately, the South Fork Dam was plagued with problems. The very fact that the dam was built from earth was a major liability, given dirt's vulnerability to erosion and seepage. The pace of construction, and perhaps the quality of the work, was slowed considerably by an epidemic of cholera during the 1850s. The dam failed for the first time in 1862, perhaps because locals had been stealing lead from the pipe joints of the water release valves. Thankfully, at the time of this early dam failure the water level in the reservoir was low, greatly limiting the impact of the resulting flood. Despite the dam's proven ability to fail, when the South Fork Club partially rebuilt the dam in 1879, they gave little thought to safety. The dam itself was reconstructed using "every manner of local rock, mud, brush, hemlock boughs, hay ... even horse manure," in the words of Johnstown Flood historian David McCullough. At the same time, the dam rebuilders declined to construct adequate spillways to release excess water on account of the high cost. The South Fork Club compounded this problem by installing wire screens on the spillways that did exist. These screens prevented the "Club's" fish from escaping downstream, but also tended to become clogged with debris during flood conditions, rendering the spillways all but useless. What is more, the Club deliberately lowered the dam in order to build an access road to the train station atop it, thereby dangerously decreasing the dam's capacity.

To worsen matters, economic development in the area surrounding the South Fork Dam was rendering the region more and more vulnerable to disastrous flooding over time. Deforestation had reduced the capacity of the surrounding mountains and hills to retain water, leading to greater run-off during rainstorms. The river downstream of the dam was becoming increasingly vulnerable to flooding as well, since Johnstown and the surrounding communities had progressively narrowed the river channel, in part to provide more land for development, but also on the mistaken belief that a narrowed river would be forced to dig a deeper channel for itself. This was wishful thinking, since the bed of the Conemaugh River was mostly solid rock.

As a result, the tragedy that occurred in 1889 was fairly predictable, at least in retrospect. Heavy rains in late May filled the dam to the top, and the spillways were inadequate to release

E. Benjamin Andrews, *History of the United States*, Vol. V (New York: Charles Scribner's Sons, 1912). Available from http://commons.wikimedia.org/wiki/Image:Johnstown_Main_Street_1889_Flood.jpg

Johnstown's main street after its disastrous 1889 flood.

the growing pressure. Eventually, water began to tumble down the front of the dam, eating away at the soil at the front of the dam. Over time, the breach grew exponentially, eventually releasing the entire contents of the lake into the Conemaugh Valley. The resulting deluge, in the words of David McCullough, was equivalent to releasing "Niagara Falls into the valley for thirty-six minutes." Witnesses downstream described the oncoming flood as "roaring like a mighty battle," punctuated with weird explosions, as temporary knots of debris were shattered forcefully by the relentless power of the flood. Several towns, including the industrial village of Woodvale just upstream from Johnstown, were entirely swept away by the scouring waters. As for Johnstown itself, it was inundated by nearly 10 meters of water for about 10 minutes, killing about well over 2000 people, about 10 percent of the valley's population. The many survivors faced a grim situation; rendered homeless by the floods, without adequate food, without sanitation, and without any chance of swift rescue, since most transportation routes into the valley had been severed. To make matters still worse, rumors spread after the flood that recent Hungarian immigrants, "fiends in human form" in the words of the New York *Herald*, were drinking, cavorting, fighting, and looting amid the ruins. Such stories should come as no surprise; as we already saw in section 3.2, the fear of disease that accompanies disasters seems to trigger temporary outbreaks of xenophobia. Thankfully, despite the lurid tales, the anti–Hungarian scare was short lived and claimed few casualties.

The ravages of the Johnstown flood, however, pales before the damage wreaked by the "August 1975 Disaster" in China. The location of this flood was the Huaihe (Huai River) watershed in China, which runs through an area of fairly steep gorges which were judged to be ideal locations for dams. Consequently, during the late 1950s and early 1960s Chinese officials constructed a slew of new dams—100 between 1957 and 1959 alone—to harness the Huai's water for agriculture, hydroelectricity, and other uses. Unfortunately, these dams were poorly designed in nearly every respect. The dam designers, working without accurate knowledge of local weather extremes, designed their dams to protect against insufficiently high flood volumes. What is more, since the years of dam construction coincided with the so-called "Great Leap Forward," there was intense pressure to build grandiose projects to increase raw resource yields without adequate regard to engineering or geological realities. Under the influence of "red experts," as communist party activists without adequate technical training were called, dams were built higher than was proper and with an inadequate number of spillways, decreasing the ability of the dams to release water from overfilled reservoirs. Trained engineers who dared to point out the design flaws in these ambitious projects were accused of being "conservatives," "right-wing opportunists," or even traitors against the Chinese people. What is more, during the Great Leap Forward, China's national mania to rack up impressive production numbers lead to the policy of "giving primacy to water accumulation," along the Huai. In practical terms, this meant collecting as much water inside the dam reservoirs for irrigation as possible. Meanwhile, resources were diverted away from flood control measures designed primarily to promote safety, such as dike maintenance and river dredging, in favor of projects that directly increased production numbers. This policy of sacrificing safety for yield continued even after the Great Leap Forward. Indeed, by the end of the 1960s another 100 dams had been built, existing dams had been redesigned to increase their capacity, and farmland was expanded steadily into large tracts of land along the Huai that had originally been left unoccupied for the purpose of floodwater diversion in peak rainfall years.

These human errors proved to be the building blocks of disaster. In August of 1975, a powerful typhoon washed ashore into central coastal China, where it encountered an unusually strong continental Asian weather system. The result was phenomenal rainfall: Witnesses described the rain as having the "force of a fireman's hose," and weather stations recorded a meter of rain over the course of just 3 days. As a result, the Shimantan and Banquiao dams on upper tributaries of the Huai River gave way, releasing a crest of water up to six meters high that surged downstream. The flood diversion areas along the Huai, which was been steadily reduced in size due to encroachment by farmers, were not sufficient to hold the flow. What is more, intensive irrigation farming along the Huai had discharged quite a bit of sediment into the Huai's normally clear waters, and these sediment deposits reduced the ability of the spillways of dams along the Huai to release pressure from dam reservoirs. As a result, the collapse of the Shimantan and Banquiao dams lead to a cascade of dam and dike failures along the Huai, triggering a flood that eventually engulfed 29 counties downstream. Those dams that did not fail, paradoxically, tended to retain the water within the channel of the Huai, meaning that the floodwaters soon collected into a vast lake 45,000 square kilometers in area that refused to drain to the sea. Chinese engineers were eventually obliged to destroy many of the surviving dams with dynamite to release the pent-up floodwaters.

The human consequences of this "natural" disaster were atrocious. Witnesses described the valley of the Huai after the dam collapses as resembling a vast lake containing with five islands, the raised urban areas of the regional county seats. Each of these "islands" were packed with desperate flood survivors. 26,000 people were killed directly by the floodwaters. Another 145,000 or so died of disease in the flood's aftermath, most commonly of diarrheal diseases, which thrived due to contaminated water supplies and the breakdown of normal sanitation measures. Thousands more contracted malaria, since mosquitoes bred in huge numbers in stagnant floodwaters, and thousands of others succumbed to influenza, which spread like wildfire due to the compromised immune systems of traumatized, malnourished, and home-less flood victims. Still others perished due to food poisoning, since they were forced by hunger to consume such questionable foods as the carcasses of drowned animals or rotting flood-borne pumpkins. Overall, at least 11 million people were adversely impacted by the "August 1975 Disaster," an astounding number. Nonetheless, as we shall see in section 6.1, the destruction wreaked by the August 1975 floods was minor in comparison to floods along the Yellow River in the last 19th and early 20th centuries.

Tsunamis

Although tsunamis and river floods are both water-based natural disasters, in many ways they are quite different. Tsunamis are usually saltwater phenomena, though freshwater tsunamis are theoretically possible if a large enough body of fresh water is impacted by a strong enough force. Moreover, tsunamis are generally the result of terrestrial disturbances, as opposed to river floods, which originate in the workings of the coupled atmospheric/oceanic water system. Despite these differences, tsunamis generally have the same overall results of freshwater flooding; in the short run they can lead to direct death by drowning and the force of water, while in the long run they can contribute to famine and epidemic disease.

A good deal of confusion surrounds ocean wave disaster terminology. In English, the term usually applied to devastating ocean waves is "tidal wave," based on the mistaken belief that tides are involved. It is true that tides can be a factor; a tsunami that strikes at high tide will likely do more damage than one that occurs at low tide. Nonetheless, the origin of these waves has nothing to do with the tides. As a result, most scientists have adopted the Japanese term *tsunami*, which technically means "great harbor wave." This term is in fact nearly as incorrect as tidal wave, since although tsunami waves are enhanced when they enter harbors, they are not intrinsically harbor phenomenon and can strike quite powerfully along any shoreline. Nonetheless, the term tsunami, although inherently misleading, does at least have the advantage of being misleading in a non–English language.

Considerable confusion also exists about what tsunamis look like. The classic artistic image of a tsunami, produced by 19th-century Japanese artist Katsushika Hokusai as part of his "36 views of Mount Fuji" woodcut series, depicts a tsunami as an exaggerated version of a normal ocean wave. In actual fact, tsunamis are quite distinct from regular ocean waves in both origin and appearance. Typical ocean waves are generated by the action of wind upon the surface of the water, and although they certainly can pack a punch, their potential force is limited by their shallow depth. The energy contained in tsunami waves, on the other hand, extends from the ocean bottom to the surface. In deep water, this vast energy may be barely perceptible, since the tsunami waves have a huge wavelength (distance between crests), a very low amplitude (height of the individual crests) and an extremely high rate of speed (tsunami waves travel at 700 km/h, approximately the speed of a jet plane). It is only when the wave approaches land and the inherent energy of the wave is concentrated into progressively shallower water that the tsunami bunches up, slows, and begins to resemble a regular ocean wave. Even then, the resemblance is not complete, since tsunami waves tend to manifest themselves as incoming shelves of water with a crest of foam rather than the breakers typically seen along ocean coasts.

The comparison between ocean waves and tsunamis is misleading in other respects as well. Normal waves are produced by the horizontal pushing action of wind, a phenomenon best illustrated by the effect of hurricanes on lakes. Because of the sustained flow of wind in one direction across the surface, the water in the lake typically becomes much higher on the leeward side

Katsushika Hokusai's famous depiction of a tsunami wave, part of his "36 Views of Mount Fuji" woodcut series.

of the lake and much lower on the windward side — a phenomenon that can trigger a disastrous flood, such as the freshwater storm surge discussed in section 5.3 that inundated the town of Moore Haven during the 1926 Miami hurricane. The motion of a tsunami wave, in contrast, is vertical. Imagine a blanket being held between two people, one of whom is shaking the blanket with an up-down motion to remove dirt; ripples will pass down the length of the cloth, even though the cloth itself will not change location. This phenomenon explains why the seawater often seems to recede before the arrival of a tsunami, since if the "downward" portion of a tsunami wave's energy arrives first, the resulting trough created in the seawater will actually drain water away from the shoreline. Indeed, throughout history many people who have been killed by tsunamis were collecting fish left high and dry by the receding waters, only to perish when the crest portion of the tsunami arrived. Some scholars even speculate that Moses' "parting" of the Red Sea described in the book of Exodus may in fact be inspired the arrival of a trough of a historical tsunami wave, though such a contention is all but impossible to prove.

Perhaps most importantly, tsunami waves are different from normal ocean waves in their sheer size. Because the energy in tsunami waves extends through the entire column of water, tsunamis have a far greater potential energy than wind-blown waves, and thus can reach stupendous heights. A 1971 tsunami that struck the Japanese island of Ryukyu reached 85 meters above sea level, a height nearly equal to the length of a football field. Tsunami waves usually reach such heights only within partially enclosed bodies of water, where surrounding headlands act as a funnel, focusing and concentrating their power. Tsunami waves can also bend around fingers of land, a feat that wind-driven waves cannot duplicate.

So what natural forces generate such powerful waves? In some cases tsunamis have been triggered by coastal or undersea landslides, which can displace vast quantities of water. Indeed, a 1958 landslide in Alaska's Lituya Bay generated an astounding tsunami wave 524 meters tall, though few people were killed due to the remoteness of the location. Tsunamis may also be caused by volcanic activity, such as the collapse of a volcano caldera or a powerful pyroclastic flow impacting the ocean. As we already saw in section 2.1, the eruption of the Krakatau volcano triggered a tsunami wave that reached 35 meters in height, though the exact mechanism that produced it remains unclear.

The most common origin of tsunami waves, however, is seismic activity. Undersea earthquakes are powerful enough to influence the entire column of water above them, leading to tsunami waves. However, not all earthquakes generate tsunamis equally. Powerful quakes are more likely to generate tsunamis than mild quakes as are earthquakes that occur relatively close to the earth's surface, since they are more likely to deform the earth's crust. What is more, the type of fault line is important for the generation of tsunamis as well. Although slip-strike or "normal" faults can generate powerful earthquakes, they tend to trigger few tsunamis, since most of the motion along such faults is horizontal rather than vertical. As a result, even in a powerful slip-strike earthquake, little water is displaced. Spreading faults, where the plates are moving apart from each other, do displace water in the process and can engender tsunamis. Indeed, some evidence exists that the Mid-Atlantic Ridge, the most extensive spreading fault on the planet, has the ability to create tsunamis. Nonetheless the relative weakness of the earthquakes along this type of fault and the distance of this fault line from most Atlantic coastal areas limits its potential to generate dangerous tsunamis.

The type of fault that generates most tsunamis is the subduction fault, where one plate is diving below another. Subduction faults are where the most powerful earthquakes occur, and also where those earthquakes create considerable vertical displacement of the earth's crust. However, it is important to recognize that the power of a tsunami is affected by factors other than the type of fault and strength of the triggering earthquake. Even a mild earthquake can give birth to an enormous tsunami if the quake causes a large undersea landslide. What is more, the topography of the seashore can exert a considerable impact on tsunami formation, blunting the impact of some tsunamis while exaggerating the size of others. Small wonder, then, that the science of tsunami prediction remains so frustratingly inexact.

The fact that tsunamis are most likely to form along subduction faults helps to explain why so many of them — perhaps 80 percent — occur along the coastlines of the Pacific Ocean. Not only is the Pacific Ocean plate moving at a fairly fast clip by seismic standards, but it is diving beneath several of the surrounding plates creating extensive zones of subduction. As already discussed in section 3.2, the junction of the Pacific, Eurasian, Philippine, and North American plates just south of Japan is one of the most seismically active areas in the world, which explains why more tsunamis strike Japan than almost anywhere else, at a rate of about one per decade. The southeastern Pacific Ocean experiences tsunamis fairly frequently as well, thanks to the subduction of the Nazca plate beneath the lighter South American plate, a process that also created the imposing Andes Mountains. The only other portion of the world that produces powerful tsunamis at predictable intervals is the Sunda Arc beneath the Indian Ocean, where the Australian Plate dives beneath the much lighter Eurasian plate. Since the plates are moving fairly slowly along the Sunda Arc with respect to each other, tsunamis in the Indian Ocean tend to occur infrequently. However, this fact is probably small comfort to the families of the 200,000 or more who perished during the Asian Tsunami of 2004, which is the subject of section 6.3.

So what can be done to mitigate the damage posed by tsunamis? Truth be told, not much; unlike river floods, which can be both caused and prevented by human behavior, tsunamis are the result of forces entirely beyond our control. The nations surrounding the Pacific Ocean collaborated to create an early tsunami warning system in the second half of the 20th century, and the Indian Ocean nations have recently begun to organize a similar system following the devastating 2004 Asian tsunami. Nonetheless, the utility of such a system is limited by the uncertainties of tsunami forecasting and by the underdeveloped transportation and communication infrastructure of some participating nations. In addition, the speed at which tsunamis travel renders the tsunami warning system all but useless in the event of an earthquake taking place immediately offshore. In Japan and elsewhere, the government has constructed seawalls up to 9 meters in height to protect coastal communities, some equipped with steel gates designed to stay open during normal conditions but swing closed when a tsunami is imminent. Nonetheless, constructing such gates along the entirety of the inhabited coastline in tsunami zones is neither economically or environmentally feasible. Perhaps the most obvious means of avoiding damage by tsunamis would be to move coastal cities in tsunami-prone areas inland, but the economic benefits — not to mention recreational advantages — of coastal living make this an unrealistic solution.

Tsunamis, therefore, are a reality that mankind is forced to live with. Unfortunately, there are indications that mankind's vulnerability to tsunamis is likely to rise over time. Human population continues to expand at a rapid pace, and as coastal cities grow so too will the number of people vulnerable to tsunami hazards. What is more, if current projections about global warming are accurate, sea levels will rise by up to a meter over the next hundred years, augmenting the destructive ability of tsunami waves by increasing the distance inland they can travel before losing their momentum. The great tsunamis of the past, therefore, may merely be preludes to greater disasters in the future.

Study Questions

1. Explain, in your own words, the most important differences between a river flood and a tsunami.

2. Which of the two phenomena discussed in this section — river floods or tsunamis — are more closely interwoven with other forms of natural disaster? Explain your answer.

3. This section implies that human beings are generally more to blame for river floods than they are for tsunamis. To what degree do you agree with this assumption? Explain your answer.

Sources/Suggested Readings

Ahmad, Emaduddin, Jahir Uddin Chowdhury, Khondaker Masoud ul Hassan, Md. Azizul Haque, Tauhidul Anwar Khan, S. M. Mahbubur Rahman, Mashfiqus Salehin. "Floods in Bangladesh and Their Processes." In K. Nizamuddin, ed., *Disaster in Bangladesh: Selected Readings*. Dhaka, Bangladesh: Disaster Research Training and Management Center, 2001, pp. 9–29.

Baker, Victor R. "The Study of Superfloods." *Science*, New Series, Vol. 295, No. 5564 (March 29, 2002), pp. 2379–2380.

Baquee, M. Abdul. "Responding to Nature's Toll: The Case of *Char*-Lands." In K. Nizamuddin, ed., *Disaster in Bangladesh: Selected Readings*. Dhaka, Bangladesh: Disaster Research Training and Management Center, 2001, pp. 9–29.

Barry, John. *Rising Tide: The Great Mississippi Flood of 1927 and How It Changed America*. New York: Simon and Schuster, 1997.

Blackhall, Susan. *Tsunami*. UK: Taj Books, 2005.

Hofer, Thomas, and Bruno Messerli. *Floods in Bangladesh: History, Dynamics, and Rethinking the Role of the Himalayas*. New York: United Nations University Press, 2006.

McCullough, David. *The Johnstown Flood*. New York: Simon and Schuster, 1968.

Montgomery, David R. *Dirt: The Erosion of Civilizations*. Berkeley: University of California Press, 2007.

Montgomery, Roger. "The Bangladesh Floods of 1984 in Historical Context." *Disasters*, Vol. 9, No. 3 (1985), pp. 163–172.

Parrinder, Geoffrey, ed., *World Religions: From Ancient History to the Present*. New York: Facts on File, 1971.

Ponting, Clive. *A Green History of the World: Nature, Pollution, and the Collapse of Societies*. New York: Penguin, 1991.

Puleo, Stephen. *Dark Tide: The Great Boston Molasses Flood of 1919*. Boston, MA: Beacon Press, 2004.

Si, Yi. "The World's Most Catastrophic Dam Failures: The August 1975 Collapse of the Banqaio and Shimantan Dams." In John G. Thibodeau and Phillip B. Williams, eds., *The River Dragon Has Come: The Three Gorges Dam and the Fate of China's Yangtze River and Its People*. Armonk, NY: M. E. Sharp, 1998.

Smith, Bruce D. *The Emergence of Agriculture*. New York: Scientific American Library, 1998.

Synolakis, Costas. "Tsunamis." In Ellen J. Prager, ed., *Furious Earth: The Science and Nature of Earthquakes, Volcanoes, and Tsunamis*. New York: McGraw-Hill, 2000.

"Tsunami, Tidal Waves and Other Extreme Waves." *National Oceanic and Aeronautic Administration*. Available from http://www.erh.noaa.gov/phi/reports/tsunami.htm.

"Tsunami — Where Next?" *National Geographic Magazine*, Geographica (April, 2005).

6.1: Yellow River Flooding, 19th and 20th Century China

The Huang He, or Yellow River, has been called both the "Cradle of Chinese Civilization" and "China's Sorrow." Both descriptions are apt. Like the Nile and Tigris-Euphrates river systems, which pump life-giving water and sediment through relatively arid lands, the Yellow River nourished an enduring civilization. At the same time, however, the specific hydrology of the Yellow River has posed enormous problems to the very same civilization that it engendered. Indeed, the two aspects of the Yellow River are intimately linked. The silt-stained waters of the Yellow River offer China enormous advantages in terms of both agriculture and transportation, but by constraining the river into an increasingly artificial channel, ever-increasing human demands on the river have repeatedly set the stage for horrific floods when human restraints on the river give way. This has been true throughout Chinese history but never with more devastating effect than the 19th and 20th centuries, when the inherent geological instability of the Yellow River combined with rising internal dissent and external military pressure to create an unprecedented series of flooding disasters.

The Yellow River's enormous influence on Chinese history is entirely out of proportion with its relatively meager annual flow. In terms of volume the Yellow River's average output is only 1,365 cubic meters per second, only 5 percent average flow of the Yangtze River in China's well-watered south. Nonetheless, the peculiar geographical realities of the Yellow River ensured that it would be crucially important to Chinese civilization. Since the headwaters of the Yellow River cut through the fine soils of China's loess plateaus, the Yellow carries an astounding amount of silt — 1.6 billion cubic meters per year, more than any other river in the world and three times as much as the much larger Yangtze River. Over time, these effusions of silt have left a definitive mark on China's landscape in the form of the North China Plain, a flat and fairly fertile alluvial deposit covering approximately 350,000 square kilometers. Indeed, this plain continues to grow seaward today at a rate of approximately 1.4 to 1.8 km/year due to continued sediment deposits. Although the North China Plain makes up less than 4 percent of China's overall territory, it accounts for nearly 19 percent of China's agricultural land. What is more, because of yearly temperature extremes, the North China Plain can support a number of different types of crops, including millet, the grain that sustained early Chinese civilization. Not surprisingly, China's first dynasties — the Xia, the Shang, and the Zhou — were all located on the North China Plain.

Unfortunately, the same river that gave rise to the fertile North China Plain also threatens the inhabitants of the plain with the constant threat of disaster. In part, this is because the Yellow River's flow is extremely variable, both between years (due to varying annual rainfall rates and different rates of snow melt) and within a year (as rainfall occurs seasonally in North China's monsoon climate). Since its upper reaches run through an area of temperature extremes, the Yellow also is subject to "ice floods" caused by the build-up and sudden break-up of river ice. The most important factor for the Yellow River's instability, however, is its high silt load. Because of annual silt deposits, the Yellow is constantly building up its own bed above the height of the surrounding plain. As a result, the Yellow River shifts its bed continuously seeking new paths of least resistance to the sea. Like many sediment-rich rivers, the Yellow River in its natural state took on a characteristically "braided" appearance, covering a large area with constantly-shifting, intertwined channels. The braided characteristic of the pre-dynastic Yellow River is hinted at by early Chinese poems and legends, which speak of the "nine rivers" or "endless flood waters" of the early North China Plain.

Not surprisingly, given the region's inherent hydraulic instability, the rise of civilization in the North China Plain was intimately connected to the development of flood control. According to early Chinese mythology the rivers of the North China Plain were first tamed by the semi-divine sage-king Yu, who imposed order on the floodplain's chaos, allowing the mountain people to begin cultivation of the fertile valleys. What is more, according to some versions of this myth, Yu was the father of mankind, further underscoring the intimate links between flood control and early Chinese civilization.

Although the story of Yu is apocryphal, it played a crucial role in the development of the Chinese institution of kingship. Successive Chinese emperors would claim that, like Yu, that they were semi-divine figures, conduits between heaven and earth charged with the task of imposing order upon a chaotic natural world. During the Zhou dynasty this political ideology was refined into "Mandate of Heaven" political theory, which held that a ruler would keep heaven's blessing so long as he kept floods and famines at bay. Should such disasters occur, the Zhou claimed, they would signal that heaven's mandate had been revoked and that a new dynasty was destined to come to power. In this way the Zhou were able to overthrow the rulers of the Shang dynasty, who claimed to be semi-divine, without destroying the sacred status of the Chinese imperial office itself.

Mandate theory greatly strengthened imperial authority in China, but it was a double-edged sword: Chinese rulers were keenly aware that their legitimacy could be weakened and they could be dethroned if caught unprepared by natural disasters. As a result, successive Chinese emperors launched ambitious plans to keep the unstable Yellow River under control. However, such efforts always proved self-defeating. The main technique used by Chinese engineers to tame the Yellow River was the construction of dikes—earthen dams running parallel to the river's flow. Unfortunately, these dikes entrapped not just the river, but also the river's sediment, which constantly built up the level of the bed. To contain the ever-higher river, government authorities were obliged to construct taller and taller dikes, to the point that the Yellow River eventually became a hanging river that ran like an aqueduct through the North China Plain. When the dikes eventually burst, usually because civil disorder, corruption, incompetence, or financial restraints compromised the efficiency of flood control measures, the Yellow River would seek an entirely new course, inundating entire districts in the process. Some would drown due to the floods, and many more would succumb to either post-flood famine or famine's constant companion, epidemic disease.

It is important to distinguish between temporary dike breaches and "avulsions"—major changes in the Yellow River's course. The dike breaches are by no means uncommon in Chinese history; researchers estimate that the Yellow River breached its dikes 1500 times before 1949. Although most breaches were soon sealed up, even a temporary breach of the Yellow River flood control measures can lead to major problems, largely because of lack of drainage in the North China Plain. In most river systems, the river itself provides passage of excess waters to the sea once the flood crest has passed. However, since the Yellow River is considerably higher than the plain through which it passes, the Yellow River is useless as a drainage mechanism. As a result, Yellow River floodwaters tend to linger for months, not only destroying the crop in the field but also preventing the planting of new crops at the appropriate time in the agricultural cycle. The resulting food shortages, unless vigorously counteracted by the Chinese central governments, can trigger horrific famines and resultant outbreaks of epidemic disease.

If the ruptured dikes are not quickly repaired the Yellow River may undergo an avulsion, a catastrophic shift to a new river channel. Avulsions have occurred only 5 times in recorded Chinese history. In 602 B.C. the dikes broke, inundating a wide swath of the North China Plain to the south of the river's old course, and weakening the already-tottering Zhou state in the process. During the "Warring States" period that followed, the barely-controlled river was frequently used as a weapon of war; flood waters were deliberately diverted to inundate the fields and cities of downstream enemies. The establishment of the Qin and Han Dynasties after 221 B.C. ushered in a new and more effective flood control regime. However, the river burst its dikes again in A.D. 11, during a period of instability in the Han Dynasty, and the river wandered throughout the North China Plain without a fixed bed for nearly 60 years.

In the period after the Han dynasty, the Yellow River behaved itself for a nearly a millennium. In fact, by the 7th century, Chinese engineers had sufficiently refined their skills that they were not only able to prevent the Yellow River from flooding, but were also able to harness the Yellow River's waters for the Grand Canal, one of the most ambitious hydraulic engineering projects in human history. The Grand Canal, which linked the Yangtze and Yellow River systems, generated enormous amounts of trade, since it provided a cheap transportation link between the people and products of China's temperate north and semitropical south. What is more, the Grand Canal effectively centralized Chinese civilization, allowing successive Chinese rulers to build unified land-based Empires around the Yangtze-Grand Canal-Yellow River navigation system. Indeed, world historian William McNeill has invoked the Grand Canal to explain the relative stability and unity of Chinese civilization over time, especially when compared to politically unstable India and politically fractured Europe. As McNeill rightly points out, "no inland waterway system in world history approaches [the Grand Canal] as a device for integrating large and productive space." Chinese history bears out McNeill's observation: In the period following the construction of the Grand Canal, China has rarely been disunited for more than a century except due to foreign intervention, while prior to the Grand Canal's construction China had suffered through successive period of chronic political instability, including one interregnum of over 500 years.

To achieve this unity, however, Chinese engineers had to maintain control over the unruly Yellow River, and this control occasionally broke down. In A.D. 1048, the sediment laden river shifted its bed again due to an accidental dike breach. Less than a century later, the river experienced an avulsion after a Song Dynasty general deliberately breached the dikes to impede the progress of an 1128 invasion by a barbarian army from the North. This drastic measure helped the Song Dynasty survive for several more generations in South China, but in the years that followed flood control on the Yellow River could not be re-established, in part because of chronic warfare between Song China and Mongol invaders. As a result, the Yellow River was free to carry out its most dramatic course change in recorded history. Over a number of years the Yellow River captured the lower course of the Huai River, and when this process was complete, the Yellow River emptied to the south rather than the north of the Shandong Peninsula, over 450 kilometers as the crow flies from its former delta at the Bo Hai Sea.

After the expulsion of the Mongols and the establishment of the Ming dynasty, Chinese engineers again turned to the problem of the Yellow River. Unfortunately, the difficulties posed by the Yellow River had only multiplied with time. As Jiongxin Xu points out in a recent article, the sediment load of the Yellow River has actually increased over the course of the past 13,000 years, in large part because rising human populations in the upriver loess plateau have increased the rate of deforestation, land degradation, and resultant soil erosion. What is more, political developments within the Chinese state greatly complicated Yellow River flood control measures. By the start of the Ming dynasty, the economic center of gravity in China had shifted from the North China Plain to the rice-growing Yangtze River basin in the south. At the same time, however, the capital of China was moved to the northern Chinese city of Peking (now Beijing) so that the Chinese Emperor could maintain a watchful eye over the ever-threatening horse nomads beyond China's northern border — not to mention the ambitious generals guarding that border.

The problem, then, was to transfer South China's vast wealth to an expensive military and administrative center located in China's relatively less prosperous north. To solve this problem, the Ming reconstructed the Grand Canal on an even more massive scale than before to link the Yangtze and Yellow river systems. This decision saddled Chinese engineers with a seemingly impossible task: Not only would they have to prevent the Yellow River from flooding, they would have to harness its waters for the Grand Canal, maintain a navigable channel for boat traffic, while somehow avoiding the perennial problem of river bed siltation in the process.

The mechanism that Ming engineers adopted to solve these problems was ingenious. Under the direction of hydraulic engineer Pan Jixun, who took control over both Chinese grain transport and Yellow River control in 1578, Chinese workers constructed two sets of dikes, "thread dikes" to keep the normal flow of the water constrained in a narrow channel and "distant dikes" capable of handling the Yellow River at full flood. Pan hoped that this twin dike system would not only prevent flooding, but would also prevent the accumulation of silt, since the narrowed Yellow River would move fast enough to "scour" the channel of silt. This strategy would have the additional benefit of maintaining a deep central channel to the Yellow River navigable to boats. As a further improvement on the old Grand Canal, Pan Jixun constructed a large dam at the confluence of the Yellow and Huai Rivers. Pan hoped that the water from behind the reservoir could be used to maintain the level of the Yellow River during dry seasons, allowing uninterrupted boat traffic along the Grand Canal river system. Perhaps even more importantly, the relatively sediment-free water of the Huai River could be used to scour the lower course of the Yellow River, thus mitigating the problem of sediment there. In addition, Pan constructed a number of diversion canals and other works designed to release the pressure on the "distant dikes" in case of a major Yellow River flood.

Pan Jixun's hydraulic system on the Yellow River was a major achievement, especially given the prevailing Confucian ethic of the Ming bureaucratic elite. During the Ming dynasty, as with earlier Chinese dynasties, entry into the official ranks of the government was limited to those able to pass a rigorous exam that mainly tested the applicant's knowledge of the Confucian classics. In general, this system worked to the advantage of the government, since it produced a loyal, homogenous bureaucratic elite well versed in a literature that stressed paternalistic duty towards inferiors and obedience to superiors. On the other hand, the exam was poor preparation for jobs requiring specialized technical skills, such as hydraulic engineering. What is more, there was little incentive for officials to acquire these technical skills once they had joined the ranks of officialdom, since moral rectitude and scholarly reputation mattered much more than technical aptitude for promotion to higher bureaucratic ranks.

The Yellow River and Grand Canal

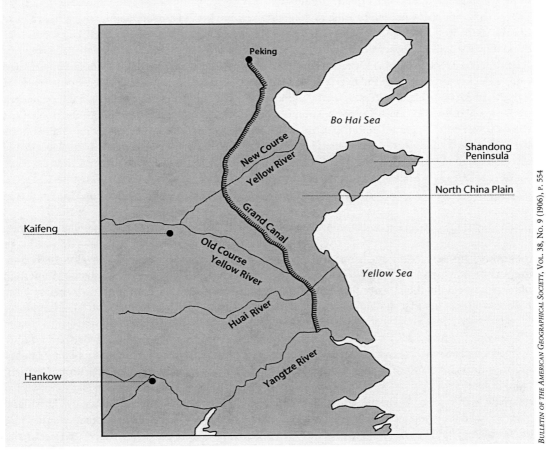

Pan Jixun's Yellow River Dikes

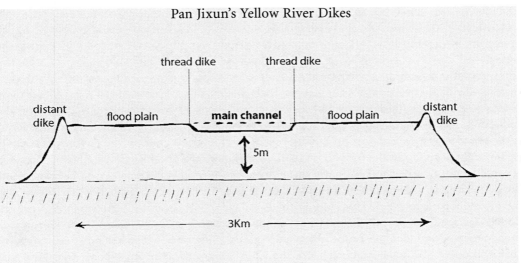

In the short run, while the silt load in the new bed of the Yellow River remained low, lack of proper training on the part of the officialdom was only a minor problem. Indeed, Pan Jixun's Yellow River–Grand Canal hydraulic system outlived the Ming Dynasty itself, which fell in during the 1640s to a Manchu invasion (despite the move of the capital to the north) and was succeeded by the Qing. However, by the 1700s Pan's flood control scheme for the Yellow River was beginning to break down. In 1761, the rising sediment load in the Yellow River bed allowed high waters to overtop the dikes in Huayuakou, leading to 27 dike breaches and an astounding flood volume of 32,000 cubic meters of water per second. Only 20 years later, another major breach in the dikes occurred, mainly due to water backed upstream by excessive sedimentation of the river's lower course. Damage to the dikes was so extensive that an entirely new diversion channel had to be built to carry the waters. Another major dike breach occurred in 1819, a year of heavy rainfall. During this event the dikes on both banks along a 50 kilometer stretch from Kaifeng to Yiyang were breached in 9 places. In each instance, however, the Chinese state was able to muster the expertise and resources to rein in the Yellow River before could carve a disastrous new path to the sea.

During the early 19th century, however, a number of factors came together that loosened the Chinese government's grip on the Yellow River. Overpopulation in China was becoming an increasing problem, forcing Chinese farmers to cultivate hillsides, colonize wastelands, or even migrate *on masse* in search of arable land. Deforestation of hillsides increased the sediment load of rivers, especially the already silt-laden Yellow. Rural land scarcity combined with native Chinese resentment against the Manchu Qing dynasty boiled over into a number of rebellions from 1796 onwards. Suppressing these various rebellions severely strained the resources of the state. Worse yet, China fared disastrously in the Opium War of 1839–41, in which Britain forcibly opened Chinese markets to her trade goods. The Qing battled heroically during this war; Manchu military units, in particular, frequently fought to the death rather than surrender to the British. Nonetheless, the Chinese could not overcome superior British weaponry, such as the iron-clad steamships that gave the British undisputed control over the rivers and coasts during their campaigns. Thanks to their technological edge, the British were able to seize the crucial river city of Zhenjiang, giving the British control over boat traffic on both the Yangtze River and the Grand Canal. With Britain's fist tightly closed around these vital trade arteries, the Chinese government had no choice but to agree to a humiliating set of trade concessions that essentially turned five Chinese cities into European trade outposts. The Chinese were also obliged to pay an exorbitant indemnity of $21 million to cover Britain's expenses and trade losses during the war.

Internal insurrection and external invasion certainly compromised China's ability to perform flood control measures, but it was the sheer weight of accumulated silt that did the most to loosen the Qing's hold on the Yellow River. In the period between the late 1500s and the mid–1800s, increasing deposits of sediment had gradually built up the level of the Yellow River to the point where the costs of building levees high enough to contain the river were escalating beyond the ability of the state to finance. Furthermore the Huai River, which was supposed to supply water to scour and maintain water levels in the Yellow River, was now below the Yellow's level due to sedimentation in that stream's bed. To compensate for this, Chinese engineers were forced to repeatedly enlarge the Gaojiayan Dam near the Yellow-Huai junction. Largely as a result, the bill for Grand Canal maintenance and Yellow River control swelled enormously, to the point that flood control was eating up as much as 10 percent of an already strained Chinese budget. To make matters worse the Chinese government, mistakenly believing that costs were rising due to corruption rather than silt accumulation, assigned Confucian scholars of great moral rectitude rather than hydraulic engineers to oversee the work. As a consequence, when the Yellow River system was struck by crisis, the men in charge had very little knowledge about hydrological engineering.

The first sign of the upcoming series of disasters occurred in 1841, when high seasonal water flow punched a hole in the dikes along the Yellow River near Kaifeng. Low-level officials had identified weaknesses in these dikes months before, but little was done due to lack of funds. What is more, Wenchong, the district official in charge of the works, had been selected by the emperor for his reputed incorruptibility rather than his abilities as an engineer. Indeed, despite his high post in the flood control bureaucracy, Wenchong had no experience whatsoever in hydraulic engineering, and proved to be entirely unequal to the task of repairing the dike. As a consequence, the small hole widened into a major breach by August, allowing the bulk of the river to pour into the Huaibei plain surrounding Kaifeng.

The 1841 flood put Kaifeng, a populous city and a former imperial capital, in a state of virtual siege. Earlier Yellow River floods had liberally deposited sediment in the surrounding plain, but the floods had been kept out of Kaifeng itself. As a result, like New Orleans before Hurricane Katrina, the city actually lay below the level of the agricultural lands that surrounded it. To ward off flooding of their low-lying city the people of Kaifeng scoured their city for rocks, bricks, and paving stones to build up the city's flood protection. Wenchong even resorted to purchasing and dismantling private residences to obtain dike-building materials. These desperate measures saved lives, but the formerly prosperous city still became an unlivable mud hole. With the crops in the surrounding fields submerged under six feet of water and sediment, the specter of famine hung over the city. Eventually the Chinese state and private citizens provided sufficient money to feed the hungry and repair the waterlogged town, but Wenhong himself was not so lucky: The Emperor ordered him to stand on the riverbank wearing a humiliating wooden collar for three months, after which he was forced into exile.

Although the dike near Kaifeng was eventually repaired — at great expense — the breach had done permanent damage to the existing flood control system. In 1845 the dikes on the Yellow River burst once again, transforming large parts of the nearby countryside into a vast sea. Worse yet, sediment-laden floodwaters from these inundations penetrated the reservoir on the Huai River, raising the water level and threatening the surrounding levees. In 1851, during an exceptional flood, these levees burst, making the Huai a temporary tributary of the Yangtze and interrupting travel on the Grand Canal. As in 1841, the government remained fixated on curbing corruption and cost overruns, and sent Confucian moralists rather than hydraulic experts to oversea the works. This was a penny wise but pound foolish strategy; the failure of the dikes probably cost the government vastly more money in lost taxation revenue and food relief than it would have cost to repair the dikes effectively. Still, even effective repairs to the dikes would only have delayed the issue for a few years, allowing more sediment to build up and thus requiring still more expensive flood control measures in the future.

Thus, the Chinese government was caught in an untenable position by the middle of the 18th century, forced to deal with rising silt levels while simultaneously holding off a rising tide of external pressure and internal insurrection. Not surprisingly, China's flood control defenses soon gave way completely. In 1855, most likely because of siltation, the course of the Yellow River within the dikes changed dramatically, forcing the full weight of the river against a previously safe section of the distant dikes. Engineers attempted to reinforce the weak point before a major breach formed, but ultimately failed, in part because the cash-strapped Chinese government was struggling to suppress three simultaneous rebellions: the Yunnan Muslim rebellion in China's southwest, the Taiping rebellion in China's center, and the Nien Rebellion in the North China Plain. Interestingly enough, the Nien rebellion, which began in earnest in 1853, was itself triggered by popular discontent following the devastating 1851 flood.

The Chinese government eventually got these human rebellions under control, but at an enormous cost. As many as 25 million Chinese perished during the Nien and Taiping rebellions alone, and the Chinese state, already near bankruptcy by 1850, became increasingly helpless against growing European influence, which in turn further discredited the government in the eyes of its people. Worst of all, while struggling to control its own people, the Qing state essentially abdicated control over the Yellow River, which was allowed to seek a new course to the sea. For two decades after 1855, the Yellow River once again became a "braided" river, wandering over a vast area of the North China Plain and inflicting enormous human suffering and economic damage in the process. It took until the 1870s for Chinese engineers to reign in the Yellow River, and because of limited resources the best the engineers could do was retain the river within its new course into the Bohai Sea. Even then, the Yellow River was by no means under control. Disastrous dike collapses in 1887, which were not repaired until 1889, inundated an enormous area and killed an estimated 2 million people, mostly by post-flood famines, cholera epidemics, and other diseases. As for the Grand Canal, the shift of the Yellow River effectively rendered it inoperable. Individual sections remained navigable, but the canal no longer provided a cheap transportation link between North and South China.

Yellow River flooding and the closing of the Grand Canal did not immediately spell the doom of the Qing Dynasty. The Chinese government compensated for the closing of the canal by opening sea shipping lanes to compensate for the loss of inland transportation and collecting cash taxes rather than grain tributes from south China. What is more, the Chinese government completed construction of a railway line between Peking and Hankow in 1899 that was intended to duplicate the functions of the now-defunct canal. However, the Imperial government could not repair the damage done to its reputation: In the eyes of many Chinese, the repeated disasters that befell the Qing dynasty were a sure sign that the Mandate of Heaven had been lifted. The tipping point occurred in 1910, when Japan formally annexed Korea to its growing overseas Empire, humiliating China, which still claimed Korea as a tributary state. In the next year, a small-scale army mutiny triggered a chain of events that led to the overthrow of the Qing Dynasty. Chinese radicals proclaimed the immediate establishment of the Chinese Republic to replace the fallen monarchy, but in actual fact the fall of the Qing ushered in an era of profound political instability in which power devolved into the hands of army commanders and local warlords. As a result, supervision over the Yellow River dikes was inherited by a myriad of local officials who did little to coordinate their efforts.

Not surprisingly, the Yellow River flood control system suffered frequent dike breaches during this period of political turmoil. A major flood in 1925 caused millions of dollars in crop loss, leading to large-scale starvation. Eight major inundations occurred between 1927 and 1938 alone. The worst was the disastrous flood of 1931, triggered by exceptionally heavy rains that caused the Yellow River to rise as much as 17 meters above normal. This flood, which may very well be counted as the single worst non-disease disaster of the 20th century, killed somewhere between 1 and 4 million people, mostly by famine. The floods also compromised China's potable water supply, contributing to the 100,000 reported cholera cases and 34,000 recorded deaths in 312 Chinese cities in the following year. The mayhem caused by the 1931 flood and 1932 cholera epidemic was compounded by an ongoing civil war between Nationalist troops and a growing Communist insurgency that prevented food relief from reaching the afflicted population. To add insult to injury, the Japanese Empire took advantage of China's natural and man-made catastrophes and invaded Manchuria in 1931. Indeed, for the next 15 years China would add Japanese invasion to its already lengthy list of woes.

The 1931 flood was perhaps the worst in Chinese history, but it was by no means the last. In 1933, the flooding river breached the dikes in 54 places, inundating the southern portion of the North China Plain; indeed, contemporaries feared that the Yellow River might re-capture the lower branch of the Huai and thus return to its pre–1855 course. Thousands of lives were lost immediately to the floods, and property damage was estimated at the time to be $250 million, or nearly $3 billion in 2006 currency. The Yellow River broke its banks once again in 1938, this time with human assistance: A commander in the Chinese Nationalist forces deliberately breached the dikes in hopes of slowing a major Japanese offensive into the North China Plain. During this disaster high waters flooded the remnants of the Grand Canal, allowing Yellow River water to penetrate as far south as the Yangtze River basin. Once again, contemporary observers worried that the Yellow River might change its course entirely and capture the riverbed of the Huai. This did not happen, but famine and disease resulting from the flood killed as many as 900,000 people. The problems caused by this flood were compounded by the Japanese invasion; not only did the Japanese restrict the movement of refugees in the territory they controlled, but the worst of the dike breaches lay in "no-man's land" between Japanese and Nationalist controlled territory, complicating the task of repairing the dikes.

In light of the half-century of disasters that preceded it, the eventual victory of the Communists over the Nationalists in the Chinese Civil war was a watershed event, not only in Chinese politics, but also in Chinese Yellow River control. In the years after the Communist Revolution the new government of the Peoples' Republic of China (PRC), well aware that its legitimacy depended on Yellow River flood control, mobilized a massive amount of manpower to build, watch over, and maintain Yellow River dikes. As a result, a possible 1949 flood was averted when strengthened dikes withstood the high water. Bolstered by their success, the Communist elite crafted an ambitious set of flood control measures designed not only to tame the Yellow River but harness its agricultural and hydroelectric potential. PRC Vice-Premier Teng Tse-Hui made this clear in a 1955 speech to the Second Session of the First People's Congress. Teng contended that "the problem of the Yellow River is the concern of the whole nation," and in the tradition of the Mandate of Heaven, he blamed its floods on the culpability of previous governments: "in the past the scourge of the Yellow River has been inseparable from the crimes of the reactionary ruling class." Now that China had liberated from its former "reactionary" rulers, Teng contended, "not only will flood and drought on the Yellow River be eliminated, full use will be made of its water resource for irrigation, power generating, and navigation." Indeed, Teng invoked the spirit of Yu, the legendary river-taming sage-king, asserting that "Yu's great ambition still fires people to this day."

"Yu's great ambition" burned particularly strong in the heart of Mao Zedong, the Chairman of the Chinese Communist Party and *de facto* dictator of China from 1949 to his death in 1976. Indeed, Teng's 1955 speech almost certainly reflected Mao's vision for the Yellow River. The centerpiece of Mao's campaign to tame the Yellow River was the construction of the Sanmenxia dam and power station, completed in 1960 after three years of work and the eviction of 400,000 people living in the area of the proposed reservoir. Sanmenxia was designed not only to generate power, but to regulate the flow of the river, entrapping floods during the high season and releasing water in months when the river ebbed low. Unfortunately, the Sanmenxia dam, like so many other Yellow River projects before, was soon undone by the River's extraordinary silt load. Within four years of completion, the reservoir behind the dam had lost 40 percent of its capacity due to siltation and the hydroelectric turbines were clogged with silt. Today, although limited hydroelectric power capacity has been restored, the reservoir has been reduced to only 10 percent of its former capacity, rendering the dam a potential liability rather than an asset in dealing with floods. Some Chinese engineers have even suggested dismantling the useless dam entirely, although the PRC government, unwilling to accept the loss of face that this surrender to the river would represent, has resisted such calls.

Despite the failure of Sanmenxia and other large-scale hydroelectric projects, the PRC government can boast of a spotless record of flood control along the Yellow River from 1949 to the present. In the past half-century, not a single breach in the Yellow River dikes as occurred, an almost unprecedented success rate. However, as always with the Yellow River, this victory has been achieved at an enormous economic and environmental cost. Because of continued silt deposits, the Yellow River has risen by approximately a meter per decade since 1855, and thus has once again become a hanging river, looming as many as 13 meters over the surrounding North China Plain. What is more, although the Yellow River has fueled productive agriculture in many regions, the flood control projects have themselves created vast sterile areas up and down the river's banks. Since the material used to build up the dikes is collected from nearby due to transportation costs, artificial depressions called "back-swamps" have formed in belts alongside the dikes where the soil was excavated. Water cannot drain from these dikes except by evaporation, so waterlogging and resultant soil salinization has occurred in an 600–700 kilometer stretch along the Yellow River, ruining .7 million hectares of formerly productive farmland. What is more, the same problem threatens the quality of the drinking water in many areas adjacent to the North China Plain.

Other problems of the modern-day Yellow River involve not overregulation of the channel, but rather under-regulation of the use of its water resources. Since Mao's death, China has implemented the so-called "Four Modernizations," which in practice have meant the decentralization of the Chinese economy and the shift from a command to a free market economy. In the Yellow River basin, this policy shift has lead to the rapid industrial and agricultural development of the Yellow River watershed. Indeed, nearly half a billion people now live in northern China, despite the fact that the region's rivers, including the Yellow, hold only 15 percent of the country's water. Far from regulating demands on the Yellow River water, however, the PRC government has actively encouraged water use. Indeed, despite its scarcity, water remains heavily subsidized in China, and until recently was provided free of charge. Not surprisingly, this policy has encouraged overuse of this precious resource, to the point that in some years the Yellow River now runs dry before reaching the Bo Hai Sea. The Chinese government is now implementing an ambitious new scheme to ameliorate the situation: the so-called North-South Water Transfer Project, a new "Grand Canal" of sorts, designed to transfer the bounty of the Yangtze Basin to the arid north. It remains to be seen if this unprecedented engineering project can solve North China's water problems, but if China's previous schemes to alter the natural landscape are any indication, this hydrological experiment may lead to disastrous long-term results.

Worse yet, North China's water problems are expected to worsen as global warming becomes a lived reality in years to come. The Qinghai-Tibet Plateau, which provides about 50 percent of the Yellow River's water, is expected to experience less rainfall in a global warming world. What is more, much of the Yellow River's water originates in mountain glaciers, which have already begun a steady retreat. In the short run, glacial melt has actually augmented the Yellow River's flow, but once these glaciers disappear entirely the Yellow River's volume will likely shrink dramatically, greatly complicating China's struggle to provide food and water to its teeming population.

Furthermore, poor regulation of Chinese industry along the Yellow River has made the Yellow River one of the most polluted waterways in the modern world, with horrible consequences for many who live along its banks. Pollution of the Yellow River began during Mao's rule, though during these years it was kept in check somewhat by Communist Party ideology that called for striking a balance between people and the environment. This ideology derived in part from old Taoist ideas of harmony between man and nature, but also reflected China's current needs, since environmental programs such as recycling fit well with Mao's dream of Chinese economic self-sufficiency. After Mao's death, the new Chinese regime promised to make environment protection a priority. However, this proved to be an empty promise due to decentralization of the economy and lack of effective enforcement measures. Indeed, the pollution levels in China in general and of the Yellow River in particular have risen dramatically since the 1970s. Today, at any given moment, up to 10 percent of the Yellow River actually consists of discharged wastewater that is often contaminated with industrial chemicals. As a result, fully 50 percent of the Yellow River is now considered biologically dead or else is so badly polluted that it cannot be used for irrigated agriculture. The Yellow River is far from unique in this regard. The drinking water of nearly 50 percent of the population of the PRC is contaminated with human or industrial waste. This is especially true in the countryside, where cancer rates have risen 23 percent since 2005 and gastrointestinal cancer is now the number one killer. However, the problem is exceptionally acute along the Yellow River, since the straightjacket of dikes that trap the river's sediment also concentrate its pollutants. The heavily polluted delta of the Yellow River is now dotted with "cancer villages" that suffer melanoma incidence rates 25 times the national average.

It remains to be seen if the Yellow River's environmental problems represent mere growing pains attending China's rise to prosperity or whether they are portents of the nation's future. Recent evidence suggests the latter — studies have found that China now loses 5.8 percent of its GDP growth to environmental damage each year. And all the while the Yellow River continues to rise ever higher in its elevated bed, waiting for engineering incompetence, governmental weakness, a powerful earthquake, or civil disorder to liberate it from its constraining dikes, allowing the Yellow River to seek a new, disastrous course to the sea.

Study Questions

1. Based on this reading, which do you think has done more to transform Yellow River flooding into a disaster — natural forces, or human economic, political, and ideological concerns?

2. Given the hydraulic realities of the Yellow River, to what degree were the great floods of the late 19th–early 20th centuries inevitable?

3. What does this section suggest about the inherent strengths — and weaknesses — of different types of government ideologies (monarchical vs. socialist, state-controlled or market economy) in dealing with natural forces?

4. "Despite repeated claims by the Chinese state that it controlled the Yellow River, in reality the Yellow River has generally controlled the Chinese state." To what degree do you agree with this statement?

Sources/Suggested Readings

Barnett, Robert W. "North China Floods Bring Large Losses." *Far Eastern Survey*, Vol. 8, No. 22 (Nov. 8, 1939), pp. 264–265.

Brush, Lucien M., M. Gordon Wolman, and Huang Bing-Wei. *Taming the Yellow River: Silt and Floods.* Boston: Kluwer Academic Publishers, 1989.

Cannon, Terry and Alan Jenkins eds., *The Geography of Contemporary China: The Impact of Deng Xiaoping's Decade.* New York: Routledge, 1990.

Chang, Chi-Yun. "Climate and Man in China." *Annals of the Association of American Geographers*, Vol. 36, No. 1 (Mar. 1946), pp. 44–74.

Chengrui, Mei, and Harold E. Dregne. "Review Article: Silt and the Future Development of China's Yellow River." *The Geographical Journal*, Vol. 167, No. 1 (Mar. 2001), pp. 7–22.

"China's Vast Flood Threatens to Unite Hwang Ho and Yangtze." *Science News-Letter*, Vol. 34, No. 1 (Jul 2, 1938), pp. 5–6.

Dakang, Zuo, and Zhang Peiyuan. "The Huang-Huai-Hai Plain." In B. L. Turner II, William C. Clark, Robert W. Kates, John F. Richards, Jessica T. Mathews, and William B. Meyer, eds., *The Earth as Transformed by Human Action*. New York: Cambridge University Press, 1990, pp. 473–477.

Dodgen, Randall A. *Controlling the Dragon: Confucian Engineers and the Yellow River in Late Imperial China*. Honolulu: University of Hawai'i Press, 2001.

"Famine Stalks after Floods on Tragic Plains of China." *Science News-Letter*, Vol. 24, No. 646 (Aug. 26, 1933), pp. 141–142.

Greer, Charles. *Water Management in the Yellow River Basin of China*. Austin: University of Texas Press, 1979.

Hu, Ch'ang-Tu. "The Yellow River Administration in the Ch'ing Dynasty." *The Far Eastern Quarterly*, Vol. 14, No. 4, Special Number on Chinese History and Society. (Aug. 1955), pp. 505–513.

Larmer, Brook. "Bitter Waters." *National Geographic*, Vol. 213, No. 5 (May 2008), pp. 146–169.

Lewis, Mark Edward. *The Flood Myths of Early China*. Albany: State University of New York Press, 2006.

Lockwood, Edward T. "Floods and Flood Prevention in China." *Far Eastern Survey*, Vol. 4, No. 21 (Oct 23, 1935), pp. 164–168.

"The Peking-Hankow Railway." *Bulletin of the American Geographical Society*, Vol. 38, No. 9 (1906), pp. 554.

Roberts, J. A. G. *The Complete History of China*. Great Britain: Sutton, 2006.

Shan-Yu, Yao. "The Chronological and Seasonal Distribution of Floods and Droughts in Chinese History, 206 BC–AD 1911." *Harvard Journal of Asiatic Studies*, Vol. 6, No. 3/4 (Feb. 1942), pp. 273–312.

Shan-Yu, Yao. "The Geographical Distribution of Floods and Droughts in Chinese history, 206 BC–AD 1911." *The Far Eastern Quarterly*, Vol. 2, No. 4 (Aug. 1943), pp. 357–378.

Tse-Hui, Teng. "Report on the Multiple-Purpose Plan for Permanently Controlling the Yellow River and Exploiting Its Water Resources." Delivered on July 18, 1955, at the Second Session of the First National People's Congress, China.

Wei, Huang. *Conquering the Yellow River*. Peking: Foreign Languages Press, 1978.

Xu, Jiongxin. "Naturally and Anthropogenically Accelerated Sedimentation in the Lower Yellow River, China, over the Past 13,000 Years." *Geografiska Annaler. Series A, Physical Geography*, Vol. 80, No. 1 (1998), pp. 67–78.

Xu, Jiongxin. "A Study of the Long-Term Environmental Effects of River Regulation on the Yellow River of China in Historical Perspective." *Geografiska Annaler. Series A, Physical Geography*, Vol. 75, No. 3 (1993), pp. 61–72.

6.2: Flooding Caused by the Asian Tsunami, 2004

In December of 2004 a massive earthquake off the Indian Ocean island of Sumatra triggered the worst natural disaster of the 21st century to date. Although the quake itself was located too far offshore to cause much damage or loss or life, the tsunami wave it created wreaked horrific destruction throughout the coastal regions of the Indian Ocean, eventually killing as many as 300,000 people in Indonesia, Sri Lanka, India, Thailand, and elsewhere. Millions more were rendered homeless and jobless by the disaster, triggering a massive humanitarian crisis throughout coastal South and Southwest Asia. In the short term, damage inflicted by the tsunami was roughly proportional to a given area's proximity to the earthquake epicenter and to the existence or absence of intervening land masses capable of deflecting the tsunami waves. In the longer term, however, the story is more complicated. In general, more affluent countries and social groups recovered more quickly from the disaster, while impoverished countries and social groups suffered more long-term affects, especially their situations were complicated by pre-quake political turmoil. Indeed, the Asian Tsunami of 2004 must be understood not only as an event unto itself but as an exacerbating factor that worsened existing political, social, gender, and economic inequalities throughout the Indian Ocean coast.

As might be expected by a recent event that affected many different nations, the Asian Tsunami goes by a number of different names in the current literature. Some names refer to the location, such as "Asian Tsunami" or "South-East Asian Tsunami." Others refer to it by the body of water that it primarily affected, and call it the "Indian Ocean Tsunami." Still others have dubbed it the "Boxing Day Tsunami" in honor of the day that it occurred: December 26th is a widely celebrated holiday in the Anglophone world outside of the United States. Since the tsunami waves reached as far as Mozambique in Africa, "Indian Ocean Tsunami" is probably the most accurate title. In this section, however, I will refer to the event as the "Asian Tsunami," partially for the sake of brevity but also because this seems to be emerging as the most popular name for the event: "Asian Tsunami" generated 529,000 Google hits in spring of 2008, as opposed to "Indian Ocean Tsunami" and "Boxing Day Tsunami," which scored only 291,000 and 59,400 hits respectively.

By whatever name, the Asian Tsunami owed its origin to the powerful Great Sumatran-Andaman Earthquake of December 24, 2006. The Sumatran-Andaman Earthquake had a magnitude of somewhere between 9.1 and 9.3, the energy equivalent to 500,000 Hiroshima-type atomic bombs. Earthquakes on this scale are extremely rare: Indeed, the Great Sumatran-Andaman Earthquake was the second highest magnitude quake ever recorded by modern seismic instruments. The Sumatran-Andaman quake was so powerful that its reverberations were felt in Singapore, nearly 1,000 kilometers away from the epicenter. Closer to the epi-

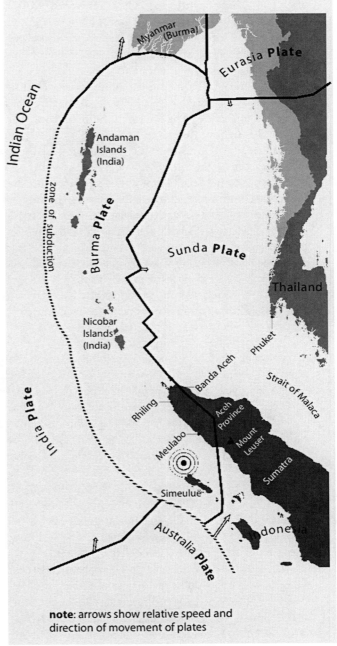

Epicenter of the Sumatran-Andaman Earthquake

note: arrows show relative speed and direction of movement of plates

USGS

center, the earthquake's powerful seismic waves seem to have re-awakened Leuser Mountain and Mount Talang, two nearby Sumatran volcanoes that were dormant at the time of the earthquake but which exhibited volcanic activity over the course of the next year.

The Great Sumatran-Andaman Earthquake quake was unusual in terms of territorial scope as well as magnitude. Although the quake did have an epicenter, located approximately 100 kilometers offshore of the Indonesian Island of Sumatra and less than 50 kilometers from the nearby island of Simeuluë, this epicenter only represented the beginning of the quake. Once begun, plate movements continued in a northwesterly direction, eventually reaching the Andaman Islands 400 kilometers from its point of origin. As a result, the earthquake itself lasted up to 10 minutes by some calculations, a remarkably long time. The length of the fault affected by the quake is important, since it played a crucial role in magnifying the destructive power of the resulting tsunami. To understand why, imagine two windowless rooms, one lit with a single incandescent light bulb, and the other illuminated by a long florescent bulb of the same candle power. The incandescent bulb will cast harsh light in exposed areas, but remote corners will be hidden in shadow. The florescent bulb, on the other hand, would distribute its light far more equally throughout the room. Because of its length, the Great Sumatran-Andaman Earthquake acted more like a florescent bulb — an exceptionally powerful florescent bulb, for that matter — that shed some light into nearly every corner of the Indian Ocean basin.

Thanks to modern seismographic equipment, the magnitude of the earthquake was almost immediately appreciated by earthquake experts around the world. However, in the vicinity of the quake itself, the Great Sumatran-Andaman Earthquake aroused fewer concerns. On nearby Simeuluë, where the quake was most strongly felt, residents abandoned the coastline for high ground and many lives were consequently saved. Indeed, the only death to occur on Simeuluë on the day of the tsunami was caused by the shaking of the earthquake itself. However, since seismic waves lose their force rapidly as they move away from the center of the event, the quake was perceived more mildly on the nearby island of Sumatra, where it caused some damage but little loss of life. Without knowing the exact epicenter of the quake, it was impossible for Sumatrans to tell whether the earthquake was a minor local tremor or a powerful but distant undersea quake capable of causing tsunamis.

In any case, few people living alongside the Indian Ocean in December of 2004 had much experience with powerful tsunamis. Unlike the Pacific Ocean, which experiences an average of 8 tsunamis a year, the Indian Ocean experiences a tsunami only every 3 years or so. Put another way, this means countries within and around the Pacific Ocean experience 24 times as many tsunamis as the countries ringing the Indian Ocean. This fact helps to answer one commonly asked question in the aftermath of the Tsunami — why had the nations on the rim of the Indian Ocean not invested into a tsunami warning system comparable to the Pacific's Tsunami Warning System (TWS)? The Pacific TWS employs satellites, buoys, and coastal measuring stations to detect oncoming tsunami waves, then utilizes public alarm systems and marked evacuation routes to get people away from endangered areas. However, given the far lower likelihood of tsunamis in the Indian Ocean and the greater poverty of these nations compared to their Pacific counterparts, it was entirely understandable — though certainly unfortunate — that no Indian Ocean equivalent of the TWS existed in 2004.

Unfortunately, while Indian Ocean tsunamis are far less common than their Pacific counterparts, when they do occur they tend to be quite powerful due to the specific tectonic characteristics of the region. Approximately 80 percent of the Indian Ocean's tsunamis are generated by the "Sunda Arc" fault system, which stretches from the Andaman Islands to Java. For the most part, the Sunda Arc fault is a subduction fault — the Indian Ocean plate is diving below the lighter Eurasian and Australian continental plates — and as we learned in chapter 2 subduction faults can generate the most powerful earthquakes. What is more, the Sunda Arc fault line is a "megathrust" fault characterized by "slip-stick" motion. In megathrusts, two fault lines may remain stuck fast for decades or centuries at a time only to "slip" when the pressure becomes overwhelming, leading to a sudden release of enormous amounts of stored-up seismic energy. As a result, megathrust faults such as the Sunda Arc fault breed not only powerful earthquakes and tsunamis but also a good deal of complacency, as many years generally pass between each major seismic event.

Height of Indonesian Tsunami 12.26.2004

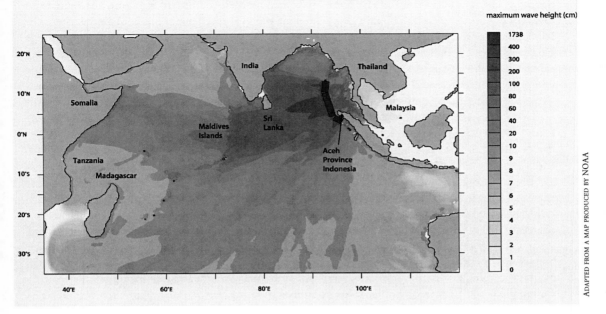

maximum wave height (cm)

ADAPTED FROM A MAP PRODUCED BY NOAA

In December of 2004, however, this complacency would prove fatal. During the earthquake, the sea floor along the fault line rose as much as 15 meters, displacing over 1000 cubic kilometers of water. Gravity quickly pulled this enormous mound of water downwards, and as the mound spread out, powerful tsunami waves began to radiate outwards from the fault line at a speed of up to 1000 kilometers per hour. At sea, these waves were barely perceptible and probably rose less than a meter above normal sea levels. However, as discussed in chapter 6, when the tsunami wave struck shallow waters the inherent energy of the wave became concentrated in a smaller and smaller volume of water. As Asian Tsunami expert Susan Blackhall eloquently explains, tsunami waves can be likened to a flick of a whip: "as the 'wave' travels down the whip from the handle to tip, the same energy is compressed in less and less material, which makes it move more violently." As a consequence, the Asian Tsunami reached as high as 50 meters above sea level when it collided with the unsuspecting settlements on the coast.

The first waves of the Asian Tsunami rolled ashore in Sumatra at 8:30 A.M. local time, or 1:30 A.M. Greenwich Mean Time (hereafter GMT). The highest wave heights recorded for the tsunami occurred on the coastline of Indonesia's Aceh province, partly because of the proximity of this region to the quake epicenter, but also because the coastline here was relatively steep, meaning that the sheer momentum of the tsunami drove the sea water high atop the shore. At Rhiting the wave reached nearly 49 meters up the coastal heights. Elsewhere along the coast to the west of Banda Aceh the wave heights averaged between 20 and 30 meters, but thankfully this area was not densely populated and the coastal hills prevented the tsunami from penetrating far inland. Banda Aceh itself was in a more protected location, since a headland shielded it from the direct impact of the tsunami wave. Nonetheless, this city of 300,000 was inundated by an average of 5 meters and a maximum of 12 meters of surging ocean water, leading to catastrophic damage. The tsunami wave then reached Thailand at 10:00 local time (GMT 3:00), where witnesses later reported hearing "a loud rumbling in the distance," followed shortly by "a white-tipped wall of water bearing down on the beach." When the wall of water reached land it inundated coastal Phuket and the surrounding islands with about 4 meters of water.

The Asian Tsunami then pulled off one of its most bizarre feats; since the wave traveled nearly as fast as the rotation of the Earth, it actually struck the Indian subcontinent earlier in local time than in Sumatra. At 3:25 GMT, the first waves washed ashore in Sri Lanka, where the local time was only 9:25 A.M. Wave height here reached as high as 11 meters, with an average height of about 5 or 6 meters. Only minutes later, at 3:35 GMT, the tsunami began to wash ashore in India's Southeastern Tamil Nadu province, where the clocks read only 9:05 in the morning, as India's clocks run 5 hours and 30 minutes ahead of GMT. The tsunami here reached a maximum height of only about 5 meters and an average height of 3.5 to 4 meters, but this is a reflection of the region's low-lying coastal topography as much as the tsunami's dwindling force, since tsunami waves reach lower vertical heights but greater horizontal distances where the coastline is flat. The tsunami then struck the Maldives, a chain of low-lying islands off India's southwest tip, where it achieved a maximum run-up height of 4.65 meters and an average height of over 2 meters, enough to completely submerge many of the archipelago's smaller islands. In the meantime, echoes from the tsunami bouncing between land masses began to wash ashore in coastal Malaysia, where run-up heights of up to 3.7 meters were reported. However, the geographic realities of the Indonesian archipelago prevented the tsunami from reaching significant heights further to the west. At around the same time, the tsunami struck Myanmar, but we know little about how the disaster affected the former Burma because the tight-lipped military junta that rules the country shared little information with the world community. Unfortunately for the Burmese people, the same junta also refused to cooperate with the international relief effort that followed.

After passing the southern tip of India, the character of the westward-traveling tsunami wave changed substantially. As it passed through the narrow passages separating the Maldive and Laccadive Islands, the tsunami's power was scattered, blunting its impact farther to the west. The worst-hit area west of the Maldives was probably Somalia, where 300 people lost their lives in Puntland on the tip of the horn of Africa. By the time that the tsunami wave reached Oman at 8:13 GMT, or just after noon at local time, its run-up height was only .28 meters. The wave was the same height when it came ashore in Kenya at 9:57 GMT or just before noon local time. The tsunami wave also penetrated the Persian Gulf, as this author knows from personal experience: On the day of the tsunami, my family and I were taking part in a desert dune-bashing expedition in the Gulf nation of Qatar, and by the time we reached the beach camp on Qatar's east coast for a late lunch an echo of the tsunami wave had washed into the campsite's tents, hurting no one but leaving the camp a soggy mess. While the Maldive and Laccadive islands for the most part reduced the power of the tsunami, they also played a cruel trick on India's southwest coast. Waves rebounding off the Laccadive Islands struck the coastline of India's densely populated Kerala province, inundating this area with up to 5 meters of water.

Although Thailand was by no means the most severely affected region struck by the tsunami, Thailand was where the world's attention was first focused upon in the aftermath of the disaster. The reason for this is simple — on the day after Christmas, Thailand was swarming with European, Australian, and American tourists, who not only gave the story immediacy for western audiences but who also recorded the tsunami in photos and movies that quickly made their way into the world's news media. The only other area to receive much coverage in the hours after the disaster was the Sri Lankan town of Galle, another resort town. Both areas did suffer considerably from the tsunami. Sri Lanka suffered over 35,000 casualties, mostly in coastal fishing villages that were all but swept clean by the sudden rising of the sea. In Galle itself, an estimated 4,000 perished. Thailand suffered fewer dead — only about 8,000 — but far higher property damage, since the coastline where the tsunami struck hardest was on or near the resort island of Phuket. The disparity in the death toll between the two areas also reflected the different construction styles used in the two regions. While most Sri Lankan dwellings in the affected region were simple wood huts, structures in Thailand consisted of a mixture of wooden houses, unreinforced concrete buildings built largely from cinderblocks, and reinforced concrete structures that proved particularly resistant to tsunami waves. What is more, many buildings on Phuket were multi-story structures, meaning that only the occupants of the ground floor were directly affected by the Tsunami impact.

Although India received considerably less attention from global media in the immediate aftermath of the tsunami, the destruction there was considerable as well. Over 12,000 people were reported dead in India's Tamil Nadu province, and given poor record keeping in rural India, the actual death toll was certainly much higher. About 50 percent of the dead were children and most the rest were adult women, which reflects the greater difficulty that women and children had keeping their heads above the surging floodwaters. Witnesses described bodies scattered throughout the coastal villages, even hanging from trees and buildings. One of the few places to suffer little damage along this coastline was Naluvedapathy, which was protected by a kilometer-thick curtain of tens of thousands of trees planted by villagers in 2002 in a successful bid to enter the Guinness Book of World Records. Southwest India's Kerala province suffered as well once the tsunami wrapped around the tip of India and rebounded off of the Laccadive Islands. Worst hit were the villages along southwest India's Kayamkulam Inlet, where 132 people were killed, most of them women and children trapped within submerged houses.

Ironically, the area that received the least initial attention was in fact the worst affected by the tsunami: Aceh province on Indonesia's island of Sumatra, which lay closest to the epicenter of the quake. The town of Meulabo, a settlement of 120,000 people located only a few dozen kilometers from the earthquake's epicenter, was struck by no less than seven waves, killing an estimated 40,000. The nearby coastal villages of Gleebruk, Calan, and Teunom were essentially obliterated, along with another 14,000 lives. Tens of thousands more were left homeless by the tsunami wave, which also inflicted about $395 million in damage to local transportation infrastructure and made recovery efforts in this fairly remote area difficult to carry out.

Worse yet, the provincial government of Aceh was in no position to provide immediate assistance to the ravaged coast as the regional capital Banda Aceh was itself devastated by the tsunami. Banda Aceh, meaning "Port of Aceh" in the local tongue, was a densely populated city of approximately 300,000 before the tsunami struck. Although Banda Aceh was shielded by a headland from the worst of the tsunami waves, a number of factors conspired to render its citizens particularly vulnerable to the Asian Tsunami. Banda Aceh was a low-lying and generally flat city cut by numerous small water channels which provided the tsunami wave easy access to the city's interior; indeed, at Banda Aceh, the tsunami waves penetrated as far as 5 kilometers inland. What is more, Banda Aceh contained relatively few multi-story structures and few reinforced concrete structures capable of withstanding the tsunami waves. It was also a prominent fishing port, so a number of large seagoing fishing vessels were docked or anchored in the harbor at the time of the tsunami. As the waves washed ashore these heavy vessels were driven into and through the streets of the town, adding to the destruction. To make matters still worse, Banda Aceh lay close enough to the quake epicenter to have been shaken by the Sumatran-Andaman Earthquake itself, weakening the city's buildings immediately before the arrival of the tsunami. As a result of these factors, Banda Aceh suffered both the most comprehensive property damage and the highest death toll: 2 out of every 3 people killed by the Asian tsunami perished on the Island of Sumatra, and the bulk of Sumatra's deaths occurred in Banda Aceh.

In terms of overall portion of the population, however, it was probably the Nicobar and Andaman Islands, low-lying island archipelagos situated atop the Sunda Arc fault line, that suffered most from the tsunami waves. These islands, which belong to India, are inhabited both

HTTP://COMMONS.WIKIMEDIA.ORG/WIKI/IMAGE:SUMATRA_DEVASTATION.JPG

Damage to a Sumatran coastal village after the Asian Tsunami.

by people from the mainland and by indigenous tribal peoples clinging to a pre-agricultural lifestyle. The Tsunami waves struck this island chain hard, inundating several islands beneath 15 meters of water; indeed, several islands were split in half or fundamentally re-shaped by the tsunami impact. Out of 50,000 inhabitants of these islands, as many as 7,000 perished during the Asian tsunami, though the exact death toll remains a mystery since the indigenous tribal people refuse to establish contact with the outside world. Indeed, according to tsunami expert Susan Blackwell, surviving islanders shot arrows at Indian government helicopters sent to check on their well-being after the disaster.

In the aftermath of the Asian Tsunami, nations throughout the Indian Ocean rim began picking up the pieces, but the challenges they faced were enormous. So many had died that the morgues were completely overwhelmed, and identifying the dead became a grueling but crucial task. Normal water supply and sanitation systems were also a casualty of the tsunami, raising the specter of epidemic disease. Much of the food in affected regions was washed away or ruined by the tsunami, and there was little chance of producing more food any time soon, since most the region's fishing boats had been wrecked by the tsunami wave and coastal farmland was quite often contaminated by salt. Thousands more who provided support services to farmers or fishermen, such as domestic servants or day laborers, became jobless overnight and unable to feed their families. What is more, in many regions the normal transportation and communication infrastructure was knocked out by the tsunami waves, meaning that the worst-affected regions were unable to get the word out about their plight. Indeed, observers reported that the small village of Sigli, only two hours by car from Banda Aceh in Indonesia's Aceh province, was still struggling to get food and medical supplies three months after the tsunami.

Although all nations on the rim of the Indian Ocean suffered similar problems, the degree to which different nations and different groups within those nations coped with these immediate problems depended largely on their pre-tsunami social and economic standing. Thailand, the wealthiest nation to be struck by the tsunami, bounced back the quickest in large part because its tourist industry proved relatively resilient. Although the number of tourists and tourist revenue dropped somewhat between 2004 and 2005, nearly 14 million foreign tourists visited Thailand in 2006, and these tourists spent over 30 percent more money than they had the year before. Indeed, the tsunami itself may have generated some tourist revenue. Many previous visitors to Thailand came back to see what had changed because of the tsunami. In addition, Thailand gained some new tourist attractions from the tsunami, including a police boat that had been washed several kilometers inland by the waves.

Despite the quick rebound of Thailand's profitable tourist industry, Thailand's rapid post-tsunami recover left many of its citizens behind. Fishing boats represent a huge capital investment, but since neither insurance nor government assistance was sufficient to compensate cash-strapped fishermen for their lost boats, the Thai fishing industry was slow to recover from the disaster. This problem was compounded by indebtedness on the part of the fishermen — while the tsunami destroyed their boats, it had left their often heavy debts intact. Many other fishermen, especially the "sea gypsy" groups of coastal areas, suffered from opportunistic land grabs. In the confusion caused by the tsunami, powerful business interests stepped in to claim ownership of the land where sea gypsy villages has been located for decades. Women also suffered discrimination in Thailand in the post-disaster period; the Thai state, for instance, provided only half as much money for funerals of deceased women as it did for deceased men.

Worst of all, however, was the plight of the estimated 7,000 Burmese migrants living in south Thailand who depended on the fishing, construction, or tourism industries for their livelihoods. In the aftermath of the tsunami, not only were these migrants out of work, many were arbitrarily rounded up and deported by the government, a process assisted by the fact that many Burmese migrants had lost their Thai government-issued identification cards during the tsunami. Stories circulated that those forcibly returned to Myanmar were arrested, imprisoned, or forced to dig graves, though given the renegade nature of the Myanmar regime such claims are impossible to verify. Whatever the reality, fear of deportation forced many Burmese migrants to hide in plantations or the jungle out of fear of arrest and deportation. Thankfully, the Thai government reversed its deportation policy within months of the tsunami, and the situation of Burmese migrants into Thailand was returning to some semblance of normality as of 2008.

In Sri Lanka, the recovery effort after the tsunami was slower than in Thailand, which is a reflection of both the high level of destruction and the fairly meager resources of the Sri Lankan government. In the short term tsunami recovery efforts were hampered by numerous pre-tsunami vacancies in the ranks of local government, prompting the Sri Lankan government to call retired officials back into service as consultants. Due to manpower problems within officialdom, the cash grant of 5000 Sri Lankan rupees (about $46 U.S. dollars) promised by the government to those affected by the disaster was slow to reach some areas. Much of the food distributed by the government in devastated areas was substandard or inedible, partly due to poor storage facilities at the distribution points. What is more, the government's efforts to combat post-tsunami homelessness were seriously flawed. In order to prevent a repeat of the tragedy, the government established a "buffer zone" near the ocean that was off-limits to home building, effectively dispossessing many Sri Lankans whose houses had stood inside the buffer zone. Those displaced were offered places in "transitional housing" camps, which writers for the Asia Pacific Forum on Women, Law, and Development condemned as "urban slums set in the middle of nowhere." Many poor Sri Lankans chose to avoid these shelters for fear of losing their jobs as well as their homes. Some Moslem Sri Lankans, in turn, did not want to move away from their mosques. Others worried that *purdah*, the customary segregation of women from men outside the family, would be impossible to practice in the crowded transitional camps.

What is more, some Sri Lankans avoided the transitional housing out of security concerns, which highlights one more factor inhibiting post–Tsunami recovery in Sri Lanka: continued harassment of the local population by the LTTE, better known as the Tamil Tigers. Since 1972, the LTTE has been waging a guerilla war on behalf of Sri Lanka's mostly–Moslem Tamil minority against the Buddhist, Sinhalese majority. As part of this campaign LTTE fighters have been employing terror tactics against Sri Lankan officials and government operations, which unfortunately includes the post-tsunami relief effort. Indeed, on August 21 of 2005, several grenades where flung into a welfare center for people affected by the tsunami in the coastal town of Kalmunai and this represents only the most egregious of a string of TLLE attacks. The TLLE has also been implicated in a number of rapes in the tsunami-stricken area. Government forces have struck back against known TLLE targets, and innocent Sri Lankan citizens have been caught in the crossfire. This level of political instability has not only hampered the government's relief effort, it has also discouraged international Non-Governmental Organizations (NGOs) from providing disaster relief in Sri Lanka. On a more positive note, the TLLE did establish its own tsunami relief efforts for political purposes, and even observers unfriendly to the TLLE have admitted that this relief was efficiently distributed. Nonetheless, the tsunami has done nothing to heal the rift between the Sri Lankan government and the Tamil independence movement.

Although a poorer country than Sri Lanka in terms of per capita GDP, India's sheer size in comparison to the relatively small zone of devastation ensured that it would have resources available — in theory, at least — to provide effective relief. India's relative political stability also made it a safe place for NGO's to operate. However, as elsewhere around the Indian Ocean, pre-existing social, political, and economic conditions have complicated India's post-tsunami recovery. Fishermen suffered particularly hard from the tsunami, since their expensive tools of the trade — boats, nets, docks, etc.— were devastated. What is more, efforts to help the needy were compromised by lingering caste tensions in India. Two groups that have been particularly singled out for poor treatment are the Dalits (the so-called "untouchables") and the Irulas, a Negrito ethnic minority group similar to the Aetas in the Philippines. Discrimination against these groups occurred during the disaster itself: In one documented incident, a pregnant Dalit woman was prevented from seeking shelter in a higher-class home, and had to force her way inside to save herself and her children. Since the tsunami disaster both groups have received less relief from aid groups, largely because higher-caste groups have diverted resources, and the Indian government has provided less financial assistance to families of deceased Dalits than to other groups. Finally, both Dalits and Irulas have suffered discrimination, if not outright intimidation, in the temporary housing camps established by the Indian government.

The area in which pre-existing problems did the most to complicate disaster recovery, however, was Indonesia's chronically unstable Aceh province. Aceh has a long history as an independent state dating to at least the 15th century, when the city of Banda Aceh was the seat of an Islamic sultanate that derived most of its wealth from trade passing through the strategic Straits of Malacca. Aceh remained wealthy into the 19th century, when it produced over half of the world's black pepper. In 1873, however, the Dutch East India Company, which already controlled most of the Indonesian archipelago, went to war to annex Aceh. The Acehnese fought back tenaciously, however, leading to nearly 3 decades of conflict that left up to 100,000 dead on the Aceh side before the Dutch claimed victory in 1903. Even after that point, guerilla fighters in the highlands fought a stubborn, if intermittent, struggle against Dutch control.

When the former Dutch East Indies became the independent state of Indonesia in 1949, Aceh was just as unwilling to give up their independence to the new Indonesian state as they had been to the Dutch, so the war of independence resumed. Indeed, if anything, the struggle for Aceh intensified, since the discovery of oil and gas reserves in Aceh during the 1970s raised the stakes. What is more, many Indonesian officers had an individual financial interest in keeping Aceh part of Indonesia, as a number of officers took advantage of military control over the region to enrich themselves through illegal logging, marijuana growing and trafficking, and other shady businesses. As a result, the Indonesian army responded to local unrest with heavy-handed tactics and alleged human rights abuses, further embittering the local population. In 2003, on the very eve of the Asian tsunami, tensions between Aceh and Indonesia reached a breaking point, and the Indonesian military launched a major offensive against Acehnese. When the tsunami struck in December 2004, the conflict was still ongoing, though as of May that year the previous declaration of martial law had been downgraded to mere civil emergency.

Unfortunately, the man-made disaster of civil emergency served to exacerbate the damage caused by the Asian Tsunami. In the immediate aftermath of the tsunami, the Indonesian government temporarily granted the U.S. military and foreign NGO's access to Aceh to provide disaster relief and recovery efforts, including the collection of bodies, distribution of food, and construction of temporary shelters to house the estimated 600,000 Indonesians displaced by the tsunami. Once the immediate crisis was over, however, the Indonesian military took quick action to curb outside interference, asking foreign troops to leave the country by March 2005 and forbidding foreign NGO's from meeting in Banda Aceh to discuss rehabilitation efforts. The Indonesian military also restricted the mobility of NGO aid workers within Aceh, ostensibly out of security concerns, though critics have suggested the real reason is to keep outsiders from observing ongoing human rights abuses by the Indonesian military.

What is more, the Indonesian military has adopted a controversial "resettlement program" for those displaced by the tsunami. Rather than allowing coastal villagers to return to their former home sites, this program has forced many tsunami refugees to dwell in large barracks-like camps far from their native villages. Indonesian authorities claim that such measures are necessary to streamline the distribution of relief supplies. However, some observers contend that the real purpose of these camps is to control a potentially rebellious population during an ongoing civil conflict. If so, the Indonesian government is certainly not the first to use a natural disaster to try to achieve political goals during a civil war. As we shall see in more detail in section 7.3, Ethiopian authorities manipulated a famine — some would argue they engineered it — in order to gain leverage over potentially restive tribal groups.

In any case, it must be admitted that as of 2008 Indonesian government seems to be employing the carrot as well as the stick to pacify Aceh province. It recently granted the region more self-governance and allowed province-wide elections in 2006, which brought former leaders of the independence movement into the provincial government. According to the authors of a 2007 Worldwatch Institute report, both the Indonesian government and the Aceh separatist leaders had good reason to be conciliatory in the months after the tsunami. The Indonesian government was keenly aware of the international scrutiny that the tsunami had brought to Aceh, and thus more inclined to resolve the matter peaceably. What is more, Aceh separatist leaders may have been predisposed to peace even before the tsunami, due to battlefield defeats against the Indonesian military, and the tsunami may have provided a face-saving excuse for separatist leaders to sit at the negotiation table. Therefore, there are reasons for optimism as well as pessimism regarding the future of Aceh province. It remains to be seen if the peace movement in Aceh following the Asian tsunami will prove to be just a short-term wave or a longer term changing of the tide.

If the overall post-tsunami relief effort has any silver lining, it is the virtual absence of epidemic disease as a wide-scale problem. In the days after the tsunami authorities worried that the destruction of normal water supply and sewage systems might provide a fertile ground for diarrheal diseases like cholera and that the destruction of housing and pools of stagnant water would lead to a spike in mosquito-borne diseases like malaria. The problem was expected to be exacerbated by widespread destruction of health care facilities in the affected area: Overall, an estimated 602 clinics and hospitals were damaged and destroyed by the tsunami around the Indian Ocean, and 700 health care workers were killed in Indonesia alone. In the end, however, the epidemics that authorities expected failed to materialize. The quick distribution of relief supplies, including enormous quantities of bottled water, largely prevented diarrheal diseases from gaining a foothold. What is more, the pools of water left behind by the tsunami tended to be too saline for breeding mosquitoes. Instead, one of the most common diseases to crop up after the Asian Tsunami was entirely unexpected: "Tsunami Lung," a general name given by doctors to respiratory infections in people who had inhaled mud and bacteria during the tsunami itself. Once the problem was identified, however, these cases were quickly remedied with standard antibiotics.

Following the tsunami, Indian Ocean countries belatedly set up a tsunami early detection system much like the TWS already in place in the Pacific. Certainly, this is a step in the right direction — had such a system been in place in 2004 it might have saved lives. However, the human and natural realities of the Indian Ocean may seriously limit the utility of such a system. Unlike the nations of the Pacific Rim, the countries facing the Indian Ocean are fairly poor, with weak transportation and communication infrastructure systems. Consequently, even if the Indian Ocean tsunami warning system detects a tsunami well in advance, this does not guarantee that the news of the impending disaster will get to the people who need it before it is too late, nor that evacuation systems will be in place to get them to safety. What is more, as we have already seen, the Sunda Arc is a "slip-stick" fault, characterized by long periods of dormancy followed by sudden movement. As a result, the Indian Ocean tsunami warning system will most likely have to combat human complacency as well as logistical shortcomings the next time the Sunda Arc fault gives rise to a powerful tsunami.

Study Questions

1. After finishing this section, to what degree do you agree with the statement that the Asian Tsunami "must be understood not only as an event unto itself but as an exacerbating factor that worsened existing political, social, gender, and economic inequalities throughout the Indian Ocean coastal region"?

2. To what degree was the Asian tsunami a "natural" disaster?

3. Overall, the Asian tsunami did not trigger the famines or disease outbreaks normally seen with large-scale natural disasters. Do you think this was due to adequate pre-disaster response, fast global action, or just luck? Explain.

4. Based on your readings and personal experience, if you UN official charged with the responsibility of advising the Indian Ocean community on safeguarding their people against the next tsunami, what advice would you offer? Explain your answer.

Sources/Suggested Readings

Asia Pacific Forum on Women, Law and Development. *Why Are Women More Vulnerable During Disasters? Violations of Women's Human Rights in the Aftermath of the Indian Ocean Tsunami and the Pakistan Earthquake.* Chang Mai, Thailand: Asia Pacific Forum on Women, Law, and Development, 2005.

Blackhall, Susan. *Tsunami*. UK: Taj Books, 2005.

Funk, Joe, Jason Hinman, and Matt Springer. *Tsunami: Hope, Heroes, and Incredible Stories of Survival*. Chicago: Triumph, 2005.

Murty, Tad S, U. Aswathanarayana, and N. Nirupama, eds., *The Indian Ocean Tsunami*. New York: Taylor and Francis, 2007.

Potera, Carol. "Infectious Disease. In Disaster's Wake: Tsunami Lung." *Environmental Health Perspectives*, Vol. 113, No. 11 (Nov. 2005), pp. A734.

Raman, Sunil. "Tsunami Villagers Give Thanks to Trees." BBC News, 2005/02/16. Available from http://news. bbc.co.uk/go/pr//1/hi/world/south_asia/4269847.stm.

Renner, Michael, and Zoë Chafe. *Beyond Disasters: Creating Opportunities for Peace*. Washington, DC: World-watch Institute, 2007.

Shangle, Robert D. *Southeast Asia Tsunami: One of the World's Greatest Natural Disasters in Modern Times*. Beaverton, OR: American Products Publishing Company, 2005.

"Special Report Asia's Tsunami: The Impact." London, UK: The Economist Intelligence Unit, January 2005.

"Tourism Situation Concerning Inbound Foreign Visitors in 2005." *Tourism Authority of Thailand*. Available from http://www2.tat. orth/stat/web/static_index.php

World Health Organization. *Responding to Communicable Diseases Following the Tsunami in South-East Asia*. New Delhi, India: World Health Organization, 2005.

6.3: Flooding Caused by Hurricane Katrina, 2005

Hurricane Katrina, which ravaged Florida and the Gulf Coast States in August of 2005, was the single most destructive natural disaster in American history. The flooding brought by Katrina killed over 1,800 Americans and inflicted over $125 billion in damage in New Orleans and along the Gulf Coast east of the city. Katrina's survivors suffered horribly from heat, deprivation, disease, and exposure in the storm's aftermath, especially those trapped in the Superdome sports stadium or the Morial Convention Center. The American public was profoundly shocked by TV images of desperate, displaced people struggling to stay alive. In some ways, however, the greatest tragedy of Katrina is that much of the death and misery could have been avoided. Poor planning, complacency, and sheer negligence on the local, state, and federal levels combined to turn a natural hazard into a true natural catastrophe.

To some degree, of course, the damage inflicted by Katrina was unavoidable, and to better understand this, it is important to distinguish between Katrina's effect in New Orleans and its effects on other parts of the Gulf coastline. Katrina's worst winds and highest seas actually missed the city of New Orleans and descended instead on coastal Mississippi, which was virtually scraped clean by a storm surge that topped over 8 meters in places. Disasters of this magnitude, though regrettable, are virtually inevitable: There is simply no cost-effective way to protect coastal towns in hurricane zones from storm surges on this scale. The situation in New Orleans, however, was different in two key respects. For one thing, since New Orleans was in the front left quadrant of the storm, where the hurricane was weakest, New Orleans suffered only a glancing blow from Katrina, experiencing winds that barely reached hurricane force and a storm surge that rose as little as 2 meters in places. Furthermore, unlike the indefensible Mississippi coastline, New Orleans was surrounded by flood control structures that were designed to protect it from a storm of Katrina's strength. The failure of New Orleans' "Hurricane Protection System," and the fatal results of that failure, will be the focus of this case study.

Why does New Orleans require a "Hurricane Protection System" (hereafter HPS) in the first place? The answer is clear from even a cursory glance at a topographical map of the area.

To best understand New Orleans' plight, imagine a normal coastal city, then turn it inside-out. Rather than sloping downward towards the sea as waterfront cities generally do, New Orleans looks upwards towards the bodies of water that surround it, namely Lake Pontchartrain, Lake Borgne, and the Mississippi River. Indeed, as science writer John McPhee has pointed out, if the ships on the Mississippi "could turn and move at river level into the city and into the [Superdome] ... they would hover above the playing field like blimps." Although a few New Orleans neighborhoods with fashionable addresses occupy the high ground near the water, most of the rest of the city lies as much as 4 meters below sea level. Without the levees and gates of the HPS, the bowl of New Orleans would quickly be filled by the surrounding waters.

New Orleans lies below sea level largely because it was built on unstable soil. Like most of lower Louisiana, New Orleans' soils consists primarily of sediment washed down the Mississippi River, and this semi-fluid earth is settling and sinking down at a rate of a little less than a meter per hundred years. To some degree this subsidence is natural, but it has been seriously exacerbated by human activities that reduce the moisture content — and thus the volume — of the soil. The subsidence is further exacerbated by the rising level of the river bottom, an unintended consequence of Mississippi River flood control.

The Mississippi is really two rivers: the upper and lower Mississippi. The upper Mississippi rises in the far northern states of Minnesota and Wisconsin and is fed by several moderate-sized rivers on its way south. The upper Mississippi is wide but fast-flowing stream by the time it nears the midpoint of its journey to the Gulf of Mexico. At this point, the Mississippi receives the waters (and sediments) of the Missouri and Ohio Rivers, which drain much of the area west and east of the upper Mississippi respectively. In addition, the river's formerly steep gradient flattens out significantly. Were it not for human intervention, the lower Mississippi would take on the characteristics of a braided river, with numerous and constantly shifting channels.

As the famous humorist, social critic, and one-time Mississippi riverboat pilot Mark Twain wrote, "ten thousand [Mississippi] River Commissions cannot tame that lawless stream." But that did not stop the U. S. Army Corps of Engineers from trying. In 1879 the Corps, with a mandate from Congress, inaugurated a program to control the course of the lower Mississippi using dikes (called levees in the United States). In keeping with the federal style of national government, oversight of the program was divided between federal, state, and local governments; the Mississippi River Commission consisted of three officers from the Corps and three civilians from the public or private sectors at the local level, whose interests frequently conflicted on multiple levels. Not surprisingly, the lower Mississippi flood control program soon became hodge-podge of existing levees that had been built and gradually extended by local governments and private individuals over the previous century combined with new levees designed and constructed under the supervision of the Corps.

The "levees only" policy eventually adopted by the Corps greatly exacerbated the problems inherent in Mississippi River flood control. In the 1850s, two prominent American engineers commissioned by Congress to study Mississippi River flood control presented rival visions on how best to tame the river. Charles Ellet, a celebrated bridge designer, proposed a system whereby flooding would be kept in check by two main mechanisms: 1) levees designed to restrain the river, and 2) reservoirs and outlets intended to drain off excess water before its pressure caused levee failure. Indeed, Elliot advocated building artificial river outlets to protect weak points of the river from Mississippi floodwaters.

Army Captain Andrew A. Humphreys, on the other hand, advocated a "Levees Only" policy. Humphrey's belief was that levees could be used to narrow the stream, speed its flow, and consequently scour dangerous accumulations of sediment from the bed of the Mississippi. Although Humphreys probably wasn't aware of it, his policy was very similar to Pan Jixun's plan for the China's Yellow River as discussed in section 6.1— a plan that ultimately failed since it could not keep pace with sediment deposits. However, Humphreys ultimately won the argument, in large part because the "Levees Only" scheme appealed to the economic interests of planters in the states along the Lower Mississippi, who were unwilling to abandon potential cropland to Ellet's proposed outlets and reservoirs but eager to acquire the riverside land that a "Levees Only" policy would produce. As a result, the Corps of Engineers and the Mississippi River Commission adopted the "Levees Only" policy clung to it doggedly for the next 50 years.

Unfortunately, the "levees only" policy failed to create the self-scouring action that its adherents anticipated, and the Mississippi River rose steadily in its bed, putting increasing pressure on the levees. After a series of major flood disasters throughout the Ohio and lower Mississippi valleys in the early 20th century, culminating the Great Mississippi Flood of 1927, Congress passed legislation that finally put Ellet's recommendations into practice. It took another half-century, but the completion of the flood gates guarding the opening to the Atchafalaya Outlet in 1977 finally brought to fruition the comprehensive flood control system envisioned by Charles Ellet, Jr., in 1852. Still, the damage had been done. Fifty years of holding the Mississippi in a narrow course had produced a "hanging river;" indeed, John McPhee has likened the modern Mississippi to a "large vein on the back of the hand." Other areas along the former Mississippi River floodplain began to subside and sink, since the soil was no longer being replenished by further deposits during flooding. This problem was particularly crucial in the New Orleans area, which was progressively slumping under its own weight into the surrounding bodies of water. So too are the freshwater marshlands surrounding New Orleans, which are being "protected" to death by the levees, since most of these wetlands are longer receiving the river sediment deposits that are a natural part of their ecology. Ironically, while New Orleans sinks, a vast quantity of sediment is guided by the levees straight through downtown New Orleans and into the depths of the Gulf of Mexico.

American commercial interests also share responsibility for New Orleans' hurricane vulnerability. In the past, New Orleans has been protected from storm surge by wetlands, which are estimated to reduce storm surge at a rate of 30 centimeters of flood crest per 4.3 kilometers of marshes and swamp. In recent years, however, the ecological integrity of Louisiana's wetlands has been eroded by the actions of the petroleum industry, which has crisscrossed the freshwater wetlands with pipelines and canals. The result has been the deadly infiltration of saltwater into formerly freshwater marshlands. The construction of the Intracoastal Waterway in 1919 also exacerbated the problem by disrupting the natural ebb and flow of waters that sustain the health of saltwater marshes. The result of these human factors has been dramatic: By 2005, Louisiana was losing wetlands at the rate of a football field every 38 minutes.

With New Orleans sinking, and protective the natural wetlands declining, the human-made structures of the HPS became more and more crucial to New Orleans' future. The HPS consists of a number of control structures, ranging from broad earthen levees, narrower T-wall and I-wall levees (which resemble steep hills topped by fences), flood gates, pumping stations, and drainage canals. In theory, these structures were designed to protect New Orleans from the "standard project hurricane," which was defined by planners as a fast-moving category 3 cyclonic storm. In practice, they proved woefully inadequate. We now know that the HPS failed not because of Katrina's strength, but despite Katrina's weakness. Indeed, Katrina's wind speed in New Orleans barely reached category 1 levels, much less category 3, and Katrina's storm surge in most parts of New Orleans did not reach category 3 standards. More significantly, many HPS storm structures failed before the hurricane was at its height, which suggests that a far weaker storm than the "standard project hurricane" might have flooded the city if it scored a direct hit.

So if Katrina wasn't the long-feared "big one," then, why did the HPS fail so spectacularly?

The answer lies in a fatal combination of resource diversion, engineering mistakes, and clashes between federal and local agencies.

In terms of resource diversion, it is important to understand that the vast majority of the HPS was constructed by the Army Corps of Engineers, but the HPS was by no means the only building project undertaken by the Corps in the New Orleans area. Under pressure from shipping interests, a great deal of the time and the budget of the Corps was diverted to such projects as harbor upgrades, canal dredging, and dock facilities, "improvements" that did nothing to protect New Orleans from disaster. Worse yet, critics charge that at least one of the Corps navigation projects—the MRGO shipping canal—probably exacerbated New Orleans' hurricane vulnerability destroying wetlands in the vitally important south and east sectors of the city, precisely where a hurricane could pose the greatest threat. In the meantime, expenditure on these elaborate shipping projects slowed the completion of the HPS. Although the HPS was originally stated for completion in the year 2008, the Corps admitted in August of 2005 that the last work on the project would not be completed until 2015 at the earliest. In the meantime, the HPS suffered from crucial weaknesses that the Katrina storm surge exploited.

Resource diversion was further exacerbated by poor engineering decisions on the part of the Corps. To save money, the Corps tended to avoid building expensive T-wall levees in favor of I-wall levies, which are half the cost. Unfortunately, I-wall levees are much more vulnerable to the two main causes of levee failure. Consisting of only a packed earth base, a single sheet of iron piling, and a narrow concrete dike, I-wall levees are prone to seepage from below during a storm surge, leading to shifts of the pilings and subsequent levee failure. T-wall levees are braced by additional iron pilings precisely to prevent this type of failure. What is more, if an I-wall levee is overtopped, the soil on its landward side is quickly eaten away by the spilling floodwaters, which can cause the dike to fall backwards and the levee to fail. Again, the more expensive T-wall levees, which feature a wide concrete base at the base of the dike, tend not to suffer this problem. The Corps' penny-pinching was further exacerbated by sheer human error; in a number of locations, especially along the 17th Street and South London drainage canals, the Corps failed to take sufficient soil samples before building levees. As a result the levees built at these locations, where the soil had the "stability of oatmeal" in Michael Grunwall's evocative phrase, did not pass the test of Katrina. At these sites the weight of Katrina's storm surge toppled the weakly-planted levees or forced water through the permeable soils underneath the levees, making levee failure a virtual inevitability.

What is more, disputes between the Corps and local agencies seriously compromised the integrity of the HPS. As a general rule, the Corps was responsible for building HPS structures in New Orleans, and then surrendering supervision and regular maintenance of the structures to the New Orleans Sewerage and Water Board and the Orleans Levee District Board. Unfortunately for New Orleans as a whole, however, these agencies had competing agendas. Consider the example of the New Orleans drainage canals, designed to pump water up and out of the city in case of rain or flooding. Thirty years before Katrina struck, the Corps proposed adding floodgates to the mouths of these canals in order to prevent them from becoming inlets for hurricane storm surge. The Sewerage and Water Board, however, wanted to spend money on more pumping capacity instead, since it was more concerned with pumping rainwater out of the city than preventing storm surge from coming in. They were supported, in turn, by the Orleans Levee District Board, which balked at the high annual cost of maintaining the floodgate structures. As a result of this resistance these crucial floodgates—which might have greatly mitigated the Katrina disaster—where never built.

Given the city's inherent geographic vulnerability and the deficiencies of the HPS, it was hardly a surprise that New Orleans flooded while Katrina passed by on August the 29th 2005.

Some of the flooding was the result of rainfall; indeed, Katrina dumped 50–90 centimeters of rain on metropolitan New Orleans. Other water entered New Orleans by overtopping the levees without destroying them. Taken however, rain and overtopping produced only about a third or less of the total volume of New Orleans floodwaters; if the levees had held, therefore, the flooding of New Orleans would have been more limited in scope and more easily reversed.

Unfortunately, the levees did not hold. Over the morning of the 29th, the HPS was breached repeatedly. First to go was a section of I-wall along the Industrial Canal, which was pushed back by the weight of the storm surge, allowing water to penetrate the weak soil at the sheet pile's base and leading to the failure of the levee. Next to fail was an I-wall on the 17th street canal, which collapsed due to essentially the same process, as did two I-walls on the London Avenue Canal, which were later proven to have been constructed atop a particularly unstable mixture of marshy fill soil and beach sand. Soon after, several more I-walls along the MRGO shipping canal breached due to overtopping, falling backwards into the trench created by water as it spilled onto the land side of the levee.

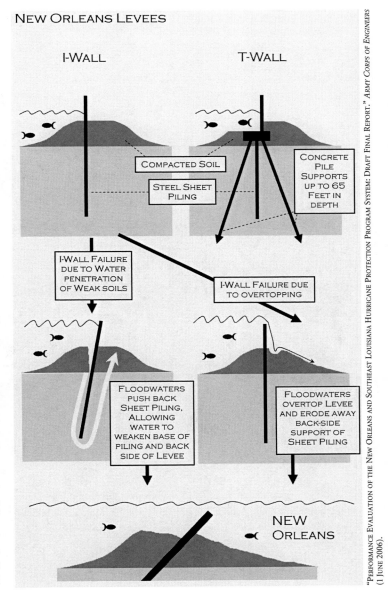

Each of these breaches represented a triple threat to the city of New Orleans. The immediate impact was profound: The water released into New Orleans advanced with steamroller force, and structures near the breaches were destroyed or washed off their foundations. In the medium term, the breaches allowed the surrounding lake waters to pour unchecked into the New Orleans bowl, eventually leaving much of the city under 2 to 3 meters of water. What is more, so long as these breaches existed, any attempts to drain the city were futile, since any water pumped into the river or surrounding lakes would simply flow back in through the breaches. As a result, the majority of flooded New Orleans homes would marinate in the increasingly contaminated water for more than a month, vastly multiplying the resulting property damage.

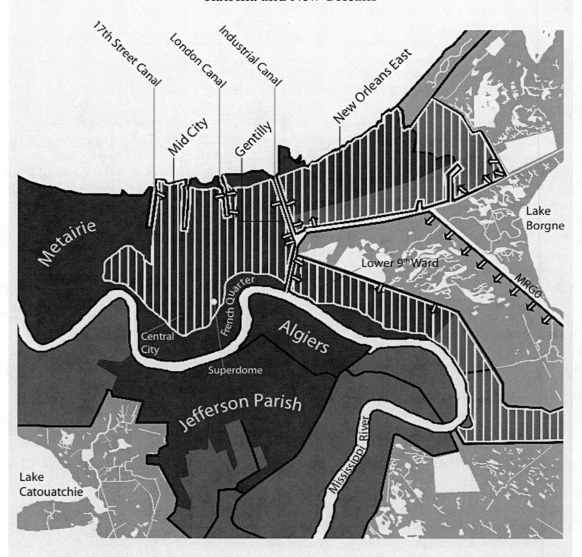

Katrina and New Orleans

17th Street Canal

London Canal

Industrial Canal

New Orleans East

Mid City

Gentilly

Metairie

Lake Borgne

Lower 9th Ward

MRGO

French Quarter

Central City

Algiers

Superdome

Jefferson Parish

Mississippi River

Lake Catouatchie

/ levee

urban areas

other protected areas

wetlands

⇨ major levee breaks

|||| white lines show areas flooded during Katrina

Of course, the greatest tragedy of Katrina was not damaged property, but wrecked lives. Katrina triggered a humanitarian crisis unmatched in recent American history. Despite the late order for mandatory evacuation — due in large part to Mayor Ray Nagin's reluctance to alienate business interests— the vast majority of the residents of New Orleans did leave before the arrival of the storm. Those who stayed behind did so for a variety of reasons. Some were hurricane partiers or else long-time residents who, come hell or high water, were not going to leave their beloved Big Easy. Others had property they wanted to protect from expected post-storm looting. Still others simply couldn't be moved, or could only be moved with difficulty, especially those homebound by medical conditions, in hospitals, or confined to nursing homes.

The vast majority of the 60,000 or so residents who remained in the city, however, were obliged to do so by sheer poverty; simply put, they didn't own a car. Indeed, New Orleans's urban population is one of the poorest in the country. According to demographers, on the eve of Katrina, no less than 25 percent of New Orleans families survived on an annual income of $15,000 or less. Although this fact was well known before Katrina, the municipal government did little to address it other than to encourage church groups to organize car pools in case of evacuation. When Katrina was on the way, the city government stirred itself into limited action, organizing bus service for city residents from their threatened neighborhoods to the Superdome, the city's main designated storm shelter, although they had neglected to stock the Superdome with much in the way of supplies. In the city's defense, there was not much else they could have done to evacuate the city's poorest residents. Although the city was widely criticized for leaving its buses idle before Katrina and allowing them to fall prey to the floodwaters, in truth the New Orleans bus fleet was not nearly up to the task of evacuating New Orleans' poor.

After the levees failed, life for those who stayed behind in New Orleans soon became a nightmare, especially for the residents of the poorest districts of the city, which not coincidentally tended to be the farthest below sea level. Many, especially the elderly and the infirm, died in the first hours of the storm as floodwaters filled their homes. Many others survived by fleeing to their attics; indeed, quite a few residents survived Katrina only by chopping holes in their attic ceiling and clambering onto the roof. Surviving the initial flood was only the half the battle, however. Katrina's victims, especially those without a boat at their disposal, found themselves trapped in their homes and unable to leave except by braving the foul, toxic floodwaters. Worse yet, the survivors soon found themselves without food and water, and in the heat and humidity that followed the storm, dehydration soon reached crisis proportions.

The fate of the 10,000 or so New Orleans residents who sought shelter in the Superdome was little better. When the power failed, the Dome quickly became a sauna, and the lack of running water made it impossible to maintain sanitary conditions; indeed, the dome soon reeked of urine and human waste. There was some food and water to be had, but not nearly enough. Medical supplies were scarce, and the small contingent of National Guardsmen stationed at the Dome was hard pressed to maintain order. Worse yet, the initial 10,000 Superdome refugees were soon joined by another 15,000 storm victims who managed to escape their flooded homes. In desperation, the already overstretched National Guard troops began to ration food supplies, and the city government closed the Dome to new refugees. As a result, many refugees gravitated to the nearby Morial Convention Center, which had the virtue of being dry, but the many vices of being entirely without food, water, electricity, medical care, or National Guard supervision. To sustain themselves, the Convention Center crowd turned to looting of local business, and this tactic of both survival — and in some cases, self-enrichment — soon became a city-wide phenomenon.

If the federal government had intervened decisively at this moment, a lot of human tragedy and quite a few additional deaths might have been averted. Unfortunately, the government's

DEADLY INTERSECTION

response was inept at best, largely because of recent changes that had been made to the Federal Emergency Management Agency, or FEMA. Under the Clinton administration, FEMA had earned bipartisan praise for its rapid response to natural disasters, partly because Clinton ensured it was well funded, and partly because the head of FEMA was both a legitimate natural disasters expert and a close confidant of the president. In the subsequent administration of George W. Bush, however, FEMA rapidly lost its ability to respond to disasters. In part this was due to Bush's budget-cutting priorities: Bush's advisors regarded FEMA as an "oversized entitlement program" and progressively drained it of funding. What is more, FEMA lost the autonomy it had once enjoyed under earlier administrations and was subsumed into the new Department of Homeland Security. The Bush administration also tried to shift FEMA's focus from natural disasters towards counter-terrorism activities, and those within FEMA who opposed this change of priorities either quit in frustration or were fired. In the meantime, the Bush administration handed out positions of leadership within FEMA to political allies with little training natural disaster prevention and mitigation. Drained of funds, refocused towards terrorism, lead by political appointees, and trapped within layers of Department of Homeland Security bureaucracy, FEMA was in no condition to come to the aid of Katrina's survivors.

In any case, even if FEMA had been better equipped, the Bush administration seemed out of touch with the realities of the situation in New Orleans, and the administration's lack of leadership would probably have blunted FEMA's effectiveness. Part of the problem was structural; Homeland Security, the office to which FEMA belonged, was receiving what later proved to be

HTTP://COMMONS.WIKIMEDIA.ORG/WIKI/IMAGE:NEW_ORLEANS_17TH_STREET_CANAL_FILLING.JPG

The 17th Street Canal Levee Breach.

misleadingly optimistic reports about Katrina's effects through its internal intelligence service. Federal inaction was also a reflection of the Bush administration's desire to trim budgets. Cost-conscious federal authorities refused to commit resources until Katrina was certified an "incident of natural significance," though what exactly constituted such an incident under new Homeland Security rules was never clearly defined. In the meantime Homeland Security officials continued to pursue pet projects: Director Michael Chertoff, for example, stayed at home working on immigration policy rather than attending an important pre–Katrina senior staff meeting on August 27th. As for President Bush, he did not deviate from his scheduled itinerary at his Crawford, Texas, ranch until late on the 30th — 36 hours after Katrina struck — and his first move was to direct Air Force One to fly over New Orleans on the way to Washington. Although Bush's aerial survey of New Orleans was intended to demonstrate his concern for the storm's victims, for many the president's belated fly-over only underscored the distance between the president and those suffering on the ground.

It has also been suggested that political wrangling further weakened the federal response. As a southern state with Democratic party governor, Louisiana is something of an anomaly, and some in the Bush administration probably saw Katrina as an opportunity to move Louisiana into the "red state" camp. To this end, Bush administration officials tried to shift blame for Katrina onto Louisiana's Governor Blanco by planting stories with the press on her state's post–Katrina failures. Furthermore, the Bush administration tried to pressure Blanco into agreeing to "federalization" of the Louisiana National Guard, presumably to ensure that the federal rather than state government got credit for rescuing New Orleans from its plight. These incidents, among others, have convinced some critics that the Bush administration's main concern in the aftermath of Katrina was avoiding negative fallout rather than saving lives.

As a result, most of the initiative for Katrina relief measures came from individual volunteers, local agencies, and private businesses rather than officials in Washington. As soon as the storm ended, some New Orleans residents lucky enough to have access to a boat began to rescue victims stranded in their houses, ferrying them to higher ground. Local sportsmen with flat bottomed fishing boats joined them, as did boat owners living hours away, including two Texans with a World War II era amphibious truck called a "duck" because of its military designation (DUKW). These private sector rescuers shared the water with boats from the Louisiana Department of Wildlife and Fisheries and the New Orleans Police Department, although the latter group had only 5 boats at its disposal and was seriously weakened by desertions. The most effective rescue group by far, however, was the U.S. Coast Guard, which eventually managed to evacuate more than 33,500 people with their helicopters and boats. In the meantime, the material needs of these refugees were met most effectively, not by FEMA, but by Wal-Mart, which turned its vast procurement and distribution network to the task of supplying supplies to Katrina's victims. Ironically, at the same time this assistance was moving into New Orleans, the few FEMA officials on the ground were being ordered to pull out, in response to overblown rumors of gunshots and violence in post-storm New Orleans.

As well-meaning as these efforts were, they did not immediately bring relief to those stranded in New Orleans. Many of those rescued by boats were dropped off at places such as the Convention Center and the I-10 overpass, where they suffered from hunger, thirst, and exposure. Worse yet, some storm victims who tried to escape the flooded city were physically prevented from doing so. In one of the more scandalous incidents to occur during Katrina, a group of about two hundred dehydrated Katrina survivors, most of whom were black, attempted to leave New Orleans via the Crescent City Connection, a bridge that lead to the relatively intact suburb of Gretna. They were prevented from doing so by armed Gretna police officers, who fired their pistols into the air to intimidate the crowd. Unwilling to return to New Orleans, the refugees camped out on the Crescent City Connection, only to be dislodged later by Gretna police, who went so far as to call in a helicopter to hover low over the refugees and essentially blow them back to New Orleans. To defend their actions, Gretna officials resorted to guilt by association, pointing out that a mall only a mile from the bridge had been looted and burned the day before, and New Orleans refugees were thought to be the culprits. As of 2008, none of the police involved in this shameful incident had been punished.

After days of misery, the situation in New Orleans finally began to improve as August gave way to September. Although the task of finding busses was bogged down by red tape, the evacuation of the Superdome refugees finally began on Wednesday, September 1st, and was completed by the 3rd. Immediately afterwards, rescue efforts were focused on the Convention Center, which was emptied of its 20,000 refugees by September 4th. In the meantime, the long awaited "cavalry" finally arrived in the form of General Honore, who promised that 30,000 federal troops would be deployed in New Orleans in the next few days—one of the few post–Katrina provinces to be kept. The real end to the acute stage of New Orleans' post–Katrina crisis, however, did not occur until September 5th, when the 17th Street Canal breach was finally filled. Within a few weeks, the floodwaters had been pumped out of the city, and New Orleans began the halting process of recovery.

Once the waters receded, New Orleans was finally able to assess Katrina's human and financial impact, and the tally was grim. In all, Katrina led to over 1,500 known deaths in Louisiana, and this is probably an underestimate of the real body count. Over 70 percent of the victims

FEMA/MARVIN NAUMAN

Stella Keasley, Katrina survivor, searches through the wreckage of her New Orleans home months after the disaster.

were elderly or disabled, and slightly more than half were black. What is more, the population of the New Orleans metropolitan area shrank dramatically because of Katrina, down from a pre-storm high of 1.4 million to 1.2 million in 2006. Indeed, former residents of New Orleans are now scattered, internal exiles in their own country: About 108,000 have moved elsewhere in Louisiana, 177,000 to Texas, 73,000 to Mississippi, and 40,000 to Georgia, and substantial communities of former New Orleanians have cropped up in places as far afield as California and Washington, DC. Since this population drain has been particularly marked in some of New Orleans' former cultural hotspots, such as the Lower Ninth Ward, academics worry that New Orleans' distinct regional culture will be diluted or lost entirely. As for property damage in New Orleans, estimates range as high as $100 billion, with a disproportional amount of damage inflicted on residential, low-income housing. Thanks to the double impact of lost people and lost property, New Orleans—never a rich city—now faces chronic financial insolvency.

Unfortunately, bankruptcy is only one of the many problems that New Orleans faces in its road to recovery. In the aftermath of Katrina, insurance is now virtually unobtainable for New Orleans properties, and without insurance, banks are unwilling to loan the money needed for reconstruction in New Orleans. As a result, very few low-income properties have been rebuilt, leading to a severe labor shortage in New Orleans that is hindering the recovery of New Orleans' businesses. Worse yet, the New Orleans utilities infrastructure suffered a mortal blow during the storm; indeed the sewage and gas lines alone carry a repair bill of approximately $5 billion dollars. Unless New Orleans receives significant financial assistance from the federal government, it is unlikely that the city will be able to solve these problems. Despite vague promises, however, so far little federal assistance has been forthcoming.

Although the tight-fisted attitude of the federal government towards New Orleans is regrettable, to a certain degree it is understandable: After all, even if New Orleans is entirely rebuilt, what is to prevent New Orleans from being flooded again by the next storm? Proposals have been put forward to protect New Orleans from even a category-5 hurricane's storm surge, but they bear a price tag of at least $30 billion. Others point out that, in an age of global warming—in other words, an age of more extreme weather and higher sea levels—the task of protecting New Orleans is becoming an increasingly futile quest. In the meantime, New Orleans is protected by essentially the same levee system that failed during Katrina, with only minor upgrades. And every year, slowly but inexorably, New Orleans sinks further and further below sea level, as the alluvial soil upon which it was built continues to subside.

Study Questions

1. Explain, in your own words, the chain of events that lead to the flooding of New Orleans on August 29, 2005.

2. Based on this reading, was the flooding of New Orleans during Katrina mainly the result of natural forces or the actions of human beings? Defend your answer.

3. On the basis of this reading and section 5.3 on Hurricane Andrew, what role does governmental ideology play in American disaster preparedness?

4. Do you believe that the federal government ought to assume financial responsibility for returning New Orleans to its pre–Katrina condition? Why or why not?

Sources/Suggested Readings

Barry, John. *Rising Tide: The Great Mississippi Flood of 1927 and How It Changed America*. New York: Simon and Schuster, 1997.

Brinkley, Douglas. *The Great Deluge*. New York: HarperCollins, 2006.

Caroll, Chris. "Deadly Delay: Katrina, Grasping for Relief." *National Geographic* (Dec. 2005), pp. 6–15.

Cooper, Christopher, and Robert Block. *Disaster: Hurricane Katrina and the Failure of Homeland Security*. New York: Henry Holt, 2006.

Grunwald, Michael. "The Threatening Storm." *Time*, August 12, 2007, pp. 28–41.

Horne, Jed. *Breach of Faith*. New York: Random House, 2006.

McPhee, John. *The Control of Nature*. New York: Farrar, Straus and Giroux, 1989.

"Performance Evaluation of the New Orleans and Southeast Louisiana Hurricane Protection System: Draft Final Report." *Army Corps of Engineers* (1 June 2006).

Steinberg, Ted. "Disasters and Deregulation." *Chronicle of Higher Regulation*, July 21 2006, p. B16.

Van Heerden, Ivor, and Bryan, Mike. *The Storm*. New York: Viking Press, 2006.

CHAPTER 7

Famines

Science and History

From the beginning of human civilization to the present famine has been a scourge of mankind. Famine affects not only a society's present, in the form of mass casualties, but also its future, by provoking psychological trauma, preventing childbirth, and compromising the normal growth of the young. Despite its prevalence in human history, however, famine is hard to define precisely. This is largely because unlike disasters like volcanoes which are unquestionably the result of natural forces, famines are essentially human phenomena and are quite often the result of political choices, ideological considerations, social relations, or market pressures. Indeed, it can be very hard to determine what factors are contributing to a given famine, or even whether or not a given situation qualifies as a famine at all. Famine is also heavily intertwined with nearly every other form of disaster, making it difficult to distinguish between famine deaths and deaths caused by flooding or disease. One fact is clear, however: Unlike most other disasters in this book, which have been rendered potentially more destructive by population expansion in the 20th century, the incidence of famine has declined over the past half century. However, if current predictions about global warming are correct, mankind's current relative freedom from famine may vanish over the course of the century to come.

The Theory and Science of Famine

Theories of Famine

At the most basic level, famine results when a given population lacks sufficient food to sustain life. But what, or who, is responsible for this deficiency? Many models of famine have been proposed, but three have proven to be especially influential: the "environmental" thesis of famine, the "Malthusian" or "FAD" theory of famine, and the "entitlement" approach. It is important to understand that these theories are not merely sterile matters of academic debate. Rather, since these theories inform policy debates they exert an enormous influence over human affairs; indeed, it is no exaggeration to say that these intellectual models can potentially be a matter of life or death for millions of hungry people. Not surprisingly, then, these theories have been the subject of intense political debate. As scholar Amartya Sen has argued, "there is no such thing as an apolitical food problem."

One often-cited explanation for famine is to ascribe it to environmental factors; famine, this theory holds, is the result of a short term or long term decline in the food-producing capacity of the environment. Harvests may fail due to drought, floods may wash out the crop, or coastal storm surge may poison the fields with salt. These problems may be exacerbated by environmental degradation. Land that is overgrazed or over farmed may become drained of nutrients, deforested, eroded, or otherwise rendered unsuitable for food production. This sort of analysis has merit — as we have already seen in section 4.2, for example, the adoption of intensive agricultural policies in the colonial and postcolonial period in West Africa led to horrific famines. Other scholars have blamed the collapse of classic Mayan civilization between A.D. 800 and 1000 on environmental factors, arguing that a combination of overpopulation, environmental degradation, and El Niño dry years caused food shortages and the collapse of Mayan urban culture.

Nonetheless, while there can be no doubt that environmental forces play an important role in food shortages, most famine experts now agree that natural phenomena are generally not a sufficient cause of famine. Even exceptionally poor harvests will not cause famine in a rich country like the United States, as the American economy has the wherewithal to buy the food it needs from external sources. What is more, famines have been observed to occur even in countries untouched by food shortage. In an influential 1982 study, Amartya Sen disproved that the Bangladesh Famine of 1974 was the direct result of flooding. In actual fact, Sen argued, food supplies in Bangladesh were actually above the level of the previous year when no famine occurred, and families were starving to death in the midst of well-stocked food markets. Clearly, environmental factors are by themselves insufficient to explain famine.

Why, then, is famine linked so tightly to natural disasters in the public's mind? In large part, this misconception has been fed by the self-serving declarations of political figures, who often blame natural forces for famine in order to divert attention from their own culpability. As we shall see in section 7.2, it was easier for Mao and his followers to invoke natural disasters to explain the famine deaths of the Great Leap Forward than it was to acknowledge the failures of their own agricultural policies. Similarly, the Ethiopian government repeatedly blamed drought for the famine deaths of the 1980s to distract attention from the regime's brutal counterinsurgency strategies, which employed food deprivation as an instrument of war. As discussed in section 7.3, the Ethiopian government went so far as to divert famine assistance to fund their military, the organization which was most responsible for causing the famine in the first place.

A second influential theory of famine argues that famine mortality is the result, not of short-term natural disasters, but rather of long-term human demographic realities. Advocates of this theory of population collapse, often called the FAD (food availability decline) thesis by its critics, postulate that the human propensity for population growth, if unchecked, will lead to periodic population crashes as human numbers overwhelm the productive capacity of their environment. This theory was articulated most clearly by 18th century economist Richard Malthus, who argued in his 1798 treatise *Principles of Population* that human population had the tendency to grow geometrically, while food stocks can increase only linearly at best, leading to inevitable shortfalls. In desperation, Malthus argues, societies attempt to cultivate marginal land, such as hillsides and swamps, but such land requires high labor inputs and produces little food. Societies also employ intensive agriculture on land already in cultivation, but each extra unit of labor added to existing plots adds less and less to food yields (a process called the law of diminishing returns). Eventually, population outstrips food supply, and the result is famine.

As with the environmental theory of famine, Malthus' theory does have some resonance with observed facts. The expansion of European farmers into marginal land during the European late Middle Ages, followed by a dramatic population collapse in the 1300s, seems to validate Malthus' insights. It should also be pointed out that Malthus' theory fits well with examples from the natural world; much as Malthus predicted, deer populations unchecked by predators have been observed to undergo cycles of rise and decline as runaway population growth peri-

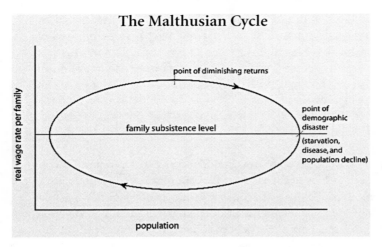

The Malthusian Cycle

odically outstrips available food. Nonetheless the Malthusian argument has many critics. Contemporaries of Malthus such as novelist Charles Dickens accused Malthus of callousness: In *A Christmas Story*, when the yet-to-be redeemed miser Scrooge is told that many of England's poor would rather die than go to a workhouse, Scrooge declares "if they would rather die they had better do it, and decrease the surplus population." More recently, scholars have accused Malthus of bad scholarship. Malthus' theory was based on a hunch rather than hard evidence, critics charge, and that the data he later collected did not support his contention. More crucially, critics charge that Malthus' theory implies that famines ought to occur where populations are most dense, while in actual fact the opposite is generally true. At least in the modern world, the area most vulnerable to famine is not densely packed East Asia, but rather rural Africa, where population density is quite low.

Indeed, this observation has led some scholarly critics, like Ester Boserup, to turn Malthus' "overpopulation" argument completely on its head. Indeed, Boserup has gone so far as to argue that high population densities actually protect societies from famine, as these societies can build the large scale public works and transportation infrastructure needed to protect themselves from food shortages. Boserup's view is not unchallenged, however. Some famine experts have doubted the universality of Boserup's argument, charging that high population densities can provide defense against famine only in areas with a sufficient resource base for industrialization. In areas without sufficient industrial resources, on the other hand, high population densities have been observed to be a hindrance rather than a help in overcoming famine.

Despite these criticisms, which have dampened the enthusiasm of modern famine scholars for the Malthusian theory of famine, Malthus' ideas have been very influential over the last two hundred years. To a certain degree this reflects the attractive simplicity of his argument, making it readily accessible even to a layman uneducated in economic theory. More importantly, Malthus' view of the world often coincided nicely with the economic and political interests of certain elite groups. This was particularly true during the 19th century, when European countries such as Britain were engaged in a grand imperialist enterprise, bending populations near (such as Ireland) and far (such as India) to their will. Malthusian economics was a useful tool during this enterprise. Indeed, as we will see in section 7.1, Malthusian economics was used to justify the British administration's hands-off approach to the Irish Potato Famine of the 1840s. Under the influence of Malthusian ideas some British administrators went so far as to view mass starvation in Ireland not as a crisis, but rather as an opportunity to remove the "excess population" from Ireland and bring needed efficiency to Irish agriculture.

So should the environmental disaster and Malthusian theories of famine be abandoned? Perhaps they should for modern incidents of famine. A strong case could be made that modern agricultural practices, increased storage capacity, and more efficient global trade networks have rendered these theories invalid, since food can be transported worldwide in sufficient quantities to prevent environmental disaster or overpopulation from causing famine. However, there is reason to believe that these theories might hold more weight for the pre-modern world, when large-scale food transfers were rare and societies were more dependent on local resources for survival.

Nonetheless, most current scholars of famine have largely abandoned these older theories in favor of Amartya Sen's "entitlement" approach. Sen argued in his 1982 book *Poverty and Famines* that famine results not from lack of food, but from lack of entitlement to existing food supplies. By "entitlement," Sen means an individual's ability to lay claim to food, a claim which can take a number of forms. A subsistence farmer's entitlement equals the nutritive value of his crop, which may be inadequate in times of drought. A commercial farmer's entitlement is tied more closely to price trends, which often reflect supply and demand in distant markets rather than local conditions. Other people earn their entitlement by selling handicrafts, providing services, or performing manual labor. Still others earn entitlements through inherited money, landlordism, or ownership of productive property like factories or means of transportation. Entitlement can also be derived from membership in a group or institution — a child's entitlement is through his family, for example, while a retired veteran's entitlement may be provided by the state. These sources of entitlement are by no means exclusive; indeed a given individual often depends on multiple sources to ensure protection against famine.

In Sen's formulation, famine results, not necessarily from lack of food, but rather from a breakdown of a given group's normal entitlement network. During the 1974 Bangladeshi famine, for example, tens of thousands of Bangladeshis found their customary entitlement critically reduced by a deadly combination of stagnant or dropping wages, fluctuating trends in seasonal labor markets, and a spike in food prices caused by speculation and rumors of shortages rather than actual lack of food. As a result, Bangladeshis who depended on wages for their food entitlement were hard hit in 1974, while farmers, who could dip into their own crop for sustenance, were much less likely to die of famine. Those farmers who did die, according to Sen, were likely to own so little land that they relied on wage labor to supplement their food entitlement, and in 1974, those wages proved insufficient to stave off famine.

As this example makes clear, Sen's theory of famine has three main advantages over the environmental and Malthusian formulations. First of all, Sen's theory allows us to understand famine that occurs in the absence of extreme overpopulation or environmental disaster. What is more, Sen's insight allows for a more fine-toothed analysis of famine, as the entitlement approach helps explain why certain groups within a society are more vulnerable to starvation than other social groups. This, in turn, leads to another advantage: By focusing on vulnerability, the entitlement approach offers the possibility of preventing famine. Unlike the Malthusian theory of famine, which regards famine as an inevitable consequence of immutable demographic laws, or the environmental theory, which blames famine on inescapable natural disasters, the "entitlement" approach can help to identify specific subsets of a population whose entitlements are most vulnerable to disruption. As a result, famines can potentially be averted before they have the power to kill.

Like the other theories of famine, however, Sen's thesis has not gone unchallenged. Sen's "entitlement" approach has been accused of being a mere repackaging of older ideas, and indeed studies of famine written over a century ago have been shown to use entitlement-like language over a century before Sen coined the phrase. Even if this is the case, however, Sen deserves credit for distilling these ideas into a useful intellectual model and for systematically demonstrating entitlement failure through case studies. In a more telling criticism, famine scholar Amrita Rangasami has accused Sen of treating famine as an "abnormal" state of affairs and ignoring the intimate link between famine and chronic poverty in the modern world. As a result, relief organizations that have adopted Sen's definition of famine tend to take action only when a food crisis has developed rather than trying to avert famines before they happen by addressing the global phenomenon of chronic poverty. What is more, famine scholar and activist Alex de Waal has criticized Sen's theory of famine on the grounds that it has little connection to how famine is defined, and experienced, by actual participants. According to de Waal, non-western societies often define famine along a sliding scale rather than absolutes, and thus consider it as an event within normal experience rather than an external "disaster."

In any case, although the three theories of famine presented above have been particularly influential, they are by no means an exhaustive list. Some famine scholars have made the case that famine is nearly inseparable from internal or external war, since conflict leads to wrecked agricultural land, disrupted food networks, and in some cases deliberate policies to use food deprivation as a weapon. This linkage between famine and war is especially clear in the Ethiopian famine of the 1970s and 1980s, as we will see in section 7.3. Other scholars believe that food scarcity often results from the misguided "economic development" policies pushed by such agencies as the World Bank and the International Monetary Fund. In general, these agencies encourage economic reforms such as the shift from subsistence to market agriculture and the abolition of protective tariffs, both of which can cause severe economic dislocation and subsequent loss of entitlement by certain groups. What is more, development schemes generally encourage exports, and this in turn leads to more intensified agriculture and resulting environmental degradation. As we saw in section 4.2, this process has been particularly notable in the Central Asian drylands, where intensive irrigated farming has caused extensive environmental degradation, if not outright famine.

Finally, there is ample evidence that governmental ideology can play a crucial role in causing or exacerbating famine. According to famine expert Andrew Natsios, for instance, North Korea suffered a famine in 1995–99 largely as a result of the regime's "*juche*" ideology — a mixture of Confucianism and Marxism — that prevented the regime from either modernizing its agriculture or appealing to outside assistance. North Korea's famine experience was by no means unique; as we shall see in section 7.2, misguided planning choices driven by Marxist ideology were a major factor in the massive famine that struck China during the so-called "Great Leap Forward." Ideology-driven famines are by no means limited to eastern Asian Marxist dictatorships, however. As mentioned above, Malthusian economic thinking on the part of the British government greatly hampered its response to the Irish Potato Famine of 1846–52. If the British government had been more willing to regulate prices, prevent food from leaving Ireland, and offer public assistance, hundreds of thousands of deaths might have been averted.

Science of Famine

Lack of sufficient food has a profound, and highly destructive, effect on the human body. The exact effect varies depending on the scale of the deficiency and the nutritional content of what food is available. If the only deficiency is calories, famine will cause progressive weight loss, as the body consumes fat reserves, muscle tissue, and eventually even internal organ tissue to keep itself alive. Adults take on a cadaverous appearance; children, in contrast, commonly get swollen bellies, as their empty stomachs are inflated by gasses emitted by bacteria in the stomach and intestines. The body's metabolism slows, and famine victims become listless and apathetic as a consequence. Psychologically, victims tend to obsess about food and are likely to suffer long-term mental disorders, such as anxiety and depression, even if they survive the famine.

In many cases, the effect of famine is compounded by specific dietary deficiencies. Lack of

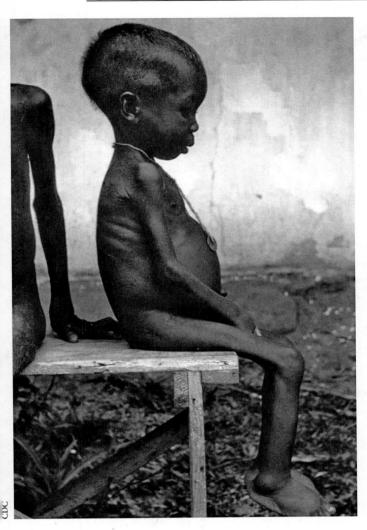

CDC

A young girl suffering from severe malnutrition. Note that, despite her overall emaciated appearance, she shows symptoms of edema, especially in her swollen belly and feet.

certain vitamins, such as A, B_3 (niacin), or C, and insufficiency of important minerals, such as iodine or zinc, can lead to specific nutritional diseases. As we shall see in section 8.1, for example, lack of vitamin B_3 can cause the debilitating disease pellagra. What is more, most famine diets are deficient in protein, and lack of protein in the blood stream causes fluid from the blood to build up in the tissues. People with this condition, called edema, suffer from grotesque swelling of the feet, then the legs and torso, and eventually the whole body. Their skin becomes doughy, and if cut, the wound will drip clear fluid rather than blood. Although edema is not in itself fatal it is generally a sign that death is not far off, often from heart failure.

One of the ironies of famine is that relatively few of the deaths it causes are directly attributable to lack of food. Rather, disease accounts for the majority of victims in nearly all famines. Starvation compromises the human immune system to the point that mild diseases like measles can become fatal and resistance to some more serious diseases, like polio and tuberculosis, is severely impaired. Famine victims also heal slowly, greatly increasing the chance of infections, like gangrene, in open wounds. In addition, the compromised immune system of a famine victim is unable to check the growth of intestinal bacteria and other parasites within the human body, sometimes leading to death. Famine can also foster disease by causing its starving, enervated victims to neglect basic matters of hygiene such as changing bedding and washing clothes, thus offering footholds for insect-borne diseases like typhus. What is more, victims of famine often congregate in refugee and/or work camps, and the resulting mixture of malnourished people and poor sanitary conditions can lead to an explosion of diarrheal diseases. One such disease is cholera, which we will discuss further in section 8.3. These famine-borne diseases, like the famine itself, generally carry away the weakest members of a community, such as pregnant or nursing women, the very young, and the very old.

As with other types of natural disaster, famine can inflict damage on a community that persists long after the immediate crisis has passed. As mentioned above, famine can lead to long-lasting psychological damage in the form of higher rates of depression and anxiety disorders, especially Post Traumatic Stress Disorder. What is more, children who survive famines generally suffer from stunted physical growth and incomplete mental development, sometimes to the point of mental retardation. In addition, famine tends to suppress population expansion in a society, partially because starving people tend to be disinterested in sex, and partly because women affected by famine often lose their fertility, a condition that can persist for years after the famine has ended. Those children who are born during famines tend to have low birth weights and are prone to sickness, especially respiratory infections. Small wonder, then, that famines can leave a lasting demographic imprint on society.

Famine in History

Famine, at least as defined by lack of food, is as old as mankind itself. It was probably relatively rare amongst hunter-gatherer societies, when human population densities were small and humans subsisted on such a variety of plants and animals that it was unlikely for all food supplies to fail in a given year. In fact, human beings probably only adopted agriculture once population pressure, combined with climate change after the end of the last ice age, compelled hunter-gatherers to gradually adopt agricultural techniques in order to feed their growing numbers in the face of dwindling natural resources. In a sense, then, human civilization can be seen as a famine avoiding mechanism, an attempt to simultaneously adapt to rising population and a changing climate.

Paradoxically, although the adoption of agriculture vastly increased the supply of food available to mankind, it also greatly increased the incidence of famine in human populations. This is in part because agricultural societies tend to became dependent on a relatively few "staple" crops for survival, so a succession of poor growing seasons for one of those crops could have catastrophic consequences. What is more, since sedentary agriculturalists can support more young children than nomadic hunter-gatherers, agriculturalists tended to have a higher birth rate, and consequently population often hovers near the limit prescribed by food supplies. As a result, in many early agricultural societies, the margin between food sufficiency and food deficiency was extremely narrow. Despite the risk of famine, however, other advantages offered by an agricultural lifestyle — such as high population densities, standing armies, relative disease immunity, and eventually metalworking technologies — meant that agriculture gradually replaced hunter-gatherer lifestyles over most of the globe after 8,000 B.C.

In the period since the adoption of agriculture in around 8,000 B.C., every world civilization has experienced famine to some degree, but the worst suffering has generally been confined to two broad "famine belts." One belt encompasses Northern Europe, Central Asia, and Northern China; in this area, excessively wet and cold weather periodically narrows the already short growing season and induces food crises. The second area stretches from West Africa through the Mediterranean, and the Indian subcontinent to southern China. Here, the seasonal monsoon exerts the greatest influence on the climate, and failure of the monsoon rains to fall can trigger disastrous droughts and consequent famine. To ward off famine, governments in both "famine belts" gradually evolved tactics designed to increase food security. The Mughal Empire, which ruled India from about 1526 to 1707, is a case in point. In times of crop failure, the Mughals employed a number of policies — such as tax relief, embargos on food exports, price regulation, and even free food distribution — to reduce the threat of mortality. What is more, the Mughal state spent considerable sums on water conservation measures, such as the construction of new wells, to lessen the impact of monsoon failures.

Other states in the famine belts employed similar measures to safeguard their subjects from famine. When faced by a horrific drought during the autumn and winter of 1743-1744, the Chinese Qing dynasty enacted a number of measures to stave off mass hunger. The "ever-normal granaries," which had been stocked with food during times of surplus, were opened to the people, and the Qing government imported food surpluses from areas in China where harvests were normal. Soup kitchens were set up throughout stricken areas, and the government handed out substantial cash grants as well. What is more, in the following spring, the government distributed seed grain and oxen to ensure a swift return to normal levels of agricultural production.

Despite these safeguards, some degree of famine was unavoidable in these vulnerable areas. Europe, for instance, suffered a series of destructive famines during the Little Ice Age of roughly 1250–1850, discussed in more detail in chapter 4. France, for instance, suffered no less than 111 famines between 1371 and 1791, with sixteen famines occurring in the eighteenth century alone. The gradual introduction of the potato and maize, extremely high yield food crops that originated in the western hemisphere, finally helped to interrupt this cycle of famine by the end of the 18th century. These crops could be a mixed blessing; as we shall see in section 7.1, the widespread cultivation of potatoes allowed Ireland's land-poor farmers to attain a population density that proved unsupportable when their potato crop failed between 1846 and 1852. Overall, however, the introduction of maize and the potato greatly reduced Europe's vulnerability to famine.

Ironically, just as Europe was beginning to escape from famine cycles, much of the non-western world was becoming far more vulnerable than before. Indeed, the two processes are closely linked. Improvements to European agriculture fueled population growth and new wealth that, in turn, helped to spark the industrial revolution. The industrial revolution, for its part, greatly increased Europe's power relative to the rest of the world, especially in terms of military power, since the industrial revolution greatly increased the rate of European technological innovation. New weapons, such as armored steamships, rifled muskets, percussion cap bullets, and the machine gun, allowed European states to progressively subjugate much of the non-western world, first taking over much of coastal Asia and North Africa, later expanding into Central Asia and Sub-Saharan Africa. European control in these territories ranged from direct administration (as in the Dutch East Indies) to rule in conjunction with local elites (as in British India) to economic domination and indirect political influence (as in China). Nonetheless, each of these strategies of control had the same general effect: They disrupted long-standing systems of famine prevention. As a result, nearly unprecedented famines raged through Asia and Africa in the second half of the 19th century.

Thanks to Mike Davis's recent book, *Late Victorian Holocausts*, historians have a much fuller understanding of this little known chapter of European imperial history. Davis claims that, despite the "civilizing" rhetoric of the European powers, their main concern was always the extraction of money and resources from their colonial possessions. To this end, the European powers enforced policies that transformed their colonies into servants of Europe's industrial and financial needs. In India, for example, Britain imposed policies that ruined the domestic weaving industry while simultaneously compelling India's farmers to increase the cultivation of crops such as cotton and indigo which were vital to England's expanding textile industry. Britain also wanted to extract cheap food from India, largely in an effort to keep factory wages low in Britain. Consequently, the British invested in grand irrigation schemes, privatized common lands, and built a railway network through the subcontinent, hoping thereby to encourage food production for export. Britain could have made up for these resource drains by taking measures to improve India's standard of living, but the high taxes Britain imposed were generally diverted to foreign policy adventures, such Britain's "Great Game" competition with Russia over Central Asia, which did nothing to benefit the average subject of the Raj. In the meantime, traditional famine reduction projects, such as water conservation schemes, withered and died from lack of funding; one contemporary British eyewitness in India was disturbed to see "many ruined tanks and disused canals in a country which has often to depend on them." The net result of these policies was the deterioration of India's traditional shields against famine.

Not surprisingly, famine soon made an appearance. As we already saw in section 4.1, the Indian Ocean monsoon failed disastrously in 1876 due to a strong El Niño. Rainfall at the Madras Weather Observatory was 75 percent lower than normal. In some districts, 94 percent of the crop was lost. Food prices rose sharply, even in areas not touched by drought, since the railway network had unified the Indian grain market. India's many poor farmers, already ground down by years of extractive British rule, were forced to sell their farm animals, tools, the thatch on their roofs, and even the wood frames of their doors and windows to buy food. In the meantime, since food prices were even higher in wealthy Europe, Indian grain exports to Europe doubled between 1875 and 1876 and doubled again between 1876 and 1877 despite the fact that food was desperately needed within India. As a result, Indians began to die by the hundreds of thousands, and the British press began to print stories of walking skeletons and dog-eaten corpses strewn by the roadside.

The official British response to the famine was purely Malthusian. Believing that famine was the inevitable consequence of Indian overpopulation, British officials initially ignored the famine and even tried to prevent private organizations from providing relief on the grounds that this would only prolong the problem posed by India's "excess population." When finally forced into action by popular pressure, the British government in India enacted a cure that was almost worse than the disease: large-scale public works. Indians who joined the work camps were fed a daily ration in exchange for heavy labor on construction projects, but these work camps rapidly came to resemble death camps as the ration fed was utterly inadequate to sustain human life — Davis claims it lower in calories than the ration given to concentration camp prisoners during the Nazi Holocaust. What is more, the congregation of so many malnourished people in a small area and the resulting hygiene and sanitation problems allowed diseases to spread like wildfire, with cholera claiming the most victims. One British official in India wrote that a roadside work project he visited "bore the appearance of a battlefield, its sides being strewn with the dead, the dying, and those recently attacked." Indeed, by some estimates, the monthly death rate in these camps was equivalent to a yearly rate of 94 percent. Small wonder, then, that many Indian famine victims begged the British to arrest them: Food rations in jail were substantially better than those in the "relief" camps.

By the time the famine abated in 1879, it had claimed 5.5 million lives, and India was far from alone in its misery. The monsoon also failed in China during the same years, and the Chinese government was unable to employ its traditional anti-famine measures to address the problem, in large part due to the economic extractions of the militarily superior European powers. As a result, between 10 and 20 million Chinese died, and the already-destabilized government became even more helpless in the face of European pressure. Mass mortality also occurred in other areas where Europeans held sway, such as Africa and the Indonesian Archipelago. Worse yet, the 1879 famine proved to be just a taste of things to come: Monsoon failures occurred again between 1899 and 1902, when deaths in India may have approached 10 million, and millions more died in China, where popular desperation overflowed into the anti–European "Boxer Rebellion" of 1900 that in turn lead to tens of thousands of Chinese deaths at the hands of Boxer insurgents or European armies. Thankfully, a combination of reduced occurrence of monsoon failure and greater European exertions to prevent famine made famine less common — though by no means unknown — in European colonies after 1900.

In contrast to the 19th century, when famine was generally the direct or indirect result of European imperialism, the worst famines of the 20th century were triggered either by war or by policy decisions of authoritarian governments. Both World War I and World War II caused spikes in famine mortality, in large part because the belligerents directly targeted each other's food supplies by means of trade embargos and submarine warfare. Famine also appeared in the wake of civil wars, such as the Igbo war for independence from the Nigerian state between 1967 and 1970, a struggle that lead to as many as a million deaths from famine and other causes. Other 20th century famines were the result not of war but of misguided or malicious government policies. Agrarian policy in Soviet Russia, for example, triggered several famines during the 20th century. The first occurred from 1918 to 1921 in part due to the disruptions caused by an ongoing civil war, but also because of a brutal policy of widespread grain appropriation by the Bolshevik government. Famine flourished again between 1929 and 1934 as a consequence of the forced collectivization of farms, political attacks on the "kulaks" or rich peasants, and massive seizures of grain used to support investment in the industrial sector. Suffering was particularly bad in the Ukraine, where Soviet Premier Stalin deliberately encouraged famine through the mass exportation of desperately needed grain in order to crush Ukrainian nationalism. Famine deaths during these years were extremely high; indeed, one study estimates that between 7.2 and 8.1 million died in the Soviet Union during 1933 alone. As we will see in section 7.2, these numbers pale before the tens of millions who died because of misguided economic policies during China's so-called "Great Leap Forward" of 1958–61.

The fact that most 20th century famines were caused by war or despotism is regrettable, but also somewhat encouraging, since it offers up the possibility that famine might one day become a thing of the past. Indeed famine scholar Alex de Waal has made the case that the spread of democracy, not the distribution of aid, is the key to overcoming famine in the modern world. Unlike authoritarian governments, de Waal argues, democratic states have an implicit "famine contract" with their citizens, who will hold the leadership accountable for any food shortages that occur. A case in point is India, which has been free of major famine since the British left in 1949 and India adopted a democratic form of government. What is more, democratic states tend to be more peaceful towards their neighbors and benevolent towards their own people than authoritarian states, reducing the chance of foreign and civil warfare respectively. Ultimately de Waal's argument supports Amartya Sen's insight — there is no such thing as an apolitical famine.

Famine and Other Disasters

Like cyclones, famines are intimately linked with other types of disasters, and occupy an intermediate place in the disaster hierarchy. Famines can result from almost any disaster, but most especially volcanic activity, earthquakes, environmental change, and floods. Famine's relationship with disease is more complex. Of course, famine almost invariably leads to some level of disease, but disease can also cause famine, or at least increase a given famine's severity.

Volcanic activity is linked to famine in several ways. Volcanic tephra can blanket nearby farmland, and since volcanic pumice is unable to absorb water like normal soil, it can ruin the fertility of that farmland for years to come. What is more, the immense volumes of ash that are emitted during a volcano can lower global temperatures and thus lead to crop failures. The eruption of Mount Tambora in 1815 catapulted as many as 50 cubic kilometers of ash and dust into the atmosphere and caused temperatures in the northern hemisphere to drop to as much as 10 degrees Celsius. The result was widespread agricultural failures, most notably in Ireland, where an estimated 100,000 died of famine and associated typhus. In addition, volcanic eruptions can trigger tsunamis, which in turn can devastate coastal farmland. Volcanoes can also cause earthquakes, and these can trigger famine by ruining the livelihoods (the "entitlements") of people nearby or by destroying the food storage and distribution infrastructure of neighboring communities.

Although volcanic activity and earthquakes have been implicated in numerous famine deaths, climate change is linked more intimately with famine and contributes to far more famine casualties. El Niño has been linked to major famines as far back as Ancient Egypt and as recently as 1982–83, when dry conditions affected tens of millions worldwide and inflicted $13 billion in damage to the global economy. El Niño has also been linked to the horrific "Victorian Holocausts" in India and China discussed earlier in this chapter and in section 4.1; both the 1879 and 1899 monsoon failures coincided with exceptionally strong El Niños. Famine is also strongly linked to desertification, especially in West Africa, where overuse of the land has caused considerable land degradation. As for global warming, there is little evidence that it has caused famine yet, but some climate scientists believe that global warming will eventually have a profound affect on mankind's capacity to feed itself. As we saw in section 4.3, computer models suggest that global warming will lead to a profound increase in the likelihood of severe weather such as droughts and floods, thus driving down agricultural yields. What is more, a warmer world will suffer from more frequent El Niños and thus more monsoon failures, threatening the food supply of the 75 percent of humanity that lives in the tropics. Indeed, many climate experts believe that the real question is not whether global warming will cause famine, but when.

Floods can also play an important contributing role in famine. River flooding can ruin the crop over huge areas, both by killing the crop in the field and by preventing the planting of new crops at the appropriate time in the agricultural cycle. The resulting harvest failures can ruin the livelihood of farmers and imperil the food entitlement of thousands more. As we saw in section 6.1, China's Yellow River, due to its high silt load and highly variable flow, has proven particularly prone to flooding, and the famines associated with these inundations have claimed millions of lives. Flooding caused by storm surges and tsunamis can also trigger famines if they destroy farmland or damage food storage or distribution infrastructure.

As discussed earlier in this chapter, famine and disease are intimately related. Famine generally leads to malnutrition, relaxed hygiene standards, and the congregation of many people into relief or refugee camps, all of which creates ideal conditions for the growth of disease. The diseases most likely to accompany famine are diarrheal in nature, such as dysentery and cholera, because these diseases most directly affect the famine victims' compromised digestive systems. Famine victims are also subject to high levels of smallpox, black death, and measles, the last of which tends to be especially deadly among the young. In addition, famine conditions favor typhus, a disease carried by human lice that thrives in the cramped, unsanitary conditions that famine often fosters. More recently, studies have shown that malnutrition increases vulnerability to HIV infection, inspiring Alex de Waal to coin the phrase "new variant famine" to describe the co-occurrence of AIDS and drought in Sub-Saharan Africa. Famine can also spawn nutritional deficiency diseases, such as scurvy (lack of vitamin C), pellagra (lack of vitamin B_3), or beriberi (lack of vitamin A). The chain of causation works in reverse as well. In some cases, disease can foster famine, for instance by debilitating or killing so many agricultural laborers in a region that there is no one left to harvest the crop, or by preventing distribution of food to needy areas. Similarly, disease can weaken a society's ability to maintain adequate flood control measures, leading to flooding and likely famine. Famine, therefore, is often just one phase of a chronic cycle of disaster mortality, especially in developing nations.

Famine and Human Agency

As this chapter has repeatedly demonstrated, famines cannot be understood outside of the context of human agency. Societies can weather out even a horrific drought if they have stored enough food from better years, and can suffer horrific famines in years of plenty if food is hoarded or exported from the country. Even overpopulation, which Malthus considered to be an immutable law of nature, reflects some degree of human choice. Societies have long known ways to limit population growth, ranging from abstinence to *coitus interruptus* to infanticide. Reliable modern contraceptive devices and medications have vastly improved this ancient arsenal. Malthus himself suggested that birth control tactics might prevent famine, but he rejected this solution as immoral. In the modern world, China's one-child policy is the best evidence that human beings do have the capacity, if the government so chooses, to tame the Malthusian monster of overpopulation.

Just as governments can take measures to avoid famine, however, they can adopt policies that favor food shortages. Britain's historical free trade policy, for example, has been implicated in exacerbating a number of famines by encouraging the exportation of food from areas of starvation to prosperous Britain, where food commanded a higher price. This occurred on a huge scale in the Victorian Holocausts discussed above, and as we shall see in section 7.1, it was a contributing factor to the Irish Potato Famine as well. Other famines have resulted not from the invisible hand of the free market but from failed attempts at social engineering (such as the Great Leap Forward, section 7.2) or from calculated attempts to increase control over potentially rebellious populations (as in the Ethiopian Famine, section 7.3). Governments can also contribute to famines by adopting policies with dire ecological consequences. As we saw in section 4.2, colonial powers in West Africa adopted an intensive cash crop economic system that contributed to severe desertification and deadly food shortages of the Sahel. Perhaps most commonly of all, famines are the result of sheer governmental inaction, due to weak leadership, lack of concern, or calculated Malthusian negligence.

It is important, however, not to heap all responsibility for famine on governments; the general public plays a role in famine as well. Famine is often triggered by speculation, which occurs when merchants withhold their stocks from the market, hoping to realize greater profits due to price increases over time. Private individuals can also trigger famine by cutting down too many trees, fostering deforestation and erosion, or by grazing too many animals on arid land, which can hasten desertification; indeed, such practices often occur in violation of governmental regulations, not because of them. What these factors have in common is the operation of the free market, which quite often encourages individuals to act in ways that sacrifice the well being of the general public for private gain. The famines that are likely to accompany global warming, should they occur, will serve as a particularly catastrophic examples of the chronic human tendency to choose short-term economic advantages and material comfort over long-term sustainability.

Study Questions

1. Based on the text, why do you think that the definition and origins of famine have been the subject of such intense debate?

2. Why has it been so difficult to distinguish between victims of famine and victims of other types of disasters?

3. Which do you think has had more of an impact historically: the actual occurrence of Malthusian crises, or the intellectual idea of Malthusian crises? Support your answer.

4. "Famines are always a human, and never a 'natural' disaster." Based on this reading, to what degree do you agree with this statement?

5. Based on this section, as well as what you learned in chapter 4, how likely do you think it is that famines will become more prevalent in the 21st century?

Sources/Suggested Readings

Cohen, Mark Nathan. *The Food Crisis in Prehistory: Overpopulation and the Origins of Agriculture.* New Haven, CT: Yale University Press, 1997.

Cuny, Frederick C. *Famine, Conflict, and Response: A Basic Guide.* West Hartford, CT: Kumarian, 1999.

Davis, Mike. *Late Victorian Holocausts: El Nino Famines and the Making of the Third World.* New York: Verso, 2001.

Devereux, Stephen. *Theories of Famine.* New York: Harvester Wheatsheaf, 1993.

De Waal, Alex. *Famine Crimes: Politics and the Disaster Relief Industry in Africa.* Irthingborough, Britain: ARIAI/Indiana University Press, 1997.

De Waal, Alex. *Famine That Kills (Revised Edition).* New York: Oxford University Press, 2005.

Newman, Lucile, ed., *Hunger in History: Food Shortage, Poverty, and Deprivation.* Cambridge, MA: Blackwell, 1990.

Sen, Amartya. *Poverty and Famines: An Essay on Entitlement and Deprivation.* New York: Oxford University Press, 1982.

Skinner, G. William. "Presidential Address: The Structure of Chinese History." *Journal of Asian Studies*, Vol. 44, No. 2 (Feb, 1985), pp. 271–292.

7.1: The Irish Potato Famine, 1846–1852

Although the Irish Potato Famine claimed far fewer lives than the massive Asian famines of the 19th and 20th centuries, in relative terms it stands out as one of the most severe in recorded history. All told the Irish Potato Famine killed approximately 1 million people out of a pre-famine population of 8 million, an astounding 12.5 percent mortality rate. More astoundingly still, this death rate occurred without any civil or domestic warfare and within the territories of what was then the wealthiest nation on earth. Some historians have interpreted the Potato Famine as a case study example of Malthusian population collapse, albeit triggered by the unexpected and unprecedented failure of the Potato crop. This interpretation has some merit, but human agency also played a crucial role in the catastrophe. The policies employed to counter the food shortages, especially work relief and the poor rates, actually served to exacerbate rather than ameliorate the famine. Indeed, the failure of these policies was predictable, since they were the work of a British government that was deeply ambivalent about the famine; although some Britons were sympathetic to the plight of the Irish, other Britons influenced by Malthusian and "providentialist" schools of thought regarded the depopulation of Ireland as acceptable or even desirable. As a result, the British did far too little to prevent an unprecedented tragedy from playing out on their very doorstep.

As implied by the name, the Irish Potato Famine was intimately linked to the fate of the potato. Although originally a New World crop, the potato was gradually adopted throughout Europe from the 17th century onward. In most of Europe, the potato was used as a "fodder" crop, meant for animal rather than human consumption, or else it was cultivated on a small scale as insurance against failure of the grain crop. Only in Ireland did the potato become a subsistence crop on a large scale. Indeed, it is estimated that by the 1840s the Irish were eating almost two and a half kilograms pounds of potatoes a day and that potatoes accounted for fully 60 percent of Ireland's food supply.

Why did the Irish rely so heavily on the potato for subsistence? In part this dependency arose from an accident of geography: Although the crop originated in the distant highlands of Peru, it grew quite well in Ireland's cool, wet climate and acidic soils. Cultural preferences played a role as well. As Cormac Ó Gráda has pointed out, the Irish love of potato that transcended space and class: Not only was the potato eaten by all ranks of Irish society, it remained the preferred food of the Irish even after they emigrated overseas where supposedly "superior" food crops were widely available.

It was sheer poverty, however, that did the most to entrench the potato in Irish diets. By the 1840s, 8 million people crowded Ireland, nearly half as many as lived in the much larger nation of England. As a consequence Ireland's limited agricultural land had become increasingly subdivided by the eve of the famine to the point that nearly 50 percent of Ireland's farms were under 20 acres in size by 1844, and fully 17 percent were under a single acre in size. Only the potato, which produced very high yields per acre, allowed the Irish to survive on such miniscule farms. Indeed, the cultivation of the potato and population growth may have been locked in a mutually reinforcing feedback loop. The potato's high yields allowed Ireland to sustain one of the fastest population growth rates in Europe, while higher population in turn made the Irish ever more dependent on the potato to feed their burgeoning numbers.

The Irish overreliance on potatoes was worsened by other economic trends in the early 19th century. The development of the British textile industry, for example, rendered the traditional Irish handicraft sector obsolete, destroying a key food entitlement mechanism of the Irish rural poor. A second negative trend was the "scissors effect" of falling real wages and rising rents, an Ireland-wide phenomenon from 1815 through 1845, which gradually reduced the relative standard of living of wage-dependent Irish. In desperation, many Irish farmers resorted to cultivating bog-land or rocky hillsides, but this unproductive land left such farmers at a chronic risk of starvation. Another sign of Irish poverty was the increased reliance of the poor on the "lumper" variety of potato, a watery, tasteless potato that nonetheless could produce impressive yields even on substandard soil. Unfortunately, this potato proved particularly vulnerable to the potato blight of 1845–52.

That being said, most Famine historians insist that the economic situation in Ireland was far from hopeless in the 1840s. During this period the Irish economy grew steadily overall thanks to the sale of

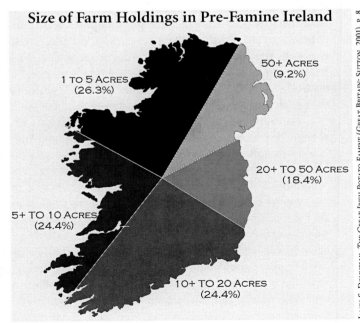

Size of Farm Holdings in Pre-Famine Ireland

1 TO 5 ACRES (26.3%)

50+ ACRES (9.2%)

20+ TO 50 ACRES (18.4%)

5+ TO 10 ACRES (24.4%)

10+ TO 20 ACRES (24.4%)

JAMES S. DONNELLY, *THE GREAT IRISH POTATO FAMINE* (GREAT BRITAIN: SUTTON, 2001), P. 8

agricultural products to neighboring Britain. Potatoes played only a small part in this market, as high transportation costs and rapid spoilage made them better suited for domestic consumption, but grain, oats, dairy products, and beef cattle were all profitable exports that lined the pockets of Irish landlords, estate agents, merchants, bankers, and other assorted middlemen. What is more, despite widespread poverty and high population densities, the Irish were generally healthier than their British counterparts, a testament to the nutritive value of the potato. Furthermore, there were grounds for future optimism about the Irish economy. Despite growing overpopulation and poverty, Ireland had not suffered a serious famine for decades. In addition, Irish population growth was finally beginning to ease off in the last few decades before the famine, prompting some historians to argue that, if the famine had not occurred in the late 1840s, Ireland may have been able to achieve economic stability or even prosperity at its current population level. As it turned out, however, this dip in population growth was too little, too late.

In any case, the Irish Potato Famine was not triggered directly by overpopulation and poverty, but rather by the importation of the fungal infection *phytophthora investans*, also known as the potato blight. Irish farmers in 1845 were dismayed to discover that their potato plants were becoming blackened and withered, while potatoes themselves rotted in the ground, giving off a terrible stench in the process. Worse yet, many apparently healthy potatoes succumbed to the rot while in storage, depleting the accumulated harvest. The overall loss of the potato crop amounted to about 30 percent of the normal harvest, rising to 40 percent in some districts of Ireland. It is important to point out that the blight was not just an Irish phenomenon; indeed, other parts of Europe suffered even worse harvest failures, in terms of percentage of the crop, than did Ireland. Nonetheless, since the potato played only a secondary role in their food supply, other countries suffered economic downturns but little famine 1840s. In potato-dependent Ireland, however, social and demographic conditions ensured that any crop loss threatened to be catastrophic.

To its credit, the British government under Robert Peel reacted decisively to the impending crisis. Peel purchased, in secret, considerable quantities of maize (corn) and maize flour from American merchants, and then resold it at cost at various points throughout Ireland. According to historians, these food imports were not large enough to make up the food deficiency, but they did serve to depress grain and potato prices, thus keeping food within the means of the Irish poor. In addition, Peel provided considerable public assistance to the Irish relief committees, allowing them to provide work relief to as many as 140,000 of Ireland's most destitute citizens. As a result of these efforts—combined with the relatively moderate loss of the potato crop—very few Irish died in 1845.

Although successful, Peel's efforts had a number of long term negative affects that would render Ireland more vulnerable to famine in the coming years. One ironic affect was the fall of Peel from power. In part because of the unpopularity of his Irish relief programs, which were seen as too generous and plagued by corruption, Peel was forced to resign in early 1846. He was succeeded as Prime Minister by the Whig leader Lord John Russell, who would prove far less effective in alleviating Irish suffering than his predecessor. What is more, the effectiveness of the famine relief in 1845 famine led to false expectations on the part of both the Irish and the British. After 1845 the Irish assumed that the British government would assist them in times of famine, a faith that soon proved to be misplaced. As for the British, they came to believe that Irish famines could be averted with only moderate expenditure. This assumption helped to limit the official British response to post–1845 Irish crop failures, with disastrous results.

As it turned out, the harvest failure of 1845 proved to be only a prelude of the true catastrophe to come. Weather in 1846 was exceptionally poor; a long winter delayed potato planting, early summer drought stunted the crop, and then heavy rains in late July and early August created perfect conditions for the potato blight to flourish. Consequently, the potato harvest of 1846 measured only 3 million tons, as compared with about 10.5 million in 1845 and 15 million in pre-blight 1844. Ireland now faced a genuine, albeit artificially created, Malthusian crisis. Ireland's population had risen far above the level that available food supplies could support.

At this point, mass starvation was all but inevitable: Even a vigorous government response could not have pumped food into Ireland fast enough to prevent some mortality from occurring. However, the British response to the famine was far from vigorous. At first the British government paid little attention to the impending Irish famine, believing that Ireland's local relief institutions were up to the task of combating the food shortage. Indeed, just as the 1846 famine was starting to fester, the famine relief measures implemented in 1845 were largely dismantled. Only after the government began to receive desperate reports from Irish officials and the British press began printing lurid tales of mass evictions and roadside deaths did the British government belatedly take action.

Unfortunately for the Irish, these actions were fatally weakened by the ideological fixations of the new Whig government of Britain. British governmental elites had a deep distaste for the Irish system of land tenure, regarding the small,

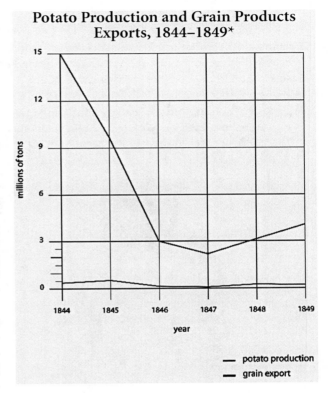

Potato Production and Grain Products Exports, 1844–1849*

subdivided Irish plots as inherently wasteful in comparison to large-scale, capitalist farming in Britain. As a consequence, some British leaders regarded the famine, not as a crisis, but rather as an opportunity to reorganize Irish farming on a more rational basis. This fed into a second British ideological mindset: belief in providence, or in other words, belief that world events are best understood as a reflection of God's will. As a consequence, many British saw the famine as a just punishment for Irish laziness, profligacy, and degeneracy, including their overreliance on the "morally inferior" potato. Not surprisingly, then, the British relief program focused too much on regenerating Irish souls and not enough on sustaining Irish bodies. Most importantly, the Malthusian mindset of many British elites convinced them that famine deaths were simply unavoidable in overpopulated Ireland; it was better, then, to let the famine burn itself out than to waste Britain's treasure on futile short-run solutions. Lord Clarendon's famous declaration on the famine expresses this attitude in a nutshell: "We shall be equally blamed for keeping [the Irish] alive," he stated, "or letting them die. We have only to select between the censure of the Economists or the Philanthropists." Ultimately the British made the tragic decision to offend the philanthropists rather than the economists.

*P. M. A. BOURKE, "THE EXTENT OF THE POTATO CROP IN IRELAND AT THE TIME OF THE FAMINE." *JOURNAL OF THE STATISTICAL AND SOCIAL INQUIRY SOCIETY OF IRELAND*, XX, PL. III (1959), PP. 1–35, AND JAMES S. DONELLY, *THE GREAT IRISH POTATO FAMINE* (GREAT BRITAIN: SUTTON, 2001), P. 61.

Rather than import food into Ireland as the Peel administration had done — a measure the free market Whigs regarded with extreme distaste — the Russell government opted to solve the famine through the traditional policy of providing work relief. This relief program was established with an eye towards cost cutting rather than effectiveness. Unlike Peel's program, which was partially funded by the public purse, Russell insisted that all money fronted to relief committees was merely a loan to be repaid out of local revenues after the famine was over. At the same time, in order to avoid the alleged corruption of Peel's work relief program, the British government kept a watchful eye over the approval of specific projects and the distribution of funds, slowing their implementation. What is more, despite the ravages of the famine, the projects chosen were not designed to increase Ireland's food supply; rather, most work relief projects centered on road and bridge construction, projects that assisted large Irish commercial farmers rather than poor subsistence farmers. In any case, in part due to local-national wrangling over funding and project approval, the works got off to a very slow start; only 26,000 Irishmen were employed on work relief in early October of 1846, rising to 441,000 by December and 714,390 (or nearly 10 percent the population of Ireland) by March 1847. For many of the Irish poor the delay between the harvest failure and the establishment of works projects proved fatal.

Even after the public works had started, they saved few lives, since they were poorly planned in the extreme. To start with, they only employed able bodied adult males, and thus provided only indirect support at best for women, children, the infirm, and the elderly. All of the work was performed outdoors during an exceptionally harsh winter, and since many of the Irish destitute had inadequate clothing, thousands died of exposure. Others succumbed to disease, especially fevers, which thrived in the densely packed labor camps. Worse yet, if outdoor conditions deteriorated to the point that work was simply impossible, the Irish were not paid at all, meaning that their survival and the survival of their families was tied to the caprices of the weather. Even when workers received wages, they were insufficient to feed a family, and they did not rise proportionally to food prices. What is more, the wages were usually paid by task rather than per hour, so workers unable to work hard due to hunger or illness earned less money over time, leading to a vicious cycle

ILLUSTRATED LONDON NEWS, DECEMBER 22, 1849

Contemporary illustration of Irish potato famine victims.

of increased hunger, greater weakness, and even less pay. Policies of this sort were all but guaranteed to produce mass mortality, and some contemporary observers came to the conclusion that Britain had designed the camps for exactly that purpose. As famine survivor Hugh Dorrian pointed out, "forcing the hungry and the half clad men to stand out in the cold and the sleet and the rain from morn till night, for the paltry reward of nine pennies a day ... meant next to slow murder."

Faced with the growing uproar over labor camp conditions, the British government changed course, and gradually closed the camps during the spring of 1846 — a decision that reflected the high financial cost of the camps as much as the high cost in human lives. To replace the camps, the government set up soup kitchens throughout Ireland, a famine relief strategy that was deemed to be not only more effective in preventing starvation but also less costly to the British exchequer. Unfortunately the transition between labor camps and soup kitchens was far from seamless: Indeed several months passed between the abolition of work relief and the institution of soup kitchens in many areas, a gap in government assistance that lead to thousands of extra deaths. What is more, not enough soup kitchens were established to feed all of Ireland's poor. Indeed the soup kitchens at their best fed a half million fewer people than were supported by the previous work relief schemes, which themselves did not reach all poor Irishmen. Furthermore, although the soup kitchens did not breed fevers like the labor camps, the monotonous gruel they dished out fostered the development of nutritional deficiency diseases, particularly scurvy. Still, most historians believe the soup kitchens were a great improvement over the labor camps that preceded them.

In the meantime, the British government refused to forbid food exports from Ireland, despite the famine raging in the country. Russell's government justified this stance on the grounds of free market economic doctrine: Prohibiting food exports would only suppress the grain trade in the long run, thus exacerbating the famine. As a consequence, shiploads of desperately needed grain were allowed to be exported from a starving nation. Admittedly, the retention of this grain would not have ended the famine. The 285,000 tons of grain exported from Ireland in 1846 would have made only a small dent in the 12 million ton shortfall in the potato harvest, even taking into consideration that grains had more nutritive value by volume than potatoes due to the potato's high water content. Still, this exported grain could have saved some lives in Ireland, and perhaps more importantly, it would have counterbalanced the upward spiral of food prices that progressively undermined the food entitlement of Irish wage-earners. Ultimately Britain's decision to allow grain exports, thus privileging ideology over human lives, was emblematic of Britain's overall behavior during the Potato Famine.

Indeed, ideology rather than philanthropy continued to characterize the British relief effort as 1846 gave way to 1847. Arguing that the indefinite free distribution of food would ruin the moral character of the Irish, the Russell government scrapped the soup kitchens in September 1847; from that point onwards, the Irish had to depend on the Poor Law for famine relief. In theory, the Poor Law should have provided some comfort to the starving Irish, as it set up work houses to provide shelter and sustenance for the indigent. Unfortunately for the Irish, however, the Poor Law proved to be an agent of misery rather than mercy. In large part this was due to two specific amendments that the Russell government added to the Poor Law in spring of that year. First of all, in order to spare the British treasury further pain, and in order to punish the Irish landlords for (supposedly) allowing Irish agriculture to become such a shambles, the amended law stipulated that all money for Irish famine relief must come from land taxes in Ireland. Secondly, the law forbade the distribution of any aid to farmers holding more than a quarter acre of land.

Taken together, these amendments proved catastrophic for the Irish small farmer, which as we have seen made up a quite substantial slice of Ireland's population. The insistence that Irish land owners pay for the poor houses threw an enormous financial burden onto the Irish landholding elite, which now faced spiraling tax burdens; indeed in some provinces the cost of caring for famine victims required annual taxes equal to 50–100 percent of the value of their property. As a result, many Irish landholders felt financially compelled to clear their estates of small holders, each of which represented a potential tax liability. Landholders were assisted in doing so by the infamous quarter-acre clause, which forced farmers to abandon all but a quarter acre of their land as a price of gaining admission to the Poor Law workhouses. If the quarter-acre clause was insufficient, landlords turned to other methods to clear out tenants, ranging from the carrot (providing funds for emigration to the Americas, for instance) or the stick (intimidating poor farmers through the police or hired muscle). At first, landlords tended to target individual "problem" tenants, but as the evictions gained force entire villages were cleared at a time, often in order to transform estates from farmland into cattle pasture since the livestock industry was becoming increasingly profitable by the late 1840s.

Irish farmers faced with evictions had few options. Emigration to the Americas was a possibility, especially if one had a family member who had left for Canada or the United States earlier in the 1830s or 1840s, but this was beyond the means of most famine-stricken Irishmen. Many Irish simply refused to surrender their land, even if that meant exclusion from the workhouses and slow death by starvation. Other Irish abandoned their houses—which were often immediately knocked down or stripped of their roofs in order to discourage the former tenant's return—and tried to survive as best they could, living in ditches, behind fences, or wherever else they could cobble together a bit of shelter. Still others moved into the already cramped houses of tenants who had not (yet) been evicted, but this only worsened the problems of unsanitary conditions and disease. This risk was further exacerbated by the traditional Irish postmortem habit of "waking the dead," the Irish funerary custom of leaving a deceased family member in the house for several days before burial. Furthermore, the evictees who sought shelter with other tenants risked the wrath of the authorities, who wanted to drive the evicted tenants out of town, partially to avoid confrontations, but also to avoid Poor Tax responsibility for the dispossessed.

As for the Poor Law workhouses, even the most desperate Irish considered them a destination of last resort. Conditions in the workhouses were deliberately kept as unpleasant as possible, largely in hopes of dissuading all but the most needy Irish from joining the workhouse rolls. As a consequence, workhouse inmates were subjected to military-style discipline and obliged to perform exhausting manual labor, such as turning mill wheels or breaking rocks. The food provided was grossly inadequate to sustain life, and the workhouses themselves were packed far beyond their intended capacity: The Femory workhouse in County Cork, for example, housed 1,800 in a space designed for 800 in March 1847. Little attempt was initially made to separate the sick from the well, and this contributed to explosive outbreaks of contagious diseases, especially typhus, relapsing fever, measles, and cholera. Indeed, the mortality rate at the Femory workhouse was so high that an estimated 24 percent of the inmates who entered the workhouse in January 1847 did not live through March. Given these awful conditions, it is hardly surprising that many Irish only entered the hell of the workhouse when they were already on the brink of death, knowing that if they passed away within the workhouse walls they would be guaranteed a coffin and Christian burial after they died.

The amendment of the Poor Law in 1847 and the soup kitchens were the last direct British interventions into the Irish Potato Famine. Indeed, British sympathy for the Irish, never strong to begin with, faded sharply over time, especially after an abortive 1848 Irish revolution which was seen as an act of profound ingratitude given all the "relief" that Britain had provided in

Disease Deaths During the Irish Potato Famine by Year

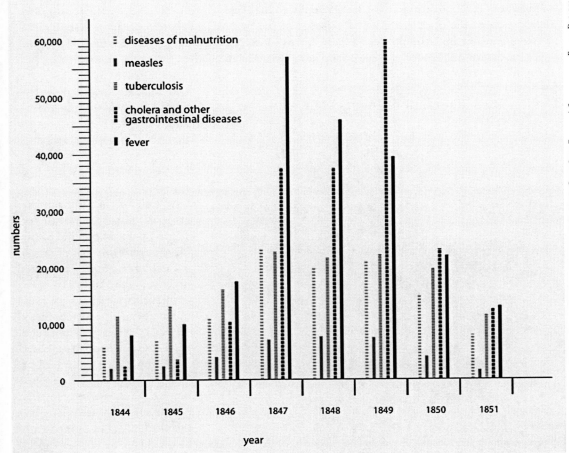

Liam Kennedy, P.S. Ell, E. M. Crawford, and L. A. Clarkson, Mapping the Great Irish Famine: A Survey of the Famine Decades (Portland, Oregon: Four Courts, 1999), p. 105

previous years. American and British philanthropic institutions continued to provide some food and money after 1847, but these efforts gradually petered out as a result of donor fatigue. In the meantime, the famine continued almost unabated. Although the potato blight spared Ireland during the 1847 harvest, the Irish had planted so little land with potatoes in 1847 that the overall harvest was still far below normal, as the crops substituted for the potatoes could not match the potato's yield. Despite lack of seed, Irish farmers made a desperate attempt to re-establish potato planting in 1848, but wet weather and a return of the potato blight devastated that harvest as well. Ultimately the famine did not abate until 1852, by which time so many people had either died or emigrated that the food supply was sufficient to sustain the remaining population.

Indeed, Ireland suffered a catastrophic drop in population as a result of the Potato Famine. According to the best estimates, almost 1.1 million Irish died between 1846 and 1851, either by starvation or through the diseases that flourished during the famine. The famine also averted about half a million births that would have occurred in non-famine years. Another 2.1 million Irish men, women, and children tried to escape the famine by emigration. Of these, about 1.5 million fled to the United States, 340,000 to Canada and other British colonies in the Americas, 200,000–300,000 to Britain itself, and thousands more to Australia and elsewhere. Some of these migrants never reached their destination: Indeed, the "coffin ships" that transported the Irish to Canada became notorious for their unsanitary conditions and rampant disease. As a result of death and emigration, Ireland entered the second half of the 19th century with only 50 percent of the population it had boasted in the first half. This demographic damage has proven long-lasting; population levels in Ireland have barely risen from the mid–1800s to the present day, and far more people of Irish decent live in the United States today than live in all of modern Ireland.

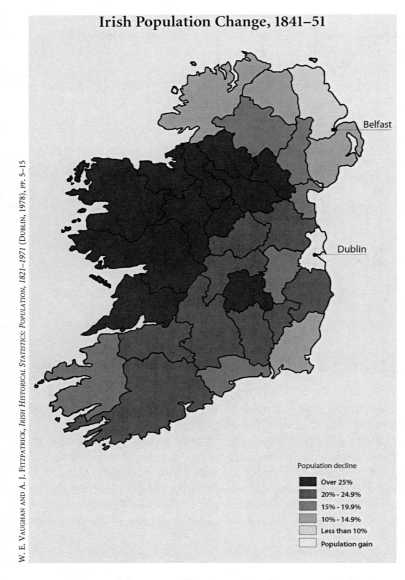

Irish Population Change, 1841–51

Belfast

Dublin

Population decline

- **Over 25%**
- **20% - 24.9%**
- **15% - 19.9%**
- **10% - 14.9%**
- Less than 10%
- Population gain

W. E. VAUGHAN AND A. J. FITZPATRICK, IRISH HISTORICAL STATISTICS: POPULATION, 1821–1971 (DUBLIN, 1978), PP. 5–15

If the Russell government's goal was to remove Ireland's excess population, therefore, that effort seems to have been crowned in success. Indeed, the British elites had cause to be pleased with the new Ireland that the famine created. The removal of "excess population" did allow for the consolidation of farms into larger, more efficient units, though the British goal of importing British-style capitalist farming was not fully realized. What is more, the Irish who survived the famine did enjoy a better standard of living compared to the pre-famine level. Of course this improvement was only relative — the Irish remained well below the British in per capita income — but given the fact that Ireland's pre-famine standard of living was roughly equivalent to that in modern-day third world nations, Ireland's post-famine economic improvement was nonetheless a step in the right direction.

Still, in the long run, the Irish Potato Famine proved to be more of a problem than a benefit to the British Empire. As we have seen, the British were not solely responsible for Ireland's sorrows; indeed even the most vigorous relief measures would not have prevented some mortality in Ireland. Nor was there any concerted British policy of "genocide," though the British certainly could have done much more to prevent the famine and could have tailored their relief efforts to Ireland's actual needs rather than their own ideological fixations. These subtle distinctions, however, were lost in the post-famine crescendo

YOUNG IRELAND IN BUSINESS FOR HIMSELF.

Punch cartoon illustrating contemporary British fears of Irish insurrection. These fears seemed to be fulfilled by the failed 1848 Young Ireland uprising, which further dampened British enthusiasm for Irish famine relief.

of voices that held Britain to be solely responsible for the Potato Famine. Indeed, in the years after the famine the false notion that the grain exported to Britain during the famine would have been more than enough to feed the starving Irish became gospel to the Irish nationalist movement, fueling virulent anti–British hatred. What is more, in the post-famine Irish mind the rebels slain and imprisoned during the inept 1848 Irish uprising rose to the status of heroes, martyrs to the cause of Irish freedom. The enduring mythology of the Irish Potato Famine, therefore, played a powerful role in shaping the Irish nationalist movement that would eventually compel Britain to accede to Irish demands for independence.

Study Questions

1. Which of the three models of famine discussed in length in this chapter — the natural disaster, Malthusian, and "entitlement" theories — do you think applies best to the Irish potato famine? Explain your answer.

2. Based on this section, which do you think did more to hamper the British relief effort in Ireland: British economic interests, of British ideological convictions?

3. "Other than geographical location, the Irish Potato Famine differs in no significant way from the "Victorian" famines in India and China described in chapter 7." Based on this section and chapter 7, to what degree do you agree with this statement?

4. "The so-called Irish Potato 'Famine' was not a famine at all, but rather an unprecedented outbreak of disease in an overpopulated country." Based on what you have read, to what degree do you agree with this statement?

Sources/Suggested Readings

Bourke, P. M. A. "The Extent of the Potato Crop in Ireland at the Time of the Famine." *Journal of the Statistical and Social Inquiry of Ireland*, Vol. 20, No. 3 (1959), pp. 1–35.
Donnelly, James S. *The Great Irish Potato Famine*. Great Britain: Sutton, 2001.
Ó Gráda, Cormac. *Black '47 and Beyond*. Princeton, NJ: Princeton University Press, 1999.
Póirtér, Catha, ed., *The Great Irish Famine*. Cork, Ireland: Mercier, 1999.
Tóibín, Colm, and Ferriter, Diarmaid. *The Irish Famine: A Documentary*. New York: St. Martin's, 2001.

7.2: Mao's Great Leap Forward

The Great Leap Forward (hereafter GLF) was a sudden shift in Communist China's economic policy, inaugurated in 1958, which led inadvertently to the largest famine in world history. At least 14 million people, and perhaps as many as 80 million, perished before the famine relented in 1962. As might be expected, such a huge disaster had numerous causes. The Chinese government's hasty collectivization of village land, crackpot agricultural theories, poor weather, and diversion of manpower away from farming all contributed to the disaster. However, the main factor driving the GLF famine was excessive governmental food requisition. The Chinese government, misled by wild exaggerations about harvest yields, extracted enormous and ultimately unsustainable quantities of food from the Chinese countryside in order to fund rapid industrialization. Indeed, the ultimate tragedy of the GLF is that the food shortfall was almost entirely avoidable; although the Chinese government later ascribed the famine deaths to three years of bad weather, in actual fact few "natural" disasters in history have been more obviously man-made than the GLF famine.

The GLF famine was far from the first famine to strike China. Indeed, food shortages have been a consistent theme in Chinese history. North China lies in the northern "famine belt," where cold snaps often cut short the growing season and disrupt harvests. Southern China, in turn, belongs to the monsoon famine belt, where the failure of the monsoon can lead to severe rainfall shortfalls and resultant crop losses. Worse yet, these famine belts overlap: North China's weather is affected by the monsoon cycle as well, further exacerbating its famine vulnerability. It is hardly surprising, then, that China has been dubbed a "land of famine" by western historians.

However, this depiction of Chinese famine history is somewhat oversimplified. As Mike Davis has demonstrated in his path breaking book *Late Victorian Holocausts*, pre-modern Chinese governments employed a number of effective measures, such as the "ever-normal granaries" and food shipments via the Grand Canal, in order to reduce mortality in times of famine. What is more, the Chinese concept of the Mandate of Heaven, which legitimized the overthrow of rulers who did not safeguard the welfare of the people, helped to ensure that Chinese Emperors kept a watchful eye over their subjects' food supply. As a consequence, Davis argues, the Chinese Empire was much more effective than European states at preventing famine during the 18th century, when the tail end of the little ice age caused widespread food failures in the northern hemisphere. China only became a "land of famine," Davis contends, after European military campaigns and economic competition undermined these anti-famine measures in the second half of the 19th century.

China grew even more vulnerable to famine as the 19th century gave way to the 20th. As we have already seen in chapter 6.1, the Qing dynasty's growing inability to control the Yellow River lead to a series of horrific inundations, many of which brought famine in its wake. The fall of the Qing dynasty in 1912, in turn, unleashed decades of warlordism, banditry, and civil war, contributing to major Chinese famines in 1924, 1927, and 1929. Matters got still worse after 1931, when the Japanese empire began a fifteen year campaign to conquer China, forcing millions of Chinese to become internal refugees who proved particularly vulnerable to the ravages of famine. Even after the defeat of Japan in 1945, continued civil war between the Kuomintang (Nationalist) government and the Communist insurgents undermined Chinese food stability, contributing to a major famine in 1946. The continuing recurrence of famine under Kuomintang rule almost certainly contributed to their defeat by the communists, as popular misery undermined the Kuomintang's "mandate" to rule the country.

The victory of the Communists in the civil war raised hopes that China would finally pull out of this vicious cycle of famine. Unlike previous regimes in China, the new Communist government had intimate ties with the Chinese peasantry, which formed its main base of support. In pure Marxist terms, this was heresy: Karl Marx had discounted the revolutionary potential of the peasantry, dismissing them as a backwards, apolitical mass. Only the industrial proletariat, Marx had argued, was a true revolutionary class. However, Mao and his comrades realized that the Chinese industrial proletariat was far too weak to serve its designated role, while the Chinese peasantry had potentially revolutionary aspirations, most especially the redistribution of Chinese agricultural land and the destruction of China's parasitical landlord class. Thus, the Chinese Communist Party (hereafter CCP) struck a deal with the peasants, promising redistribution of China's farmland and freedom from famine after Communist victory in return for peasant support against the Kuomintang.

After the fall of the Kuomintang, the CCP at first kept its end of the bargain. Starting as early as 1949, the CCP and its local agents launched a campaign against rich peasants and landlords, rural elites who controlled the lion's share of both land and political power in agricultural villages. Although this often-violent political program lead to a disturbingly high death toll — at least 200,000 people were killed — it also had the positive effect of removing a class of middlemen and thus raising the efficiency of Chinese agricultural production. Indeed, China's agricultural sector grew by 12.6 percent immediately after the end of the civil war, though whether this rise was predominantly due to land redistribution or to post-war economic recovery is a matter of conjecture. However, one fact is clear: By seizing the wealth of rich farmers and adding it to the land of the poor, the CCP was potentially reducing the danger of famine in China, since the food entitlement of the average farmer rose in proportion with his gains in cropland.

In the meantime, in order to strengthen Communist China's underdeveloped industrial sector, the CCP adopted the centralized planning techniques of the Soviet Union, China's ally and fellow communist state. Following the Soviet model, the CCP enacted a "five-year plan" in 1953, during which the CCP established complete oversight and control over China's industrial economy in order to achieve rapid economic growth, especially in the industrial sector. During this five-year plan, the CCP focused on the development of industries, most especially metallurgy, electronics, and chemicals, which were deemed important to China's security. Hard workers received capitalist-style cash rewards for their extra effort, a policy that demonstrated that productivity was given a higher value than ideological purity during the five-year plan. What is more, China depended heavily on technical experts, mostly in the form of Soviet economic advisors or Soviet-trained Chinese students, to overhaul outdated practices and construct modern facilities. The results of this five-year plan were impressive: Electricity production rose by 166 percent, chemical fertilizer 249 percent, and steel 297 percent. However, the expansion of Chinese industry was limited by stagnation in the agricultural sector, which after 1952 just barely kept up with population growth, and which failed to meet the rising demand for raw materials in China's burgeoning industrial sector.

Why did China's agricultural sector fail to keep pace with industry? Two key problems were holding Chinese farmers back: the dispersion of their land into numerous small holdings, and continued rural poverty, which limited the ability of Chinese farmers to invest in agricultural improvement. The solution to both problems, the CCP believed, was the adoption of collectivized farming on the Soviet Union's model. Under this scheme, a sizable chunk of each peasant's land would be seized by the state and amalgamated together into a cooperative farm, jointly tended by all peasants in the community. Many within the party opposed the idea on the grounds that it risked alienating the peasantry, the main source of the CCP's political support. However, the Soviet Union's leadership strongly supported this strategy on ideological grounds, despite the fact that collectivization had caused food shortages and political unrest in the Soviet Union. More importantly, collectivization received the all-important blessing of CCP chairman Mao Zedong, who dominated politics in China up to his death in 1976. In any case the debate was moot: Other than capitalist market farming, which was anathema to the CCP, collectivization was the only economic model available that promised desperately-needed improvements in Chinese crop yields.

In theory, collectivization seemed like a perfect solution for China's agricultural woes. Large collective farms were far better suited to modern agricultural techniques, such as mechanized farming with tractors and chemical fertilizers, than the small, scattered holdings of traditional Chinese farmers. What is more, CCP officials were disturbed to find that their successful political campaign against rural elites was being undermined by a new class of rich peasants who were busily repurchasing land previously distributed to their poorer compatriots. Most members of the CCP were concerned by the resurgence of this "inherently capitalistic" rich peasant class and saw collectivization as a way to eliminate a possible threat. Collectivization also fit well with the CCP's Marxist dreams of socialist utopia. In the words of Mao Zedong, collectivization offered the possibility of "the socialist transformation of agriculture as a whole through co-operation." As a result of these considerations, the CCP enacted a program of gradual collectivization between 1954 and 1956.

In practice, however, collectivization failed to fix China's agricultural woes. Rather than leading to improved economies of scale, collectivization actually hurt Chinese farm efficiency since peasants laboring on collectively-owned land lacked work incentives. High government procurement targets further hurt farm efficiency, since peasants had little incentive to produce a surplus they knew would only be seized by the government. Chinese agricultural production also suffered from a shortage of draft animals, as their owners often slaughtered their livestock rather than surrender it to the collective, and those draft animals that did become property of the collective were often poorly cared for. If farm machinery was widely available, the lack of livestock might not have been a problem, but in actual fact few collectives received the tractors they had been promised. Indeed, China's first tractor factory only came on line in 1958, and in any case the Soviet-style tractors it produced were poorly suited to rice paddy cultivation. Farmers did receive heavy plows that were a pet project of Chairman Mao, but these expensive plows proved to be all but useless and had to be scrapped. Overall, collectivization did nothing to increase China's agricultural production and may very well have reduced it substantially.

Faced with these problems, economic planners in the CCP did the sensible thing, and tried to reign in collectivization in order to minimize the damage to the Chinese economy. Mao, however, refused to adopt a more moderate policy, and insisted instead that China speed up the pace of economic change. Mao's motives in doing so have been the subject of fierce debate. Some historians believe that Mao was a starry-eyed dreamer who legitimately believed that rhetoric and mass mobilization of labor could achieve any goal. According to these authors, Mao's world view was shaped by his experience as military leader of the Communists against the Japanese and Kuomintang, which taught him to think in terms of mobilizing the enthusiasm of his subordinates to achieve sudden breakthroughs rather than the steady achievement of rational economic targets using available resources. Despite his rise to head of state, these authors argue, Mao's mindset was still essentially that of a guerilla soldier, valuing improvisation and instinct rather than careful planning.

On the other hand, some historians see Mao in a more cynical light, and have argued that Mao's "Great Leap Forward" (hereafter GLF) was really a political tactic designed to break the power of the

AP/WORLD WIDE PHOTOS

A 1950 official photograph of Chinese Communist Party Chairman Mao Zedong, architect of the Great Leap Forward famine.

CCP economic planners. These planners tended to be influential and well educated CCP veterans, and collectively they represented the greatest potential political threat to Mao's domination of China. Furthermore, some historians argue the GLF was Mao's preemptive assault against the de–Stalinization campaign that Nikita Khrushchev launched in Russia 1956. Mao worried that Khrushchev's campaign against Stalin's "cult of personality" might prompt critics of Mao to do the same within China, greatly weakening his authority. This fear led directly to the "anti-rightist" campaign of 1957, which Mao used to silence opposition both inside and outside of the CCP by persecuting intellectuals who had criticized the CCP. Indeed, some historians have argued that the GLF was hardly about economics at all, but rather was an unfortunate intrusion of Mao's "anti-rightist" political campaign into the economic sphere.

Whatever the case, Mao started the ball of the GLF rolling in the fall of 1957. In October Mao adopted the slogan "more, faster, better, cheaper," which many took as a sign that China was abandoning its previous policy of careful planning along the Soviet model in favor of more dramatic change. What is more, Mao publicly attacked the top-down approach of the Soviet economic system in favor of a decentralized, popular approach, in which worker congresses and political rallies would replace cash incentives to Chinese laborers. Expertise in agriculture and industry took second place to Communist enthusiasm; in the language of the time, it was more important to be "red" than "expert." Mao also called for the creation of People's Communes, large-scale amalgamations of collective farming communities that included an average of 5,000 families. The purpose of these communes was twofold; not only did they represent yet another step towards socialism, a process already begun through collectivization, but they would command sufficient resources for large-scale investments into such projects as land improvement and water conservation. In addition, the communes were told to invest in small-scale furnaces capable of smelting steel, so as to fulfill Mao's goal of matching British and American industrial output in just a few years. In the process, Chinese peasants were stripped of what little farmland that remained to them following the first push towards collectivization, further reducing work incentives and the labor productivity of the Chinese agricultural sector.

The CCP's economic planners had serious reservations about these reforms, so Mao took steps to neutralize their opposition. Rather than continue to work through the planners, Mao bypassed them and reached out directly to local party leaders, who tended to be far more enthusiastic about rapid economic advancement than the more cautious central planners. Indeed, in a crucial economic conference held in Nanning in January 1958, Mao shunned the economic planners entirely and worked with a handpicked group of 25 high Chinese officials, many of whom were provincial leaders. When Mao did address the economic planners in Nanning, he attacked their performance and accused them of having "rightist leanings." As a result, the blindsided economic planners capitulated entirely to Mao's demands and were forced to make humiliating self-criticisms. Consequently, by the time of the important Chengdu conference in March 1958, Mao's position was unassailable; indeed one participant in the conference declared that "we have to trust the Chairman to the degree of blind faith, we should obey the Chairman to the extent of total abandon." Following this conference, Mao's public declarations and even offhand remarks were increasingly regarded as binding, and local officials scrambled to enact Mao's latest directives even though they often contradicted each other. According to Chinese historian Alfred Chan, during the GLF "decision-making became a slipshod and haphazard affair; hunches, improvisations, and 'oral' instructions replaced planning and calculation of costs and benefits."

Unfortunately for the Chinese, Mao's "hunches" and "improvisations" were almost invariably ill-considered, and as a consequence Mao's intervention into the economy would have disastrous consequences. The "backyard" steel furnaces that Mao insisted on building in the countryside, for example, were grossly inefficient, and generally produced inferior-grade steel at almost four times the cost of conventional steel works. They also sucked up enormous amounts of labor both to build and to operate, leading to a severe labor shortage at the height of the 1958 harvest. What is more, Mao insisted that they be built throughout China, even in areas without iron ore deposits, forcing many peasants to sacrifice their bicycles, iron bed frames, kitchen utensils, and even farming tools to the furnaces in a vain attempt to meet the high steel quotas set by the government. In areas without coal reserves, Chinese peasants were forced to cut down trees to provide fuel for the furnaces, leading to serious deforestation. Chinese Environmental historian Judith Shapiro believes that as much as 10 percent of China's remaining forestland was cut down in the 3 years of the GLF, triggering long-term erosion, sedimentation, and desertification problems.

In agriculture, Mao's policies were even more unrealistic. Mao was an ardent admirer of the Soviet scientist Trofim Denisovich Lysenko, who based his scientific discoveries on Marxist doctrine in general, and Stalinist ideology in particular. For example, Lysenko rejected the Darwinian theory of evolution, which insisted that the characteristics of living beings are determined by genetics, in favor of his own crackpot theory which held that the characteristics of living things can be forced to change by abruptly changing their environment — just as the Communist Party had transformed Russia from a backwards autocracy to a modern socialist state by top-down social engineering. As a consequence, Lysenko's students wasted their time on fruitless experiments, such as scattering seed on snow in an attempt to teach it to sprout out of season. Similarly, in China Mao insisted on "close planting" in agriculture. Just as people of the same social class have common interests, Mao decreed, so too seeds of the same variety will support rather than impede each other's growth, making the traditional Chinese agricultural practice of spacing out rice plants in a paddy unnecessary. Mao also hoped to encourage Chinese agricultural production by borrowing the Soviet idea of "deep plowing," in which the soil is plowed to a depth of up to 4 meters by specially-designed machinery. Not only did deep plowing require an enormous expense of time and effort — indeed, in some areas lack of machinery forced peasants to dig these enormous furrows by hand — it probably reduced yields by allowing sterile subsoil to mix with the fertile topsoil. These nonsensical notions would probably have withered in the face of informed criticism, but as most of China's agricultural experts had been incarcerated in labor reform camps due to Mao's "anti-rightist" campaign, few voices were raised to challenge his pseudo-scientific notions.

Other Maoist ideas about agriculture were even more destructive. Mao insisted that the communes build dams for the purpose of water and soil conservation, and although this was a good idea in theory, in practice the poorly-built dams constructed of packed soil by unskilled peasant labor were more dangerous than useful. Indeed as we already saw in chapter 6, the August 1975 failure of two GLF–era dams, the Shimantan and Banqiao dams on the Huai River watershed, is still on record as the most catastrophic dam collapse in history. Most GLF dams did not last nearly that long and washed away in the first few seasons after they were built. Other public works of the GLF period, for instance the dramatic expansion of irrigation systems into semi-arid land, proved equally disastrous, as most of these irrigation schemes were built with insufficient attention to drainage and as a consequence soil salinization soon became a serious problem.

Worse of all, Mao's slogan of "plant less, produce more, harvest less" called upon Chinese farmers to reduce the area they planted by ⅓ in hopes of turning "the whole [of China] ... into a garden." This scheme was inspired by the agricultural experiments of Vasily Williams, another influential Soviet scientist, who claimed that leaving a third of the land fallow each year would have the twin benefits of allowing for more intensive agriculture on the land that was harvested and the natural rejuvenation of the land left unplowed. The actual amount of land left untilled in China came nowhere close to ⅓ because many officials recognized that the full implementation of this policy would lead to a disastrous reduction in yields, but nonetheless enough communes adopted Mao's "plant less" policy to have a negative impact on the 1958 harvest.

As a result of this combination of collectivization, poorly conceived agricultural practices, and diversion of resources to industrial development, it soon became clear to many local officials that the 1958 harvest would be disastrously low. However, since any notes of pessimism would be attacked as "rightist" sentiments, local officials were under intense pressure to report high yields; indeed, local officials competed with each other to issue increasingly exaggerated harvest statistics. In Judith Shapiro's words, the mindset of the time was one of "utopian urgency." Fantastic lies were reported to the central government, such as harvests that exceeded those of the previous year by 200 or even 300 percent. Those officials who resisted the peer pressure and who submitted more realistic yield estimates risked being denounced as "rightists," "tide-watchers," or "dogmatists." What is more, since these new agricultural policies had received the stamp of support from Mao, who was regarded as almost a godlike figure by most Chinese, local officials were reluctant to report results that would cause the Chairman to lose face. In fact, local CCP leaders devised elaborate schemes to hide the scale of the developing food crisis from Mao, for instance by stacking food on the side of the road as he passed to create an illusion of prosperity.

As a result of such deceptions, Mao legitimately believed that the 1958 harvest was a bumper crop, and consequently instituted several policies that would further exacerbate the coming famine. Mao increased China's grain exports to the Soviet Union by 50 percent and even provided free grain to the Communist governments of North Korea, North Vietnam, and Albania, while importation of foodstuffs into China was scaled back. To celebrate the supposedly phenomenal harvest, Mao ordered that the communal kitchens in China's rural communes provide unlimited amounts of free food to peasants, to the point that "everyone blinked like an owl as if drunk from eating." Most important of all, Mao revised the state's grain appropriation figures to match the new, exaggerated harvest estimates. As a result, local officials who had boasted about their bumper crops were now directed to deliver absurdly high amounts of food to the central government, in many cases far more food than the communities could support. As a result, many local officials all but stripped the countryside bare in order to cover up their earlier exaggerations. When food was not forthcoming despite these measures, Mao assumed the shortfall was the result of hoarding rather than poor harvests, and directed officials to extract the food by force from what he called the "privately dividing-the-grain movement."

As signs of famine continued to mount in early 1959, a small group of Chinese officials, led by Minister of Defense Peng Dehuai, finally dared to raise the subject of the famine with Mao in the form of a private letter. Mao's response reinforces the charge that his GLF campaign was as much about politics as economics. Rather than addressing Peng's concerns, Mao circulated the letter amongst high Chinese officials as proof of a developing conspiracy. Matters soon escalated: Peng accused Mao of acting despotically in a Politburo meeting, whereupon Mao labeled Peng a "rightist" and charged that he was trying to divide the CCP. In the end, few deputies were willing to support Peng, and the humiliated defense minister was formally condemned as an "anti-party element" and put under house arrest. Nor did the matter end there. In the months that followed, a large number of CCP members were accused of being "little Peng Dehuais" and were arrested on charges of "right opportunism," effectively silencing any party opposition to the GLF. As a consequence, local officials competed to issue even more extravagant claims about production figures before the 1959 harvest, and grain procurements were set at an even higher level than in 1958.

As a result of this procurement, the food shortages triggered by the 1958 harvest exploded into full-blown famine in 1959. Peasants already weakened in 1958 entered the 1959 planting season with few farm implements (due to the demands of the steel-making campaign) and little seed to plant, since farmers had been forced to dip into their seed crop in early 1959 to sustain themselves. In an attempt to grow more food in 1959, farmers planted high-yield sweet potatoes rather than grain and ignored Mao's directive to leave more land fallow. What is more, officials quietly shifted labor away from the "backyard furnaces" and back to agriculture, knowing that as much as 10 percent of the 1958 harvest had rotted in the fields due to lack of laborers to harvest it. Despite these measures, there was simply not enough food to go around in 1959. Desperate peasants tried to collect wild foods to survive, but in densely-packed eastern China there were few uncultivated stretches of land and thus limited opportunities for forage. Even if wild foods were available, many peasants no longer had the proper cooking utensils to prepare them. Local officials tried to compensate for lack of food by adding various food substitutes, such as dirt, ground-up corn cobs, and dried swamp algae, to the daily food ration. Unfortunately, such substitutes not only provided little nutrition, they were also potentially deadly, since they could tear or block up the digestive tract. According to some reports, some individuals or even entire communities resorted to cannibalism, to the point of cooking and serving the flesh of "counter-revolutionary" prisoners.

Despite these measures, China suffered mass mortality in 1959–1961. Deaths were not equally distributed throughout the country; indeed, certain professions and geographic regions proved to have higher levels of food "entitlement" than others. Cities received comparatively more food than rural communities, largely as a by-product of the CCP's decision to shift resources to cities in an effort to stimulate industrial production. Northern China tended to suffer much higher mortality than the south, in part due to the occurrence of drought in the north during the GLF, but more probably due to the north's relative poverty compared to the more prosperous south, which meant that the northern Chinese were already living closer to the subsistence level when the GLF started. As with most famines, the very young and the very old suffered a disproportionably high number of deaths, as did women; indeed, demographic studies of China's population after the GLF famine suggest that a high level of female infanticide occurred from 1958 to 1961. So-called enemies of the people, such as criminals and people arrested during the anti-rightist campaign, fared worst of all, receiving a meager ration that in practice amounted to a slow death. The only group that suffered little during the GLF were members of the CCP, who received the highest food rations in China.

As for the total number of deaths, there is little agreement amongst the available sources. Indeed, death estimates range from a low of 14 million to a staggering high of 80 million. This ambiguity is partially the result of an active Chinese campaign to hide the existence of the GLF famine from outsiders. It also reflects different measuring criteria used by GLF researchers. Should averted births be included in famine death statistics, or should the death toll only include the already-born? How reliable are China's census figures? How much weight should we give to the oral accounts of former Chinese officials, such as Chen Yizi, who claimed China suffered 80 million "unnatural deaths"? Despite these various measures of GLF mortality, or perhaps because of them, the GLF famine's death toll remains a matter of conjecture. Nonetheless, most estimates fall between 16 million to 30 million, so it is likely the real death toll lies somewhere within that range.

Just as hotly debated as the death toll is the relative impact of different factors in producing the GLF famine. Simply put, what factors contributed the most to the mass mortality? Although most studies of the GLF are content simply to list the causes of the famine without weighing their relative importance, two recent studies have given precise (though somewhat

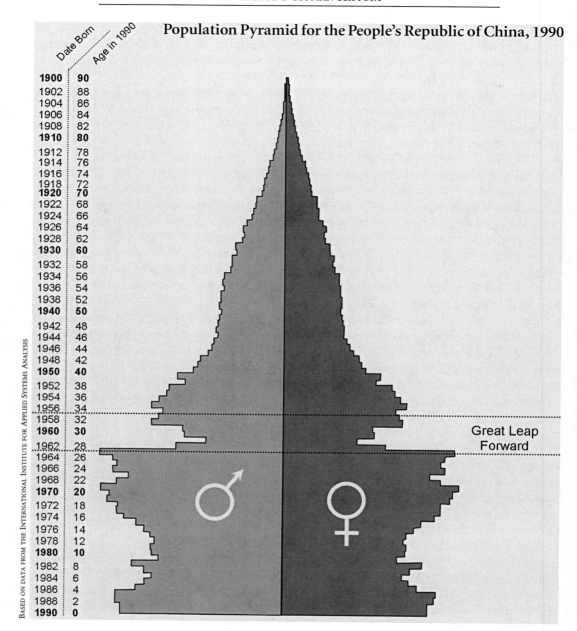

Population Pyramid for the People's Republic of China, 1990

Date Born	Age in 1990
1900	90
1902	88
1904	86
1906	84
1908	82
1910	80
1912	78
1914	76
1916	74
1918	72
1920	70
1922	68
1924	66
1926	64
1928	62
1930	60
1932	58
1934	56
1936	54
1938	52
1940	50
1942	48
1944	46
1946	44
1948	42
1950	40
1952	38
1954	36
1956	34
1958	32
1960	30
1962	28
1964	26
1966	24
1968	22
1970	20
1972	18
1974	16
1976	14
1978	12
1980	10
1982	8
1984	6
1986	4
1988	2
1990	0

Great Leap Forward

BASED ON DATA FROM THE INTERNATIONAL INSTITUTE FOR APPLIED SYSTEMS ANALYSIS

As this diagram shows, China had a disproportionately low number of men and women aged between 28 and 32 in 1990, due to averted births and high infant mortality rates during the Great Leap Forward famine.

conflicting) assessments of the relative influence of different causal factors. According to a 1995 assessment by Y. Y. Kueh, for instance, poor weather accounted for 75 percent of the poor harvests from 1959 to 1961, and the other 25 percent loss is attributable to state interference, especially Mao's "plant less" policy and the excessive procurement of the 1958 harvest, which left the peasants with little to plant in 1959–1960. Despite these findings, Kueh nonetheless insists that the 25 percent loss due to state policy was the most crucial causative factor in the GLF famine, and that without state interference peasants could have survived the poor weather relatively comfortably. What is more, Kueh insists that state interference during the GLF would have caused a demographic disaster even without bad weather, a conclusion that is hard to reconcile with his claim that bad weather was 75 percent responsible for the food shortfall.

A more recent published article has come up with a more balanced assessment of the factors reducing harvest yields during the GLF. In a 2001 discussion paper, Mark Yuying An, Wei Li, and Denis Tao Yang determined that the fall of grain output in 1959 and 1960 was due primarily (51.7 percent) to the weakening of the physical strength of the peasantry due to malnourishment caused by excessive harvest procurement. Resource diversion of agricultural labor to industrial tasks accounted for another 28.6 percent, excessive consumption of food following the 1958 harvest 17.5 percent, and bad weather 16.2 percent. These losses were somewhat counterbalanced by the increased use of modern chemical fertilizers, which helped to offset the damage to the 1959 and 1960 harvests by about 15.8 percent. Both studies agree, therefore, that poorly thought out government policy was by far the most important factor in causing the GLF famine.

Just as governmental policy drove the famine forward, a change in governmental policy after 1960 eventually led to the end of the famine. By that time, enough high officials had been exposed to the horrors of the famine that a consensus grew that China would be depopulated or the government overthrown unless fundamental changes were instituted. As a consequence, a cabal of high officials, including Liu Shaoqui, Zhou Enli, and Chun Yen, tried to find ways to end the famine without embarrassing Mao. To that end, they scaled back collectivization and allowed peasants to grow food for themselves on small plots of wasteland, a measure that gradually increased the Chinese food supply. Mao's policy of selling food abroad was overturned, and vast quantities of both grain and chemical fertilizers were imported from overseas. The Lysenkoists who dominated universities during the GLF were turned out and educated professionals were slowly reinstated in their jobs. Perhaps most importantly, state requisition of food from the countryside was dramatically decreased. Recognizing that the excessive extractions of the past few years amounted to "draining the pond to catch the fish," Chinese economic planners vastly lowered their requisitions in order to give the peasantry time to recover.

These measures eventually ended the GLF famine, but in the long run they perpetuated the political infighting that had contributed to the GLF in the first place. In 1966, Mao had recovered sufficiently in authority to launch his Cultural Revolution campaign, which encouraged the new generation of young communist party members to strike out against "party persons in power taking the capitalist road." The resulting violence and persecution claimed about half a million lives, including a large number of officials who had opposed Mao's GLF. Indeed, in an ironic twist, Liu Shaoqui was accused by young radicals of causing the GLF famine he in fact had helped to end, and died in prison from torture and neglect. Similarly, Peng Dehuai was humiliated in front of the Chinese army he used to lead, tortured and imprisoned, and kept under house arrest until he died 8 years later. As a result of such tactics, all party officials who had opposed the GLF were either killed, imprisoned, or intimidated, and Mao once again reigned supreme in Chinese politics until his death in 1976.

Although Mao's death signaled the end of an area of Chinese political history, the long-term demographic and economic damage wrought by the GLF lingered on. One Chinese economic expert wrote in 1980 that "for nearly twenty years ... there was little or no rise in living standards," largely due to Mao's perennial campaign to collectivize agriculture and tamp down rural capitalism. Indeed, Chinese agricultural productivity had fallen to levels lower than during the Han dynasty, which had ruled China two thousand years before. What is more, Chinese peasants were forced to contend with the environmental problems that had been created by the GLF, such as crumbling dams, erosion resulting from deep plowing, and salinization of poorly-irrigated fields. China's agricultural production only began to recover after 1979, when the its government tacitly abandoned collectivization and reintroduced private land ownership. In addition, the new Chinese Premier Deng Xiaoping encouraged Chinese peasants to use agricultural techniques that Mao had suppressed, such as improved grain varieties, cheap chemical fertilizers, and small "walking tractors" that were ideally suited to Chinese farming. As a result of these measures, China finally regained the level of agricultural prosperity it had enjoyed in the early 1950s, before collectivization and the Great Leap Forward.

Study Questions

1. Based on this reading, which model of famine (Malthusian, environmental collapse, or entitlement) do you think is the most useful in explaining the Great Leap Forward famine? Provide evidence for your answer.

2. Which factor do you think played a greater role in the Great Leap Forward famine — Marxist ideology, or struggles for political power?

3. To what degree was the Great Leap Forward famine linked to other natural disasters?

4. To what degree was the role played by the government in the Great Leap Forward famine comparable to the role played by the government in the Irish Potato Famine, as discussed in section 7.1? Defend your answer.

Sources/Suggested Readings

An, Mark Yunying, Li Wei, and Denis Tao Yany. "China's Great Leap: Forward or Backward? Anatomy of a Central Planning Disaster." Discussion Paper Series, Centre for Economic Policy Research, June 2001.

Becker, Jasper. *Hungry Ghosts: Mao's Secret Famine*. New York: Henry Holt, 1996.

Chan, Alfred. *Mao's Crusade: Politics and Policy Implementation in China's Great Leap Forward*. New York: Oxford University Press, 2001.

Kane, Penny. *Famine in China: 1959–61*. New York: St. Martin's, 1988.

Roberts, J. A. G. *The Complete History of China*. Great Britain: Sutton, 2006.

Shapiro, Judith. *Mao's War Against Nature: Politics and the Environment in Revolutionary China*. New York: Cambridge University Press, 2001.

Teiwes, Frederick C., and Sun, Warren. *China's Road to Disaster*. Armonk, New York: East Gate, 1999.

Xianliang, Zhang. *Grass Soup*. Boston: David R. Godine, 1993.

7.3: Famine in Ethiopia, 1973–Present

In the past quarter of a century, the African nation of Ethiopia has become virtually synonymous with famine, and for good reason: Over 1 million Ethiopians have died of famine in the last 30 years alone. Why so many have died in Ethiopia is a matter of lively debate. Some scholars have argued that there is nothing "natural" about Ethiopia's food shortages, especially the great famine of 1983–85, which they contend was created by the ideologically-driven agricultural policies and the harsh counter-insurgency tactics of Ethiopia's Marxist regime. Other scholars, while conceding that war and public policy have played some role in Ethiopian famines, contend that environmental factors such as deforestation and soil erosion have been the chief causes of famine in recent Ethiopian history. Still other scholars have dusted off the old Malthusian theory of famine and have blamed Ethiopia's food shortages on overpopulation, contending that Ethiopia's population has recently begun to outstrip the food supply. Whatever the cause of Ethiopia's past famines, it is likely that continued political instability, escalating environmental degradation, and souring population growth will ensure that Ethiopia will remain exceptionally vulnerable to famine as we move into the 21st century.

Although hunger in Ethiopia only came to the world's attention in the mid–1980s, famine has been a constant theme in Ethiopian history. Researchers have identified 70 likely incidents of famine in Ethiopia between 153 B.C. and A.D. 1987, a rate of 3.5 famines per century. Ethiopia's special vulnerability to famine is to some degree a consequence of the El Niño global weather phenomenon described in chapter 4.1, which usually brings drought to the Horn of Africa. During the "Cruel Days" of 1888 and 1892, for instance, back-to-back El Niños so devastated the Ethiopian peasantry that lions, leopards, and hyenas reportedly preyed on starving farmers, who were too weak from hunger to protect themselves. In their desperation, the Ethiopians turned to cannibalism; indeed, a popular song dating back to the "Cruel Days" is titled "His Wife Gave Him Indigestion." Overall, the death toll in Ethiopia may have been as high as 3.6 million, or about a third of the country's population.

As a result of these predictable, periodic droughts, Ethiopian highland farmers adopted a set of traditional practices designed to avoid or reduce famine. Many Ethiopian farmers cultivated "guaro" gardens near their houses, and although small, these gardens tended to produce high yields, since they benefited from constant attention by the landowner as well as fertilizer in the form of household waste. In times of drought, the extra food produced from these hand-watered gardens could mean the difference between starvation and mere hunger. The traditional land-holding system in the Ethiopian highlands helped mitigate famine as well. In Ethiopian villages, farmers tilled a number of disconnected plots of land, and since these scattered strips were often at different elevations and suitable for different crops, they helped farmers avoid complete crop loss. Another common Ethiopian anti-famine tactic was to earn money as petty traders, in hopes of producing a meager but life-saving cash income. Other Ethiopians turned to economic migration in times of famine, abandoning their withered fields for industrial or agricultural work in other parts of Ethiopia. Still another tactic was to sell livestock in exchange for grain, since cash value of an animal generally purchased more calories in grains than the animal's meat could provide. The most common overall tactic, however, was for farmers to store the surplus from years of plenty to sustain them through the inevitable years of dearth.

These tactics occasionally sufficed against El Niño drought, but they were less effective against a second cause of famine in Ethiopia: the high tax and crop demands of the parasitical Ethiopian monarchy. Even more than most pre-industrial governments, the Ethiopian state was built on the backs of the peasants, who paid heavy taxes and as much as half of their harvest to support a large standing army. As monarchy expanded from its core territories in highlands of northern Ethiopia into the more arid lowland provinces to the south, the conquered population was reduced to serfdom and parceled out like cattle amongst the victorious Ethiopian soldiers, a system that both ensured that the soldiers would be fed (at the expense of the serfs) and that each conquered subject would be closely supervised by a member of the Ethiopian military. The burden on peasants within the Ethiopian Empire became even worse in wartime, when the Ethiopian state called up a huge conscript army that sustained itself through pillaging and forcible food requisitions, leaving hunger in its wake. Indeed, the military objective of the Ethiopian mass army was often the food stores of the enemy, in part to feed itself, but also to deny food to the enemy, thereby employing famine as an instrument of war.

Given the strong link between the Ethiopian monarchy and food shortages, it seems only just that famine played a significant role in finally toppling the 17-century reign of the Ethiopian kings. During the 1970s, a number of factors conspired to weaken the Ethiopian state. Ethiopia's

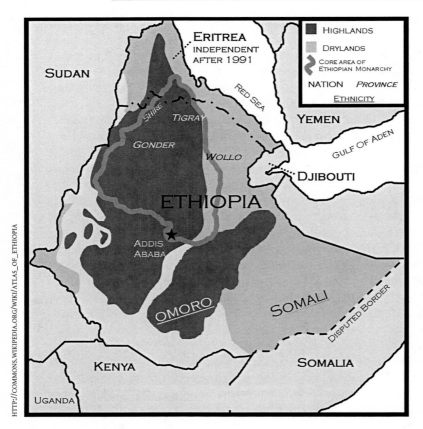

emperor was growing senile, and the crown prince was debilitated by a stroke. A rebellion was festering in the Ethiopian province of Eritrea, a formerly Italian colony that predominately Christian Ethiopia had unilaterally annexed in 1962 much to the dismay of the mostly Muslim local population. The closure of the Suez Canal during the Yom Kipper War of 1973 led to a dramatic spike in Ethiopian commodity prices. Technological change conspired against Ethiopia too: Orbiting satellites rendered a once vital American communication center in Ethiopia obsolete, weakening the long-standing alliance between Ethiopia and the United States. What is more, a new generation of young army officers who had been trained abroad were becoming increasingly impatient with the backwards political and economic systems of their homeland. Perhaps most importantly, large parts of Ethiopia were suffering famine due in part to the powerful El Niño of 1972. By 1973, nearly 2 million peasants were starving, and having eaten both their reserves and their seed grain, they had begun flocking into large towns in a desperate quest for food. The government belatedly directed resources towards famine relief, but much of the money was swallowed up by corruption, which was raging out of control due to the weakness of the central government. As a result, an estimated 100,000 to 200,000 Ethiopians died of hunger and hunger-related diseases, greatly discrediting and destabilizing the Ethiopian state.

Due to this growing economic and political chaos, large sections of Ethiopian society rose in rebellion against the government during 1973, and the army eventually sided with the rebels. Over the course of 1974, a council of army officers seized control of the state, deposed the Emperor, and established a government called the *derg*. That the army would hijack leadership of the revolution against the monarchy came as no surprise, since the army was by far the most powerful institution within the Ethiopian state. More surprising was fact that the *derg* came to be dominated by radical Marxist military officers, who declared Ethiopia a socialist state and nationalized the banks, most of the industry, and all of the foreign-owned companies. What is more, the *derg* redistributed the country's agricultural lands, seizing it from rich landowners and redistributing it to local peasant associations.

The *derg* regarded land redistribution not as an end in itself, but rather as a means to a greater end: the socialist transformation of Ethiopia's agriculture. Like the Chinese Communists described in chapter 7.2, the *derg* intended to completely overhaul the rural economy.

Ethiopia's patchwork of small holdings was slowly replaced with producer cooperatives or even collectivized farms using heavy machinery. The grain trade was heavily regulated by the government, not only because the Marxist *derg* regarded merchants as unproductive parasites, but also to ensure that the government controlled both the grain trade and the profits it generated. When the peasants defied the government and tried to smuggle food for sale into cities, the *derg* countered with checkpoints on major roads to interdict the flow of grain. Worst of all, the government requisitioned enormous amounts of food from the countryside in order to support the cities and the army, whose goodwill was crucial to the survival of the *derg* regime.

The eventual result of these policies would be disastrous. The cooperative and collectivized farms suffered from low productivity and high levels of environmental degradation, since collectivized peasants had little motivation to work hard and little reason to conserve land that wasn't theirs. The government's excessive grain requisitions left many Ethiopians with the bare minimum of food they needed to survive, preventing peasants from storing away the surplus they needed to get through drought years. Even more damaging were the government's restrictions on the grain trade. Because of its geographic complexity, Ethiopia is divided into regions of grain surplus and regions of grain deficiency which exist in symbiotic relationship with each other, with grain surplus areas supplying food to the deficit areas in return for animal products or crafts. The government restrictions on the grain trade, however, shattered Ethiopia's traditional trade pathways, effectively fragmenting the national economy and reducing the incentive of grain producing reasons to produce a surplus for the market.

Thankfully for Ethiopia, however, changes to the agricultural sector proceeded slowly, since in its early years the *derg* was forced to focus its attention on war. Indeed, the newborn government was threatened on three fronts. Although the rebels in Eritrea were largely Marxist themselves, they fought just as hard against Ethiopia's new socialist government as they had against the former monarchical state. The *derg* also had to contend with a number of internal insurgencies, often fueled by ethnic tensions within the Ethiopian state. The most notable such rebel groups in the early years of the *derg*'s rule were the Omoro and Somali tribes of southeastern Ethiopia, which had been conquered but not fully subdued by the Ethiopian monarchical state. The Ethiopian campaign against the ethnic Somali rebels, in turn, served as a pretext for the opening of a third front against the *derg*: an invasion by the Somali army, which formally invaded Ethiopia in July 1977 after over a year of behind-the-scenes meddling in Ethiopian affairs.

Thanks to an infusion of military equipment from the Soviet Union, which was eager to expand its influence in a country formerly tied to the United States, the Ethiopians gradually began to enjoy success against all three threats. By March 1978 Somali troops had been forced to retreat from Ethiopia back to Somalia, accompanied by tens of thousands of ethnic Somali refugees. The *derg* then focused its forces against the Eritrean insurgency and managed to seize all of Eritrea outside of a few impenetrable mountain strongholds. However, the problem of insurgent groups in southeast Ethiopia proved harder to solve. As a result, the *derg* turned to brutal measures. The Ethiopian army slaughtered livestock and firebombed villages, hoping to crush the rebellion by starving the rebels and their civilian supporters into submission. Food stores were seized and crops were burnt in the fields. Worst of all, the *derg* began to implement a population displacement program, called villagization by the government, to control the civilian populace and thus deny guerrillas essential supplies. More than two million people were forcibly relocated between 1978 and 1982 and were packed into guarded communities that were virtual concentration camps, complete with armed guards. Worse yet, the state seized all food they produced and instead provided daily rations in order to ensure total dependence on the government. To discourage villagized farmers from returning to their original homes, the *derg* set up settlers from northern Ethiopia in their former dwellings or else burned them to the ground.

In the meantime, a powerful new rebellion against the *derg* had flared up in the northern province of Tigray. The sources of this rebellion are complex. To some extent the growth of a Tigrayan insurgent group in Ethiopia was a spin off of similar insurgent groups in neighboring Eritrea. The Tigrayan revolt was also fueled by nationalism, since the people of Tigray were fiercely devoted to their ethnic traditions and outraged by the government's suppression of regional culture as "counterrevolutionary." Furthermore, many Tigrayan peasants were unhappy about how land had been redistributed after the fall of the monarchy and the extremely low prices offered by the government to Tigrayan food producers. Tigrayans were also upset by the government's restrictions on the grain trade, especially since much of Tigray was either a food surplus or food deficit zone, making the grain trade indispensable to Tigrayan survival. To make matters worse, the *derg* attempted to prevent Tigrayan peasants from engaging in seasonal migratory agricultural or industrial labor in other provinces on the grounds that economic migration was an outmoded, counterrevolutionary practice. Since these tactics were an essential economic strategy in the grain-poor parts of Tigray, the government in effect gave the Tigrayans no choice but to rebel.

As a result, while the government was distracted with the Omoro and Somali rebellions in the late 1970s and early 1980s, a rebel group called the TPLF (Tigrayan People's Liberation Front) grew in strength and eventually asserted effective control over Tigray province. By 1982, the TPLF and their allies were strong enough to go on the offensive, and even managed to seize several towns and block several roads in the neighboring province of Wollo. Ethiopian counteroffensives against the TPLF met with little success, largely because TPLF guerilla fighters tended to disappear into the civilian population whenever government troops arrived, only to regroup and counterattack once government troops had left the area.

Unable to engage the rebels in the field the *derg* once again employed harsh measures to quell the insurgency. The Ethiopian army seized control of the food surplus "Shire" region of Tigray, hoping thereby to starve the rebellion into surrender. Cattle were slaughtered, grain stores were destroyed, crops were burnt or trampled in the fields, and farmers were displaced from their homes. The movement of people within Tigray and Wollo was increasingly regulated through a "pass" system, effectively strangling the grain trade. The army also used land mines to discourage the movement of both TPLF rebels and grain merchants. Worst of all, the Ethiopian air force was employed to bomb grain markets in an attempt to starve the TPLF and its civilian supporters into surrender. There was a calculated logic behind these brutal tactics: According to famine expert Alex de Waal, since the rebels moved through the civilian population "like a fish through water," the Ethiopian army reasoned that the best counterstrategy was to "[drain] the sea to catch the fish." Indeed, the *derg* foreign minister candidly admitted to a U.S. official in 1974 that "food is a major element of our strategy against the secessionists."

These atrocities did little to weaken the TPLF. They did, however, play a significant role in triggering the worst Ethiopian famine of the 20th century. The Ethiopian government would later deny responsibility for causing the famine, laying blame instead on unusually dry conditions in the first half of the 1980s. Some historians of Ethiopia have endorsed this claim, and there is some evidence to back it up. There can be no doubt that 1982 was a strong El Niño year — indeed, crop losses reached almost 50 percent in some countries worldwide and overall economic damage topped $13 billion — and rainfall in Ethiopia was substantially below normal in the next two years as well. What the government failed to mention (and these historians failed to consider) is that such droughts are normal rather than exceptional circumstances in Ethiopia. Knowing this, Ethiopians store away excess food in years of surplus in preparation for dry years, and since 1980 and 1981 were years of bumper crops in Ethiopia, in the normal course of things enough food should have been available to prevent or reduce famine from 1983 to 1985. Unfortunately, the high food requisitions of the *derg*, its suppression of the grain trade, its brutal anti-insurrectionary campaigns, and its policies such as villagization and collectivization prevented the normal storage of surplus grains in those years of plenty. As a result, in the words of Alex de Waal, "by the time the drought struck, the famine was already well under way."

The famine of 1983–1985 began in Tigray, where food became virtually unavailable at any price, but soon radiated outwards. The food shortage in Tigray drove up prices elsewhere; the price of grain more than quadrupled in neighboring North Gonder province and nearly quintupled in North Wollo. Ethiopian peasants turned to their traditional famine relief strategies, but these strategies met with limited success between 1983 and 1985. The small "guaro" gardens, which traditionally provided food of last resort in case of famine, were in decline, as the Marxist *derg* had discouraged such farming practices as individualistic and counterrevolutionary. This was especially true in the new "villagized" communities under direct government control, where famine often struck hardest. Some peasants turned to the proven tactic of setting themselves up as petty traders, but faced persecution or even execution at the hands of the army, since the *derg* had outlawed such "exploitive" and "parasitical" trading practices. Other starving farmers turned to the old tactic of economically motivated migration, but once again, the government frowned on such activity and persecuted the migrants. To make matters worse, the TPLF rebels also restricted economic migration, since like the government they ascribed to Marxist ideology, albeit of a more Maoist stripe than the Leninism of the *derg*. In any case, due to the nation-wide nature of the famine, the wage labor market was soon flooded with unwanted workers, so wages rapidly fell below food prices. Still other Ethiopian farmers sold their livestock to buy grain, but since the famine rapidly became national, Ethiopian markets soon became glutted with animals and livestock prices plummeted while grain prices soared. In desperation, some farmers were even forced to sell or eat their plow oxen, but since animal muscle was vital to Ethiopian farming practices, these farmers were purchasing short-term survival at the price of long-term poverty and desperation.

As a result of this perfect storm of woes, Ethiopia suffered famine on an epic scale between 1983 and 1985. Estimates for the total population effected by famine range from 6 to 7.2 million, and the number deaths may have exceeded 1 million. As with most famines, the bulk of those who died were children under the age of 5, and many people were carried off by opportunistic disease—chiefly measles, typhus, relapsing fever, cholera, and malaria—rather than by starvation. These deaths, it is important to note, were not limited to Ethiopia itself. The Ethiopian famine had a ripple effect into Eritrea, where warfare between the *derg* and rebel groups continued, and into the crowded refugee camps in neighboring countries that were filled with Ethiopians who had fled the *derg*. What is more, the famine did not affect all of Ethiopia equally, but was disproportionably concentrated in Tigray and surrounding provinces, as well as the "villagized" Omoro and ethnic Somali areas of Ethiopia's south and east. The famine was relatively less deadly in other provinces of Ethiopia where the *derg* was firmly in control, for reasons that will be discussed below.

Despite the severity of 1983–85 famine, which was considerably worse than the famine which had helped topple the Ethiopian monarchy in 1973, the *derg* was able to survive the crisis. Indeed, the *derg* managed to turn the suffering caused by the famine to its own advantage. At first, the Ethiopian government tried to downplay the extent of the starvation, but eventually western journalists brought the famine to international attention. Aghast at the scale of Ethiopia's hunger, western governments swallowed their distaste for the Marxist *derg* and contributed huge amounts of food aid to the Ethiopian people. The private sector chipped in as

AP/WORLD WIDE PHOTOS

An emergency feeding center set up north of Addis Ababa during late 1984.

well, most notably through "Band Aid," a charity album recorded by mostly–British musicians in 1984 to raise money for famine relief. Unfortunately, the *derg* managed to channel much of this food and monetary aid to its own purposes. Quite a bit of the food aid was diverted to feed the army, which of course had helped to cause the famine in the first place. What is more, as much as a third of the aid to Eritrea was used to pay the salaries of pro–Ethiopian government militia groups, which were dubbed "wheat militias" as a consequence. At the same time, the *derg* systematically attempted to prevent relief supplies from reaching rebel-controlled areas. Tigray, for example, received only 5.6 percent of the grain directly distributed by the Ethiopian government, despite containing as much as 33 percent of all Ethiopian famine sufferers. What is more, the Ethiopian government repeatedly threatened to expel aid agencies from its own territories if they also supplied food to areas held by insurgent groups, effectively employing its own starving populace as a bargaining chip in its zero-sum game against the insurgency. Aid agencies were also threatened with expulsion if they spoke out against the *derg*'s human rights violations, and were even directly attacked by the government if they operated in rebel-held areas. On April 8 1986, for instance, the Ethiopian army bombed a food distribution center and an orphanage run by the International Committee of the Red Cross in the rebel-held town of Wukro. The rebels groups also targeted the international relief agencies, though on a smaller scale.

Worse yet, the *derg* directly used food aid as a tool of population pacification. In some rebel areas, such as Eritrea, families received aid only if they lived in "protected" villages—where movement was restricted by curfews and land mines—and aid was dispensed frequently in small amounts in order to foster dependence on the Ethiopian government. A disproportionate amount of aid was given to the collectivized farms or the "settlements" established by the *derg* as part of the counter-insurgency campaign in Ethiopia's south. In an act of unbelievable cynicism, the *derg* went so far as to seize trucks from the Save the Children Fund to transport settlers from the north, many of whom may have been taken against their will or coerced, to its resettlement camps in the south. Indeed, Alex de Waal claims that "in effect [the relief effort] served as an enormous subsidy for the titanic social engineering that the government was implementing in the southern and central parts of the country."

Ultimately the *derg* would be defeated, not by the famine, but by a combination of internal rebellions and external diplomatic developments. Starting in December 1987, the Eritrean rebels won a series of victories in northern Eritrea and steadily began to drive the Ethiopian army from the province. When the Ethiopian army moved troops from Tigray to deal with the Eritrean menace, the TPLF returned to the offensive and inflicted several more defeats on the Ethiopian army, seizing vital military equipment in the process. Worse yet, the *derg* lost the diplomatic and material support of the Soviet Union, which under President Gorbachev was moving in the direction of internal political and economic reforms and thus had little sympathy for the *derg*'s old-school Leninist philosophy. As the *derg* weakened, the TPLF became stronger, expanding its territorial control within Ethiopia, building ties of trust with the Ethiopian peasantry, and even successfully courting American diplomats. Finally, in May of 1991, the leader of the *derg* fled into exile, and the TPLF and its allies assumed effective control over Ethiopia — minus Eritrea, which had *de facto* become an independent state in 1991, though it would be two more years before the new Ethiopian government would officially recognize this fact.

With the fall of the *derg*, many observers hoped that Ethiopia would be able to wriggle free from its crushing burden of famine, but these hopes proved to be misplaced. Although the new TPLF–headed government did liberalize the economy somewhat, the economic reforms it embraced arguably hurt Ethiopia's farmers by subjecting them to the vagaries of the market. In years of plenty, Ethiopian farmers got little for their produce. On the other hand, in drought years, prices of food skyrocketed, but since many farmers in such years become food purchasers rather than sellers due to poor crop yields, rising food prices can lead to rural hunger rather than prosperity. Ironically, bumper crops in Ethiopia encourage food shortages as well, since low prices following a plentiful harvest often lead Ethiopian farmers to produce less grain and more cash crops or livestock, reducing food production in the following year.

Post-*derg* Ethiopia's increasing integration into the global economy has also produced mixed results. Ethiopia's farmers are at a decided disadvantage compared to farmers in developed nations, who benefit both from superior agricultural techniques and from generous government subsidies. At the same time, Ethiopia has benefited little from the modern global phenomenon of outsourcing — the movement of industrial and service sector jobs from high-wage to low-wage countries — due to Ethiopia's underdeveloped infrastructure and low rates of literacy. Indeed, the International Monetary Fund's insistence that Ethiopia balance its budgets has forced the government to strip resources from programs such as health care, despite the chronic link between famine and disease. As a result, despite the liberalization of the economy, Ethiopia remains extremely vulnerable to famine.

Indeed, many observers believe that, despite relative political stability in recent years, Ethiopia is becoming more and more vulnerable to catastrophic famine with the passage of time. Two factors in particular combine to undermine food security in Ethiopia: overpopulation and environmental degradation. Ethiopia's population, which was recorded at 42 million in 1982, had soared to 73 million by 2005. Surprisingly, this spike in population has occurred despite a high level of AIDS, since deaths caused by AIDS have so far been counterbalanced by Ethiopia's very high 2.76 percent population growth rate. It is now expected that the population growth rate will decline to 2.38 percent by 2010, but even at this lower rate of population growth, Ethiopia will be burdened with more than a million new mouths to feed each year.

Experts disagree somewhat about the impact high population growth will have on Ethiopia's future. Some scholars deny that overpopulation will necessarily breed famine, arguing that, despite Malthus' gloomy predictions, there is little hard evidence to link rising population with hunger. Other scholars argue that a clear link does exist, pointing out that rising population leads to increased subdivision of the land, larger families with more dependent children to feed, and increased rates of cultivation in less fertile soils such as steep hillsides and arid lowlands. However, all are in broad agreement that Ethiopia's population growth is increasingly outstripping the food supply and that Ethiopia has become far too dependent on imported food, especially foreign aid grants.

Experts also disagree as to how closely population growth is linked to environmental degradation. Some Ethiopian famine scholars see no clear causal linkage between high population and high rates of environmental damage, arguing that socio-cultural, technological, and institutional factors play a greater role than burgeoning numbers in triggering deforestation and erosion. Other authors, however, have made a convincing case for just such a link. In a detailed 1990 study of environment, famine, and politics in the Wollo province of Ethiopia, Alemneh Dejene sketched out a number of ways in which overpopulation breeds environmental problems. Faced with the daunting task of feeding their families, Dejene argues, Ethiopian farmers have adopted more intensive agricultural methods and abandoned the traditional practice of leaving land fallow. As a result, much of Ethiopia's cropland is being choked with stones as topsoil erodes away or else is crisscrossed with steep erosion gullies, making cultivation all but impossible. Indeed, the fertility of Ethiopia's soil is declining by approximately 1–2 percent a year. Human population growth has also accelerated deforestation by creating a higher demand for wood for building and fuel, and deforestation in turn accelerates soil erosion, especially in the Ethiopian highlands that host over 80 percent of the country's population. Deforestation has also obliged Ethiopia's swelling population to use dung as a household fuel rather than as an agricultural fertilizer, further reducing the soil's fertility.

Clearly, overpopulation has played a significant role in modern Ethiopia's environmental problems, but conscious human decisions are to blame as well. Ethiopian farmers place a great deal of value on maintaining as much livestock as possible, partially as a reserve against famine, but also because large livestock herds are considered synonymous with wealth and status. However, excessive livestock ownership leads to a myriad of problems. Overgrazed hillsides quickly lose their vegetation cover and the soil washes into neighboring farms, often burying productive farmland under a choking layer of infertile subsoil. The overgrazed soil also tends to dry out and form a hard crust, leading to desertification. Finally, large livestock herds tend to impinge on good agricultural land, reducing crop yields. Since cultivated land produces many more calories for human consumption than the same acreage of grazing land, the Ethiopian cultural preference for large herds may directly contribute to food shortages and famine.

Other Ethiopian cultural and political choices have also combined to make the country more vulnerable to famine. To compensate for Ethiopia's chronic rate of high infant mortality, Ethiopians tend to have very large families, to the point that by 1990 fully 47 percent of the population was under the age of 15. Since children of that age must be fed, but are economically less productive than adults, they represent a large potential drain on Ethiopia's resources. Another self-destructive choice made by many Ethiopians is to abandon food cultivation in favor of growing qat, a mild stimulant drug that is popular throughout the Horn of Africa and southern parts of the Arabian Peninsula. While individual farmers may be able to earn respectable incomes from the production and sale of qat, Ethiopia as a whole suffers from the qat trade, both because less food is produced and because the drug itself leads to a reduction of work efficiency. Finally, the new government has decided for political reasons to retain the *derg*'s principle of state ownership of the land, in spite of their other liberalizing reforms. Unfortunately, this has greatly exacerbated the problems of environmental degradation, since Ethiopian farmers lack an incentive to practice environmentally sound agriculture on land they do not themselves own.

What is more, Ethiopia's food supply faces increasing jeopardy from climate change. Ethiopia is a dry country — indeed, almost 60 percent of its land area is classified as hyper-arid, arid, or semi-arid — and indications are that it is likely to become even dryer over time. Much of Ethiopia lies in the African Sahel, and as discussed in chapter 4.2, the Sahel is subject to extreme cyclical rainfall variations. The fact that Ethiopia's weather is so closely tied to El Niño poses further problems. El Niño activity is projected to increase in frequency as global warming worsens, meaning that Ethiopia will likely face more and more years of reduced rainfall in the 21st century. Worse yet, any rain that does fall will likely evaporate more quickly due to the higher temperatures brought by global warming, further increasing Ethiopia's aridity and therefore its vulnerability to famine.

As a result of these environmental problems and poor human choices, Ethiopia's ability to feed itself is looking increasingly doubtful. Since the 1970s, Ethiopia has lost at least a billion tons of topsoil to erosion each year, far more than is replaced by natural process. Thanks to this and to other factors, Ethiopian food production has fallen by 3.45 percent over the past three decades despite an increase in population of as much as 50 percent. Worse yet, the productivity of the livestock sector has started to decline as well; Ethiopia's output of meat, milk, and eggs declined by an average of 2.5 percent over the last decade. As a result, Ethiopia is now more vulnerable to famine than ever before in her history. Indeed, an estimated 10 million Ethiopians were threatened by famine during the 1999/2000 agricultural cycle, and no less than 14 million were faced with famine in 2003 because of poor and erratic rainfall in 2002.

Thankfully, Ethiopia received massive amounts of international aid in 2003 in the form of 1.5 million tons of food assistance and $65 million in cash aid, so widespread mortality was prevented. Nonetheless, international assistance to Ethiopia poses dangers of its own. Ethiopian scholar Fassil G. Kiros has condemned his country's "addiction to food handouts," which, although generous, have disinclined Ethiopia from seeking a lasting solution to its food shortage crisis. Kiros reports that many of his countrymen have developed the attitude that "it doesn't matter if the rains fail in Wollo as long as they don't in Canada." The only way to shake this addiction, Kiros argues, is for international agencies to switch from food grants to work relief programs that may be of long term benefit to Ethiopia's farmers. However, Kiros admits that previous attempts to do so have failed, largely because Ethiopian aid recipients tend to seek short term gain over long term benefits. He cites several instances when farmers paid to terrace hillsides later tore the terraces down, and farmers paid to reforest degraded land planted trees upside-down so that they could be paid twice for doing the same work. Given the horrific specter of famine that hangs over Ethiopia, it is hard to fault these farmers for trying to make as much money for their families in the short run as they can, even at the cost of Ethiopia's long-term development.

When considering Ethiopia's many problems, it is all too easy for we inhabitants of the developed world to feel sympathy, but not empathy. The problems Ethiopia faces, we tell ourselves, are certainly tragic, but just as certainly not applicable to us. However, this attitude is extremely short sighted. Indeed, in many ways, Ethiopia is a microcosm of our modern global society. The problems that modern Ethiopia faces — overpopulation and environmental degradation — are fast becoming world problems as the global population continues to rise and cropland continues to be lost to desertification, urbanization, and soil erosion. In that sense, we are all Ethiopians, and unless we can find a sustainable balance between population growth and agricultural productivity, Ethiopia's famines may just be a sneak preview to horrific global food shortages in the 21st century.

Study Questions

1. Which factor do you think has done more to cause famine in Ethiopia: environmental forces, or poor human decisions? Explain your answer.

2. How important are other types of disaster — particularly climate change and disease — in triggering famine in Ethiopia?

3. "Although they occurred in different decades and on different continents, the Ethiopian famine of 1983–85 was almost identical to the Great Leap Forward famine described in chapter 7.2." To what degree do you agree with this statement?

4. Based on this chapter and other readings in this book, how convincing do you find the claim that Ethiopia is a "microcosm" of the modern world? Explain your answer.

Sources/Suggested Readings

Dejene, Alemneh. *Environment, Famine, and Politics in Ethiopia.* Boulder, CO: Lynne Rienner, 1990.
De Waal, Alex. *Evil Days: Thirty Years of War and Famine in Ethiopia.* New York: Human Rights Watch, 1991.
Marcus, Harold G. *A History of Ethiopia.* Berkeley: University of California Press, 1994.
Kiros, Fassil G. *Enough with Famines in Ethiopia: A Clarion Call.* Hollywood, CA: Tsehai, 2006.
Rahmato, Dessalegn. "Peasant Survival Strategies in Ethiopia." *Disasters: Journal of Disaster Studies and Management,* Vol. 12, No. 4 (1988), pp. 326–344.

CHAPTER 8

Disease

Science and History

Of all natural disasters, disease arguably enjoys the most intimate relationship with mankind. While other forms of disaster, such as earthquakes and hurricanes, are the result of natural forces unrelated to our species, many diseases would cease to exist entirely without their human hosts. What is more, diseases, like mankind itself, have evolved considerably over the passage of time. As mankind has passed through progressive stages of material development — the adoption of agriculture, the founding of cities, the growth of long distance trade, and the dawn of the industrial age, and the age of imperialism — diseases have kept pace, opportunistically exploiting changes in their human environment. Diseases are opportunistic in a shorter time frame as well. Epidemics frequently flare up in the aftermath of nearly every other type of natural disaster, taking advantage of the chronic malnutrition, displacement, and overcrowding that is the lot of many disaster victims. As a result of this opportunism, combined with their prevalence throughout history, diseases have probably accounted for more human misery and more human deaths than all other forms of natural disaster combined.

The Science of Disease

The term "disease" is a shockingly imprecise term, encompassing a number of different pathologies. Technically, any condition that impairs the health or disrupts the normal functioning of the human body is a disease. Some diseases, such as cholera, are the result of infection by bacteria, one-celled organisms that colonize and proliferate in the human body. Other diseases, such as AIDS and influenza, are caused by viruses, tiny packages of genetic material that reproduce themselves by infiltrating and taking control of human body cells. Still other diseases, such as the misleadingly named ringworm infection, are caused by fungal growths upon or within the human body. Disease can also be caused by malnutrition; the debilitating and deadly plague of pellagra, for example, is caused by insufficient dietary niacin. Still other diseases have a genetic component. Sickle cell anemia occurs when a child receives a specific recessive gene from both parents, leading to deformation of red blood cells and a host of related problems ranging from severe chest pain to stroke. On the brighter side, sufferers of sickle cell tend to be resistant to malaria, which helps to explain the prevalence of this otherwise disadvantageous gene in the human population. Other genetic diseases, such as Down's syndrome, result from mutations during conception. Many types of cancer, on the other hand, are the result of cellular mutation during childhood or adulthood. Another set of diseases result from environmental causes. Black lung, a crippling respiratory disease, is caused by inhalation of particles such as coal dust and can lead to deterioration of the lung tissues. Mental disorders, such as post-traumatic stress disorder, are often related to environmental conditions as well.

What is more, diseases rarely fit easily into clearly-defined typologies. Some cancers are apparently triggered by viral infections: the human papillomavirus has been linked to cervical cancer in women, for example, while Kaposi's sarcoma cancer is caused directly by the human herpesvirus 8 and more indirectly by HIV infection, which can weaken the immune system, giving human herpesvirus 8 an opportunity to fester. The heavy toll taken by HIV on the immune system allows a number of diseases to flourish, both bacterial and viral. What is more, diseases with a genetic component such as cancer can encourage the proliferation of viruses and bacteria. Leukemia patients, for example, tend to have few healthy white blood cells, which are the body's main defense against bacterial infection.

Further complicating the issue of disease is the variety of ways by which diseases can be contracted. Some diseases, such the HIV virus that causes AIDS, must be transmitted through bodily fluids, either through sexual contact, intravenous needle use, transfusions, or in rare cases through open wounds. Other viruses are spread through aerosol particles, which invade the body through the respiratory or digestive system. Indeed, a number of diseases induce the human body to cough or sneeze, thus manipulating a natural bodily process normally used to expel dangerous substances into a means of their own propagation. Similarly, diarrheal diseases spread by hijacking the body's excretory system, forcing it to expel large volumes of fluid containing viral or bacterial pathogens. Other diseases make use of a host animal to propagate themselves. The malaria parasite, for example, makes itself at home in the salivary glands of certain mosquitoes, thus transforming the mosquitoes into unwilling carriers of the parasite into human populations. Diseases can propagate themselves using larger host animals as well. The rabies virus, which is transmitted through mammalian saliva, causes its victims to drool excessively and display hyperagressive and hypersexual behavior, thus maximizing the chance of spreading the infection. Indeed, the rabies virus may have inspired the vampire legend; like vampires, rabies victims tend to fear water, avoid strong smells such as garlic, and feel compelled to bite others. What is more, the animals that are traditionally associated with vampires—wolves and bats—are quite often the vector through which rabies is transmitted to humans.

Still other diseases are caused not by the presence of a malicious pathogen, but by a surfeit or surplus of nutrients. Scurvy, the rickets, pellagra, and anemia are caused by the dietary deficiency of vitamin C, vitamin D, niacin, and iron, respectively. Populations that are dependent on rice for their subsistence are often plagued by beriberi, a debilitating disease characterized by paralysis or heart failure resulting from thiamin deficiency. Dietary diseases can be triggered by ingesting too much food as well. People or cultures which ingest large amounts of red meat tend to suffer from colon cancer, heart disease, and the hardening of the arteries, which in turn can trigger heart attacks or a stroke. Excessive food consumption and lack of exercise can also cause obesity, which in turn helps to cause heart disease and diabetes. Unfortunately, dietary diseases are becoming more and more common over time, in part due to the global spread of American fast food cuisine, but also due to ever more sophisticated techniques of food processing. The process of "polishing" crude grains of rice may create a more attractive snow-white product, but it also removes 70 percent of the thiamin from the rice.

Just as the causes of disease are various and many, so to are the means used to cure or prevent them. Nutritional diseases are in theory the easiest to cure, since they require only changes to the diet. In practice, however, human cultural preferences may prevent people from changing their eating habits, and some impoverished societies simply cannot afford to buy the necessary dietary supplements to stave off disease. Bacterial disease is also easy to cure, in theory, now that several classes of antibiotic medications are available to physicians. Once again, though, the reality is more complicated. Overuse or misuse of antibiotics has lead to the development of a number of antibiotic-resistant disease strains, for example drug resistant tuberculosis. What is more, the routine administration of antibiotics to cattle as part of the fattening-up process is creating antibiotic-resistant versions of common bacterial pathogens, such as salmonella and E. coli, which are then passed on to the consumer after the cattle are butchered. Bacterial epidemics can also be forestalled through the use of vaccinations, described in more detail below.

The problems of disease prevention are even more imposing if the illness is caused by a virus. Unlike bacteria, which are single-celled organisms visible under a microscope, viruses are miniscule packets of genetic material protected by a simple protein sheath. Viruses are unaffected by antibiotics since they operate by hijacking normal cells within the human body, and these cells are not damaged by the toxins that are the active agents of antibiotics. Indeed, the only effective treatment for most viral diseases, once they develop, is to counteract the symptoms of the disease such as fever and dehydration that are harmful to the life of the afflicted organism. People afflicted by viruses are sometimes given antibiotics as well, not to eradicate the virus, but to preempt opportunistic infection by harmful bacteria. Given that there are few effective antiviral agents, the best way to counter viral infection is to prevent the pathogen from taking hold in the human body in the first place. Good hygiene is a crucial weapon in this struggle, as is an ample diet, since viruses have trouble overwhelming the immune system of healthy, well-fed patients. In addition, medical authorities can take action to prevent the animal hosts of the virus from spreading the disease. In the case of human hosts, this generally means putting afflicted individuals in quarantine until they are no longer capable of transmitting the illness. If animals host the disease, authorities generally slaughter and burn the affected animals to prevent its spread.

The most effective way of containing or even eliminating viral infections, however, is through the use of vaccinations. In this procedure, doctors deliberately inculcate patients with a weakened form of a viral or bacterial infection. The patient's immune system generally makes short work of the weakened disease, and in the process develops antibodies capable of fighting off more virulent strains of the pathogen, giving the patient immunity or resistance to the disease for a period of time. Vaccinations have allowed medical authorities to obliterate several diseases, most notably smallpox, and to greatly reduce the incidence of other infections, such as polio and measles. Unfortunately a number of viruses, most notably AIDS and influenza, have so defied all attempts to develop an effective vaccine.

The relationship between mankind and diseases is further complicated by the various ways in which they can co-exist alongside their human hosts. In densely settled and long-established human populations, diseases tend to take the form of "endemics," a Greek term meaning "among the people." Also called "childhood diseases," endemic diseases tend to be constantly present, though at a low level, within a given population. If the disease has a long incubation period, human beings may be the host; alternatively, the disease may be harbored either by domesticated animals or by wild animals living in the vicinity of human communities. Either way, endemics chiefly affect the young, who either die of the ailment or else survive with antibodies against the pathogen. As a result, endemic diseases rarely strike adults, and thus present little threat to the economic and social fabric of the societies that host them. Endemic diseases in the modern West include measles, mumps, whooping cough, and chicken pox.

While endemic diseases smolder in human societies at a constant, low level, epidemic diseases have more in common with wildfires. Diseases generally become epidemics when a human population is afflicted with a "new" disease against which they have no immunological defense.

Of course, no disease is ever really "new" — viruses and bacteria are the result of thousands of years of evolution. Nonetheless, there are a number of different ways by which an old disease can become "new" to humans. As we shall see in section 8.1, new diseases can accompany the adoption of an unfamiliar type of food; pellagra, for example, followed close upon the heels of the corn plant as it spread across the globe. Diseases can also appear "new" if they suddenly jump from an animal host to humans, as was the case with HIV/AIDS, which scientists now believe spread to mankind from an isolated population of chimpanzees in southern Cameroon sometime in the early 20th century. In addition, "new" epidemics can result if a disease inflicting only animals mutates in such a way that it gains the capacity to infect humans. Scientists are worried that avian flu, a disease affecting both wild and domestic birds, may be on the verge of just such a transformation. As of the summer of 2007, 200 people had died of avian (bird) flu, and leading disease experts have warned that, should it mutate into a form that is readily transmissible between humans, the result would be a pandemic capable of killing a substantial fraction of the human population.

The most common way that epidemics originate, however, is through the transfer of an ailment from one human population to another. As agricultural societies develop, they gradually "domesticate" a number of epidemic diseases to the point they become endemics, forming what plague historian William McNeill has dubbed "disease pools." This is especially true if the agricultural society also engages in animal husbandry, since the majority of human diseases originated first in domesticated animals. When these endemic diseases of agriculturalists spill over into hunter-gatherer or nomadic populations, the results can be disastrous. Since the non-agriculturalists have no experience with the endemics of their farming kin, the agriculturalists' endemics generally explode into virulent epidemics that rage through hunter-gatherer communities. Worse yet, non-agriculturalists generally do not have the population density necessary to host endemic diseases, so once the epidemic runs out of susceptible victims, the disease — and resistance to the disease — vanishes from the non-farming populations, setting the stage for future epidemics. As a result, non-agricultural populations are at a real disadvantage against agriculturalists, who engage in constant though usually unintentional biological warfare against their non-farming neighbors.

Epidemics can also erupt explosively when previously isolated "disease pools" are put in contact with each other due to exploration, conquest, or trade. At this point, one society's endemics become the other's epidemics, which run riot through a virgin population. Since it may take centuries for the newly-acquired epidemics to be domesticated, the sudden expansion of diseases into new disease pools can have truly apocalyptic results. As we shall see below, the spread of bubonic plague out of East Asia in the 14th century, and the expansion of European childhood diseases to the Americas in the 16th century, led to two of the most spectacular known episodes of mass human mortality.

Disease in History

Human diseases are as old as mankind itself; indeed, as the human species has evolved, the various bacteria, viruses, and other parasites that afflict mankind have adapted to fit mankind's changing condition. Despite this, diseases probably played a relatively small role in the life, or the death, of prehistoric man. During most of the lifespan of *Homo sapiens*, human beings lived in relatively small hunter-gatherer bands that were constantly in motion from place to place in search of food resources. Although our ancestors did sometimes contract parasiti-

The "Dance of Death," a theme that became common in Europe following the ravages of the Bubonic Plague.

cal organisms like worms or flukes from the wild game they ate, low population density severely curtailed the risk of epidemic disease.

As mankind abandoned hunting and gathering in favor of a more "civilized" lifestyle, mankind's relationship with disease changed as well — though not to the same degree worldwide. Indeed, recent research suggests that different regional levels of disease may have exerted a profound influence on the most basic level of human culture. Scholars of human behavior have long classified human societies into two rough groups, those espousing "individualist" values, and those adhering to "collectivist" forms of behavior, where tradition and conformity are valued over innovation and deviation is discouraged. Some scholars have gone so far as to claim that the individualist/collectivist divide may be the single most important characteristic defining human cultural variation. This basic cultural division of humanity has repeatedly been supported by research, but up until now no fully satisfactory explanation has been proposed to explain the phenomenon.

However, a new article published by the *Proceedings of the Royal Society B* and co-authored by a team of biologists from the University of New Mexico and psychologists in the University of British Columbia claims that the individualist/collectivist divide is correlated strongly with differing levels of disease. According to these authors, "individualist" behavior can lead to rewards, such as new foods, ideas, or production technologies. On the other hand, a culture's willingness to tolerate outside individuals and novel behaviors can lead to profound risks, since many traditional practices are designed as firewall against environmental diseases and "outsiders" can carry infectious diseases against which a community has no defense. As a result, societies such as India, China, and Japan which historically were at a high risk of disease due to tropical climate or high population density tended to adopt a "collectivist" mindset out of an instinct for self-preservation. This is an attractive theory for historians, since it not only helps to explain Imperial China's relative lack of interest in overseas exploration, but also Japan's historical tendency for xenophobic behavior, such as its refusal to trade with the outside world until forced to do so by western pressure. Western societies, on the other hand, lived in a less disease-prone environment and thus retained a more individual mindset, with its accompanying potential for discovery and innovation. Although this theory is not without problems— most notably, it does little to explain why many disease-prone African societies tend towards an individualist ethos— but it is certainly worthy of future investigation.

Just as disease has left a fundamental stamp on human behavior, so to have changes in human behavior made a mark on disease. Indeed, as human beings have achieved new levels of technological and organizational sophistication, they inevitably offered new opportunities for the proliferation of disease. Four human developments in particular have lead to fundamental changes with mankind's relationship to disease: 1) the adoption of agriculture, 2) the rise of empires, 3) the rise of industrialization, and 4) the advent of the modern "global" age.

Diseases of Agriculture

The adoption of agriculture was by far the most important step in the transformation of the human/disease relationship. Agriculture allowed humans to remake the natural environment to suit their own interests, replacing species of plants with no nutritive value to mankind with plants that have edible leaves, roots, or seeds. Jared Diamond argues in his seminal book *Guns, Germs, and Steel* that edible plant and animal species make up 90 percent of the biomass in farmed land, as opposed to only 0.1 percent in land that is in its natural state. As a result, agriculturalists could support far more people on each unit of land than their hunter-gatherer ancestors. Agriculture also required mankind to abandon nomadism and live permanently in one place, since cropped fields must be tended constantly by farmers, not to mention defended against hungry natural or human predators. Consequently, human beings began to gather together in permanent settlements, ranging in size from small villages to bustling cities. Densely populated and often unsanitary, these early settlements offered a perfect breeding ground for disease, first of the epidemic variety, and later endemics as human resistance built up and the ailments settled down as "childhood diseases."

Agriculture also fostered the growth of disease by putting human beings in regular and intimate contact with domesticated animal species. Farm animals were of enormous value to early farmers, since they offered mankind meat, dairy products, useful fibers, farm labor, and manure, which farmers discovered could increase the productivity of the fields. On the other hand, each animal species suffers from its own intrinsic diseases, so when farm animals began to live in close contact with mankind, these diseases had the opportunity to jump to human populations. Indeed, measles and smallpox probably spread to human beings from cattle, while influenza seems to have originated in domesticated fowl or pigs.

One of the ironies of agriculture is the fact that, despite the dramatic expansion in food production that accompanied farming, the adoption of agriculture also made mankind far more vulnerable to nutritional diseases. Most scholars now believe that the first civilizations turned to agriculture not out of a conscious desire to change their lifestyle, but rather as a response to population growth since only the gradual adoption of agricultural practices could provide sufficient food for their ever-increasing numbers. Population pressure forced early man to adopt some features of an agricultural lifestyle, which in turn allowed for even higher human populations and consequently the need for ever more technological and organizational breakthroughs. Agriculture also increased the fertility rate, since sedentary women could have children more frequently than wandering nomads, which further drove up population numbers. As a result of this viscous feedback loop, human populations in pre-modern farming societies generally hovered just below the threshold of starvation, to the point that historian R.H. Tawney quipped that "the position of the rural population is that of a man standing permanently up to his neck in water, so that even a ripple is sufficient to drown him." Although written to describe the Chinese peasantry, this observation is broadly true for most subsistence farming societies, which were often just a bad harvest or two away from famine and all the nutritional diseases which accompanied it.

What is more, as human beings adopted agriculture and reduced the biological variety of the surrounding lands, they lost much of the variety in their diets in the process. For all its faults, hunter-gathering did at least provide humans with a relatively balanced diet consisting of roots, nuts, leaves, insects, fish, and game animals. With the adoption of agriculture, human beings turned increasingly to a few "staple" crops, such as wheat in West Asia, rice in East Asia, and corn (maize) in North America. These carbohydrate-rich foods provided plenty of energy but were potentially deficient in both proteins and certain vitamins. In fact, most staple grains actually hinder the absorption of key nutrients; chemicals called phytates present in most cereal grains bind to metals in the human intestine, ensuring they pass out of the body rather than being absorbed. What is more, the hard work required by early agriculture meant that farmers had higher food requirements than their hunter-gather neighbors, who could generally sustain themselves on only four hours of labor per day. Indeed, archeological evidence suggests that human beings initially became less healthy as they made the switch from hunter-gathering to agriculture. Skeletal evidence suggests that early agriculturalists were shorter in stature and far more susceptible to nutritional diseases like rickets and scurvy than their non-farming counterparts.

Not surprisingly, given the various opportunities that agriculture afforded to disease, references to disease appear early in the historical record. The literature of Mesopotamia and Egypt — the two earliest cradles of human civilization — are filled with references to disease and plague. One of the first recorded diseases was malaria, a mosquito-borne parasite that thrived in the agricultural canals and irrigation channels of early farmers. Sumerian and Indian texts dating to the 17th century B.C. bear witness to a disease that clearly resembles malaria, and references to malaria in China may be even older. Another early killer was smallpox, which thrived in the densely packed settlements of early agricultural society. Indeed, some archeologists claim that a well preserved Egyptian mummy dated to 12th century B.C. shows telltale signs of smallpox infection. Typhus, a deadly fever passed to humans by body lice, is also an old human disease, dating as far back as the 5th century B.C., when it may have caused the mysterious "Plague of Athens" that ended Athenian dominance in ancient Greece. Like smallpox, typhus would have thrived in the overcrowded and unsanitary towns and cities of early agricultural society.

Diseases of Empire

As agricultural societies grew larger and more sophisticated, two related developments gradually changed humanity's relationship with disease. Over time, each of the world's "civilized" regions became increasingly integrated, in part due to the physical growth and expansion of agricultural society but also due to the establishment of regional trade networks. In the process, the epidemics that plagued each region gradually declined to the status of endemic childhood diseases as regional populations rose high enough to support them. William McNeill claims in *Plagues and Peoples* that, because of this process, four discrete "disease pools" had developed by 500 B.C.: the "Fertile Crescent" of Mesopotamia and Egypt, the Mediterranean basin, India, and China. Within each region, McNeill claims, diseases were "on the way to arriving at a mutually tolerable accommodation to their human hosts."

In the period after 500 B.C., however, the relative equilibrium between man and pathogen was upset by the development of a new phenomenon: the establishment of large regional empires. These powerful states, such as the Persian Empire of the Fertile Crescent, the Han Empire of China, and the Roman Empire of the Mediterranean Sea, boasted large populations and were highly aggressive, constantly seeking to add more territory on the frontiers to their domain. What is more, these states were characterized by an unprecedented degree of wealth, fueling in turn a keen demand for luxury goods. Desire for trade goods, in turn, led to the establishment of long-distance trade, most especially between the Han and Roman Empires. At the heyday of this trade, in the 1st century A.D., caravans plodded constantly along the Silk Road, a constantly-shifting trade route connecting China and Syria. In addition, Greek merchants began to navigate the Indian Ocean, employing the seasonal monsoon winds to reach the trade cities of India and beyond.

Unfortunately, the same caravans and ships that carried merchants and their goods also carried infections. Indeed, one of the unforeseen results of long distance trade was the explosive mixture of the Mediterranean and Chinese disease pools. Since these disease pools had developed in virtual isolation from each other, each civilization's endemics quickly blazed into epidemics when transplanted to the other civilization's virgin population. The Roman Empire suffered a terrible epidemic which began in 165 and which raged on for 15 years, carrying off as much as a quarter to a third of the inhabitants of stricken cities in the process. Another nightmarish plague struck Europe from A.D. 251 to 266, hastening the decline and the eventual disintegration of the western half of the Roman Empire. In the meantime, China was experiencing horrific plagues of its own, especially between A.D. 161–162 and 310–312. In part because of epidemic disease, the Han state collapsed at the start of the 3rd century A.D., ushering in over four centuries of decentralization.

The rise of later Eurasian empires would trigger further outbreaks of epidemic disease in surrounding territories. By the 14th century, the Mongols had carved out the largest empire in the history of the world, encompassing China, almost all of Russia, central Asia, and present day Iraq and Iran. In the process, they created unprecedented opportunities for long-distance travel, epitomized by the globetrotting career of Marco Polo, an Italian who traversed Mongol lands and may have even have served as a government official in Mongol China. Long distance trade reawakened as well, including a new Silk Road passing through the heart of the Mongol steppes. Unfortunately, this route happened to traverse the territory of burrowing rodents that harbored the *Yersinia pestis* bacteria, an organism better known as the causative agent of the bubonic plague. Hosted by rats, and carried by fleas to human hosts, the bubonic plague kills both quickly — often within a 10 days of infection — and efficiently, slaying an estimated 60 percent of those infected. Worse yet, some victims develop pneumonic plague, which can be passed directly from person to person by aerosol particles and causes an even more rapid and certain death.

Not surprisingly, when this plague spread east and west along the Silk Road, the results were catastrophic. As many as 25 million died in China, and another 25 million are estimated to have died in Europe, or approximately a third of Europe's population. In some areas of Europe, such as England, the fatality rate probably topped 70 percent. This unprecedented level of mortality to some extent reflects the virulence of the *Yersinia pestis*, but it is also a testimony to Europe's vulnerability at the time; by 1300 Europe's climate had begun to cool due to the "Little Ice Age" of the 13th–19th centuries, and severe overpopulation meant that Europe was both thickly settled and badly nourished. Indeed, some historians have viewed Europe's "Black Death" as a Malthusian collapse, and have interpreted the bubonic plague as the means by which Europe's population was knocked back down to a supportable level. North Africa and the Middle East also suffered terrible losses, though not quite on the same scale as Europe.

As might be expected, mortality on this scale left an enormous imprint on world history. The plague created such a labor shortage in Europe that it empowered European workers, who demanded higher wages. In Eastern Europe, the landed elite effectively fought back against these demands and succeeded in keeping peasants tied to the land, perpetuating the system of land tenure called serfdom — a system, incidentally, which has been blamed for the long-term economic stagnation of Eastern Europe. In Western Europe, however, the ties binding lords and peasants were somewhat weakened. Indeed, some historians have argued that competition between landlords for peasant labor, and the resulting creation of a labor market, helped fuel the development of capitalism. The plague also contributed enormously to European history by stirring up anti–Semitism. As the plague progressed, rumors spread throughout Europe that Jews had poisoned the wells, a rumor given credence by the fact that European Jews mostly avoided the use of public wells out of a religious obligation to be clean. As a result, at least 350 massacres of Jews took place across Western Europe, reinforcing a vein of anti–Semitism in Europe that would later find its fullest expression during the Holocaust. Many of the surviving Jews traveled eastwards, where they joined and strengthened the growing Ashkenazi community of Yiddish-speaking Jews.

HTTP://COMMONS.WIKIMEDIA.ORG/WIKI/IMAGE:1349_BURNING_OF_JEWS-EUROPEAN_CHRONICLE_ON_BLACK_DEATH.JPG

Medieval European manuscript illustration depicting the burning of Jews during the Bubonic Plague.

Perhaps the most important role played by the Black Death in European history, however, was the toll it took on the authority of the Catholic Church. The Black Death brought out the best in some clergymen, who diligently administered to their ailing flocks, and quite often contracted the Plague as a reward for their services. Other priests shirked their duties out of fear of infection and thus lost the respect of their congregations. With its best and bravest gone, the post–Plague Catholic Church began a long decline into peculation and corruption, which in turn lead to new challenges to the authority of the Church. In the short term the Church was undermined by the establishment of lay flagellant orders, religious zealots who marched from town to town scourging themselves with whips and rods in an attempt to assuage God's apparent displeasure with mankind. Believing that they had a special connection with Christ, the flagellants frequently clashed with the church hierarchy, going so far as to drive priests from churches and condemn the Church hierarchy. In the medium term the Black Death inculcated Europe with a more secular, live-for-the-moment ethos that contributed to the European Renaissance. Indeed, Boccaccio's *Decameron*, one of the first literary works of the early Renaissance, takes the form of a collection of secular stories told to each other by Italian aristocrats who had fled from Florence to the countryside in an attempt to avoid the Black Death. In the long run, popular European discontent with the Catholic Church helped to fuel the Reformation, which resulted in the rise of Protestantism and the fragmentation of the formerly unified European church.

The Black Death, however, pales in significance when compared to the most spectacular outbreak of "imperial" diseases: the "Columbian Exchange" plagues that broke out after A.D. 1500. When Christopher Columbus "discovered" the Americas in 1492, he initiated an era of European contact with Amerindian cultures that had been effectively out of contact with their Eurasian ancestors for over 10,000 years. As a result, these Amerindians had no previous exposure to the endemic diseases that had developed in Eurasia and Africa following the rise of agricultural society. When European explorers, missionaries, and soldiers began to penetrate the American continents, they carried along their endemic diseases such as measles and smallpox, and these ailments soon exploded into epidemics in the virgin populations of the Amerindians. Worse yet, as the native American labor pool dried up, the Spaniards and Portuguese turned to African slave labor to fill the mines and plantations of their American colonies, and this in turn allowed African diseases, most notably yellow fever and malaria, to reach the tropical regions of the Americas. The overall death toll these various epidemics reaped in the Americas is a matter of conjecture due to varying estimates of the pre–Columbian Amerindian population. Nonetheless some scholars believe that European and African diseases may have killed over 100 million people between 1500 and 1650, a figure that represents 90 percent to 95 percent of the pre–Columbian population of the American continents.

Not surprisingly, mass mortality on such an enormous scale dramatically altered the course of world history. The indigenous Amerindian states, which included large empires such as that of the Aztecs and Mayans, were quickly swept away, unable to withstand the dual attack by European weaponry and Old World pestilence. Traditional Amerindian culture was by and large swept away as well, outside of a few remnant cultural practices such as Mexico's Day of the Dead celebration. As for the Amerindians themselves, they were pushed to the margins of the New World. In temperate areas such as North America and Argentina, where the climate resembled that of Europe, European settlers armed with guns and germs all but exterminated the native Amerindian populations. In the tropical lowlands such as Brazil and the Caribbean, where African diseases took hold, the Amerindian population generally melted away and was replaced mainly by African slaves and their descendants. Substantial Amerindian populations only survived to the present day in highland areas such as Mexico and the Andes mountains that had boasted dense populations before Columbus arrived and were relatively sheltered from the onslaught of the diseases from the Old World tropics.

As a result of the near obliteration of the Amerindian population, there was little to stop Europeans from remaking the New World in their own image — and in their own interests. European Christianity and European languages became firmly established throughout the Americas, vastly increasing the extent, and influence, of "Western" civilization. This was true even in areas where substantial Amerindian populations survived, in part because of the forcible imposition of European cultural norms, but also because of the psychic shock of the European diseases themselves. The fact that Europeans seemed immune to epidemic diseases, while the Amerindians died by the thousands, must have strained the religious convictions of the Amerindians, facilitating their conversion to European Christianity.

Diseases and depopulation allowed Europeans to remake the economy of the Americas as well. To exploit the vast agriculture resources of the New World, Europeans set up plantations — large farms worked with slave labor — to grow crops that fetched a good price in Europe. Chief amongst these crops was sugar, which could be grown only a few places in Europe but which was extremely well suited to the climate of the Americas, particularly in the Caribbean and Brazil. Later on other crops, including indigo, rice, and the addictive American plant tobacco were sold at great profit in European markets. These new resources, and the trade they generated, allowed the European economy to expand dramatically after the year 1500 to the point that it rivaled and soon exceeded the wealth of the large empires of Asia and North Africa. The wealth generated by the "Atlantic Economy" also helps to explain why Europe, and not some other continent, was the birthplace of the industrial revolution.

The near extinction of the Amerindian population when confronted with Eurasian diseases begs the question: Why were Europeans not equally devastated by the diseases of the Americas? After all, Eurasians would be just as vulnerable to American ailments as Amerindians were to Eurasian plagues. Europeans, however, benefited enormously from the fact that Amerindian civilizations domesticated only a few animal species and as a result the opportunities for diseases to jump from animal hosts to the Amerindians were quite circumscribed. What is more, productive agriculture developed much later in the Americas than in other regions of the world, giving Amerindian farmers less time to develop endemic diseases than the civilizations of Eurasia. Nonetheless, the European colonization of the Americas did have a significant affect on the disease history of Eurasia. As we shall see in section 8.1, the American food plant corn (Maize) lead to deadly outbreaks of pellagra as it spread throughout Eurasia and Africa. What is more, smallpox, long endemic in Europe, suddenly evolved into a more vicious endemic during the time of the Columbian Exchange, though it is unclear whether this new strain was the result of European smallpox mutating as it raged through the Amerindian population, or whether it was a virulent African strain of smallpox carried to Europe after the establishment of the American slave plantation economy.

The American disease that left the greatest impact on Europe, however, was syphilis. Although the origins of syphilis have been the subject of considerable controversy, it is now widely believed that syphilis was an Old World disease carried by the ancestors of the Amerindians to the American continent. Once there, syphilis evolved into a highly contagious and deadly disease transmitted mainly through sexual contact. Columbus' men apparently brought it back to Europe following the "discovery" of the Americas and it soon became a Europe-wide pandemic, earning itself the title the "Great Pox" due to the disfiguring skin pustules that often covered most of the victim's body. In the first half century following Columbus' voyage, syphilis proved to be extremely deadly, killing most victims in a matter of months. As syphilis spread, however, the more virulent strains died off with their victims, and syphilis evolved into its modern form: a milder, endemic disease with a long incubation period in the human body.

Early Renaissance German depiction of syphilis, which was called the "Great Pox" when it first exploded through Europe following the discovery of the Americas.

Diseases of Industry

The age of industrialization marked the start of a new age of human economic productivity, but also the beginning new relationships between man and disease. Industrialization brought dramatic changes in human society, especially in terms of urbanization, pollution, and improved transportation, which provided new opportunities for disease. A case in point is the bacterial infection typhoid. Although typhoid fever is probably as old as mankind itself, it prospered as never before in the filthy, overcrowded cityscapes of industrial Europe. A waterborne bacterium, typhoid invades the human body through contaminated water, and then causes extreme diarrhea, which in turn can perpetuate or even spread the contagion if the fecal matter reaches drinking water supplies. As might be expected, given the extremely primitive sanitation facilities of the haphazard neighborhoods built up around industrial factories, typhoid deaths were common in early industrial Europe. Ironically, some early attempts by European and American authorities to tackle the problem of poor sanitation only made the problem worse: As we shall see in section 8.3, misguided British attempts to discharge sewage from early 19th century London served only to contaminate the Thames River and thus set the stage for cholera, another disease spread through sewage. These waterborne killers only faded away with the construction of sophisticated urban sewer and water treatment systems in the late 19th and early 20th centuries.

Dietary diseases flourished in the industrial age as well. Like the agricultural revolution, industrialization unlocked vast new resources for mankind, but in the short term it led to a distinct decline in human welfare, as the workers in early industrial factories were less well fed, less well housed, and more overworked than their rural compatriots. Not surprisingly, various types of nutritional disease thrived under these conditions. Probably the most debilitating such disease was osteomalacia, better known as rickets. Rickets is caused by lack of vitamin D, which leads to insufficient levels of the bone growth hormone calcitriol and as a consequence severely deformed bones. In the normal course of things, human beings receive the vitamin D they need from the ultraviolet rays in sunlight, which react with a type of cholesterol in the skin and synthesize the vitamin. During the industrial revolution, however, human beings progressively shifted from agriculture to factory work, which required them to be indoors for much if not all of the working day. Workers were further deprived of sunlight by the haze of coal smoke that shrouded most industrial cities, and the sheer bulk of the tall brick tenements and row houses where they lived, which cast a shadow over the narrow urban streets. Small wonder, then, that the incidence of rickets rose to as high as 90 percent in industrial Europe before researchers discovered that sun exposure and dietary supplements like fish oil could ameliorate the disease.

The most characteristic diseases of the industrial era, however, were undoubtedly tuberculosis and cholera. Although an old disease, tuberculosis only reached epidemic status in the new industrial cities of the 19th centuries, where it became the single most common cause of death in American and European urban areas. An airborne bacterial infection, tuberculosis found fertile ground in the dirty and overpopulated slums of industrial cities, where families lived cheek and jowl in poorly ventilated single-room tenements. The smoke and dust that was characteristic of 19th century industrial centers often damaged the lungs of urban residents, offering further opportunities for tuberculosis infection. What is more, 19th century workers also tended to be malnourished due to the low wages they received, and this facilitated the epidemic by compromising the victims' immune systems. Once stricken, slum-dwellers developed a wracking and bloody cough and often wasted away, becoming thin pale, listless, and feverish as the disease progressed. As a result of these symptoms, the disease was popularly dubbed "consumption" at the time. Although a vaccine of limited effectiveness — the BCG vaccine — was later introduced to counter tuberculosis, the best form of preventing tuberculosis both then and now is the alleviation of poverty: spacious and well-ventilated housing, sufficient food, and access to health care all serve as bulwarks against tuberculosis epidemics.

Like tuberculosis, cholera thrived in the crowded slums of the early industrial era, claiming hundreds of thousands of victims in urban Europe over the course of the 19th century. Unlike tuberculosis, however, cholera killed extremely quickly, reducing apparently healthy men to shriveled corpses in as little as a day. As we shall see in section 8.3, cholera's swift onset, grotesque symptoms, and high mortality combined to make it the most feared epidemic of the 19th century.

Diseases of Globalization

More recently, the dawn of the "global" era of world history has once again changed mankind's relationship with disease. In the modern age, people and information can travel all but instantly around the globe, creating new relationships between previously isolated peoples. The result has been the increasing integration of the world's economy — the local prices of a commodity can now be determined by market fluctuations or crop failures half a world away — as well as the world's peoples, who have come under the homogenizing influence of western media and, more recently, the Internet. What is more, globalization has led to unprecedented population shifts, both within countries (from villages to cities, for example) and between countries, as demonstrated by the scale of immigration from Asia into Europe and from Latin America into English-speaking North America. Finally, air travel has made long-distance movements of population both far quicker and far more common, in the form of increased levels of tourism.

Needless to say, changes in human behavior on such a massive scale have created inevitable new opportunities for disease, as best epitomized by the 1918-1919 pandemic, or global epidemic, of influenza. By the 1910s, the world had become integrated to a degree that had never been possible before. European states ruled far-flung patchworks of territories in Asia, Africa, and the Americas, stitched together by railroads, telegraph lines, and fast steamship transportation. What is more, the opening of the Suez Canal in 1869 and the Panama Canal in 1914 effectively shrunk the world, vastly reducing travel time between the world's continents. Even more importantly, the influenza epidemic coincided with the final years of the First World War, and as the name implies, this conflict was truly global in scale, involving the transcontinental movement of an unprecedented number of people — mostly soldiers— over a short period of time. During World War I, West Africans rubbed shoulders with African-Americans from Alabama on the fields of France, Japanese soldiers seized German strong points in China, British-led Indian soldiers shivered through Belgian winters, and British, and Australian, and New Zealand infantrymen died together on the Turkish peninsula of Gallipoli. This sudden co-mingling of previously isolated populations, combined with wartime stress and malnutrition, set the stage for an epidemiological nightmare.

In fall of 1918, a particularly virulent strain of influenza broke out at three separate points: Boston in the United States, Freeport in West Africa, and Brest in France, all of which were military transportation centers for the Allied forces. From there the influenza spread to nearly every corner of the earth; indeed, blood tests performed later suggest that over half the world's population may have contracted the viral infection. Unlike the milder flu strains endemic to the modern world, the 1918-1919 influenza was exceptionally virulent, killing healthy adults as well as the elderly and the young. The official death toll is usually put at 21 million, but this is probably a low estimate, and recent scholars have put the death toll as high as 100 million, with 20 million perishing in India alone. Worst hit were isolated populations with little exposure to previous flu strains, such as Pacific Islanders and North American Inuits, who suffered double digit mortality rates. Following the 1918-1919 pandemic, the influenza reverted to its original status as a mild endemic disease, but given the influenza virus' extraordinary rate of mutation, the return of a more deadly form of influenza remains a distinct possibility in the modern world.

The legacy of the 1918-1919 influenza pandemic helps explain why scientists and health professionals were so concerned about the flu-like disease SARS, which threatened to become a worldwide epidemic during the first years of the 21st century. The virus that causes the Severe Acute Respiratory Syndrome, or SARS, seems to have jumped to human beings from Chinese bats, either directly or through the intermediary of the civet cat, a gourmet delicacy in China. Soon after the first human victims contracted the disease in Southern China, SARS spread rapidly, manifesting itself as a severe flu-like disease with nearly a 10 percent mortality rate. In the past, SARS might have remained a mere local phenomenon, but the advent of air travel allowed a number of infected persons to leave China before the symptoms manifested themselves and return to their own countries, carrying the infection with them. As a result, outbreaks of SARS blossomed worldwide, especially in Taiwan, Singapore, the Philippines, Europe, and Canada, where the cosmopolitan city of Toronto hosted the highest number of SARS cases outside of Asia and served as a base for the further dissemination of SARS throughout the Western Hemisphere. Thanks to an unprecedented effort by the World Health Organization to identify and quarantine SARS victims, in the end only about 8,000 people were infected by SARS, which proved not to be the pandemic that health officials had initially feared. Nonetheless, the possibility remains that a future pandemic, such as the widely feared avian flu, might spread too fast for quarantine measures to be effective.

Despite — or perhaps because of— the development of a worldwide food trade, globalization has also contributed to the spread of nutritional diseases. Because of globalization, local cuisines are breaking down and being replaced by a fairly homogenous diet of American style fast food, salty snacks, sugary colas, and processed food manufactured in a factory setting. Unfortunately, this high-carbohydrate, high-fat diet contributes to a number of nutritional diseases. Developed nations increasingly suffer from heart disease, which has been linked to excess fat intake, and diabetes, which can be triggered by an appetite for sugary, carbohydrate-rich foods. In addition, developed countries tend to suffer high rates of obesity, putting their citizens at risk of heart problems, diabetes, and certain types of cancers such as colon cancer. In addition, the higher rates of meat consumption associated with American-style diets means greater exposure to carcinogenic (cancer-causing) agents that are often present in grilled meat, such as benzopyrene, which has been linked to stomach cancer, breast cancer, colon cancer, and cancer of the pancreas. On the other hand, the globalization of the food trade can cause worldwide price spikes that lead, in turn, to severe malnutrition. While this book was being written, soaring global food prices forced many poor Haitians to subsist on cakes consisting mainly of dirt. As we saw in chapter 7, people starved to death during the Bangladeshi famine of 1974 in the very midst of well-stocked supermarkets. During the 21th century, we may see the same juxtaposition of famine and plenty on a global scale.

The most well-known pandemic of the modern global era, however, is undoubtedly AIDS. Indeed, in the past 100 years, AIDS has been transformed from an endemic disease in a remote African chimpanzee population to a global pandemic. By 2007, AIDS had killed an estimated 25 million people, and another 40 million people worldwide thought to be infected by HIV, the virus that causes AIDS. As we shall see in section 8.3, a number of factors have contributed to the explosive growth of AIDS in the modern era, and all are linked directly or indirectly to globalization.

Disease and Other Disasters

Bacterial, viral, and nutritional diseases are intimately tied to other types of natural disasters. Since natural disasters tend to break down the normal infrastructure, cultural norms, political stability, and economic underpinnings of a society, they tend to create opportunities for diseases to flourish. As a result, diseases often serve as the proximate, or immediate, cause of death and destruction, even when the original disaster was the result of tectonic forces, cyclonic weather, or famine. In rare cases, diseases can play a causative role as well, serving as the indirect or direct trigger of natural disasters.

Volcanic eruptions and earthquakes, for example, frequently trigger outbreaks of disease. People displaced by a volcanic eruption or a quake often accumulate in urban areas or refugee camps, where poor hygiene and malnutrition are common. What is more, the intermingling of refugees from previously isolated populations, which often occurs in the aftermath of eruptions or earthquakes, creates an ideal environment for the proliferation of disease. Volcanic emissions also emit toxic chemicals, such as sulfur, that can induce illness in both people and their livestock. In rare cases, volcanic eruptions can even spawn diseases worldwide by exerting a measurable effect on the world's climate. As we saw in chapter 2, for instance, the cataclysmic eruption of Tambora in 1816 was implicated in famine and associated disease outbreaks throughout the northern hemisphere, most notably in Ireland, where the death toll may have reached 100,000.

Climate change can lead to disease outbreaks as well. El Niño can tamper with the African and Asian monsoon cycle, leading to lack of rain, famine, and associated nutritional or epidemic diseases, if a large number of people are displaced by the disaster. Excessive monsoon rains can bring about the same circumstances, plus the additional threat of diarrheal disease (due to floodwaters contaminating water supplies) and mosquito-born epidemics. As for global warming, scientists fear that it might exacerbate future disease outbreaks by extending the range of many mosquito species into adjacent subtropical and even temperate climate zones. The likely consequence will be the expansion of mosquito-hosted diseases, such as yellow fever, dengue fever, and malaria, into virgin territories.

In the shorter term, both river flooding and cyclonic weather can lead to profound epidemiological consequences. The physical damage wrought by these disasters can destroy food crops, wash away food stores, and disrupt trade infrastructure, breeding famine and associated diseases. What is more, both river flooding and cyclonic downpours can contaminate water supplies by allowing polluted waters to intermingle with previously safe freshwater supplies. In addition, mosquitoes tend to thrive in the stagnant pools left behind by major flooding, exacerbating the risk of mosquito-borne infection.

The form of natural disaster most intimately linked with disease, however, is famine. Lack of food compromises the human immune system, which creates an opportunity for many types of epidemic disease. Famine victims also tend to eat a limited variety of foods, often leading to diseases associated with dietary deficiencies: beriberi, pellagra, rickets, and scurvy. What is more, lack of dietary iron, usually due to low meat consumption or exclusive consumption of cereal crops, leads to anemia, a condition that weakens the body's skeletal structure and may also compromise brain development an the immune system. Perhaps most importantly, famine breeds diseases by causing large scale displacement of the affected population. Unable to feed themselves in their home communities, many famine sufferers flee to urban centers, work camps, or refugee camps. As overcrowding sets in, hygienic conditions break down. Airborne diseases pass swiftly through the overpopulated camps, as do diseases carried from person to person via insect vectors, such as bubonic plague and typhus. Worst of all, in all but the most sanitary refugee camps, water supplies are soon tainted by human feces, leading to the proliferation of diarrheal diseases such as typhoid and cholera. Indeed, as discussed in chapter 7, the bulk of deaths attributed to famine are actually the work of disease running riot through a hunger-weakened population.

Although disease is normally the consequence of other disasters, and not the cause, disease has occasionally been implicated in worsening or even triggering natural disasters that are normally higher in the disaster hierarchy. There is evidence, for instance, that disease created a feedback loop with famine during the great famines of the Victorian age. In India, epidemic malaria so weakened farmer populations that, even once the rains returned in 1878, farmers proved to be too enervated to sow seeds on their fields. During the same drought, northern Chinese farmers weakened by famine succumbed to dysentery — the inflammation of the intestinal lining — by overeating when food became available once more. As a result, in the words of one European observer, "fields of millet stood unharvested, sagged, and decayed," perpetuating the famine. Most controversially of all, one author has suggested that famine can actually lead to climate change. As discussed in section 4.3, William Ruddiman has speculated that large-scale epidemics, such as the bubonic plague and the plagues attending the Columbian Exchange, can lead to the contraction of agricultural populations, fostering the regrowth of forests. Forest growth, in turn, leads to the sequestration of carbon from the atmosphere, which has the effect of cooling the climate and initiating a feedback loop of lowered temperatures, resultant famine and disease, and yet more regrowth of forest.

Disease and Human Agency

As we have seen repeatedly throughout this chapter, human beings play a crucial role in the development and propagation of disease; indeed, many diseases would not even exist in the absence of their human hosts. What is more, each new era in human society from agriculture to globalization has provided new opportunities for disease. Human beings also influence the development of disease in a more subtle way: by imbedding disease in a network of religious, cultural, social, and political practices that shape the way in which disease is experienced by a community.

In a clinical sense, a disease is a condition caused by a specific pathogen, mutation, or dietary condition that has a negative impact on the human body. Since these changes to the body work on the cellular or even the molecular level, however, they were largely invisible to premodern humans. As a result, human societies were forced to understand disease using the intellectual tools available to them: religion, tradition, folklore, ideology, philosophy, etc. Indeed, disease scholar Sheldon Watts goes so far as to distinguish between "disease," by which he means an actual physiological condition, and "disease Construct," which he defines as the "complex of cultural filters" through which the disease is perceived by a society. Simply put, Watts believes that the way that disease is viewed — and sometimes manipulated by those in power — is just as important as the disease itself.

A case in point for Watts is the skin affliction leprosy. In a clinical sense, leprosy is caused by a bacterium akin to the tuberculosis germ which causes progressive nerve degeneration followed by soft tissue damage, especially in extremities such as the nose, hands, and feet. The actual pathology of leprosy, however, matters less than the way in which different cultures understood the disease. Islamic societies considered leprosy to be a disease like any other and did not regard it with any particular terror; indeed, most Moslems followed the example of the Prophet Mohammed, who made a point of eating with a leper and remarking, "the disease will not catch me unless Allah wants it." Judeo-Christian society, however, saw leprosy in a far more sinister light. Their leprosy Construct was built around passages taken from the Old Testament book of Leviticus, which declared leprosy a punishment for offenses against God and prescribed that lepers "shall dwell alone without the camp." As a result, generations of Jews and Christians regarded leprosy as a disease of the soul rather than the body, for which the only "cure" was to segregate the sinner from society at large.

This attitude towards leprosy reached its apogee during the European Middle Ages, especially between 1090 and 1363. During these years, Europe embarked on what one historian has dubbed the "Great Leper Hunt": Thousands of individuals were accused of leprosy, tried and convicted, deprived of their possessions, and herded into specially built "lazar houses," where presumably they would live out their days contemplating the moral failings that caused them to contract the disease. Ironically, it is likely that relatively few of these "lepers" actually had leprosy. Rather, Medieval European priests and magistrates routinely accused troublemakers and malcontents as "lepers" as a means of social control, or else accused the rich of leprosy as a ploy to seize their property. What is more, accusations of leprosy were a money-making scheme for the Christian Church, which collected considerable sums for the creation and maintenance of lazar houses, which also provided appointments for the swollen ranks of the Christian clergy.

Just as the origins of the "leprosy" epidemic were tied to the economic and social priorities of Medieval European elites, Watts argues, the end of the "leprosy" epidemic reflected a shift in those priorities. By the late Medieval period, the Catholic Church developed the doctrine of instant entry upon death into heaven, hell, or purgatory. Previously, European Christians had been taught that the soul only ascended to heaven or descended to hell at the end of the world, as suggested by the Book of Revelations. Now, however, Europeans had reason to fear that their dead relatives were suffering from hellfire during their own lifetimes, encouraging massive donations to the Church on behalf of the dearly departed. With such a potent new means of encouraging donations at their disposal, Watts reasons, the leprosy Construct was no longer needed, and not surprisingly accusations of leprosy dropped sharply thereafter.

Leprosy is far from the only disease to be perceived very differently by people of different cultures. In a fascinating article published in 1992, disease historian Lawrence Conrad argued that the bubonic plague's cultural impact in the Arabic world was much less than that in Europe largely due to a different set of beliefs about epidemic disease. Over time, Arabic thought on epidemics underwent a number of notable changes. Old Arabic tradition ascribed diseases to semi-divine *jinn*, but with the advent of Islam, this superstitious belief fell into disfavor. In fact, Mohammed went so far as to virtually deny the existence of epidemics altogether; the Prophet was associated with the pronouncement "no contagion," which was interpreted as meaning that epidemics were not spread between individuals but rather were the will of Allah. This belief was not fully satisfying, however, partly because it conflicted with the observed reality of disease infection, but also because it did not answer the question as to why diseases — and presumably the will of Allah — struck down believers and unbelievers alike. To solve this problem, Islamic thinkers began to posit that disease serves different functions in the faithful and the faithless. Islamic theologians speculated that Allah created epidemics to separate the wheat from the chaff, punishing the infidel with everlasting torment just as it rewarded good Moslems with paradise. Indeed, death by disease became accepted as a form of martyrdom; Moslem plague victims ascended directly to heaven upon death. This articulation of the meaning of epidemic disease proved enduring, and held sway in the Arabic world from the 9th century A.D. onwards.

Thanks to this reassuring theological formulation about epidemic disease, Conrad argues, Moslems were far better mentally equipped to handle the ravages of the bubonic plague than their European Christian contemporaries. While the bubonic plague instituted a new era of self-doubt and intellectual crisis in Europe, the plague was accepted with more equanimity in the Islamic world, despite similarly high levels of plague mortality. Some historians have seen this lack of self-reflection as a failing of Islam, and argue that it demonstrates a relative lack of cultural creativity. Conrad, however, turns this argument on its head, and asserts that Islam's more sedate reaction to the plague demonstrates the Arab world's intellectual maturity — the difficult questions that Europe was forced to ask itself, in Conrad's opinion, had long been answered to everyone's satisfaction in the Islamic East.

As we shall see in the sections to follow, leprosy and bubonic plague are far from the only ailments in which "disease Constructs" play an important role. Pellagra, for example, was long seen as a moral disease associated with slovenliness and degeneracy. Much the same was true of cholera, which arose in England just as a new middle class was flexing its political muscle. Indeed, the rising middle class used cholera as a means of differentiating themselves from the "ignorant rabble," which was supposedly predisposed to cholera infection by their idleness, immorality, alcoholism, and general lack of respectability. Tragically, this assumption encouraged the British establishment to deny that cholera was a contagious disease, and Britain's hands-off approach served to facilitate the spread of the cholera epidemics. What is more, despite recent advances in medical technology, the phenomenon of "construct disease" is still alive and well today, as best demonstrated by public attitudes towards AIDS. Many people persist in regarding AIDS as a "gay" or "junkie" disease, and therefore a disease of moral failure. Unfortunately for society as a whole, such assumptions are not only incorrect, they are potentially deadly.

Study Questions

1. Based on this reading, why is the term "disease" so difficult to define?

2. "Disease has exerted a more powerful impact on human history than any other type of natural disaster." Based on this reading and other chapters in this text, to what degree would you agree with this statement?

3. Based on the information presented, to what degree would you argue that disease is really a "natural" disaster?

4. "Unlike other forms of natural disaster, human culture plays a major role in determining how disease affects an afflicted population." Based on this reading and readings from other chapters, to what degree would you agree with this statement?

Sources/Suggested Readings

Barry, John. *The Great Influenza: The Epic Story of the Deadliest Plague in History.* New York: Viking, 2004.

Bollet, Alfred J. *Plagues and Poxes: The Impact of Human History on Epidemic Disease.* New York: Demos Medical Publishing, 2004.

Cantor, Norman. *In the Wake of the Plague: The Black Death and the World It Made.* New York: Free Press, 2001.

Cohen, Mark Nathan. *Health and the Rise of Civilization.* New Haven, CT: Yale University Press, 1989.

Cohen, Mark Nathan. "Prehistoric Patterns of Hunger." In Lucile F. Newman, ed., *Hunger in History: Food Shortage, Poverty, and Deprivation.* Cambridge, MA: Blackwell, 1990.

Crosby, Alfred W. *The Columbian Exchange: Biological and Cultural Consequences of 1492.* Westport, CT: Praeger, 2003.

Davies, Pete. *The Devil's Flu: The World's Deadliest Influenza Epidemic and the Scientific Hunt for the Virus That Caused It.* New York: Henry Holt, 2000.

Diamond, Jared. *Guns, Germs, and Steel: The Fates of Human Societies.* New York: W. W. Norton, 1997.

Fincher, Corey L., Randy Thornhill, Damien R. Murray, and Mark Schaller. "Pathogen Prevalence Predicts Human Cross-Cultural Variability in Individualism/Collectivism." *Proceedings of the Royal Society B,* Vol. 275, No. 1640 (June 7, 2008), pp. 1279–1285.

Katz, Jonathan M. "Poor Haitians Resort to Eating Dirt," *Associated Press* (Jan. 30, 2008). Available from http://news.nationalgeographic.com/news/2008/01/080130-AP-haiti-eatin_2.html.

Kelly, John. *The Great Mortality.* New York: Harper Perennial, 2005.

Kiple, Kenneth F., ed., *Plague, Pox, and Pestilence.* London: Barnes and Noble Books, 1997.

McNeill, William. *Plagues and Peoples.* New York: Anchor Books, 1976.

Oldstone, Michael B. A. *Viruses, Plagues, and History.* New York: Oxford University Press, 1998.

Ranger, Terence, and Slack, Paul eds., *Epidemics and Ideas: Essays on the Historical Perception of Pestilence.* New York: Cambridge University Press, 1992.

Tawney, R. H. *Land and Labor in China.* London: G. Allen & Unwin, 1931.

Watts, Sheldon. *Epidemics and History: Disease, Power, and Imperialism.* New Haven, CT: Yale University Press, 1997.

Webster, R. G., and Walker, E. J. "The world is teetering on the edge of a pandemic that could kill a large fraction of the human population." *American Scientist* Vol. 91 No. 2, (2003), p. 122.

8.1: Disease of Agriculture: Pellagra

Technically speaking, pellagra is a nutritional disease associated with low levels of nicotinic acid, or niacin. In real life terms, however, the story of pellagra is inextricably intertwined with the history of the cultivation of the niacin-deficient crop maize, better known to Americans as corn. The story of pellagra is also intimately tied to the existence of poverty. Throughout human history, pellagra has almost always been a disease of the poor, to the extent that the telltale "butterfly" facial rash caused by pellagra has served as a social stigma marking its bearer

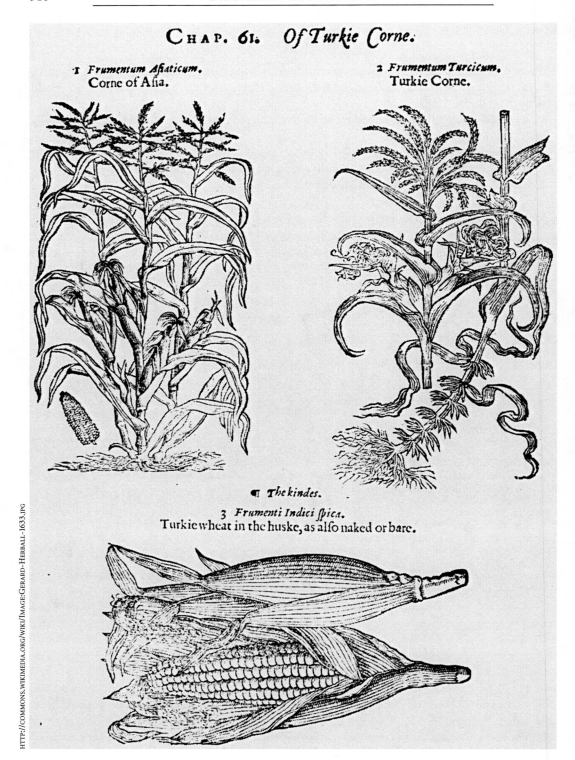

Illustration of the maize plant from John Gerard's *Herball*, written in 1633.

as the member of an inferior caste. Pellagra's close association with poverty has also made it a difficult disease to treat, largely because eradication of the disease required an overhaul of the social system that rendered the effected population vulnerable to the disease in the first place. Thankfully, pellagra has all but disappeared today, largely due to the practice of "enriching" bread and other foodstuffs with missing vitamins. Nonetheless, the increasing global popularity of maize as a subsistence and industrial crop suggests that pellagra may yet make a return appearance.

Pellagra is often termed the "disease of the three D's" as a result of its characteristic symptoms. Pellagra patients, or "pellagrins" as they used to be called, commonly suffer from *dermatitis*, or skin inflammation. The skin reddens and peels, especially on the face, upper chest, and throat, and feels rough to the touch. Pellagra also leads to severe *diarrhea*, which in turn worsens the disease by preventing the human body from absorbing the nutrients it needs from food. As pellagra further progresses, it often leads *dementia* in the form of psychotic or severely depressed behavior. Indeed, pellagra patients tend to suffer from low levels of the neurotransmitter serotonin, which in turn has been linked to mental illnesses ranging from insomnia to panic attacks to depression to chronic anxiety. Untreated pellagra can lead to a fourth D: death, which typically claims the life of about 5–10 percent of pellagrins.

Pellagra was an uncommon disease worldwide before 1500, since at that time maize was grown only in the Americas, and the Amerindians had adopted methods of cooking maize that effectively staved off niacin deficiency. Amerindians traditionally softened the hard kernels of maize by soaking them in a lime or ash solution, which serendipitously converted the niacin in the maize into a form usable by the human body. Amerindians also tended to eat maize with other crops, such as squash and beans, which either contained niacin or facilitated the digestion of the niacin in maize. Furthermore, Amerindians frequently ate maize "green" off the stalk, when if often was infested with various insect pests rich in dietary vitamins. When Americans, Asians, and Africans adopted maize, however, they generally incorporated the new crop into their older culinary traditions, substituting maize for the wheat, rye, or millet that had formerly served as the staple crop. Maize enjoyed substantial advantages over these traditional crops, since it produced far greater yield per acre that traditional Old World grains could achieve, and it could be grown in areas too well-watered to be suitable for wheat. However, since Europeans did not adopt New World strategies of maize preparation, maize's additional yield came at the potentially deadly price of niacin deficiency.

Evidence suggests that Europeans were aware of maize's shortcomings as early as the 17th century, when English botanical treatises complained that eating too much maize caused "itches and scabbes." Maize caused these symptoms, it was believed, by overheating the blood, an explanation that made sense in the context of 17th century medical theory, which ascribed diseases to an excess of bodily "humours" linked to primary elements such as fire. Other herbalist complained that "Turky wheat," as maize was then called, "doth nourish far less than either wheat, rie [rye], barley, or otes [oats]." Nonetheless, maize cultivation was actively encouraged by governments impressed by the high yields, and correspondingly high tax revenues, that maize cultivation could produce. What is more, sheer Malthusian population pressure obliged farmers in the poorer areas of Europe, such as southern France, the mountainous country of central and northern Italy, and the territory now known as Romania, to adopt maize cultivation. Maize also spread beyond Europe, most notably into Egypt and South Africa, where it became a staple crop.

It was in northern Spain, however, that the disease now known as pellagra was first identified by medical science. In 1735 Dr. Gaspar Casal of the town of Oviedo noted a new ailment among his patients that was popularly known as the "*mal de la rosa*" due to the distinctive reddish skin symptoms it caused. Casal noted that this illness was common among the poorest laborers who ate mainly maize bread, and claimed that the disease could be cured by adding milk and cheese to the diet. As it turned out, Casal's observations about both the origins and cures of pellagra were spot on, though it would take nearly 200 years for the world's medical community to embrace his insights. It is worth noting that maize cultivation in Spain predated the appearance of pellagra by many years, and that corn cultivation alone was not sufficient to cause pellagra. Rather, "*mal de la rosa*" was the result of the growing rural poverty of the 18th century, caused in part by the collapse of the Spanish wool industry, but also by the breakdown of traditional landlord paternalism towards their tenants as Spain increasingly adopted a market economy.

Soon after "*mal de la rosa*" appeared in northern Spain, a similar malady began to afflict northern Italy. Doctors there noted a new disease characterized by "seizures" (*agra* in Latin) of the skin (*pelle* in Italian). The victims of the strange ailment would become "repulsively disfigured," subject to a "diarrhea most resistant to all remedies," and finally "trouble in the head" including "mania," "sadness," "wakefulness," and "vertigo." Interestingly enough, it was noted that the disease tended to develop in the late winter or spring, only to fade away with the summer and autumn harvests. Italian doctors of the time, noting that pellagra symptoms resembled sunburn, speculated that pellagra was caused by the strengthening springtime sun. In actuality, pellagra appeared in spring largely because spring was the leanest time in the agricultural cycle, as last year's stored harvest was beginning to run out and next year's harvest was not yet ready for consumption. When summer finally arrived, it would bring with it a variety of fresh foods and a respite from pellagra symptoms until the following spring, when pellagra would inevitably reappear in vulnerable populations.

As in Spain, pellagra in Italy was a function of poverty as much as maize consumption. The peasants most vulnerable to pellagra in Italy were those laboring under the "*mezzadria*" labor system, in which peasants received a plot of land from a landowner in exchange for half of his yearly produce. Extractions on this scale meant that peasants had no capital with which to improve the land; indeed, they could barely feed themselves, and relied on a monotonous diet of cheap corn meal, called polenta, to survive the lean winter and spring months. Worse yet, while peasants in France and England could make use of village "commons" to graze a cow or two, no such tradition existed in Italy, denying peasants access to relatively niacin-rich milk and meat. The situation of Italian peasants was worsened even further by high taxes imposed by the Austrian empire, which ruled northern Italy for much of the 18th and 19th centuries, and by periodic outbreaks of malaria, which further weakened an already downtrodden peasant class.

At around the same time, a similar drama was playing out in the sun-soaked fields of southern France. Maize cultivation began slightly later in France than Italy, but by the late 1700s, the crop's high yields had won over farmers in the southern half of the country. Indeed, during his 1790 survey of French agriculture, British agronomist Arthur Young found that maize was the staple crop south of a line running from Bordeaux in the west to Lorraine on the Rhine River. Once again, however, maize cultivation only led to pellagra in the presence of poverty. The first French pellagrins, who came to the attention of doctors in the first half of the 19th century, were nearly all "poor and uncleanly who subsist on course food." French physicians were at first largely silent about the malady, perhaps because of misplaced national pride: Few Frenchmen wished to admit that a disease associated with poverty and human misery had appeared within the hexagon. This changed, however, after French doctor Théophile Roussel published *De la pellagre* in 1845. Roussel noted that the common linkage between French, Italian, and Spanish pellagra outbreaks was corn, particularly the moldy maize meal that sustained the poorest peasants through the hungry spring. To combat pellagra, Roussel argued, the French state must discourage the planting of maize in favor of potato cultivation and animal husbandry. He also advocated improving the living conditions of the rural poor to break their abject dependency on rapacious landlords. To France's credit, these suggestions were largely carried out, and pellagra all but disappeared from France by the first decades of the 20th century.

Unfortunately, Roussel's apparent success in combating French pellagra lent credence to his theories about the disease, which were a mixture of half-truths and unwarranted assumptions. Roussel's belief that mold in the maize, rather than the maize itself, was the causative factor in pellagra served to shift the blame for the disease onto the poor peasants, who brought the disease upon themselves by improperly storing the maize. Alternatively, his theories allowed authorities to defend local maize harvests while condemning inferior imports—a claim that served both the economic interests and the regional pride of officials in pellagra-prone locales. Worst of all, Roussel speculated that pellagrins were susceptible to the disease because of intrinsic genetic weakness, or "bad blood" as he called it. Later authors expanded upon this theme, and linked pellagra to "a bad formation of the skull," particularly elongated or shortened heads, "badly set ears, asymmetry of the face, and abnormalities of the genitalia." Such beliefs were probably comforting to middle-class physicians, who wanted to distance themselves genetically as well as socially from the pellagra-ridden poor, but hindered attempts to effectively counteract the disease.

Instances of pellagra were by no means limited to Europe; as maize spread throughout the Old World, pellagra followed close behind. British epidemiologist Fleming Sandwith discovered numerous cases of Pellagra while serving at the Kasr el Ainy Hospital in Cairo. Nearly all victims, Sandwith noted, came from Lower Egypt, where maize was a common food crop. Upper Egypt, where millet was the staple grain, was relatively pellagra free. As elsewhere, Egyptian pellagra was closely associated with poverty. Sandwith found that the pellagra rate in prosperous villages was only about 15 percent, while up to 62 percent inhabitants of poor villages showed symptoms of the disease. British doctors discovered pellagra elsewhere in Africa as well, particularly in South Africa, where pellagra was reported in maize-growing Bantu populations impoverished by the ravages of the Boer War. Elsewhere in Africa the incidence of pellagra was lower, in part because African farmers tended not to rely exclusively on maize, but rather treated it as a supplement to their regular crop repertoire. As we shall see below, this attitude towards maize is changing in modern Africa, with potentially destructive consequences.

It was in the United States, however, that pellagra exerted its greatest impact upon public health, especially in the post–Civil War period. Before the Civil War, the economy of the southern United States was closely tied to the fortunes of cotton, which was in great demand due to the rapid expansion of the British textile industry. Since picking cotton is exhausting, unpleasant work, the South relied on slaves of African descent to plant, harvest, and process the cotton crop. Slaves were an expensive investment—indeed, the cost of a slave was roughly equivalent to the price of a piece of factory equipment today—so southern landowners generally ensured their slaves were well fed. This attitude of self-interested paternalism, fueled by the vast profits generated by high cotton prices, helped to ensure that the slaves of the South, although miserably treated and denied even the most basic human rights, were at least generally pellagra-free. Indeed, the main outbreak of pellagra in the South before 1865 occurred among white inmates in the infamous Andersonville, Georgia prison camp, where pellagra, starvation, exposure, and other diseases combined to kill as many as 13,000 Northern prisoners during the Civil War.

Following the Civil War, the South underwent a number of transformations that fostered the development of pellagra. One unexpected side effect of the war was the entry of new cot-

Picking cotton on a plantation in the Southern United States, c. 1920. Southern farm workers were plagued by pellagra, especially sharecroppers.

ton-producing areas, especially India, Egypt, Turkey, and Brazil, into the international cotton trade, driving down international cotton prices. The opening of the Suez Canal after 1869 further depressed cotton prices by allowing Indian cotton to compete more competitively in European markets with the American-grown product. Far from discouraging American cotton production, however, lower cotton prices compelled the South to produce still more cotton, in hopes of recovering their pre-war prosperity. To produce this cotton in a post-slavery economy, the South relied on a new labor system: sharecropping. Poor laborers, both black and white, were given parcels of land by landlords in exchange for a portion of the cotton crop. As with Italy's similar "*mezzadria*" labor system, sharecropping led to crushing poverty on the part of the poor farmers, who lived from harvest to harvest and were plagued by perpetual debt. Harsh anti-vagrancy laws effectively tied these sharecroppers to the land, as did a brutal penal system that rivaled the horrors of slavery. Worst of all, the chief form of wealth in a sharecropper economy was now farmland rather than slave laborers. As a result, planters no longer had an economic incentive to look after the health of their work force. Taken together, these economic and social changes led to almost unfathomable levels of poverty — and as in Europe, poverty and pellagra went hand in hand.

Cotton cultivation favored the development of pellagra in other ways as well. Since the goal of every sharecropper was to produce as much cotton as possible for the market, sharecroppers had little time or acreage to spare for growing food crops. Indeed, contemporary witnesses to the South's poverty noted that sharecroppers often planted cotton up to the very doorways of their meager cottages. Unfortunately, since uninterrupted cotton cultivation drains nutrients from the soil, sharecroppers faced declining cotton production over time, and consequently growing poverty. What is more, since cotton was inedible sharecroppers were extremely vulnerable to market fluctuations; unlike planters of grain or vegetables, cotton growers could not feed themselves from their own harvest if market prices dropped. If sharecroppers did plant some food on their land, they almost always raised maize, which had the advantage of yielding a large volume of calories with relatively little effort, allowing sharecroppers to expend the lion's share of their labor on the cotton crop. Sharecroppers relied on local grocery stores for the rest of their food, which collectively became known as the "three M" diet: meat (mostly in the form of fat-rich, protein deficient pork fat), meal (cornmeal), and molasses. This diet became so pervasive that some poor southerners preferred it even when alternative foods, such as milk and dairy products, were available for sale. Unfortunately this monotonous food regimen, which was ubiquitous among the Southern poor until at least the Second World War, was a perfect recipe for pellagra.

Nor was pellagra limited to sharecroppers. After the Civil War, prominent politicians had promised to build an economically prosperous "New South," and central to this vision was the establishment of textile factories throughout Dixie. Unfortunately, these textile towns proved to be just as pellagrous, if not more so, than rural areas. Because factory wages in the South were quite low, factory workers were forced to subsist on the same "three M" diet that sustained sharecroppers. What is more, many factories obliged their workers to make their purchases at the "company store," which sold a limited inventory of food at inflated prices. Worse yet, in comparison to their rural kin, urban dwellers often had less access to alternate food sources that might have added variety to their diet. Some mill towns, for instance, banned the ownership of cattle within city limits for sanitary reasons, a decision that reduced the availability of pellagra-preventive dairy products to the industrial poor.

What is more, the South suffered from structural problems with its food production and distribution infrastructure. In some ways, the South lagged behind the rest of the country: The South Carolina mill town of Spartanburg, for example, had only one slaughterhouse and no cold storage facilities in 1914, severely limiting the resident population's access to fresh meat, especially in comparison to the cities of the American north. At the same time, the South adopted new food production technologies that actually exacerbated the pellagra problem. Soon after the turn of the century, southern millers adopted a new machine for grinding maize, the "Beall degerminator," which removed the fatty "germ" or embryo from the rest of the corn kernel. This new equipment was a boon for millers, since the degerminated flour resisted spoilage, and the maize germ could be processed to produce corn oil. However, the resulting corn flour was even more deficient in niacin than regular corn meal. Indeed, pellagra researcher Alfred Bollet has argued that the rapid appearance of pellagra in the South after 1900 was no coincidence, but rather was predictable consequence of the Beall degermination process further impoverishing an already nutritionally deficient diet.

As a result of these changes to the rural and urban landscapes of the American South, reports of pellagra became increasingly frequent as the 19th century gave way to the 20th. By 1909, the year of the first National Conference on Pellagra, approximately 1,000 cases of pellagra were occurring yearly in the United States. This is probably a low estimate. Many doctors did not know how to identify pellagra symptoms at this early stage, and the extremely poor who were most susceptible to the ailment were less likely to seek medical treatment. The number of pellagra patients climbed quickly afterwards, to 75,000 in 1915 and 100,000 per year over the course of the 1920s. Pellagra cases spiked in 1921 due to a dramatic fall in world cotton prices, and then again in 1927 following the disastrous floods along the Mississippi River discussed in section 6.3. Pellagra cases climbed once again from 1930 to 1931, when dry weather and reckless farming practices led to the "dust bowl" drought described in section 4.2. Ironically, pellagra cases actually declined during the Great Depression of the 1930s, in part because cotton prices fell so low that southern farmers gave up on cotton and instead grew more food for domestic use. The food relief distributed by the Federal Emergency Relief Administration to impoverished communities during the worst ravages of the Great Depression also helped to check pellagra by adding new foods to the Southern diet.

All told, pellagra afflicted approximately 4.5 million and killed about 150,000 Americans between 1906 and 1940. Above and beyond this human cost, pellagra represented an enormous drain on the Southern economy. Researchers in Mississippi estimated that pellagra cost the state $2,280,111 in 1914 alone, a sum equal to almost half a billion dollars in 2007 currency. Indeed, pellagra probably contributed significantly to the relative economic stagnation of the American South compared to the prosperous north in the first half of the 20th century.

Not surprisingly, given the demographic and economic damage pellagra inflicted on the South, American doctors worked feverishly from 1909 onward to discover a "cure." Nonetheless, progress was slow, in part because of widespread misunderstanding about the nature of pellagra. Many southern physicians and politicians were persuaded by Roussel's claim that pellagra was caused by moldy corn rather than nutritional defects in the maize itself, and as a consequence focused their attention on regulating supposedly inferior imported maize rather than diversifying the Southern diet. What is more, a bewildering array of alternate theories ascribed pellagra to anything from poor sanitation to cottonseed oil to blackbirds to the bite of the simulium fly. One popular theory was that "Italian leprosy," or pellagra, was an infectious disease brought to the United States by Italian immigrants, a belief that tells us more about American prejudices in the early 1900s than about the realities of pellagra transmission. As a result of the public panic over pellagra, some Italians suffering from pellagra symptoms were refused entry into the United States from public health reasons. Had Americans been less hostile to Italian immigrants, they might have realized that recently-arrived Italians, who avoided the "three M" cuisine of the South in favor of a more varied diet, were generally pellagra free despite their relative poverty.

Still other authorities believed that certain people were born with an innate vulnerability to pellagra. Woman were said to be particularly susceptible because of the "delicacy" of their nervous systems. In actual fact, women did get pellagra more often than men, but this was a reflection of their relative lack of earning capacity and the tendency of male household heads to eat the best foods at given meal rather than women's supposed physiological weakness. Other prominent scientists, especially those influenced by the American scientific racist movement of the early 20th century, argued that pellagra was an inheritable genetic deficiency, much like insanity, poverty, and low IQ scores, traits that were supposedly much more prevalent among the non Anglo-Saxon portion of the American population. The evidence for a genetic component to pellagra was fundamentally flawed; as historian Allan Chase has pointed out, pellagra ran in families due to shared experience rather than genetics, and to argue for pellagra genetic lineages was tantamount to claiming that French children spoke French because of their genes rather than learning it in the nursery. Nonetheless, since the genetic explanation resonated with the prevailing racial prejudices of the time, it remained persuasive to many American elites well into the 20th century.

Progress against pellagra was also hampered by the obstructionism of some Southern elites. Many Southerners tried to deny that pellagra, a disease associated with poverty and backwardness worldwide, could possibly exist in Dixie. Pellagra denial was particularly vehement in Florida, where it was feared that the scourge might deflate the Sunshine State's thriving tourist and real estate industries. Some southern politicians went so far as to blame their neighbors to the North for pellagra, especially the "Yankee" railroad companies who siphoned off the South's wealth through unjust railroad rates. In a fit of southern nationalism, other Dixie politicians went so far as to refuse offers of free food assistance from Northern business concerns, such as the American Meat Packers and the Borden Milk Company. The strongest backlash against pellagra studies, however, came from the maize industry and its political defenders, who worried that associating corn with pellagra would cripple the domestic and export earnings of one of America's most profitable agricultural products.

Due in part to this combination of pseudoscience, ingrained prejudices, economic motivations, and wounded regional pride, American scientists did not conclusively prove that pellagra was caused by diet until the mid–1930s. By 1938, however, scientists had identified a miracle cure for the disease: nicotinic acid, renamed "niacin" under pressure from the American baking industry, which did not want the public to associate nicotinic acid with the tobacco chemical nicotine. Nonetheless, despite a growing understanding of the disease and free distribution of niacin-rich baker's yeast throughout the South, pellagra rates remained high through the second half of the 1930s.

Ultimately, what stopped pellagra was not medical science so much as social change triggered largely by the experience of World War II. War meant the end of a decade of depression and the advent of an era of full employment, putting much more money into the pockets of formerly pellagra-ridden Southerners. Even more importantly, during World War II the American government intervened actively in food production and distribution, with salutary effects. During the war all food was rationed, which had the effect of democratizing the American diet, allowing poor southerners access to previously unavailable pellagra-preventive foods. What is more, under pressure from the American government, bakers began to "enrich" their bread with vitamins, putting back the niacin which was removed from the corn during the milling process. Since most bakers continued to enrich their products even after wartime government oversight of their industry ended, World War II proved to be a lasting turning point in the history of pellagra. Indeed pellagra is all but unknown in present day America, though it can occur as a side effect to other diseases, most notably alcoholism and anorexia.

The United States was one of the last "developed" nations to wipe out pellagra. As we have already seen, thanks to the theories of Roussel, France had halted its own pellagra epidemic by the turn of the century. Pellagra in Italy began to decline during the latter half of the 19th century due to the increasing importation of lower-priced cereal grains from Eastern Europe, which gradually began to replace maize in the diets of the poor. Pellagra incidents rose briefly around 1890, when government protectionist policies drove up the price of imported grains, but then fell again after 1896, when Italian industrial growth helped to soak up Italy's jobless laborers. At around the same time, Italian labor groups launched a series of strikes that eventually provided higher wages for both urban and rural workers, raising incomes and thus potential access to pellagra-preventive foods. The First World War also reduced Italian pellagra cases, in part by raising wages, and in part by providing increased employment opportunities to women and the young. Pellagra reappeared in Italy briefly during the Great Depression of the 1930s, but disappeared entirely soon afterwards. As for Spain, pellagra lingered there for years, and cases spiked dramatically due to the dislocation caused by the Spanish Civil War of the 1930s. Soon after, pellagra declined in Spain thanks to the same constellation of factors that reduced its incidence elsewhere.

Indeed, since the Second World War, pellagra has shifted almost entirely to the developing world. Pellagra was common among Bantus in South Africa through at least the 1950s and 1960s, thanks to a high rate of maize consumption and the grinding economic exploitation of the black population by the South Africa's apartheid regime. Pellagra also lingered on in Egypt during the same period, where it was closely associated with the most miserable peasant communities in maize-growing districts. Interestingly enough, pellagra has also been noted in recent years in areas where little maize is planted. In India, for example, large regions are dependent on "jowar" millet for their staple food, and since this particular millet subspecies is niacin deficient, those Indians unable to supplement their diet with meat, eggs, and milk often suffer pellagra. Overdependence on sorghum, another niacin deficient staple grain, has produced pellagra in both India and Africa. Pellagra also occurs during modern famines in every part of the world. Still, the incidence of pellagra worldwide is far lower today than it was before the Second World War.

Nevertheless, the increasing cultivation of maize as a food and industrial crop in the modern world raises the possibility that pellagra may become more prevalent in the 21st century. Maize is now the third most widely grown grain crop in the world, in large part because advances in modern science have allowed chemists to extract maize's constituent chemicals and then recombine them to form a bewildering array of useful compounds. Food researcher Michael Pollan estimates that a quarter of all supermarket items—from cake mixes to salad dressings to disposable diapers to trash bags—contain extracts from the maize plant. No other crop, with the possible exception of soybeans, is as well adapted to modern chemical and manufacturing technology. One unexpected disease outcome of this "industrial" corn in developed nations has been obesity, largely because high fructose corn syrup is commonly used as an inexpensive substitute for sugar. On the other hand, industrial corn poses little pellagra threat, since it is easy to add niacin to the finished product at the food processing factory. The popular snack food Twinkies, for example, contains artificial niacin manufactured from water, air, and petroleum.

More troubling is the increasing dependency on the world's poor on maize crops, particularly in modern Africa. For most of the modern period, maize has been a real boon to Africa; maize can grow in all but the wettest or driest parts of Africa, it produces far higher yields than traditional African crops, and it could be grown in cleared rainforest environments suitable to no other crops. Indeed, the rise of several African states, most notably the Asante kingdom of West Africa, has been linked to the adoption of maize cultivation. In recent years, however, maize has changed its role in Africa diets—maize used to be a valuable supplement to existing crops, but is now a indispensable staple crop in many parts of Africa. Two recent developments help to explain this phenomenon. In some parts of Africa, such as Ethiopia, population has risen to such a degree that no other crop can come close to fulfilling the caloric requirements of the nation's population. What is more, in African states that mainly grow export crops, such as cocoa or coffee, maize is grown as a supplemental food crop since it produces the most possible calories with the least amount of labor. As a result, according to food historian James McCann, a "tidal wave of maize ... engulfed Africa" in the last decade of the 20th century to the point that some African countries now count on maize for more than 50 percent of their calories. Indeed, 16 of the world's 23 most maize-dependent countries are in Africa. Since 95 percent of the African maize crop is eaten by people, rather than fed to animals or processed industrially, this maize dependency leaves modern Africans chronically vulnerable to pellagra.

Even more worrisome is the recent trend in global crop prices. At the end of the first decade of the 21st century, when this book was written, global food began to rise dramatically. For the most part, this price spike was a function of rising petroleum prices, since not only does petroleum play a crucial role in producing fertilizer, machine harvesting the crop, and transporting the crop to market, it also is a mutually substitutable commodity with food due to advances in biofuel technology. If this trend continues, high food prices will almost certainly force more and more of the world's poorest inhabitants to economize by reducing variety in their diets, consuming more cheap staple grains and less vegetables, milk, meat, and oil. The result will likely be a spike in vitamin deficiency diseases, including beriberi, scurvy, and of course pellagra.

Study Questions

1. Based on this section, to what degree would it be fair to label pellagra a "disease of agriculture?" See beginning of chapter for a definition of an "agricultural" disease.

2. To what degree is pellagra a "natural" disaster?

3. Based on this section, how did actual pellagra differ from "Construct pellagra" in the 19th and early 20th centuries? See beginning of chapter for a definition of "Construct" disease.

4. "Although pellagra is commonly seen as a nutritional disease, it is better understood as a social disease, endemic to failed or inequitable societies." After reading the text, to what degree to you agree with this statement?

Sources/Suggested Readings

Brandes, Stanley. "Maize as a Culinary Mystery." *Ethnology*, Vol. 31, No. 4 (Oct., 1992), pp. 331–336.

Chase, Allan. *The Legacy of Malthus: The Social Costs of the New Scientific Racism.* New York: Alfred A. Knopf, 1977.

Crosby, Alfred W. Jr. *The Columbian Exchange: Biological and Cultural Consequences of 1492.* Westport, CT: Praeger, 2003.

Etheridge, Elizabeth W. *The Butterfly Caste: A Social History of Pellagra in the South.* Westport, CT: Greenwood Publishing Company, 1972.

McCann, James. "Maize and Grace: History, Corn, and Africa's New Landscapes, 1500–1999." *Comparative Studies in Society and History*, Vol. 43, No. 2 (Apr., 2001), pp. 246–272.

Pollan, Michael. *The Omnivore's Dilemma: A Natural History of Four Meals.* New York: Penguin, 2006.

Roe, Daphne A. *A Plague of Corn: The Social History of Pellagra.* Ithaca, NY: Cornell University Press, 1973.

Whittaker, Elizabeth D. "Bread and Work: Pellagra and Economic Transformation in Turn-of-the-Century Italy." *Anthropological Quarterly*, Vol. 65, No. 2 (Apr., 1992), pp. 80–90.

8.2: Disease of Imperialism: Malaria

Malaria is one of mankind's oldest ailments, and is arguably the disease that has left the deepest imprint on human history. This is not because malaria is a particularly deadly disease; indeed the direct death rate from even the most virulent strain of malaria, *Plasmodium falciparum*, rarely exceeds one in ten. Rather, malaria exerts its greatest impact as an endemic disease: shortening the human life span, rendering fertile land uninhabitable, reducing worker productivity, and otherwise debilitating any society living within the breeding zone of malaria mosquitoes. Worse yet, malaria infections tend to initiate a feedback loop: The bodily weakness and social dislocation produced by malaria leads to poverty, which tends to breed poor quality housing and poor nutrition, and this in turn makes societies more susceptible to malaria. Despite its importance as a public health threat in the tropical world, malaria is currently not seen as a major problem by most modern industrial states, and thus has received little attention either from either western governments or, perhaps more importantly, from western pharmaceutical companies. As we shall see in this chapter, however, global warming's projected ability to increase both global poverty and global temperatures may force the western world to pay greater attention to the dire threat posed by the modern malaria plague.

The disease malaria is caused by single-celled parasites called plasmodia found in stomachs of female *Anopheles* mosquitos. The life cycle of malaria plasmodia is complex. After sexually combining within a mosquito's stomach, malaria plasmodia create "sporozoites," specialized plasmodia cells which infiltrate the mosquito's salivary glands. When the mosquito bites a human victim, the sporozoites are injected into the host's bloodstream. Eventually they find their way into liver cells, where they multiply rapidly. Once a critical mass is reached, the infected liver cells burst simultaneously, releasing a wave of "merozoites"—immature plasmodia cells—into the bloodstream. When this occurs the human immune system responds by raising the body temperature to up to 106 degrees Fahrenheit (41.4 degrees Celsius) in an attempt to kill the invading plasmodium, giving rise to the sudden cycles of fever that are characteristic of malaria infection. The human body also tries to kill the merozoites by attacking them with white blood cells, which are specialized cells designed to engulf invading microbes. The merozoites avoid this defensive mechanism by infiltrating the body's red blood cells, where they feed and multiply asexually. Since these red blood cells have the task of carrying oxygen throughout the human body, the depredations of the malaria plasmodia can lead to anemia (low red blood cell counts) and consequent shortness of breath, weakness, and fatigue.

The body has one more line of defense against malaria plasmodia: the spleen, which filters defective or infected red blood cells from the blood stream. Unfortunately, the malaria plasmodium has evolved a tactic against this defensive mechanism as well. Malaria parasites force infected red blood cells to put out sticky protein strands, making the infected cells more likely to adhere to blood vessel walls rather than circulate throughout the body. This behavior by malaria parasites is particularly dangerous, because if "sticky" red blood cells congregate in the brain, the resulting interruption in blood flow can lead to a coma or even death, especially in young victims. Children who avoid death from this condition, called cerebral malaria, often suffer lifelong brain damage, mental retardation, or even epilepsy. Thankfully, cerebral malaria normally only develops during infections by *Plasmodium falciparum*, malaria's most virulent strain.

Despite the best efforts of the human immune system, malaria tends to linger in the human body for months or even years, depending on the strain. Once established, the plasmodia

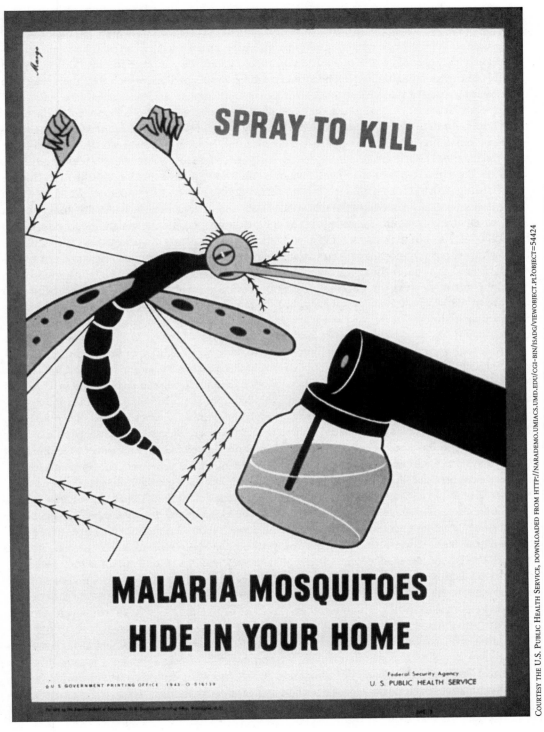

During World War II, it was estimated that malaria incapacitated as many as 30 American soldiers for every 1 killed on the battlefield, so the U.S. military campaigned vigorously to inform its servicemen about the dangers posed by malaria.

undergo transformations designed to spread the infection to yet more hosts. Some of the malaria merozoites in the bloodstream transform into gametocytes, plasmodia specialized for sexual reproduction. When the next *Anopheles* mosquito bites an infected victim, some of these gametocytes are transported to the mosquito's stomach, where they engage in plasmodial sex and multiply enormously. This mating eventually produces sporozoites, which find their way into the salivary glands of the mosquito, beginning the cycle again.

It is important to note that the life cycle of malaria described above is mostly characteristic of *Plasmodium falciparum* malaria, a heat-loving malaria strain which flourishes in the tropics where mosquito populations can thrive year-round. Indeed, it is believed that the virulence of *P. falciparum* is an indirect consequence of its environment: Since mosquitoes breed constantly in the tropics, *P. falciparum* has developed the ability to multiply ferociously in its human host, trading short-term virulence for long-term staying power. In temperate climates, where mosquitoes feed and breed seasonally, malaria strains have traded lethality for longevity in order to ensure that a human reservoir for the infection persists even if the host mosquitoes have died off. Indeed, the common malaria strain *P. vivax* implants "hypnospores" in the human liver, which can burst months or years after the initial infection and begin a new cycle of recurrent fever and anemia. If the relapsing malaria victim is then bitten by an *Anopheles* mosquito, if the mosquito survives the 10–21 day gestation period needed for the malaria sporozoites to migrate to the mosquito salivary glands, and if the mosquito then goes on to bite further victims, a single human carrier of malaria hypnospores can be the source of a new malaria epidemic.

Although *P. vivax, P. falciparum,* and other malaria strains differ in both range and virility, they have a similar impact on human demographic patterns. Populations where malaria is endemic suffer high rates of child mortality, since children lack resistance to the disease. Adults are more likely to survive malaria infections, in part because they likely contracted the disease as children and thus enjoy some immunity, though this immunity does tend to fade over time. The exception to this rule is pregnant women, who are more to vulnerable to malaria since their immune systems have been partially shut off during pregnancy in order to prevent the mother's immune system from treating the fetus as an alien organism. To save itself, the body of a malarial mother aborts the fetus in as many as 50 percent of cases, greatly reducing a malarial society's fertility. What is more, children who are born to malarial mothers tend to have a low growth rate and, as a consequence, weakened immune systems, greatly reducing their life expectancy. Worst of all, since malaria itself dampens the immune system, malarial adults are more likely to die of other infections, especially gastrointestinal diseases, typhoid, tuberculosis, cholera, and HIV/AIDS. Medical scholars estimate that malaria plays a role in three or four times the number of deaths than are directly attributed to malaria in a given society. Indeed, in some areas where malaria was eradicated during the 20th century, the overall death rate dropped by 50 percent — an astoundingly high number, given the unlikelihood of death from even the most virulent "pure" malaria infection.

Vulnerability to malaria differs by region as well as by age group. Since malaria plasmodia do better in hot climates— though this differs somewhat by species— malaria is more likely in torrid tropical zones than in cooler temperate zones, and more common in hot lowlands than in chill highlands. Even minor elevations can serve as effective barriers to malaria, since *Anopheles* mosquitoes are poor flyers and have trouble traveling uphill. Indeed, hills are doubly safe from malaria, since they tend to be breezier than lowland areas, and *Anopheles* mosquitoes have trouble flying in windy conditions. The degree of malaria in any given community is also intimately tied to the region's hydrology, since all *Anopheles* mosquitoes lay their eggs in still or slow-moving water. As a result, malaria is most commonly associated with wetlands, where pools of stagnant water offer ideal breeding conditions. In fact, the term "malaria" is derived from an Italian phrase meaning "bad air," as the disease was initially thought to be caused by the foul stenches emitted by rotting plant matter in swamps.

Depending on the species of *Anopheles* mosquito, however, malaria can thrive even in areas that are normally quite dry. Some of the most deadly malaria outbreaks, for example, have occurred in the Indian province of Punjab, which normally gets little rain. As a result, in normal years malaria is "hypoendemic" in the Punjab: It infects barely enough victims to retain a toehold in the human population. In 1929, however, exceptionally heavy rains flooded the Punjab, creating ideal breeding opportunities for *Anopheles* mosquitoes. However, since few Punjabis had acquired the disease as children and since in any case resistance to malaria fades over time unless the individual is continuously exposed, the death toll was atrocious: Overall 40,000 Punjabis lost their lives. What is more, malaria can penetrate dry areas if given a little help by man. Malaria mosquitoes can thrive in agricultural irrigation canals, roadside drainage ditches, water retention ponds, and other bodies of water that are intentionally or unintentionally created in the course of "developing" dry landscapes.

Although heat and moisture are the most obvious factors determining whether a given region is malarious or not, the types and characteristics of local mosquito populations can play an important role as well. Only *Anopheles* mosquitos can host the malaria plasmodia, and some *Anopheles* sub-species prefer biting animals over humans. In regions where such mosquitoes thrive, malaria epidemics may only start when most domesticated or wild animals of an area have been wiped out. Alternatively, endemic malaria may peter off in societies which adopt large numbers of farm animals, since local mosquitoes may switch from human to animal blood. In other cases, *Anopheles* mosquitoes may prefer to live in specific microenvironments, such as the treetop canopy of forests, and will only become a major problem for humankind if these forests are cleared for agriculture.

Finally, the degree of malaria in a given region is strongly linked with the presence, or absence, of competing non-malarial mosquitoes in the ecosystem. If malaria-carrying mosquitoes are edged out of a given environment by more competitive non-malarial mosquitoes, malaria cases in a given region may decline or disappear entirely. The sudden intrusion of a previously unknown species of *Anopheles* mosquito into virgin territory, on the other hand, can trigger sudden and disastrous malaria epidemics. Case in point was the 1942 invasion of Egypt by the *Anopheles gambiae* mosquito, a species that feeds almost exclusively on human beings. By 1943, these exotic invaders had colonized over 4,000 square kilometers of the Nile River Valley and had transmitted to malaria to over 750,000 people; the death rate is unknown, but may have topped 25,000 victims. It took 4,600 workers six months to finally evict this alien species from Egyptian soil.

As might be expected, given the various biological, demographic, and geographical factors that influence any given malaria outbreak, malaria has presented a constantly changing face throughout human history. Disease researchers now believe that mankind picked up malaria very early in its history, perhaps from primate species in Southeast Asia, but more likely in Africa. Indeed, it is now widely accepted that the most virulent malaria strain, *P. falciparum*, originated in Africa. During mankind's hunter-gatherer stage, malaria played relatively little role in human affairs, since population levels were too low for malaria to reach endemic status. However, man's relationship to malaria changed markedly after the adoption of agriculture, which altered the ecosystem in ways that favored the proliferation of malaria. Forests were cut down throughout the tropical world, forcing mosquitoes that formerly inhabited the forest into human homes. Gouged by the plow and by erosion, agricultural land was far more likely than forest land to develop the small puddles of still water where mosquitoes like to breed. Humans further fostered malaria by building agricultural canals, paddies, and other "improvements" that in fact provided ideal mosquito habitats. What is more, agriculture allowed human numbers to expand dramatically, and since each new human added to the population is a potential host for the malaria plasmodia, malaria soon assumed endemic status in most human agricultural societies where *Anopheles* mosquitoes thrived. Indeed, the first written texts produced by human beings, the cuneiform tablets of the Sumerian civilization, describe fevers that closely match modern clinical descriptions of malaria as early as the 4th millennium B.C.

As agriculture spread, so did malaria. The first record of malaria in Chinese civilization dates to approximately 2,700 B.C., but at this point China's struggle with malaria had barely begun; malaria mosquitoes breed relatively poorly in cold, dry northern China, but quite well in semitropical southern China, an area that would increasingly become China's economic and population center over time. Indeed, environmental historian William McNeill believes that Chinese settlement of the Yangtze River Valley was delayed until nearly the 3rd century A.D. by malaria and other diseases present in warm, humid Southern China. In India, the first clear references to malaria appear in Vedic texts dated to approximately 1,600 B.C., and there are suggestive references to malaria in the Hebrew Bible — for instance, some scholars believe that the "Angel of Death" that ravaged the Assyrian army invading Judah in 701 B.C. might well have been malaria.

Malaria also plagued nearby Greek civilization, which probably picked up the plasmodia from trade with Asia and Africa. The prevalence of malaria in Greek civilization is attested to by the frequency of the "thalassemia" trait in the modern Mediterranean gene pool. Like the sickle-cell gene, this recessive condition creates blood abnormalities that render its carriers more vulnerable to anemia. On the other hand, it confers some advantage to people living in malarial areas, since the same blood cell abnormalities make it harder for malaria plasmodia to survive in the human body. In any case, malaria played an important role in Greek history, most notably in the defeat of Athenian forces on the island of Sicily in 413 B.C. — a disastrous setback that led to the unraveling of the Athenian empire. Some historians have gone so far as to claim that malaria, which was well established in Greece by the 4th century B.C., contributed substantially to the decline of Greek civilization. However, this argument seems unconvincing. Although malaria no doubt brought considerable misery to Greece, "decline" must be judged in reference to other civilizations, and the evidence suggests that both Macedonia and Rome, which conquered the Greeks in the 4th century B.C. and the 2nd century B.C. respectively, suffered from similar levels of malaria.

Indeed, hundreds of years before the Roman Empire conquered Greece, malaria plasmodia had already invaded Italy, perhaps in the bodies of the Greek settlers who migrated to southern Italy and Sicily in the 8th century B.C.. Malaria thrived in Italy; ample rainfall favored mosquito proliferation, and the temperatures were warm enough to support both *P. vivax* and *P. falciparum*, which were known to the Romans as "spring fever" and "harvest fever" respectively. What is more, historians now believe that Italy of two thousand years ago was both wetter and hotter than it is today due to natural cycles of climate change, creating perfect conditions for both malaria plasmodia and their mosquito hosts.

It is important to note that malaria by no means exerted a uniformly negative influence on Roman history; indeed, some scholars believe that malaria helped to protect Rome from invaders from the north, such as the Volci tribe, during the early, vulnerable years of Roman history. However, over time, the Romans inadvertently altered the environment of Italy in ways that favored malaria. By the time of the Roman Empire, Italy was suffering considerable deforestation, leading in turn to high levels of soil erosion. As a result, Italy's rivers, which had formerly been deep and fast moving, became increasingly shallow and languid, greatly increasing their suitability as mosquito breeding sites. Italy's sediment-choked rivers were also flooded frequently, and malaria mosquitoes tended to thrive in the puddles left behind by retreating floodwaters. What is more, sediment washed downstream choked Italy's tidal salt marshes and transformed them brackish swamps, which were better suited than moving salt water to mosquito proliferation. The Romans worsened this problem further by studding their coasts with artificial fish ponds, which supplied fish for the dinner tables of the Roman aristocrats. Unfortunately, the still and brackish water of these ponds provided ideal havens for *Anopheles* mosquitoes. Furthermore, the replacement of forests with agricultural lands in Italy had the same effect that it had elsewhere in the world: It exacerbated malaria by creating more depressions in the soil that could be colonized by mosquitoes following seasonal rains.

The Romans unintentionally fostered malaria within Italy in other ways as well. Rome is rightfully famous for its road building program, but Rome's storied roads facilitated the spread of malaria as well as people, as mosquitoes thrived in roadside drainage ditches and in quarries left behind in the construction process. Rome's large-scale agricultural schemes worsened malaria as well by creating pools of stagnant or slow-moving water, perfect nurseries for mosquitoes. Finally, the Roman practice of setting aside land for household gardens, even within large cities like Rome itself, further contributed to malaria by providing nighttime resting spots for *Anopheles* mosquitoes.

Admittedly, the Romans did take some positive steps to mitigate the risk of malaria. Although the Romans had no idea that mosquito bites caused malaria, they did observe that people who slept above the ground were less susceptible to the illness, so Roman houses were often constructed with bedrooms on the second floor or higher. What is more, many Roman house compounds were built around a central courtyard, with few doors or windows facing outwards. This made it more difficult for mosquitoes to enter Roman dwellings, though admittedly the safety of these houses was compromised by the Roman habit of building a rain catch basin, called an *impluvium*, within the central courtyard. Romans also tended to build their houses upon hills, on the premise that high and breezy places had healthier air — such locations, of course, also provided some protection against *Anopheles* mosquitoes. It is important to note that these precautions against malaria were mainly available to the middle and upper classes. The Roman poor tended to have inferior housing, especially the rural population, whose crude thatch huts offered little protection against the mosquitoes that carried malaria.

Given the prevalence of malaria in ancient Italy, it comes as no surprise that malaria exerted a strong influence on Roman history. Some historians believe that malaria led to the gradual decline of the Roman smallholding farmer class, which dwindled as the land became progressively more malarious over time. As a result, Roman smallholders were increasingly replaced by slaves, especially on the most fertile land, which tended to be the same flat coastal land that was most subject to malaria. Since mortality among these slaves was high, demand for slaves was high for well, which helps to explain Rome's expansionist tendencies. At the same time, the displacement of smallholding farmers by large slave-worked farms meant that Rome was increasingly forced to draft the landless poor into its armies, and this in turn strengthened the political power of Rome's successful generals, who could win the loyalty of their impoverished soldiers with promises of land or other financial rewards. As a result, malaria probably helps to explain the overthrow of the Roman Republic by Julius Caesar and his successors and the subsequent establishment of the Roman Empire. Perhaps most importantly of all, since malaria depresses the human immune system, it likely worsened the damage inflicted by the Asian diseases that were brought to Rome via the Indian Ocean and Silk Road trade routes after c. A.D. 200. In this way, malaria probably hastened the collapse of the Roman Empire.

Even after the fall of the Roman Empire, however, malaria continued to play important role in European history. In part, this is because malaria had become endemic throughout Europe, even as far north as England, where *P. vivax* severely shortened the life expectancy of people dwelling in marshy regions. Perhaps even more importantly, even after the fall of the Roman Empire, the city of Rome retained its status as the religious and cultural center of Europe, and as a result attracted hundreds or thousands of visitors a year. Unfortunately, Rome and the surrounding areas also retained its status as a breeding ground for mosquitoes that carried the deadly *P. falciparum* strain of malaria. As a consequence, through much of European history, Rome played the role of the legendary will-o'-the-wisp, a shining light that lured nighttime travelers into deadly marshes. Attracted by the reflection of ancient glory, Rome received a constant flow of pilgrims, scholars, political figures, and other social elites from throughout Europe, and every year a certain portion of these illustrious visitors were slain by *P. falciparum*. In 1623, for instance, malaria infected nearly every cardinal who visited Rome for the election of a new pope, and six cardinals succumbed to the infection, along many of their scribes, advisors, and other attendants. Foreign visitors who survived would take *P. falciparum* with them in their blood, perhaps triggering new malaria epidemics when they returned home.

Indeed, given the importance of "Roman Fever" in European history, it is tempting to speculate about possible links between malaria, the Protestant Reformation, and the growing dominance of the Northern states over European affairs. As a result of the Protestant Reformation, which was sparked by German monk Martin Luther's 1517 protest against Church doctrine, much of northern Europe effectively declared religious independence from the Rome-based Catholic Church. One of Luther's complaints is that the Catholic Church was a parasite on Northern Europe, exacting heavy tithes and peddling instant sin forgiveness to fund an ambitious building program in Rome. But what about the demographic drain that Rome exerted, the deaths of northern notables who were drawn to the Eternal City, only to be ensnared by *P. falciparum*'s fatal trap? Does Northern Europe's break with Rome, and with it *P. falciparum*, help to explain why the center of gravity in Europe gradually shifted northwards—to Holland, England, and later Germany—in the years after 1517? Perhaps, though this thesis remains unproven.

One fact that is certain is that malaria played an important role in the European colonization of the Americas. Europeans probably carried *P. vivax* and other malaria strains in their own bloodstreams, and since many species of *Anopheles* mosquitoes are native to the New World, it was not long before epidemic malaria spread to the Americas. Thanks in part to *P. vivax*, the Amerindian population of the Americas fell by as much as 95 percent in the 150 years following Columbus' voyage to the Americas. The resulting labor shortage obliged Europeans to tap into the slave markets of Africa, and in the process, the more virulent *P. falciparum* strain of malaria reached the Americas, probably carried over the Atlantic in the blood of African slaves.

These strains of malaria, combined with other endemic diseases brought by Europeans, had a profound impact in shaping the demographics of the modern Americas. European diseases ravaged the population of temperate zones in the Americas, such as the future United States and Argentina, allowing land-hungry colonists of European descent to progressively displace the surviving Amerindian population. In tropical areas, most notably Brazil and the Caribbean, these European infections were augmented by *P. falciparum* malaria and yellow fever, rendering these zones fatal to Amerindians and dangerous even for Europeans. Indeed, Europeans were extremely lucky that native American *Anopheles* mosquitoes were less efficient transmitters of *P. falciparum* to humans than the *Anopheles* of Africa, or else the tropical portions of the Americas, like Africa during that time period, might have become all but uninhabitable for people of European descent. However, since both *P. falciparum* malaria and yellow fever were common childhood diseases in Africa, Africans slaves proved to be relatively resilient to these infections. What is more, many Africans carried the sickle-cell trait in their genes, giving them further resistance to New World malaria outbreaks. Perhaps most importantly, 95 percent of sub–Saharan Africans carry the gene for the "negative Duffy antigen," which gives its bearer total immunity to *P. vivax* malaria. Indeed, European colonizers cynically twisted Africa's resistance to malaria into a justification of the institution of slavery. Tropical diseases like malaria and yellow fever, it was thought, were diseases of savage climates, and the fact that Africans could withstand these illnesses proved that they were "lower animals" with an inherently savage nature. Thus the very fact that slaves survived in climates where whites could not was spun into a justification for their enslavement.

The varying resistance by Indians, Africans, and Europeans to malaria and other tropical diseases has left a strong impact on the map of Africa up to and including the present day. Due to first-generation African resistance to tropical infections, lowland tropical America soon came to be inhabited disproportionately by people of African descent, with a smaller number of mixed race settlers and an even smaller ruling elite of whites. Large numbers of Amerindians managed to survive only in highland areas like Mexico and Peru which boasted sufficient population to support malaria as an endemic infection and which were too high and cold to host epidemics of yellow fever and *P. falciparum* malaria. Whites, in turn, tended to thrive in temperate America, most especially North America and Argentina, where the climate suited both the crops and the diseases that Europeans brought over from Europe.

Malaria also influenced New World history by inhibiting the economic development of potentially resource-rich areas of the Americas. Case in point is the Amazon River Basin, which became intensely malarial soon after the European colonization of Brazil. Between 1890 and 1910, as many as a million Brazilians migrated into the Amazon region, some attracted by high prices world prices of rubber, others displaced from their homes in the northeastern provinces of Brazil by a series of horrific El Niño–induced droughts which struck between 1888 and 1902. These internal migrants came to the Amazon in search of opportunity, but discovered *P. falciparum* instead. Indeed, malaria plasmodia found perfect conditions in which to thrive. The Amazon Basin was the right temperature for *P. falciparum*, it hosted large numbers of *Anopheles* mosquitoes, and the river's seasonal floods and many stagnant pools provided year-round mosquito breeding opportunities. What is more, the Amazon Basin was inundated with a dense population of heavily exploited immigrants who could barely afford enough food to survive, who lived in substandard housing, and who had no previous exposure to *P. falciparum* infection. It was a perfect storm of circumstances for the proliferation of malaria, and indeed, the *P. falciparum* was discovered in the blood of approximately 75 percent of the test samples from the migrant workforce. Although statistics are scanty in this frontier zone, the death toll must have been atrocious, perhaps topping 50,000 for malaria alone, and perhaps four times that number if we include deaths to other diseases—like pneumonia—that were worsened by chronic malaria. Small wonder, then, that contemporary Brazilian researchers claimed that "every kilo of rubber extracted [from the Amazon] represented one human death."

Brazil was far from the only part of the world during this period where "development" was associated with higher rates of malaria. During the mid–19th century, for example, the British managed to transform the Indian Ocean island of Mauritius from an exotic island paradise to a malarial hellhole in the name of economic progress. Before the British arrived, there were no malaria plasmodia in Mauritius. Neither were there any *Anopheles* mosquitoes, largely because the closest *Anopheles* species to Mauritius—the African mosquitoes *Anopheles gambiae* and *Anopheles funestus*—preferred high human population densities and lots of open, sun-drenched land, qualities that the heavily forested and lightly inhabited island of Mauritius originally lacked. Soon after the British seized Mauritius from the French, however, they set out to transform the island into a vast sugar plantation, worked by indentured servants recruited from India. These workers brought various strains of malaria in their bloodstreams or in the form of hypnospores, but without a mosquito vector to transmit the plasmodia from person to person, no malaria outbreaks were possible.

In the mid–1860s, however, human "development" reached a crucial level in terms of both population density and deforestation, and *Anopheles* mosquitoes managed to colonize Mauritius. The result was an explosion of malaria mortality: 32,000 died in up to 1867 and another 10,000 fell to malaria in 1868 alone. The death toll was worsened by the mixed nature of the Indian work force: Imported Indian workers had resistance only to the strains of malaria found in the areas in India where they themselves had grown up, so when they swapped malaria strains their previous exposure to different strains of the plasmodia offered little protection. The death toll slackened considerably after 1868, not because malaria had vanished, but because nearly every possible victim on the island had been infected and the survivors enjoyed some immunity. Thereafter malaria assumed the status of an endemic disease in Mauritius, and killed mainly children and new Indian recruits to the island colony.

If things were bad in Mauritius, they were far worse in British controlled India, where malaria killed between 1 million and 5.5 million a year from 1881 to 1939. The British claimed that epidemic malaria in India was a product of the "ignorance and even hostility of the masses of [Indian] people" toward proper sanitary habits, but this was just blaming the victim; in actual fact, the spike in Indian malaria during these years was largely a consequence of ill-planned British agricultural development schemes. By 1929, the British had irrigated 12 percent of the country's agricultural land by means of 75,000 miles of main and branch canals, mainly to grow cotton for the export market. These canals proved wildly profitable for Britain; according to disease historian Sheldon Watts, the average yearly return on investments in these canals was nearly 10.5 percent. Consequently the British elites of the day used their considerable influence to support the construction and maintenance of these agricultural works, even in the face of protest over the health hazard they represented.

Unfortunately, the epidemiological cost of these irrigation works was staggering. Built largely by inexperienced engineers who knew little about Indian climatic conditions, and constructed with an eye toward getting maximum financial return from minimal investment, these agricultural works were not well designed for drainage and thus provided many breeding opportunities for *Anopheles* mosquitoes. What is more, in order to get the necessary manual labor to build the canals and cultivate the irrigated land, the British organized mass internal migrations of workers within India. In the process, the British took people out of areas where certain malaria strains were endemic and mixed them with people from regions with different endemic strains. The result was predictable: One group's endemic become another group's epidemic, and the death toll skyrocketed. Thanks to the yearly harvest of epidemic malaria that the British cultivated in India, in conjunction with the horrific El Niño famines that ravaged the country at the turn of the century, Indian life expectancy actually dropped by two years from 1891 to 1911. It is important to note, incidentally, that the British were far from the only colonial powers to spread malaria under the banner of empire. The French, for example, greatly worsened malaria in Algeria by introducing rice farming, which exponentially multiplied the potential breeding spots for Algeria's native *Anopheles* mosquitoes.

European imperial powers worsened malaria in their colonies in other ways as well. Forest clearance for export agriculture predictably created more breeding opportunities for *Anopheles* mosquitoes. The European penchant for forcing nomadic herders to settle down in permanent villages, so as to better control and tax them, served to create concentrated populations susceptible to malarial infection. Europeans further increased colonial population density by providing health care innovations, such as antiseptics, which served to increase Africa and Asian populations. At the same time, massive European extractions of money and resources led to widespread colonial malnourishment, which in turn led to further vulnerability to malaria. Indeed, the British Colonial Department conducted a study of native malnutrition in 1936 which came to the conclusion that Europe's insistence on growing crops for exports led to "inadequate production of food crops, low wages, and poor yields," rendering colonial populations so susceptible to disease that the commissioners recommended tackling poverty rather than proving band-aid programs directed towards particular illnesses. Unfortunately, under the pressure of European economic interests, the findings of this commission where sanitized and whitewashed before being released to the general public.

This phenomenal death toll in Europe's colonies due to malaria is all the more unforgivable given the fact that, by the turn of the 20th century, scientists had identified both the mosquito mechanism of malarial infection and a possible cure: quinine, an anti-fever drug derived from the bark of the South American cinchona tree. Indeed, doctors working for the Catholic Church had discovered the beneficial properties of quinine as early as the 1630s, shortly after the highly malarial papal conclave in 1623 that had claimed the lives of six cardinals. The discovery of quinine was a monumental medical advance, but in the short term run its benefit was tempered by the fact that the quantity of quinine in the bark of a given cinchona tree was highly variable. As a result, good quality quinine did not become available in large qualities until the mid–1800s, when the quinine-rich cinchona subspecies *ledgeriana* was identified and cultivated commercially.

Unfortunately, the discovery of quinine had the paradoxical effect of increasing rather than reducing human misery, especially for Europe's imperial subjects. Europeans made little effort to use quinine to control malaria within their imperial holdings, partly because of the cost, but also due to the Malthusian belief that taming malaria would only encourage unsupportable population growth. Rather, Europeans used quinine to bring yet more territory under their control. Before the mid–1800s, tropical fevers like malaria and yellow fever rendered most of Africa extremely unhealthy for Europeans, and as a consequence European presence was mostly limited to North Africa and Africa's temperate south. The 19th-century sailor's rhyme—*"the Bight of Benin. The Bight of Benin. Few go out but many go in"*—amply expresses Europe's fear of the diseases of tropical sub–Saharan Africa. With the advent of quinine, however, it became far safer for Europeans to travel to Africa, first as traders, explorers, and missionaries, and later as conquerors. Indeed, in the years between 1880 and 1914, a veritable "scramble for Africa" took place, during which Africa was carved up between the European Imperial powers. By 1914, only the Christian kingdom of Ethiopia—an imperial state itself—managed to survive the European onslaught.

Despite the West's success in taming malaria in Africa—at least among the soldiers, missionaries, and colonists of the imperial powers—malaria remained a chronic problem in the heartland of many imperialist countries well into the 20th century. Europe suffered from malaria infections until at least mid-century, especially in the warmer states of Southern Europe, which suffered from both *P. vivax* and heat-loving *P. falciparum*. What is more, malaria remained a recurrent problem within the United States well into the 20th century. Although most Americans think of malaria as a disease of the distant tropics, if they think of it at all, malaria is deeply imbedded into U.S. history. Early European settlers brought *P. vivax* plasmodia in their bloodstreams, and African slaves contributed *P. falciparum*. These strains of malaria were soon picked up by North American *Anopheles* mosquitoes, particularly *A. quadrimaculatus*, which liked to invade houses at night. According to disease historian Margaret Humphreys, malaria in the early United States followed a distinctive bell curve pattern. At first, after a virgin tract of land was settled, malaria cases would be fairly rare, as low population density precluded a widespread epidemic. However, as farmsteads multiplied human populations would reach a critical threshold that allowed uninterrupted cycles of malaria transmission between people and mosquito, and a protracted malaria epidemic would set in. What is more, as population increased, humans would increasingly alter the environment in ways that facilitated mosquito breeding, for instance by building mill ponds, quarry pits, and roadside drainage ditches. Once a district reached urban status, however, malaria cases would decline, since the high tax base of urban areas allowed for improvements— such as swampland drainage — that inhibited the breeding of *Anopheles* mosquitoes.

Malaria was a national scourge of the United States; indeed, *P. vivax* malaria extended even into Canada, and *P. falciparum* could penetrate as far north as Kentucky and Tennessee. Nonetheless, some areas were more vulnerable than others, and perhaps nowhere in America was more malarial than the cotton-growing districts of the South. Indeed, the post Civil War institution of sharecropping provided a perfect environment for malaria plasmodia. In these regions, most sharecroppers lived in atrocious housing that provided little defense against nightly invasions by mosquitoes, and since they tended to rent rather than own their housing, they had no incentive for improvement. Nor did their planter landlords, who found it easier to replace sick workers than to keep their croppers healthy. For the most part, these inadequate cottages were relegated to marginal, swampy land unsuitable for cotton farming, though quite suitable for the breeding of *Anopheles* mosquitoes. What is more, since cotton is a labor intensive crop, sharecroppers occupied cotton country in sufficient density to sustain chains of malaria infection. As discussed in section 8.1, sharecroppers often suffered from pellagra infection, which left them both biologically and economically vulnerable to malaria. Indeed, cotton-growing sharecroppers were predisposed to malaria by sheer poverty, which ensured that croppers were poorly clothed and malnourished. Interestingly, this poverty was intensified by malaria itself. Unfortunately for cotton farmers, the peak times for *P. vivax* and *P. falciparum* malaria corresponded with the cotton planting season and harvest season respectively, weakening the labor force at the most crucial moments in the agricultural cycle.

Not surprisingly, malaria in the United States disappeared at the same time as sharecropping, the institution that sustained it. During the late 1930s, the U.S. government pushed agricultural policies that favored the increased mechanization of agriculture, and as a result the institution of sharecropping declined precipitously. As sharecroppers migrated to the cities, Margaret Humphreys argues, rural populations declined to the point that they could no longer sustain the constant human/mosquito infection chains required to perpetuate malaria in a given region. This process was helped along by increasing use of insecticides, especially DDT, as well as more systematic use of quinine and related drugs to clean malaria plasmodia from the bloodstreams of infected individuals. As a result, the United States became essentially malaria free by the early 1940s.

Emboldened by these successes, Europeans and Americans now began to dream about wiping out malaria for good. In the heady days of the mid–20th century, in fact, this goal increasingly seemed attainable. Quinine was found to be effective in not just treating malaria fevers, but in killing off the malaria parasites itself. What is more, Europeans were enjoying increasing success in land drainage schemes, most notably in Italy, where Italian dictator Benito Mussolini managed to tame malaria in the Pontine Marshes, a notoriously unhealthy marshland south of Rome. In fact, during World War II, the Germans deliberately destroyed the pumps and canals that drained the Pontine Marshes in hopes that resurgent malaria would slow the American advance up the Italian peninsula, an act that disease historian Frank M. Snowden calls "the only known case of biological warfare in Europe in the twentieth century." Europeans and

Americans also discovered the effectiveness of spreading oil or insecticide to kill mosquito lar-
vae in areas near human settlements. Most encouraging of all, a Swiss chemist added DDT to
mankind's anti-malarial arsenal during World War II. When it first came out, DDT seemed like
a miracle — it was seemingly harmless to man, but extremely toxic to insects, and a single treatment on a surface retained its effectiveness for up to six months. DDT seemed to offer up hope
of eradicating *Anopheles* mosquitoes and, with them, the malaria plasmodia that has plagued
mankind since the dawn of human history.

Indeed, starting in 1955, the newly-established World Health Organization (WHO)
launched a global campaign to wipe out malaria once and for all. The idea was to attack malaria
on all fronts; DDT would be applied continuously to all houses in malarial zones, all cases of
malaria would be aggressively treated with quinine and other anti-malarial drugs, and blood
screens would be used to seek out any remnant plasmodia within the human population. If all
went well, both human beings and *Anopheles* mosquitoes worldwide would be free of malaria
within just five years. To ensure success, governments worldwide were encouraged to spend up
to 35 percent of their medical funding budget on anti-malarial programs, and the United States
kicked in another $790 million through the U.S. Agency for International Development, or
AID.

For a short while after the Second World War, it appeared that malaria was in retreat on
all fronts. Malaria disappeared entirely from most areas in the developed world after 1945, in
part due to anti-mosquito campaigns, but also due to increased quality of housing and nutri-

tion, which reduced the number
of malaria plasmodia carriers to
such a low level that the disease
essentially petered out. This
process was helped along by
European and American urbanization, which meant that rural
human populations were
replaced increasingly by large
numbers of dairy and meat animals; since many *Anopheles*
mosquitoes species prefer to bite
animal rather than human hosts,
this effectively severed the mos-
quito-human infection chain
needed to perpetuate endemic
malaria. Even in the developing
world, where poverty levels
remained high, WHO–organ-
ized prevention campaigns
seemed to be scoring notable
successes. In India, for example,
where annual malaria infections
had traditionally numbered in
the tens of millions and deaths
in the millions, only 50,000 cases
were reported in 1961, just six
years into the program.

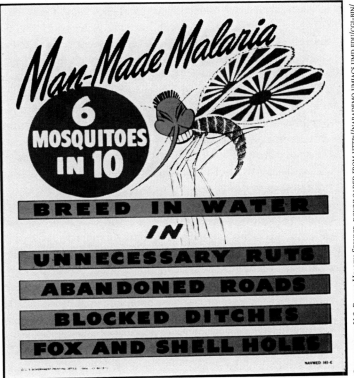

Another World War II era anti-malaria poster. Note that the
mosquito has been given distinctively Japanese features by
the artist.

Unfortunately, these gains proved to be short lived, and by the late 1960s it was clear that malaria was on the rebound, at least within the developing world. In retrospect, the WHO campaign was hopelessly flawed and naïve. The DDT spraying program, for example, only worked against mosquitoes whose genetic programming disposed them to rest on a house wall after eating, and did nothing against *Anopheles* species genetically wired to fly away after taking their blood meal. The blood screen and DDT spraying program also proved to be beyond the financial means of the cash-strapped nations of the tropics, and as a result many corners were cut, if these measures were carried out at all. Both programs also ran into considerable resistance from the people they were supposed to help. Malayan villagers, for example, refused to cooperate with malaria workers because DDT spraying caused their house roofs to collapse about a month after being treated. Bizarrely, DDT had little effect on the caterpillars that fed on the palm fronds of Malayan roofs, but was highly toxic to the wasps that fed on the caterpillars. With nothing to check their numbers, caterpillars kept eating until the weakened roofs collapsed under their own weight. Worst of all, both *Anopheles* mosquitoes and the malaria plasmodia proved to be more resilient than expected. After years of overuse of DDT, especially by western commercial farmers who considered it a perfect pesticide, *Anopheles* mosquitoes became increasingly resistant to DDT. The malaria plasmodia, in turn, developed a growing resistance to chloroquine, a quinine derivative that was the most effective and most widely-used antimalarial drug. In recent years, malaria has also demonstrated increasing tolerance of later-generation drugs, most notably mefloquine and sulfadoxine-pyrimethamine.

This is not to say that the WHO's anti-malarial campaign was a complete failure. Malaria has been entirely abolished in some areas where it was long endemic, for instance Italy and the United States, though socioeconomic advances were probably more important to this victory than the WHO's campaign. Nonetheless, despite all the expense of resources, malaria continues to rage almost unabated throughout much of the tropical world, most especially in Africa, where 90 percent of present day cases occur. Science is still looking for a magic bullet against malaria, either in the form of a new drug, or a vaccine, or perhaps by deciphering the genetic code of the deadly *P. falciparum*. In the meantime, inexpensive bed nets treated with insecticide hold the hope of significantly reducing infection in malarial zones. However, distribution of the nets and education about their proper usage still poses considerable logistical problems, especially in rural Africa where they are needed the most.

Indeed, it could be argued that malaria remains one of the most dangerous foes of the human species in the modern world. Today, 300–500 million people globally catch malaria each year, and between 1.1 million and 2.7 million die of it, making malaria the world's third most deadly infectious disease after AIDS and tuberculosis. As is normal with an endemic disease, most victims who are killed outright by malaria are children; indeed, in sub–Saharan Africa, an estimated 20 percent of all childhood deaths are blamed on malaria. Malaria also plays an important contributing role in the deaths of adults by worsening other infections, especially AIDS, tuberculosis, and gastrointestinal disease. Malaria also seriously impacts national economies. Because of the health care costs and lost work hours associated with malaria, the disease is estimated to reduce the annual GDP growth rate by up to 1 percent a year in areas where it is hyperendemic, and since the malarial season in most areas overlaps with the harvest season, malaria plays a contributing role in causing famine as well. Worst of all, indications are that malaria will become even more dangerous in the future. The adaptable malaria plasmodium is becoming tolerant of anti-malaria drugs faster than new drugs can be developed. Anopheles mosquitoes, in turn, are becoming increasingly adapted to life in Africa's teeming cities, especially *A. gambiae*, a human-preferring mosquito species which is malaria's most efficient transmission vector.

Most worrying of all, it is widely suspected that global warming will further exacerbate mankind's malaria problem. The steady rise of global temperatures will lead to a gradual spread of the malaria plasmodia, especially the heat-loving *P. falciparum* strain, into higher latitudes and higher altitudes worldwide. What is more, since malaria-infected mosquitoes produce sporozoites quicker when it is warm, higher global average temperatures will speed up the mosquito-to-human malaria transmission cycle. Global warming is also likely to cause more extreme weather events, such as flooding, which will likely provide more opportunities for *Anopheles* mosquitoes to breed. What is more, global warming combined with rising populations will likely generate higher levels of poverty, depriving populations in the developing world of the adequate diets and proper housing that are the best protection against malaria. Finally, global warming will almost certainly increase the number of economic refugees worldwide, and fast modern transportation may allow carriers of malaria plasmodia to reach the developed world before the malaria burns itself out within the human body. As a result, malaria will probably get worse — perhaps much worse — before it gets better.

Study Questions

1. Based on this section, to what degree would it be fair to label pellagra a "disease of imperialism?" See beginning of chapter for a definition of an "imperial" disease.

2. To what degree is malaria a "natural" disaster?

3. "Malaria is the 'best supporting actor' among natural disasters, always playing a subtle, though crucial, background role." To what degree do you agree with this statement?

4. Given limited funding, do you think that governments of nations in malarial zones should spend money to try to eradicate malaria, or rather improve the economic wellbeing of their citizenry? Defend your answer.

Suggested Readings

Desowitz, Robert S. *The Malaria Capers*. New York: W. W. Norton, 1991.

Harrison, Gordon. *Mosquitoes, Malaria, and Man*. New York: E. P. Dutton, 1978.

Hume, Jennifer C. C., Emily J. Lyons, and Karen P. Day. "Malaria in Antiquity: A Genetics Perspective." *World Archeology*, Vol. 35, No. 2, Archeology of Epidemic and Infectious Disease. (Oct., 2003), pp. 180–192.

Humphreys, Margaret. *Malaria: Poverty, Race, and Public Health in the United States*. Baltimore, MD: John Hopkins University Press, 2001.

Kiple, Kenneth F. *The Caribbean Slave: A Biological History*. New York: Cambridge University Press, 1984.

Marshall, Eliot. "A Renewed Assault on an Old and Deadly Foe." *Science*, Vol. 290, No. 5491. (Oct. 20, 2000), pp. 428–430.

Packard, Randal M. *The Making of a Tropical Disease: A Short History of Malaria*. Baltimore, MD: John Hopkins University Press, 2007.

Rocco, Fiammetta. *Quinine: Malaria and the Quest for a Cure That Changed the World*. New York: HarperCollins, 2003.

Roger, David J., and Sarah E. Randolph. "The Global Spread of Malaria in a Future, Warmer World." *Science*, Vol. 289, No. 5485. (Sep. 8, 2000), pp. 1763–1766.

Sallares, Robert. *Malaria and Rome: A History of Malaria in Ancient Italy*. New York: Oxford University Press, 2002.

Snowden, Frank M. "From Triumph to Disaster: Fascism and Malaria in the Pontine Marshes, 1928–1946." In John Dickie, John Foot, and Frank M. Snowden, eds., *Disastro! Disasters in Italy Since 1860: Culture, Politics, Society*. New York: Pelgrave, 2002.

Stepan, Nancy Leys. "'The Only Serious Terror in These Regions': Malaria Control in the Brazilian Amazon." In Diego Armus, ed., *Disease in the History of Modern Latin America*. Durham, NC: Duke University Press, 2003.

Takken, Willem, Pim Martens, and Robert J. Bogers, eds., *Environmental Change and Malaria Risk: Global and Local Implications*. The Netherlands: Springer, 2005.

Teklehaimanot, Awash, Burt Singer, Andrew Spielman, Te_im Tozan, and Allan Schapira. *Coming to Grips with Malaria in the New Millennium*. Sterling, VA: Earthscan, 2005.

Watts, Sheldon. "British Development Policies and Malaria in India 1897–c.1929." *Past and Present*, No. 165. (Nov., 1999), pp. 141–181.

Watts, Sheldon. *Epidemics and History: Disease, Power, and Imperialism*. New Haven, CT: Yale University Press, 1997.

8.3: Disease of Industry: Cholera

Cholera, a deadly gastrointestinal disease, was to the 19th century what AIDS is to the modern world: an apparently new and highly deadly disease that provoked widespread terror. The cholera bacterium is itself quite old, and is endemic to the Ganges River Delta, though there are indications that there might be oceanic reservoirs of the cholera bacteria as well. Despite its antiquity, cholera only exploded into the consciousness of most humans in the 1800s, when British hydrological engineering and rapid global transportation, combined with the urban overpopulation and woeful sanitary conditions of the early industrial age, allowed it to become a worldwide pandemic. Cholera causes spectacular physical symptoms, including pro-fuse diarrhea, the shriveling of the body due to dehydration, and frequently death, often within hours. Although no vaccine for cholera has yet been developed, cholera is now easily treatable, and sanitary measures have banished cholera from the developed world. Nonetheless, cholera remains a real threat in the developing world, where poverty not only helps to create the unsani-tary conditions it needs to thrive, but deprives sufferers of the simple medical treatments needed to preserve life. Thus, a disease that was the archetypical ailment of industrial cities in the 1800s became a scourge of the developing world's poor in the 20th and 21st centuries.

Until recently, scientists believed that cholera afflicted only human beings, and that its per-manent reservoir was in the groundwater of the area now known as Bangladesh. Recent research, however, suggests that cholera bacteria are an organic part of south Asian river delta ecosys-tems, where they flourish among chitinaceous zooplankton and shellfish living in brackish to highly saline water. The bacterium can survive water of low salinity if that water contains enough organic matter, however, which helps to explain why cholera can persist for weeks in sewage. Cholera can even survive for long periods of time in deep ocean water by becoming dormant, much like malaria plasmodia can survive for years in the human liver in the form of a hypno-spore. These findings not only explain why cholera epidemics keep recurring, but also why cholera epidemics seem to be associated with coastal cities. Indeed, in modern years, disease researchers theorize that the ballast water discharged by oceangoing vessels may play a role in spreading cholera from one part of the world to another. After being introduced into local seawaters, these researchers posit, cholera can reach the human population through contaminated seafood.

Once cholera enters the human population, it generally passes from person to person by hijacking the human excretory system. Much like a cold virus spreads by inducing sneezing and then traveling as aerosol particles into new hosts, the cholera bacteria propagates by forcing the human intestines to release rather than absorb fluid from the digestive system As a result, cholera victims generally discharge enormous amounts of watery diarrhea, often called "rice-water" diarrhea due to resemblance to water in which rice has been soaking. Cholera victims generally release an average of 36 liters of body fluid over the course of the infection, and may lose more than 10 percent of their body mass in a matter of hours. Without treatment, this dra-matic fluid loss often leads to organ failure and death.

As far as cholera is concerned, however, the death of the host is largely irrelevant. Only a million or so of the trillion bacteria emitted by a cholera victim need to find their way into a new host in order to continue the infection chain, and these bacteria can enter a new host in a number of ways. People who touch the soiled clothing or bedding of a cholera victim, and then touch their own mouths, may pick up enough cholera bacteria to cause an infection. Food items which are exposed to the diarrhea of human victims, for instance crops irrigated with cholera-laden water, can also transmit cholera. The most common way that cholera is transmitted, however, is through contamination of drinking water. Given the sheer volume of fluid discharged by a cholera

CHOLERA PATHWAYS

victim, it is almost inevitable that cholera victims will foul the drinking water of a community that is not protected by a modern sanitation system.

It is important to note that cholera is by no means a unique infection; quite a number of human diseases, from typhoid to dysentery, are transmitted through human feces. Indeed, some scientists argue that the prevalence of such diseases, called gastrointestinal diseases as a group, has left an important mark on genetic makeup of agriculturalist man. Unlike nomadic man, who could simply walk away from his feces, agriculturalist man lived in densely packed and permanent settlements, where sanitary disposal of human waste was a constant difficultly. As a result, the incidence of diseases of the human gastrointestinal tract rose markedly after the transition of agriculture. Those agriculturalists who drank alcohol, however, tended to suffer lower mortality from these diseases, since alcohol has natural antimicrobial properties. Alcohol does have significant drawbacks, however: It is both potentially addictive and poisonous in large quantities. As a result, through a process of natural selection, people in sedentary societies gradually developed enzymes capable of breaking down alcohol efficiently. The peoples of the world who never or only partially adopted agriculture, however, did not develop these genes. This fact may explain both why the original inhabitants of North America had a reputation of being unable to "hold their liquor," and why alcoholism is so rife among Amerindian populations today. In any case, it is clear that gastrointestinal infections have been extremely important to human development, and have left a mark on both human history and the human genetic code itself.

Cholera differs from other gastrointestinal diseases mainly by virtue of its sheer virulence. Although some victims of cholera fight the disease several days before succumbing to dehydration, other victims die in a matter of hours; indeed, a man who appears perfectly healthy in the morning can be dead by nightfall due to cholera. In the absence of treatment, cholera has a mortality rate of nearly 50 percent, which again distinguishes it from its somewhat less virulent gastrointestinal cousins. By way of contrast typhoid, the second most deadly gastrointestinal infection, kills in only about 10 percent to 20 percent of cases. Thankfully, one side effect of cholera's virulence is that infections tend to be short in duration, raging through susceptible members of a given population over the course of a few months or years, and then petering out after running out of potential victims. Mankind is also fortunate insofar as cholera, at least of the "classical" variety, is not a good traveler. The incubation period of the disease in the human body is only 2–3 days, after which the patient either dies or else gains some immunity to cholera. In addition, cholera bacterium can only survive for about four weeks on plant matter, three weeks in sewage, and even less time in groundwater. As a result, for most of history, slow sea and overland transportation combined with a very short latency time in the human body meant that cholera was generally unable to spread outside of its home territory in the Ganges Delta.

In the early 19th century, however, British economic "development" in India allowed cholera to escape from its original homeland. As discussed in section 8.2, the British constructed a large number of irrigation canals during the 19th century in order to tap the agricultural potential of their Indian colony, and these canals eventually watered about 20 percent of India's agricultural land. Unfortunately, these poorly designed canals led to salinization, which in turn created a hospitable environment for the saline-tolerant cholera bacteria. Furthermore, India's canals had a habit of flooding over adjacent land, and as a result, they tended to pick up cholera bacteria from infected villages and spread them over a wide area. The British further worsened the problem by insisting on the compulsory settlement of Indian subjects alongside these canals, meaning that semi-nomadic pastoral and agriculturalist people were forcibly obliged to adopt a full-fledged agricultural lifestyle, and all the diseases that went with it.

British imperialism in India fostered cholera in other ways as well. The railway system that Britain constructed in India greatly sped ground transportation, and thus allowed people infected with cholera to travel hundreds of miles during the disease's 2–3 day incubation period. As we saw in chapter 7, this same railway system allowed Britain to extract considerable quantities of food from India even in years of drought. Consequently, India suffered a series of devastating famines in the second half of the 19th century, and since the digestive systems of malnourished people are low in the stomach acids which are the body's initial defense against cholera, Britain's policy of food extraction indirectly worsened Indian cholera. The work relief programs that Britain instituted during famine years further exacerbated India's cholera problem. This was in part because the water sources in these closely-packed and unsanitary camps quickly became infected with cholera bacteria. It also reflected the starvation wages paid by the British that all but ensured that the Indian poor would be malnourished and thus vulnerable to epidemic cholera.

The British further exacerbated the death toll of cholera in India through sheer callousness towards the suffering of the Indian population. Instead of taking responsibility for worsening cholera through their "development" program, the British created a myth that epidemic cholera was "timeless" in India. According to Sheldon Watts, the British went so far as to actively suppress information linking their canal programs to disease outbreaks for fear of scaring off investors and dampening profits. The British also insisted that cholera was not contagious, despite considerable evidence to the contrary, since if cholera was labeled a contagious disease then quarantine measures would have been implemented, and British business interests considered such measures to be an insufferably expensive violation of the sacred principles of free trade. Instead, the British insisted that cholera was caused by the vice, torpor, and "filthy habits" of the Indian people. As we shall see below, this would not be the last time that the British elites responded to cholera deaths by blaming the victim. Overall, the epidemiological consequences of British meddling in India were atrocious; disease historian Sheldon Watts believes that as many as 25 million Indians died of cholera in the years of British imperialism, severely retarding India's demographic and economic growth in the 19th and 20th centuries.

Worse yet, British imperialism allowed cholera to break out of South Asia and to embark on a series of global killing sprees. The first global pandemic began when British troops moved from Bombay to Muscat in 1817, carrying cholera with them. From Oman, cholera followed the shipping lanes in every direction, reaching as far north as Southern Russia, as far west as Syria, as far east as Japan, and as far south as the African port of Zanzibar, which at the time was still dominated by Omani traders. Cholera spared Europe and the Americas during this first pandemic, probably because transportation was not yet swift enough for the disease to travel a sufficient distance. Whatever barriers that existed in the 1810s were gone by the 1830s, when a second pandemic began to spread worldwide, this time from an epicenter in Southern Russia. Cholera spread from there to the Arabian Peninsula, most likely following the movement of pilgrims during the traditional Moslem Hajj. Indeed, Mecca suffered an outbreak of cholera so devastating that "the living ceased to bury the dead singly." Pilgrims returning home from the Hajj carried the disease throughout the Islamic world and later to southern Europe. In the meantime, the disease also spread overland from Russia into northern Europe, spread in part by the movement of troops during regional warfare.

Cholera's impact in Europe was epitomized by the horrific outbreak in Paris, which by the early 1830s was one of Europe's largest and most densely populated cities. Indeed, Paris in 1830 offered almost ideal conditions for cholera's spread. Over 700,000 people crowded within the medieval walls of Paris by 1830, living alongside narrow streets that doubled as the city's sewer system. Like the malnourished poor of India, Paris' inhabitants were chronically underfed, as suggested by Parisian death records, which indicate that only 17 percent of Parisians during this period could even afford their own funerals. Population density reached 1 person per 7 square meters in some areas, and sanitary standards were so atrocious that one contemporary authority quipped that poor neighborhoods were essentially "encased in ... garbage."

Not surprisingly, the overcrowded and unsanitary slums were the first areas to be overwhelmed by epidemic cholera, and this allowed the Parisian authorities to blame cholera on the immorality and vice of the Parisian underclass. Indeed, the French elites went so far as to claim that their posh lifestyle made them immune to cholera: "the best tea for protecting yourself against cholera," a theatre journal of the period advised, "is champagne." The Parisian aristocracy had cause to regret this arrogance, however, when cholera began to spread to the rich as well. Regrettably, cholera's lack of class consciousness only served to further worsen the plight of the poor, since many rich employers fled the city, talking jobs with them. As a result, the unemployed workers left behind in the city became increasingly malnourished and thus increasingly prone to cholera. All told, 1 out of every 19 Parisians contracted the disease during the 1832 Paris outbreak, and half of the victims—18,000 Parisians—died of cholera.

Thanks to increasingly swift sea transportation, the second cholera pandemic even managed to reach the Americas, striking the major cities of Canada before moving southwards along the Great Lakes, Erie Canal, and Hudson River into the United States. Many Americans had assumed that the United States would not be impacted by cholera, since it was widely believed that America lacked the overcrowding, filth, and bad morals of Europe. Indeed, quite a few

Americans professed that cholera was a manifestation of God's wrath, and that Americans, who were supposedly more God fearing than their European contemporaries, would escape harsh punishment.

Such hopes soon proved misplaced: Indeed, large American cities proved to be just as vulnerable to cholera as the industrial capitals of Europe. New York, for example, was densely populated by impoverished people living in squalid apartments, drinking bad water from easily contaminated urban wells. Indeed, the nasty flavor of New York's well water probably saved some lives, since wealthy New Yorkers were in the habit of purchasing hogsheads of drinking water from pure springs outside of Manhattan, a preference that proved prophylactic once New York's groundwater was contaminated by cholera. This was doubtless small comfort to New York's poor, such as the inhabitants of the notorious Five Points district, who could not afford imported water and thus sickened and died in huge numbers. Overall, the death toll in New York City topped 3,000, and at its height cholera was killing about 100 New Yorkers each day. Nor was that the end of it. Cholera then jumped from port to port down the U.S. eastern seaboard and followed the railroads into the American interior, eventually reaching almost every part of the young United States. New Orleans suffered particularly high casualty figures, no doubt due to its combination of high population density, a high water table, high vulnerability to flooding, and high levels of urban poverty.

As in Europe, many Americans continued to regard cholera as a moral failing rather than an epidemic disease. Cholera was a "rod in the hand of God," most American clergymen agreed, which providence used to "promote the cause of righteousness" by "drain[ing] off the filth and scum which contaminate and defile human society." Americans acknowledged that cholera spread from place to place in the manner of an infectious disease. Nonetheless, it was generally argued that people only fell sick in a "choleraic" atmosphere if they were predisposed towards illness by intemperate living, impiety, sexual excess, and personal uncleanliness. The fact that most cholera victims were poor only bolstered this belief, since during the first half of the 19th century it was common for Americans to ascribe poverty to moral rather than socioeconomic causes.

After the second pandemic, cholera pandemics began to occur with increasing frequency, a development that probably reflects the rising efficiency of global transportation networks due to steamships, railroads, and the opening of the Suez Canal. A third cholera pandemic broke out in 1852, and unlike the first two pandemics, the exact source was hard to determine: In some cases local outbreaks during this pandemic were probably caused by sudden flare ups of cholera left behind by the first two pandemics. Although the third pandemic was the worst in Russia, where it may have claimed 1 million lives, it was also quite deadly in Europe's growing industrial cities, where extreme overpopulation and poor sanitation created perfect conditions for cholera bacteria to thrive. In London, for example, the population density had reached up to 100,000 people per square kilometer by 1851, and according to cholera historian Steven Johnson, this figure represents four times the population density of present-day Manhattan. As would be expected, disposal of human waste was an almost insurmountable problem for mid–19th-century London. For the most part, human waste accumulated in the London's cesspools, which due to infrequent emptying were often full to overflowing and emitted an indescribable stench. In some cases human waste was simply allowed to pile up in the basement, or else was dumped into empty lots, where it collected in stagnant pools that were "more like watery mud than muddy water ... the colour of strong green tea." Worst of all, the very same sewers that collected human wastewater also served as the source of drinking water for many Londoners. According to contemporary eyewitness accounts, poor Londoners slaked their thirst by scooping up the contents of the sewer and "put[ting] the mucky liquid to stand, so that they

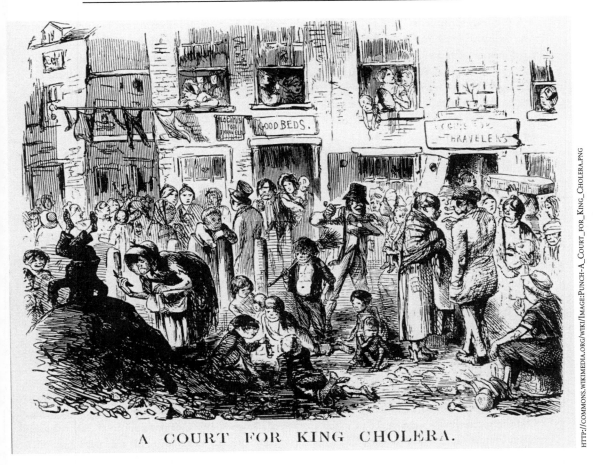

A COURT FOR KING CHOLERA.

Punch cartoon from 1852 that clearly reflects the British elite's association of cholera with urban filth and disorder.

may, after it has rested for a day or two, skim the fluid from the solid particles of filth, pollution, and disease." It is hard to imagine a more surefire method of acquiring cholera.

The transmission of cholera in London was further facilitated by mistaken medical ideas and counterproductive "public health" engineering measures. The very idea of a waterborne disease would have seemed heretical to a mid–19th-century European doctor, since most people in the medical profession clung to the traditional Galenic belief that disease could be caused by overpowering, offensive smells. To some degree this belief was natural; human beings have a deep instinctual aversion to the smell of feces and rotting flesh, which may reflect the inherited genetic wisdom of thousands of generations of human beings who survived by keeping their distance from such odors. However, in this case, the elites of London followed their noses directly towards civic disaster. Believing that London would be a healthier place to live if the bad smells were removed, London city commissioners had waged a war against urban cesspools during the 1840s, advocating instead that human waste be discharged via sewer systems directly into the Thames River. As a result, in the words of contemporary London builder Thomas Cubbitt, "the Thames is now made a great cesspool instead of each person having one of his own." Since many London water companies piped their water out of the Thames, the sewers built in the 1840s essentially delivered cholera directly into the mouths of London water consumers.

Other contemporary beliefs further predisposed the people of London to death by cholera. As in Paris and New York City, the elite class of London widely regarded cholera as a moral failing. Of course diseases were caused by bad, foul-smelling air, a belief about disease that was known as the time as "miasma theory." But who gets disease, and what specific ailment do they get? The conventional wisdom in mid–19th century London was that certain people — especially the poor and debauched — were especially vulnerable to cholera because of their flawed constitutions. As a result, the London elites typically regarded cholera as an inevitable consequence of immoral behavior rather than as a public health problem that needed to be solved.

Indeed, disease historian Sheldon Watts believes that "Construct cholera," which he defines as the ideological and social beliefs surrounding cholera rather than the biological organism itself, served as a marvelous way for the emerging middle class of England to distinguish itself from the working class poor. Watts goes so far as to claim that some British elites, under the influence of Richard Malthus, regarded cholera as an unpleasant necessity, since without cholera the working poor would expand beyond the ability of British agriculture to support. Furthermore, as in India, British business interests predisposed the authorities to adopt a moral rather than epidemiological understanding of cholera. After all, if cholera was an epidemic disease rather than moral failing, the British would have to put expensive quarantine measures into place. As a result, the British elites generally adopted a "do-nothing" attitude towards cholera within Britain, exacerbating the death toll. In all, as many as 15,000 Londoners died during the third cholera pandemic.

There was a silver lining to this cloud, however: It was during the third pandemic that British doctor John Snow convincingly demonstrated that cholera was a waterborne disease. Snow was able to clearly link a cholera outbreak in Golden Square in London to the Broad Street Pump, which served as a local epicenter of a neighborhood-wide epidemic. Snow's work was further confirmed by the fact that the Golden Square cholera epidemic petered off soon after the handle from the Broad Street Pump was removed. Snow then managed to collect data demonstrating that cholera cases in a specific London neighborhood correlated almost perfectly with houses supplied with water by a single supplier, the East London Water Company, whose reservoir had been tainted by river water containing human feces. The British medical community remained skeptical, but Snow's theory received yet more confirmation during the "Great Stink" of 1858, when a summer heat wave transformed the Thames River into almost a solid mass of reeking human waste. The sheer intensity of the Great Stink's odor shut down parliament, but contrary to the predictions of the "miasma" theory, the disease death toll during the "Great Stink" was no higher than normal.

John Snow's great contribution to European epidemiological history, then, was to demonstrate indisputably that the cholera problem in Europe's great industrial cities was inextricably tied to poor sanitation — and once the problem had been clearly identified, Europe's great industrial cities had the resources at their disposal to craft solutions. During the 1860s, for example, London's civil engineers constructed a new sewer system for the city that ran parallel to the Thames, flushing London's sewage into the ocean downstream of the city rather than directly into the river. Thanks to this sewage system, which was completed in 1865, London's wastewater was now segregated from its drinking water, effectively severing the person-to-person transmission of cholera. As a result, Britain suffered from a number of cholera casualties during the fourth cholera pandemic, which began in 1863, but hardly any during the fifth pandemic, which began in 1881. Indeed, the last known case of cholera to arise in Britain occurred in 1893; since then, Britain has been effectively cholera-free, with all cholera cases originating outside of the country.

London's example soon proved contagious. New York started building modern sewers as

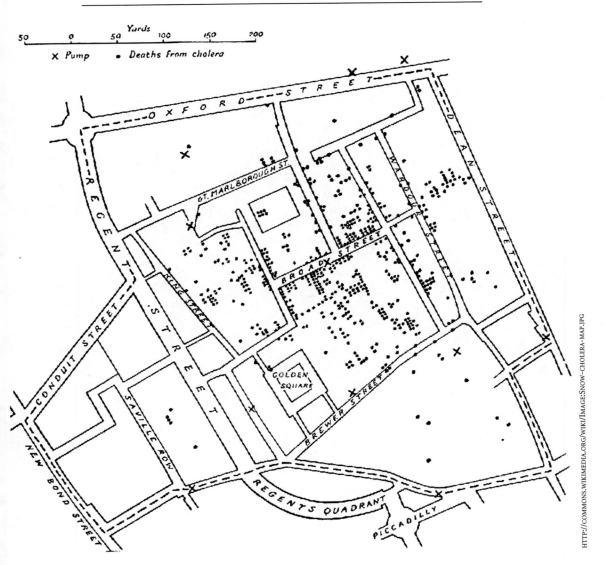

John Snow's famous map of the Golden Square region of London, which clearly illustrates that the neighborhood's cholera cases were clustered around the Broad Street water pump.

early as the 1850s, and by the turn of the century, nearly every building in New York could dispose of its waste in a sanitary fashion. Paris began constructing its own sewer system in the 1850s under the direction of urban planner Baron Haussmann, and by 1878, 360 miles of pipe in Paris ensured that wastewater remained strictly segregated from drinking water supplies. These sewers did not entirely prevent cholera outbreaks in Paris during the fifth pandemic, but greatly reduced the incidence and spread of the disease. Indeed, the fifth pandemic provided further evidence that modern sanitation could counter cholera: European cities that had not constructed sewers, such as Moscow, Saint Petersburg, and Hamburg, suffered atrocious casualty figures during the fifth pandemic, while cities with improved sanitation suffered only sporadic cases. By the sixth pandemic, which began in 1899, European sanitation had improved still further, and as a consequence deaths due to cholera were far less than in previous epidemics,

FATHER THAMES INTRODUCING HIS OFFSPRING TO THE FAIR CITY OF LONDON.

(*A Design for a Fresco in the New Houses of Parliament.*)

Punch Cartoon printed at the time of London's "Great Stink."

GEOGRAPHICAL REVIEW, VOL. 41, NO. 2 (APRIL 1951), PP. 272–273

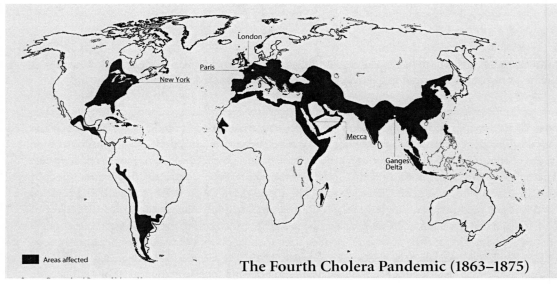

The Fourth Cholera Pandemic (1863–1875)

especially in Western Europe. Much the same was true of the United States, which all but eliminated domestic cholera cases by 1911.

In the meantime, cholera continued to rage almost unabated outside of Europe and the Americas. This was especially true of the Islamic world, largely because one of the most important religious traditions in Islam, the Hajj pilgrimage to the sacred city of Mecca, was almost perfectly suited to the proliferation and distribution of cholera bacteria. The Hajj attracted Moslems from throughout the world, including the heavily Moslem Ganges Delta where cholera is endemic. By the mid–19th century, and especially after the opening of the Suez Canal, most Hajjis traveled to the Arabian Peninsula on steamships, which generally suffered atrocious overcrowding and thus provided excellent conditions for transmission of cholera bacteria. These steamships, moreover, traveled fast enough to reach their destination before the cholera cases on board had fully burnt themselves out. Because most Hajjis hailed from European controlled colonies, where the prevailing policies favored resource extraction rather than the native people's well being, they tended to be malnourished, and thus susceptible to the cholera. Furthermore, since all Moslems are supposed to perform the Hajj before they die, the Hajj attracted people in ill health to start with, many of whom hoped they could complete their spiritual duty before their deaths. Once the Hajjis reached Mecca, they concentrated in huge numbers in areas with limited sources of water. As a result, drinking water and wash water of the pilgrims quite often became infected with cholera bacteria. Worst of all, at the end of the Hajj, pilgrims returned to their various countries of origin, often carrying cholera with them as a deadly souvenir.

Not surprisingly, therefore, the Hajj pilgrimages of the 19th and early 20th centuries were frequently marred by devastating outbreaks of cholera. In 1865, an estimated 15,000 of the 90,000 Hajjis in Mecca died of cholera, and returning pilgrims carried the bacteria to Egypt,

HTTP://COMMONS.WIKIMEDIA.ORG/WIKI/IMAGE:BURTON_CROWD.GIF

An image of the 19th century Hajj, taken from the second edition of Richard Burton's *Pilgrimage.*

where cholera carried away 60,000 more victims in only three months. During an even worse epidemic in 1893, the Arabian port city of Jidda was transformed into "a vast cemetery," in the words of a contemporary observer, and Arabia as a whole counted 33,000 corpses. In 1908, still another terrible epidemic erupted in Mecca, which during the Hajj was so overcrowded that the "entire area" where the pilgrims camped was "covered with excrement," and so many people died that some bodies decomposed before they could be buried. All told, the Mecca pilgrimage was marred by a total of 27 epidemics between 1850 and 1931, and infected Hajjis carried cholera with them to areas as far-flung as Nigeria, Indonesia, and France.

In the early 20th century, several turning points occurred in the relationship between mankind and the cholera bacteria. Improvements to the Hajj infrastructure and the imposition of strict quarantine measures finally shut down cholera infections in Mecca, eliminating one major vector for the survival and global proliferation of cholera bacteria. Soon after, Eastern Europe joined Western Europe in banishing cholera, and thereafter suffered only sporadic cases which originated from outside of Europe. Perhaps most importantly, a new, milder cholera strain, called "El Tor" after the Egyptian quarantine camp where it was first identified, began to replace classical cholera strains worldwide. The origins of El Tor cholera are a matter of some dispute: The first epidemic of El Tor seems to have originated in Celebes, Indonesia, but cholera scholar Kerrie L. MacPherson has identified El Tor cholera as *Huoluan*, a fairly ancient disease in China. Whatever its origin, El Tor is a hardier organism than the classic cholera biotype, and as a result has replaced older versions of the cholera bacteria in India and other areas where cholera is endemic. Furthermore, El Tor cholera produces many cases of long-lasting infections that are not debilitating to the victims, greatly facilitating the spread of the disease. El Tor cholera is also less fatal than classic cholera, killing only about 14 percent of its untreated victims rather than 50 percent, and can survive longer than classical cholera both inside and outside of the human body.

Some public health authorities hoped that the emergence of a new, milder form of cholera might bring the era of deadly global pandemics to an end. This optimistic projection, however, was dashed by the outbreak of a seventh cholera pandemic in 1961. As with all pandemics since the fourth, the sixth pandemic largely afflicted the developing world, raging through Indonesia, Southern China, Bangladesh, India, Pakistan, Iran, Iraq, Southeast Asia, and Asiatic Russia. The bacteria later reached West Africa, which had been spared by earlier pandemics, and spread quickly through the continent's developing road and water infrastructure. Indeed, there is evidence that African cholera was greatly facilitated by traditional West African funeral rites, which involve large, regional funeral feasts and the ceremonial washing of the dead. Together, these practices greatly facilitate the transmission of cholera to large numbers of people, especially if the dearly departed was infected by cholera.

The seventh global pandemic struck hard in other areas as well. Cholera made an appearance in the Persian Gulf monarchies, and spread from there to New Zealand, which suffered a small outbreak after airline passengers contracted the bacteria from an in-flight meal prepared in the Gulf state of Bahrain. In 1974, the pilgrimage city of Mecca suffered its first cholera outbreak in many years, though only about 90 of a million pilgrims fell ill, and even fewer transported cholera back to their native soil. A number of cases cropped up in Europe, most of which were found to be the result of uncooked, contaminated seafood, suggesting that cholera had infiltrated local sea ecosystems. Infections linked to tainted seafood also emerged in the United States after 1987, which suggests to some scientists that El Tor cholera has colonized the Gulf of Mexico. Even areas as remote as the Maldives in the Indian Ocean and the Gilbert Islands in the Pacific Ocean reported cholera cases, most likely a side effect of tourism and rapid air transportation.

The seventh global pandemic also witnessed two important medical developments, one negative and the other highly positive. In an attempt to stem the rising tide of cholera, many nations relied on the large-scale distribution of antibiotics. Although antibiotics did provide some protection against cholera, overuse soon led to the creation of several antibiotic-resistant strains, greatly complicating the task of health workers in areas where cholera is endemic. At the same time, however, the development of oral rehydration therapy, or ORT, provided medical professionals with an invaluable tool in the fight to save the lives of cholera victims. In previous years, health care workers had used intravenous saline drips to try to restore the fluids and salts lost by cholera victims, but with only limited success, in part because intravenous treatment can only be administered by trained professionals. Attempts to rehydrate victims orally with water proved ineffectual, in part because cholera victims lose vital salts as well as water in their "rice-water" diarrhea, and in part because the small intestine absorbs pure water rather inefficiently. During the seventh global pandemic, however, Indian and Bangladeshi doctors experimented with administering mixtures of water, sugar, and salt to counter fluid loss due to diarrhea. This treatment was first put into effect on a large scale in 1971, when Bangladesh was suffering a horrific cholera pandemic thanks to the Great Bhola Cyclone (described in section 5.1) and the bloody war of independence that followed. Although doctors resorted to oral hydration only out of desperation, the results were spectacular: Only 3 percent of the 3000 patients given ORT died, as compared to 20 percent–30 percent of the patients given more traditional intravenous fluid treatment. Thanks to ORT, which has been described as the most important medical breakthrough of the 20th century, nearly every patient who is brought to a hospital with a diarrheal disease now survives.

It is important to note that ORT is not a cure-all; in particular, ORT does nothing to break cholera's person-to-person transmission chain. Mankind will only get true freedom from cholera when every human being has access to pure, uncontaminated water for drinking and cooking. Unfortunately, as the recent outbreak of cholera in Latin America demonstrates, this goal is depressingly far off. The Latin American cholera epidemic began in January of 1991, and like many outbreaks in the 20th century, it was likely triggered by cholera-infested seafood. Latin America had managed to escape cholera infection since 1885, but researchers posit that cholera reentered Latin America when a ship from a cholera zone discharged ballast water or human sewage into the water, allowing it to colonize local fish populations and shellfish beds. Cholera then entered the human body through seafood, perhaps by means of *ceviche*, a popular Peruvian dish consisting of fish and shellfish marinated in lemon juice and served nearly raw. Once transferred into the human population, cholera spread rapidly through the coastal slums of Peru, where sanitary facilities are nearly nonexistent. Areas fortunate enough to be serviced by running water proved to be no better off than areas with no water pipes, since tap water was frequently contaminated at its source, effectively delivering cholera directly into people's mouths. Even those who were careful not to drink the tap water contracted the disease through ice made with tap water, fruit or vegetables grown using contaminated water, and other means.

The Latin American cholera epidemic of the 1990s was worsened by a number of human factors, both internal and external. The inhabitants of Latin America had the misfortune of belonging mainly to the O blood group, which for some reason suffers a disproportional number of severe cases when exposed to cholera. Worse yet, the inhabitants of Peru and other Latin American countries were saddled with a bad government that exacerbated rather than ameliorated the cholera problem. Government mismanagement led to hyperinflation, which contributed to loss of tax revenue and the resultant deterioration of water and medical infrastructure at the eve of the epidemic. Anxious to avoid blame for the epidemic, not to mention avoid paying for expensive state-funded health care options, the cost-conscious government of Peru largely blamed cholera on poor individual hygiene, and tacitly encouraged the popular belief that the cholera epidemic was God's will, punishing the sinful for their wicked ways. President Fujimori even purged the competent health minister Carlos Vidal from his cabinet in the midst of the epidemic due to Vidal's entirely reasonable desire to expand the government's health services in the face of the epidemic. Given these complications, it is surprising that epidemic cholera killed relatively few: Of the 322,562 known cholera cases in Peru in 1991, only 2,909 died of the disease, a testimony to the effectiveness of ORT therapy.

Although Peru was the epicenter of the Latin American cholera epidemic, the plague of cholera soon spread elsewhere in the Americas, even to the United States. Both Ecuador and Chile had epidemics of their own, most likely spawned by contaminated sea foods. Cholera jumped from country to country in the bodies of perennial migrants, including shrimp farm workers, itinerant preachers, and even drug runners, who may have transported the epidemic to Mexico in their treetop-flying drug smuggling planes. Cholera also jumped from country to country in more conventional aircraft: In early 1992, a cold seafood salad served in an Argentinean plane that took off from Peru touched off a small cholera epidemic in Los Angeles. Several more Americans contracted cholera from contaminated crabs which family members had carried from Latin America in their luggage. All told, 18 Western Hemisphere countries recorded cholera cases by February 1992, and by the time the Latin American cholera epidemic played itself out in 1994, over a million people in the Americas had fallen ill and about 10,000 had died. Interestingly, although coastal urban areas suffered by far the most overall cholera cases, the fatal cases tended to occur in remote jungle and mountain areas, where the salt packets used to prepare ORT were unknown or in short supply.

Although the Latin American cholera epidemic has now abated, cholera continues to pose a threat to global populations, especially in areas afflicted with chronic poverty. Cholera experts Eugene J. Gangarosa and Robert V. Tuaxe have pointed out that, in the modern world, "cholera has come to be a metaphor for underdevelopment," and the facts of the matter bear this out: Indeed, the nations that suffered cholera cases between 2005 and 2007 — Angola, Chad, Cameroon, Senegal, Niger, and the Sudan — are almost all among the world's most impoverished countries. The 2006 outbreak of cholera in the Sudan, a country currently wracked by civil conflict, also demonstrates how cholera can thrive in the dislocation and confusion created by modern war. Further proof of this point is provided by a small cholera epidemic in northern Iraq in 2007, caused by the breakdown of regional water supplies during a time of intense civil disorder, forcing families to dig shallow wells near their own homes (and by consequence near their own sewage) to obtain water.

Furthermore, many experts fear that there will be a resurgence of cholera cases in the 21st century. As the world's burgeoning population puts increasing pressure on the natural environment, it will likely become increasingly difficult to provide clean water to all the world's peoples. Moreover, cholera bacteria tend to thrive in warm water, and thus can be expected to be one of the net gainers from global warming. As discussed in section 4.3, global warming is also likely to cause increasing rainfall variation, and thus more instances of flooding, a disaster which often causes wastewater and drinking water to intermingle and thus brings cholera in its wake. Finally, cholera outbreaks often correspond with El Niño events, especially in areas where El Niño brings with it warmer water temperatures. The Latin American cholera epidemic of 1991–1994, for example, may have been triggered by the El Niño event of 1991–1993, one of the most protracted El Niños in recorded history. El Niño's role as a handmaiden of cholera was further demonstrated in 1997–1998, when El Niño returned and Peru suffered a simultaneous uptick in cholera cases. Since global warming may increase the frequency of El Niño events, as we saw in section 4.1, it is probable that cholera will become even more common in the undeveloped world in the years to come. Of course, since cholera can now be successfully treated in almost all patients using ORT, it is unlikely that more cholera cases will lead to sudden spikes in human mortality. Nonetheless, the heavy expense posed by cholera, in terms of medical treatment and sewage control mechanisms, will probably take an increasing toll on the already scanty economic resources of the developing world in years to come.

Study Questions

1. Based on the information presented in this section, to what degree would it be fair to characterize cholera as a "disease of industrialization?" See beginning of chapter for a definition of an "industrial" disease.

2. "Unlike many other diseases, cholera is more likely to be caused by human decisions than by other forms of natural disaster." To what degree do you agree with this statement?

3. Based on the information presented in this section, in what key ways did the actual course of cholera differ from the "Construct" cholera during the 19th century? See beginning of chapter for a definition of a disease "construct."

Sources/Suggested Readings

Barua, Dhiman, and William B. Greenough III, eds. *Cholera.* New York: Plenum Medical Book Company, 1992.

Briggs, Charles L. and Clara Mantini-Briggs. *Stories in the Time of Cholera: Racial Profiling During a Medical Nightmare.* Berkeley: University of California Press, 2003.

Charmichael, Ann G. "Cholera: Pandemic Pestilence." In Kenneth F. Kiple, ed., *Plague, Pox, and Pestilence.* New York: Barnes and Noble Books, 1997.

Colwell, Rita R. "Global Climate and Infectious Disease: The Cholera Paradigm." *Science,* Vol 274, No. 5295 (Dec. 20, 1996), pp. 2025–2031.

Cueto, Marcos. "Stigma and Blame During an Epidemic: Cholera in Peru, 1991." In Diego Armus, ed., *Disease in the History of Modern Latin America.* Durham, NC: Duke University Press, 2003.

Glass, R. I., M. Libel, A. D. Brandling-Bennett. "Epidemic Cholera in the Americas." *Science,* Vol. 256, No. 5063 (Jun. 12, 1992), pp. 1524–1525.

Johnson, Steven. *The Ghost Map: The Story of London's Most Terrifying Epidemic — and How It Changed Science, Cities, and the Modern World.* New York: Riverhead Books, 2006.

Kudlick, Catherine J. *Cholera in Post-Revolutionary Paris: A Cultural History.* Berkeley: University of California Press, 1996.

MacPherson, Kerrie L. "Cholera in China, 1820–1930." In Mark Elvin and Liu Ts'ui-jung, eds., *Sediments of Time: Environment and Society in Chinese History.* New York: Cambridge University Press, 1998.

Peters, F. E. *The Hajj: The Muslim Pilgrimage to Mecca and the Holy Places.* New Jersey: Princeton University Press, 1994.

Rodó, Xavier, Mercedes Pascual, George Fuchs, and A. S. G. Farugue. "Enso and Cholera: A Nonstationary Link Related to Climate Change?" *Proceedings of the National Academy of Sciences of the United States of America,* Vol. 99, No. 20 (Oct. 1, 2002), pp. 12901–12906.

Rosenberg, Charles E. *The Cholera Years: The United States in 1832, 1849, and 1866.* Chicago: University of Chicago Press, 1962

Watts, Sheldon. *Epidemics and History: Disease, Power, and Imperialism.* New Haven, CT: Yale University Press, 1997.

8.4: *Disease of Globalization: AIDS*

Acquired immunodeficiency syndrome, or AIDS, is on track to become the most prolific killer in human history. In many ways, however, AIDS is an unlikely candidate for this dubious honor: Not only is AIDS relatively new to mankind, it generally takes many years for AIDS to kill its victim, and infection by the virus that causes AIDS is almost completely preventable if individuals take proper precautions. Despite these facts, AIDS continues to rage almost unabated today, not only in the impoverished developing world, but also in developed western countries, where complacency and misinformation has opened opportunities for AIDS infection. Indeed, as we shall see throughout this chapter, HIV the disease thrives in part because human beings have created an AIDS "Construct" that helps rather than hinders the spread of the pathogen. Real progress in eradicating AIDS is only possible if the world's various nations can get past the misinformation and fully appreciate the specific social, cultural, and economic mechanisms at work within each society that perpetuate this horrifying modern epidemic.

In a strict sense, "AIDS" is not a disease per se, but a description of the consequences that the human immunodeficiency virus, or HIV, eventually produces within the human body. Furthermore, in a strict sense, HIV itself rarely kills people. Rather, HIV progressively destroys the human immune system to the point that victims are overcome by opportunistic infections that are normally harmless or easily treatable. Case in point is tuberculosis, a bacterial infection of the lungs that can usually be treated successfully in non–HIV positive patients, but which often produces fatal cases in HIV patients. Indeed, medical personnel often refer to HIV and TB as "the terrible twins" or "Bonnie and Clyde." Research suggests that HIV patients are also more likely to be infected by, and die of, malaria parasites. Even more commonly, HIV patients die of Pneumocystis pneumonia, a respiratory infection caused by the uncontrolled growth of yeast-like fungus in the human lungs that is extremely uncommon in individuals with uncompromised immune systems. Individuals with HIV also suffer the uncontrolled growth of malignant gastrointestinal bacteria, leading to diarrhea and the inability of the patient to absorb nutrients from food. Furthermore, AIDS patients also suffer disproportionably from cancers, especially those cancers linked to viral infections like Kaposi's sarcoma, lymphoma, and cervical cancer. Worse of all, perhaps, is AIDS–related dementia, caused by the proliferation of viral, bacterial, or parasitical organisms in the brain. Although any one of these secondary opportunistic infections may be the direct cause of death in an AIDS patient, the real killer is HIV.

The damage that AIDS inflicts on the human immune system is a deadly side effect of the virus' quest to replicate and perpetuate itself within the human body. When the AIDS virus enters the body, it infiltrates the body's CD4 immune cells, also called "T cells," and duplicates the T cell's DNA. As a result of this ingenious invasion mechanism, HIV doubly compromises the body's immune system: HIV not only destroys cells normally used to fight off infections, it actually hides in plain sight by lurking within the very cells that are designed to counter invading diseases. Once inside the body's T cells, HIV manipulates those cells into manufacturing countless more copies of the AIDS virus, and once a critical mass is reached, the T cells erupt, releasing the virus into the blood and other bodily fluids. Indeed, researchers estimate that HIV invades, corrupts, and destroys about 5 percent of the body's T cells each day, severely compromising the human immune system over the long term. In the short run, however, HIV is kept in check by the body's other immune system defenses, which prevent HIV from completely wiping out human T cells. During this early stage of AIDS, the human host of HIV will likely be unaware of the war being raged within his or her body — the only symptoms typically reported are short in duration and similar to the flu. Unfortunately, this is also the period in which the majority of AIDS sufferers are most infectious to others.

Following this initial stage of HIV infection, often called the "window period" by researchers, the HIV virus goes into seeming quiescence for about 10 years, during which the AIDS suffer typically report no symptoms whatsoever. However, appearances are deceiving. Within the body, HIV continuously wears down the immune system, causing an inexorable drop in the T cell count, which typically decreases from about 1,200 cells per microliter of blood to

THE TYPICAL PROGRESSION OF AIDS

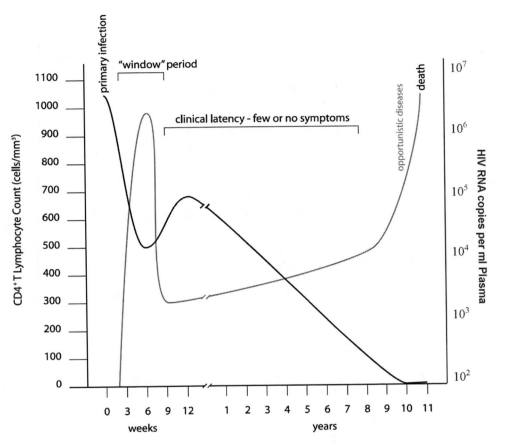

virtually none by the infections' tenth and eleventh years. If antiviral medication is administered during this period, it can considerably slow down the work of HIV in the human body, extending the patient's lifespan by years or decades. However, all too often, the HIV virus goes undiagnosed due to lack of symptoms; indeed many people only discover they are HIV–positive when they are administered routine blood tests, such as pregnancy tests, blood sugar level tests, or tests on the safety of donated blood.

In the meantime, HIV hijacks the body's normal functioning to spread to new hosts. Unlike influenza, which exploits the body's respiratory system, and cholera, which manipulates the human digestive and excretory systems, AIDS spreads primarily by taking advantage of human sexual behavior. The sperm and other fluids of HIV carriers contain millions of copies of the virus, so if these materials come into contact with another human's bloodstream, HIV may be able to jump to a new host. The likelihood of infection depends on the exact nature of the sexual contact between two partners. AIDS transmission is most common if an HIV–positive man penetrates a partner — man or woman — through the anus, since this form of sex frequently results in torn tissue and exposed blood vessels. Vaginal sex is only about ⅕ as likely to transmit the AIDS virus, since this form of intercourse less likely to involve torn tissue, but even normal sex involves some risk of creating fissures in the wall of the vagina, and the likelihood of damaging the vagina rises significantly in the case of rough sex or rape. The chance of contracting HIV through oral sex is smallest of all, though the receiving partner is at some risk, especially if he or she suffers from abrasions in the mouth or gum disease. In addition, the penetrating partner in all three forms of the sex act is at a small risk of acquiring HIV as well, since the virus may be present in the vaginal secretions, the saliva, and most especially the blood of the penetrated partner. However, since the penis has a relatively small surface area compared with the anus, vagina, and throat, the insertive partner in the sex act is considerably less likely to catch the virus from an HIV–positive receptive partner.

The HIV virus can spread to new victims through non-sexual means as well. The reuse of unsterilized hypodermic needles is a common route of transmission — if an intravenous drug user with HIV injects himself or herself and then shares the needles with others, all subsequent users of the hypodermic needle have about a 1 in 150 chance of acquiring HIV. The improper use of hypodermic needles for legitimate medical uses, such as blood donations and vaccinations, can also transfer AIDS from person to person. HIV can also survive on instruments used to cut the human skin for ornamental or religious reasons, for instance tattoo needles, body piercing needles, and blades used for ritual circumcision or scarification. It is also possible to acquire HIV from blood transfusions if one or more of the blood donors is HIV positive. What is more, HIV–positive mothers have about a 25 percent chance of passing the virus on to their children during pregnancy, and about a 10 percent–15 percent chance of infecting their children through breast milk after birth, though in both cases the administration of anti-viral drugs can significantly reduce the chance of infection.

It is important to understand the variety of the ways that AIDS can be transmitted, since the diversity of transmission mechanisms helps to counter one of the prevailing myths about AIDS — that it is a "gay" disease. AIDS gained this reputation because the first identified AIDS epidemic, which began in 1981, was located in the U.S. homosexual community. This accident of history is extremely unfortunate, for two main reasons. First of all, within the developed world AIDS became associated with male homosexuals, leading to complacency on the part of the heterosexuals. Indeed, some western Christian groups positively welcomed the news of AIDS, declaring it a "rightful and cleansing plague" inflicted upon a morally undesirable group. There is nothing new to such language; as we have already seen in section 8.3, earlier generations of American clergymen had welcomed cholera as divine retribution against the sinful. Although few mainstream Americans regarded AIDS in such cold-hearted terms, there was a widespread assumption that "gay cancer" (as AIDS was sometimes known) was a disease of America's "sexual third world," not of its mainstream straight population. Ironically, this very attitude towards AIDS facilitated its jump to the heterosexual community of the developed world.

The location of the "original" outbreak of AIDS was even more unfortunate as far as the developing world was concerned. Because the first well-publicized cases involved the Los Angeles homosexual community, AIDS fast gained the reputation of being a disease of degenerate Americans. This perception was reinforced after AIDS cases rose among American drug users, allowing the leaders of the developing world to dismiss AIDS as a side affect of distinctively American forms of sordid behavior. As a result, when AIDS cases did begin to surface in the developing world, many nations were trapped by their own rhetoric, forced to deny the existence of the epidemic out of a sense of national pride. As we shall see below, this phenomenon is particularly notable in China, which now faces a national AIDS catastrophe due to past and present denials about the scale of AIDS within China's borders. African leaders were loath to admit the existence of AIDS within their countries as well, even as late as the 1985, when the World Health Organization (WHO) held a conference on African AIDS. It was difficult for Africans to accept the existence of a disease associated with American gays and drug users—

ESTIMATED PER ACT RISK OF ACQUIRING HIV

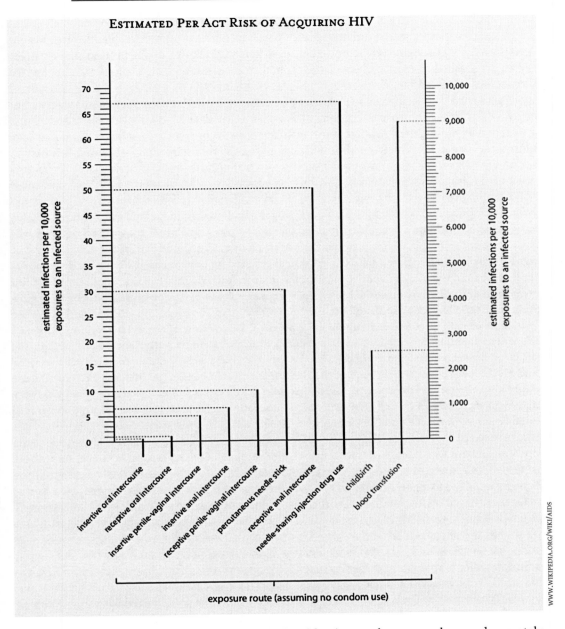

exposure route (assuming no condom use)

and in any case, confessing to an African AIDS epidemic may have scared away desperately needed tourist dollars.

Africa's denial of AIDS notwithstanding, modern science now agrees that Africa was the epicenter of the AIDS epidemic. Like most other human ailments, AIDS was originally a disease of animals. Indeed, the ancestral progenitors of the human immunodeficiency virus—or more properly viruses, since two main variants exist—has been located in specific monkey species found in the forests of Cameroon and surrounding central African nations. Exactly how the virus jumped to humans is unknown. It is quite possible that Africans became infected by AIDS through the "bush meat" trade—in other words, the African practice of hunting wild animals, including monkeys, and then selling their flesh in town or city markets. The original monkey carriers of HIV may have bitten their hunters, transferring the virus. More likely, monkey blood may have come into contact with wounds, nicks, or abrasions on a hunter's body. Alternatively, HIV might have jumped species when a butcher in the bush meat market inadvertently splashed himself or herself with blood from an HIV positive monkey, allowing the virus to enter through an open cut.

The scenario described above could explain how AIDS entered the human population, but not why HIV infection rose to epidemic levels. Unlike malaria and yellow fever, diseases that are carried by mosquitoes, AIDS requires intimate human contact to spread, and humans unlike mosquitoes are fairly selective about with whom they share their fluids. Although it is easy to see how AIDS might run through the family of a bitten bush meat hunter, marriage institutions or traditional sexual morality — not to mention spousal jealousy — may have prevented AIDS from spreading to the wider village. Even if AIDS did jump to the village level, transportation difficulties, distrust of outsiders, or social taboos could easily have contained AIDS to a single location and prevented it from rising to epidemic status. As with all diseases, the mere existence of a pathogen is not sufficient to trigger an epidemic or pandemic; rather, the right constellation of economic, social, political, and technological conditions must exist to foster its spread. Unfortunately for mankind, a situation favorable to the proliferation of HIV did emerge in central Africa after 1885, when King Leopold of Belgium founded the Congo Free State in the Congo River basin of Africa.

Belgian rule transformed almost all aspects of life in the Congo forest region. Politically, the entirety of the Congo River basin was unified under a single authority, greatly facilitating the large-scale transfer of people beyond their native villages. Economic changes further transformed the lives of the inhabitants of the Congo. During their rule, the Belgians organized mass migrations of workers to labor on railroad construction and to collect the rubber and the ivory that were the Congo's most valuable export commodities. Belgian economic activity also fostered the growth of cities in the Congo River basin, such as Kinshasa and Kisangani, and these cities proved to be fertile ground for the AIDS virus, since transient populations, organized prostitution, and the breakdown of traditional village values all created favorable conditions for the wide dissemination of the virus. In technological terms, the Belgians greatly facilitated the movement of the Congo's inhabitants by introducing the railroad and, even more importantly, the steamship, allowing relatively swift transportation through the Congo River and its many large tributaries. Ironically, the introduction of modern medical technology by the Belgians also facilitated the spread of AIDS. To combat disease, such as sleeping sickness, smallpox, and polio, the Belgians resorted to mass vaccination of their African work force. However, the hypodermic needles employed in these vaccination campaigns were often used repeatedly and without sterilization, meaning that a single individual's HIV could be spread to many other Africans.

This scenario for the genesis of the African AIDS epidemic is supported by available genetic evidence. Since the rate of mutation of viruses is relatively predictable, it is possible for researchers to date a given strain of a virus by comparing how far a given virus' genes have diverged from those of its ancestral strain. In the case of HIV, the number of differences between the human viruses and the ancestral viruses in the monkey populations indicates that the AIDS virus jumped to humans from monkeys sometime around the 1930s. Again, this is not to say that the HIV virus never jumped to the human species before that time. However, until the era of European imperialism, the social and economic environment within central never allowed AIDS to become a regional epidemic, much less a worldwide plague.

Once AIDS emerged from the forests, it spread rapidly throughout sub–Saharan Africa, though for the most part its ravages went undetected. Indeed, since AIDS usually kills by proxy, by means of TB, malaria, pneumonia, or some other infection, it is hardly surprising that Africa's chronically under funded medical sector was only vaguely aware of the growing pandemic. Furthermore, given Africa's low life expectancy compared with the developed world, many African AIDS infections went undetected when HIV–afflicted Africans died before the symptoms of AIDS became manifest. AIDS did not go completely unnoticed — in Uganda, for example, AIDS symptoms became so prevalent that local people began to speak of "slim," a disease that causes progressive wasting of the human body. Nonetheless, since AIDS symptoms masqueraded as other ailments, since its long incubation time made it difficult to connect cause and effect, and since no specific pathogenic agent was identified, the world's most deadly modern disease went largely undetected.

Once established, AIDS began to spread through Africa by a variety of means. As we have already seen, forced levies of migrant laborers by European authorities during the colonial period probably played a role in spreading AIDS. Even during the post-colonial period, long-distance economic migration remained a common phenomenon in Africa. In some areas, it was customary for rural farmers to emigrate seasonally to towns and cities after the harvest season was over in search of craft or industrial jobs. Large-scale economic migration was also a common survival mechanism during famines, which are a fact of life in underdeveloped but over-populated areas in sub–Saharan Africa. In addition, many Africans would spend years at a time working as mine laborers or farm hands in export-oriented plantations, often hundreds of miles from their homes and their families. In all of these situations, long absences from home encouraged many laborers to employ the services of prostitutes, who quickly became reservoirs of HIV within Africa.

Other human agents played equally important roles in disseminating the HIV virus within Africa. Long-distance truck drivers in Africa, who often relied on prostitutes or informal wives to satisfy their sexual desires on the road, became a potent vector for the spread of HIV. The prostitutes themselves, many of whom traveled from place to place or even country to country, also played a crucial role in dispersing AIDS throughout Africa. Indeed, one study found that 50 percent of prostitutes in Abidjan, the capital of the West African nation of Côte D'Ivoire, were HIV–positive in 1989. In addition, the rapid movement of Africa's population into cities, due to the pull of economic opportunity and the push of rural poverty and starvation, has also created a favorable situation for the spread of the virus. Unlike traditional villages, where religion or custom keeps extramarital sex in check, the growing cities of modern Africa created more opportunities for recreational sex and havens for prostitution.

African armies became a potent mechanism for spreading the HIV virus as well. Soldiers often served far from their home, meaning that they could easily carry HIV from their homelands to distant villages or vice versa. While away from their families, soldiers made frequent use of prostitutes, further exposing them to the disease. What is more, during wartime African soldiers often participate in rapes, creating yet more opportunity for soldiers to contract HIV. Unfortunately, rape is a particularly effective means of transferring HIV from person to person. The tissue damage that often accompanies rape (both on the part of the victim and victimizer) heightens the likelihood of HIV infection. Rapists rarely use condoms, further exacerbating the risk of catching the disease. Not surprisingly, African soldiers today are as likely or likelier to harbor HIV as African sex workers: According to Tony Barnett and Alan Whiteside, the HIV–positive rate in Tanzania's army was as high as 30 percent, Angola and Congo's army 60 percent, and Zimbabwe's army up to 80 percent. As a consequence, HIV infections in Africa follow closely on the wake of both foreign and civil war.

Furthermore, sheer poverty greatly facilitates the spread of AIDS throughout Africa. Because of chronic economic underdevelopment, Africa's health care system is feeble at best, and consequently treatable sexually transmitted diseases like syphilis and gonorrhea frequently

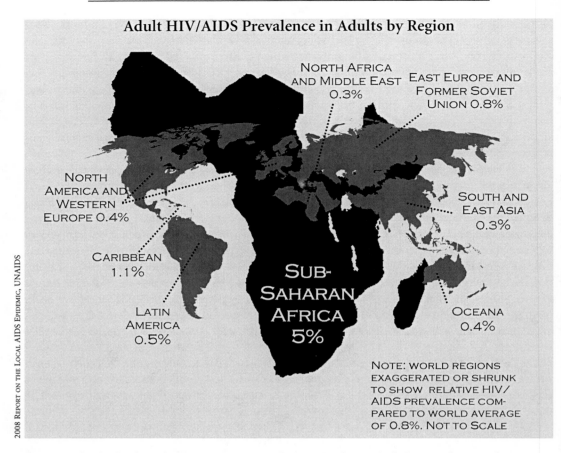

2008 REPORT ON THE LOCAL AIDS EPIDEMIC, UNAIDS

fester unchecked. These infections can cause lesions in the genital tissues, thus vastly increasing the chance of transmitting HIV during sex. Africa's poverty also obliges many doctors to reuse hypodermic needles: One recent study, for instance, found that a mission hospital in Zaire used just 5 needles to inject 400 patients over the course of a single day. AIDS in Africa is also facilitated by the fact that the most common means of preventing HIV infection, the condom, was and remains simply too expensive for day-to-day use in most African nations. Those condoms that do exist are often washed and reused, reducing their effectiveness. Of course, poverty also plays a role in forcing Africans to try to survive by resorting to prostitution or migrant labor, which as we have already seen creates opportunities for AIDS infection.

Economic factors, then, clearly predispose Africa for an AIDS epidemic. It is less clear whether African cultural practices, especially African sexual mores, play an exacerbating role as well. Some scholars do advocate this position; disease scholar W. A. Rushing, for example, argues that Africans have "little guilt" about sex and that "social norms permit and even encourage sex with multiple partners." However, the available evidence provides only limited support for the thesis that intrinsic African sex practices are at the root of Africa's AIDS problem. It is true that most African ethnicities practice polygamy, a habit they share with roughly 85 percent of the world's population. Like most supposedly polygamous societies, however, monogamy is the *de facto* norm, and in almost all regions of Africa, traditional values strongly discourage extramarital sex. In some parts of Islamic Africa, in fact, draconian law codes proscribe death by stoning for unfaithful wives, while male adulterers face only slightly less harsh punishment. In reality, the microcultures in Africa where frequent multi-partner sex are most common tend to be areas where traditional African cultures have weakened under the assault of social and economic forces impinging on Africa from the outside.

Indeed, the colonial and post-colonial European powers must bear a considerable portion of the blame for fostering AIDS in Africa. Like many other ailments, AIDS is exacerbated by poverty and social disorder, and Africa's modern-day economic and social problems are to a significant degree legacies of the brutalities of the era of European colonialism. Furthermore, the post-colonial economic policies of international organizations like the World Bank and the International Monetary Fund, which are dominated by the former European imperial powers, are playing an indirect role in worsening the AIDS crisis in modern Africa. Both institutions provide loans to developing African nations, but in return insist that those nations adopt SAPs— Structural Adjustment Policies—which often do more harm that good to the continent's people. Most African nations, for example, are under pressure to repay their foreign debts and balance their budgets. As a result, African nations have little money to pay the rising cost of AIDS treatment, and even less money to spend on AIDS prevention. As a result, AIDS debilitates the work force, further deepening African poverty. The World Bank and IMF also insist that African nations maximize their exports, but since the export trade generally benefits the rich few rather than the struggling many, these policies perpetuate the economic inequality and instability that provides fertile ground for AIDS. Both institutions also insist that developing nations make regular installments on their crushing burden of debt, payments that jeopardize the economic growth that the original loans were supposed to foster. In the words of Salih Brooker, an expert on global human rights in the modern world, the World Bank and IMF "must be made accountable for their role in causing the worst health crisis in human history, which Africa now faces."

Given all the facts that we have discussed so far—that AIDS originated in Africa, that European colonialism and neo-colonialism have fostered its growth, and that crushing poverty

Mike Keefe THE DENVER POST 2001 www.cagle.com

creates a favorable climate for its perpetuation — it is hardly surprising that Africa was and remains the continent most strongly impacted by the modern AIDS pandemic. As of 2003, 26 million Africans had died of AIDS — a staggering statistic, especially given that only 2 million people had died of AIDS outside of Africa by that time. Worse yet, failing the discovery of some miraculous cure, at least 18 and perhaps as many as 30 million Africans will die of AIDS by 2010. Nearly all of the countries with the highest domestic AIDS rates are in sub–Saharan Africa, and at the very top sits Botswana, where almost 40 percent of the population is HIV–positive. Even in countries that are relatively prosperous by African standards, such as South Africa, the HIV rate is closing in on 25 percent. AIDS exerts such a drain on South Africa's economy that its growth in GDP is expected to reach only 1.5 percent by 2010, nearly two percentage points lower than it would have been without AIDS. Also by 2010, five African countries are expected to have negative population growth, and the life expectancy in eleven African nations will dip below 30 years. Indeed, AIDS is poised to wipe away a century of demographic progress in Africa; as AIDS expert Susan Hunter points out, negative population growth on this scale has "not been seen since the end of the 1800s."

This is not to say that the AIDS picture in sub–Saharan Africa is universally bleak. AIDS is concentrated in areas where migrant labor has been common, such as South Africa and Botswana, where thousands of workers were attracted to the relatively high wages offered by mining companies. Other countries, such as Somalia and Nigeria, have been less affected, though Nigeria is beginning to suffer from regional "microepidemics" that may be the prelude to a future explosion of AIDS. As a rule, Islamic Africa has been less impacted than areas with large populations of Christians or followers of traditional African religions, most likely because of harsher penalties for extramarital sex in societies following Islamic *shari'a* law. Furthermore, Western Africa has been less badly affected by AIDS. This is not because HIV is absent, but rather because the prevalent local strain of HIV is HIV 2, which develops more slowly than HIV 1 in the human body and which usually provides the victim some degree of protection from infection by HIV 1. Furthermore, aggressive treatment and prevention campaigns in some African countries have successfully stemmed the tide of AIDS. Case in point is Uganda, which some scholars believe was the epicenter of the modern AIDS epidemic, but which has nonetheless managed to reduce HIV positivity levels from a high of about 15 percent to only about 6.7 percent today by means of a public information campaign generously funded by the United States.

Despite such minor successes, the AIDS situation in Africa remains dire. Worse yet, there is reason to believe that Africa's AIDS plight may just be the first act of a much larger world tragedy, since new AIDS cases outside of Africa are now rising at a far higher rate than new African cases. Indeed, while HIV prevalence rose by 30 percent in Africa between 1996 and 2001, it expanded by an estimated 40 percent in Latin America, 60 percent in the Indian subcontinent, 100 percent in the Middle East and North Africa, 160 percent in East Asia, and a staggering 1300 percent in Russia. In each of these regions, as in North America and Europe, AIDS remains largely a disease of "risk groups," though there are signs that AIDS is fast becoming established as a disease of the mainstream heterosexual population.

For many people worldwide, AIDS is strongly associated with the homosexual community of the United States. While it is true that the first well studied and documented AIDS cases did occur in this group, genetic studies suggest that the HIV strain that infected North American homosexuals first passed through Haiti, a Caribbean island nation which had the reputation of being a gay-friendly vacation destination. AIDS probably reached Haiti, in turn, in the bodies of educated Haitians who traveled to the former Congo Free State in the 1960s after Belgium granted it independence. In the meantime, HIV 2 entered Europe from West Africa, which had close ties to Europe, especially France, due to the legacies of the imperial era. HIV probably spread from person to person in the Caribbean, North America, and Europe for about 10 years before carriers of the virus began to become symptomatic during the final stages of the disease. In 1981, American doctors began to detect puzzling outbreaks of Pneumocystis carinii pneumonia and Kaposi Sarcoma cases in the American homosexual community. Although the original concentration was in Southern California, by July of 1982 a total of 452 cases had been identified in 23 states, with New York City increasingly becoming a focal point of these unusual syndromes. Since at first the disease seemed limited to homosexuals, the disease was widely dubbed Gay Related Immune Deficiency, or GRID.

Almost immediately after the term GRID was adopted, new cases demonstrated that the disease was not limited to homosexual men after all. By late July of 1982, "GRID" cases began to turn up among hemophiliacs, suffers of a blood disorder that requires patients to receive frequent transfusions of donated blood products. In response, medical researchers agreed to rename the disease AIDS, though this did little to counter the public's perception that AIDS was a "gay" disease. The next group in which AIDS symptoms was noted was Haitian immigrants, and in late 1982, the first case of mother-child transmission of the disease was observed. By early 1983, AIDS cases were beginning to crop up among users of intravenous drugs. As a result, people began to speak of AIDS as an endemic disease of the "4-H club": Hemophiliacs, Heroin addicts, Haitians, and Homosexuals. Since the disease seemed limited to those groups, few people yet worried about the epidemic, and the U.S. government took few steps to address the growing plague. Nonetheless, it soon became clear that HIV had no intention of remaining inside the "risk group" box in which it had been placed: In June of 1983, doctors determined that a 71-year-old heterosexual woman had acquired AIDS, and the only reasonable way she could have contracted the illness was through sex with her 74-year-old hemophiliac husband.

Further evidence that AIDS more than a "gay plague" was soon forthcoming from Europe. Researchers there detected two distinct AIDS epidemics. The first epidemic, which mainly afflicted the UK, West Germany, and Denmark, resembled the American outbreak on the main, since it involved almost exclusively the male homosexual community. Studies determined that most AIDS patients in these regions had participated in homosexual sex with North American partners. In France and Belgium, however, AIDS patients were rarely homosexual. Rather, AIDS appeared in patients who had personal links to Central Africa. AIDS also began to appear among European hemophiliacs; indeed French officials later came under heavy criticism for continuing to distribute potentially tainted blood products to hemophiliacs even after these products were determined to be a source of AIDS infection. On a brighter note, French medical researchers identified the virus that caused AIDS in May of 1983, opening the way to detection and prevention of the illness. However, the development of a blood test for AIDS was slowed somewhat by a bitter fight between French researchers and an American research team which pressed the case — ultimately without success— that U.S. scientists had discovered the virus first.

While scientists quibbled, the epidemic expanded exponentially through the human population of Europe and the Americas. By the end of 1984, a total of 7,699 cases of AIDS had been reported in the U.S., and 3,665 people had died. Of course, since AIDS was such a new disease, it is quite possible that many other AIDS victims went undiagnosed, especially since doctors tended to look for AIDS cases primarily among patients in the "4-H" categories. In Europe, 762 cases had been reported by the end of 1984, but once again, this was probably just the tip of the iceberg. In any case, confirmed AIDS cases in both Europe and the Americas skyrocketed thereafter: Within just one year, the number of known AIDS cases more than doubled, and by 1990, the number of AIDS cases in Europe and America was estimated to be over 300,000, in addition to another 2.5 million pre-symptomatic patients infected by HIV.

As in Africa, the dramatic growth of AIDS cases during this period was by no means inevitable: The mere presence of an infective agent is not enough to trigger a pandemic. Unfortunately for the developed world, however, a number of factors conspired in the mid–20th century to greatly facilitate the spread of epidemic AIDS. By the 1970s, homosexuals in the west were beginning to "come out of the closet," despite continued cultural disapproval and sometimes even legal prosecution. In some areas "gay culture" achieved virtual institutional status: In San Francisco, for example, gay-friendly bath houses became hot spots for homosexual sex, and potentially HIV infection as well. However, homosexuals were hardly the only group during this period to indulge in more frequent sexual encounters. The 1960s and 1970s also witnessed a sexual revolution among heterosexuals, leading to more frequent sexual behavior and more numerous sexual partners among the young.

Other factors set the stage for HIV infections in the developed world as well. Fast and relatively cheap air travel greatly increased the popularity of long-distance tourism and thus facilitated the spread of diseases between continents. The increasing popularity of the addictive drug heroin in the 1970s also helped to spread HIV, since unlike marijuana and LSD, the classic drugs of the 1960s, heroin is most infrequently administered by injection. The use of heroin, in turn, received a boost in the technological changes: By the 1970s, cheap and disposable plastic syringes had appeared on the market, so many more people had access to drug injection equipment. Unfortunately, heroin users frequently reuse and share supposedly "disposable" syringes, providing numerous opportunities for AIDS infections. Many heroin users also resort to prostitution to feed their drug habits, further increasing the chance of acquiring or disseminating the virus.

Modern social changes in the West have created a favorable environment for the spread of HIV as well. The de-industrialization of many Western cities and the explosive growth suburban populations has tended to concentrate poverty in inner city areas, and since these inner cities are hot spots for drug use and prostitution, they often serve as reservoirs for the HIV virus. Poverty is also strongly correlated to high levels of rape and low levels of condom use, both of which contribute to the AIDS epidemic. Furthermore, the burgeoning American prison system has become, in the words of AIDS scholar Susan Hunter, a "virtual infection pump of HIV into the general population." In part due to the "war on drugs," the American prison population has quadrupled in the last two decades, to the point that 2.1 million Americans were incarcerated by 2001. Unfortunately, since both anal sex and intravenous drug use is common within prison walls, America's soaring prison population also suffers from a soaring rate of HIV infection, and when these prisoners are eventually released into the general population, HIV is effectively released as well.

AIDS infections have also been fostered in the modern West by certain ideological beliefs. Most obvious in this regard is the widespread assumption that AIDS is a disease of "risk populations" such as the so-called 4-H club. Not only does this attitude help spread the virus by disinclining people to protect themselves during heterosexual sex, it has also blunted the political will to fight the disease. After all, why waste public money on a disease that drug users, prostitutes, and homosexuals bring upon themselves with their immoral and often illegal behaviors? For many American and European conservatives, active governmental steps to combat AIDS infection were tantamount to government support for immoral and dangerous lifestyles. For the same reason, the Religious Right in the United States has actively opposed sexual education classes, insisting that if schools offer any sexual guidance to young people at all, it ought to take the form of advocating abstinence rather than training students in condom use. Advocates of abstinence education argue that teaching the use of condoms implicitly encourages premarital sex, though there is little evidence to support this contention, while there is ample

NEW AIDS DIAGNOSIS IN THE US, 2005

exposure category	male	female	total	change in total cases since 1980
male-to-male sexual contact	18,939	-	18,939	↘
injection drug use	5,806	3,179	8,985	↘
male-to-male sexual contact and injection drug use	2,190	-	2,190	↘
high-risk hetero-sexual contact	5,208	8,278	13,486	↗
other/risk not identified	287	253	540	↘
total	32,430	11,710	44,140	
change since 1980	↘	↗		

evidence that condom use is very effective in preventing HIV infection. One particularly disastrous outcome of abstinence education is that it can lead to girls trying to preserve their virginity for marriage by agreeing only to anal sex, and as we have already seen, anal sex is a considerably more effective vector for AIDS transmission than vaginal intercourse.

The greed of western pharmaceutical companies has played a role in worsening the epidemic as well, not only within the West but on a global scale. U.S. Drug companies keep the price of medications, including those for AIDS, artificially high on the grounds that money for drug sales pay for new research. In actuality, drug companies spend far more money marketing their existing products than they do researching new medications, while in the meantime raking higher profits than almost any other sector of the American economy. "Big Pharm" also insists that American AIDS patients take handfuls of high-price, name-brand pills rather than the generically manufactured fixed-dose combination drugs available at a fraction of the cost overseas. As a result, a given American AIDS patient's annual drug bill often tops $10,000, while the generic drugs available in the non-western world cost only about $400 a year. Worse yet, American drug companies have enlisted the help of the U.S. Federal Government and the World Trade Organization in putting pressure on overseas pharmaceutical countries to desist making generic copies of AIDS drugs. Because of American bullying, for example, Brazil has refused to sell its inexpensive generic AIDS drugs to other Latin American countries. Heavy-handed pressure of this sort not only hurts AIDS victims, but also their wives, lovers, and even newborn children, since people receiving antiviral therapy are far less likely to transmit HIV through sex, childbirth, or breast feeding.

Perhaps most tragic of all, advances in medical science have themselves created a favorable condition for the spread of HIV. The transfusion of blood products offers the possibility of greatly extending the life of the seriously ill, especially hemophiliacs, who lack blood platelets and thus bleed profusely from even small cuts. During the mid–20th century, doctors discovered that occasional transfusions of donated blood platelets can add clotting agents to hemophiliacs' blood. However, since the blood of thousands of donors is used manufacture a single batch of clotting agent, blood transfusions served, in the words of AIDS researcher Mirko

Grmek, as a "royal road" for HIV into the human body. Furthermore, since the sale of blood products is an international business, blood products became mechanism for the intercontinental dissemination of HIV. Furthermore, the advanced medical technique of plasmapheresis, in which blood is drained, broken down into component products, and then selectively reinjected into the donor, also poses a risk of transmitting HIV. Plasmapheresis can save the lives of people suffering from autoimmune disorders and other diseases, but if multiple patients use the same machine and the machine is not properly sterilized between uses, this advanced procedure can serve as a potent vector of AIDS. Indeed, a single plasmapheresis center in Valencia, Spain infected a number of patients with AIDS, some of whom subsequently traveled as far away as Australia.

As a result of the various factors listed above, AIDS in the developed world is rapidly losing its character as a disease of only "risk populations." Although AIDS used to be predominantly (but no means exclusively) found in white male homosexual populations, AIDS in America has increasingly become a disease of minority groups. Indeed, African-Americans and Hispanics, who are generally poorer than the national average and thus has less access to health care, are increasingly becoming the focus of the American and European AIDS epidemics. Furthermore, as in Africa, women in the developed world are increasingly becoming the focal point of the AIDS epidemic. In part this is because women are biologically more susceptible to the virus than men given the mechanisms of HIV transmission. This fact also reflects the continued disempowerment of women in the United States, especially low-income women, who are more likely to be raped or coerced into sex. In Europe, the situation is similar. In Britain today, for instance, less than half of new AIDS cases result from homosexual sex, non-whites are disproportionally affected, and 60 percent of the known carriers of HIV are women. As a result, the AIDS epidemic in the developed world increasingly resembles the African epidemic: AIDS is no longer a disease of "risk groups," but rather a generalized concern for the population at large, especially society's most poor and oppressed.

Nonetheless, the AIDS situation in Europe and the United States is relatively bright by world standards. The percentage of North Americans with HIV today is only .8 percent, a far cry from the 5.9 percent HIV infection rate in sub–Saharan Africa. In Western and Central Europe, only .3 percent of the population is HIV positive. Better yet, the rate of new infections is holding at about 20 percent per year, a far cry from the 100 percent or more yearly growth rate of AIDS cases that was observed in these regions at the very beginning of the epidemic. Unfortunately, in other areas, the explosive growth of AIDS seems to have just begun. Three regions of the world in particular worry AIDS researchers: Russia, India, and China.

Russia acquired AIDS at a relatively late date, largely due to the fact that contact between people within the "Warsaw Pact" countries and the outside world was fairly limited during the Cold War. The authoritarian government of the USSR also strongly discouraged prostitution, homosexual behavior, and drug use, which were seen as decadent artifacts of the capitalist West that had no place in Soviet society. Furthermore, Soviet citizens had access to a health care system that, although not without its problems, was free to all. As a result, by 1995, barely over a thousand HIV infections had been reported in Russia. In the period of turmoil and chaos following the collapse of the Soviet Union, however, the incidence of HIV rose dramatically. The break-down of Soviet authority led to an explosion of illicit drug use, especially intravenous drugs, which served as a potent vector of AIDS. Post-Soviet Russia also experienced a belated sexual revolution, while at the same time sexual education continued to lag in the Russian school system. As a result, over a million people in Russia are HIV positive today. AIDS is still especially prevalent among intravenous drug users and prostitutes, groups that often overlap each other, but recent trends are disturbing: The number of new HIV transmissions through heterosexual sex rose from just over 5 percent in 2001 to 20 percent in 2003. This suggests that AIDS in Russia, though still limited mainly to "risk groups," may soon follow the African pattern of becoming epidemic in the population at large.

The AIDS situation in India gives even more cause for concern. Currently "only" 2.5 million Indians are HIV positive, a number that is absolutely large but relatively small given India's vast population of over 1.1 billion people. Nonetheless, AIDS is growing at an astounding rate. It was probably inevitable that AIDS would find its way to India, given that a vast number of Indian workers are employed overseas, some in areas like South Africa which are hot spots of AIDS. Once AIDS became established in India, the government's response was blunted by the tendency to examine the disease through the "risk group" model. As a result, prostitutes, truck drivers, drug users, and homosexuals came under particular scrutiny. Unfortunately, as disease scholar Niranjan S. Karmak points out in a recent essay, the western "risk group" model proved highly misleading in the Indian context. The western model of homosexuality, for instance, does not apply well to the Indian context, while India has sexual categories, such as eunuchs, which do not exist in the developed world. Furthermore Indian women have even less power over sexual relations than they do in the developed world, and are frequently unable to make choices about the timing of sex, not to mention whether or not condoms are used. Women's lack of power in sexual relations is matched only by the dominance of men, who by and large consider sex on demand to be the right of a husband in marriage, and who don't face the same public opprobrium as women for extramarital sex. Not surprisingly, then, the AIDS epidemic in India greatly resembles the African epidemic: Although HIV remains more prevalent among "risk groups," heterosexual sex is increasingly becoming the most important transmission mechanism, suggesting that AIDS may soon become an established epidemic within India's mainstream population.

As in India, the HIV–positive population of the Peoples Republic of China is high in an absolute sense — approximately 650,000 — though low relative to the country's vast population of over 1.3 billion. However, this number is expected to rise dramatically over time, in part due to the government's fairly woeful record thus far of tackling the AIDS epidemic. Initially the Chinese government argued that AIDS posed no threat to China: In 1987, for instance, the Chinese health minister declared that China's AIDS risk was "slim" as both homosexuality and "abnormal" sexuality were only a "limited" problem in China. Since the disease was seen fundamentally as a western epidemic, the early Chinese response to AIDS largely consisted of advising Chinese women not to have sex with foreign men. Furthermore Chinese exchange students and other travelers were rigorously examined upon returning to China lest they introduce this "Western" contagion into Communist China. In the meantime, AIDS staged an unanticipated assault following the so-called "Road of Death," a heroin trafficking route that runs from Yunnan on China's southern border all the way to Beijing. Nonetheless, AIDS was still seen as an "outsiders" disease. Indeed the Chinese popularly dubbed AIDS the "loving capitalism disease," since both homosexuality and drug use were seen as artifacts of western capitalism.

In the early 1990s, however, AIDS took advantage of poorly managed Chinese blood donation schemes to make a definitive leap into the mainstream Chinese population. During this decade, in response to the high price of blood products, unscrupulous traders called "bloodheads" offered the rural poor cash for blood at a rate of $5 a pint, but made little effort to sterilize their equipment between blood extractions. As a result, in some areas, up to 65 percent of the inhabitants of rural communities contracted HIV, and villages like Wenlou in Henan province became a "waiting room for death." Furthermore, China's prostitute population increasingly became a reservoir for AIDS, in part because government oppression forces prostitutes to keep such a low profile that the sex industry is almost entirely unregulated. In addition, the government has only recently provided education about AIDS to the general population, to the point that by 2003 only about 1 out of 4 Chinese knew that condom use could provide protection against AIDS and 1 out of 6 Chinese had never heard of the disease. Only recently has China recognized the AIDS problem and implemented the commonsense approach, already adopted successfully by other countries, of advocating widespread condom use as a prophylactic against AIDS.

The AIDS problem in China is likely to get worse over time as Chinese women, even more than their Indian counterparts, have little leverage over their sex lives. Studies find that Chinese women are generally not in a position to compel their husbands to use condoms, even when they know that their husband has a "second wife," a common practice when Chinese males have jobs that oblige them to travel. The inferiority of women in Chinese society is further illustrated by the shocking rate of sex crimes against women: No less than a third of Chinese women report being victims of rape or child abuse. Furthermore, China's "one child policy" led to a high rate of female infanticide, leading in turn to a modern-day deficit of women as compared to men — and this in turn has led to the phenomenon of criminal gangs abducting and then selling women as "brides" to men with poor marriage prospects. Needless to say, such "commodified" women have little say about whether or not condoms are used. Chinese women are also paid less well than their male counterparts in the workforce, and like elsewhere, poverty is strongly correlated to AIDS transmission.

As a result, it is hardly surprising that the pattern of AIDS transmission in China beginning to follow the same trajectory that we have seen in North America and elsewhere while AIDS might have begun as a disease of "risk groups," AIDS in China is fast becoming an affliction of the general population. Studies show that heterosexual sex, which accounted for only about 7 percent of known HIV infections in 1998, is now responsible for about 20 percent of new HIV infections, and this number is expected to continue rising over time. Indeed, Peter Piot, the head of the UN AIDS program, estimated in 2001 that there might be as many as 50 million HIV–positive Chinese by 2010. More recent data collected by the AIDS charity AVERT suggests that Piot's doomsday scenario was a severe overestimation: The HIV–positive population in China was set at only 700,000 in 2007, though due to underreporting in rural areas it is likely the true number is quite a bit higher.

Even if the death toll proves to be fairly modest in coming years, however, demographic realities in China will likely magnify the social costs of AIDS to the society at large. In Chinese culture, the young of the family are supposed to provide support for their elderly parents. China's one-child policy, which effectively makes the support of two elderly parents the responsibility of a single individual, is already putting this tradition under considerable strain. If AIDS curtails the lives of millions of young Chinese, then, it will further disrupt an already tenuous intergenerational social contract in China, and may force the Chinese state into a financial crisis as it tries to support millions of destitute, childless Chinese elders. Despite the urgency of this demographic disaster, China continues to invest little money in prevention campaigns, and the government has even been accused of harassing or censoring Chinese anti–AIDS activists. Perhaps as a result, some observers expect China to host the world's largest HIV–positive population in the near future.

The global pandemic AIDS, therefore, represents an enormous threat to both present and future generations. Perhaps the greatest significance of AIDS, however, is not the disease itself, but what the disease represents. HIV is a modern disease that jumped to the human species as a result of the specific characteristics of the modern world: Fast transportation, urbanization, increased migration, changing social and sexual mores, and growing social inequality. Since all of these characteristics of modernity are likely to grow more pronounced over time, AIDS may just prove to be the first of a series of unprecedented 21st century pandemics. Indeed, AIDS may be just the first of a series of epidemics to arise from mankind's current push into previously undisturbed tropical forest ecosystems. Tropical forests host a far denser concentration of unique species than anywhere else on the planet, and since each animal species hosts its own endemic diseases, each square meter of cleared forest could potentially host dozens of harmful bacteria and viruses against which human immune systems have no defense. AIDS already passed from animals to man in the 20th century, as did Ebola, a terrifying hemorrhagic fever with a 90 percent mortality rate. Thankfully, Ebola proved to be only moderately infective, as did AIDS, but mankind may not be so lucky the next time a disease of the tropical forest jumps the species barrier to mankind.

Study Questions

1. Based on this section, to what degree is it fair to label AIDS a "disease of globalization?" Support your answer.

2. To what degree does "construct" AIDS play a role in worsening the modern AIDS epidemic? See beginning of chapter for a definition of a disease "construct."

3. "Unlike such diseases as malaria and cholera, because of its mode of transmission, AIDS is unlikely to be worsened by other natural disasters." Based on the text and your own reasoning, how convincing do you find this statement?

4. "Mainly because of cultural factors, AIDS in America and Europe has little in common with the AIDS epidemics of Africa and Asia." How convincing do you find this statement?

Suggested Readings

"AIDS and HIV Information." *AVERT.* Available from http://www.avert.org/

Amirkhanian, Yuri A., Dennis V. Tiunov, and Jeffrey A. Kelly. "Risk factors for HIV and Other Sexually Transmitted Diseases Among Adolescents in St. Petersburg, Russia." *Family Planning Perspectives*, Vol. 33, No. 3 (May-June, 2001), pp. 106–112.

Barnett, Tony, and Alan Whiteside. *AIDS in the Twenty-First Century: Disease and Globalization.* New York: Palgrave Macmillan, 2002.

Berridge, Virginia. "The Early Years of AIDS in the United Kingdom 1981–6: Historical Perspectives." In Terence Ranger and Paul Slack, eds., *Epidemics and Ideas.* New York: Cambridge University Press, 1992.

Desai, Sapna. "HIV and Domestic Violence: Intersections in the Lives of Married Women in India." *Health and Human Rights*, Vol. 8, No. 2, Emerging issues in HIV/AIDS. (2005), pp. 140–168.

Grmek, Mirko D. *History of AIDS: Emergence and Origin of a Modern Pandemic.* Princeton, NJ: Princeton University Press, 1990.

Hansen, Keith. "A Plague's Bottom Line." *Foreign Policy*, No. 137. (July-Aug. 2003), pp. 26–27.

Hunter, Susan. *AIDS in America.* New York: Palgrave Macmillan, 2006.

Hunter, Susan. *Black Death: AIDS in Africa.* New York: Palgrave Macmillan, 2003.

Kalipeni, Ezekiel, Susan Craddock, Joseph R. Oppong, and Jayati Ghosh. *HIV and AIDS in Africa: Beyond Epidemiology.* Malden, MA: Blackwell, 2004.

Karnik, Niranjan S. "Locating HIV/AIDS and India: Cautionary Notes on the Globalization of Categories." *Science, Technology, & Human Values*, Vol. 26, No. 3. (Summer, 2001), pp. 322–348.

Renwick, Neil. "The 'Nameless Fever': The HIV/AIDS Pandemic and China's Women." *Third World Quarterly*, Vol. 23, No. 2, Global Health and Governance: HIV/AIDS (Apr., 2002), pp. 377–393.

"2008 Report on the Global AIDS Epidemic." *UNAIDS.* Available from http://www.unaids.org/en/KnowledgeCentre/HIVData/GlobalReport/2008/2008_Global_report.asp.

Weinhold, Bob. "Infectious Disease: The Human Costs of Our Environmental Errors." *Environmental Health Perspectives* Volume 112, Number 1 (Jan. 2004), pp. A34–A39.

Conclusion

In the past chapters, we have explored how human behaviors and beliefs have interacted with natural forces to produce repeated disasters throughout history, particularly over the course of the past 150 years. So what lessons can we draw from these findings about our shared human future? Is the record of past disasters a reliable guide for the environmental hazards that lie ahead in the 21st century? As a scholar trained in the profession of history, it would be tempting to answer this question with a resounding yes. However, the available evidence suggests otherwise. Indeed, both modern human beings and the planet they occupy are currently experiencing previously unknown rates of change.

The present rate of technological advance, for example, is utterly unprecedented in human history. Only a century and a half ago, the main forms of transportation were the horse and the sailing ship, just as they had been for thousands of years. Today, horses and sail-driven boats are restricted to isolated populations of the economically disadvantaged and, ironically, to the leisure pursuits of the affluent. What is more, humanity's pace of change is increasing over time. The coal-powered steam engine, first developed by Thomas Newcomen in 1712, was an enormous breakthrough for its time, but nonetheless it was not altered substantially for sixty or seventy years. In the past fifty years, by way of contrast, computers have progressed from monstrosities the size of a room to "microcomputers" equipped with tiny processers capable of doing millions of times the work of their room-size forbearers— and the speed of these microprocessors is still doubling every 18 months or so. Given mankind's current headlong dive into an increasingly advanced future, it is small wonder why so many modern college students believe that the study of our historical past has little meaning to their present lives.

The population of human beings, like the advance of technology, has also experienced an unprecedented growth spurt in recent years. It took all of human history up to the early years of the 19th century for the population of people on the planet to reach one billion, but now humans add another billion to their population every decade and a half or so. Human population doubled between the 1960s and the first years of the 21st century, an astounding rate of growth. Human population density, as opposed to overall population, is also reaching previously unseen levels. According to environmental historian J. R. McNeill, the percentage of the world's surface covered by urban areas jumped from .1 percent to 1 percent between 1900 and 1990, a trend that continues into the 21st century. Sometime in 2008, there will be more people will be living in urban than rural areas for the first time in human history. What is more, urban areas themselves are becoming larger in scale. As geographer James K. Mitchell points out in a recent book, human beings are increasingly becoming concentrated in "megacities," sprawling urban areas with millions of residents. Although this trend has slowed somewhat in the developed world, it continues unchecked in the developing world, where sprawling urban centers continue to soak up excess rural population. The Bangladeshi capital of Dhaka, for example, has topped 11 million in population and continues to grow at a rate of nearly 4 percent annually.

The parallel explosion of technological and demographic growth in the modern age is by no means accidental; indeed, there are reasons to believe that the two processes are intimately linked. Possibly the most underappreciated scientific breakthrough of the 20th century was Fritz Haber's discovery that of an efficient industrial method of creating artificial fertilizer by breaking the strong bond between the atoms of an atmospheric N_2 molecule. As a result, since the 1920s, humanity has been able to extract nitrogen fertilizer from the atmosphere itself, greatly increasing the amount of food available to mankind. Geographer Vaclav Smil has gone so far as to claim that 40 percent of the world's population today is owes its existence to the additional food that has become available to human populations thanks to the discovery of synthetic nitrogen fertilizer. Pesticides, motorized farm machinery, and genetic engineering of crops and livestock has also increased mankind's food supply, as have improved transportation and storage mechanisms. Technology contributes to the megacity phenomenon as well. Skyscrapers would be inconceivable without elevators, and without modern sewer systems megacities would be hives of disease rather than centers of human political, cultural, and economic life. In return, population expansion almost certainly contributes to technological advances, since the swelling global population means that there are more potential innovators alive today than at any time in humanity's past.

Clearly, population expansion and technological advancements are complimentary processes. Unfortunately both processes are also linked to a third phenomenon: unprecedented rates of natural resource depletion on a global scale. Since 1800, for example, escalating human demands for fuel, housing, and agricultural land have led to steadily increasing rates of deforestation. Indeed, the planet is now losing up to 120,000 square kilometers of forest a year to logging, herding, or agriculture. Much of this deforestation is in the tropics, where nutrients lost due to deforestation cannot easily be replaced, and where the chance of previously unknown infections crossing the species barrier is particularly high. As discussed in sections 8.2 and 8.4 respectively, Malaria and AIDS both jumped to the human species as a result of human intrusion into tropical forest ecosystems, and these deadly epidemics may just be a taste of things to come.

Deforestation, in turn, is linked to another present day catastrophe: soil erosion, which is now occurring at a previously unseen rate. As David Montgomery points out in his recent work, *Dirt: The Erosion of Civilizations*, soil is created very slowly by nature but can quickly be destroyed by human agriculturalists employing unsustainable farming practices. Montgomery goes so far as to claim that modern farmers are "skinning our planet," reducing the Earth's soil deposits by as much as 24 billion tons a year, or about 4 tons for each person alive in 2008. In part, this soil loss is due to the increasing exploitation of marginal hillsides and prairies by land-hungry farmers in developing nations. However, developed nations bear some responsibility for soil loss as well, since mechanized farming renders soil particularly susceptible to erosion. Although soil erosion is by no means a new problem in human history, the current rate of global soil loss is unprecedented: Mankind is currently stripping away the soil at 20 times the natural erosion rate, a process that is likely to have catastrophic impact in the future.

The current rate of technological and demographic advance has also endangered the world's supply of water, which is arguably our most vital natural resource. As we saw repeatedly throughout chapter 7, short-term or localized drought has wreaked havoc on human populations throughout history. However, human population pressure means that large parts of the world are now in real danger of exceeding available water resources, not only in rare years of low rainfall but even during normal years. As of 2008, 35 percent of the world's renewable freshwater is already diverted from the ecosystem for human use, mostly in agriculture, which requires enormous water inputs. In some arid countries, such as Egypt and Israel, this statistic is nearing 100 percent, further undermining the stability of this already volatile region. What is more, some Middle Eastern nations are already "mining" their water sources, withdrawing considerably more water from the ecosystem than is replaced by natural sources. The nation of Qatar, where this book was written, is currently consuming 6 times as much water as is replenished by natural processes. In the neighboring United Arab Emirates, which hosts the boom town of Dubai, the rate of water consumption is about 17 times annual replenishment.

So far, human beings have had some success in staving off the looming water crisis through various forms of technology. Underground aquifers have been located and tapped, river water has been piped to distant cities hundreds of kilometers away, and desalinization plants have converted saltwater into fresh. Perhaps most importantly of all, water-poor or overpopulated countries have sustained themselves by importing "virtual water" in the form of food. The world's largest exporter of virtual water is the United States, which ships out billions of liters of "water" annually in the form of grain, allowing importing nations to support higher populations than they could with their limited domestic water supplies. However, none of these techniques are likely to cope with increasing global populations in the long run. Desalinization is expensive, while rivers have only a limited annual capacity, and aquifers that are drained faster than they are replenished will eventually disappear. Already some of the world's great rivers, most notably America's Colorado and China's Yellow, sometimes run dry before reaching the sea due to escalating demands on their water.

Worse yet, virtual water is inextricably tied to the price of petroleum, another finite resource. The price of virtual water depends in large part on the cost of transportation, which in turn is determined largely by fuel costs. In addition, food and fuel are increasingly becoming interchangeable commodities due to advances of biofuel technology. Much of the consumer gasoline in the United States, for example, contains a percentage of ethanol, a motor fuel distilled from maize. As a consequence, when the price of crude oil reached unprecedented levels in the second half of the first decade of the third millennium — largely as a result of economic boom in China — the price of corn in the U.S. rose threefold. American consumers felt the pain mainly at the gas pumps, but people in the developing world felt it in their bellies, since food represents a far higher fraction of the household budget in poor as opposed to wealthy countries. Nations that depend primarily on "virtual water" for their water needs, therefore, are courting disaster.

The world's water problems, in turn, are worsened by another unprecedented modern problem: the unintended environmental consequences of human technological and economic advances. Deforestation and road building has reduced the ability of the world's soils to absorb rainfall, lowering the rate of replenishment in many of the world's aquifers. As we saw on a small scale in section 6.1, industrial pollutants continue to render some of the world's fresh water unusable by man. Worst of all, global warming due to anthropogenic greenhouse gas emissions will likely wreck havoc with the world's water supply. Glaciers are already retreating worldwide, and when they vanish, many of the world's great rivers will flow more intermittently. What is more, global warming will lead to more erratic weather patterns, meaning that there will likely be less "average" rainfall — the sort of steady rain that refills aquifers and sustains rivers. Rather, the world will experience more "extreme" weather conditions, such as downpours that lead to floods and soil erosion, interspersed with more dry spells that trigger drought. Higher global temperatures will also increase evaporation rates, meaning that many areas may suffer from drier soil conditions and thus reduced agricultural production even if the local annual rainfall is technically higher. As we saw in section 4.3, the scientific understanding of global warming remains incomplete, but the main question is not whether these things will happen but rather how quickly they will occur and to what an extent.

The rapidity of climate change in the present age of global warming will cause other problems in the future as well. The ecologist Jeffrey S. Dukes estimates that the fossil fuels that human beings consumed between 1751 and 1998 were equivalent to the amount of sunlight that the world's plants captured in the preceding 13,300 years. The energy contained in this ancient plant matter has fueled mankind's advance from the age of agriculture through the industrial and into the technological age, but it also released thousands of years of buried carbon dioxide back into the atmosphere. Never before, outside of catastrophic volcanic eruptions, has a similar volume of greenhouse gas been released as rapidly into the ecosystem. Indeed, meteorologist Paul Crutzen has gone so far as to claim that world has entered a new geological age, the "Anthropocene," defined by the fact that human beings (*anthropo* in Greek) are now exerting the primary influence upon the world's climate.

The result will almost certainly be dramatic environmental change in the next few hundred years—and unfortunately, the human species is not well suited to rapid environmental fluctuations. As already discussed in chapter 4, biologists classify *homo sapiens* as a K-selection organism, where "K" stands for "constant." Organisms of this type produce relatively few young, but those young are extremely well adapted to the environment in which they are born. As a result, K strategy organisms thrive in a constant environment but have trouble surviving rapid environmental changes. Rapid environmental change, in turn, favors r-selection organisms, where "r" stands for random. Such organisms produce a very large number of offspring, on the hopes that a few will survive and pass on their genetic material even if their environment fluctuates. Unfortunately for mankind, the quintessential "r" organisms are bacteria and viruses, which react to a flickering climate by rapid mutation. It remains to be seen if the rapid medical advances that the human species achieved in the 20th century will be able to keep up with the new epidemic diseases that are likely to arise over the course of the 21st.

Given the recent rapid changes in technology, population, and the environment, therefore, it is quite possible that the disasters of the future might look quite different from the disasters of the past. True, earthquakes and volcanoes will likely occur much as before, though human population growth in general—and in megacities in particular—will magnify their effects. Other disasters are likely to change more dramatically in the 21st centuries and beyond. Population pressure and a changing climate will likely produce unprecedented levels of deforestation, desertification, soil erosion, and consequent famine. Indeed, in an age of soaring food prices and declining water availability, famine may become endemic in some parts of the world, no longer held in check by the cheap transportation of large food surpluses that curbed the ravages of famine in the late 20th century. As we saw in chapter 5, tropical cyclones may become more violent in the future, though the science is uncertain. El Niño may become a constant, much as it was three million years ago, when jungle stretched to the poles. Finally, unprecedented population density, near instantaneous modern transportation, and a rapidly changing environment will create a host of new opportunities for infectious disease.

Advances in technology might ameliorate the effects of these supercharged modern disasters. However, as has been the case repeatedly in the past, advances in technology will almost certainly create new disasters in mankind's future. As mankind's need for energy continues to increase, fossil fuels reserves continue to dwindle, and CO_2 continues to accumulate in the atmosphere, the pressure will build for humanity to exploit nuclear power for its energy needs. Indeed, this process has already begun; more than 90 nuclear plants are under construction or in the planning stage in the nation of China alone. Nuclear power has a worse reputation than

it deserves, but the reality is bad enough — nuclear meltdowns can cause both immediate death and long-term cancer rates, and nuclear waste can be extremely harmful if improperly stored. In addition, nuclear waste could be used by terrorists to craft a "dirty bomb," capable of spreading harmful radioactive material — and death — over a large area. Another potentially harmful technology is genetic engineering. Genetically Engineered (GE) crops offer enormous advantages in terms of yield, pest resistance, nutrition, and other desirable characteristics, but these engineered crops can interact with natural ecosystems in unpredictable and potentially harmful ways. What is more, since GE crops by their very nature lack diversity, they may prove less resilient to plant diseases, adverse weather conditions, or environmental change than our current repertoire of food crops, raising the specter of a genetically engineered future famine.

The future disasters we should probably fear the most, however, are disasters arising from the unintended consequences of well-meaning applications of technology. A case in point is chlorofluorocarbon, or CFC as it is commonly called for simplicity's sake. CFCs, which were first discovered in the late 1920s, are relatively inert compounds used as a propellant in spray cans and as a fire retardant. By the 1980s, however, it was becoming increasingly clear that the chlorine in CFCs was eating away at the world's ozone layer, and as a result, dangerous amounts of ultraviolet radiation were bathing our planet's southern hemisphere. The use of CFC's has been sharply curtailed since the 1980s, but the damage has been done: Populations throughout the southern hemisphere are reporting higher than normal rates of skin cancer.

However, the truly frightening thing about CFCs is that the damage could have been far, far worse. If the chemical bromine had been slightly less expensive when CFCs were put on the market, industrial chemists might have manufactured BFCs (Bromofluorocarbons) instead, since BFCs and CFCs are virtually identical as far as industrial uses are concerned. Had that occurred, we would be living in a very different planet today. According to meteorologist Paul Crutzen, bromine in the atmosphere destroys ozone 45 times more efficiently than chorine.

Therefore, in addition to causing much higher rates of cancer, BFCs would have triggered famine on an enormous scale, since both marine fisheries and many types of crop plants would have been devastated by the UV radiation bombardment. It is somewhat disquieting to think that a seeming technological advance could have led to an environmental nightmare if not for a singular stroke of dumb luck.

So what can the disasters of the past tell us about the disasters of the future? Perhaps not much. In terms of population, technological development, and environmental change, we are all moving into uncharted territory. However, it is likely that two crucial lessons that we have learned from previous chapters will remain valid in the future: 1) apparently different types of natural disaster are in fact intimately linked, and 2) natural disasters are often created, or at least badly exacerbated, by human agency.

It is likely that the disasters mankind faces will become even more intimately linked in the 21st century and beyond. In particular, global warming may play the role of the "master disaster" of the post–20th century, indirectly influencing nearly almost every other type of natural event. Rising global temperatures may lead to altered tropical cyclone activity, more frequent El Niño events, and the spread of tropical diseases beyond their current boundaries. Rising sea levels will swallow coastal agricultural land and concentrate more and more people into squalid megacities, heightening their vulnerability to disease. Furthermore, the poverty bred by global warming may worsen even terrestrial disasters such as earthquakes and volcanic eruptions, since poverty plays a crucial role in determining the vulnerability of human populations to all natural hazards. Worst of all, if current projections hold true, global warming may precipitate the worst famine in human history as rising human populations run headlong into declining agricultural productivity. The result may be a new Malthusian crisis on a regional or even global scale.

It may be that the human species will find ways to extricate itself from the mess that it finds itself in today, but the lessons of the historical record are not encouraging. The word disaster is derived from an Italian word that means "unfavorable to one's stars," since the astrology-minded Romans

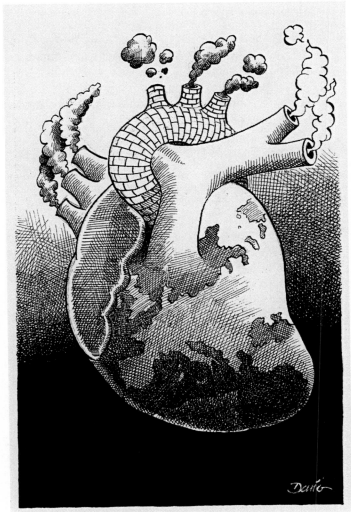

believed that disasters arose from unknowable, supernatural causes. In reality, as we have seen repeatedly throughout this book, most "natural" disasters are partially or wholly man-made, and this truism will likely become even truer as we move further into the Anthropocene era. Human beings, especially those living in capitalist economic systems, tend to make choices that favor short-term gains and comforts rather than long-term sustainability and stability. This impetus has caused us to make disastrous choices. We continue to build suburbs on fault lines, construct vacation homes on storm-swept coastlines or volcano slopes, and inundate poorly drained fields with scarce river water, leading to inevitable soil salinization. In an age where population control provides the surest means of mitigating future disasters, the world's wealthiest state refuses to fund programs that offer birth control for fear of offending the moral scruples of certain American interest groups. Perhaps most damaging of all, human beings are still slow to make sacrifices in the short term that might mitigate the environmental damage of global warming in the long run. As a society, we have faith that the technologies of tomorrow will defuse the future disasters that we are creating by our actions today. We had better hope that we are not misplacing our faith.

Study Questions

1. "Before the year 2000, most disasters arose from natural causes, but in the 21st century and beyond disasters are likely to result from human uses of technology." How convincing do you find this statement?

2. After reading this chapter, and this book, what is your next step? In other words, to what degree, and how, will the issues in this book influence your behavior and decisions in the future?

Sources/Suggested Readings

Allan, T. "Moving water to satisfy uneven global needs: «Trading» water as an alternative to engineering it." *ICID Journal*, 47(2), 1998, pp. 1–8.

Crosby, Alfred W. *Children of the Sun: A History of Humanity's Unappeasable Appetite for Energy.* New York: W. W. Norton, 2006.

Crutzen, P. J., and E. F. Stoermer. "The 'Anthropocene.'" *Global Change Newsletter.* 41 (2000), pp. 12–13.

Crutzen, P. J. "The Geology of Mankind." *Nature*, 415(23), 2002.

Dukes, Jeffrey S. "Burning Buried Sunshine: Human Consumption of Ancient Solar Energy." *Climactic Change*, 61 (Nov. 2003), pp. 31–44.

McNeill, J. R. *Something New Under the Sun: An Environmental History of the Twentieth-Century World.* New York: W. W. Norton and Company, 2000.

Montgomery, David R. *Dirt: The Erosion of Civilizations.* Berkeley: University of California Press, 2007.

"Nuclear Power in China." World Nuclear Association, accessed 5/13/08. Available from http://www.world-nuclear.org/info/inf63.html

Pollan, Michael. *The Omnivore's Dilemma: A Natural History of Four Meals.* New York: Penguin Press, 2006.

Ryan, Frank. *Virus X: Tracking the New Killer Plagues.* New York: Little, Brown, 1997.

Walters, Mark Jerome. *Six Modern Plagues and How We Are Causing Them.* Washington, DC: Island Press/Shearwater Books, 2003.

Bibliography

Books

Anderegg, C. R. *The Ash Warriors*. Washington, DC: Air Force History and Museums Program, 2005.

Armus, Diego ed. *Disease in the History of Modern Latin America*. Durham, NC: Duke University Press, 2003.

Asia Pacific Forum on Women, Law and Development. *Why Are Women More Vulnerable During Disasters? Violations of Women's Human Rights in the Aftermath of the Indian Ocean Tsunami and the Pakistan Earthquake*. Chang Mai, Thailand: Asia Pacific Forum on Women, Law, and Development, 2005.

Banerjee, Dipankar, and D. Suba Chadran, eds., *Jammu and Kashmir After the Earthquake*. New Delhi, India: Samskriti, 2007.

Bankoff, Greg. *Cultures of Disaster: Society and Natural Hazard in the Philippines*. New York: RoutledgeCurzon, 2003.

Barnes, Jay. *Florida's Hurricane History*. Chapel Hill: University of North Carolina Press, 1998.

Barnett, Tony, and Alan Whiteside. *AIDS in the Twenty-First Century: Disease and Globalization*. New York: Palgrave Macmillan, 2002.

Barry, John. *Rising Tide: The Great Mississippi Flood of 1927 and How It Changed America*. New York: Simon and Schuster, 1997.

_____. *The Great Influenza: The Epic Story of the Deadliest Plague in History*. New York: Viking, 2004.

Barua, Dhiman, and William B. Greenough III, eds., *Cholera*. New York: Plenum Medical Book Company, 1992.

Bawden, Garth, and Richard Martin Reycraft, eds., *Environmental Disaster and the Archeology of Human Response*. Albuquerque, NM: Maxwell Museum of Anthropology, 2000.

Becker, Jasper. *Hungry Ghosts: Mao's Secret Famine*. New York: Henry Holt, 1996.

Belknap, Reginald Rowan. *American House Building in Messina and Reggio*. New York: G. P. Putnam's Sons, 1910.

Benjamin, Sandra. *Sicily: Three Thousand Years of Human History*. Hanover, New Hampshire: Steerforth, 2006.

Blackhall, Susan. *Tsunami*. UK: Taj Books, 2005.

Bollet, Alfred J. *Plagues and Poxes: The Impact of Human History on Epidemic Disease*. New York: Demos Medical Publishing, 2004.

Briggs, Charles L., and Clara Mantini-Briggs. *Stories in the Time of Cholera: Racial Profiling During a Medical Nightmare*. Berkeley: University of California Press, 2003.

Brinkley, Douglas. *The Great Deluge*. New York: HarperCollins, 2006.

Brush, Lucien M., M. Gordon Wolman, and Huang Bing-Wei. *Taming the Yellow River: Silt and Floods*. Boston: Kluwer Academic Publishers, 1989.

Bunbury, Bill. *Cyclone Tracy: Picking Up the Pieces*. South Freemantle, Australia: Freemantle Arts Press Centre, 1994.

Cannon, Terry, and Alan Jenkins eds., *The Geography of Contemporary China: The Impact of Deng Xiaoping's Decade*. New York: Routledge, 1990.

Cantor, Norman. *In the Wake of the Plague: The Black Death and the World It Made*. New York: Free Press, 2001.

Castro, Eddee. *Pinatubo: The Eruption of the Century*. Quezon City, Philippines: Phoenix, 1991.

Chan, Alfred. *Mao's Crusade: Politics and Policy Implementation in China's Great Leap Forward*. New York: Oxford University Press, 2001.

Chase, Allan. *The Legacy of Malthus: The Social Costs of the New Scientific Racism*. New York: Alfred A. Knopf, 1977.

Chen, Lincoln C., ed., *Disaster in Bangladesh: Health Crises in a Developing Nation*. New York: Oxford University Press, 1973.

Cline, William R. *Global Warming and Agriculture: Impact Estimates by Country*. Washington, DC: Center for Global Development, 2007.

Cohen, Mark Nathan. *Health and the Rise of Civilization*. New Haven, CT: Yale University Press, 1989.

_____. *The Food Crisis in Prehistory: Overpopulation*

and the Origins of Agriculture. New Haven, CT: Yale University Press, 1997.

Cooper, Christopher, and Robert Block. *Disaster: Hurricane Katrina and the Failure of Homeland Security.* New York: Henry Holt and Company, 2006.

Crosby, Alfred W. *The Columbian Exchange: Biological and Cultural Consequences of 1492.* Westport, CT: Praeger, 2003, originally published 1972.

_____. *Children of the Sun: A History of Humanity's Unappeasable Appetite for Energy.* New York: W. W. Norton, 2006.

Cuny, Frederick C. *Famine, Conflict, and Response: a Basic Guide.* West Hartford, CT: Kumarian Press, 1999.

Davies, Pete. *Inside the Hurricane: Face to Face with Nature's Deadliest Storms.* New York: Henry Holt and Company, 2000.

_____. *The Devil's Flu: The World's Deadliest Influenza Epidemic and the Scientific Hunt for the Virus That Caused It.* New York: Henry Holt, 2000.

Davis, Mike. *Late Victorian Holocausts: El Nino Famines and the Making of the Third World.* New York: Verso, 2001.

De Boer, Jelle Zeilinga, and Theodore Donald Sanders. *Volcanoes in Human History.* Princeton, NJ: Princeton University Press, 2002.

_____. *Earthquakes in Human History.* Princeton, NJ: Princeton University Press, 2005.

De Waal, Alex. *Evil Days: Thirty Years of War and Famine in Ethiopia.* New York: Human Rights Watch, 1991.

_____. *Famine Crimes: Politics and the Disaster Relief Industry in Africa.* Irthingborough, Britain: ARIAI/Indiana University Press, 1997.

_____. *Famine That Kills (Revised Edition).* New York: Oxford University Press, 2005.

Dejene, Alemneh. *Environment, Famine, and Politics in Ethiopia.* Boulder, CO: Lynne Rienner Publishers, 1990.

Del Moral, Roger and Lawrence R. Walker. *Environmental Disasters, Natural Recovery, and Human Responses.* New York: Cambridge University Press, 2007.

Denham, Tim and Peter White. *The Emergence of Agriculture: A Global View.* New York: Routledge, 2007.

Desowitz, Robert S. *The Malaria Capers.* New York: W. W. Norton, 1991.

Devereux, Stephen. *Theories of Famine.* New York: Harvester Wheatsheaf, 1993.

Diamond, Jared. *Collapse: How Societies Choose to Fail or Succeed.* New York: Penguin Books, 2005.

_____. *Guns, Germs, and Steel: The Fates of Human Societies.* New York: W. W. Norton, 1997.

Dickie, John, John Foot, and Frank Snowden, eds., *Disastro! Disasters in Italy since 1860.* New York: Palgrave, 2002.

Dodgen, Randall A. *Controlling the Dragon: Confucian Engineers and the Yellow River in Late Imperial China.* Honolulu, HI: University of Hawai'i Press, 2001.

Donnelly, James S. *The Great Irish Potato Famine.* Great Britain: Sutton Publishing, 2001.

Dow, Kirstin, and Thomas E. Downing. *The Atlas of Climate Change: Mapping the World's Greatest Challenge.* Berkeley: University of California Press, 2006.

Dressler, Andrew E., and Edward A. Parson. *The Science and Politics of Global Climate Change: A Guide to the Debate.* New York: Cambridge University Press, 2006.

Duesberg, Peter H. *Inventing the AIDS Virus.* Washington, DC: Regnery Publishing, 1996.

Durisch, Peter, Robert Howarth, and Kenneth Stevens. *Cyclone! Christmas in Darwin 1974.* Sydney, Australia: Sydney Morning Herald, 1975.

Durrani, Jan Ahmad, Amr Salah Elnashai, Youssef M. A. Hashash, Sung Jig Kim, and Arif Masud. *The Kashmiri Earthquake of October 8, 2005: A Quick Look Report.* Urbana-Champaign, IL: Mid-America Earthquake Center, 2005.

Elvin, Mark, and Liu Ts'ui-jung, eds., *Sediments of Time: Environment and Society in Chinese History.* New York: Cambridge University Press, 1998.

Emanuel, Kerry. *Divine Wind: The History and Science of Hurricanes.* New York: Oxford University Press, 2005.

Engels, Friedrich. *The Condition of the Working Class in England.* 1845. Reprint, New York: Oxford University Press, 1993.

Etheridge, Elizabeth W. *The Butterfly Caste: A Social History of Pellagra in the South.* Westport, CT: Greenwood, 1972.

Fagan, Brian. *Floods, Famines, and Emperors: El Nino and the Fate of Civilizations.* New York: Basic Books, 1999.

_____. *The Great Warming: Climate Change and the Rise and Fall of Civilizations.* New York: Bloomsbury, 2008.

_____. *The Little Ice Age: How Climate Made History, 1300–1850.* New York: Basic Books, 2000.

Flannery, Tim. *The Weather Makers: How Man Is Changing the Climate and What It Means for Life on Earth.* New York: Atlantic Monthly, 2005.

Fleming, James Rodger. *Historical Perspectives on Climate Change.* New York: Oxford University Press, 1998.

Fondevilla, Emma F. Sr. *Eruption and Exodus: Mt. Pinatubo and the Aytas of Zambales.* Quezon City, Philippines: Claretian, 1991.

Fradkin, Philip L. *The Great Earthquake and Firestorms of 1906.* Berkeley: University of California Press, 2005.

Friedrich, Otto. *The End of the World.* New York: Coward, McCann and Geoghegan, 1982.

Funk, Joe, Jason Hinman, and Matt Springer. *Tsu-*

nami: Hope, Heroes, and Incredible Stories of Survival. Chicago, IL: Triumph, 2005.

Geist, Helmut. *The Causes and Progression of Desertification.* Burlington, VT: Ashgate Publishing Company, 2005.

Greer, Charles. *Water Management in the Yellow River Basin of China.* Austin: University of Texas Press, 1979.

Grmek, Mirko D. *History of AIDS: Emergence and Origin of a Modern Pandemic.* Princeton, NJ: Princeton University Press, 1990.

Hammer, Joshua. *Yokohama Burning: The Deadly 1923 Earthquake and Fire That Helped Forge the Path to World War II.* New York: Free Press, 2006.

Harrison, Gordon. *Mosquitoes, Malaria, and Man.* New York: E. P. Dutton, 1978.

Haque, C. Emdad. *Hazards in a Fickle Environment: Bangladesh.* Boston: Kluwer Academic Publishers, 1997.

Hofer, Thomas, and Bruno Messerli. *Floods in Bangladesh: History, Dynamics, and Rethinking the Role of the Himalayas.* New York: United Nations University Press, 2006.

Horne, Jed. *Breach of Faith.* New York: Random House, 2006.

Houghton, John. *Global Warming: The Complete Briefing.* New York: Cambridge University Press, 2004.

Howe, Maud. *Sicily in Shadow and in Sun: The Earthquake and the American Relief Work.* Boston: Little, Brown, and Company, 1910.

Humphreys, Margaret. *Malaria: Poverty, Race, and Public Health in the United States.* Baltimore, MD: John Hopkins University Press, 2001.

Hunter, Susan. *AIDS in America.* New York: Palgrave Macmillan, 2006.

_____. *Black Death: AIDS in Africa.* New York: Palgrave Macmillan, 2003.

Johnson, Marc Pierre, Karel Mayrand, and Marc Paquin eds., *Governing Global Desertification.* Burlington, VT: Ashgate, 2005.

Johnson, Steven. *The Ghost Map: The Story of London's Most Terrifying Epidemic — and How It Changed Science, Cities, and the Modern World.* New York: Riverhead, 2006.

Kalipeni, Ezekiel, Susan Craddock, Joseph R. Oppong, and Jayati Ghosh. *HIV and AIDS in Africa: Beyond Epidemiology.* Malden, MA: Blackwell Publishing, 2004.

Kane, Penny. *Famine in China: 1959–61.* New York: St. Martin's, 1988.

Kedrick, T. D. *The Lisbon Earthquake.* New York: J. B. Lippincott, 1955.

Kelly, John. *The Great Mortality.* New York: Harper Perennial, 2005.

Keys, David. *Catastrophe: An Investigation into the Origins of the Modern World.* New York: Ballantine, 1999.

Kiple, Kenneth F. *Plague, Pox, and Pestilence.* London: Barnes and Noble Books, 1997.

_____, ed., *The Caribbean Slave: A Biological History.* New York: Cambridge University Press, 1984.

Kiros, Fassil G. *Enough with Famines in Ethiopia: A Clarion Call.* Hollywood, CA: Tsehai, 2006.

Kolbert, Elizabeth. *Field Notes from a Catastrophe: Man, Nature, and Climate Change.* New York: Bloomsbury, 2006.

Kudlick, Catherine J. *Cholera in Post-Revolutionary Paris: A Cultural History.* Berkeley: University of California Press, 1996.

Kunstler, James Howard. *The Long Emergency.* New York: Grove, 2005.

Larson, Erik. *Isaac's Storm.* New York: Vintage Books, 1999.

Lewis, Mark Edward. *The Flood Myths of Early China.* Albany: State University of New York Press, 2006.

Li, Lillian M. *Fighting Famine in North China: State, Market, and Environmental Decline, 1690–1990's.* Stanford, CA: Stanford University Press, 2007.

Linden, Eugene. *The Winds of Change: Climate, Weather, and the Destruction of Civilizations.* New York: Simon and Schuster, 2006.

Longshore, David. *Encyclopedia of Hurricanes, Typhoons, and Cyclones.* New York: Checkmark, 2000.

Lourensz, R. S. *Tropical Cyclones in the Australian Region July 1909 to June 1980.* Canberra, Australia: Australian Government Publishing Service, 1981.

Lovejoy, Thomas E., and Lee Hannah, eds., *Climate Change and Biodiversity.* New Haven, CT: Yale University Press, 2005.

Marcus, Harold G. *A History of Ethiopia.* Berkeley: University of California Press, 1994.

McCullough, David. *The Johnstown Flood.* New York: Simon and Schuster, 1968.

McKay, Gary. *Tracy: The Storm That Wiped Out Darwin on Christmas Day 1974.* Crows Nest, Australia: Allen and Unwin, 2001.

McNeill, J. R. *Something New Under the Sun: An Environmental History of the Twentieth-Century World.* New York: W. W. Norton, 2000.

McNeill, William. *Plagues and Peoples.* New York: Anchor, 1976.

_____. *The Rise of the West: A History of the Human Community.* Chicago: University of Chicago Press, 1963.

McPhee, John. *The Control of Nature.* New York: Farrar, Straus and Giroux, 1989.

Middleton, Nick. *Desertification.* New York: Oxford University Press, 1991.

Mitchell, James K., ed., *Crucibles of Hazard: Mega-Cities and Disasters in Transition.* New York: United Nations University Press, 1999.

Montgomery, David R. *Dirt: The Erosion of Civilizations.* Berkeley: University of California Press, 2007.

Murnane, Richard J., and Liu, Kam-Biu, eds., *Hurri-*

canes and Typhoons: Past, Present, and Future. New York: Colombia University Press, 2004.

Murty, Tad S., U. Aswathanarayana, and N. Nirupama, eds., *The Indian Ocean Tsunami*. New York: Talyor and Francis, 2007.

Nash, J. Madeleine. *El Nino: Unlocking the Secrets of the Master Weather-Maker*. New York: Warner, 2002.

Newhall, Christopher G., and Raymondo S. Punongbayan, eds., *Fire and Mud: Eruptions and Lahars of Mount Pinatubo, Philippines*. Seattle: University of Washington Press, 1996.

Newman, Lucile, ed., *Hunger in History: Food Shortage, Poverty, and Deprivation*. Cambridge, MA: Blackwell, 1990.

Nizamuddin, K., ed., *Disaster in Bangladesh: Selected Readings*. Dhaka, Bangladesh: Graphtone, 2001.

Ó Gráda, Cormac. *Black '47 and Beyond*. Princeton, NJ: Princeton University Press, 1999.

Oldstone, Michael B. A. *Viruses, Plagues, and History*. New York: Oxford University Press, 1998.

Packard, Randal M. *The Making of a Tropical Disease: A Short History of Malaria*. Baltimore, MD: John Hopkins University Press, 2007.

Parrinder, Geoffrey, ed., *World Religions: From Ancient History to the Present*. New York: Facts on File, 1971.

Peacock, Walter Gillis, Betty Hearn Morrow, and Hugh Gladwin, eds., *Hurricane Andrew: Ethnicity, Gender, and the Sociology of Disasters*. Chapter New York: Routledge, 1997.

Peters, F. E. *The Hajj: The Muslim Pilgrimage to Mecca and the Holy Places*. Princeton, NJ: Princeton University Press, 1994.

Philander, George S. *Our Affair with El Nino*. Princeton, NJ: Princeton University Press, 2004.

Póirtér, Catha, ed., *The Great Irish Famine*. Cork, Ireland: Mercier, 1999.

Pollan, Michael. *The Omnivore's Dilemma: A Natural History of Four Meals*. New York: Penguin, 2006.

Ponting, Clive. *A Green History of the World: Nature, Pollution, and the Collapse of Societies*. New York: Penguin, 1991.

Prager, Ellen. *Furious Earth: The Science and Nature of Earthquakes, Volcanoes, and Tsunamis*. New York: McGraw-Hill, 2000.

Provenzo, Eugene F., Jr., and Asterie Baker Provenzo. *In the Eye of Hurricane Andrew*. Gainesville: University Press of Florida, 2002.

Puleo, Stephen. *Dark Tide: The Great Boston Molasses Flood of 1919*. Boston: Beacon, 2004.

Ranger, Terence, and Slack, Paul, eds., *Epidemics and Ideas: Essays on the Historical Perception of Pestilence*. New York: Cambridge University Press, 1992.

Reardon, Leo Francis. *The Florida Hurricane and Disaster*. Coral Gables, FL: Arva Parks, 1986 edition, originally published 1926.

Reese, Joe Hugh. *Florida's Great Hurricane*. Miami, FL: Lysle E. Fesler, 1926.

Reilly, Benjamin. *Tropical Surge: A History of Ambition and Disaster on the Florida Shore*. Sarasota, FL: Pineapple, 2005.

Renner, Michael, and Zoë Chafe. *Beyond Disasters: Creating Opportunities for Peace*. Washington, DC: Worldwatch Institute, 2007.

Ritchie, David. *The Encyclopedia of Earthquakes and Volcanoes*. New York: Facts on File, 1994.

Roberts, J. A. G. *The Complete History of China*. Great Britain: Sutton, 2006.

Roberts, J. M. *A Short History of the World*. New York: Oxford University Press, 1993.

Rocco, Fiammetta. *Quinine: Malaria and the Quest for a Cure that Changed the World*. New York: HarperCollins, 2003.

Roe, Daphne A. *A Plague of Corn: The Social History of Pellagra*. Ithaca, NY: Cornell University Press, 1973.

Rosenberg, Charles E. *The Cholera Years: The United States in 1832, 1849, and 1866*. Chicago: University of Chicago Press, 1962.

Ruddiman, William F. *Plows, Plagues, and Petroleum: How Humans Took Control of Climate*. Princeton, NJ: Princeton University Press, 2005.

Ryan, Frank. *Virus X: Tracking the New Killer Plagues*. New York: Little, Brown, 1997.

Sallares, Robert. *Malaria and Rome: A History of Malaria in Ancient Italy*. New York: Oxford University Press, 2002.

Samad, M. A. *Cyclone of 1970 and Agricultural Rehabilitation*. Dacca, Bangladesh: Agricultural Information Service, 1971.

Savino, John, and Marie D. Jones. *Supervolcano: the Catastrophic Event That Changed the Course of Human History*. Franklin Lakes, NJ: New Page Books, 2007.

Scarth, Alwyn. *La Catastrophe: The Eruption of Mount Pelée, the Worst Volcanic Disaster of the 20th Century*. New York: Oxford University Press, 2002.

_____. *Vulcan's Fury: Man Against the Volcano*. New Haven, CT: Yale University Press, 1999.

Seidensticker, Edward. *Low City, High City: Tokyo from Edo to the Earthquake*. New York: Alfred A. Knopf, 1983.

Sen, Amartya. *Poverty and Famines: An Essay on Entitlement and Deprivation*. New York: Oxford University Press, 1982.

Shangle, Robert D. *Southeast Asia Tsunami: One of the World's Greatest Natural Disasters in Modern Times*. Beaverton, OR: American Products, 2005.

Shapiro, Judith. *Mao's War Against Nature: Politics and the Environment in Revolutionary China*. New York: Cambridge University Press, 2001.

Shimizu, Hiromu. *Pinatubo Aytas: Continuity and Change*. Manila, Philippines: Ateno de Manila University Press, 1989.

Simkin, Tom, and Richard S. Fiske. *Krakatau 1883*. Washington, DC: Smithsonian Institution Press, 1983.

Smith, Bruce D. *The Emergence of Agriculture.* New York: Scientific American Library, 1998.

Soriquez, Tessa, and Ruben Maria Soriquez. *Mount Pinatubo and the Saga of the Megadike.* Quezon City, Philippines: Jade Asia Group, 2006.

Steinberg, Ted. *Acts of God: The Unnatural History of Natural Disaster in America.* New York: Oxford University Press, 2000.

Stommel, Henry, and Elizabeth Stommel, *Volcano Weather: The Story of 1816, The Year Without a Summer.* Newport, RI: Seven Seas, 1983.

Stone, Bailey. *The Genesis of the French Revolution: A Global Historical Interpretation.* New York: Cambridge University Press, 1994.

Takken, Willem, Pim Martens, and Robert J. Bogers, eds., *Environmental Change and Malaria Risk: Global and Local Implications.* The Netherlands: Springer, 2005.

Tawney, R. H. *Land and Labor in China.* London: G. Allen & Unwin, 1931.

Teiwes, Frederick C., and Sun, Warren. *China's Road to Disaster.* Armonk, NY: East Gate, 1999.

Teklehaimanot, Awash, Burt Singer, Andrew Spielman, Teşim Tozan, and Allan Schapira. *Coming to Grips with Malaria in the New Millennium.* Sterling, VA: Earthscan, 2005.

Terry, James P. *Tropical Cyclones: Climatology and Impacts in the South Pacific.* New York: Springer, 2007.

Thibodeau, John G., and Phillip B. Williams, eds., *The River Dragon Has Come: The Three Gorges Dam and the Fate of China's Yangtze River and Its People.* Armonk, NY: M. E. Sharp, 1998.

Tóibín, Colm, and Ferriter, Diarmaid. *The Irish Famine: A Documentary.* New York: St. Martin's, 2001.

Toomey, David M. *Stormchasers: The Hurricane Hunters and Their Fateful Flight into Hurricane Janet.* New York: W. W. Norton, 2003.

Turner, B. L. II, William C. Clark, Robert W. Kates, John F. Richards, Jessica T. Mathews, and William B. Meyer, eds., *The Earth As Transformed by Human Action.* New York: Cambridge University Press, 1990, pp. 473–477.

Van Heerden, Ivor, and Bryan, Mike. *The Storm.* New York: Viking, 2006.

Walters, Mark Jerome. *Six Modern Plagues and How We Are Causing Them.* Washington, DC: Island Press/Shearwater Books, 2003.

Watts, Michael. *Silent Violence: Food, Famine, and Peasantry in Northern Nigeria.* Berkeley: University of California Press, 1983.

Watts, Sheldon. *Epidemics and History: Disease, Power, and Imperialism.* New Haven, CT: Yale University Press, 1997.

Wei, Huang. *Conquering the Yellow River.* Peking: Foreign Languages Press, 1978.

Winchester, Simon. *Krakatoa: The Day the World Exploded August 27, 1883.* New York: HarperCollins, 2003.

World Health Organization. *Responding to Communicable Diseases Following the Tsunami in South-East Asia.* New Delhi, India: World Health Organization, 2005.

Xianliang, Zhang. *Grass Soup.* Boston: David R. Godine, 1993.

Zebrowski, Ernest, Jr. *The Last Days of St. Pierre: The Volcanic Disaster That Claimed Thirty Thousand Lives.* New Brunswick, NJ: Rutgers University Press, 2002.

Articles

Ali, Tanvir, Babar Shahbaz, and Abid Suleri. "Analysis of the Myths and Realities of Deforestation in Northwest Pakistan." *International Journal of Agriculture and Biology*, 2006.

Allan, T. "Moving water to satisfy uneven global needs: «Trading» water as an alternative to engineering it." *ICID Journal*, Vol. 7, No. 2 (1998), pp. 1–8.

Ambrose, Stanley H. "Late Pleistocene human population bottlenecks, volcanic winter, and differentiation of modern humans." *Journal of Human Evolution*, Vol. 34, No. 6 (1998), pp. 623–651.

Amirkhanian, Yuri A., Dennis v. Tiunov, and Jeffrey A. Kelly. "Risk factors for HIV and Other Sexually Transmitted Diseases Among Adolescents in St. Petersburg, Russia." *Family Planning Perspectives*, Vol. 33, No. 3 (May-June, 2001), pp. 106–112.

An, Mark Yunying, Li Wei, and Denis Tao Yany. "China's Great Leap: Forward or Backward? Anatomy of a Central Planning Disaster." Discussion Paper Series, Centre for Economic Policy Research, June 2001.

Baker, Victor R. "The Study of Superfloods." *Science*, New Series, Vol. 295, No. 5564 (March 29, 2002), pp. 2379–2380.

Bankoff, Greg. "Time Is of the Essence: Disasters, Vulnerability, and History." *International Journal of Mass Emergencies and Disasters*, Vol. 22, No. 3 (Nov. 2004), pp. 23–42.

Barnett, Robert W. "North China Floods Bring Large Losses." *Far Eastern Survey*, Vol. 8, No. 22 (Nov. 8, 1939), pp. 264–265.

Bourke, P. M. A. "The Extent of the Potato Crop in Ireland at the Time of the Famine." *Journal of the Statistical and Social Inquiry of Ireland*, Vol. 20, No. 3 (1959), pp. 1–35.

Bourne, Joel K. Jr. "Green Dreams." *National Geographic*, Oct. 2007, pp. 41–59.

Brandes, Stanley. "Maize As a Culinary Mystery." *Ethnology*, Vol. 31, No. 4 (Oct., 1992), pp. 331–336.

Caroll, Chris. "Deadly Delay: Katrina, Grasping for Relief." *National Geographic* (Dec. 2005), pp. 6–15.

Chang, Chi-Yun. "Climate and Man in China." *Annals of the Association of American Geographers*, Vol. 36, No. 1 (Mar. 1946), pp. 44–74.

"China's Vast Flood Threatens to Unite Hwang Ho and Yangtze." *Science News-Letter*, Vol. 34, No. 1 (Jul 2, 1938), pp. 5–6.

Chengrui, Mei, and Harold E. Dregne. "Review Article: Silt and the Future Development of China's Yellow River." *The Geographical Journal*, Vol. 167, No. 1 (Mar. 2001), pp. 7–22.

Colwell, Rita R. "Global Climate and Infectious Disease: The Cholera Paradigm." *Science*, Vol 274, No. 5295 (Dec. 20, 1996), pp. 2025–2031.

Crossley, Stella. "Real Estate vs. Human Lives in Florida," *The Nation*, Oct. 13 (1926), pp. 341–342.

Crutzen, P. J. "The Geology of Mankind." *Nature*, Vol. 415, No. 23 (2002).

_____, and E. F. Stoermer. "The 'Anthropocene.'" *Global Change Newsletter*. 41 (2000), pp. 12–13.

Cueto, Marcos. "Stigma and Blame During an Epidemic: Cholera in Peru, 1991." In Diego Armus, ed., *Disease in the History of Modern Latin America*. Durham, NC: Duke University Press, 2003.

Davison, Charles. "The Japanese Earthquake of 1 September 1923." *The Geographical Journal*, Vol. 65, No. 1. (Jan. 1925), pp. 41–61.

Desai, Sapna. "HIV and Domestic Violence: Intersections in the Lives of Married Women in India." *Health and Human Rights*, Vol. 8, No. 2, Emerging Issues in HIV/AIDS. (2005), pp. 140–168.

Dukes, Jeffrey S. "Burning Buried Sunshine: Human Consumption of Ancient Solar Energy." *Climactic Change*, 61 (Nov. 2003), pp. 31–44.

Emanuel, Kerry. "Increasing Destructiveness of Tropical Cyclones Over the Past 30 Years." *Nature*, Vol. 436, No. 4 (August 2005), pp. 686–688.

_____, Ragoth Sundararajan, and John Williams. "Hurricanes and Global Warming: Results from Downscaling IPCC AR4 Simulations." *Bulletin of the American Meteorological Society* (2008).

"Famine Stalks After Floods on Tragic Plains of China." *Science News-Letter*, Vol. 24, No. 646 (Aug. 26, 1933), pp. 141–142.

Faulkner, Jason, Mark Schaller, Justin H. Park, and Lesley A. Duncan. "Evolved Disease — Avoidance Mechanism and Contemporary Xenophobic Attitudes." *Group Processes and Intergroup Relations*, Vol. 7, No. 4 (2004), pp. 333–353.

Federov, Alexey V., and S. George Philander. "Is El Nino Changing?." *Science*, Vol. 288, No. 5473. (June 16, 2000), pp. 1997–2002.

Fincher, Corey L., Randy Thornhill, Damien R. Murray, and Mark Schaller. "Pathogen Prevalence Predicts Human Cross-Cultural Variability in Individualism/Collectivism." *Proceedings of the Royal Society B*, Vol. 275, No. 1640 (June 7, 2008), pp. 1279–1285.

Fitzgerald, Alice. "Experiences in Naples After the Messina Disaster." *The American Journal of Nursing*, Vol. 9, No. 7 (Apr. 1909), pp. 482–492.

Glass, R. I., M. Libel, A. D. Brandling-Bennett. "Epidemic Cholera in the Americas." *Science*, Vol. 256, No. 5063 (Jun. 12, 1992), pp. 1524–1525.

Glick, Daniel. "The Big Thaw." *National Geographic*, Sept. 2004, pp. 13–33.

Gore, Rick. "Andrew Aftermath." *National Geographic*, Vol. 183, No. 4 (April 1993), pp. 1–37.

Gross, Eric. "Somebody Got Drowned, Lord: Florida and the Great Okeechobee Hurricane Disaster of 1926." Ph.D. Thesis, Florida State University, 1995.

Grunwald, Michael. "The Threatening Storm." *Time*, August 12, 2007, pp. 28–41.

Hamilton, William. "An Account of the Earthquakes Which Happened In Italy..." *Philosophical Transactions of the Royal Society of London*, Vol 73. (1783), pp. 169–208.

Hansen, Keith. "A Plague's Bottom Line." *Foreign Policy*, No. 137. (July-Aug. 2003), pp. 26–27.

Haque, C. Emdad and Danny Blair. "Vulnerability to Tropical Cyclones: Evidence from the April 1991 Cyclone in Coastal Bangladesh." *Disaster*, Vol. 16, No. 3 (Sept. 1992), pp. 217–229.

Hobbs, W. H. "The Messina Earthquake." *Bulletin of the American Geographical Society*, Vol. 41, No. 7 (1909), pp. 409–422.

Hopkins, Richard. "Long-Term Effects of Hurricane Andrew: Revisiting Mental Health Indicators. *Diasters*, Vol. 19, No. 3 (Sept. 1995), pp. 235–245.

Hu, Ch'ang-Tu. "The Yellow River Administration in the Ch'ing Dynasty." *The Far Eastern Quarterly*, Vol. 14, No. 4, Special Number on Chinese History and Society. (Aug. 1955), pp. 505–513.

Hume, Jennifer C. C., Emily J. Lyons and Karen P. Day. "Malaria in Antiquity: A Genetics Perspective." *World Archeology*, Vol. 35, No. 2, Archeology of Epidemic and Infectious Disease. (Oct., 2003), pp. 180–192.

Jacobsen, Thorkild, and Robert M. Adams. "Salt and Silt in Ancient Mesopotamian Agriculture." *Science*, Vol. 128, No. 3334 (Nov. 21, 1958), pp. 1251–1258.

Karnik, Niranjan S. "Locating HIV/AIDS and India: Cautionary Notes on the Globalization of Categories." *Science, Technology, & Human Values*, Vol. 26, No. 3. (Summer, 2001), pp. 322–348.

Kerr, Richard A. "Volcanic Blasts Favor El Nino Warmings." *Science* 17 January 2003, 336–337.

Kipling, Rudyard. "White Man's Burden." (1899).

Knutson, Thomas R. and Robert E. Tuleya. "Impact of CO_2–Induced Warming on Simulated Hurricane Intensity and Precipitation." *Journal of Climate*, Vol. 17, No. 18 (Sept. 15, 2004), pp. 3477–3495.

Kumar, K. Krishna, Balaji Rajagopalan, and Mark A. Cane. "On the Weakening Relationship Between the Indian Monsoon and ENSO." *Science*, Vol. 284, No. 5423. (June 25, 1999), pp. 2156–2159.

Larmer, Brook. "Bitter Waters." *National Geographic*, Vol. 213, No. 5 (May 2008), pp. 146–169.

Lockwood, Edward T. "Floods and Flood Prevention in China." *Far Eastern Survey*, Vol. 4, No. 21 (Oct. 23, 1935), pp. 164–168.

Maclure, Malcolm. "Inventing the AIDS Virus Hypothesis: An Illustration of Scientific vs. Unscientific Induction." *Epidemiology*, Vol. 9, No. 4 (July, 1998), pp. 467–473.

Mann, Charles C. "Our Good Earth." *National Geographic*, Vol. 214, No. 3 (Sept. 2008), pp. 180–106.

May, Jacques M. "Map of the World Distribution of Cholera." *Geographical Review*, Vol. 41, No. 2 (Apr. 1951), pp. 272–273.

Marshall, Eliot. "A Renewed Assault on an Old and Deadly Foe." *Science*, Vol. 290, No. 5491. (Oct. 20, 2000), pp. 428–430.

McCann, James. "Maize and Grace: History, Corn, and Africa's New Landscapes, 1500–1999." *Comparative Studies in Society and History*, Vol. 43, No. 2 (Apr., 2001), pp. 246–272.

McDonnell, Sharon, Richard P. Troiano, Nancy Barker, Eric Noji, W. Gary Hlady, and Richard Hopkins. "Long-Term Effects of Hurricane Andrew: Revisiting Mental Health Indicators. *Disasters*, Vol. 19, No. 3 (Sept. 1995), pp. 235–245.

McKibben, Bill. "Carbon's New Math." *National Geographic*, Oct. 2007, pp. 33–37.

Monastersky, R. "Unusual Weather Spurred Andrew's Growth." *Science News*, Vol. 142, No. 19 (Sept. 5, 1992), p. 150.

Montgomery, Roger. "The Bangladesh Floods of 1984 in Historical Context." *Disasters*, Vol. 9, No. 3 (1985), pp. 163–172.

Morrow, Betty Hearn, and Elaine Enarson. "Hurricane Andrew Through Women's Eyes: Issues and Recommendations." *International Journal of Mass Emergencies and Disasters*, Vol. 14, No. 1 (March 1996), pp. 5–22.

Oldham, R. D. "The Italian Earthquake of December 28, 1908." *The Geographical Journal*, Vol. 33, No. 2 (Feb. 1909), pp. 185–188.

"Pakistan Earthquake: International Response and Impact on U.S. Foreign Policies and Programs." Staff Trip Report to the Committee of Foreign Relations, United States Senate. Washington, DC: U.S. Government Printing Office, 2005.

Palaca, S. and R. Socolow. "Stabilization Wedges: Solving the Climate Problem for the Next 50 Years with Current Technologies." *Science*, Vol. 305 (August 13, 2004), pp. 968–972.

"Performance Evaluation of the New Orleans and Southeast Louisiana Hurricane Protection System: Draft Final Report." *Army Corps of Engineers* (1 June 2006).

Pielke, R. A. Jr., C. Landsea, M. Mayfield, J. Laver, and R. Pasch. "Hurricanes and Global Warming." *American Meteorological Society* (Nov. 2005), pp. 1571–1575.

Potera, Carol. "Infectious Disease. In Disaster's Wake: Tsunami Lung." *Environmental Health Perspectives*, Vol. 113, No. 11 (Nov. 2005), pp. A734.

Rahmato, Dessalegn. "Peasant Survival Strategies in Ethiopia." *Disasters: Journal of Disaster Studies and Management*, Vol. 12, No. 4 (1988), pp. 326–344.

Renwick, Neil. "The 'Nameless Fever': The HIV/AIDS Pandemic and China's Women." *Third World Quarterly*, Vol. 23, No. 2, Global Health and Governance: HIV/AIDS (Apr., 2002), pp. 377–393.

Rodó, Xavier, Mercedes Pascual, George Fuchs, and A. S. G. Farugue. "Enso and Cholera: A Nonstationary Link Related to Climate Change?" *Proceedings of the National Academy of Sciences of the United States of America*, Vo. 99, No. 20 (Oct. 1, 2002), pp. 12901–12906.

Roger, David J., and Sarah E. Randolph. "The Global Spread of Malaria in a Future, Warmer World." *Science*, Vol. 289, No. 5485. (Sep. 8, 2000), pp. 1763–1766.

Ryang, Sonia. "The Great Kanto Earthquake and the Massacre of Koreans in 1923: Notes on Japan's Modern National Sovereignty." *Anthropological Quarterly*, Vol. 76, No. 4. (Autumn 2003), pp. 731–748.

Schmuck, Hanna. "'An Act of Allah': Religious Explanations for Floods in Bangladesh as Survival Strategy." *International Journal of Mass Emergencies and Disasters*, Vol. 18, No. 1 (March, 2000), pp. 85–95.

Seitz, Stefan. "Coping Strategies of an Ethnic Minority Group: The Aeta of Mount Pinatubo." *Disasters*, Vol. 22(1) 1998, 76–90.

Shan-Yu, Yao. "The Chronological and Seasonal Distribution of Floods and Droughts in Chinese History, 206 BC–AD 1911." *Harvard Journal of Asiatic Studies*, Vol. 6, No. 3/4 (Feb. 1942), pp. 273–312.

_____. "The Geographical Distribution of Floods and Droughts in Chinese History, 206 BC–AD 1911." *The Far Eastern Quarterly*, Vol. 2, No. 4 (Aug. 1943), pp. 357–378.

Skinner, G. William. "Presidential Address: The Structure of Chinese History." *Journal of Asian Studies*, Vol. 44, No. 2 (Feb, 1985), pp. 271–292.

Smith, Stanley K., and Christopher McCarty. "Demographic Effects of Natural Disasters: A Case Study of Hurricane Andrew." *Demography*, Vol. 33, No. 2 (May, 1996), pp. 265–275.

"Special Report Asia's Tsunami: The Impact." London, UK: The Economist Intelligence Unit, January 2005.

Steinberg, Ted. "Disasters and Deregulation." *Chronicle of Higher Regulation*, July 21 2006, p. B16.

"The Peking-Hankow Railway." *Bulletin of the American Geographical Society*, Vol. 38, No. 9 (1906), pp. 554.

"Tsunami — Where Next?" *National Geographic Magazine*, Geographica (April, 2005).

Tse-Hui, Teng. "Report on the Multiple-Purpose Plan for Permanently Controlling the Yellow River and Exploiting Its Water Resources." Delivered on July 18, 1955, at the Second Session of the First National People's Congress, China.

Watts, Sheldon. "British Development Policies and Malaria in India 1897–c.1929." *Past and Present*, No. 165. (Nov., 1999), pp. 141–181.

Webster, R. G., and Walker, E. J. "The world is teetering on the edge of a pandemic that could kill a large fraction of the human population." *American Scientist* Vol. 91 No. 2, (2003), p. 122.

Weinhold, Bob. "Infectious Disease: The Human Costs of Our Environmental Errors." *Environmental Health Perspectives*, Vol. 112, No. 1 (Jan. 2004), pp. A32–A38.

White, Lynn Jr. "The Historical Roots of Our Ecologic Crisis." *Science*, Vol. 155, No. 3767 (March 10, 1967), pp. 1203–1207.

Whittaker, Elizabeth D. "Bread and Work: Pellagra and Economic Transformation in Turn-of-the-Century Italy." *Anthropological Quarterly*, Vol. 65, No. 2 (Apr., 1992), pp. 80–90.

Wright, Charles W. "The World's Most Cruel Earthquake." *National Geographic*, Vol. 20 (1909), pp. 373–396.

Xu, Jiongzin. "A Study of the Long-Term Environmental Effects of River Regulation on the Yellow River of China in Historical Perspective." *Geografiska Annaler. Series A, Physical Geography*, Vol. 75, No. 3 (1993), pp. 61–72.

_____. "Naturally and Anthropogenically Accelerated Sedimentation in the Lower Yellow River, China, over the Past 13,000 Years." *Gografiska Annaler. Series A, Physical Geography*, Vol. 80, No. 1 (1998), pp. 67–78.

"Hurricane Andrew: South Florida and Louisiana, August 23–266, 1992." National Disaster Survey Report, U.S. Department of Commerce, National Oceanic and Atmospheric Administration, National Weather Service, Silver Spring, Maryland, November 1993. http://www.nws.noaa.gov/om/assessments/dfs/andrew.pdf.

Katz, Jonathan M. "Poor Haitians Resort to Eating Dirt" *Associated Press* (Jan. 30, 2008). http://news.nationalgeographic.com/news/2008/01/080130-AP-haiti-eatin_2.html.

"Nuclear Power in China." World Nuclear Association. http://www.world-nuclear.org/info/inf63.html.

Raman, Sunil. "Tsunami Villagers Give Thanks to Trees." BBC News, 2005/02/16. http://news.bbc.co.uk/go/pr/fr/1/hi/world/south_asia/4269847.stm.

"Significant Earthquakes of the World, 2005." *United States Geological Service*, http://earthquake.usgs.gov/eqcenter/eqarchives/significant/sig_2005.php.

"Tourism Situation Concerning Inbound Foreign Visitors in 2005." *Tourism Authority of Thailand.* http://www2.tat.orth/stat/web/static_index.php.

"Tsunami, Tidal Waves and Other Extreme Waves." *National Oceanic and Aeronautic Administration.* http://www.erh.noaa.gov/phi/reports/tsunami.htm.

"2008 Report on the Global AIDS Epidemic." *UNAIDS.* http://www.unaids.org/en/KnowledgeCentre/HIVData/GlobalReport/2008/2008_Global_report.asp.

"Volcano Hazards Program." *United States Geological Service.* http://volcanoes.usgs.gov/.

Wikipedia: The Free Encyclopedia. http://www.wikipedia.org.

Wikimedia Commons. http://wikimedia.org/wiki/Main_Page.

On-Line Resources

"AIDS and HIV Information." *AVERT.* http://www.avert.org/.

Index

385